MENTAL HEALTH, LEGAL CAPACITY, AND HUMAN RIGHTS

Since adoption of the Convention on the Rights of Persons with Disabilities and the interpretive General Comment 1, the topic of legal capacity in mental health settings has generated considerable debate in disciplines ranging from law and psychiatry to public health and public policy. With over 180 countries having ratified the Convention, the shifts required in law and clinical practice need to be informed by interdisciplinary and contextually relevant research as well as the views of stakeholders. With an equal emphasis on the Global North and Global South, this volume offers a comprehensive, interdisciplinary analysis of legal capacity in the realm of mental health. Integrating rigorous academic research with perspectives from people with psychosocial disabilities and their caregivers, the authors provide a holistic overview of pertinent issues and suggest avenues for reform.

Michael Ashley Stein is the Executive Director of the Harvard Law School Project on Disability, and a visiting professor at Harvard Law School. Considered one of the world's leading experts on disability law and policy, Stein participated in the drafting of the UN Convention on the Rights of Persons with Disabilities; works with disabled peoples' organizations and non-governmental organizations around the world; actively consults with governments on their disability laws and policies; advises an array of UN bodies and national human rights institutions; and has brought landmark disability rights litigation globally.

Faraaz Mahomed is a research associate at the Harvard Law School Project on Disability, and a visiting research fellow at the Centre for Applied Legal Studies, University of the Witwatersrand, Johannesburg, South Africa. Mahomed self-identifies as a person with a psychosocial disability and has worked in mental health practice, in community-based as well as institutionalized settings, as a clinical psychologist. He now works in the human rights field, supporting rights-based approaches to mental health in Africa at the Open Society Foundations. He received a Fulbright scholarship in 2008.

Vikram Patel is The Pershing Square Professor of Global Health in the Department of Global Health and Social Medicine at Harvard Medical School. Vikram's work has focused on the burden of mental health problems, their association with social disadvantage, and the use of community resources for their prevention and treatment. He has been awarded the Chalmers Medal, the Sarnat Prize, the Pardes Humanitarian Prize, an honorary OBE, and the John Dirk Canada Gairdner Award in Global Health for his leading work in the field.

Charlene Sunkel is the Founder and CEO of the Global Mental Health Peer Network. She is a global mental health lived-experience advocate, and she has authored or co-authored a number of papers related to mental health and human rights. Sunkel also serves on or advises several international boards and committees.

Mental Health, Legal Capacity, and Human Rights

Edited by

MICHAEL ASHLEY STEIN

Harvard Law School

FARAAZ MAHOMED

University Of The Witwatersrand, Johannesburg

VIKRAM PATEL

Harvard Medical School

CHARLENE SUNKEL

Global Mental Health Peer Network

Editorial Assistant

JULIANA LYNN RESTIVO

Harvard Medical School

CAMBRIDGE UNIVERSITY PRESS

Shaftesbury Road, Cambridge CB2 8EA, United Kingdom

One Liberty Plaza, 20th Floor, New York, NY 10006, USA

477 Williamstown Road, Port Melbourne, VIC 3207, Australia

314–321, 3rd Floor, Plot 3, Splendor Forum, Jasola District Centre, New Delhi – 110025, India

103 Penang Road, #05–06/07, Visioncrest Commercial, Singapore 238467

Cambridge University Press is part of Cambridge University Press & Assessment, a department of the University of Cambridge.

We share the University's mission to contribute to society through the pursuit of education, learning and research at the highest international levels of excellence.

www.cambridge.org
Information on this title: www.cambridge.org/9781108972451

DOI: 10.1017/9781108979016

© Cambridge University Press & Assessment 2021

This publication is in copyright. Subject to statutory exception and to the provisions of relevant collective licensing agreements, no reproduction of any part may take place without the written permission of Cambridge University Press & Assessment.

First published 2021
First paperback edition 2024

A catalogue record for this publication is available from the British Library

Library of Congress Cataloging-in-Publication data
NAMES: Stein, Michael Ashley, editor. | Mahomed, Faraaz, 1985– editor. | Patel, Vikram, editor. | Sunkel, Charlene, editor.
TITLE: Mental health, legal capacity, and human rights / edited by Michael Ashley Stein, Harvard Law School, Massachusetts; Faraaz Mahomed, Wits University; Vikram Patel, Harvard Medical School; Charlene Sunkel, Global Mental Health Peer Network.
DESCRIPTION: Cambridge, United Kingdom ; New York, NY : Cambridge University Press, 2021. | Includes bibliographical references.
IDENTIFIERS: LCCN 2021010113 (print) | LCCN 2021010114 (ebook) | ISBN 9781108838856 (hardback) | ISBN 9781108972451 (paperback) | ISBN 9781108979016 (ebook)
SUBJECTS: LCSH: Mental health laws. | Mental health policy. | Convention on the Rights of Persons with Disabilities and Optional Protocol (2007 March 30)
CLASSIFICATION: LCC K3608 .M468 2021 (print) | LCC K3608 (ebook) | DDC 346.01/30874–dc23
LC record available at https://lccn.loc.gov/2021010113
LC ebook record available at https://lccn.loc.gov/2021010114

ISBN   978-1-108-83885-6   Hardback
ISBN   978-1-108-97245-1   Paperback

Cambridge University Press & Assessment has no responsibility for the persistence or accuracy of URLs for external or third-party internet websites referred to in this publication and does not guarantee that any content on such websites is, or will remain, accurate or appropriate.

Contents

List of Figures		page viii
List of Tables		ix
List of Boxes		x
List of Contributors		xi
Preface		xxxi
Foreword by António Guterres, The Secretary-General, United Nations		xxxvii
	Introduction: A "Paradigm Shift" in Mental Health Care *Faraaz Mahomed, Michael Ashley Stein, Vikram Patel, and Charlene Sunkel*	1
1	The Alchemy of Agency: Reflections on Supported Decision-Making, the Right to Health and Health Systems as Democratic Institutions *Alicia Ely Yamin*	17
2	Redefining International Mental Health Care in the Wake of the COVID-19 Pandemic *Benjamin A. Barsky, Julie Hannah, and Dainius Pūras*	29
3	Reparation for Psychiatric Violence: A Call to Justice *Tina Minkowitz*	44
4	Divergent Human Rights Approaches to Capacity and Consent *Gerald L. Neuman*	56
5	From Pipe Dream to Reality: A Practical Legal Approach Towards the Global Abolition of Psychiatric Coercion *Laura Davidson*	70

6	The 'Fusion Law' Proposals and the CRPD *John Dawson and George Szmukler*	95
7	Contextualising Legal Capacity and Supported Decision Making in the Global South: Experiences of Homeless Women with Mental Health Issues from Chennai, India *Mrinalini Ravi, Barbara Regeer, Archana Padmakar, Vandana Gopikumar, and Joske Bunders*	109
8	The Potential of the Legal Capacity Law Reform in Peru to Transform Mental Health Provision *Alberto Vásquez Encalada*	124
9	Advancing Disability Equality Through Supported Decision Making: The CRPD and the Canadian Constitution *Faisal Bhabha*	140
10	Decisional Autonomy and India's Mental Healthcare Act, 2017: A Comment on Emerging Jurisprudence *Soumitra Pathare and Arjun Kapoor*	155
11	Towards Resolving Damaging Uncertainties: Progress in the United Kingdom and Elsewhere *Adrian D. Ward*	171
12	'The Revolution Will Not Be Televised': Recent Developments in Mental Health Law Reform in Zambia and Ghana *Heléne Combrinck and Enoch Chilemba*	184
13	Supported Decision-Making and Legal Capacity in Kenya *Elizabeth Kamundia and Ilze Grobbelaar-du Plessis*	199
14	Seher's "Circle of Care" Model in Advancing Supported Decision Making in India *Bhargavi V. Davar, Kavita Pillai, and Kimberly LaCroix*	213
15	The Swedish Personal Ombudsman: Support in Decision-Making and Accessing Human Rights *Ulrika Järkestig Berggren*	230
16	Strategies to Achieve a Rights-Based Approach through WHO Quality Rights *Michelle Funk, Natalie Drew Bold, Joana Ansong, Daniel Chisholm, Melita Murko, Joyce Nato, Sally-Ann Ohene, Jasmine Vergara and Edwina Zoghbi*	244

17	The Clubhouse Model: A Framework for Naturally Occurring Supported Decision Making *Joel D. Corcoran, Cindy Hamersma, and Steven Manning*	260
18	Mind the Gap: Researching 'Alternatives to Coercion' in Mental Health Care *Piers Gooding*	273
19	Psychiatric Advance Directives and Supported Decision-Making: Preliminary Developments and Pilot Studies in California *Christopher Schneiders, Elyn R. Saks, Jonathan Martinis, and Peter Blanck*	288
20	Community-Based Mental Health Care Delivery with Partners In Health: A Framework for Putting the CRPD into Practice *Stephanie L. Smith*	302
21	Lived Experience Perspectives from Australia, Canada, Kenya, Cameroon and South Africa – Conceptualising the Realities *Charlene Sunkel, Andrew Turtle, Sylvio A. Gravel, Iregi Mwenja and Marie Angele Abanga*	316
22	In the Pursuit of Justice: Advocacy by and for Hyper-marginalized People with Psychosocial Disabilities through the Law and Beyond *Lydia X. Z. Brown and Shain M. Neumeier*	332
23	The Danish Experience of Transforming Decision-Making Models *Dorrit Cato Christensen*	349
24	The Use of Patient Advocates in Supporting People with Psychosocial Disabilities *Aikaterini Nomidou*	364
25	Users' Involvement in Decision-Making: Lessons from Primary Research in India and Japan *Kanna Sugiura*	378
26	Involvement of People with Lived Experience of Mental Health Conditions in Decision-Making to Improve Care in Rural Ethiopia *Sally Souraya, Sisay Abyaneh, Charlotte Hanlon, and Laura Asher*	396

Figures

2.1	Risk and protective factors for mental health promotion	page 40
5.1	Key provisions to ensure legal compliance with Article 12 CPRD	89
5.2	Study of the impact of various organised and informal peer support practices on the exercise of legal capacity and the reduction of coercive practices	90
10.1	Elements of decisional capacity	156
10.2	Presumption of decisional capacity	160
10.3	Decisional capacity and right to health	166
14.1	The Mental Health Spectrum	218
14.2	The Eight-point Framework	219
14.3	What is the Eight-Point Framework?	220
14.4	Circle of Care	221
14.5	Circles of Support	224
20.1	Partners In Health mental health service delivery planning matrix to achieve universal health coverage	307
23.1	Police actions against the mentally ill, Denmark	358
23.2	Forced admissions, Denmark, 2009–16	360
25.1	The world view of a service user	380

Tables

7.1	Procedures for CTIs (Adapted from The Banyan's structure and process document)	*page* 119
8.1	Support in the Peruvian legal system	129
15.1	POs: four modes of action	236
16.1	WHO QualityRights training materials	248
16.2	QualityRights e-training questionnaire	250
25.1	Criteria for psychiatry admission and frequency	382
25.2	Included service users	385
26.1	Research studies on service user involvement in rural Ethiopia	399

Boxes

23.1 Danish Legislation   page 356
26.1 Rehabilitation Intervention for people with Schizophrenia
     in Ethiopia (RISE) project   401

Contributors

Marie Abanga is a woman, mother, author, and lawyer. She is a person with a lived experience of a mental illness; she is the Global Mental Health Peer Network Country Executive for Cameroon, and was recently elected as the first regional representative for Africa. Marie is the founder of the association Hope for the Abused and Battered in Cameroon, and is a certified cognitive behavioral therapist with a budding private practice. She can be contacted at www.marieabanga.com or www.hope4abusedbattered.com.

Sisay Abayneh is a lecturer at the College of Education and Behavioral Studies at Madda Walabu University in Ethiopia and a PhD student in mental health epidemiology at Addis Ababa University. His PhD focuses on developing mental health service user and caregiver involvement in mental health system strengthening (policy making, planning, service development and delivery, service evaluation and improvement, advocacy, mental health research, and education) in Ethiopia. Sisay has a BA in psychology and in development management and an MA in educational psychology. He is also currently pursuing another degree in social work.

Joana Ansong is the National Professional Officer for Health Promotion in the WHO Ghana Country Office. She is responsible for noncommunicable diseases risk factors/mental health as well as social determinants of health. She provides support for programs such as immunizations, epidemic-prone diseases, the Urban Health Initiative, and maternal and child health, among others. She also provides technical and programmatic support to the Ministry of Health, multi-sectoral national stakeholders, UN agencies and other development partners in planning, policy and guideline development and program implementation.

Laura Asher is a clinical associate professor in Public Health at the University of Nottingham and Honorary Consultant in Public Health Medicine at Public Health England. Dr. Asher's main area of research is the design and evaluation of complex interventions for people with psychosis in low- and middle-income countries. She was principal investigator of the Rehabilitation Intervention for People with Schizophrenia in Ethiopia (RISE) cluster randomized trial. Dr. Asher is a principal investigator for the Psychosocial Rehabilitation through Peer Support for People with Schizophrenia in South Africa (PRIZE) pilot trial and is also coinvestigator in the National Institute for Health Research (NIHR) global health research group on the development and piloting of packages of care for the mental health of survivors of violence in South Asia. Dr. Asher also has an interest in mental health and human rights. She has conducted qualitative work on the physical restraint of people with mental illness, involvement in decision-making about care, collaboration between biomedical and traditional mental healthcare providers, and experiences of recovery.

The Banyan Authors – Chapter 7 is authored by five human service professionals from The Banyan. All five of us are engaged with mental health systems in one way or the other as mental health professionals, peer leaders, policy level contributors, researchers, and social entrepreneurs.

Benjamin A. Barsky is a PhD student in health policy at Harvard University, He is also a Legal Research Fellow at the Scattergood Program for Applied Ethics of Behavioral Health Care at the University of Pennsylvania. Ben researches in the areas of health law and justice, mental health policy, and disability rights. He is currently working on a project that explores how law and policy can offer solutions to the systematic mistreatment of people with mental health conditions involved in the criminal justice system. Before pursuing his doctoral studies, Ben served as a judicial law clerk for a federal judge in Memphis, Tennessee, and occupied various positions in law and mental health policy.

Faisal Bhabha is an associate professor at Osgoode Hall Law School in Toronto, Canada. He also serves as the Faculty Director of the Canadian Common Law LLM degree program. He has researched and published in the areas of constitutional law, multiculturalism, law and religion, disability rights, national security, and access to justice. He teaches constitutional law, human rights, legal ethics, and appellate advocacy. Previously, he sat as Vice-chair of the Human Rights Tribunal of Ontario (2008–11). He maintains a varied public and private law practice, appearing before administrative boards and tribunals and at all levels of court, including the Supreme Court of Canada. He advises and represents a variety of individuals and public interest organizations in matters pertaining to constitutional law and human rights. He has appeared as an expert witness before Canadian parliamentary committees and served as a member of the Equity Advisory Group of the Law Society of Ontario. He has lived and worked in the Middle East and South Africa, and has lectured and taught in many countries.

Peter Blanck, University Professor and Chairman, and **Jonathan G. Martinis**, Legal Director, are affiliated with the Burton Blatt Institute at Syracuse University in Syracuse, New York. **Elyn R. Saks**, Distinguished Professor of Law and Founder and Faculty Director, and **Christopher Schneiders**, Director, are affiliated with the Gould School of Law, Saks Institute for Mental Health Law, Policy, and Ethics, at the University of Southern California in Los Angeles.

Natalie Drew Bold, who holds a master's in human rights from the School of Advanced Study, University of London, is the Technical Officer within the WHO Policy, Law and Human Rights team. As part of her work she supports countries to reform national policies, plans and laws and services in line with international human rights standards. In addition, she works closely with government and civil society actors in countries in the implementation of WHO QualityRights. She oversees several WHO online platforms including the WHO QualityRights country implementation portal, the WHO QualityRights e-training platform and the WHO MiNDbank online database. Natalie is also the WHO's mental health and human rights focal point.

Lydia X. Z. Brown is an advocate, organizer, attorney, strategist, and writer whose work focuses on interpersonal and state violence against disabled people at the intersections of race, class, gender, sexuality, faith, language, and nation. They are Policy Counsel for Privacy & Data at the Center for Democracy & Technology, focused on algorithmic discrimination and disability, as well as Director of Policy, Advocacy, & External Affairs at the Autistic Women & Nonbinary Network. Lydia is also adjunct lecturer and core faculty in Georgetown's Disability Studies Program, and adjunct professorial lecturer in American University's Department of Critical Race, Gender, and Culture Studies. They serve as a commissioner on the American Bar Association's Commission on Disability Rights, chairperson of the ABA Civil Rights & Social Justice Section's Disability Rights Committee, board member of the Disability Rights Bar Association, and representative for the Disability Justice Committee to the National Lawyers Guild's National Executive Committee. Lydia founded the Fund for Community Reparations for Autistic People of Color's Interdependence, Survival, and Empowerment, and they are creating Disability Justice Wisdom Tarot. Previously, they served as Chairperson of the Massachusetts Developmental Disabilities Council, Visiting Lecturer at Tufts University, and Justice Catalyst Legal Fellow at the Bazelon Center for Mental Health Law. They have received numerous awards for their work, including from the White House, American Association of People with Disabilities, and Society for Disability Studies, and written for several community and academic publications. Often, their most important work has no title, job description, or funding, and probably never will.

Joske Bunders is Professor Emeritus of biology and society, Vrije Universiteit Amsterdam, and Chair Professor of transdisciplinary studies in sustainable development, Faculty of SIPC, MIT-WPU, Pune. She was the founder and director of the

Athena Institute for research on innovation and communication in the health and life sciences, Faculty of Science, Vrije Universiteit Amsterdam. Her specific field of interest is the linking of the knowledge and expertise of end users (e.g. small-scale farmers or patients) with developments in modern science and (inter)national policy. Dr. Bunders has published widely on the role of users in shaping the innovation process. In particular, she has conducted research on methodology development to stimulate and facilitate interactive and transdisciplinary processes of problem solving in which various stakeholders engage in a deliberative mutual search and learning process. Much of her research is focused on low- and middle-income countries, such as India, Bangladesh, South Africa, Tanzania, Indonesia, Vietnam, and Kenya.

Daniel Chisholm is Programme Manager for Mental Health at the WHO Regional Office for Europe (based in Copenhagen, Denmark). He works with WHO Member States and other partners to develop and implement national mental health policies and plans, as well as provide guidance, tools, and advocacy for the promotion of mental health and the development of prevention, treatment, and recovery services across the life-course. He was formerly a health systems adviser in the Department of Mental Health and Substance Abuse at the WHO Headquarters Office in Geneva, Switzerland.

Enoch M. Chilemba holds a bachelor of laws (honours) degree, master of laws degree, and doctor of law degree. He is Deputy Dean, Coordinator of Disability Rights Clinic, and Senior Lecturer in human rights, disability rights, and international law at the University of Malawi, Faculty of Law. He has previously worked as Senior State Advocate in Malawi, and also served as a researcher at the Dullar Omar Institute and the Centre of Disability Law and Policy at the University of the Western Cape. He is involved in teaching, research, and consultancy in human rights, disability rights, and international law.

Dorrit Cato Christensen worked as a pediatrician for ten years, then as teacher of Danish as a foreign language at a school for refugees and the Danish Center for Torture Victims. In 1972 she gave birth to her lovely daughter Luise, who would be in the psychiatric treatment system for twelve years. Ms. Christensen participated in all sorts of forums around Luise's treatment. For many years she was a member of the municipal psychiatric forum in Copenhagen, representing as a relative of a mentally ill person. She set up relatives' groups – for example, at Luise's different residential centers. All that stopped when Luise sadly died in 2005. A few years after Luise's death she started an association called Dead in Psychiatric Care (DiP), where she was chair. Her presidency lasted until she stepped down in November 2020. As chair, she was a member of three different public associations on psychiatry. In 2017 DiP became a member of Mental Health Europe (MHE) (Ms. Christensen is now an individual member of MHE). Over her ten years as chair of DiP, Ms. Christensen was consulted by countless desperate users of psychiatry and their relatives about poor treatment in psychiatry. As a result, she has been involved in many sad cases. In 2011 her book *Dear Luise – A Story of Power and Powerlessness in Denmark's Psychiatric Care System* was published. She wrote the book to tell the world about how bad treatment in psychiatry can be for a large group of people with mental health issues. The book has been translated into English.

Heléne Combrinck is an associate professor at the Faculty of Law, North-West University, South Africa. She previously worked as a senior researcher at the Centre for Disability Law and Policy, University of the Western Cape, Cape Town. Her publications focus on disability rights as well as gender equality. She has been a coeditor of the *African Disability Rights Yearbook* since its launch in 2013. Current research interests include the rights of persons with psychosocial disabilities and the development of disability rights in Africa.

Joel D. Corcoran has been Executive Director of Clubhouse International since 1997. Prior to that he worked in various positions in the field of mental health since 1981. Clubhouse International is an organization working to end social and economic exclusion for people with mental illness. The Clubhouse model provides pathways to meaningful social inclusion, work, and wellbeing. Clubhouses are voluntary and empowering organizations where individual choice and multiple opportunities to succeed are the standard. The model has gained international recognition, scaling to more than 300 Clubhouses in thirty countries. In 2014 Clubhouse International and its partner Fountain House were recognized as an exemplary organization working to "alleviate human suffering" with the Conrad N. Hilton Humanitarian Prize. Joel is a passionate champion for the rights of people living with mental illness, and the importance of their involvement in the design of services and systems that support dignity, opportunity, and recovery.

Bhargavi Davar has survived childhood exposure to mental asylums and enduring trauma for more than three decades. She has worked extensively in the area of nonmedical healing and advocacy since 1993. Her publications include *Psychoanalysis as a Human Science* (1995); *Mental Health of Indian Women* (1999); *Gender from a Mental Health Perspective* (2001); and *Gendering Mental Health: Knowledges, Identities, Institutions* (with Sundari Ravindran, 2015). She founded the Bapu Trust in 1999, which has been in the forefront of service innovations, training, and advocacy in the Asia Pacific region. She is an arts-based therapist and teacher.

Laura Davidson is a London human rights Barrister and a noted authority on mental health, capacity and disability law. She is also an international development consultant, providing advice to the United Nations, governments and NGOs. In 2013 she worked as a consultant for the Government of Rwanda and drafted the country's first mental health law. She has advised the UN in Timor-Leste and in Zimbabwe on international legal requirements under the Convention on the Rights of Persons with Disabilities. Dr. Davidson also has an interest in gender justice and women's empowerment, and is currently a consultant for UN Women analysing Uganda's international legal compliance with its gender equality commitments. In addition, she works as an independent researcher, and has published peer-reviewed research on trauma services in East Africa. In 2008 Dr. Davidson co-founded the UK's first charity dedicated to funding research into the causes of mental illness in order to develop better treatments with fewer side-effects (Mental Health Research UK), of which she remains a Trustee.

John Dawson is a professor of law at the University of Otago, New Zealand. Since the 1980s, he has published extensively on law governing outpatient commitment, privacy of health information, and health research. He was a member of the OCTET team that conducted a randomized controlled trial of the English outpatient commitment scheme. With George Szmukler, he has proposed the 'fusion' of mental health and adult guardianship legislation. He has engaged extensively in evaluation research and consults to law reform bodies. He is a barrister and solicitor and member of the NZ Law Society.

Michelle Funk holds a master's degree in clinical psychology from the University of New South Wales and a postdoctoral degree in public health from the University of Sydney, Australia. She is the Unit Head of the WHO Policy, Law and Human Rights team. She is responsible for cross-cutting work related to policy, planning, service development, human rights and legislation across the mental health, brain health and substance use units of the Department of Mental Health and Substance Use. She leads the WHO QualityRights Initiative, which builds capacity of stakeholders to understand and promote human rights and recovery approaches, and supports countries to develop services, policies, and laws in line with international human rights standards.

Piers Gooding is a research fellow at the University of Melbourne Law School, where he focuses on the law and politics of mental health and disability. He is the author of *A New Era for Mental Health Law and Policy: Supported Decision-Making and the UN Convention on the Rights of Persons with Disabilities* (Cambridge University Press, 2017) and is an editorial associate of the *International Journal for Mental Health and Capacity Law*. Dr. Gooding completed postdoctoral research at the Centre for Disability Law and Policy at the National University of Ireland, Galway. He has collaborated with the UN Special Rapporteur for the Rights of People with Disabilities, the UN Special Rapporteur on the right to physical and mental health, the UN Economic and Social Commission for Asia and the Pacific, and the World Psychiatric Association.

Vandana Gopikumar has worked extensively with homeless and poor persons with severe mental illness for three decades. She cofounded The Banyan and The Banyan Academy of Leadership in Mental Health, which have serviced over 3,000 homeless individuals and a million low-income households, including those from indigenous communities. Models developed at The Banyan are located within a social justice framework and are therefore collaborative and informed significantly by the wisdom of experiential experts. She uses case studies, ethnographies, and oral histories to better understand mental ill health attributions, identity, "social withdrawal," "recovery" and hope. She is passionate about promoting peer-led care, leadership, advocacy and research.

Staff Sergeant (ret'd.) Sylvio (Syd) A. Gravel, MOM, is a former police officer, having served thirty-one years. In 2007 the Governor General of Canada inducted him as a member of the Order of Merit in Policing, and he was awarded the Order of Ottawa in 2020. He has authored the books *56 Seconds* and *How to Survive PTSD and Build Peer Support*, and co-authored *Walk the Talk*. Syd co-leads the Peer and Trauma Support Systems Team for the Mood Disorders Society of Canada, is an advisor to Badge of Life Canada and a representative for the Global Mental Health Peer Network.

Ilze Grobbelaar-du Plessis is an Associate Professor in the Department of Public Law, Faculty of Law from the University of Pretoria. She lectures Constitutional Law for the LLB undergraduate students, and the multi-disciplinary LLM / MPhil (Disability Rights in Africa) in collaboration with the Centre of Human Rights for the post graduate students. She also co-lectures Constitutional Law for the LLM (Advanced Constitutional Law) and is a guest lecturer in the MPhil (Medical Law and Ethics) in the module Medico-legal issues on the analysis of disability rights in an international and domestic context. Prof Grobbelaar-du Plessis also lectures in the Advanced Human Rights Course on Disability Rights in an African Context at the Centre of Human Rights at the University of Pretoria, was the co-editor of Aspects of Disability Law in Africa (PULP, 2011) with the late T. P. van Reenen and was a co-editor of the African Disability Rights.

Cindy Hamersma is an expert by experience in mental healthcare. She's a member, board member and coach in two different clubhouses in the Netherlands. In 2019 she became a faculty member of Clubhouse International, working on a global scale to improve mental health care. Besides textbook knowledge, she brings to the table her own experience, to support and coach others who find themselves in situations similar to the one she faced several years back. Therefore, multiple organizations, including local government, are using her knowledge to gather information aiming to improve different aspects of policy and treatment of mental health issues.

Charlotte Hanlon is a reader in global mental health and co-director of the WHO Collaborating Centre for Mental Health Research and Training, IoPPN, at King's College London and an adjunct associate professor at the Department of Psychiatry, Addis Ababa University (AAU) in Ethiopia, where she lives. The main focus of Dr. Hanlon's work is on service interventions, implementation research and systems strengthening to support increased access to mental health care in low- and middle-income countries, particularly for people with severe mental conditions. Ensuring involvement of people with lived experience and local communities is a key part of her work.

Julie Hannah is a lecturer in law at the University of Essex, where she is also a member of the Human Rights Centre. Since 2014, she has served as the Director of the International Centre on Human Rights and Drug Policy, a leading center of research on the subject. She previously served as Senior Advisor to the former UN Special Rapporteur on the right to health. Her current research focuses on the right to mental health, structural transformation and human rights, the intersection of medicalization and criminalization with human rights, and international drug policy.

Ulrika Järkestig Berggren currently holds the position of Associate Professor in the Department of Social Work at Linnaeus University, Sweden. She is an experienced clinical social worker with special training in the field of disability. She works with nongovernmental organizations and disabled people's organizations in Sweden on issues of welfare services. In her previous capacity as Coordinator of Research at the Swedish Family Care Competence Centre, she consulted the government on issues of welfare support for children and their families living with disabilities. In this capacity she also founded the national research network "Children as Next of Kin" in Sweden and coedited an anthology written by the scholars of the research network for students and professionals. Her research, published in leading journals, focuses on services for persons with disabilities and children. She has received funding from national grants on disability support for families and on the organization of child support.

Elizabeth Kamundia works as an assistant director in the Research, Advocacy and Outreach Directorate at the Kenya National Commission on Human Rights and leads the Commission's work on rights of persons with disabilities. She holds an LLD from the Faculty of Law, University of Pretoria (2019). Her thesis is entitled "Supported decision-making as a human rights principle in mental health care: An international and comparative analysis". She holds an LLM in international and comparative disability law and policy from the Centre for Disability Law and Policy National University of Ireland, Galway (NUI Galway). Elizabeth has worked as a disability rights consultant with users and survivors of psychiatry in Kenya. In this role, she led research on the link between peer support and the exercise of legal capacity by persons with psychosocial disabilities in the Kenyan context. In addition to a research background, Elizabeth also approaches mental health from the perspective of a family member. Elizabeth has worked at the Centre for Disability Law and Policy, NUI Galway (Legal Researcher) and the Centre for Human Rights, University of Pretoria (Disability Rights and Law Schools Project Coordinator). She has also worked at the Commission on the Implementation of the Constitution of Kenya (Consultant on Disability) and the Committee of Experts on Constitutional Review, Kenya (Legal Researcher). Elizabeth is an advocate of the High Court of Kenya.

Arjun Kapoor is a Research Fellow at the Centre for Mental Health Law & Policy at the Indian Law Society, Pune, India. He holds a bachelor's degree in law from NALSAR University of Law, Hyderabad and a master's degree in psychology (psycho-social clinical studies) from Ambedkar University, Delhi. Previously, he was appointed as Law Clerk to the Supreme Court of India and assisted the Court in matters of constitutional law and public law. Subsequently, he worked with community lawyers and paralegals in Gujarat, India to develop socio-legal interventions on access to justice and socio-economic rights. At the Centre, he co-leads various projects on law, policy, and services reform for mental health and youth suicide prevention. He provides technical support and leads capacity initiatives for a range of stakeholders on implementation of the Mental Healthcare Act, 2017 and National Mental Health Policy, 2014 using rights-based approaches. He also works with various stakeholders in India's mental health system to build a repository of data and information on mental health laws, policies, and services to promote evidence-based policy making for mental health and suicide prevention.

Kimberly Lacroix has been leading the Seher Community Mental Health and Inclusion Program for the last three years. Having trained in psychoanalytic psychotherapy and clinical thinking, she engages with the question of community mental health from an intersectional and social justice perspective. Her research is informed by both practice and thinking about practices in mental health from a critical feminist and, more recently, disability rights perspective. Through her work under the Seher program she has been engaging in questions about disabilities and cross-disability research and advocacy.

Faraaz Mahomed is a clinical psychologist and public health scholar working in the field of mental health and human rights. He received an MA in clinical psychology from the University of the Witwatersrand, Johannesburg, South Africa and an MA in international policy from the Middlebury Institute of International Studies in Monterey, California as a Fulbright Scholar. He received a Doctor of Public Health degree from the Harvard School of Public Health, is a research associate at the Harvard Law School Project on Disability and the FXB Center for Health and Human Rights at Harvard, and a visiting research fellow at the Center for Applied Legal Studies at the University of the Witwatersrand. He has worked as a researcher with the Office of the UN Special Rapporteur on the Right to Health and as a research consultant on financing for rights-based approaches to mental health in the Global South with the Open Society Foundations. He previously held the positions of Senior Researcher for Equality at the South African Human Rights Commission and Clinical Psychologist in community health settings in Johannesburg and Cape Town, South Africa, and currently holds the position of Program Officer in Mental Health and Rights at the Open Society Foundations.

Steven Manning is a Fort Wayne, Indiana native who has been a member of the Carriage House Clubhouse in Fort Wayne since 2002. Prior to joining the clubhouse, he was hospitalized several times. He went through a stint of homelessness, and there were about four suicide attempts. After becoming involved regularly at Carriage House, Mr. Manning experienced a wonderful transformation; in about ten years he was able to complete his master's degree in secondary education. He also started a video production company, a business venture that continues to grow and improve. Steven's love for performance on stage and screen has resulted in him receiving roles in feature-length movies. His most recent film, entitled *I Only Want You*, is currently in production in southern Indiana. Steven will play the role of Sheriff Hap Jenkins in this intense drama. It will be his fourth movie and largest role so far. Steven says, "without my faith and without the love and support from members and staff at the Carriage House, there's absolutely no way I would be living such a wonderful life. It will be my life's work to be an advocate for men, women, and children, who suffer from severe and persistent mental illness; helping them experience all the love, support, and opportunities that they deserve to have."

Jonathan Martinis is the Senior Director for Law and Policy for the Burton Blatt Institute at Syracuse University, leading its efforts to ensure that older adults and people with disabilities have access to the services and support they need to lead independent, inclusive lives.

Tina Minkowitz is a lawyer based in the United States who works on the international human rights of persons with disabilities, focusing on the rights of persons with psychosocial disabilities and the universal right to legal capacity. She contributed significantly to the drafting of the Convention on the Rights of Persons with Disabilities, in particular to Articles 12 and 14, among others, and was among the leaders of the International Disability Caucus. Ms. Minkowitz participates in the global movement of users and survivors of psychiatry and persons with psychosocial disabilities, and represented the World Network of Users and Survivors of Psychiatry in the CRPD drafting process and in other UN processes for some years afterwards. In 2009 she founded the Center for the Human Rights of Users and Survivors of Psychiatry, which she still serves in the capacity of President. She regularly contributes to the work of the Committee on the Rights of Persons with Disabilities and other UN human rights mechanisms, and has contributed to the work of the OAS on legal capacity and support measures. She maintains contact with networks in all parts of the world and provides advice and support to disabled people's organizations in their work of implementing and monitoring the Convention. She received an LLM in Public International Law from the University of Oslo, and has written numerous articles, blog posts, and advocacy papers related to legal capacity and related issues.

Melita Murko is a psychologist from Bosnia and Herzegovina with over twenty years of experience in the field of mental health at the national, regional and international level. Two largest projects she worked on in the past were the Mental Health Project for south-eastern Europe, implemented under the Stability Pact's Social Cohesion Initiative from 2002 to 2008, and the WHO European Declaration *Better health, better lives: children and young people with intellectual disabilities and their families*, endorsed by the Regional Committee in Azerbaijan in 2011. Since June 2016 Melita has been working for the WHO Regional Office for Europe as a technical officer with the Mental Health Programme.

Iregi Mwenja is a mental health advocate with childhood lived experience. He grew up in rural Kenya where he faced the social challenges of growing up with undiagnosed ADHD. He received his diagnosis as an adult, a revelation that became a turning point in his life. Though an accomplished wildlife biologist, he left a well-paid job as a country director of an international NGO to establish a mental health nonprofit: Psychiatric Disability Organization (PDO). PDO works to foster mental healthcare for the socially disadvantaged in Kenya. Through PDO, thousands of Kenyans have received affordable mental healthcare and the much-needed social support.

Joyce Nato obtained her MD degree from the University of Nairobi (Kenya) and an MMeD (Psych) from the University of Nairobi (Kenya). She worked with the Ministry of Health at all levels, including national level, where she was head of the division of noncommunicable diseases (NCDs). She later joined the WHO Country Office as the National Professional Office (NPO) in charge of prevention and control of NCDs, mental health, disability, tobacco control, and violence and injury prevention. In 2006, she held brief for the Regional Advisor on Tobacco Control for a period of seven months (April to October 2006) in Brazzaville, Congo. She has supported the government to prioritize NCDs. Some of the achievements include ratification, domestication and implementation of the WHO Framework Convention on Tobacco Control. Documents in place include the National NCDs Prevention and Control Strategy, Mental Health Policy, Injury and Violence Prevention Strategy, Cancer Control Strategy and Cancer Treatment Guidelines, and the Physical Activity Action Plan. She's a member of the recently launched Mental Health Task Force to look into issues of mental health in the country following a presidential directive.

Shain Neumeier is a lawyer, activist, and community organizer, as well as an out-and-proud member of the disabled, trans, queer, and asexual communities. Their passion on the issue of ending abuse and neglect of youth with disabilities in schools and treatment facilities stems from their own experiences with involuntary medical treatment and bullying, and led them to go to law school. They have pursued their goal of using legal advocacy to address these problems ever since. Currently, Shain is a Trial Attorney in the Commitment Defense Unit of Massachusetts' Committee for Public Counsel Services' Mental Health Litigation Division. Shain previously worked with the Intersex & Genderqueer Recognition Project, the Autistic Women & Nonbinary Network, and the Community Alliance for the Ethical Treatment of Youth. They have volunteered with the Southern Immigrant Freedom Initiative, the People's Parity Project, and Capital Area Against Mass Incarceration. As a solo practitioner in Massachusetts, they specialized in defending disabled people against involuntary commitment and guardianship, and earlier worked on a series of cases against an abusive residential treatment facility in Oregon. Shain's writing appears in *Autistic Activism and the Neurodiversity Movement: Stories from the Frontlines, Resistance and Hope: Essays by Disabled People: Crip Wisdom for the People, Rewire News*, and *Loud Hands: Autistic People, Speaking*. Their work has been featured by the New England Center for Investigative Reporting, *American Bar Association Journal, Pacific Standard, The Nation*, WGBH, and MassLive. Among other honors, they were named the Massachusetts Bar Association's Outstanding Young Lawyer in 2018, the Self Advocacy Association of New York State's Self Advocate of the Year in 2017, and the Association of University Centers on Disabilities' Leadership in Advocacy Awardee in 2015. When not working, they're probably crafting, playing Dungeons & Dragons, listening to history podcasts, or watching Netflix with their partner and three feline roommates.

Gerald L. Neuman is the J. Sinclair Armstrong Professor of International, Foreign, and Comparative Law at Harvard Law School, and Director of its Human Rights Program. He teaches human rights, constitutional law, and immigration and nationality law. From 2011 to 2014, he was a member of the Human Rights Committee, the treaty body that monitors compliance with the International Covenant on Civil and Political Rights. He served previously on the faculty of Columbia Law School (1992–2006), and the University of Pennsylvania Law School (1984–1992). He is a member of the American Academy of Arts and Sciences.

Aikaterini Nomidou – Being an active carer to her brother who lives with schizophrenia and seeing the problems faced by families trying to cope with mental illness consequences – and the unfairness of the situations service users find themselves in – prompted Aikaterini to become actively involved in the mental health issues that affect vulnerable people and society as a whole. Following a degree in Italian language and literature at Aristotle University and a degree in law at Democritus University of Thrace, she received a postgraduate degree in mental health, law and human rights from the Indian Law Society. Her area of passion and expertise includes the use of the WHO QualityRights toolkit and package of training and guidance modules to assess quality and human rights in mental health and social care facilities, and to build capacity among key stakeholders. Aikaterini is a practicing lawyer; WHO PFPS Champion for Greece; Secretary General of the Global Alliance of Mental Illness Advocacy Networks, GAMIAN-Europe; President of the Greek Federation of Associations/Organizations for Mental Health, POSOPSI; Vice-president of the Association for Mental Health and Alzheimer's disease, SOFPSI N.SERRON; and a visiting lecturer in compassionate care and course coordinator in health law at the Faculty of Medicine, University of Crete. She serves on the Mental Health Committee of the Greek Central Board of Health and the Permanent Mental Health Committee for monitoring the implementation of Greece's mental health strategic and operational plan, and is a member of EC Chafea and the Innovative Medicines Initiative (IMI) pool of patient experts. Aikaterini has worked with governments and organizations on mental health policies and legislation, including in Afghanistan, Qatar, United Arab Emirates, and Sierra Leone, and was a Fulbright scholar and fellow at the Salzburg Global Seminar on Health and Health Care Innovation in the 21st Century, Session 587: "Changing Minds: Innovation in Dementia Care and Dementia-Friendly Communities."

Sally-Ann Ohene is the National Professional Officer for Disease Prevention and Control in the WHO Ghana Country Office. She is responsible for noncommunicable diseases including mental health conditions and epidemic-prone diseases and provides technical and programmatic support to the Ministry of Health, multisectoral national stakeholders, UN agencies and other development partners in planning, policy and guideline development and program implementation.

Archana Padmakar has been a clinical psychologist working in the mental health sector for fifteen years. She has a doctorate from Vrije University, Amsterdam. Her PhD thesis focused on developing a framework for adaptive mental health systems for homeless women with mental health issues. She has completed MPhil in clinical psychology from Kasturba Medical College, Manipal. She has a licensing certification from the Rehabilitation Council of India. She has specialization in treating children, adults, and adolescents, utilizing a wide range of holistic psychological interventions and techniques that can provide every client with an individualized experience. She has experience of working in diverse clinical settings, such as with homeless persons with mental health issues, including in underprivileged communities; in inpatient and outpatient centers; with homeless women with mental health issues; and with support groups comprising caregivers. She also practices low-cost therapy for individuals, couples, and families. She currently heads the Emergency Care and Recovery Centre at The Banyan and its replication model across five districts in Tamil Nadu. Archana's expertise in recovery pathways for people with mental health issues led her to research models of long-term care, continuity of care, and support structures that families would require as part of her PhD. She also works as a teaching faculty in Department of Applied Psychology at Banyan Academy of Leadership in Mental Health, teaching the masters of clinical psychology course.

Vikram Patel is the Pershing Square Professor of Global Health and Wellcome Trust Principal Research Fellow at the Harvard Medical School. He co-leads the GlobalMentalHealth@Harvard initiative. His work has focused on the burden of mental health problems, their association with social disadvantage, and the use of community resources for their prevention and treatment. He is a cofounder of the Movement for Global Mental Health; the Centre for Global Mental Health (at the London School of Hygiene & Tropical Medicine); the Mental Health Innovations Network; and Sangath, an Indian NGO which won the WHO Public Health Champion of India prize. He is a fellow of the UK's Academy of Medical Sciences and has served on the committee which drafted India's first National Mental Health Policy and the WHO High-Level Independent Commission for NCDs. He has been awarded the Chalmers Medal, the Sarnat Prize, the Pardes Humanitarian Prize, an Honorary OBE, and the John Dirk Canada Gairdner Award in Global Health. He was listed in *TIME Magazine*'s 100 most influential persons of the year in 2015.

Soumitra Pathare is a consultant psychiatrist and Director of the Centre for Mental Health Law and Policy at the Indian Law Society, Pune, India. His primary interests are in the areas of mental health policy, scaling up mental health services, rights-based care, and legislation. He was a member of the Mental Health Policy Group appointed by Government of India to draft India's first National Mental Health Policy, released in October 2014. He has provided technical assistance to the Ministry of Health and Family Welfare, Government of India in drafting India's new Mental Health Care Act 2017, which takes a rights-based approach to mental health care and provides for publicly funded universal mental health care. He has served as a WHO consultant in many low- and middle-income countries, assisting in developing mental health policy and drafting and implementing mental health legislation. He was the Principal Investigator of QualityRights Gujarat project (2014–16), which implemented the WHO QualityRights program in six public mental health facilities in Gujarat. He has recently (2013–19) been involved in scaling up Atmiyata across Mehsana district, Gujarat, with a population of 1 million. Atmiyata is a project to improve access to mental health services in rural areas by training and mentoring women leaders of microcredit self-help groups to provide basic psychological interventions and access to social benefits for a defined rural population.

Kavita Pillai is Assistant Director, Training, at Bapu Trust for Research on Mind & Discourse, Pune. Her practice is informed by engagement with Eastern mind traditions, rights-based perspectives, and practices in psychosocial disability. She is a certified arts-based therapy practitioner and educator.

Dainius Puras is Professor of child psychiatry and public mental health at Vilnius University, Lithuania. From 2018 he is also Director of the Human Rights Monitgoring Institute – NGO based in Lithuania. Positions he has held have included President of the Lithuanian Psychiatric Association, Dean of Medical Faculty of Vilnius University, President of the Baltic Association for Rehabilitation, and Chair of the Board of Human Rights Monitoring Institute. From 2007 to 2011 Puras was a member of the UN Committee on the Rights of the Child. From 2014 to 2020, Puras has been a UN Special Rapporteur on the right to physical and mental health. Puras has been actively involved in national and international activities in the field of developing and implementing evidence-based and human rights-based health-related policies and services, with special focus on children, persons with psychosocial and intellectual disabilities, other groups in vulnerable situations, and issues related to promotion of mental health and prevention of all forms of violence. His main interest is the management of change in the field of health-related services regionally and globally, with a main focus on operationalization of a human rights-based approach through effective policies and services.

Mrinalini Ravi is Co-lead for the Sundram Fasteners Centre for Social Action and Research at The Banyan Academy. She holds bachelor's and master's degrees in psychology and mental health services research respectively. She's held several portfolios in the past decade, but holds her five-year stint managing a shelter for homeless men with mental health issues closest to her heart. Much of her learning comes from her clients, who were kind and patient enough to share their journeys with her and helped her to navigate her interests in working with vulnerable populations meaningfully. Her dream is to establish a recovery college and enable more students like her to benefit from peer-led education and research.

Barbara Regeer is Associate Professor of transdisciplinary strategies for sustainable development and system transformation at the Athena Institute for research on innovation and communication in the health and life sciences, Vrije Universiteit Amsterdam. Her research interests are in emerging innovative strategies for (sustainable) development, with a specific focus on the facilitation of multi-stakeholder processes, knowledge co-creation, social change, and mutual learning between all actors involved, in such areas as mental health care, child and youth care, disability mainstreaming, sustainable food systems, and integrated rural development. Besides publications in the mentioned areas in international peer-reviewed journals, she has (co)authored books on approaches to knowledge co-creation for sustainable development. She coordinates, and teaches in, various courses on (transdisciplinary) research methodology, science communication, policy processes and (social) innovation. She is director of the Graduate School for Transdisciplinary PhD Education at the Athena Institute.

Elyn R. Saks is Orrin B. Evans Distinguished Professor of Law, Psychology, and Psychiatry and the Behavioral Sciences at the University of Southern California Gould School of Law; Adjunct Professor of Psychiatry at the University of California, San Diego, School of Medicine; and Faculty at the New Center for Psychoanalysis. Professor Saks received a BA in philosophy from Vanderbilt University, where she graduated first in her class; an MLitt in philosophy from Oxford University, where she was a Marshall Scholar; a JD from Yale Law School, where she was an editor on the *Yale Law Journal* and recipient of the Francis Wayland Prize for her clinical work; and a PhD in psychoanalytic science from the New Center for Psychoanalysis, where she received the Jacques Brien prize. Saks has also received honorary doctorate degrees from Pepperdine University and from the Chicago School of Professional Psychology. Professor Saks teaches law and mental health to law students and psychiatry and psychology fellows at the USC Keck School of Medicine. She writes extensively in the area of law and mental health, having published some sixty articles and book reviews and four scholarly books. She has also published an award-winning memoir describing her life with schizophrenia, called *The Center Cannot Hold: My Journey Through Madness*. She is on a number of mental health boards. And she has been elected to the American Law Institute and she is a winner of a MacArthur Fellowship, also known as "the genius grant."

Christopher Schneiders is the Director of the Saks Institute for Mental Health Law, Policy, and Ethics at USC Gould School of Law. He leads the development, planning, and implementation of the institute's research and activities, including the annual spring symposium and the current supported decision-making research study for people with psychiatric disabilities. He also contributes to the academic efforts of Distinguished Professor Elyn Saks and the Saks Student Scholars. He is a founding member of the USC Alliance for Civic Engagement and serves on Pearson, Inc.'s Corporate Disability Mentoring Advisory Council.

Stephanie L. Smith is the Co-Director of Mental Health at Partners in Health (PIH), an Associate Psychiatrist at Brigham and Women's Hospital (BWH), and an Instructor in Psychiatry at Harvard Medical School (HMS). She also holds affiliations with the Division of Global Health Equity at BWH, and the Department of Global Health and Social Medicine at HMS. In her role at PIH, Dr. Smith provides clinical, programmatic, and research support for mental health integration across all the PIH sites, including Rwanda, Liberia, Lesotho, Malawi, Mexico, Sierra Leone, Peru, and Haiti. Dr. Smith's current research interests focus on evaluating outcomes and impact of task-sharing endeavors for mental health care across the PIH sites. Dr. Smith continues to provide clinical care as a consultation-liaison psychiatrist at the BWH, and actively teaches and mentors trainees at all levels, including psychiatry residents and fellows, medical and other professional students, and other allied health professionals.

Sally Souraya is a senior service development manager at Implemental. She is involved in systems evaluations and capacity-building programs supporting the development and implementation of mental health strategies and services in different countries. Sally's areas of interest are advocacy, rights-based approaches, and models of empowerment and participation of people with lived experience. Her experience includes working as an occupational therapist, Mental health Technical Advisor, CRPD Trainer and Advocacy Consultant with local and international organizations in the Middle East and North Africa (MENA) region and China. Her work focused on empowering people with disabilities, promoting their rights and enhancing their social participation and involvement in their care. She also conducted research on involvement of people with schizophrenia in decision-making relating to their care in Ethiopia. Sally is involved in policy analysis and research on Stigma as part of the INDIGO network. She is also supporting the implementation of the mental health law in Qatar. Sally has an MSc in global mental health from King's College London and the London School of Hygiene and Tropical Medicine, and an international master's in public health from Tsinghua University in China.

Michael Ashley Stein is the Cofounder and Executive Director of the Harvard Law School Project on Disability, and a visiting professor at Harvard Law School since 2005. Considered one of the world's leading experts on disability law and policy, Dr. Stein participated in the drafting of the UN Convention on the Rights of Persons with Disabilities; works with disabled peoples' organizations and nongovernmental organizations around the world; actively consults with governments on their disability laws and policies; advises a number of UN bodies and national human rights institutions; and has brought landmark disability rights litigation globally. Professor Stein has received numerous awards in recognition of his transformative work, including the inaugural Morton E. Ruderman Prize for Inclusion; the inaugural Henry Viscardi Achievement Award; and the ABA Paul G. Hearne Award. His authoritative and pathbreaking scholarship has been published worldwide by leading journals and academic presses, and has been supported by fellowships and awards from the American Council of Learned Societies, the National Endowment for the Humanities, and the National Institute on Disability Rehabilitation and Research, among others. Dr. Stein holds an extraordinary professorship at the University of Pretoria's Centre for Human Rights, is a visiting professor at the Free University of Amsterdam, and teaches at the Harvard Kennedy School of Government. He earned a JD from Harvard Law School (where he became the first known person with a disability to be a member of the *Harvard Law Review*), and a PhD from Cambridge University. Professor Stein previously was Professor (and

Cabell Professor) at William & Mary Law School, taught at New York University and Stanford law schools, and was appointed by President Obama to the United States Holocaust Memorial Council.

Kanna Sugiura has an MD (Tokyo Women's Medical University), MScPH (London School of Hygiene and Tropical Medicine, and PhD (the University of Tokyo). As a psychiatrist and a researcher, she took part in a randomized controlled trial on suicide prevention, quantitative research on physicians' attitudes towards coercion, and qualitative research on involuntary psychiatric admission and supportive decision-making. Her global work was in Fiji, Equatorial Guinea and India, and she also worked at the WHO and the Japanese Ministry of Foreign Affairs, where she developed a toolkit on a rights-based approach to mental health services (WHO MINDbank, QualityRights, and WHO PROmind), drafted Japanese Global Health Policy, and chaired the G7 Progress Report health chapter. She is currently working as a psychiatrist, researcher, and a university lecturer (medical anthropology) in Japan.

Charlene Sunkel is a globally active voice for the rights of people with lived experience of mental health conditions and disorders. She's been working in the field of mental health, advocacy, and human rights since 2003. She authored several papers from a lived experience perspective published in renowned international medical journals. She has written and produced theatre plays and a short feature film on mental disorders to raise public awareness. Ms Sunkel had been involved in the review and drafting of various policies and legislation in South Africa and provided technical assistance to international mental health-related reports and documents. She serves on a number of national and international boards and committees. She is the Principal Coordinator for the Movement for Global Mental Health. Ms Sunkel is the Founder/CEO of the Global Mental Health Peer Network, which was officially launched at the fifth Global Mental Health Summit in 2018. Ms Sunkel was diagnosed with schizophrenia in 1991, which led to her passion and work in mental health advocacy and human rights. She received a number of awards for her work, with the latest award for Outstanding Achievement in Mental Health from the Swiss Foundation and the WHO.

George Szmukler is Emeritus Professor of Psychiatry and Society at the Institute of Psychiatry, Psychology and Neuroscience at King's College London. He was previously a consultant psychiatrist at the Maudsley Hospital (1993–2013), Medical Director of the Maudsley and Bethlem NHS Trust (1997–2001), and Dean of the Institute of Psychiatry, King's College London (2001–2007). He was a visiting professor in the Department of Sociology (BIOS Centre) at the London School of Economics (2005–2014). From 2007 to 2015, he was an associate director of the National Institute for Health Research Mental Health Research Network, with lead responsibility for Patient and Public Involvement. A major aim was to increase the involvement in mental health research of service users and carers as partners in the conduct of research. His key research interests concern mental health law reform, methods of reducing coercion in psychiatric care, and questions posed by risk assessment in mental healthcare.

Andrew Turtle is a mental health consumer, thought leader and advocate. Along with degrees in Chinese medicine and public health, Andrew has designed the successful website known as the Mental Health Navigation Tool and has been on numerous committees on a local, state, and global level. Andrew is currently the chairperson of the Nepean Blue Mountains Primary Health Network (NBMPHN) Consumer and Carer Committee at a local level and the Australian representative on the Global Mental Health Peer Network (GMHPN) on a global level, and works as an intensive support worker with One Door Mental Health at Frangipani House, a drop in centre providing a range of individual and group based activities for people with severe and persistent mental health.

Alberto Vásquez Encalada works as Senior Advisor at the Center for Inclusive Policy (CIP). Previously, he was the Research Coordinator for the Office of the UN Special Rapporteur on the rights of persons with disabilities. He is a Peruvian lawyer and holds a LLM in disability law and policy from the National University of Ireland, Galway. He has worked extensively on disability rights and mental health law at national, regional, and international levels. As the president of the Peruvian NGO Society and Disability, SODIS, he participated in the Peruvian Congress' Special Committee for reviewing the legislation related to the legal capacity of persons with disabilities, and was actively involved in the drafting and advocacy related to the adoption of that milestone reform. He is also a member of the Latin-American Network of Psychosocial Diversity.

Adrian D. Ward is a recognized national and international expert in adult incapacity law. While still practising, he acted in or instructed many leading cases in the field. He has been published in several languages, and his books include the standard texts on adult incapacity law in Scotland. He has been continuously involved in law reform processes. As consultant to the Council of Europe, he completed in 2018 a review of implementation throughout Europe of Council of Europe Recommendation (2009)11 on principles concerning powers of attorney and advance directives for incapacity. His report "Enabling Citizens to Plan for Incapacity," which includes proposals for future action and initiatives at European level, was adopted and accepted, and published by the Council at www.coe.int/en/web/cdcj/activities/powers-attorney-advance-directives-incapacity. Prior to that he was a member of the core research group of the Three Jurisdictions Project, which assessed compliance of the UK jurisdictions with the UN Convention on the Rights of Persons with Disabilities, and made recommendations to UK government bodies. He has addressed the UN Committee on the Rights of Persons with Disabilities at the UN in Geneva and has had ongoing contact with members of the Committee. He is frequently in demand as keynote speaker at major international conferences. He is an expert adviser to the Centre for Mental Health and Capacity Law, Edinburgh Napier University, and a research affiliate with Essex Autonomy Project. He has been founder chairman of NHS Trusts and a Mental Health Association, and has also engaged in service delivery projects overseas. He has been convener of the Mental Health and Disability Committee of the Law Society of Scotland since 1989. His awards include an MBE for services to the mentally handicapped in Scotland; national awards for legal journalism, legal charitable work, and legal scholarship; and the lifetime achievement award at the 2014 Scottish Legal Awards. At the 2017 Law Society AGM he was the first person since 2009 to be made an honorary member of the Law Society of Scotland. He has advised in several countries as Expert Adviser on Mental Health Law and Practice to the WHO, and as Expert in Incapacity Law in projects promoted by European Union. He has assisted and acted as adviser to various projects at home and abroad, including with the Hague Conference on Private International Law and the European Law Institute. He is one of the four principal authors and editors of *The International Protection of Adults* (Oxford University Press), the principal international textbook on its subject. He assisted with the planning and delivery of all Judicial Institute (previously Judicial Studies Committee) courses on adults with incapacity since the Act of 2000 was passed.

Alicia Ely Yamin is currently a Lecturer on Law and Senior Fellow on Global Health and Rights at the Petrie-Flom Center for Health Law Policy, Biotechnology and Bioethics at Harvard Law School and Adjunct Senior Lecturer on Health Policy and Management at the Harvard TH Chan School of Public Health. She devotes much of her time to advocacy as Senior Advisor on Human Rights at the global health justice organization, Partners In Health. Yamin's 25+-year career at the intersection of global health and human rights has bridged academia and activism, as well as law and global health/development. She has lived and worked in Latin America and East Africa for half of her professional life, working with and through local advocacy organizations.

Edwina Zoghbi is a public health professional whose work focuses on matters of mental health and noncommunicable diseases. Edwina has been working at the WHO in Lebanon since 2013. She provides support in the development and implementation of the national mental health strategy, in particular the integration of mental health into primary health care, the Quality Rights project, national awareness campaigns, and various capacity building for health and mental health professionals. Edwina holds a BA in psychology, BS in nutrition, and MPH in public health from the American University of Beirut.

Preface

The aim of this volume is to engage critically with the subjects of legal capacity and human rights for people with psychosocial disabilities, and the closely related subjects of coercion in mental health and supported decision-making. Our book is the culmination of an effort to solicit multiple, diverse, and often varying perspectives on an issue that intersects with numerous academic disciplines, clinical practices, and lived experience perspectives.

Since the adoption of the United Nations Convention on the Rights of Persons with Disabilities (CRPD), a number of academic works have engaged with subjects such as law reform, rights-based clinical practice and supported decision-making in light of the provisions of Article 12 of the CRPD and General Comment 1 on Article 12 issued by the Committee on the Rights of Persons with Disabilities. However, to our knowledge, our use of an interdisciplinary and global approach with engagement of the academy, clinical practitioners, legal scholars, and people with lived experience (with a resultant total of sixty-three authors from twenty-one countries, ten of which are low- and middle-income countries) to engage critically with issues of legal capacity and supported decision-making is unique, and especially so for the divergence of views presented. Such an approach is also necessary because, as the chapters illustrate, the provisions of Article 12 and General Comment 1 have implications for law and policy, for economics, for clinical practice, for community-driven practices, for research, and – most important of all – for rights-based advocacy.

We were especially careful to include – and feel very fortunate to have a pathbreaking section dedicated to – the voices and perspectives of people with psychosocial disabilities and their caregivers. In fact, at least twenty-two authors represented in this volume, including editors, count themselves as people with psychosocial disabilities or as caregivers. Participation is a central tenet of the CRPD, embodied by the principle of "Nothing About Us Without Us," and we hope that we have given due attention to this principle, and centralized it at the core of this volume. Certainly, this work would be not be complete without the lived experiences of individuals with psychosocial disabilities. The book is intended to be critical and dialogical; to simultaneously engage with conceptual thinking as well as practical implementation; to expound on existing research while also recognizing the need to be forward looking. As editors, we have endeavored to help individual chapter authors make their arguments as clearly and strongly as they could, while remaining agnostic as to the content of their contributions. We are grateful to each of the contributors but do not endorse, as editors, any particular view presented.

Our contribution exists in a continuum of efforts that have been undertaken in recent years, heavily influenced by an interdisciplinary workshop held at the Harvard Law School Project on Disability and sponsored by the Weatherhead Center for International Affairs, which was attended by many of the authors represented in the volume's chapters. The workshop was a useful precursor to the work presented here, because it embraced a similar dialogical approach, and sought to build an interdisciplinary and diverse community of thought partners who continue to grapple with the tensions around issues of legal capacity, as is evident in the book, and in the individual and collective work of contributors. As was clear then, this volume makes equally clear: there are no formulaic answers to many of the questions that have arisen in recent years. Even so, it is also abundantly clear that there is no shortage of critical engagement, constructive dialogue and innovation in the field of mental health practice free of all forms of coercion and inclusive of supported decision-making, and this will ultimately be the determinant of progress in a field that is rapidly evolving.

The book begins with an introduction by the coeditors, exploring the many unanswered questions and providing a background for what follows. Thereafter, the volume is divided into four parts. In the first, our contributors have focused on legal and conceptual issues related to universal legal capacity. Alicia Yamin has provided a thoughtful account of the way in which Article 12 interacts with the right to health, recognizing that the two are interdependent and indivisible. Likewise, Benjamin Barsky, Julie Hannah, and Dainius Puras have engaged with the way in which the universal right to legal capacity interacts with broader conceptual and practical reforms in thinking in the mental health field, illustrating the urgency of the need for a shift to noncoercive mental health models in the context of the COVID-19 pandemic. The chapter by Tina Minkowitz illustrates the way in which Article 12 symbolizes a broader recognition of the humanity and dignity of people with psychosocial disabilities, and issues a call for reparations from the psychiatric community.

Of course, there are many perspectives which view the provisions of Article 12 and General Comment 1 in a different light, and we have sought to include those as part of our commitment to dialogue. Examples include the chapter by Gerald Neuman, who suggests that the absolutist approach to legal capacity evident in Article 12 and General Comment 1 is tenuous and not in keeping with other approaches, including the approach of the United Nations Human Rights Council. Laura Davidson, meanwhile, makes a case for 'interim' legislation that would reduce and potentially abolish coercive mental health practices, but which would likely be in tension with General Comment 1's assertion that the right to equal recognition before the law is not subject to progressive realization.

Another counterargument is provided by Szmukler and Dawson, who argue that incapacity is a concept that extends beyond mental health and therefore suggest that laws and policies ought to focus on legislation related to the subject of incapacity on any ground, rather than being the purview of mental health law specifically. Similarly, Mrinalini Ravi and colleagues have argued that the binary between capacity and incapacity and between coercion and non-coercion is an acontextual and an asocial one, suggesting that while autonomy is indeed a fundamental right, it should not be viewed in isolation from the interdependence of people, the ways in which communities and families function, and the ways in which social contexts support or undermine it.

The second section of the book focuses on legal and policy reforms that have sought to domesticate the provisions of the CRPD. Alberto Vasquez shares an exposition of the content of reforms in the civil code in Peru, while also providing a very pragmatic account of barriers to the realization of the right to equal recognition before the law, including in national legislation in that country. Faisal Bhabha's chapter engages with the subject of supported decision-making provisions at federal and provincial levels in Canada, illustrating the disparate nature of reforms and providing a clear indication of what can be done to mitigate these concerns. Similarly, the chapter by Pathare and Kapoor offers insight into the ways in which India sought to domesticate legal capacity provisions into the national Mental Health Care Act and examines the practicalities of implementation of the Act now that it has passed.

In providing an exposition of the reforms evident in Scottish legislation, Adrian Ward has shed light on some of the complexities that arise in regulating supported decision-making, while also demonstrating how Scotland has sought to navigate them. The role of civil society and disabled peoples' organizations in driving legal reform is also evident in the chapter by Helene Combrink and Enoch Chilemba, which focuses on the complexities of introducing CRPD-compliant legislation in Zambia and Ghana. Similarly, Elizabeth Kamundia and Ilze Grobbelaar-du Plessis have noted the significance of consultative processes in the development of the Kenyan Mental Health Amendment Bill, while nonetheless expanding on the shortcomings of the Bill itself.

The third section of the book is dedicated to the practice of supported decision-making and noncoercive mental health care. It highlights innovative practices, while also expounding on research underway and research that is still needed. Bhargavi Davar and colleagues have shared their experiences of working in non-coercive, community-oriented ways to develop the practice they call the "circle of care" in Pune, India, illustrating the utility of this approach in crisis-support intervention as well as decision-making. Likewise, Ulrike Jarkestig Berggren outlines the model of the "personal ombudsman" in Sweden, examining both its utility and the critical elements which make it useful. Two chapters have a transnational focus: Michelle Funk and colleagues provide an account of the World Health Organization's Quality Rights Initiative, which aims to transform mental health systems to become rights affirming, including a specific emphasis on noncoercive measures. Similarly, the Clubhouse model is showcased in the chapter by Joel Corcoran, Cindy Hamersma, and Steven Manning. The model is an approach to psychosocial support in a community context, which the authors suggest can be adapted to various contexts and can be utilized as a means of supported decision-making.

Piers Gooding's chapter is a useful illustration of the ways in which research can and has contributed to progress in this field. It is also a useful indicator of what research is still required and what barriers exist in its conduction. The chapter by Schneiders et al. also focuses on research, particularly in relation to supported decision-making, conducted by the Saks Institute at the University of Southern California. It demonstrates the utility of the research itself, as well as its potential for broader transformation of mental health care systems. Stephanie Smith, meanwhile, demonstrates that much more needs to be done in the way of research and standard setting to make the CRPD a reality, particularly in resource-limited settings as far afield as Haiti, Rwanda, Liberia, Sierra Leone, Malawi, Lesotho, Peru, and Mexico.

The fourth section of our book focuses on the voice of lived experience in decision-making, both by documenting research efforts related to the experience of people with psychosocial disabilities and by accounts of their experience provided directly. Charlene Sunkel and colleagues in the Global Mental Health Peer Network provide first-person narratives of their experiences of coercion in mental health systems, of recovery, and of the value of peer support and collective advocacy from South Africa, Cameroon, Kenya, Australia, and Canada. Lydia Brown and Shain Neumeier illustrate the value of collective lived experience advocacy as well, but they focus on the United States and demonstrate very effectively how ableism and sanism collude with various other forms of discrimination to create "hyper-marginalization."

Dorrit Cato Christensen's account of her daughter's experience of involuntary treatment in Denmark is interspersed with an exploration of noncoercive methods that align with the CRPD, offering an emotional account that also calls for practical reforms. Similarly, Aikaterini Nomidou's chapter focuses on the author's own experience as a caregiver for a family member with a psychosocial disability and as an advocate for change in Greece and beyond. The chapter by Kanna Sugiura is a useful exploration of the varied perspectives of people with psychosocial disabilities in relation to coercion, decision-making, and involuntary admission into mental health institutions in Japan and India, while the chapter by Sally Souraya and colleagues provides a similar account in the context of Ethiopia.

Through this breadth of chapters covering many countries and perspectives, we have sought to explore issues of legal capacity, supported decision-making, and coercive mental health treatment in a cross-cutting, comprehensive, and interdisciplinary manner. We acknowledge that it is not possible to engage with all perspectives in the space of one volume, but as the exegeses above demonstrate, there are vast amounts of knowledge and expertise contained in the chapters that follow. It is a testament to the significance of the subject matter that we have solicited work from so many parts of the world, and that we have garnered perspectives from practitioners and policymakers alike, and from advocates, researchers, and people with psychosocial disabilities alike too.

We express our sincere thanks to the colleagues and friends who have contributed to this volume, and to the editors and publishers at Cambridge University Press. We reiterate our gratitude to the Weatherhead Center for International Affairs for their workshop sponsorship. Special thanks are due to Juliana Restivo, Program Coordinator for the GlobalMentalHealth@Harvard Initiative for invaluable contributions made in coordinating both the volume and the workshop, and for superb work as our editorial assistant, and to Juliet Bowler, Senior Program Manager of the Harvard Law School Project on Disability for supporting the workshop. Readers are invited to learn more about these two research and advocacy centers and their work by visiting their respective websites: https://globalhealth.harvard.edu/domains/global-mental-health-harvard/; https://hpod.law.harvard.edu/.

Finally, we express also our very sincere hope that this volume will contribute to realizing a world in which people with psychosocial disabilities enjoy the same freedoms, rights and responsibilities as any other members of their communities and that coercion and discrimination in all experiences, most notably health care, are eliminated altogether. In the final analysis, this was – and remains – our singular aspiration.

Foreword

In times of pandemic, we should especially consider those who are most likely to be overlooked and left behind. Historically, persons with disabilities have been among those most excluded. Many persons with disabilities – including those with psycho-social disabilities – have been exposed to serious human rights violations, had their legal agency substituted by guardians and been denied the right to choose what is best for them.

Mental health systems that intimidate or coerce those that need help the most are bound to fail. Change will only come with equal recognition before the law of the legal agency of persons with disabilities. This must be combined with the availability of community-based services, including those that work to prevent sexual violence, and with concrete steps on ending institutionalization. Community-based services enable persons with disabilities to remain in their communities and to contribute to their own well-being.

Having legal agency allows for valid, free, and informed consent. It is the key to ending coercive treatment and ensuring that an individual can decide on services they can trust to support them best.

Realizing the rights of persons with disabilities is a matter of justice and an investment in our common future. We should be guided by human rights, and by persons with disabilities themselves, in line with the disability community's motto: "Nothing about us, without us".

I welcome the initiative of the group of scholars, mental health practitioners, human rights experts and persons with disabilities that has led to the publication of *Mental Health, Legal Capacity, and Human Rights*. Only by working together can we succeed. Building knowledge is the path to drawing the roadmap towards more just and inclusive societies.

António Guterres, *The Secretary-General, United Nations*

Introduction

A "Paradigm Shift" in Mental Health Care

Faraaz Mahomed, Michael Ashley Stein, Vikram Patel, and Charlene Sunkel

Abstract

The passage of the United Nations Convention on the Rights of Persons with Disabilities (CRPD or the Convention) has been hailed as the culmination of a "paradigm shift" from the biomedical model of disability to the social and human rights-oriented model. The CRPD's assertion of equal recognition before the law applying to all persons with disability, including mental health and psychosocial disability, and thus amounting to universal legal capacity, in Article 12 and in the subsequent General Comment, Number 1 on Article 12 issued by the Committee on the Rights of Persons with Disabilities (CRPD Committee), has been the subject of considerable debate. While many have argued that this is a long overdue protection and a manifestation of nondiscrimination and freedom from coercion on the basis of disability, some have raised concerns based on perceived impracticality or risk. Among the obligations of States parties to the Convention is the mandate to shift from coercion, in the form of substitute decision-making models, to supported decision-making regimes, relying on a "will and preference" standard rather than a "best interests" standard. Even while debate around the exact nature and scope of Article 12 and General Comment 1 continues, efforts to end coercion in mental health and to promote supported decision-making have been gaining momentum in laws, policies, and practices around the world.

1 INTRODUCTION

The CRPD is an extraordinary instrument that potentially has unprecedented implications for social, economic, political, and legal systems as well as for practitioners in policy, health, education, and numerous other fields. Mental health law, policy, and practice are particularly affected by the need to domesticate the provisions of the CRPD into national frameworks. For example, the Indian Mental Health Care Act of 2017 (Ministry of Law and Justice, 2017) states explicitly that it was drafted because "it is necessary to align and harmonise the existing laws with [the CRPD]." Indeed, similar processes have taken place, or are in motion, in various corners of the world, ranging from Scotland to Colombia, Kenya, Ghana,

Hungary, Ireland, Zambia, Costa Rica, Peru, Northern Ireland, and parts of Canada and Australia (El Congreso de Colombia, 2019; Kenya National Commission on Human Rights, 2018; Hoffman and Könczei, 2010; Department of Justice and Equality, 2013; Disability Rights Watch, 2015; Disability Rights Fund, 2012; ASAN, 2016; Asemblea Legislativa de la Republica Costa Rica, 2016; Australian Law Reform Commission, 2017; Northern Ireland Human Rights Commission and Equality Commission for Northern Ireland, 2017; see also Chapter 9 by Faisal Bhabha, Chapter 11 by Adrian D. Ward, and Chapter 12 by Heléne Combrinck and Enoch Chilemba).

In 2017, the United Nations (UN) Special Rapporteur on the rights of persons with disabilities reported that at least thirty-two countries had either undertaken reforms or were in the process of implementing reforms to their legal frameworks to incorporate the paradigm advanced by the CRPD (UN General Assembly, 2017b). It is indeed worth highlighting these examples as indicating the very significant potential for change that has arisen in the aftermath of the adoption of the CRPD. Notwithstanding this potential, however, challenges remain in realizing the CRPD's provisions to its fullest extent. In this respect, one particular topic is repeatedly cited as a challenge: the issue of acknowledging and implementing legal capacity for people with psychosocial disabilities.[1] In this chapter, we outline the provisions related to legal capacity in the CRPD, while also examining the controversies that have arisen related to these provisions and the continuing impediments to implementation thereof.

2 THE CRPD AS A CULMINATION OF A "PARADIGM SHIFT"

The CRPD was adopted by the UN General Assembly in 2006 and, at the time of writing, has gained 181 State ratifications. The Convention has been credited with shifting the manner in which disability rights are conceived of and operationalized.

---

[1] In practice, the evolving debates around legal capacity also apply to what are often referred to as intellectual or cognitive disabilities and some degenerative conditions, such as dementia. Intellectual and cognitive disabilities are distinct from psychosocial disabilities in that the etiology of the former is primarily related to biological determinants and the disability is evident from birth or early life and endures throughout the life of the person; on the other hand, the etiology of the latter is thought to derive from an interaction of psychological and environmental factors with biological factors; the disability appears most commonly during one's youth; and it is often not enduring. Dementia, which typically begins in older age and is a progressing neurodegenerative condition, has multiple biological etiologies ranging from vascular incidents to Alzheimer's disease, and does significantly alter the ability of an individual to function independently. All of these conditions are likely to be affected by changes in decision-making regimes and should, therefore, be considered in debates related to legal capacity. In practical terms, this was not possible for this particular book; as a result, the book focuses on psychosocial disabilities. That being said, it is conceivable that many of the findings and assumptions relating to mental health may apply to intellectual disabilities, dementia, and other conditions which affect capacity. However, this is not a universal truth, and conclusions drawn here about the mental health care system should be interrogated further before being applied to social care models for the intellectually disabled or for those whose condition may not improve with time.

It is the first treaty of its kind and one of the most widely ratified international conventions in history, illustrative of a broader "paradigm shift" from an impairment-focused, "biomedical" model to a socially-oriented, human rights-focused model (Stein and Lord, 2010; Pearl, 2013). The former view suggests that disability is an individual impairment, a function of the organic deficit or illness in a particular person, which can be addressed largely through a medical intervention. More recent iterations of this model have, however, incorporated critical elements and made mention of the need to address various social determinants that cause or exacerbate mental health challenges. Nonetheless, critics argue that its primary emphasis remains a focus on a biomedical conceptualization of "illness" (Deacon, 2013).

The social model views disability as a product of an individual's interaction with his or her environment. The impairment is the result of a lack of an accommodating environment and the "disability" is actually a result of a context which denies a differently abled person the same rights and opportunities afforded to others (Shakespeare, 2006). While the social model is seen as a useful explanatory model for disability, it has been critiqued for not offering substantial guidance for how to go about changing circumstances that marginalize people with disabilities. Moreover, the needs for disability to be valued as a facet of human diversity and for social justice to be a cornerstone of thinking around disability were highlighted as important shortcomings that later came to be addressed through the human rights-based model embodied by the CRPD (Stein, 2007). It is these shifts in thinking – and the requirement that these shifts also see realization in law and policy – that have led authors to view the CRPD as the culmination of a "revolution" in disability discourse (Pearl, 2013).

The relationship between human rights-based approaches and biomedical or public health approaches to mental health has brought into view some inherent tensions, with even the terminology of "mental illness" being critiqued and replaced by the CRPD-informed construct of psychosocial disability. Differing approaches to psychosocial disability or mental health can influence policies, interventions, and potentially even public attitudes (see also Chapter 1 by Alicia Ely Yamin). By its nature, mental health interacts with various disciplines that include psychiatry, psychology, public health, anthropology, economics, law, and public policy. These disciplines and their practitioners face the daunting task of interpreting and implementing the paradigm shift alluded to above, while also incorporating various discipline-specific objectives and ethical considerations.

3 LEGAL CAPACITY THEN AND NOW: THE SIGNIFICANCE OF ARTICLE 12 OF THE CRPD

Since the adoption of the CRPD, the area that has arguably spurred the most considerable debate is around the issue of legal capacity, or the capacity to be recognized as a "legal person" before the law, incorporating both the holding of rights and duties (legal standing) and the actual exercise those rights and duties (legal agency). The recognition (or lack thereof) of legal capacity can have important implications, including affecting the right of people living with psychosocial disabilities to make decisions about treatment, to live independently, to vote, and to enter into contracts (Dhanda, 2006). Traditional approaches to capacity have been rooted in millennia-old conceptions of mental health challenges as spiritual deficits, with resultant practices of chaining, exorcism, incarceration, and sometimes even execution, with decision-making based largely on the judgments of spiritual or religious counselors or medical practitioners of the day (Kroll and Bachrach, 1984). With the movement to the "illness" theory of etiology of mental health conditions evident in the development of the biomedical model, many of these practices were somewhat reified, allowing for what is now known as "substitute decision-making" or the judgment of a clinician or family member or other judicially recognized individual to supersede that of the person affected when that person is deemed to be incapacitated due to their mental state (Ossa-Richardson, 2013; Dunn et al., 2005). This has led to a history of numerous forms of abuse and maltreatment. At the onset of the CRPD negotiations, the World Network of Users and Survivors of Psychiatry demonstrated that a wide range of unnecessary and harmful coercive measures have been implemented at the hands of professionals in whose power resided the adjudication of an individual's "competence" to make decisions for themselves, in the process suggesting that coercive treatment amounts to a violation of the right to freedom from torture and cruel, inhumane, and degrading treatment (World Network of Users and Survivors of Psychiatry, 2001; see also Chapter 3 by Tina Minkowitz), a position later also adopted by the UN Special Rapporteur on torture (United Nations General Assembly, 2013).

In large part because of the history of the abuse of declarations of incapacity, and because of the discriminatory nature of laws that discriminate against people with psychosocial disabilities (sometimes referred to as "sanism;" see Perlin, 1992), the global disability rights movement has been vocal in its campaign for the right to equal recognition before the law, a campaign which was successful in the drafting of Article 12 of the CRPD. Paragraph 2 of Article 12 provides that:

> States Parties shall recognize that persons with disabilities enjoy legal capacity on an equal basis with others in all aspects of life . . .

This provision is viewed by many as a crucial tool to end discrimination on the basis of psychosocial disability, and a key achievement of the CRPD (Arstein-Kerslake and Flynn, 2016).

Further interpretation of Article 12 takes the form of General Comment 1 on Article 12 by the CRPD Committee, issued to clarify the scope and application of Article 12 (CRPD, 2014). The General Comment asserts that equal recognition before the law, and, by extension, legal capacity, are universally applicable rights which cannot be derogated because of a disability. The Committee further recognizes the right to supported decision-making where necessary and requires state parties to the CRPD to eliminate substitute decision-making with immediate effect. It is important to note that the General Comment states explicitly that the principle of progressive realization does not apply to the issue of legal capacity. It therefore obligates States to roll out supported decision-making mechanisms and to engage in law reform without delay (see Chapter 5 by Laura Davidson). Yet, as demonstrated below, it is not without its detractors.

4 OPPOSITION TO THE ADOPTION OF ARTICLE 12

According to the UN Special Rapporteur on the rights of persons with disabilities, thirteen countries[2] "issued reservations and declarations upon ratification or accession, with the intention of limiting the implementation of Article 12 and other related articles" (United Nations General Assembly, 2017b: 9–10). Germany and Norway argued that it is not contrary to the CRPD to restrain legal agency when a person cannot make a decision in their own interests, even in the event of the best possible support being made available, because such an action does not diminish legal standing (Federal Republic of Germany, 2014; Government of Norway, 2014). Similarly, Denmark and France suggested that, while legal standing is an absolute and universal right, legal agency can be restrained when necessary (Ministry of Foreign Affairs of Denmark, 2014; Republique Francaise, 2014; see also Chapter 23 by Dorrit Cato Christensen). This goes to show, then, that there has been substantial controversy regarding the right to equal recognition before the law since the very inception of the CRPD.

Article 12 of the Convention and General Comment 1 have, moreover, been criticized as potentially damaging flaws in the treaty (Ward, 2011; Freeman et al., 2015; Appelbaum, 2016), with some even calling for revisions to the treaty (Appelbaum, 2019). A particular controversy exists with regard to involuntary treatment and with respect to the implications for people living with psychosocial disabilities. Clinicians have argued that, as key participants in the implementation of any provisions relating to the care, support, and treatment of people living with psychosocial disabilities, sufficient consultation and engagement did not take place (Freeman et al., 2015). A universalist approach to legal capacity has been argued to be unhelpful because of the ethical difficulties visited upon clinicians who have a duty to protect mental health care users who might be considered vulnerable and because of the potential for abuses at the hands of "supporters" (Ward, 2011; Scholten and Gather, 2017; Weich, 2017). While the General Comment requires State parties to the CRPD to adhere to these principles, it does not offer substantive guidance on how States can harmonize their laws, including mental health laws, with its thinking.

---

[2] Australia, Canada, Egypt, Estonia, France, Georgia, Kuwait, Malaysia, Netherlands, Norway, and Poland, Singapore and Venezuela (Bolivarian Republic of).

The General Comment mandates that supportive regimes become a standard feature of systems which interact with people living with psychosocial disabilities, prioritizing the will and preference of the individual concerned as opposed to the traditional "best interests" standard that critics of a biomedical approach have argued can be construed as paternalistic (Browning, Bigby, and Douglas, 2014) In instances where that will and preference is unknown, States should require adherence to the "best interpretation of the individual's will and preference." Dhanda (2017), for example, notes that legal capacity is intrinsically linked to personhood, because it is through one's ability to act autonomously that they are able to exercise their personhood. Other scholars, still, have argued that the suggestion that a right such as dignity is derived from capacity or that personhood is dependent on autonomy is, itself, flawed, because dignity, personhood, and equality are derived from humanity alone (Bilchitz, 2016). Whether this can satisfy mental health service users who view "legal control" as a central feature of their own dignity is, however, a complex question (Kogstad, 2009).

Some clinicians and legal scholars, while not questioning the content of the right articulated in the CRPD, have questioned whether this vision of legal capacity can be realized in practical terms, because of the difficulty – and perhaps even the impossibility – of reaching a best interpretation of every patient's will and preference; commentators have suggested that there will always be some individuals for whom such an interpretation cannot be elicited – so-called "hard cases" (Quinn, 2010; Dawson, 2015; Gooding, 2015; see also Chapter 18 by Piers Gooding). Others consider universal legal capacity as the possible dereliction of the duty to protect people living with psychosocial disabilities from maltreatment, neglect or exploitation (Dawson, 2015; Scholten and Gather, 2017), citing examples such as mania or rare cases of violent psychosis, or women with mental health challenges who live on the street (see Chapter 7 by Ravi et al.). Detractors of the CRPD approach have also argued that there is a moral or ethical duty to engage in coercive mental health interventions when the person with a psychosocial disability might pose a risk of harm to self or others (Scholten and Gather, 2017). Defenders of the CRPD position, however, have suggested that a reluctance to relinquish power over the lives of those affected is a significant driving factor behind these concerns, and suggest that this power, which has undoubtedly been left open to abuse, requires urgent and systematic checking if the abuses of the past are not to be repeated (Spandler, Anderson, and Sapey, 2015; Series, 2015). Similarly, defenders of the CRPD approach also note that the "risk of harm" argument, when applied solely to people with psychosocial disabilities, constitutes unfair discrimination on the grounds of disability (Callaghan, Ryan, and Kerridge, 2013; in this volume, see also Chapter 4 by Gerald L. Neuman and Chapter 8 by Alberto Vásquez Encalada). Others argue also that diagnoses of mental health conditions and concomitant involuntary treatment are themselves applied disproportionately to marginalized groups, thus reflecting systemic and structural barriers to equality that coercion only exacerbates

(Bennewith et al., 2010; see also Chapter 22 by Lydia X. Z. Brown and Shain M. Neumeier).

Linked to the debate regarding involuntary treatment is also the debate regarding the so-called "insanity defense," which would, according to some commentators, be considered untenable if universal legal capacity were to be operationalized. While the claim of universal legal capacity can go some way to addressing the stigmatization of psychosocial disabilities in criminal justice systems, some authors question whether it leaves those affected vulnerable to abuse and amounts to a violation of due process, fair trial, and dignity mandates. Michael Perlin (2015) argues that this represents an oversight of the drafters, in that the implications of universal legal capacity never discussed this particular challenge, suggesting that it may have been an unintended consequence of the broader shift towards universal legal capacity. However, the General Comment (2014) is clear on the need for criminal law to be "disability-neutral," thereby precluding a defense based on disability status. Others have argued that the defense of inability to judge the rationality of one's own actions need not be based on disability but, instead, criteria ought to be applied which are suitable for disabled and non-disabled alike (Slobogin, 2014). It is therefore worth noting that questions which apply to treatment bear significance for this realm of criminal justice as well.

5 WHAT NOW? (NON)IMPLEMENTATION OF ARTICLE 12 AND GENERAL COMMENT 1

Some 181 States parties are bound by the provisions of the CRPD, and many have already begun the process of seeking to ensure its domestication into national laws and policies, including those relating to mental health. Yet, despite the desire to see this "new" paradigm gain traction, there remain significant questions about how the provisions of the CRPD and General Comment 1 to Article 12 can be implemented, even among proponents of the universalist approach to legal capacity (Szmukler, Daw, and Callard, 2014; Dhanda, 2017; see also Chapter 6 by John Dawson and George Szmukler). Numerous scholars, generally supportive of the paradigm of supported decision-making, have nonetheless raised questions about the need for exceptions or nuanced interpretations that take into account the proportionality of a particular disability and accommodate interventions to avoid "serious adverse effects" (Bach and Kerzner, 2010) or to address the risk of "imminent and grave harm" (De Bhailis and Flynn, 2017). Yet it has been noted that these very exceptions then reawaken the possibility of abuse and maltreatment that Article 12 and General Comment 1 were intended to put an end to (Dhanda, 2017). Likewise, calls for a "radical reduction and eventual elimination" of coercive treatment, including by the UN Special Rapporteur on the right to health (United Nations General Assembly, 2017a; see also Chapter 2 by Benjamin A. Barsky, Julie Hannah, and Dainius Pūras), have been viewed as insufficient by those seeking complete abolition on the basis of its potential for abuse and because it is seen as the gradual implementation of a step that ought to be taken without any reservations or equivocations (Minkowitz, 2017).

The literature in recent years has shown that these questions remain largely unresolved, despite the obligations incumbent upon state parties to domesticate the CRPD (Gooding, 2015; Dhanda, 2017; Series, 2015). Laws that have been enacted since the issuance of the CRPD and General Comment 1 have struggled to find a balance between the call for supported decision-making regimes and established clinical, legal, and social practices. In 2016, Costa Rica adopted Law No. 9379, which abolished all forms of guardianship and created the legal figure of "guarantor for the equality before the law of persons with disabilities," whose role is to ensure the full enjoyment of legal capacity by all persons with disabilities; but appointment of a guarantor is itself dependent on the adjudication of a court (United Nations General Assembly, 2017b). In India, the Mental Health Care Act of 2017 allows for an advanced directive to be taken into account, although it may be applied when an individual is deemed to have "ceased" to have capacity (Ministry of Law and Justice, 2017), thus suggesting that the determination of capacity still relies on the judgment of a substitute (see Chapter 10 by Soumitra Pathare and Arjun Kapoor).

In Peru, strong advocacy from disabled people's organizations led to reform of the civil code, which asserted the right to universal legal capacity (see Chapter 8). Even so, this instrument continues to allow exceptional pronouncements of incapacity, such as when an individual is deemed to be under the influence of a substance (Minkowitz, 2018). At the time of writing, the country is considering mental health legislation, parts of which have been determined to be in contravention of the CRPD (Personal communication with Alberto Vásquez Encalada, 2020). Similarly, provisions in the draft Kenyan Mental Health Amendment Bill and the draft Mexican Mental Health Amendment Bill have also been the subject of debate because they contain provisions which allow for substitute decision-making or because they fail to adequately implement supported decision-making (Health Rights Advocacy Forum, 2019; Human Rights Watch, 2017; see also Chapter 13 by Elizabeth Kamundia and Ilze Grobbelaar-du Plessis).

To counter the discriminatory application of incapacity law to people living with psychosocial disabilities as a group, others have sought broader attempts at "capacity legislation" that focuses not on the impairment per se but, rather, on the ability of individual to make a decision for him or herself, regardless of the reason for any perceived incapacity (Szmukler, Daw, and Dawson, 2010; see also Chapter 6). In keeping with this argument, the Northern Irish Mental Capacity Act provides a single legislative framework governing situations where a decision needs to be made in relation to the care, treatment (for a physical or mental illness), or personal welfare of a person aged sixteen or over, who lacks capacity to make the decision for themselves. The Act, assented to in 2016, continues to provide for substitute decision-making, while also requiring that an assessor or supporter pay "special regard" to the individual's past and present wishes and beliefs (Northern Ireland Human Rights Commission and Equality Commission for Northern Ireland, 2017).

Similar to the issue of laws and policies, clinical protocols and norms continue to grapple with the challenge of engaging health professionals on this subject of involuntary treatment. In 2016, the World Psychiatric Association (WPA) issued a Bill of Rights, in which it states:

> When the patient is gravely disabled, incapacitated and/or incompetent to exercise proper judgment because of a mental disorder, the psychiatrists should consult with the family and, if appropriate, seek legal counsel, to safeguard the human dignity and the legal rights of the patient (cited in Lewis and Callard, 2017).

This is indicative of the fact that the CRPD's thinking at the time did not necessarily align with that of the WPA, with potentially widespread implications for public health practice. The WPA published a 'consultation paper' in June 2020 entitled 'Implementing Alternatives to Coercion in Mental Health Care' in which states the following:

> The passage of the ... CRPD and subsequent statements from international human rights bodies have challenged nations worldwide to improve access to voluntary mental health supports and reduce, prevent and potentially even end coercive interventions. Some clinicians and other commentators have expressed reservations about (and in some cases, outright rejection of) moves to avoid coercion in mental health services. These include arguments that compulsory treatment must be available to protect individuals and/or those around them from harm, to protect individuals' other rights, and to ameliorate the negative impacts of certain mental disorders on individuals' wellbeing ... These different views are reflected in debates by policymakers, government agencies and civil society organisations all over the world as well as among service users and persons with associated psychosocial disabilities. There is a risk that these debates are becoming intractable. What is often lost is the considerable agreement that exists across diverse perspectives, and the pathway that this creates for positive change. There is widespread agreement that coercive and compulsory practices are often over-used, and there is an evidence base to support the implementation of alternatives to coercion (World Psychiatric Association, 2020: 1).

This is perhaps a signifier that while the provisions of Article 12 and General Comment 1 continue to spur debate, the field of clinical practice is shifting substantially in favor of efforts to reduce or end coercion. In a similar vein, the World Health Organization (WHO) has developed a set of best practice guidelines under the rubric of the Quality Rights initiative, which states that all people possess legal capacity at all times, and which encourages States and healthcare practitioners to engage with efforts aimed at realizing the right to supported decision-making (WHO, 2017). The WHO has also invested significantly in capacity building for this model of care in various parts of the world, engaging with policymakers as well as disability rights advocates (WHO, 2017). There is therefore some potential for reforming health systems in part through this initiative (see Chapter 16 by Funk et al.). Another source for optimism is the increasing proliferation of supported decision-making mechanisms in various parts of the world. This is the subject turned to next.

6 SUPPORTED DECISION-MAKING AND THE NEED FOR CONTEXTUALLY RELEVANT RESEARCH

Efforts to engage with supported decision-making have been gaining traction in various parts of the world. "Ulysses contracts," or mental health advance directives, have pre-dated the CRPD in statutes or in practice in England, Wales, Scotland, Germany, the Netherlands, Switzerland, Austria, and parts of Canada (including in British Columbia, where advance directives are considered binding) and the United States, and have since been incorporated into such legislation as the Indian Mental Health Care Act (Ministry of Law and Justice, 2017; see also Chapter 10). These directives have demonstrated utility, but they also leave open the question of "which will" applies – that is, the contemporary preference or that contained in the directive, with ethicists noting that this remains an area that can be more opaque in practice than it seems in law and policy (Davis, 2008; Zelle, Kemp, and Bonnie, 2015; see also Chapter 6 and Chapter 11).

Peer support initiatives have also been gaining in popularity as alternative models of care that are user-driven and that meet CRPD standards (Pathare and Shields, 2012; see also Chapter 21 by Charlene Sunkel et al. and Chapter 17 by Joel D. Corcoran, Cindy Hamersma, and Steven Manning). In Britain, the "circle of support" model has been utilized to bring together groups of family members and friends of people living with psychosocial disabilities to engage with them on their will and preferences where needed (Circles Network, 2011). Similarly, the process of "open dialogue," whereby mental health care users are treated in their own homes and dialogue is generated in family and treatment systems as a means of understanding the user's experience (and, by extension, his or her preference), has been proposed as a potential solution, based on its demonstrated utility in Finland (Seikkula et al., 2006; see also Chapter 25 by Kanna Sugiura and Chapter 18). In Sweden, the introduction of a personal ombudsman for an individual with psychosocial disabilities has also been seen as a potential model, whereby the individual's will is the primary consideration (National Board of Health and Welfare of Sweden, 2008; see also Chapter 15 by Ulrika Jarkestig Berggren). Likewise, a 2016 study investigated the utility of "crisis cards" as a means of documenting the treatment preferences of mental health care users, finding that such a method can be of utility if utilized regularly (Drack-Schonenberger et al., 2016).

Importantly, a review conducted in 2012 found that supported decision-making provisions were particularly wanting in low- and middle-income countries, raising questions about scalability and resourcing, in addition to those posed by the paradigm shift alluded to earlier (Pathare and Shields, 2012). There have been some efforts to engage with supported decision-making, however, as highlighted by a study outlining various initiatives aimed at providing non-coercive mental health care around the world (Gooding et al., 2018). These efforts include models such as the "circle of care" model implemented in Pune, India, which uses "non-formal caregivers" in socioeconomically disadvantaged areas to provide support to individuals with psychosocial disabilities in their communities (Satyamev Jayate, 2018; see also Chapter 14 by Davar et al.) and pilot projects are currently being undertaken in numerous countries from Bolivia to Kenya, according to the UN Special Rapporteur on the rights of people with disabilities (UN General Assembly, 2017b). The Special Rapporteur also highlighted the need for both formal and informal substitute decision-making regimes that cater to varied needs based on the extent and complexity of disability, incorporating efforts at "will interpretation" as well as providing the support of "trusted others" in the decision-making process (UN General Assembly, 2017b; see also Chapter 24 by Aikaterini Nomidou). As Chapter 7, by Ravi et al., Chapter 26 by Souraya et al., Chapter 14, and Chapter 18 illustrate, efforts are increasingly being undertaken in low- and middle-income countries to involve service users in decision-making, and this has the potential to substantially improve outcomes. What these existing models illustrate is that supported decision-making regimes need to be contextually relevant, recognizing the significance of local resource availability and cultural norms that may have a bearing on relationships and relational autonomy. This has therefore required further effort towards innovation and development of contextually relevant models, rather than wholesale importation of existing approaches.

The efforts at realizing the CRPD's conception of legal capacity notwithstanding, it is clear that innovations in the field of legal capacity and supported decision-making remain obscure, with the dominance of the biomedically oriented substitute decision-making paradigm still extant (Mahomed, Stein & Patel, 2019). Research into non-coercive models of mental health care, particularly those that are contextually relevant, is still very much needed (see also Chapter 19 by Christopher Schneiders et al. and Chapter 18). Nevertheless, it is encouraging to see these mechanisms take hold, with innovative rights-affirming practices not only showing relevance but also clinical validity (Bergström et al., 2018; Newton-Howes, Pickering and Young, 2019).

7 CONCLUSION

Clinical practice and policymaking continue to struggle with questions relating to the exact scope of legal capacity for people living with psychosocial disabilities, with the nature of supports that might be appropriate and contextually relevant, and with how to go about regulating these matters. However, what is also clear from the proliferation of supported decision-making initiatives, academic inquiry, and legal reforms, as well as the growth and empowerment of lived experience advocates, is that realizing the aspiration of Article 12 and General Comment 1 is a widely accepted paradigm shift in the experience of mental health care by persons with psychosocial disabilities. Support for non-coercive practices in mental health is growing substantially, and while this may or may not invoke the provisions of the CRPD, it is clear that efforts to render Article 12 and General Comment 1 implementable and to engage with unresolved tensions will only add to this momentum.

REFERENCES

Arstein-Kerslake A & Flynn A. (2016). The General Comment on Article 12 of the Convention on the Rights of Persons with Disabilities: a roadmap for equality before the law. *The International Journal of Human Rights*, 20(4), 471–90.
Appelbaum PS. (2016). Protecting the rights of people with disabilities: an international convention and its problems. *Psychiatric Services*, 67(4), 366.
Appelbaum PS. (2019). Saving the UN Convention on the Rights of Persons with Disabilities – from itself. *World Psychiatry*, 18(1), 1–2.
Asemblea Legislativa de la Republica Costa Rica. (2016). Ley Para La Promocion de la Autonomia Personal de las Personas con Discapacidad, No. 9379. www.tse.go.cr/pdf/normativa/promocionautonomiapersonal.pdf
Australian Law Reform Commission. (2017). Equality, Capacity and Disability in Commonwealth Laws. www.alrc.gov.au/publication/equality-capacity-and-disability-in-commonwealth-laws-ip-44/
Autistic Self-Advocacy Network (ASAN). (2016). The right to make choices: International Laws and Decision-Making by People with Disabilities. http://autisticadvocacy.org/wp-content/uploads/2016/02/Easy-Read-OSF-5-Guardianship-and-SDM-Laws-v3.pdf
Bartlett P (2014). Implementing a paradigm shift: implementing the CRPD in the context of mental disability law. In Torture in Healthcare Settings: Reflections on the Special Rapporteur on Torture's 2013 Thematic Report. Washington: Centre for Human Rights and Humanitarian Law, American University Washington College of Law, 169–80.
Bennewith O, Amos T, Lewis G, Katsakou C, Wykes T, Morriss R, Priebe S. (2010). Ethnicity and coercion among involuntarily detained psychiatric in-patients. *BJPsych*, 196(1), 75–6.
Bergström T, et al. (2018). The family-oriented open dialogue approach in the treatment of first-episode psychosis: nineteen–year outcomes. *Psychiatry Research*, 270, 168–75.
Bilchitz D. (2016). Dignity, fundamental rights and legal capacity: moving beyond the paradigm set by the General Comment on Article 12 of the Convention on the Rights of Persons with Disabilities. *South African Journal on Human Rights*, 3, 410.
Browning M, Bigby C & Douglas J. (2014). Supported decision making: understanding how its conceptual link to legal capacity is influencing the development of practice. *Research and Practice in Intellectual and Developmental Disabilities*, 1(1), 34–45.
Callaghan S, Ryan C & Kerridge I. (2013). Risk of suicide is insufficient warrant for coercive treatment for mental illness. *International Journal of Law and Psychiatry*, 36, 5–6, 374–85.
Carney, T & Beaupart Fleur (2013). Public and private bricolage: challenges balancing law, services and civil society in advancing the CRPD supported decision making. *University of New South Wales Law Journal* 36(1), 175–201.

Circles Network. (2011). Circles of support. www.youtube.com/watch?v=w6RX_WQmSf4& feature=youtu.be&t=54
Craigie J, et al. (2019). Legal capacity, mental capacity and supported decision-making: Report from a panel event. *International Journal of Law and Psychiatry*, 62, 160–168.
Davis JK. (2008). How to justify enforcing a Ulysses contract when Ulysses is competent to refuse. *Kennedy Institute of Ethics Journal*, 18(1), 87–106.
Dawson J. (2015). A realistic approach to assessing mental health laws' compliance with the UNCRPD. *International Journal of Law and Psychiatry*, 40, 70.
Deacon BJ. (2013). The biomedical model of mental disorder: a critical analysis of its validity, utility, and effects on psychotherapy research. *Clinical Psychology Review*, 33, 846.
De Bhailis C & Flynn E. (2017). Recognising legal capacity: commentary and analysis of Article 12 CRPD. *International Journal of Law in Context*, 13(1), 6.
Department of Justice and Equality, Ireland. (2013). Assisted Decision-Making (Capacity) Bill, 2013. www.oireachtas.ie/documents/bills28/bills/2013/8313/b8313d.pdf
Dhanda A. (2006). Legal capacity in the Disability Rights Convention: stranglehold of the past or lodestar for the future. *Syracuse Journal of International and Comparative Law*, 34, 429.
Dhanda A. (2017). Conversations between the proponents of the new paradigm of legal capacity. *International Journal of Law in Context*, 13(1), 87.
Disability Rights Fund. (2012). Law No. 29973, Peru, General Law on Persons with Disabilities. http://disabilityrightsfund.org/resources/law-no-29973-peru-general-law-on-persons-with-disabilities/
Disability Rights Watch. (2015). Legal Capacity in Zambia. http://disabilityrightswatch.net/wp-content/uploads/2015/08/Legal-Capacity-for-Persons-with-Mental-and-Intellectual-Disabilities-in-Zambia1.pdf
Drack-Schonenberger T, Bleiker M, Lengler S, et al. (2016). Crisis cards for the prevention of compulsory hospitalization: signs of a crisis, treatment-specific demands and coping strategies from the patients' perspective. *Psychiatrische Praxis*, 43, 5, 253.
Dunn MC, Clare ICH, Holland AJ & Gunn MJ. (2007). Constructing and reconstructing 'best interests': an interpretative examination of substitute decision-making under the Mental Capacity Act 2005. *Journal of Social Welfare and Family Law*, 29(2), 117.
El Congreso de Colombia. (2019). Ley 1996: Por Medio de la Cual se Establece el Regimen Para el Egercicio de la Capacidad Legal de las Personas con Discapacidad Mayores de Edad. https://dapre.presidencia.gov.co/normativa/normativa/LEY%201996%20DEL%2026%20DE%20AGOSTO%20DE%202019.pdf
Federal Republic of Germany. (2014). German Statement on the Draft General Comment on Article 12 CRPD, Committee on the Rights of Persons with Disabilities.
Gooding P. (2015). Navigating the "flashing amber lights" of the right to legal capacity in the United Nations Convention on the Rights of Persons with Disabilities: responding to major concerns. *Human Rights Law Review*, 15(1), 45.
Gooding P, McSherry B, Roper C, Grey F. (2018). Alternatives to Coercion in Mental Health Settings: A Literature Review. Melbourne: University of Melbourne. https://socialequity.unimelb.edu.au/__data/assets/pdf_file/0012/2898525/Alternatives-to-Coercion-Literature-Review-Melbourne-Social-Equity-Institute.pdf
Government of Norway. (2014). Draft General Comment No. 1 on Article 12 of the Convention on the Rights of Persons with Disabilities – submission by the Norwegian Government, Committee on the Rights of Persons with Disabilities.
Health Rights Advocacy Forum. (2019). Civil society submission to the Parliament of Kenya on the Mental Health Amendment Bill of 2018.

Henderson C, Swanson JW, Szmukler G. (2008). A typology of advance statements in mental health care. *Psychiatric Services*, 59(1), 63.

Hoffman I & Konczei G. (2010). Legal regulations relating to the passive and active legal capacity of persons with intellectual and psychosocial disabilities in light of the Convention on the Rights of Persons with Disabilities and the impending reform of the Hungarian Civil Code. *Loyola of Los Angeles International and Comparative Law Review*, 33, 143.

Human Rights Watch. (2017). Mexico: Mental Health Bill Undermines Disability Rights. www.refworld.org/docid/59e5f7d84.html

Kenya National Commission on Human Rights. (2018). The Many Faces of Mental Health in Kenya. www.knchr.org/DesktopModules/EasyDNNNews/DocumentDownload.ashx?portalid=0&moduleid=2432&articleid=1086&documentid=18

Kogstad RE. (2009). Protecting mental health clients' dignity – the importance of legal control. *International Journal of Law and Psychiatry*, 32(6), 383.

Kroll J & Bachrach B. (1984). Sin and mental illness in the Middle Ages. *Psychological Medicine*, 14, 507–514.

Lewis O & Callard F. (2017). The World Psychiatric Association's 'Bill of Rights': A curious contribution to human rights. *International Journal of Mental Health*, 46(3), 157.

Mahomed F, Stein MA & Patel V. (2019). Involuntary mental health treatment in the era of the United Nations Convention on the Rights of Persons with Disabilities. *PLoS Med*, 15(10). https://doi.org/10.1371/journal.pmed.1002679

Ministry of Law and Justice, India. (2017). The Mental Health Care Act, No. 10 of 2017. www.prsindia.org/uploads/media/Mental%20Health/Mental%20Healthcare%20Act,%202017.pdf

Ministry of Foreign Affairs of Denmark. (2014). Response from the Government of Denmark with regards to Draft General Comment on Article 12 of the Convention – Equal Recognition before the Law, Committee on the Rights of Persons with Disabilities.

Minkowitz T. (2006). The United Nations Convention on the Rights of Persons with Disabilities and the right to be free from nonconsensual psychiatric interventions. *Syracuse Journal of International and Comparative Law*, 34, 405.

Minkowitz T. (2012). CRPD advocacy by the World Network of Users and Survivors of Psychiatry: the emergence of a user/survivor perspective in human rights. http://dx.doi.org/10.2139/ssrn.2326668

Minkowitz T. (2017). New UN report: steps forward, but no end to impunity. *Mad in America*. www.madinamerica.com/2017/05/steps-forward-but-no-end-to-impunity/

Minkowitz T. (2018). Peruvian legal capacity reform – celebration and analysis. *Mad in America*. www.madinamerica.com/2018/10/peruvian-legal-capacity-reform-celebration-and-analysis/

Morse JM. (1995). The significance of saturation. *Qualitative Health Research*, 5(2), 147.

National Board of Health and Welfare of Sweden. (2008). A New Profession Is Born: Personligt ombud, PO. www.personligtombud.se/publikationer/pdf/A%20New%20Proffession%20is%20Born.pdf

Newton-Howes G, Pickering N & Young G. (2019). Authentic decision-making capacity in hard medical cases. *Clinical Ethics*, 14(4), 173–7.

Northern Ireland Human Rights Commission/Equality Commission for Northern Ireland. (2017). Disability Rights in Northern Ireland. www.equalityhumanrights.com/sites/default/files/northern_ireland_supplementary_submission_to_crpd_uk_loi_-_ecni_nihrc.pdf

Ossa-Richardson A. (2013). Possession or insanity? Two views from the Victorian lunatic asylum. *Journal of the History of Ideas*, 74(4), 553–75.

Pathare S & Shields LS. (2012). Supported decision-making for persons with mental illness: a review. *Public Health Reviews*, 34, 15.
Pearl AL. (2013). Article 12 of the United Nations Convention on the Rights of Persons with Disabilities and the Legal Capacity of Disabled People: the way forward? *Leeds Journal of Law and Criminology*, 1(1), 1.
Perlin M. (1992). On sanism. *SMU Law Review*, 46, 373–93.
Perlin M. (2015). "God said to Abraham/kill me a son": why the insanity defense and the incompetency status are compatible with and required by the Convention on the Rights of Persons with Disabilities and basic principles of therapeutic jurisprudence. Paper delivered at the 5th International Therapeutic jurisprudence Conference at the University of Auckland, New Zealand. www.researchgate.net/publication/286775785_God_Said_to_AbrahamKill_Me_a_Son_Why_the_Insanity_Defense_and_the_Incompetency_Status_Are_Compatible_with_and_Required_by_the_Convention_on_the_Rights_of_Persons_with_Disabilities_and_Basic_Principles
Quinn G & Arstein-Kerslake A. (2010). Restoring the "human" in "human rights": personhood and doctrinal innovation in the UN disability convention. In C Gearty & C Douzinas (eds.) *The Cambridge Companion to Human Rights Law*. Cambridge: Cambridge University Press, 36–55.
Republique Française. (2014). Commentaire de la France sur le projet d'observations générales du Comité des droits des personnes handicapées, relative à l'article 12 de la Convention relative aux droit des personnes handicapées, Committee on the Rights of Persons with Disabilities.
Satyamev Jayate. (2018). Circles of care. www.satyamevjayate.in/nurturing-mental-health/episode-5article.aspx?uid=s3e5-ar-v1
Scholten M & Gather J. (2017). Adverse consequences of article 12 of the UN Convention on the Rights of Persons with Disabilities for persons with mental disabilities and an alternative way forward. *J Med Ethics*, 0, 1–8, https://doi.org/10.1136/medethics-2017-104414.
Seikkula J, Aaltonen J, Alakare B, et al. (2006). Five-year experience of first episode nonaffective psychosis in open-dialogue approach: treatment principles, follow-up outcomes and two case studies. *Psychotherapy Research*, 16, 2, 214.
Series L. (2017). Relationships, autonomy and legal capacity: mental capacity and support paradigms. *International Journal of Law and Psychiatry*, 40, 80.
Shakespeare T. (2006). The Social Model of Disability. In LJ Davis (ed.) *The Disability Studies Reader*. New York: Routledge, 195–203.
Slobogin C. (2015). Eliminating mental disability as a legal criterion in deprivation of liberty cases: the impact of the Convention on the Rights of Persons With Disabilities on the insanity defense, civil commitment, and competency law. *International Journal of Law and Psychiatry*, 40, 36.
Spandler H, Anderson J & Sapey B. (2015). Advancing the rights of users and survivors of psychiatry using the UN Convention on the Rights of Persons with Disabilities. In H Spandler, J Anderson & B Sapey (eds.) *Madness, Distress and the Politics of Disablement*. Bristol: Policy Press, 171–82.
Stein MA. (2007). Disability human rights. *California Law Review*, 95, 75–121.
Stein MA & Lord JE. (2010). Monitoring the Convention on the Rights of Persons with Disabilities: innovations, lost opportunities, and future potential. *Human Rights Quarterly*, 32, 689.
Szmukler G, Daw R & Dawson J. (2010). A model law fusing incapacity and mental health legislation. *Journal of Mental Health Law*, 20, 11.

Szmukler G, Daw R & Callard F. (2014). Mental health law and the UN Convention on the Rights of Persons with Disabilities. *International Journal of Law and Psychiatry*, 37, 245–252.

United Nations Committee on the Rights of Persons with Disabilities. (2014). General comment No. 1: Article 12, Equal recognition before the law. 11th session, March 31–April 11, 2014. www.ohchr.org/EN/HRBodies/CRPD/Pages/DGCArticles12And9.aspx

United Nations Convention on the Rights of People with Disabilities. (2007). General Assembly resolution 61/106 of 24 January 2007.

United Nations General Assembly. (2013). Report of the Special Rapporteur on torture and other cruel, inhuman or degrading treatment or punishment, Juan E. Méndez. UN Doc A/HRC/22/53. www.ohchr.org/Documents/HRBodies/HRCouncil/RegularSession/Session22/A.HRC.22.53_English.pdf

United Nations General Assembly. (2017a). Report of the Special Rapporteur on the right of everyone to the enjoyment of the highest attainable standard of physical and mental health. UN Doc A/HRC/35/21. https://documents-dds-ny.un.org/doc/UNDOC/GEN/G17/076/04/PDF/G1707604.pdf?OpenElement

United Nations General Assembly. (2017b). Report of the Special Rapporteur on the rights of persons with disabilities. UN Doc A/HRC/37/56. www.un.org/en/ga/search/view_doc.asp?symbol=A/HRC/37/56

Ward A. (2011). Adults with incapacity: freedom and liberty, rights and status: Part 1. *Scots Law Times*, 5, 21.

Weich S. (2017). The Maudsley Debate: Has the Mental Health Act had its day? No. *BMJ*, 359. https://doi.org/10.1136/bmj.j5248

World Health Organization. (2017). Protecting the Right to Legal Capacity in Mental Health and Related Services – WHO QualityRights Training to Act, Unite and Empower for Mental Health (Pilot Version). WHO/MSD/MHP/17.5, Licence: CC BY-NC-SA 3.0 IGO. Geneva: World Health Organization.

World Network of Users and Survivors of Psychiatry. (2001). Human Rights Position Paper of the World Network of Users and Survivors of Psychiatry. https://d3gqux9sloz33u.cloudfront.net/AA/AG/chrusp-biz/downloads/256093/wnusp_mexico_statement.doc

World Psychiatric Association. (2020). Implementing alternatives to coercion in mental health care. Discussion Paper from the World Psychiatric Association Task Force.

Zelle H, Kemp K & Bonnie RJ. (2015). Advance directives for mental health care: innovation in law, policy and practice. *Psychiatric Services*, 66(1), 7.

1

The Alchemy of Agency: Reflections on Supported Decision-Making, the Right to Health and Health Systems as Democratic Institutions

Alicia Ely Yamin

Abstract

There has been little interdisciplinary discussion between the global health and disability rights fields regarding the relevance of article 12 of the Convention on the Rights of Persons with Disabilities (CRPD) to States parties' obligations to respect, protect and fulfill the right to health under international law. While disability rights advocacy has focused largely on coerced treatment and abuses in facilities, the global health and development communities' attention has been focused on unmet need for mental health care. This chapter argues that conceptualizing health in terms of rights, just as disability, requires upending aspects of the biomedical and conventional public health paradigms. In turn, once the incompatibility of health and disability rights is dispelled, implementing supported decision-making (SDM) for persons with psychosocial disability reveals important aspects needed for constructing health systems as inclusive democratic social institutions more broadly. SDM and substituted decision-making should not be seen as dichotomous options when a crisis arises, but rather in terms of a range of options available for a range of disabilities, which is supported by the financing and organization of the health system.

INTRODUCTION

The following two truths can and do coexist: on the one hand, mental illness imposes real suffering on individuals (and their loved ones), and there is a severe lack of available, accessible, acceptable and quality health facilities, goods and services across contexts of varying resource levels.[1] For example, after surveying

---

I am deeply grateful to Neil Thivalapill for his research assistance and help in preparing this chapter for publication.

[1] Ramage, W. E. (1992). The pariah patient: The lack of funding for mental health care (Special Project: Caring for the Nation – Current Issues in Health Care Reform). *Vanderbilt Law Review*, 45(4), 951–976. Amerio, A., Starace, F., Costanza, A., Serafini, G., Aguglia, A., Odone, A., Ghaemi, S. N., & Amore, M. (2020). Putting Codman's lesson to work: Measuring and improving the quality of Italian mental health care. *Acta Psychiatrica Scandinavica*, 141(1), 91–92. https://doi.org/10.1111/acps.13112. Candiago, R., Silva Saraiva, S., Gonçalves, V., & Belmonte-de-Abreu, P. (2011). Shortage and underutilization of psychiatric beds in southern Brazil: Independent data of Brazilian mental health reform.

fifty low- and middle-income countries, Lora and colleagues determined that unmet need for schizophrenia treatment was as high as 96 percent in Eritrea.[2] While these estimates signal the profound need for greater attention to vast human suffering, the methodological construction of "unmet need" raises both conceptual and statistical problems.[3] At the same time, persons with psychosocial disabilities face widespread abuses and violations of their dignity in health systems under the justification of medical "treatment."[4] Systemic neglect and abuse are in fact two sides of the same coin: a failure to respect the rights and dignity of persons with psychosocial disabilities in health systems. When we focus on only one of these truths we tend to obscure the other, and in turn to lose a significant dimension of understanding the drivers of neglect and abuse, as well as how to advance the health rights of persons with psychosocial disabilities.

This chapter attempts to contribute to bridging that gap by exploring the implications for the right to health of General Comment 1 from the Committee on the Rights of Persons with Disabilities (CRPD Committee),[5] which asserts that supported decision-making (SDM), as opposed to substitute decision-making, is required in order to ensure respect for the legal capacity of persons with any form of impairment.[6] Both the CRPD model of disability generally and General Comment 1's call for replacing substitute decision-making with SDM depart from the biomedical model of mental health in which disability and mental capacity are taken as facts, to be assessed through professional expertise.[7] In Part I, I argue that in

---

[1] *Social Psychiatry and Psychiatric Epidemiology*, 46(5), 425–429. https://doi.org/10.1007/s00127-010-0207-1. Slade, E., & Goldman, H. (2015). The dynamics of psychiatric bed use in general hospitals. *Administration and Policy in Mental Health and Mental Health Services Research*, 42(2), 139–146. https://doi.org/10.1007/s10488-014-0554-4

[2] Lora, A., Kohn, R., Levav, I., Mcbain, R., Morris, J., & Saxena, S. (2012). Service availability and utilization and treatment gap for schizophrenic disorders: A survey in 50 low- and middle-income countries. *Bulletin of the World Health Organization*, 90(1), 47–54B. https://doi.org/10.2471/BLT.11.089284

[3] Pathare, S., Brazinova, A., & Levav, I. (2018). Care gap: A comprehensive measure to quantify unmet needs in mental health. *Epidemiology and Psychiatric Sciences*, 27(5), 463–467. https://doi.org/10.1017/S2045796018000100

[4] Stanley, N., & Penhale, B. (1999). *Institutional Abuse: Perspectives across the Life Course*. Routledge. Cadwallader, J. R., Spivakovsky, C., Steele, L., & Wadiwel, D. (2018). Institutional violence against people with disability: Recent legal and political developments. *Current Issues in Criminal Justice*, 29(3), 259–272. https://doi.org/10.1080/10345329.2018.12036101

[5] Convention on the Rights of Persons with Disabilities, Jan. 24, 2007 G.A. Res 61/106, U.N. GAOR, 61st Sess., Supp. No. 49, U.N. Doc. A/RES/61/106 (2007) at art. 12 [hereinafter CRPD]. *General Comment No. 1: Article 12: Equal recognition before the law*, U.N. Committee on the Rights of Persons with Disabilities, 11th Sess. U.N. Doc. CRPD/C/GC/1 (2014). [hereinafter CRPD, *General Comment No. 1*]

[6] Ibid.

[7] Scholten, M., & Gather, J. (2018). Adverse consequences of Article 12 of the UN Convention on the Rights of Persons with Disabilities for persons with mental disabilities and an alternative way forward. *Journal of Medical Ethics*, 44(4), 226–233. https://doi.org/10.1136/medethics-2017-104414 . Gooding, P. (2013). Supported decision-making: A rights-based disability concept and its implications for mental health law. *Psychiatry, Psychology and Law*, 20(3), 431–451. https://doi.org/10.1080/13218719.2012.711683.

order to harmonize the right to health and SDM, it is important to understand the ways in which treating "health" as a matter of rights requires departing from biological individualism and conventional public health utilitarianism as well.

Part II then goes on to consider the implications for health systems of putting in place contextually appropriate models of SDM in order to ensure full and informed consent. In keeping with other scholars, I suggest that informed consent is better thought of as an intersubjective process requiring varying degrees and modes of SDM, both in the context of persons with psychosocial disabilities and in health more generally. Further, implementing varying forms of SDM requires fostering changes in upstream health financing and service delivery more broadly, rather than appending SDM to current health systems in crisis situations exclusively in the context of psychosocial disabilities. In short, embedding SDM in health systems, across contexts of varying resources, both requires and facilitates a rethinking of how health systems can function as core social institutions that enhance democratic norms.

I DEFINING QUESTIONS: CONSIDERING HEALTH AND DISABILITY AS MATTERS OF RIGHTS

The starting point for mapping the intersections of health and disability rights requires understanding how defining health (as well as disability) in terms of rights challenges the biological individualism of mainstream medicine and the utilitarian assumptions of conventional public health. That is, with respect to disability, the logic of the biomedical model first defines certain physical and mental states as defective. For example, Freeman et al state: "In the case of mental illness ... by definition, their decision-making faculties are compromised" In turn, that assertion is then used to justify violence in controlling them: "If a person having a severe exacerbation of affective or psychotic illness is not provided proven, effective treatment, can he or she be said to be receiving the highest attainable standard of health?"[8] This argument seems based on General Comment 14 from the CESCR which recognizes that contained in obligations to *respect* the right to health is the obligation of States to refrain "from applying coercive medical treatments, *unless on an exceptional basis for the treatment of mental illness*"[9] However, General Comment 14 was issued well before the CRPD was promulgated. Indeed, I argue here that in a clinical setting the ostensible trade-off between rights – between the autonomy of a person experiencing an emotional crisis and her "right to health" – is generally misplaced and fallacious.

[8] Freeman, M. C., Kolappa, K., de Almeida, J. M. C., Kleinman, A., Makhashvili, N., Phakathi, S., Saraceno, B., & Thornicroft, G. (2015). Reversing hard won victories in the name of human rights: A critique of the General Comment on Article 12 of the UN Convention on the Rights of Persons with Disabilities. *The Lancet Psychiatry*, 2(9), 844–850. https://doi.org/10.1016/S2215-0366(15)00218-7

[9] *General Comment 14: The Right to the Highest Attainable Standard of Health*, U.N. Committee on Economic, Social and Cultural Rights, 20th Sess., 12, U.N. Doc. E/C.12/2000/4 (2000). [hereinafter ICESCR *Gen. Comment No. 14*] [emphasis added].

Indeed, just as a disability rights framework challenges the biomedical paradigm, both epistemically and politically, so too does treating *health* as a matter of rights. In the biomedical paradigm, health is defined as the "normal" on the liver or the kidney function test, etc. – that is, the absence of disease or infirmity, or slightly more broadly, the absence of pathology. This negative definition of health, including mental health, is simultaneously (1) abstracted from social context (and therefore permits standardization in research and classification of disease); and (2) appraised exclusively through a specialized scientific expertise. The extension of this definition to populations through mainstream public health examines deviations from "species typical functioning"[10] or "normal functioning."[11] The health system in turn is conceptualized in terms of a technical apparatus delivering medical goods and services. In the World Health Organization framework, for example, the apparatus is composed of "building blocks" – service delivery, workforce and information systems, among others – and its functioning is measured through technical indicators.[12]

By contrast, conceptualizing health as a right requires accepting that: (1) health has special moral value because of its relationship to dignity – variously and not mutually exclusively understood as self-governance, a preservation of a range of opportunities, and the ability to participate fully in one's community and society; and (2) health is *not* merely an individual biological issue. On the contrary, understanding health as a right requires understanding it to be not a natural good, but a social good, dependent upon the just arrangement of important institutions in society.[13] Just as with disability, our conception of health and well-being is also constructed in interaction with social norms and institutions, including health systems.[14] Health systems in a rights framework are not merely technical delivery apparatuses for goods and services, but rather core social institutions that also play normative roles and embed social values.[15] For example, remedying inequalities in health access and status often calls for changing normative frameworks and institutional practices, not merely medical interventions to be prescribed by clinicians, nor

---

[10] Imrie, R. (2004). Demystifying disability: A review of the International Classification of Functioning, Disability and Health. *Sociology of Health & Illness*, 26(3), 287–305. https://doi.org/10.1111/j.1467-9566.2004.00391.x

[11] Daniels, N. (2008). *Just Health: Meeting Health Needs Fairly*. Cambridge University Press, 36.

[12] World Health Organization. (2010). *Monitoring the Building Blocks of Health Systems: A Handbook of Indicators and Their Measurement Strategies*. https://www.who.int/healthinfo/systems/WHO_MBHSS_2010_full_web.pdf?ua=1

[13] Daniels, N. (2008). *Just Health: Meeting Health Needs Fairly*. Cambridge University Press.

[14] Sen, A. (2004). Elements of a Theory of Human Rights. *Philosophy & Public Affairs*, 32(4), 315–356. https://doi.org/10.1111/j.1088-4963.2004.00017.x

Rawls, J. (1971). *A Theory of Justice*. Belknap Press of Harvard University Press.

[15] Yamin, A. E. (2020). *When Misfortune Becomes Injustice: Evolving Human Rights Struggles for Health and Social Equality*. Stanford University Press 187–193,

Lynn P Freedman. (2005). Achieving the MDGs: Health systems as core social institutions. *Development*, 48(1), 19–24. https://doi.org/10.1057/palgrave.development.1100107

conventional public health interventions of the sort that focus on changing behavior and specific practices but take status quo social parameters as a given.[16]

The core formulation of *the right to health* in international human rights law was set out in Article 12(1) of the International Covenant on Economic, Social and Cultural Rights (ICESCR), which asserts that there is a "right of everyone to the enjoyment of the highest attainable standard of physical and mental health."[17] The "highest attainable standard" has both a societal and an individual dimension. However, the right to physical *and mental* health for individuals inherently involves self-governance, and therefore choice. Just as there is not a violation of the right to food if a person chooses to fast, as opposed to starving from lack of food, adults can by and large choose what health treatments they undergo, even if their choices are deemed ill advised.[18] For example, when an adult cancer patient decides to forego treatment even though it could save her life, or a Jehovah's Witness rejects a blood transfusion which could do the same out of religious conviction, it would be inconsistent with human rights and most domestic law, as well as immoral, to force that person to undergo involuntary treatment. Indeed, the "Dignity of Risk" – the dignity inherent in being able to take a calculated risk about one's own destiny – is not merely a question of private decisional autonomy, but an important public value in a plural, democratic society.[19]

On a societal level, respecting the right to the highest attainable standard of physical and mental health, like all rights, requires both formal nondiscrimination (treating similarly situated people equally) and substantive nondiscrimination (treating differently situated people in ways that give them equal enjoyment in practice).[20] However, substantive equality with respect to the right to health necessarily requires navigating multiple dimensions of heterogeneity that go beyond socioeconomic status, ethnicity, gender, race and the like. Substantive equality in health – in both access to and appropriateness of public health preconditions and health services – calls for considering severity of condition, as well as "conversion gaps," in Sen's terminology (i.e., those factors that change the ability to convert income into the capability for health achievements) that interact in people's lived realities.[21] To be

---

[16] Gostin, L. O., Monahan, J. T., Debartolo, M. C., & Horton, R. (2015). Law's power to safeguard global health: A Lancet–O'Neill Institute, Georgetown University Commission on Global Health and the Law. *The Lancet*, 385(9978), 1603–1604. https://doi.org/10.1016/S0140-6736(15)60756-5

[17] International Covenant on Economic, Social and Cultural Rights, Dec. 16, 1966 G.A. Res. 2200, U.N. GAOR, 21st Sess., Supp. No. 16, at 49, U.N. Doc. A/6316 (1966), 993 U.N.T.S. 3 at art. 12(1) [hereinafter ICESCR].

[18] *Report of the Special Rapporteur on the Rights of Persons with Disabilities*, U.N. HRC, 37th Sess. Agenda Item 3, U.N. Doc. A/HRC/37/56 (2017). [hereinafter *Report of the Special Rapporteur*]

[19] Gooding, Supported decision-making.

[20] *General Comment No. 20: Non-discrimination in economic, social and cultural rights (art. 2, para. 2, of the International Covenant on Economic, Social and Cultural Rights)*, Committee on Economic, Social and Cultural Rights, 42nd Sess., U.N. Doc. E/C.12/GC/20 (2009) [hereinafter ICESCR *Gen. Comment No. 20*].

[21] Voorhoeve, A., Ottersen, T., & Norheim, O. F. (2016). Making fair choices on the path to universal health coverage: A précis. *Health Economics, Policy and Law* 11(1), 71–77. https://doi.org/10.1017/S1744133114000541. Sen, A. (1995). *Inequality Reexamined*. Oxford University Press

clear: this does not mean that priority must automatically be given to addressing the particular health needs of persons with severe illness nor those with chronic impairment. However, showing everyone equal moral consideration does demand starting with a premise of heterogeneity in people's specific needs at given times in given contexts, which will often include additional measures for persons with significant impairments, either because of additional health needs or because of ancillary services required for them to effectively enjoy rights in practice.[22] This starkly contrasts with the prevalent public health starting point of homogeneous health needs, which leads to allocation of interventions through metrics of cost-effectiveness. These distributionally indifferent metrics automatically disfavor persons with expensive chronic conditions (e.g., severe psychiatric disorders) and disfavor certain treatments (e.g., talk therapy, for which it is difficult to standardize assessment) as opposed to others (e.g., pharmaceuticals).

Thus Article 25 of the CRPD can be read as deepening our understanding of the challenges posed by prevalent clinical and public health assumptions for the effective enjoyment of the right to health by *all* persons.[23] Article 25 calls for States Parties to take all appropriate measures to ensure access for persons with disabilities to health services, which include providing persons with disabilities:

> the same range, quality and standard of free or affordable health care and programmes as provided to other persons ...
>
> ...*those health services needed by persons with disabilities specifically because of their disabilities*, including early identification and intervention as appropriate, and services designed to minimise and prevent further disabilities ...
>
> ... health services as close as possible to people's own communities ...
>
> ... the same quality [services] as to others, including on the basis of free and informed consent by, inter alia, raising awareness of the human rights, dignity, autonomy and needs of persons with disabilities through training and the promulgation of ethical standards for public and private health care.[24]

As Amartya Sen notes: "since a disabled person, or one who is chronically ill, and thus disadvantaged in general, also receives less medical attention for other ailments, the exercise of DALY minimization ... has the effect of adding to the relative disadvantage of a person who is already disadvantaged."[25]

To be consistent with the requirements of substantive nondiscrimination in relation to health rights generally, *as well as with Article 25 of the CRPD*, the measure of disease burden would at a minimum take account of the way in which individual and social resources can compensate for the level of impairment

---

[22] Yamin, *When Misfortune Becomes Injusticee*, 175–201.
[23] ICESCR *Gen. Comment No. 20, supra* note 27.
[24] Interpreting nondiscrimination in the context of Article 25 should in turn be read in conjunction with Article 17's protections for mental and physical integrity. CRPD, *supra* note 10, at arts. 17, 25.
[25] Sen, A. (2002). Why health equity? *Health Economics*, 11(8), 659–666. https://doi.org/10.1002/hec.762.

experienced.[26] Further, in a rights framework, the rules for defining the contours of a right to health must be subject to justification to those who are affected by those decisions. Thus, the process of setting priorities in relation to health must incorporate the meaningful participation of diverse users of the health system, including persons with psychosocial and other disabilities, as opposed to being left to technical experts behind closed doors.[27] In short, taking seriously the rights of persons with disabilities has implications for construing definitions and metrics for health and structuring health systems in ways that respect, protect and fulfill the right to health for *all* people.[28]

Unfortunately, the implications of taking health and disability rights seriously for structuring health systems around norms of participation, inclusion and substantive nondiscrimination contrast sharply with neoliberal privatization and marketization of health finance and health provision, which in turn reinforce both biological individualism, as well as inequalities.[29] For example, multinational pharmaceutical companies control the supply, and promote the demand for, pharmaceutical remedies to treat mental (and all) illness. Likewise, marketized insurance systems foster precisely the discrimination against persons identified as having psychosocial disabilities called out in Article 25 of the CRPD, as well as other "non-productive" populations. On a global level, the effects of receding fiscal space and in turn the political capacity of many states – especially those in the Global South – hollow out the possibilities for fulfilling claims for health and social protection by persons with disabilities, and more broadly.

II THE IMPLICATIONS OF SUPPORTED DECISION-MAKING FOR HEALTH SYSTEMS

In General Comment 1, the CRPD Committee directly challenges the authority of psychiatrists and other mental health professionals constructed through the biomedical paradigm: "Mental capacity is not, as is commonly presented, an objective, scientific and naturally occurring phenomenon. Mental capacity is contingent on social and political contexts, as are the disciplines, professions and practices which

---

[26] Anand, S., & Hanson, K. (1997). Disability-adjusted life years: A critical review. *Journal of Health Economics*, 16(6), 685–702. https://doi.org/10.1016/s0167-6296(97)00005-2.

[27] Baltussen, R., Jansen, M. P., Bijlmakers, L., Tromp, N., Yamin, A. E., & Norheim, O. F. (2017). Progressive realisation of universal health coverage: What are the required processes and evidence? *BMJ Global Health*, 2(3), e000342. https://doi.org/10.1136/bmjgh-2017-000342.

[28] ICESCR *Gen. Comment No. 14*, *supra* note 16. *General Comment No. 22: On the Right to Sexual and Reproductive Health (Art. 12)*, Committee on Economic, Social and Cultural Rights, UN Doc. E/C.12/GC/22 (2016).

[29] Global Initiative for Economic, Social and Cultural Rights and University of Essex Human Rights Centre Clinic. (2019). *Private Actors in Health Services: Towards a human rights impact assessment framework*. https://www.gi-escr.org/publications/private-actors-in-health-services-towards-a-human-rights-impact-assessment-framework.

play a dominant role in assessing mental capacity."[30] The Committee distinguishes mental capacity from legal capacity, which encompasses both legal standing (recognition as subject of rights) and legal agency (ability to act on and claim rights).[31] The Committee's General Comment has had significant norm-diffusion effects even while generating controversy.[32]

From a health rights perspective, the question is how SDM might be implemented as a means to achieve full and informed consent in health systems, which is a critical component of the right to health for *all* persons. Piers Gooding's insight that the value of the SDM model in relation to disability lies in its reframing of autonomy as an *inter*dependent concept, rather than an independent concept, is an important place to start.[33] SDM should not be understood as a unique or rigidly defined mechanism, but rather as a process to promote optimal communication between patient and provider on the basis of mutual respect, given extreme asymmetries in power. The advocacy for SDM by the disability rights community, and its (often imperfect) inclusion in law reform, reflects the realization that in order to communicate on the basis of rough equality, patients require an array of different forms of support in practice.[34]

For example, in Canada, there has been a formalization of support networks constituted by informal supporters (peers, family members, partners, and so on from beyond the health system itself), who are invited by the individual to support her in both making and effectively communicating decisions. Gooding writes that in addition to helping with practical tasks, "[t]he network also holds a crucial symbolic value ... affirm[ing] to everyone involved, that the person being supported is an equal and a peer – a subject with rights rather than an object of care and welfare."[35] Weller has pointed to psychiatric advance directives as a practical method for formalizing SDM in mental health law,[36]

---

[30] CRPD, *General Comment No. 1*, *supra* note 11, at para. 14.
[31] Ibid.
[32] See, e.g., *General Comment No. 35 of United Nations Human Rights Committee clarifying interpretation of Article 9 (Liberty and security of person)* para 19. CCPR/C/GC/35 (2014). See also, e.g., *General Observation of the Committee for the Elimination of all Forms of Discrimination Against Persons with Disabilities (CEDDIS), on the Need to Interpret Article 1.2(B) in Fine of the Inter-American Convention on the Elimination of All Forms of Discrimination Against Persons with Disabilities in the Context of Article 12 of the United Nations Convention on the Rights of Persons with Disabilities*, Committee for the Elimination of All Forms of Discrimination Against Persons with Disabilities (CEDDIS), CEDDIS/RES.1 (I-E/11) (2011). Likewise, a draft protocol to the African Charter on Human and People's Rights recognizes the right to legal capacity of all persons with disabilities. *Protocol to the African Charter on Human and People's Rights on the Rights of Persons with Disabilities in Africa*, African Commission on Human and People's Rights (2018).
[33] Gooding, Supported decision-making.
[34] Jeste, D., Dunn, L., Palmer, B., Saks, E., Halpain, M., Cook, A., Appelbaum, P., & Schneiderman, L. (2003). A collaborative model for research on decisional capacity and informed consent in older patients with schizophrenia: Bioethics unit of a geriatric psychiatry intervention research center. *Psychopharmacology*, 171(1), 68–74. https://doi.org/10.1007/s00213-003-1507-x.
[35] Gooding, Supported decision-making.
[36] Weller, P. (2008). Supported decision-making and the achievement of non-discrimination: The promise and paradox of the Disabilities Convention. *Law in Context: A Socio-Legal Journal*, 26(2), 85–110.

which could be done so as to "take account of varying mental health conditions and the specific institutional contexts in which mental health treatment is provided."[37] In Sweden, personal ombudsmen are often trained social workers or lawyers who are supposed to support the patient's negotiations in the health system and when necessary "argue effectively for the client's rights in front of various authorities or in court." In the UK, the Centre for the Human Rights of Users and Survivors of Psychiatry has advocated "Intentional Peer Support" by other persons with psychosocial disability as a form of SDM. Such family-based and informal support networks already exist throughout much of the Global South and may make SDM more feasible in contexts of limited resources in health systems as well. However, the UN Special Rapporteur on Disability Catalina Devandas cautions that SDM must accommodate not only variability in the extent of support required, but also variability in where this support comes from: "while peers and social networks often make for trustworthy supporters, many individuals in the disabled community do not have access to these networks. To that end, it is the state's responsibility for ensuring that those requiring supported decision-making receive the support they need regardless of severity of disability or extent of social network."[38]

It is important to underscore that the same insights regarding both the variation in modes and sources, as well as the state's responsibility, apply more broadly to decision-making with respect to health by diverse persons. For example, in a case involving the involuntary sterilization of an indigenous woman, *I. V. v Bolivia*, the Inter-American Court of Human Rights recognized that:

> Given the power imbalance that is typical of the relationship between health professionals and their patients ... the contextual needs for truly informed consent has meant that a change in the paradigm of the doctor-patient relationship, in that free and informed decision-making requires a participatory process with the patient and not the paternalistic model in which the doctor was the one to decide what was best for the person with regard to undergoing a specific treatment.[39]

Additional factors the Inter-American Court takes into account are the level of education and poverty, etc., which – among other things – could make absorbing information and communication more difficult and exacerbate power imbalances.[40] In short, implementing SDM for persons with psychosocial disabilities requires specific innovations and considerations to be balanced which in no way should be minimized. Nonetheless, it is not a stretch to assert informed consent for *all persons* requires a range of different support modes that can vary with personal characteristics and the specific health issue, as well as over a person's lifetime.

It would be naïve to argue that there will not be emergencies in which, as Freeman et al put it, "a person with mental illness is a danger to self or to others,

---

[37] Ibid.
[38] *Report of the Special Rapporteur*, supra note 25.
[39] *I. V. v. Bolivia*, Report No. 72/14, Merits, Inter-American Commission on Human Rights Case 12.655 (2014), para. 122.
[40] Ibid., para. 130.

[such as] hearing voices that tell him or her to hurt themselves or another person."[41] All rights require balancing in the context of a democratic society; similarly the rights of a particular subject with psychosocial disabilities must be considered in the context of respecting the rights of others, who have equal claims to dignity. Nonetheless, these exceptional circumstances must be confined carefully. Just as the allocation of health entitlements in a democratic health system should be done through a process that accords users equal moral consideration and is subject to justification, so to should any process that deprives an individual of freedoms. Indeed, Article 12(4) of the CRPD sets out a process that balances the need to intervene with a range of protections for the will and preferences of the person, proportionate and sensitive to background discrimination that can affect determination of capacity. And, as Weller writes, "in the absence of an examination of the substance of the decision-making process, [the] traditional legal safeguards of second medical opinion, review or appeal are useful but insufficient strategies to ensure CRPD compliance."[42]

More broadly, facilitating meaningful SDM processes requires identifying supporters for persons with psychosocial disabilities within and beyond the system *before crises arise*. Gooding suggests the "Open Dialogues" approach pioneered in Finland, "wherein care decisions are made in the presence of the individual and their wider networks, even during severe psychosis."[43] Gooding writes that:

> preliminary results of a two-year follow up found that a group of people with a first instance diagnosis of schizophrenia who used the approach 'were hospitalized for fewer days, family meetings were organized more often and neuroleptic medication was used in fewer cases ... [and] participants experienced fewer relapses and less residual psychotic symptoms and their employment status was better than in the (non-participating) comparison group.'[44]

Likewise, "joint crisis plans" are advance agreements that have been piloted in England and developed in consultation with national service-user groups. Henderson, Flood, Leese, Thornicroft, Sutherby and Szmukler found that the "use of joint crisis plans reduced compulsory admissions and treatment in patients with severe mental illness."[45] The usefulness of these different mechanisms are subject to debate.[46] Nonetheless, these and many other examples make clear that SDM and substitute decision-making should not be seen as binary options that

---

[41] Freeman, et al., Reversing hard won victories in the name of human rights.
[42] Weller, P. (2014). The Convention on the Rights of Persons with Disabilities and the social model of health: New perspectives. *International Journal of Mental Health and Capacity Law* 21, 74. https://doi.org/10.19164/ijmhcl.v0i21.234.
[43] Gooding, Supported decision-making.
[44] Ibid.
[45] Flood, C., Byford, S., Henderson, C., Leese, M., Thornicroft, G., Sutherby, K., & Szmukler, G. (2006). Joint crisis plans for people with psychosis: Economic evaluation of a randomised controlled trial. *BMJ*, 333(7571), 729–732. https://doi.org/10.1136/bmj.38929.653704.55.
[46] Freeman et al., Reversing hard won victories in the name of human rights.

emerge in a moment of crisis. Innovative practices can be developed across contexts of varying resources, which allow for ensuring adequate support, ranging from minimal to very extensive.

However, such experimentalism requires stepping back from the moment of crisis to address issues embedded in mental health service delivery models more broadly. For example, health delivery systems based on primary care, where providers are closer to the communities they serve, and have personal knowledge of people in the catchment area, are more likely to produce processes of communication that most accurately reflect individuals' will and preferences. Unfortunately, as Weller notes, in the economic North, "the chronic under-resourcing of mental health systems following global deinstitutionalization in the context of neoliberal economic policies has compounded the inadequate provision of appropriate community services, placed stress on acute services resulting in inappropriate discharge practices and limited access to appropriate general health care."[47] Likewise, in the Global South, in addition to low priority on mental health in general, the shackles of austerity have caused health systems to impose cost barriers and retract community health promotion activities that could enable greater identification and use of support.

III CONCLUDING REFLECTIONS

There is an alchemy by which some assertions of agency are considered valid while others are not. Constructing health rights, and all human rights, has meant enlarging our understanding of *agency* and the actors who are entitled to assert it – in the private sphere as well as public domain, in relation to democratic deliberation and accountability, and as requiring communication between embodied social beings, not an abstract autonomy.[48] Patricia Williams famously likened rights to a "magic wand of visibility and invisibility, of inclusion and exclusion, of power and no power."[49] In health systems, people's well-being and sometimes even lives qualitatively depend on those vested with authority regarding them as fully human. On the one hand, the real needs of persons with psychosocial disabilities are systematically marginalized and invisibilized in health financing and priority setting. On the other, persons experiencing emotional crises are still regularly treated as *situations* to be resolved by biomedical means, reinforcing their invisibility, "thingness," and lack of power. Recognizing the need to guarantee the effective enjoyment of health rights for all persons, including those with psychosocial disabilities, therefore calls for

---

[47] Ibid.
[48] Yamin, *When Misfortune Becomes Injustice*, 175–201.
[49] Williams, P. J. (1987). Alchemical notes: Reconstructing ideals from deconstructed rights (Minority critiques of the critical legal studies movement; selected papers written for a panel discussion at the 10th National Critical Legal Studies Conference, January 7, 1987). *Harvard Civil Rights-Civil Liberties Law Review*, 22(2), 433.

dramatically modifying how agency is defined and protected in the institutional practices in our health systems.

Throughout this chapter, I have suggested that the challenges faced by persons with psychosocial disabilities both in terms of abuses within health systems and a lack of appropriate mental health care provide insights into the ways in which health systems more broadly reinforce patterns of exclusion and marginalization in our overall societies, as opposed to upholding fundamental normative commitments to equality and dignity for diverse human beings. In this context, as well as others, challenges relate not just to entrenched discrimination and prejudice, often enshrined in law, but also to epistemic premises that stem from the biomedical paradigm, which are reflected in clinical training and practice, as well as in conventional public health programs and metrics. Additionally, I have argued that there is a toxic synergy between the logic of biological individualism and the increasing marketization of health systems and societies more broadly that stem from neoliberal economic paradigms, which further exacerbates both the denial of care and the challenges to SDM. In short, realizing the effective enjoyment of health rights of persons with psychosocial disabilities as well as other diverse human beings, including rights to SDM within health systems, may call for nothing less than reshaping the political economy of global health.

2

Redefining International Mental Health Care in the Wake of the COVID-19 Pandemic

Benjamin A. Barsky, Julie Hannah, and Dainius Pūras

Abstract

The COVID-19 pandemic has exacerbated inequities for people with psychosocial disabilities producing in its wake a serious obstacle for mental health policymakers and advocates committed to upholding Article 12 of the Convention on the Rights of Persons with Disabilities. To overcome this obstacle, stakeholders must resist a common tendency in international mental health policymaking: to over-invest in interventions that arise from a biomedical conception of mental illness. Instead, the pandemic is an opportunity to look beyond the dominant biomedical framework in international mental health care – which has a record of undermining Article 12 principles like legal capacity, autonomy, and self-determination – toward one based on human rights. This shift in positionality will serve to uphold Article 12 and help fulfill the spectrum of human rights for people with psychosocial disabilities.

INTRODUCTION

The COVID-19 pandemic has brought the global community to its knees, laying bare severe inequities in societies of all kinds.[1] By many measures, these inequities arise from social and institutional legacies that have undermined the dignity and worth of certain population groups, including people with psychosocial disabilities. Regrettably, research so far shows that policy responses to COVID-19, such as lockdowns, physical distancing, and the associated breakdown of social connections, have worsened risk factors associated with mental health conditions (Torales et al. 2020; Rajkumar 2020; Holmes et al. 2020). The pandemic thus represents a significant obstacle for mental health policymakers and advocates committed to upholding Article 12 of the Convention on the Rights of Persons with Disabilities

---

[1] The authors wrote this chapter during the summer of 2020. Although they had the opportunity to review this chapter before publication in 2021, they decided not to alter the substance in an intention to preserve what they had experienced and learned approximately six months into the COVID-19 pandemic.

(CRPD), particularly its principles of legal capacity for all and equal recognition before the law.

To overcome this obstacle, however, we caution international actors – including governments, service providers, and researchers – against a temptation that has pervaded mental health policymaking in the last several decades: to overinvest in biomedical interventions at the detriment of social and human rights-oriented services (Chapman et al. 2020). In this chapter, we offer insights on how these actors should instead use the pandemic as an opportunity to pivot away from the dominant biomedical paradigm – which often compromises autonomy and opportunities for individual self-determination – in favor of one based on human rights. By integrating human rights norms, reforming international mental health practice, and moving past unduly coercive practices, this paradigm shift will serve to uphold Article 12 and its promises for people with psychosocial disabilities around the world.

This chapter proceeds in two parts. First, we discuss current practices in international mental health care, calling attention to the fact that the biomedical status quo often results in coercive and asymmetrical patient–provider relationships, stigma, and an arbitrary hierarchization of fundamental rights. Second, we argue that framing the mental health consequences of the pandemic as a crisis of individual conditions, as opposed to one of communal responsibility, will constitute a missed opportunity to make the changes needed to achieve the aims of Article 12. We thus call for human rights-oriented change within and beyond international mental health services. Within international mental health care, stakeholders should seek to bolster innovative forms of support and care, including through remote ways of providing services, dismantling untherapeutic environments, and reconceptualizing universal healthcare coverage. Beyond, they should look to align their actions more closely with international law and the CRPD more specifically, while addressing social determinants that threaten mental health.

1 THE BIOMEDICAL PARADIGM, COVID-19, AND CURTAILING ARTICLE 12

Research on how to address the mental health consequences of the pandemic is still underway. Yet, a consensus may already be coalescing around the idea that nations should focus their investments on biomedical advances and interventions. In an already widely cited position paper in *Lancet Psychiatry*, for instance, Emily A. Holmes and her colleagues emphasize the need to study the neurotoxic effects of COVID-19, including through "building pathology and molecular neuroscience networks to enable brain and other tissue to be collected at autopsy and examined for viral infection and damage" (Holmes et al. 2020). They also push for the "discovery, evaluation, and refinement of mechanistically driven interventions to address the psychological, social, and neuroscientific aspects of this pandemic" (Holmes et al. 2020).

Holmes and her colleagues, along with the broader mental health academic community, have not ignored how the pandemic has exacerbated certain social determinants associated with mental illness, to be sure (Holmes et al. 2020; Galea, Merchant, & Lurie 2020; Ghebreyesus 2020; Khoo & Lantos 2020; United Nations 2020). They recognize that by upending employment, educational, and social support systems, the pandemic has worsened pre-existing vulnerabilities for many population groups, including people with intellectual and developmental disabilities; marginalized groups like incarcerated people, the homeless, and refugees; and lower-income, majority-minority, and Indigenous communities. We agree with this aspect of the analysis and we hope and hope that competing biomedical priorities will not crowd it out. Unfortunately, prevailing practices in international mental health care render us doubtful that this hope will be realized.

The history of medicine is a narrative of great progress, achievement, and breakthrough. But it is also one of expansive human rights violations, illustrated by practices that have subjugated, harmed, and even killed vulnerable individuals receiving care (Pūras 2017). Perhaps unsurprisingly, the history of psychiatric and mental health care has followed a similar course. Stakeholders calling for the prioritization of widespread mental health treatment have successfully argued for a conceptual model that frames mental health conditions in biomedical terms (*The Lancet* 2011). What has emerged is a policy orientation that focuses on the development of neuroscience and pharmaceutical treatment options that, like other medical treatments, result in narrow and often immediately measurable outcomes.

At the same time, however, this orientation has led to problematic practices that may continue unabated, even once the pandemic is under control. First, it has led to coercive treatment practices that undermine service users' rights to autonomy, capacity, and dignity protected under Article 12 of the CRPD. Providers have also become gatekeepers of the well-being of people with psychosocial disabilities, legally entrusted to assess legal capacity and administer treatment without consent, frequently in violent and degrading circumstances. Second, asymmetrical power relationships between providers and patients, often fueled by paternalistic attitudes carried by conventional psychiatry adherents, have served to contribute to the stigma associated with psychosocial disabilities. Third, mental health services have tended to prioritize certain rights (e.g., treatment and access to care) while neglecting others (e.g., autonomy, liberty, family and community care). In the next sections, we explore each of these problems in more detail.

1.1 *Coercion and Power Asymmetries*

In international mental health care, coercive practices like forced treatment and substituted decision-making have contributed to what Natalie Drew and her colleagues have called "an unresolved global practice" (Drew et al. 2011). Medical experts generally agree that, as compared to other health care settings, coercion happens most often in mental health care. This widespread reliance on coercion is due in part to the traditional psychiatric view that providers should determine the direction of treatment. Under this understanding, decision-making, priority-setting, and the organization of care often fall in the hands of mental health care specialists and occur in settings that are isolated from the lives of service users. As a result, providers unilaterally decide what is best for people diagnosed with mental health conditions, which jeopardizes the ability of service users to participate in their treatment course.

Coercion in mental health care takes on different forms, including treatment pressures (e.g., incentives and sanctions), interpersonal leverage, threats, and the legally sanctioned use of force to make a person accept treatment (Szmukler 2015). Treatment over objection – the most drastic of these measures – frequently necessitates the use of behavioral controls, "including different forms of restraint (mechanical, physical or pharmacological), forcible seclusion in confined spaces, treatment by administration of medication without the person's consent and restrictive conditions imposed as part of treatment and supervision in the community" (Sashidharan, Mezzina, & Pūras 2019). Coercive practices also occur in several types of settings, notably inpatient psychiatric institutions, where there can be "an absence of recovery-oriented treatment, with people with mental and psychosocial disabilities chained to beds or posts and made immobile for long periods of time" (Drew et al. 2011). These practices also occur in non-clinical and punitive settings, such as jails, prisons, and other detention facilities, which raises the risk of having abusive practices left unchecked by clinical, legal, and democratically accountable oversight mechanisms.

From a human rights standpoint, undue coercion is problematic for multiple reasons. Most basically, the etiology and phenomenology of mental illness remain a subject of much scholarly attention and debate. The biological processes behind mental health conditions are also poorly understood. Yet, coercive practices like forced medicalization and pharmaceutical interventions often transpire under the guise of evidence-based practice, even though available evidence showing their clinical benefits is debatable (D'Lima 2017; Luciano et al. 2014; Sailas & Fenton 2000; Wright 2003). If anything, research has shown that coercive practices can adversely impact quality of life for people with psychosocial disabilities, leaving many traumatized and disempowered (Corrigan et al. 2003; Kallert, Glöckner, & Schützwohl 2008; Paksarian et al. 2014).

What is more, people with mental health conditions often have to confront power asymmetries with their providers, leaving them at the mercy of paternalistic decision-making. The former United Nations Special Rapporteur on the right to health has included these forms of asymmetries as part of a "global burden of obstacles" to promoting human rights-based mental health policies and practices (UN Human

Rights Council 2017; Pūras 2017). Power asymmetries between providers and service users weaken therapeutic relationships and dissuade "people from seeking further treatment thus increasing the risk of non-adherence and involuntary treatment, particularly those with long-term mental health problems" (Sashidharan, Mezzina, & Pūras 2019). Given the positive influence that the social sciences, humanities, and other disciplines (e.g., community and social psychiatry) have had on conventional psychiatry throughout the twentieth century, we would hope that this kind of show of power would become a thing of the past (Bracken 2014; Priebe, Burns, & Craig 2013). But the use of paternalistic and coercive practices persists, revealing one of many paradoxes in mental health practice, and one of the central barriers to fulfilling Article 12's commitment to promoting autonomy and self-determination for people with psychosocial disabilities.

1.2 Stigma and Abnormalizing the Normal

Stigma represents another persistent obstacle to protecting equal rights and legal capacity for people with mental health conditions (Randall 2010; McDaid 2008). Conventional psychiatry adherents have long held that people with psychosocial disabilities are "ill" and thus unable to participate fully in social, political, or economic pursuits. This labeling, exacerbated by the biomedical model's flawed equivalence between mental health conditions and physical illnesses, has contributed to perceptions of incapacity, preventing individuals with psychosocial disabilities from integrating into society and enjoying decision-making capacity (Sashidharan, Mezzina, & Pūras 2019). And yet, as international systems prepare for the predicted rising tide of mental health issues caused by the pandemic, we fear that certain behavioral reactions like stress and anxiety will be overpathologized, a response that may only serve to marginalize further those in need. That risk is particularly salient in areas of the world that continue to use colonial-era psychiatric asylums, as coercive interventions perpetuate the impression that people with mental health conditions are unpredictable and dangerous (Mascayano, Armijo, & Yang 2015).

Furthermore, overestimating the prevalence of mental illness through the pathologization of certain behaviors and emotional reactions will provide a biased picture of the pandemic's impact. This approach will blur the line between people who need clinical attention and those whose conditions may attenuate through non-clinical interventions. The kind of "mass pathologization" might force vulnerable people into traditional mental health care systems, even if they stand to derive more benefit from employment, educational, and social support systems (Horwitz & Wakefield 2007). The latter issue in particular might have the perverse distributional effect of burdening already weakened healthcare systems while simultaneously reinforcing a system that has a history of perpetuating stigma.

1.3 *The Arbitrary Hierarchization of Fundamental Rights*

International mental health care has also tended to uphold certain fundamental rights while undermining others. For example, although mental health systems offer care to people in need, it may come at the cost of other rights (e.g., informed consent), particularly when it occurs under conditions of coercion. For many, this arbitrary prioritization of rights can cause harm. It also undercuts a bedrock principle of Article 12 – that is, the ability of people with disabilities to "[fend] off others purporting to make decisions for us" (Quinn 2011). Person-centered mental health care is thus necessary to protect the autonomy and dignity of individuals with psychosocial disabilities, and it serves as an ethical orientation that aligns with the CRPD.

One of the authors here has already observed that this problematic phenomenon runs in parallel to the human rights travesties that have occurred in some orphanages and other types of residential institutions in Central and Eastern Europe (UN Human Rights Council 2015). These orphanages came into being during an era of charity and paternalism, when the state was expected to take over the upbringing of children who grow up in at-risk families, so to provide essential needs like nutrition and shelter. But evidence started to emerge showing that institutionalized children often had at least one parent from whom they had suffered separation, and that massive institutionalization of children did more harm than good. The orphanage system's choice to prioritize one set of rights (e.g., nutrition and shelter) over others (e.g., living in family and community) meant overlooking the right to a supportive family environment. This failure caused many institutionalized children irreparable physical and mental health harm.

2 CHANGING PARADIGMS

In light of the pandemic, international systems must look for opportunities to redefine how to care for people with psychosocial disabilities within and beyond mental health services. In so doing, they should aim to put people with psychosocial disabilities "at the center of the discourse" (United Nations Enable). This orientation will fulfill the obligation under Article 12 "to take appropriate measures to provide access by persons with disabilities to the support they may require in exercising their legal capacity."

2.1 *Within Mental Health Services*

2.1.1 Expanding Access to Remote Forms of Care

Given the mass isolation caused by the pandemic, offering remote forms of mental health care must become a priority for countries across the world. The delivery of such care can occur via videoconferencing, internet forums, phone applications, text messaging, and emails (Zhou et al. 2020). A robust tele-mental health care infrastructure would ideally ensure that service users – particularly the most vulnerable – can access care under their own terms and from the comfort of their homes or other dedicated care facilities. Research has already shown that such care will assist people with mental health conditions to "maintain psychological well-being and cope with acute and post-acute health requirements more favorably" (Zhou et al. 2020). Moreover, as John Torous and Til Wykes have explained, "digital health platforms could be important developments from this pandemic, but the most enduring will be investment in the people, process, and support to ensure telehealth cycles of interest are not tied to disasters but rather improve care every day" (Torous, & Wykes 2020).

Several countries (e.g., the Netherlands, Sweden, and the United States) have facilitated the widespread use of tele-mental health care services through the lifting of legal and regulatory barriers (Wind et al. 2020; Torous & Wykes 2020). In the United States, for example, the Coronavirus Aid, Relief, and Economic Security Act helped expand insurance coverage for people with mental health conditions who required immediate tele-behavioral health services (P.L. 116–136). Nevertheless, most countries lack the resources or the will to develop the technological and policy infrastructure necessary to deploy remote mental health care services at scale (Ohannessian, Duong, & Odone 2020). For example, despite being one of the countries hardest hit by the pandemic, Italy did not include telehealth as an essential health care service covered by the *Servizio sanitario nazionale*, the country's universal healthcare system (Ohannessian, Duong, & Odone 2020). Furthermore, access to the Internet is often stratified across racial and economic lines, resulting in what many call the "Digital Divide" (Van Dijk 2017; Fairlie 2004). Addressing these gaps through best practices and laws that ensure access and the protection of service users' privacy will not only make countries more resilient to future crises. It will also offer an alternative, less restrictive avenue of support for people with psychosocial disabilities, bolstering their ability to readily access care. An expansion of the scope of mental health care services beyond those traditionally offered in clinical settings is a necessary step forward in addressing the pandemic and fulfilling the aims of Article 12.

2.1.2 Dismantling Untherapeutic Environments

International mental health care policymakers must also take accountability for the gaps in care in non-clinical settings, such as carceral institutions and immigration detention centers. As the pandemic continues to unfold, this obligation becomes all the more urgent because places of detention house a disproportionate amount of people with mental illness (Liebrenz et al. 2020). These places are also "epicenters for infectious diseases because of the higher background prevalence of infection, the higher levels of risk factors for infection, the unavoidable close contact in often overcrowded, poorly ventilated, and unsanitary facilities, and the poor access to health-care services relative to that in community settings" (Kinner et al. 2020).

In times of crisis like the current pandemic, these issues coalesce in making places of detention inhumane. One part of the problem involves the heightened risk of preventable death caused by the high rates of infection and the lack of adequate clinical infrastructure. In the United States, estimates suggest that around 108,000 inmates had contracted COVID-19 as of August 2020, and almost 900 had already died due to complications associated with the virus (The Marshall Project 2020). Similarly eerie numbers were captured in the United Kingdom, where epidemiologists predicted that the pandemic could cause more than 800 preventable deaths in the country's prison system (Institute of Epidemiology and Health Care 2020). Another part of the problem is that individuals feel unsafe in institutional settings, leading them to experience unrest and outrage. In Mexico, for instance, a riot broke out in an immigration detention center over fears that overcrowding and unsanitary conditions would expose the detained population to infection. This incident left one person dead and others severely injured (The Associated Press 2020).

One of the authors here has already argued for the diversion of people with mental illness away from the criminal legal system (Barsky, Cucolo, & Sisti 2020). The idea underlying of this argument is that non-clinical institutional settings like jails and prisons lack the resources, expertise, and accountability mechanisms necessary to respond to the needs of people with mental illness, resorting reflexively and discriminatorily to drastic and punitive practices like solitary confinement. The pandemic has magnified the need to both eliminate unduly punitive practices and dismantle untherapeutic environments (UN Human Rights Council 2018). Indeed, if people with mental health conditions cannot receive minimally appropriate attention in these kinds of settings, opportunities for rehabilitation and self-determination are rendered impossible. This result is repugnant to the principles of Article 12.

2.1.3 Humanizing Universal Health Coverage and Access

As part of its 2030 *Agenda for Sustainable Development*, the World Health Organization (WHO) has made it a priority to "achieve universal health coverage and access to quality health care" (UN General Assembly 2015). But, in the wake of the pandemic, achieving "physical and mental health and well-being," as the WHO has set out to do, will involve more than health care coverage and access (UN General Assembly 2015). To achieve this goal, and to overcome the mental health challenges caused by the pandemic, international mental health care systems must adopt a person-centered, human rights-based understanding of universal health care that eschews a narrow biomedical conceptualization of health. Strengthening global mental health systems based on principles of legal capacity, self-determination, nondiscrimination, and participation is vital for people with mental health conditions, as they are particularly at risk of coming into prolonged and repeated contact with such systems throughout their lives.

One facet of this expansive understanding of universal health coverage will involve research on the critical role played by what the CRPD defines under Article 27 as the right to work and employment – that is, "the opportunity to gain a living by work freely chosen or accepted in a labour market and work environment that is open, inclusive and accessible." According to recent research from Bangladesh and India, several suicides have occurred due to work deprivation and other forms of economic distress (Bhuiyan et al. 2020; Dsouza et al. 2020). These troubling events corroborate past research that has found that "economic recession, unemployment, and poverty are strongly associated with severe psychological comorbidities such as suicidal behaviors" (Bhuiyan et al. 2020). Thus, if global mental health systems are to prevent increased incidences of mental illness and suicide, they must look beyond clinical interventions and into preventive economic relief programs, which can help protect people who lose their income and are otherwise in financially precarious positions. A corollary benefit of this proposal also centers on ensuring that people with psychosocial disabilities can "control their own financial affairs," which is an objective of Article 12.

A critical assessment of how mental health systems have responded to the needs of homeless people and others who have lesser or no means for self-determination is also necessary. For a long time, researchers have recognized that homelessness is a risk factor for mental illness (Bassuk, Rubin, & Lauriat 1984). Plus, as Jack Tsai and Michal Wilson have warned, people experiencing homelessness are particularly at risk of COVID-19 exposure because many "congregate in living settings – be it formal (i.e., shelters or halfway houses) or informal (i.e., encampments or abandoned buildings) – and might not have regular access to basic hygiene supplies or showering facilities" (Tsai & Wilson 2020). Global mental health stakeholders must, therefore, take account of the need to offer sheltering services, where the priority is both to offer basic living services and to connect people with needed community-based services.

2.2 Beyond Mental Health Services

The pandemic has exacerbated certain social determinants (e.g., inequality and discrimination) that contribute to mental illness (Compton & Shim 2015). Rolling back this damage will require ingenuity and creativity on the part of global mental health stakeholders. But, doing so will require that governments design social policy and invest in services beyond mental health care that aim to maximize the improvement of social determinants that contribute to mental health conditions. No one-size-fits-all solution exists, to be sure. But certain human rights principles, including those enunciated in Article 12 and other provisions in the CRPD, can serve as guideposts as countries continue to coordinate with global mental health stakeholders in setting up an infrastructure capable of weathering the pandemic. Two of the authors here have contributed to producing a set of critical elements for rights-based supports for crisis response, setting an important starting point for how human rights standards can translate into operational elements at the practical level (Stastny et al. 2020). What follows is thus less of a formula and more of an evidence-based exercise in understanding how services beyond mental health care can help people with mental illness cope with the pandemic.

One obvious area of concern relates to how countries provide supported decision-making, integration, and community-based services to elderly people. Article 12 espouses a person-centered policy framework, one in which all people should have the ability to care for themselves autonomously and free of unduly coercive constraint (Barsky 2021). Furthermore, Article 19 of the CRPD recognizes the right of "all persons with disabilities to live in the community" and requires that countries "take effective and appropriate measures to facilitate full enjoyment by persons with disabilities of this right." But the pandemic has made clear that the institutional model of care for the elderly – namely nursing homes and other senior housing facilities – is a failure and has isolated this vulnerable segment of the population while establishing conditions propitious for mass infection, suffering, and death (Armitage & Nellums 2020). To fulfill the rights to self-determination, independence, and community inclusion, systems of elderly care must change. But who will bear this burden? Governments? Innovators in the private sector? The public? As the pandemic continues to affect communities across the world, and as global mental health stakeholders continue to address not only the current pandemic, but also future crises, these questions will only grow in importance. What is clear, however, is that the status quo has favored practices of isolation and marginalization. These practices are a sure way to short-circuit hope for a more inclusive future.

Another urgent area concerns the development of supportive and preventive services for children, especially those with psychosocial and intellectual disabilities. Article 7 of the CRPD requires that countries "take all necessary measures to ensure the full enjoyment by children with disabilities of all human rights and fundamental freedoms on an equal basis with other children." But, by upending the provision of social services like schools, which have traditionally operated as "a de facto mental health system for many children and adolescents," the pandemic has impacted the attainment of developmental milestones. Moreover, as Louise Dalton and her colleagues have stated, rapid COVID-19 spread has required "caring for a predominantly adult patient population, magnifying the invisibility of children's urgent psychological needs" (Dalton, Rapa, & Stein 2020). Solutions to these problems can only come through initiatives rooted in access (e.g., tele-mental health and online learning platforms), inclusion (e.g., financial packages for economically distressed families and universal education), and non-discrimination (e.g., robust legal protections for children with disabilities).

Evidence also shows that adverse childhood experiences (ACE) contribute to a high prevalence of physical and mental health conditions that can persist through life (Monnat & Chandler 2015; Schilling, Aseltine, & Gore 2007). Starting from infancy, children can suffer from different forms of violence, including emotional abuse and neglect. When such forms of violence reach the level of toxic stress, the brain and body will learn to react to any stressful event in harmful ways. Given research showing a relationship between the pandemic and increased instances of family violence – a phenomenon that may have to do with the stress caused by measures like lockdowns and social distancing – more children will be vulnerable to suffering adverse childhood experiences (Usher et al. 2020). But pathologization and medicalization of effects of ACEs and toxic stress would be counterproductive. Instead, we suggest that there should be more investments to promote healthy holistic development and positive parenting, so that children are protected from any forms of violence.

Although important, these issues are far from exhaustive. But the approach we propose here – that is, enhancing social determinants of mental health while promoting human rights principles in tackling problems caused by the pandemic – should apply in all areas of social policy. In the context of global mental health care, this approach is of particular importance. Resorting to a biomedical conception of mental health, as well as the coercive and other problematic practices that have long stemmed from it, will not assist the millions of people whose mental health and well-being have deteriorated because of the pandemic. Turning to the CRPD and other sources of international human rights policy and law will best calibrate policy interventions.

3 CONCLUSION

The COVID-19 pandemic has created conditions that may very well increase the incidence of mental health conditions in communities across the world. To address this generation-defining challenge, however, international mental health systems need to look beyond a biomedical conception of mental health and toward an orientation predicated on the kinds of human rights principles embedded in Article 12. By humanizing mental health treatment services and investing in policies that prioritize social determinants, this approach will enable the design of interventions that place people – and their well-being – first.

The pandemic – a global catastrophe that has caused the death of millions, and the suffering of millions more – thus represents a moment of reflection and learning for stakeholders committed to upholding Article 12 and the principles it enshrines. In this spirit, we are reminded of what the late Dr. Martin Luther King, Jr. told a crowd in Memphis, Tennessee, at the height of the Civil Rights Movement, the day before his assassination: "that only when it is dark enough can you see the stars."

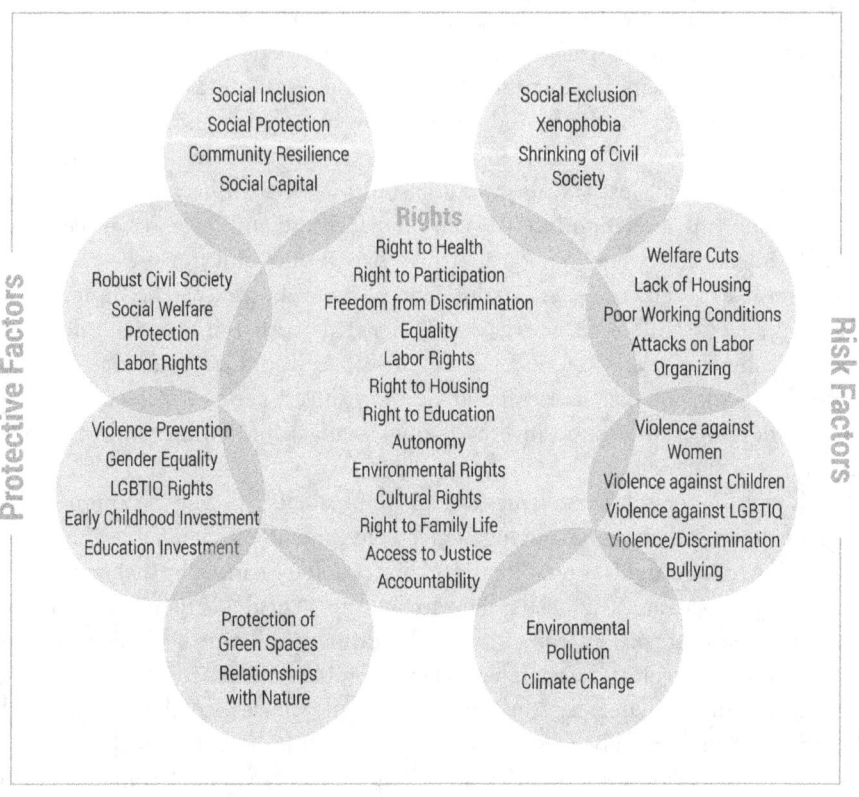

FIGURE 2.1 Risk and protective factors for mental health promotion
Source: University of Essex Human Rights Centre

The stars here represent a new way of caring for people with psychosocial disabilities, a population group that continues to suffer discrimination, oppression, and subjugation. And only in moments of deep change – like those in which we live at this moment – can an honest, introspective process of reform occur. Now is a time like no other to change paradigms.

REFERENCES

Armitage, R., & Nellums, L. B. (2020). COVID-19 and the consequences of isolating the elderly. *The Lancet Public Health*, 5(5), 256.
Barsky, B. A. (2021). Dual federalism, constitutional openings, and the Convention on the Rights of Persons with Disabilities. *University of Pennsylvania Journal of Constitutional Law* (In Press).
Barsky, B. A., Cucolo, H., & Sisti, D. A. (2020). Expanding therapeutic jurisprudence across the federal judiciary. *Journal of the American Academy of Law and Psychiatry*. https://doi.org/10.29158/JAAPL.200040-20

Bassuk, E. L., Rubin, L., & Lauriat, A. (1984). Is homelessness a mental health problem? *American journal of psychiatry*, 141(12), 1546–50.
Bhuiyan, A., Sakib, N., Pakpour, A. H., Griffiths, M. D., & Mamun, M. A. (2020). COVID-19-related suicides in Bangladesh due to lockdown and economic factors: case study evidence from media reports. *International journal of mental health and addiction*, 1–6. Advance online publication.
Bracken, P. (2014). Towards a hermeneutic shift in psychiatry. *World Psychiatry*, 13(3), 241.
Chapman, A., Williams, C., Hannah, J., & Pūras, D. (2020). Reimagining the mental health paradigm for our collective well-being. *Health and Human Rights*, 22(1), 1.
Compton, M. T., & Shim, R. S. (2015). The social determinants of mental health. *Focus*, 13(4), 419–25.
Coronavirus Aid, Relief, and Economic Security Act, P.L. 116–136.
Corrigan, P., Markowitz, F., Watson, A., Rowan, D., & Kubiak, M. (2003). An attribution model of public discrimination towards persons with mental illness. *Journal of Health and Social Behavior*, 44(2), 162–79.
Dalton, L., Rapa, E., & Stein, A. (2020). Protecting the psychological health of children through effective communication about COVID-19. *The Lancet Child & Adolescent Health*, 4(5), 346–7.
D'Lima, D., Crawford, M. J., Darzi, A., & Archer, S. (2017). Patient safety and quality of care in mental health: a world of its own? *BJPsych Bulletin*, 41(5), 241–3.
Drew, N., Funk, M., Tang, S., et al. (2011). Human rights violations of people with mental and psychosocial disabilities: an unresolved global crisis. *The Lancet*, 378(9803), 1664–75.
Dsouza, D. D., Quadros, S., Hyderabadwala, Z. J., & Mamun, M. A. (2020). Aggregated COVID-19 suicide incidences in India: fear of COVID-19 infection is the prominent causative factor. *Psychiatry Research*, https://doi.org/10.1016/j.psychres.2020.113145
Fairlie, R. (2004). Race and the digital divide. *The B.E. Journal of Economic Analysis & Policy*, 3(1), 1–40.
Galea, S., Merchant, R. M., & Lurie, N. (2020). The mental health consequences of COVID-19 and physical distancing: the need for prevention and early intervention. *JAMA Internal Medicine*, 180(6), 817–8.
Ghebreyesus, T. A. (2020). Addressing mental health needs: an integral part of COVID-19 response. *World Psychiatry*, 19(2), 129.
Holmes, E. A. et al (2020). Multidisciplinary research priorities for the COVID-19 pandemic: a call for action for mental health science. *The Lancet Psychiatry*, 7(6), 547–60.
Horwitz, A. V., & Wakefield, J. C. (2007). *The Loss of Sadness: How Psychiatry Transformed Normal Sorrow into Depressive Disorder*. Oxford University Press.
Institute of Epidemiology and Health Care (April 9, 2020). Preventing and containing Covid-19 outbreaks in prisons. Retrieved from www.ucl.ac.uk/epidemiology-health-care/news/2020/apr/preventing-and-containing-covid-19-outbreaks-prisons.
Kallert, T. W., Glöckner, M., & Schützwohl, M. (2008). Involuntary vs. voluntary hospital admission. *European Archives of Psychiatry and Clinical Neuroscience*, 258(4), 195–209.
Khoo, E. J., Lantos, J. D. (2020). Lessons learned from the COVID-19 pandemic. *Acta Paediatrica*, 2, 1323–5.
Kinner, S. A., Young, J. T., Snow, K., et al. (2020). Prisons and custodial settings are part of a comprehensive response to COVID-19. *The Lancet Public Health*, 5(4), 188–9.
Liebrenz, M., Bhugra, D., Buadze, A., & Schleifer, R. (2020). Caring for persons in detention suffering with mental illness during the Covid-19 outbreak. *Forensic Science International: Mind and Law*, 1. https://doi.org/10.1016/j.fsiml.2020.100013

Luciano, M., Sampogna, G., Del Vecchio, V., et al. (2014). Use of coercive measures in mental health practice and its impact on outcome: a critical review. *Expert Rev Neurother*, 14(2):131–41.

Mascayano, F., Armijo, J. E., & Yang, L. H. (2015). Addressing stigma relating to mental illness in low- and middle-income countries. *Frontiers in Psychiatry*, 6, 38.

McDaid, D. (2008). Countering the Stigmatisation and Discrimination of People with Mental Health Problems in Europe. Luxembourg: European Commission, 1–20.

Monnat, S. M., & Chandler, R. F. (2015). Long-term physical health consequences of adverse childhood experiences. *The Sociological Quarterly*, 56(4), 723–52.

Ohannessian, R., Duong, T. A., & Odone, A. (2020). Global telemedicine implementation and integration within health systems to fight the COVID-19 pandemic: a call to action. *JMIR Public Health and Surveillance*, 6(2), 18810. https://doi.org/10.2196/18810

Paksarian, D., Mojtabai, R., Kotov, R., et al. (2014). Perceived trauma during hospitalization and treatment participation among individuals with psychotic disorders. *Psychiatric Services*, 65(2), 266–9.

Priebe, S., Burns, T., & Craig, T. K. (2013). The future of academic psychiatry may be social. *The British Journal of Psychiatry*, 202(5), 319–20.

Pūras, D (2017). Human rights and the practice of medicine. *Public Health Reviews*, 38 (9), 1–5.

Quinn, G. (2011). Legal capacity law reform: the revolution of the UN Convention on the Rights of Persons with Disability. *Frontline*. Retrieved from https://frontline-ireland.com /legal-capacity-law-reform-the-revolution-of-the-un-convention-on-the-rights-of-persons-with-disability/.

Rajkumar, R. P. (2020). COVID-19 and mental health: a review of the existing literature. *Asian Journal of Psychiatry*, 52, 102066.

Randall, J., Thornicroft, G., Brohan, E., et al. (2012). "Stigma and Discrimination: Critical Human Rights Issues for Mental Health." In M. Dudley, D. Silove and F. Gale (eds.) Mental Health and Human Rights: Vision, Praxis, and Courage. Oxford: Oxford University Press, 113–24.

Sailas, E., & Fenton, M. (2000). Seclusion and restraint for people with serious mental illnesses. *The Cochrane Database of Systematic Reviews*, 2000(2), CD001163. https://doi .org/10.1002/14651858.CD001163

Sashidharan, S., Mezzina, R., & Pūras, D. (2019). Reducing coercion in mental healthcare. *Epidemiology and Psychiatric Sciences*, 28(6), 605–12.

Schilling, E. A., Aseltine, R. H., & Gore, S. (2007). Adverse childhood experiences and mental health in young adults: a longitudinal survey. *BMC Public Health*, 7(1), 30.

Stastny, P., Lovell, A. M., Hannah, J., et al. (2020). Crisis response as a human rights flashpoint: critical elements of community support for individuals experiencing significant emotional distress. *Health and Human Rights*, 22(1), 105.

Szmukler, G. (2015). Compulsion and "coercion" in mental health care. *World Psychiatry*, 14(3), 259.

The Associated Press (April 1, 2020). Migrant dies in Mexico detention center riot over virus fear. Retrieved from https://apnews.com/e8f0224caf612cf1e7bcf28500a01fae.

The Lancet (October 18, 2011). Global mental health 2011. Retrieved from www.thelancet.com /series/global-mental-health-2011.

The Marshall Project (August 28, 2020). A state-by-state look at Coronavirus in prisons. Retrieved from www.themarshallproject.org/2020/05/01/a-state-by-state-look-at-coronavirus-in-prisons.

Torales J., O'Higgins M., Castaldelli-Maia J. M., Ventriglio A. (2020). The outbreak of COVID-19 coronavirus and its impact on global mental health. *Int J Soc Psychiatry*, 66(4), 317–20.

Torous J., Wykes T. (May 11, 2020) Opportunities from the coronavirus disease 2019 pandemic for transforming psychiatric care with telehealth. *JAMA Psychiatry*. Published online.

Tsai, J., & Wilson, M. (2020). COVID-19: a potential public health problem for homeless populations. *The Lancet Public Health*, 5(4), 186–7.

UN General Assembly (2015). Resolution adopted by the General Assembly on 25 September 2015. A/RES/70/1.

UN Human Rights Council (2015). Report of the Special Rapporteur on the right of everyone to the enjoyment of the highest attainable standard of physical and mental health. A/70/213.

UN Human Rights Council (2017). Report of the Special Rapporteur on the right of everyone to the enjoyment of the highest attainable standard of physical and mental health. A/HRC/35/21.

UN Human Rights Council (2018). Report of the Special Rapporteur on the right of everyone to the enjoyment of the highest attainable standard of physical and mental health. A/HRC/38/36.

United Nations (2020). Policy Brief: COVID-19 and the Need for Action on Mental Health.

United Nations Enable (January 18, 2006). Daily summary of discussion at the seventh session. Retrieved from www.un.org/esa/socdev/enable/rights/ahc7sum18jan.htm.

University of Essex Human Rights Centre (n.d.). UN Mandate on the Right to Health. Retrieved from www.essex.ac.uk/research-projects/un-mandate-on-the-right-to-health.

Usher, K., Bhullar, N., Durkin, J., Gyamfi, N., & Jackson, D. (2020). Family violence and COVID-19: increased vulnerability and reduced options for support. *International Journal of Mental Health Nursing*, 29(4), 549–52.

Van Dijk, J. A. (2017). "Digital Divide: Impact of Access." In P. Rössler (ed.) *The International Encyclopedia of Media Effects*, 1–11.

Wind, T. R., Rijkeboer, M., Andersson, G., & Riper, H. (2020). The COVID-19 pandemic: the "black swan" for mental health care and a turning point for e-health. *Internet Interventions*, 20, 100317. https://doi.org/10.1016/j.invent.2020.100317.

Wright, S. (2003). Control and restraint techniques in the management of violence in inpatient psychiatry: a critical review. *Medicine, Science and the Law*, 43(1), 31–8.

Zhou, X., Snoswell, C. L., Harding, L. E., et al. (2020). The role of telehealth in reducing the mental health burden from COVID-19. *Telemedicine and e-Health*, 26(4), 377–9.

3

Reparation for Psychiatric Violence: A Call to Justice

Tina Minkowitz

Abstract

Grounded in my personal experience as a survivor of psychiatric violence, I take a historical approach to the recent development of norms that support a demand for reparations for psychiatric violence. I introduce the reader to the advocacy by the World Network of Users and Survivors of Psychiatry (WNUSP) that led to the establishment of norms in international law that require the abolition of forced psychiatric interventions, and discuss the confirmation by international human rights mechanisms of our position that such interventions are acts of ill treatment and/or torture. Following that, I share key advances and challenges in national implementation, and my proposal for a social model of crisis support to fill a gap in our advocacy and to respond to current challenges. Finally I set out the argument for reparations and indicate the forms it might take.

Personal experience of psychiatric violence[1] led me to join in an advocacy movement for the abolition of these practices, and to work in particular to change and then to utilize the norms of international law. I was one of the key protagonists involved in changing relevant norms through the Convention on the Rights of Persons with Disabilities (CRPD or the Convention), which was adopted by the UN General Assembly in 2006 and entered into force in 2008. The CRPD reversed centuries of discrimination to require respect for the legal capacity of persons with disabilities on an equal basis as others, and to prohibit deprivation of liberty based on the existence of a disability. As I will discuss below, these norms are interpreted in light of the treaty's purpose and its governing principles in a manner that strictly prohibits substitute decision-making and any form of involuntary admission or treatment in mental health settings. States parties to the Convention are, of course, obligated to change their own laws and practices accordingly.

---

[1] I will not elaborate on the nature of my personal experience. By the term "psychiatric violence" I mean any or all of the following: enforced or nonconsensual medication or electroshock; restraint; solitary confinement; other inhuman and degrading practices, including any enforced or non-consensual measures in psychiatric settings; and the imposition of detention itself, which entails these practices and is itself violent for being based on an allegation of personal defect, amounting to disability-based discrimination. The definition can also include symbolic and epistemic violence. This is illustrative and is not intended to be an exhaustive definition.

Despite some phenomenal achievements in international law, we face resistance – as expected with any movement for social justice and equality – and there are wide disparities in power and resources that make it hard to find institutional support for the realization of our full human rights. In this article I present an introduction to the international norms and present circumstances of this movement, and advance the right to reparation as a suitable framework to shape the next phase of implementation.

As I was finalizing this paper, the UN Special Rapporteur on Torture issued a report to the Human Rights Council on psychological torture,[2] in which he acknowledges that "involuntary ... psychiatric intervention based on 'medical necessity' of the 'best interests' of the patient," among other practices "may well amount to torture" if other defining elements are present. I have written a preliminary analysis of the report's significance in a blog post and refer readers there for more information.[3]

CRPD TRANSFORMS INTERNATIONAL LAW

The advocacy by users and survivors of psychiatry to shape the CRPD text and its application by the designated monitoring body has brought the standpoint of a population victimized by law into the formulation of new legal norms that assumes our equal worth, dignity, rights, and capacity to represent ourselves.[4] As a result of our work,[5] the CRPD requires States parties to recognize the legal capacity of persons with disabilities on an equal basis with others, including the right to make healthcare decisions; to prohibit the deprivation of liberty based on disability; and to guarantee the physical and mental integrity of persons with disabilities, including their right to be free from torture and other ill treatment, on an equal basis as others.[6]

---

[2] UN Doc. No. A/HRC/43/49, Advance Unedited Version. Available at www.ohchr.org/EN/HRBodies/HRC/RegularSessions/Session43/Documents/A_HRC_43_49_AUV.docx [hereafter SRT 2020].

[3] Minkowitz, T, (2020) UN Report: Involuntary Psychiatric Interventions "May Well Amount to Torture," *Mad in America*, available at www.madinamerica.com/2020/03/report-psychiatric-interventions-torture/.

[4] Minkowitz, T, (2012) CRPD Advocacy by the World Network of Users and Survivors of Psychiatry: The Emergence of an User/Survivor Perspective in Human Rights, available at www.ssrn.com/abstract=2326668 [hereafter Minkowitz, WNUSP Advocacy].

[5] This is evident from the Negotiation Archive, which can be studied at www.un.org/development/desa/disabilities/resources/ad-hoc-committee-on-a-comprehensive-and-integral-international-convention-on-the-protection-and-promotion-of-the-rights-and-dignity-of-persons-with-disabilities.html. WNUSP advocacy in later sessions of the Ad Hoc Committee was merged into joint International Disability Caucus submissions.

[6] Convention on the Rights of Persons with Disabilities, UNTS vol 2515 p 3, adopted in resolution 61/106 of 2006, UN Doc. No. A/RES/61/106, December 13, 2006 (New York), entered into force May 3, 2008, available at https://treaties.un.org/doc/source/docs/A_RES_61_106-E.pdf, Articles 12, 14, 15, 16 and 17. See also General Comment No. 1 on Article 12, UN Doc. No. CRPD/C/GC/1, available at https://tbinternet.ohchr.org/_layouts/15/treatybodyexternal/Download.aspx?symbolno=CRPD/C/GC/1&Lang=en [hereafter GC1], and Corrigendum, UN Doc. No. CRPD/C/GC/1/Corr.1, available at

As early as 1986 the UN Special Rapporteur on Torture included among the forms of physical torture, "the administration of drugs, in prisons or psychiatric institutions, including ... neuroleptics, which cause shivering, trembling and contractions, but mainly make the subject apathetic and dull his [or her] intelligence."[7] Yet in 1991, the United Nations General Assembly adopted a declaration of "Principles for the Protection of Persons with Mental Illness and for the Improvement of Mental Health Care," which legitimized involuntary treatments (as a matter of routine practice emphasizing those same neuroleptic drugs) as a series of exceptions to the right to informed consent.[8] The 1991 Principles also legitimized guardianship and involuntary admissions in mental health facilities, and contained a general limitations clause that in effect situated persons deemed to have a mental illness for all purposes as wards of the health system.[9] At the domestic level, laws abound that authorize involuntary commitment and involuntary treatment in mental health settings,[10] and until recently the World Health Organization urged countries that lacked such laws to enact them in order to regulate what they considered to be a legitimate practice that merely required safeguards.[11] This meant that people like me had no recourse against acts that amounted to torture, unless there was a blatant violation of domestic procedures or we could demonstrate that we were not in fact "mentally ill" and were placed in the psychiatric system for extraneous motivations such as political dissidence. For the vast majority of us, that is not possible.[12]

---

https://tbinternet.ohchr.org/_layouts/15/treatybodyexternal/Download.aspx?symbolno=CRPD/C/GC/1/Corr.1&Lang=en; and Guidelines on Article 14, Annex to Bi-Annual Report 2016, UN Doc. No. A/72/55, available at https://tbinternet.ohchr.org/_layouts/15/treatybodyexternal/Download.aspx?symbolno=A/72/55&Lang=en [hereafter GA14].

[7] Report by the UN Special Rapporteur on Torture Mr P Kooijmans, UN Doc. No. E/CN.4/1986/15, available at https://undocs.org/E/CN.4/1986/15, paragraph 119.

[8] UN General Assembly Resolution 46/119 of 1991, UN Doc. No. A/RES/46/119, available at https://undocs.org/en/A/RES/46/119, principle 11.

[9] Ibid., principles 1, 16, and General Limitations Clause. (This does not exhaust the problematic features of the document.)

[10] See e.g., New York State Mental Hygiene Law, Article 9 – Hospitalization of the Mentally Ill, available at www.nysenate.gov/legislation/laws/MHY/TBA9; Ley Nacional de Salud Mental (Argentina), Ley 26.657 (2010), particularly Capítulo VII – Internaciones, available at http://servicios.infoleg.gob.ar/infolegInternet/anexos/175000-179999/175977/norma.htm; Mental Healthcare Act of 2017, available at www.prsindia.org/uploads/media/Mental%20Health/Mental%20Healthcare%20Act,%202017.pdf. The latter two are examples of mental health laws enacted subsequent to the entry into force of the CRPD for the respective countries; despite invoking human rights terminology and concepts such as "support for decision-making," involuntary treatment cannot be made compatible with the Convention (see CRPD Concluding Observations to India of 2019, UN Doc. No. CRPD/C/IND/CO/1 paragraphs 27(a) and 31(a), and Concluding Observations to Argentina of 2012, UN Doc. No. CRPD/C/ARG/CO/1 paragraphs 41–42).

[11] www.who.int/mental_health/policy/legislation/en/.

[12] I refer here to the substantive norms of domestic mental health legislation that deny justice even to those who can make use of available processes. The failure of mental health legislation to eliminate psychiatric violence is a tautology; mental health legislation is designed to legitimize such violence, when carried out according to certain rules, which typically specify bureaucratic procedures to be followed and criteria for

As the World Network of Users and Survivors of Psychiatry (WNUSP)[13], our advocacy for the Convention on the Rights of Persons with Disabilities was designed to counter the 1991 Principles and to bring ourselves fully into the light of day of human rights and fundamental freedoms on an equal basis with everyone else.[14] To do that, the abolition of those practices of the mental health system that violated our human rights – not incidentally, but deliberately, as a matter of policy – had to be addressed as a priority both in the text and in the subsequent interpretation and implementation of the Convention. We needed to find textual equivalents for the abolition of these violent and coercive practices that would place us squarely in the mainstream of disability discourse, to establish our rights within the context of the Convention.

We advocated for the text to prohibit "forced interventions aimed at correcting, alleviating or improving an actual or perceived impairment" under the article on torture and other cruel, inhuman, or degrading treatment or punishment.[15] Although this strategy did not succeed in the end,[16] we achieved the underlying goal through an obligation on free and informed consent in the Article on health, and a legally innovative guarantee of equal legal capacity, which transformed disability human rights law by allowing only support – not substitution – of a person's will when they may face difficulty carrying out legal acts or making decisions.[17] In addition, we secured a prohibition of disability-based deprivation of liberty.[18] These provisions were sufficient to require the abolition of all three dimensions of the involuntary mental health system – substitute decision-making, forced interventions, and detention – and we supported the text.

In 2008, the Special Rapporteur on Torture adopted our original approach and recognized that medical interventions of an intrusive and irreversible nature, aimed at correcting or alleviating a disability, when enforced or carried out without the free and informed consent of the person concerned, can amount to torture or other ill

---

applying them. The subjection of these measures to rule of law, by legally specifying the procedures and criteria for their application and providing for an adjudicative process (in most cases after the measures have already begun to be applied), restricts the scope of legal dispute in individual cases to the question of whether the terms of that law have been met. The adjudication therefore denies justice to those who are found to deserve the ongoing violence imposed on them, and to an even wider group who forgo the humiliation of risking such a likely outcome. The CRPD opens up new possibilities for a different kind of access to justice that can be effective to end the violations, but only if domestic courts and tribunals are empowered to apply its provisions and do apply them. See Guidelines on Article 14, paragraphs Basic Principles and Guidelines on Remedies and Procedures on the Right of Anyone Deprived of Their Liberty to Bring Proceedings Before a Court, A/HRC/30/37, Principle 20 and Guideline 20.

[13] For history and background of the WNUSP, see www.wnusp.net.
[14] Statement of WNUSP – the World Network of Users and Survivors of Psychiatry, for the Meeting of Experts on the International Convention to Promote and Protect the Rights and Dignity of Persons with Disabilities in Mexico City, 11–14 June 2002, available with further information at www.wnusp.net/index.php/wnusp-and-a-new-human-rights-treaty.html.
[15] Contribution by the WNUSP (text proposal), available at: www.un.org/esa/socdev/enable/rights/wgcontrib-wnusp.htm; for context, see www.un.org/esa/socdev/enable/rights/comp-elemento.htm.
[16] SRT2020 paragraph 37.
[17] CRPD Articles 25 and 12, respectively. See GC1 paragraphs 7, 8, 40–42 and GA14 throughout, for detail of interpretation.
[18] CRPD Article 14; see Guidelines on Article 14.

treatment.[19] The Committee on the Rights of Persons with Disabilities similarly acknowledges that forced treatment, including forced psychiatric interventions, violates the right to legal capacity and also violates the right to be free from torture and other cruel, inhuman, or degrading treatment or punishment.[20]

The recent report of the Special Rapporteur on Torture in February 2020 synthesizes the work of his predecessors and makes explicit not only that involuntary psychiatric intervention cannot be justified by claims of "medical necessity" or the individual's "best interests," but that this practice "may well amount to torture."[21] This is significant for the moral and legal posture of victims, who are faced with national laws that make use of those justifications. It underscores the argument I am making in this article about the necessity for moral and legal recognition of the status of victims of psychiatric violence as an aspect of our right to legal capacity, which is foundational to accessing justice.

NATIONAL IMPLEMENTATION AND THE POTENTIAL FOR BREAKTHROUGHS

In national implementation of the CRPD, in contrast to the drafting and negotiations, survivors and users of psychiatry were often absent and our issues left behind, notwithstanding the spotlight placed on legal capacity as a pivotal issue in the Convention through the proposal and subsequent removal of a footnote distinguishing "capacity for rights" from "capacity to act."[22] Our marginalization in national implementation resulted from the shift from our role as organized global protagonists to influencers of others' policymaking and interpretive activities, as academics and donor agencies took the initiative, along with governments and NGOs that had financial capacity but were not controlled by people with disabilities. These actors supported legal capacity reform that prioritized the introduction of supported

---

[19] Report of the Special Rapporteur on Torture Manfred Nowak, UN Doc. No. A/63/175 (2008) [hereafter SRT2008], available at https://undocs.org/A/63/175, paragraphs 40 and 47; see also paragraphs 37–41, 42–44, 46–50, 61–65.

[20] GC1 paragraph 42; GA14 paragraph 12.

[21] See Footnote 2 above. The Special Rapporteur on Torture subsequent to Manfred Nowak, Juan E. Méndez, had both advanced and set back the standard, from the point of view of survivors, with his 2013 report and commentaries related to it; see Washington College of Law, Center for Human Rights and Humanitarian Law Anti-torture Initiative (2014) *Torture in Healthcare Settings: Reflections on the Special Rapporteur on Torture's 2013 Thematic Report*, available at http://antitorture.org/torture-in-healthcare-publication/, including my own response, Minkowitz, T, A response to the report by Juan E. Méndez, Special Rapporteur on Torture, dealing with torture in the context of healthcare, as it pertains to nonconsensual psychiatric interventions [hereafter Response to Special Rapporteur on Torture]. The 2020 report resolves most of the uncertainty about the standard currently upheld by that mandate.

[22] See discussion in Minkowitz, WNUSP Advocacy. See also United Nations (April 4, 2008) Arbour welcomes entry into force of "ground-breaking" convention on disabilities, available at: www.un.org/development/desa/disabilities/arbour-welcomes-entry-into-force-of-ground-breaking-convention-on-disabilities.html. This statement by then-UN High Commissioner for Human Rights Louise Arbour on entry into force of the Convention mentions "recognition of the capacity to make decisions."

decision-making while relegating the abolition of involuntary treatment to a later stage. Furthermore, in many countries we lacked a robust movement of people with lived experience of psychosocial disability or psychiatric oppression.

The WNUSP was only a year old when the CRPD negotiations began, and despite the presence of some strong activists from Global South countries, the dominant representation and perspectives were from the Global North. After the adoption of the Convention, many activists prioritized the creation of national and regional organizations, national implementation, and the creation of theory and practice that was counter-hegemonic not only to the narratives of psychiatry and the law but also to those from the Global North.[23] We remain in this phase at the present time, and continue to work towards global cooperation that is based in equal leadership and mutual respect. Despite a wide range of differences in national circumstances, leaders from all regions promote the abolition of forced interventions and the implementation of a full human rights agenda within the CRPD framework, and reject the placement of our human rights issues under the policy leadership of the mental health system.[24]

Some national legal capacity reforms have recently been implemented that substantially comply with central features of the CRPD's stringent standards,[25] by recognizing the full legal capacity of people with all types of disabilities and eliminating restrictions to legal capacity based on either the status of having a disability or a person's decision-making skills, sometimes called "mental capacity."[26] Instead of allowing the person's will

---

[23] The regional organizations developed in the Global South are, in order of their creation, the Pan-African Network of People with Psychosocial Disabilities, Transforming Communities for Inclusion-Asia Pacific, and RedEsfera Latinoamericana de la Diversidad Psicosocial (Locura Latina). The European Network of (ex-)Users and Survivors of Psychiatry pre-existed WNUSP and remains active.

[24] Consultation on human rights and mental health: "Identifying strategies to promote human rights in mental health," held by the Human Rights Council on May 14–15, 2018. UN Doc. No. A/HRC/39/36, available at https://ap.ohchr.org/documents/dpage_e.aspx?si=A/HRC/39/36; see in particular the presentations of Ms Yeni Rosa Damayanti, Ms Bhargavi Davar, Mr Michael Njenga, and Ms Olga Runciman, and intervention from the floor by the WNUSP, available at www.ohchr.org/EN/Issues/ESCR/Pages/ConsultationHRandMentalhealth.aspx.

[25] See in particular GC1 paragraphs 13–15, 18, 19, 21, 22, 29(g) and (i), and GC1Corr (paragraph 27), for the key features that eliminate "mental capacity" assessment and protect the right to make decisions according to one's own will and preferences. As background describing the debates on Article 12 in the context of the negotiations and its interpretation by the Committee, see Series L, Nilsson A (2018), Article 12 CRPD: Equal Recognition before the Law, in Bantekas, I, Stein, MA, Anastasiou, D, eds. *The UN Convention on the Rights of Persons with Disabilities: A Commentary* [Select Chapters]. Oxford: Oxford University Press, available at www.ncbi.nlm.nih.gov/books/NBK539188/.

[26] Peruvian reform is contained in Decreto Legislativo 1384, available at: https://busquedas.elperuano.pe/normaslegales/decreto-legislativo-que-reconoce-y-regula-la-capacidad-jurid-decreto-legislativo-n-1384-1687393-2/; see also Minkowitz, T, (2018) Peruvian legal capacity reform: celebration and analysis, *Mad in America*, available at www.madinamerica.com/2018/10/peruvian-legal-capacity-reform-celebration-and-analysis/; my analysis includes a link to English translation of the Legislative Decree. Colombian reform is contained in Ley 1996, available at https://dapre.presidencia.gov.co/normativa/normativa/LEY%201996%20DEL%2026%20DE%20AGOSTO%20DE%202019.pdf. Notaries are working out the implications of the new framework for their professional obligations and practices; see especially Mejía Rosasco, Rosalía (2019), *La Implementación de la Convención de las Personas con Discapacidad en la Función Notarial*, Lima: Colegio de Notarios de Lima Fondo Editorial, available at www.onpi.org.ar/

to be substituted by that of a guardian or court, they promote the availability of support that can be formally designated by an individual for assistance in understanding information, weighing options, or communicating a decision; only when it is not possible to determine a person's will, despite significant effort, can a court designate supports based on a best interpretation of the person's will. Nevertheless, these reforms failed to repeal all the provisions in national law that permit detention and forced treatment in mental health settings. In Colombia, a residual derogations clause may allow for litigation to overturn any remaining provisions.[27] In Peru, current provisions allow involuntary admission and treatment only for a period of twelve hours in a situation defined as a "psychiatric emergency" in the noncriminal context,[28] along with the usual provision for hospitalization as a security measure in penal cases.[29] Even this short period is contrary to CRPD Articles 12 and 14, which prohibit any detention based on a mental health condition and any restriction of the legal capacity to make decisions about treatment, including in crisis or emergency situations.[30]

SOCIAL MODEL FOR CRISIS SUPPORT

The stereotype of incompetence is negated by Article 12, General Comment No. 1, and the emergence of credible reforms at national level in Peru and Colombia. Long-term institutionalization has few defenders. What remains is the defense still commonly put forward of short-term detention and compulsory treatment, based either on a purely medical analogy of "emergency" (still contrary to the General Comment);[31] or on the notion of risk assessment, which is also contrary to the General Comment as well as the Guidelines on Article 14.[32]

[27] documentos/publicaciones/publicaciones-del-notariado-internacional/la_implementacion_de_la_conven cion_de_las_personas_con_discapacidad_en_la_funcion_notarial.pdf.
Ley 1996, artículo 61.
[28] Ley No 30947, available at https://busquedas.elperuano.pe/normaslegales/ley-de-salud-mental-ley-n-30947-1772004-1/, Artículos 5.2, 5.3, 9 y Disposición Complementaria Modificatoria 1.
[29] Ibid., Artículo 29. This too is contrary to CRPD, see GA14 paragraphs 16–18, 20 and 21. See also Minkowitz, T, Rethinking Criminal Responsibility from a Critical Disability Perspective: The Abolition of Insanity/Incapacity Acquittals and Unfitness to Plead, and Beyond, *Griffith Law Review*, 23(3), 2014, available at https://papers.ssrn.com/sol3/papers.cfm?abstract_id=2930530.
[30] GC1 paragraphs 18 and 42; GA14 paragraphs 10, 22–23.
[31] In situations where, despite significant effort including accessible communication and reasonable accommodations, it is not feasible to obtain an expression of will from the person, a "best interpretation of will and preferences" must be used rather than a "best interests" determination; see GC1 paragraph 21; LD 1384 (Perú) Artículos 659-B and 659-E; Ley 1996 (Colombia) Artículos 4.3, 38, 47, 48. As Hege Orefellen points out in a personal communication, "due to the intrusive, controversial and potentially irreversible and harmful nature of psychiatric interventions, there has to be a high requirement for consent, and an affirmative expressed consent should be required for such procedures to be carried out, also in 'crisis' situations. In situations where it after significant efforts have been made is not practicable to determine the persons will and preferences, psychiatric treatment should not be inflicted based on presumed or hypothetical consent (as might happen with other medical procedures), and should not without an advance directive or earlier expressed preferences be interpreted as the will of the person."
[32] GC1 paragraph 22, GA14 paragraphs 13–15.

Experiencing a sense of impasse, I began to develop a social model framework to conceptualize the support needed in crisis situations from a phenomenological descriptive standpoint that rejects both medicalization and judicialization of services as either "treatments" or mandated interventions, and instead obligates the state to make available on-call, trustworthy forms of support that are "artisanal" in the sense of having flexibility to meet the specific needs presented by the person,[33] always adhering to the obligation to respect the person's will and preferences. We may require support to make decisions related to the crisis itself – to decide how we can get through this day and this night, as well as how we need to move towards accommodation or transformation in the longer term – and practical support to maintain ourselves in our daily lives without too much disruption during this time. These two kinds of support are contemplated by the Convention in Article 12 (informal support for the exercise of legal capacity, broadly understood to encompass large and small life decisions, and not only the performance of legal acts),[34] and in Article 19 (support to live independently in the community and prevent unwanted isolation). The notion of risk is reversed in such a framework to look at safety from the perspective of the person concerned, to ensure an environment free from aggression and violence. It is understood that everyone has duties towards one another that complement human rights, and the availability of nondiscriminatory, community-based mechanisms to resolve conflict and intervene to stop acts of interpersonal violence is complementary to crisis support.

This model develops the logic of the CRPD paradigm for autonomy, plus support that recursively respects such autonomy, informed by the premise that our crisis experiences belong to ourselves as part of our agency and subjectivity, to be respected and supported and not dissociated from us narratively or in their unfolding. It is these experiences, in which a person may reach out for support and need an immediate, constructive response, that psychiatry has met with detention, violence, and subjection to the control of others. By promoting an alternative conceptualization, we lay the groundwork for a discourse of crisis, distress, and unusual states of consciousness that are part of human diversity and neither feared nor segregated, and for practices that are fully human rights-based and congruent with the justice needs of people with lived experience of psychosocial disability and psychiatric oppression.

[33] Thanks to Víctor Lizama, justice facilitator with Documenta A.C. (Mexico) for the term "artisanal" as description of his own work, due to the strong human interaction required to build procedural adjustments according to the needs of each person. It fits well for all types of support offered in the context of psychosocial distress, crisis and disability. See https://www.documenta.org.mx/discapacidad-y-justicia/.

[34] The broad scope of Article 12 and of support is reflected in GC1 paragraph 52, which urges states to combat informal as well as formal substitute decision-making; in paragraph 17, which describes various types of informal as well as formal forms of support; and in paragraph 42, which requires that nonmedical options be made available along with ensuring respect for decision-making, in contrast to forced psychiatric interventions.

The potential value and policy implications of approaching crisis support from a fully social model standpoint, and the multidimensional context of life and society that this vision engages with, are developed in my work in progress, tentatively titled *Reimagining Crisis Support: Matrix, Roadmap and Policy*. The basic elements of this model, as briefly illustrated above and in my earlier schematic paper,[35] can serve as a starting point for those who want to carry out such reforms or begin to rethink policy.

REPARATION AND RENEWAL

Finally, I return full circle to my experience and its impact on me as a survivor. Forced psychiatric interventions, including both deprivation of liberty and administration of a neuroleptic drug against my will, harmed me greatly. The harm was profound, extensive, and life-altering. It was physical, mental, social, and spiritual. I have worked on healing throughout my life, while also bearing witness to the violations and working to end them – and that is not enough. A social dimension of healing and justice is required for victims of human rights violations to be reconciled with the state and society that acquiesced in that harm and abandoned the victims to their fate. Social healing and justice are encompassed in the obligation of reparation for gross violations of international human rights law.[36] Forms of reparation include satisfaction, guarantees of non-repetition, restitution, compensation, and rehabilitation.

Meaningful reparation in my case would begin with an acknowledgment that in fact what was done to me, and to others like me who had no particularized individual claim to be taken out of the "mental patient" category, constitutes torture – no less than the drugging with neuroleptics meted out to political prisoners that in all likelihood was the concern of the Special Rapporteur on Torture in 1986. No one should have to prove their exceptional status in order to be recognized as deserving the most fundamental of human rights: the right to be secure in one's mental and physical integrity. Indeed, as the Special Rapporteur on Torture said in 2008, the existence of a disability is a factor to be taken into account in assessing the level of

---

[35] Minkowitz, T (2019), Positive policy to replace forced psychiatry, based on the CRPD, available at www.academia.edu/39229717/Positive_policy_to_replace_forced_psychiatry_based_on_CRPD.

[36] Basic Principles and Guidelines on the Right to a Remedy and Reparation for Victims of Gross Violations of International Human Rights Law and Serious Violations of International Humanitarian Law, UN Doc. No. A/RES/60/147 (2005), available at https://undocs.org/en/A/RES/60/147; see also Committee against Torture, General Comment No. 3, UN Doc. No. CAT/C/GC/3, available at https://undocs.org/CAT/C/GC/3; CRPD Guidelines on Art 14; SRT2008 paragraph 45. I have promoted reparation for psychiatric violence in the following materials; see Minkowitz, T, Forced psychiatric interventions: right to remedy and reparation, in *Open Mind*, (January & February 2012); Minkowitz, T (2012) Reparations: It is Conceivable, *Mad in America*, available at www.madinamerica.com/2012/12/reparations-it-is-conceivable/; and Response to Special Rapporteur on torture. Hege Orefellen has also addressed reparation for psychiatric violence; see https://absoluteprohibition.org/2016/02/06/hege-orefellen-on-reparations/.

suffering or pain, as well as "the acquisition or deterioration of an impairment as result of the treatment or conditions of detention of the victim."[37] When we are at our most vulnerable, the highest protection should be assured to create a space of trust and potential for healing; instead, in the name of protection, and abusing the trust placed in the medical profession by society, the greatest harms are perpetrated, which can lead to lifelong victimization.[38] It is only by confronting the profound discrimination that has allowed this to happen, and exploring its consequences, its rationalizations, and its functioning throughout society and culture, that we can uproot it and create the space for justice and healing. (This is the opposite of therapeutic jurisprudence;[39] it is not a managed healing but a political exercise in participatory democracy that makes possible mutual understanding based in a fundamental commitment to equality.) An acknowledgement that routine psychiatric practices amount to torture and arbitrary detention, and a process to explore what that has meant for victims-survivors,[40] the mental health system, and society would constitute the first element of reparation, "satisfaction."

Guarantees of non-repetition in this case begin with the obligations that states parties to the CPRD have already undertaken, and not yet complied with, to abolish legislative provisions that authorize acts of torture and arbitrary detention either directly (e.g., mental health acts that authorize involuntary admissions and involuntary treatment) or indirectly (e.g., legislation that allows a person to be declared incapable of consent and a substitute decision-maker to consent on their behalf). Legislative reform will only succeed if it is undertaken with an appreciation of its purpose – that is, to eliminate these regimes as a matter of policy and practice and not to reform them or reestablish their justification on grounds supposed to be "disability-neutral."[41] A framework of reparation is the surest way to maintain clarity and focus and a moral standpoint in solidarity with victims-survivors.

Restitution, compensation, and rehabilitation are individual measures but require systemic support and policy to be put into practice, and need to be contextualized in a broad project of social justice in order to promote social harmony

---

[37] SRT2008 paragraph 47.
[38] For an exploration of this contradiction, see Whitaker, Robert (2010) *Anatomy of an Epidemic: Magic bullets, psychiatric drugs, and the astonishing rise of mental illness in America*, New York: Crown Publishers/Random House. See also Whitaker, Our Psychiatric Epidemic – A Historical Overview, speech at the conference Psychiatric Drugs Do More Harm Than Good in Copenhagen, September 15, 2015, available at www.youtube.com/watch?v=Wd3_Iq8P3Fo.
[39] For an explanation of "therapeutic jurisprudence" see Chesser, Brianna (2020) Therapeutic Jurisprudence, *Oxford Bibliographies*, available at www.oxfordbibliographies.com/view/document/obo-9780195396607/obo-9780195396607-0203.xml.
[40] I use the term "victims-survivors" to honor individual self-identification as victims, which emphasizes the fact that they have been victimized and seek justice, and/or as survivors, which emphasizes that they did not perish and they go on constructing their lives after victimization.
[41] See my commentary on this question in Minkowitz, T, CRPD and Transformative Equality, *International Journal of Law in Context*, 13(1) (March 2017) pp. 77–86, available at https://papers.ssrn.com/sol3/papers.cfm?abstract_id=2930553.

through congruence and mutual solidarity. Otherwise such regimes may be resented by others, who view them as competing with other needs. Restitution may be seen to encompass social measures as well as individual, in particular the removal of additional discriminatory provisions from legislation (e.g. with respect to marriage, voting, child custody, and professional licenses)[42] to ensure equal rights in all civil, political, economic, social, and cultural fields. Rehabilitation needs to include the availability of support to heal from trauma incurred in the mental health system, taking a solidarity approach that gives the victim-survivor space to articulate her narrative and its meaning. Options include autonomous mutual support groups designed for this particular purpose,[43] trauma-informed counseling with particular sensitivity to healing from psychiatric violence, and other means that victims-survivors can devise to meet their own needs. Such support should be located outside the mental health system, for those who want no part of the system that abused them, and should be done in any case only through an agency or practitioner that has fully accomplished its own process of accountability and reparation for violations. In addition, rehabilitation should include knowledgeable, nonjudgmental, and sensitive support to withdraw from psychiatric drugs.

Compensation is difficult to explore from a policy standpoint, given the large number of individuals affected in a large number of countries. Monetary compensation should not be the only way of confronting the particularities of individual harm, and can lead to unnecessary resentment as one person's harm is measured against that of another. However, it must be acknowledged that impoverishment is a consequence of institutionalization, of pervasive discrimination in employment, housing, and social spaces generally against people known to have a psychiatric history, and of the accumulated impact of repeated instances of institutionalization, other violations, and discrimination over the course of people's lives. Even those who survive and thrive after psychiatric abuse will have lost opportunities, had their relationships impaired, and had their reputation undermined; they will also have to live with the memories of being placed in a state of defenselessness against harm in which one's subjectivity itself is objectified as a fitting object for mechanical alteration. States, with input from the general public as well as from victims-survivors of psychiatry, need to come up with appropriate ways of making amends, to end the cycle of abuse, misunderstanding, resentment, and discrimination, in which intersectional discrimination and generalized social and political harms are also implicated.

To concretize the proposal, a commission on truth and justice for victims of psychiatric violence could be convened by the United Nations, by regional

---

[42] These rights are substantively guaranteed without discrimination in CRPD Articles 23 (marriage and child custody), 29 (voting) and 27 and 30 (professional licenses, through the right to work and right to develop and utilize one's creative, artistic and intellectual potential, respectively).

[43] "Autonomous" refers to being constituted by and for the members of the group to meet their own needs, and independent of any outside influences.

intergovernmental mechanisms, and/or by states. Such a commission must be independent from government influence (similarly to the functioning of a national human rights institution) and governed by terms of reference adhering to the CRPD and the standards elaborated in General Comments and in the Guidelines on Article 14. Victims-survivors of psychiatric violence and their representative organizations need to have an influential role in setting the terms for a responsive process, as this is both required by the CRPD[44] and itself an element of reparations, reversing the negation of subjectivity.

---

[44] Article 4.3; see also General Comment No. 7, UN Doc. No. CRPD/C/GC/7, available at https://tbinternet.ohchr.org/_layouts/15/treatybodyexternal/Download.aspx?symbolno=CRPD/C/GC/7&Lang=en.

4

Divergent Human Rights Approaches to Capacity and Consent

Gerald L. Neuman

Abstract

The institutional dialogue among the Committee on the Rights of Persons with Disabilities and other human rights tribunals has led to greater protection of rights. But not all courts and treaty bodies have accepted the Committee's absolutist position on legal capacity. The chapter illustrates the multiple human rights-based approaches to capacity and decision-making, and describes how the Committee's absolutism endangers many of the people living with moderate or severe dementia whom it supposedly benefits.

INTRODUCTION

The Committee on the Rights of Persons with Disabilities (CRPD Committee, or the Committee) has successfully influenced other human rights bodies over the past decade to strengthen their standards for the protection of people with disabilities. While some institutions have followed the CRPD Committee's absolutist interpretations on issues of legal capacity and consent, others such as the Human Rights Committee and the European Court of Human Rights have declined to fully incorporate these interpretations into their own human rights approaches. Instead they have recognized the possibility that certain limitations may be justified by the interests of the individual in question or by the rights of third parties.

This chapter describes some examples of this divergence, and examines some of the arguments in favor of less absolutist standards, including reasons that have been articulated in dialogue between the Human Rights Committee and the CRPD Committee. The chapter proceeds in three sections, first by pointing out some of the features of the CRPD Committee's approach (A); then by describing some of the interplay between the CRPD Committee and other human rights institutions (B); and then by illustrating the implications of the absolutist approach for people living with moderate or severe dementia (C).

The author is 100 percent grateful for expert advice on this chapter. He thanks Professor Stein and the Harvard Program on Disability for long-continued collaboration. All errors are the author's own.

A THE CRPD COMMITTEE AND ITS GENERAL COMMENT ON LEGAL CAPACITY

The CRPD Committee is the treaty body created by the Convention on the Rights of Persons with Disabilities. A human rights treaty body is a committee of independent experts, elected by the states that have ratified a particular human rights treaty, for the purpose of monitoring compliance with the obligations under the treaty. There are currently nine other treaty bodies at the global level, including the Human Rights Committee, which despite its generic name actually monitors compliance with the International Covenant on Civil and Political Rights (ICCPR).[1] Among other activities, treaty bodies commonly engage in the review of states' overall reports, the adjudication of "communications" submitted by individuals alleging a violation by a state, and the issuance of texts known as general comments, which address legal issues of substance or procedure under the treaty without being focused on any particular state. Treaty bodies' interpretations of their governing conventions have been described as "authoritative," given the bodies' expert character and functions, but they are not legally binding in international law, unlike the judgments of international courts.[2]

The CRPD Committee issued its first general comment in 2014, on CRPD Article 12, entitled "Equal recognition before the law."[3] The main theme of the General Comment is the Committee's account of the right to legal capacity and the requirement of supported decision-making.

General Comment No. 1 calls for a shift from substituted decision-making, where outsiders make a decision that should be based on the best interests of the person with disability, to supported decision-making, where the person with disability receives support in order to make a decision freely. The core of this argument, referring to the disrespect and dangers involved in older systems of substituted decision-making, has considerable force. The argument is less persuasive, however, in the full generality that General Comment No. 1 actually asserts.

Tracing a path through the text of the General Comment illustrates the extreme range of its prescriptions. Legal capacity is the (juridical) ability both to hold rights and duties and to exercise those rights and duties (para. 13). Mental capacity, in contrast, refers to the decision-making skills of a person (para. 13). Actual deficits in mental capacity must not ever be used as justification for denying legal capacity (para. 13). An assessment of whether a person can understand the nature and consequences of a decision can never be taken as legitimate grounds for denying the person's legal capacity (para. 15). That is prohibited discrimination (para. 15).

---

[1] See Gerald L. Neuman, "Giving Meaning and Effect to Human Rights: The Contributions of Human Rights Committee Members," in *The Human Rights Covenants at 50: Their Past, Present, and Future*, ed. Daniel Moeckli, Helen Keller and Corina Heri (Oxford: Oxford University Press, 2018), 31.
[2] Neuman, "Giving Meaning," 33–34.
[3] Committee on the Rights of Persons with Disabilities, General Comment No. 1 (2014): Article 12: Equal recognition before the law, UN Doc. CRPD/C/GC/1 (2014).

Instead, support must be provided for the exercise of legal capacity (para. 15). Nonetheless, taking advantage of support is wholly optional – a person with disability always has the right to refuse any support (paras. 19, 29(g)). In other words, a person who cannot understand the nature and consequences of a decision has the absolute right to make the decision without assistance, and have full legal consequences attributed to the decision. Moreover, the person has "the right to take risks and make mistakes" (para. 22).

Forbidden regimes of substitute decision-making include systems where even a single decision is removed from the scope of a person's legal capacity (para. 27). Supported decision-making must totally replace substituted decision-making, which cannot be maintained as a parallel option at all (para. 28). Supported decision-making must be available to all, no matter how high their support needs (para. 29 (a)). The right to support in the exercise of legal capacity cannot be limited by a claim of disproportionate or undue burden; states have "an absolute obligation to provide access to support in the exercise of legal capacity" (para. 34). The individual must have the right to refuse support and to terminate or change the support relationship at any time (para. 29(g)). Individuals may never be detained in an institution or placed in a residential setting without their specific consent; that constitutes arbitrary detention and is prohibited (para. 40). Forced treatment by psychiatric and other health and medical personnel is always a violation of the right to equal recognition before the law, and indeed of the right to freedom from torture; the right to choose or reject medical treatment must be respected at all times, including in crisis situations (para. 42).

It might also be observed that in the General Comment the right to free exercise of one's legal capacity apparently includes the right to make decisions that have consequences for others, indeed to exercise power over others.[4] Persons with disabilities have wrongfully been excluded from key roles in the justice system as lawyers, judges, or members of a jury (para. 38). Actual defects in a person's decision-making ability cannot be a justification for any exclusion from the right to stand for election or serve as a member of a jury (para. 48). States should guarantee the right of all persons with disabilities to stand for election, to hold office effectively, and to perform all public functions at all levels of government, with reasonable accommodation and support, where desired (para. 49). That is, support can be provided where the officeholder desires it – persons with disabilities, including those in office, have an absolute right to refuse all support.

The Committee on Persons with Disabilities describes these far-reaching conclusions as necessitated by "the human rights-based model of disability" (para. 3). For the Committee, there is only one human rights-based approach.

---

[4] This feature deserves a study of its own, but will not be further explored here. See also David Bilchitz, "Dignity, fundamental rights and legal capacity: moving beyond the paradigm set by the General Comment on Article 12 of the Convention on the Rights of Persons with Disabilities," *South African Journal on Human Rights* 32 (2016): 418.

The Committee's absolutist rejection of any diminution in the right to exercise legal capacity in any circumstance is consistent with other absolutist features in the Committee's interpretation of the Convention, and in particular with the Committee's absolutist conception of discrimination. In Article 12, the right to legal capacity "on an equal basis with others" means on exactly the same basis; there is no room for justified differentiation. The Committee's General Comment No. 6 on discrimination similarly sets forth an absolute conception of prohibited discrimination.[5] There should be no laws that allow for specific denial, restriction, or limitation of the rights of persons with disabilities (para. 14). The Committee defines direct discrimination as including any less favorable differential treatment for a reason related to disability, regardless of motive (para. 18(a)). Direct discrimination must be comprehensively prohibited; the General Comment does not contemplate any circumstances under which differential treatment could be justified. In fact, the final version of the General Comment also eliminates any possibility of justifying facially neutral practices that have negative differential effects on persons with certain disabilities. Language in the first reading draft of the General Comment would have recognized that practices with differential effects do not amount to such indirect discrimination if they are "objectively justified by a legitimate aim, and the means achieving that aim are appropriate and necessary,"[6] but the Committee deleted that clause on second reading.[7] In the final version, only the separately listed requirement of reasonable accommodation includes a possibility of justification.[8]

The absolutist notion of discrimination is not the usual human rights-based approach to direct discrimination. The Committee was doubtless aware of the discrepancy. It had previously been pointed out to the Committee by members of the Human Rights Committee, and the present author made a written submission to the CRPD Committee's day of general discussion in preparation for General Comment No. 6, urging the Committee to align its definition with the standard definition in international human rights law. The submission quoted examples from the Human Rights Committee, the Committee on Economic, Social and Cultural Rights, the Committee on the Elimination of Racial Discrimination, the European Court of Human Rights, and the Inter-American Court of Human Rights, all defining direct discrimination in terms that require an inquiry into the objective justification for differential treatment.[9] The CRPD Committee instead continued on its chosen path.

---

[5] Committee on the Rights of Persons with Disabilities, General Comment No. 6 (2018) on equality and non-discrimination, UN Doc. CRPD/C/GC/6 (2018).

[6] Committee on the Rights of Persons with Disabilities, General Comment on Equality and Non-discrimination (Article 5): First draft as at August 31, 2017, para. 20(b), available at https://www.ohchr.org/EN/HRBodies/CRPD/Pages/CallPersonsDisabilitiesEqualityResponsability.aspx.

[7] General Comment No. 6, para. 18(b).

[8] Ibid., para. 18(c).

[9] See Submission of Prof. Gerald L. Neuman regarding draft General Comment on article 5, Equality and non-discrimination, available at https://www.ohchr.org/EN/HRBodies/CRPD/Pages/

Several states have attempted to preserve some exceptional use of substituted decision-making by accompanying their ratification of the CRPD with reservations, or understandings in the nature of reservations. However, the validity of such reservations has been challenged for deviating from the absolutist approach. The CRPD Committee's concluding observations on Canada in April 2017 claimed that Canada's reservation "contradicts the object and purpose of the Convention," and did not comply with "the human rights model of disability."[10] Later the same year, the Special Rapporteur on the rights of persons with disabilities devoted a report to legal capacity, in which she asserted that reservations to Article 12 are incompatible with the object and purpose of the Convention and therefore not permitted, because they "hinder and/or deny the full and equal enjoyment" of CRPD rights.[11]

B THE DIALOGUE AMONG HUMAN RIGHTS INSTITUTIONS

Even before issuing General Comment No. 1, the Chairperson of the CRPD Committee called the attention of the Human Rights Committee to a passage in one of the latter's General Comments from the 1990s, describing "established mental incapacity" as a permissible basis for denying the right to vote, which contradicted the CRPD Committee's understanding of the subsequent Convention. The Human Rights Committee did not undertake a revision of the General Comment, but after deliberations on state reports it adopted concluding observations superseding that passage by a stricter standard for finding an inability to vote. The stricter standard allowed for individualized determinations of the relevant mental capacity, and did not impose the absolute prohibition favored by the CRPD Committee and later embodied in that committee's General Comment No. 1.[12]

WSEqualityArt5.aspx (quoting from Human Rights Committee, General Comment No. 18, Non-discrimination, para. 13 (1989), reprinted in Compilation of General Comments and General Recommendations Adopted by Human Rights Treaty Bodies, UN Doc. HRI/GEN/1/Rev.9 (2008); Committee on Economic, Social and Cultural Rights, General comment No. 20, Non-discrimination in economic, social and cultural rights (art. 2, para. 2, of the International Covenant on Economic, Social and Cultural Rights), UN Doc. E/C.12/GC/20 (2009); Committee on the Elimination of Racial Discrimination, General recommendation No. 32, The meaning and scope of special measures in the International Covenant on the Elimination of All Forms [of] Racial Discrimination, UN Doc. CERD/C/GC/32 (2009); Inter-American Court of Human Rights, Advisory Opinion OC-18/03, *Juridical Condition and Rights of the Undocumented Migrants*, 18 Inter-Am. Ct. H.R. (ser. A) (2003); and *Biao v. Denmark* [GC], No. 38590/10 (ECHR 2016) [GC]).

[10] CRPD Committee, Concluding observations on the initial report of Canada, UN Doc. CRPD/C/CAN/CO1 (2017), para. 7.

[11] Report of the Special Rapporteur on the rights of persons with disabilities, UN Doc. A/HRC/37/56 (2017), para. 37.

[12] See Human Rights Committee, Concluding observations on the third periodic report of Hong Kong, China, UN Doc. CCPR/C/CHN-HKG/CO/3 (2013), para. 24; Human Rights Committee, Summary Record of the 2,950th meeting, UN Doc. CCPR/C/SR.2950 (2012), para. 1; Human Rights Committee, Summary Record of the 2,978th meeting, UN Doc. CCPR/C/SR.2978 (2013), para. 14.

The Human Rights Committee also revised its approach to nonconsensual psychiatric treatment, in concluding observations adopted in March 2014. It recommended that "[n]on-consensual psychiatric treatment may only be applied, if at all, in exceptional cases as a matter of last resort, where absolutely necessary for the benefit of the person concerned, provided that he or she is unable to give consent, for the shortest possible time, without any long-term impact and under independent review."[13] Again, the standard was not an absolute prohibition, and it assumed that nonconsensual treatment might exceptionally be necessary for the individual's own benefit.

The most extensive consultations between the two treaty bodies at this period occurred in connection with the Human Rights Committee's adoption of its General Comment No. 35 on the right to liberty and security, which included a paragraph on involuntary hospitalization.[14] Human Rights Committee members also benefited from meetings with disability rights advocates. The Human Rights Committee made several modifications to its draft to take into account concerns expressed by the CRPD Committee, but it became clear that the two treaty bodies disagreed fundamentally about the meaning of the right to non-discrimination and the limits of the right to physical liberty. There was also disagreement about whether the insanity defense in criminal law should simply be abolished without anything available to replace it. The Human Rights Committee ultimately declined to adopt the CRPD Committee's absolutist definition of discrimination on grounds of disability as an interpretation of the ICCPR, or to regard involuntary hospitalization as always per se arbitrary detention. Once more, the Human Rights Committee tightened its prior standard, insisting that deprivation of liberty must be applied only as a last resort, accepting unconsented hospitalization that is proportionate and necessary "for the purpose of protecting the individual in question from serious harm or preventing injury to others."[15] The CRPD Committee countered by issuing a public statement, and subsequently "Guidelines," reiterating its view that it is never permissible to detain persons with disabilities based on perceived danger to themselves or to others.[16]

[13] See Human Rights Committee, Concluding observations on the fourth periodic report of the United States of America, UN Doc. CCPR/C/USA/CO/4 (2013), para. 18 (citing articles 7 and 17 of the ICCPR); Human Rights Committee, Concluding observations on the third periodic report of Latvia, UN Doc. CCPR/C/LTV/CO/3 (2013), para. 16. The present author took part in the deliberations on the Latvia report, but not in the deliberations on the USA report, being recused by reason of his nationality.

[14] See Human Rights Committee, General comment No. 35: Article 9 (Liberty and security of person), UN Doc. CCPR/C/GC/35 (2014); Gerald L. Neuman, "Arbitrary Detention and the Human Rights Committee's General Comment 35," in *Justice et droits de l'homme: Mélanges en hommage à Christine Chanet*, ed. Emmanuel Decaux, Patrice Gilibert and Iulia Motoc, Paris: Editions A. Pedone, 2019, 118–22.

[15] Human Rights Committee, General Comment No. 35, para. 19.

[16] See CRPD Committee, Statement on Article 14 of the Convention on the Rights of Persons with Disabilities, reprinted in Report of the Committee on the Rights of Persons with Disabilities on its twelfth session (September 15, 2014–October 3, 2014), UN Doc. CRPD/C/12/2 (2014), at 14–15; CRPD Committee, Guidelines on the right to liberty and security of persons with disabilities (2015), reprinted in Report of the Committee on the Rights of Persons with Disabilities, UN Doc. A/72/55 (2017), at 16–21.

Other treaty bodies and UN special procedures have varied in their approaches to such issues.[17] The Committee Against Torture, the Subcommittee for the Prevention of Torture, and the Special Rapporteur on torture and other cruel, inhuman or degrading treatment or punishment have declined to consider involuntary hospitalization or nonconsensual treatment as always per se violations of the rights within their mandates. The UN Special Rapporteur on the rights of persons with disabilities has, not surprisingly, followed the CRPD Committee's interpretation.[18] The Working Group on Arbitrary Detention, which ostensibly applies the prohibition of arbitrary detention contained in the ICCPR and its analogue in customary international law, knowingly diverged from the Human Rights Committee's interpretation of the ICCPR when it adopted "Basic Principles and Guidelines on Remedies and Procedures on the Right of Anyone Deprived of Liberty to Bring Proceedings Before a Court,"[19] condemning in all circumstances unconsented medical treatment, involuntary hospitalization, and substituted decision-making.

Meanwhile, at the regional level the European Court of Human Rights has issued a series of judgments over the past decade that pursue a non-absolute human rights-based approach to legal capacity, despite explicit reminders of the CRPD Committee's understanding.[20] For example, the 2019 Grand Chamber judgment in *Rooman v Belgium*, upholding the current detention of a convicted offender for psychiatric treatment, explained:

> in the light of the developments in [the Court's] case-law and the current international standards which attach significant weight to the need to provide treatment for the mental health of persons in compulsory treatment... it is necessary to acknowledge expressly, in addition to the function of social protection, the therapeutic aspect of the aim referred to in Article 5 § 1(e), and thus to recognize explicitly that there exists an obligation on the authorities to ensure appropriate

---

[17] See Suzanne Doyle Guilloud, "The right to liberty of persons with psychosocial disabilities at the United Nations: a tale of two interpretations," *International Journal of Law and Psychiatry* 66 (September–October 2019), https://doi.org/10.1016/j.ijlp.2019.101497.

[18] See, e.g., Report of the Special Rapporteur on the rights of persons with disabilities, UN Doc. A/HRC/40/54 (2019).

[19] UN Doc. A/HRC/30/37 (2015), para. 106. This is not the only respect in which the "Basic Principles" diverge from the Human Rights Committee's interpretation of the ICCPR.

[20] See, e.g., *A.M.-V. v Finland*, App. no. 53521/13 (ECtHR 2017), paras. 74, 90 (taking into account the CRPD Committee's rejection of substituted decision-making but "mindful of the need for the domestic authorities to reach, in each particular case, a balance between the respect for the dignity and self-determination of the individual and the need to protect the individual and safeguard his or her interests, especially under circumstances where his or her individual qualities or situation place the person in a particularly vulnerable position."); *Hiller v. Austria*, App. no. 1967/14 (ECtHR 2016), paras. 54–44 (finding that placement of an involuntarily hospitalized individual in an open ward was consistent with the requirement that the deprivation of liberty "must be scaled down to the extent which is absolutely necessary under the given circumstances," and that his subsequent escape and suicide did not demonstrate a failure of state protection); *J.D. and A. v United Kingdom*, App. nos. 32949/17, 34614/17 (ECtHR 2019), paras. 82–89 (explaining that very weighty reasons would be required for differential treatment of people with disabilities, but maintaining the possibility of justification).

and individualized therapy, based on the specific features of the compulsory confinement, such as the conditions of the detention regime, the treatment proposed or the duration of the detention. On the other hand, the Court considers that Article 5, as currently interpreted, does not contain a prohibition on detention on the basis of impairment, in contrast to what is proposed by the UN Committee on the Rights of Persons with Disabilities in points 6–9 of its 2015 Guidelines ...[21]

The same day another Grand Chamber judgment, in *Fernandes de Oliveira v Portugal*, addressed the duty of a public hospital to prevent a voluntary patient from leaving the premises and killing himself. The majority explained:

> The Court considers that a psychiatric patient is particularly vulnerable even when treated on a voluntary basis. Due to the patient's mental disorder, his or her capacity to take a rational decision to end his or her life may to some degree be impaired. Further, any hospitalization of a psychiatric patient, whether involuntary or voluntary, inevitably involves a certain level of restraint ... [which] may take different forms, including limitation of personal liberty and privacy rights ... [T]he Court considers that the authorities do have a general operational duty with respect to a voluntary psychiatric patient to take reasonable measures to protect him or her from a real and immediate risk of suicide.[22]

The majority rejected the mother's claim of a substantive violation of the right to life, finding that there had not been sufficient evidence of risk to trigger this positive obligation. The majority had noted without explicit discussion the contrasting views at the international level on the permissibility of involuntary hospitalization.[23]

The German Federal Constitutional Court, which has often been influential in European human rights thinking, has also confronted the interaction between protection of life and legal capacity. In 2016, the Court held unconstitutional the absence from the Civil Code of provisions that would permit life-saving medical treatment to be administered involuntarily to patients who lack the mental capacity to "recognise the necessity of the medical measure or cannot act in accordance with that realization," but who were too impaired physically to meet the standards for a civil commitment order.[24] The Court addressed the contrary position of the CRPD Committee, asserting that a treaty body's interpretations of its convention "have

---

[21] *Rooman v Belgium*, App. No. 18052/11 (ECtHR 2019) [GC], para. 205 (citations omitted).

[22] *Fernandes de Oliveira v Portugal*, App. No. 78103/14 (ECtHR 2019) [GC], para. 124. The Court did find a subsequent violation of procedural obligations in the proceedings to investigate responsibility for his death. Two judges dissented in part, arguing among other reasons that the hospital's obligation to prevent suicide should have been defined more strongly. *Fernandes de Oliveira* (opinion of Judge Pinto de Albuquerque joined by Judge Harutyunyan). Although the two judgments were issued the same day, the composition of the two Grand Chambers differed.

[23] See *Fernandes de Oliveira*, paras. 68–79.

[24] Judgment of July 26, 2016, 1 BvL 8/15 (BVerfG), para. 103 (official translation), available at www.bundesverfassungsgericht.de/SharedDocs/Downloads/EN/2016/07/ls20160726_1bvl000815en.pdf?__blob=publicationFile&v=2. Under the relevant law, unconsented treatment could be directed only for patients who were legally ordered into a closed environment, and patients who were too physically weak to remove themselves would not meet the standard for such an order.

significant weight, but they are not binding under international law for international or national courts."[25] It also argued that the Committee's statements were vague and did not "give an answer to the question of what, according to its understanding of the text of the Convention, should happen to persons who cannot form a free will and are in a helpless situation."[26] For similar reasons, the Court has rejected the Committee's reading of the CRPD as absolutely prohibiting the use of physical or chemical restraints for "persons who cannot (or no longer) be reached by means of communication and who pose an immediate danger to themselves or others."[27]

The German court's opinions make explicit a problem that the CRPD Committee's penchant for absolute rules repeatedly raises. The Committee demands immediate abolition of existing practices and institutions without providing implementable answers to the question of what should replace them. The issue can be illustrated in a hypothetical interaction between a member of the Human Rights Committee and a member of the CRPD Committee regarding the latter Committee's position that the CRPD requires abolition of the insanity defense and normal criminal trials with support for persons with psychosocial disabilities. The first member asks whether that means that defendants with severe disabilities should be convicted and punished even if they cannot understand their trials, and whether they should be eligible for execution in countries that still retain the death penalty (which would be contrary to the Human Rights Committee's current interpretation of the ICCPR). The second member replies that we need an entirely new understanding of criminal responsibility, which is yet to be developed. The first member concludes that it is no benefit to such defendants to dismantle existing protections completely before alternative solutions that respond to their situations have been found.

C DILEMMAS OF THE ABSOLUTIST APPROACH TO DECISION-MAKING IN DEMENTIA

The example that I will focus on here is moderate or severe dementia, which can involve what the Committee calls a high level of support needs. For people of my own age, this is a not-too-remote concern. According to the World Health

---

[25] Ibid., 2016, para. 90.
[26] Ibid., para. 91.
[27] Judgment of July 24, 2018, 2 BvL 309/15 (BVerfG), para. 92 (official translation), available at https://www.bundesverfassungsgericht.de/SharedDocs/Entscheidungen/EN/2018/07/rs20180724_2bvr030915en.html. Later, in relation to the right to vote, the Court contradicted at length the Committee's interpretation of Articles 12 and 29 of the CRPD, and insisted that the treaty does not absolutely prohibit exclusion from voting rights of persons who lack "the cognitive skills necessary to make a free and self-determined electoral decision," while finding unconstitutional a statute that imposed too broad a disenfranchisement of persons under guardianship as a violation of the constitutional provision against discrimination on grounds of disability. Judgment of January 29, 2019, 2 BvC 62/14 (BVerfG), paras. 69–77 (official translation), available at www.bundesverfassungsgericht.de/SharedDocs/Entscheidungen/EN/2019/01/cs20190129_2bvc006214en.html.

Organization, "[i]n 2015, dementia affected 47 million people worldwide (or roughly 5 percent of the world's elderly population), a figure that is predicted to increase to 75 million in 2030 and 132 million by 2050."[28]

Dementia is not one disease but an umbrella term covering a variety of forms of nontemporary significant decline in multiple cognitive abilities that significantly impair social or occupational functioning.[29] Different categories of dementia may involve different types of damage to the brain and produce different typical patterns of cognitive impairment, and the same individual may also experience more than one of these categories. The most common form of dementia recognized at present is Alzheimer's Disease. Other examples include vascular dementia (caused by strokes), Parkinsonian dementia, frontotemporal dementia, dementia with Lewy bodies, and other, less common forms.

My goal in this discussion is not to overgeneralize, and definitely not to conflate a diagnostic category with a present loss of ability. Nonetheless there are frequent consequences of dementia that many, perhaps millions of individuals will experience, and a doctrinal approach to decision-making by people with dementia cannot simply ignore those consequences when they do occur.

One symptom, particularly frequent with Alzheimer's Disease, is progressive loss of memory function, causing increasing difficulty in forming new memories and retaining them even for short periods of time.[30] In later stages, loss of older memories often follows, which may extend to the identities of close relatives. Another common symptom is impairment of "executive functions,"[31] higher level operations by which the brain controls the carrying out of complex mental tasks.[32] Deteriorating temporal and spatial orientation makes it more difficult for individuals to keep track of the passage of time, or to remember where they are going or even where they are.[33] They often lack understanding or memory of their own mental limitations, and may become deeply suspicious of others.

Such declines in cognitive abilities with moderate or severe dementia seriously undermine the ability of the affected individuals to make decisions on their own

---

[28] World Health Organization, *Global action plan on the public health response to dementia 2017–2025* (Geneva: World Health Organization, 2017), 3.

[29] See Elissa L. Ash, "What Is Dementia?", in *The Law and Ethics of Dementia*, ed. Charles Foster, Jonathan Herring and Israel Doron, London: Hart Publishing, 2014, 4; Alzheimer's Association, "2020 Alzheimer's disease facts and figures," *Alzheimer's & Dementia* 16 (2020), 392; see also Nancy L. Mace and Peter V. Rabins, *The 36-Hour Day: A Family Guide to Caring for People Who Have Alzheimer Disease, Other Dementias, and Memory Loss*, 6th ed. (Baltimore: Johns Hopkins University Press, 2017).

[30] Alireza Atri, "Alzheimer's Disease and Alzheimer's Dementia," in *Dementia: Comprehensive Principles and Policies*, ed. Bradford Dickerson and Alireza Atri (Oxford: Oxford University Press, 2014); Alzheimer's Association, "2020 facts and figures," 395–96.

[31] Ibid., 373.

[32] Kirk R. Daffner and Kim C. Willment, "Executive Control, the Regulation of Goal-Directed Behaviors, and the Impact of Dementing Illness," in *Dementia: Comprehensive Principles*.

[33] Atri, "Alzheimer's Disease," 374.

behalf, or even to follow explanations of complex matters by people attempting to support them. They can also lead persons with dementia to reject support.

Some people with dementia are fortunate enough to have close relatives whom they trust, and when they are no longer able to understand decisions that need to be made, they can engage in what the Committee would call supported decision-making. This may really amount to decision-making by the relative, with uninformed acquiescence. The foundation of trust may be destroyed for reasons caused by the illness, for example when the person can no longer recognize the relative, or when the person imagines that the relative is an impostor who merely looks like the relative. Under the absolutist approach, the person must be free to terminate the support relationship and make decisions without support at any time, which are entitled to legal effect, regardless of the danger they pose to the person's own interest.

Other people with dementia are not so fortunate, and have no close relatives who care for them, and no close friends who would take on the support responsibility. Their support can only come from strangers, and they may be unable to recognize or trust strangers as their dementia progresses. Under the absolutist approach, they must be free to reject the support of strangers at any time, regardless of the consequences.

With moderate dementia, the person may retain older memories while having great difficulty in forming new memories or comprehending current circumstances. Physical ability and mobility often remain while mental ability is declining. Often individuals with dementia cannot recognize or remember their own mental impairments, and do not understand why they should not engage in activities that put them in danger. Ordinary daily activities of routine life such as cooking, walking outside alone, and driving become risky. People who retain enough skill to drive badly, but cannot remember that they are prohibited from driving, or why, endanger themselves as well as others.[34] (Treating such drivers just like other drivers by punishing them for driving without a license, as the Committee's approach to discrimination would suggest, is not a useful solution.) Simply taking a walk outside may result in "wandering" away from the home (which the person may not understand as home) and create a range of risks depending on the situation, such as getting lost, exposure to the elements, criminal attack, and dangerous physical conditions that the person does not appreciate.[35]

Countermeasures against these dangers, such as hiding the car keys, selling the car,[36] putting complicated locks on doors,[37] getting GPS finders in shoes,[38] and

---

[34] See Desmond O'Neill, "Driving and Dementia," in *Law and Ethics of Dementia*; Mace and Rabins, *36-Hour Day*, 56–60.

[35] See Mace and Rabins, *36-Hour Day*, 141-50; L. Robinson et al., "Balancing rights and risks: conflicting perspectives in the management of wandering in dementia," *Health, Risk & Society* 9(4) (December 2007), 389–406.

[36] Ibid., 59.

[37] Ibid., 148.

[38] Ibid., 144; see Julian C. Hughes, "The Use of New Technologies in Managing Dementia Patients," in *Law and Ethics of Dementia* (arguing for balance between risks and benefits in tracking dementia patients who "wander").

disarming the stove³⁹ are all questionable under the absolutist approach to legal capacity. Under that approach, individuals should always have the right to make their own decisions, with or without support, and to make later decisions inconsistent with earlier ones. People with dementia should have the right to leave the premises at any hour of day or night in any weather, as people without dementia generally do, and preventing them would be arbitrary detention.⁴⁰

Advance care planning and durable powers of attorney may provide partial solutions to some of the dilemmas created by the absolutist approach. These legal instruments, adopted prior to the onset of dementia or in its early stages or before one's judgment is impaired, allow individuals to make choices for the future, or to designate people they trust to decide as they would wish.⁴¹ But these documents have limitations, and the absolutist approach undermines their usefulness.

To begin with, many people who are already living with moderate or severe dementia lack these documents. Prospectively, healthy individuals who have less income or live in less developed societies face barriers to acquiring instruments tailored to their preferences. Even with resources, specifying future courses of action is difficult when unforeseen problems or new alternatives may arise.⁴² There may also be cultural barriers to these forms of legalized future planning.⁴³

Next, the CRPD Committee's General Comment appears to contemplate a highly restricted role for advance directives, only for individuals who *cannot* communicate their current wishes, such as those in a coma, or those whose ability to communicate is severely obstructed and who have no one who can interpret for them. Otherwise, the individual's current preference is what counts, and the individual must be free to override a directive at any time, or terminate it, by expressing a contrary choice. And of course all choices can be made with or without support.

---

³⁹ See Mace and Rabins, *36-Hour Day*, 70–71.
⁴⁰ I recall the eloquent plea by a member of the Subcommittee on the Prevention of Torture, at a consultation convened by the Working Group on Arbitrary Detention in September 2014, that individuals in group facilities cannot be simply allowed to go out in winter without coats. The Working Group nonetheless chose to follow the absolutist approach of the CRPD Committee. See "Basic Principles," para. 106.
⁴¹ See Barak Gaster, Eric B. Larson and J. Randall Curtis, "Advance directives for dementia: meeting a unique challenge," *Journal of the American Medical Association* 318(22) (December 12, 2017), 2175–76; cf. Pablo Nicaise, Vincent Lorant and Vincent Dubois, "Psychiatric advance directives as a complex and multistage intervention: a realist systemic review," *Health and Social Care in the Community* 21(1) (2013), 1–14 (on advance planning in the mental health field); Ruth Dukoff and Trey Sunderland, "Durable power of attorney and informed consent with Alzheimer's disease patients: a clinical study," *American Journal of Psychiatry* 154(8) (August 1997), 1070–75 (on powers of attorney for consent to research participation); Adrian Thorogood et al., "Consent recommendations for research and international data sharing involving persons with dementia," *Alzheimer's & Dementia* 14 (2018), 1334–43.
⁴² That reality is particularly vivid to an author writing in the midst of the COVID-19 pandemic.
⁴³ See Leigh Turner, "From the local to the global: bioethics and the concept of culture," *Journal of Medicine and Philosophy* 30 (2005), 305–20; Bolatito A. Lanre-Abass, "Cultural differences in advance directives relating to end of life decision making," *Prajñā Vihāra* 9 (2008) 23–49.

Experts on the CRPD Committee's jurisprudence also explain that advance directives and similar documents cannot be drafted so that they become effective when the individual's mental capacity reaches a particular level of impairment.[44] Making the legal effect of the document depend on a finding about functional capacity is said to be forbidden discrimination, and individuals cannot be permitted to adopt such an instrument.

As an "older person,"[45] I do not want to be condemned to the uncomprehending freedom of action that some disability advocates on and off the CRPD Committee would impose on people with moderate to severe dementia. If it should come to pass that my memory and my reasoning abilities are so severely damaged that I cannot perceive obvious consequences of my actions, I do not want every insistent impulse to be indulged as an exercise of my absolutely equal right to take risks. Nor do I want my freedom to plan against such a future to be limited by the CRPD Committee's vision of absolute equality and the irrelevance of functional capacity to the ability to perform every particular act with legally binding effect. Nor would I impose that state of affairs on others.

To be clear, I do not contend that the current wishes of a person with moderate or severe dementia are irrelevant, or that they should always yield to someone else's estimate of the person's best interests. Rather, I am arguing that there are situations of serious harm where the individual's uncomprehending choice should not be given the exclusive focus that the absolutist approach demands.

Moreover, the failings of the absolutist approach in dealing with dementia are indicative of a wider methodological problem in the CRPD Committee's construction of doctrines to implement its Convention. The Committee's absolutism is not the usual human rights approach, and certainly not the only human rights approach.

D Conclusion

The advent of the Convention on the Rights of Persons with Disabilities and the work of the CRPD Committee have contributed greatly to the protection of persons with disabilities and to the human rights system. Other courts and treaty bodies have gained insights from textual and oral dialogue with the CRPD Committee and have revised their own interpretations of other treaties to reflect those insights, though not always by accepting its conclusions.

Regrettably, the CRPD Committee has adopted an unrealistic and rigid absolutist approach to issues such as legal capacity and discrimination, and has insisted that

---

[44] See, e.g., Report of the Special Rapporteur on the rights of persons with disabilities, UN Doc. A/HRC/37/56 (2017), para. 44 (citing General Comment 1, para. 17); Elionoir Flynn and Anna Arstein-Kerslake, "Legislating personhood: realising the right to support in exercising legal capacity," *International Journal of Law in Context* 10 (2014), 89.

[45] See Inter-American Convention on Protecting the Human Rights of Older Persons, June 15, 2015, O.A.S.T.S. No. A-70, art. 2.

this absolutism constitutes the only human rights-based approach. As the example of dementia illustrates, the absolutist approach to decision-making can undermine the rights of many people it purports to serve. One can only hope that the dialogue will continue and that the learning will be mutual.

5

From Pipe Dream to Reality: A Practical Legal Approach Towards the Global Abolition of Psychiatric Coercion

Laura Davidson

Abstract

Psychiatric coercion is prima facie discriminatory and unlawful under the Convention on the Rights of Persons with Disabilities (CRPD), according to its Committee. However, significant disagreement about the Convention's interpretation remains, even within the UN, and many argue that a complete coercion ban will exacerbate harm to persons with disabilities in certain circumstances. Thus, the called-for paradigm shift away from the current biomedical model remains unrealised. Rather than debating the correctness of the Committee's position, this chapter proposes escape from the impasse towards the global abolition of psychiatric coercion through a practical process endorsed by the Committee. It must issue a general comment which gives tacit approval for the progressive realisation of rights under Articles 12 and 14 and provides a clear and reasonable deadline for total abolition – such as by 2030, which would align with the UN Sustainable Development Agenda. To meet that goal, states should be required to (i) introduce new policy and interim legislation significantly improving rights' protection for those with psychosocial disabilities; (ii) set clear time-bound milestones towards introducing a complete ban on psychiatric coercion; and (iii) end lawful psychiatric coercion in accordance with the Committee's deadline. The chapter also proposes and discusses four essential ingredients as foci for any new mental health laws.

INTRODUCTION

"Everyone, regardless of their diagnosis, the voices they hear, the substances they use, their race, nationality, gender, sexual orientation or gender identity, or other status, is guaranteed the right to non-discrimination in accessing care and support for their mental health. However, discrimination de jure and de facto continues to influence mental health services, depriving users of a variety of rights, including the rights to refuse treatment, to legal capacity and to privacy, and other civil and political rights.'"

This chapter arose from a longer article by the author published in the *Harvard Health and Human Rights Journal*.

[1] D. Pūras, Report of the UN Special Rapporteur on the right of everyone to the enjoyment of the highest attainable standard of physical and mental health, UN Doc. A/HRC/44/48 (2020), para. 61. Available at https://undocs.org/A/HRC/44/48. See also Chapter 20.

So stated Dainius Pūras in his final report as Special Rapporteur on the right of everyone to the enjoyment of the highest attainable standard of physical and mental health (SR on health) before stepping down at the end of his term. However, is a world free from psychiatric coercion a pipe dream? The right to liberty is a dichotomy. It remains subject to exceptions, despite being a fundamental right enshrined in numerous international treaties (including the Convention on the Rights of Persons with Disabilities (CRPD)).[2] Such exceptions include punishment for certain criminal offences, and hospitalisation to treat mental illness. Coercive hospital admission and treatment on the basis of perceived risk and/or the severity of mental illness is permitted globally in mental health legislation. This use of force has been so normalised that its lawfulness is rarely questioned, much less whether or not it succeeds in its purpose. The Committee on the Rights of Persons with Disabilities (CRPD Committee) has repeatedly criticised non-consensual psychiatric care as discriminatory, and hence a violation of the treaty,[3] amounting to torture and cruel, inhuman or degrading treatment or punishment under Article 15 of the CRPD.[4] Compulsory hospitalisation often leads to other restrictive practices such as physical, chemical and mechanical restraint, seclusion, 'over-medicalization and treatment practices that fail to respect... autonomy, will and preferences'.[5] There is significant evidence that '[e]mpowerment and recovery cannot happen in closed settings',[6] with

---

[2] See, e.g., Article 3(a): 'Respect for inherent dignity, individual autonomy including the freedom to make one's own choices, and independence of persons' (a CRPD general principle).

[3] The CRPD Committee prefers the term 'psychosocial disability' for those with a mental health diagnosis, which the author adopts for this chapter.

[4] Committee on the Rights of Persons with Disabilities, General Comment No. 1 on Article 12: Equal recognition before the law (GC1), UN Doc. CRPD/C/GC/1, 19 May 2014, para. 42. Available at https://undocs.org/en/CRPD/C/GC/1. See, also, e.g., Committee on the Rights of Persons with Disabilities, Concluding Observations: Australia, UN Doc. CRPD/C/AUS/CO/1 (2013), paras. 35–36. Available at https://undocs.org/en/CRPD/C/AUS/CO/1; J. Mendez, Report of the Special Rapporteur on torture and other cruel, inhuman or degrading treatment or punishment, A/HRC/22/53, 1 February 2013 (SR on torture), paras. 62–65 and para. 89. Available at www.ohchr.org/documents/hrbodies/hrcouncil/regularsession/session22/a.hrc.22.53_english.pdf.

[5] D. Pūras, Report of the Special Rapporteur on the right of everyone to the enjoyment of the highest attainable standard of physical and mental health, UN Doc. A/HRC/29/33 (2015), para. 98. Available at https://undocs.org/en/A/HRC/29/33; Human Rights Council, Resolution on Mental Health and Human Rights, A/HRC/32/L.26, 29 June 2016. Available at https://undocs.org/A/HRC/32/L.26.

[6] D. Pūras, Report of the Special Rapporteur on the right of everyone to the enjoyment of the highest attainable standard of physical and mental health, UN Doc. A/ HRC/38/36 (2018), para. 52 and para. 85. See also, e.g., Wallsten, T., Kjellin, L., Lindström, L. (2006), 'Short-term outcome of inpatient psychiatric care – impact of coercion and treatment characteristics', *Soc Psychiatry Psychiatr Epidemiol*, 41(12): 975–980; Kallert, T. W., Katsakou, C., Adamowski, T., et al. (2011), 'Coerced hospital admission and symptom change – a prospective observational multi-centre study', *PLoS One*, 6(11): e28191. Available at https://doi.org/10.1371/journal.pone.0028191; Molodynski, A., Khazaal, Y., and Callard, F. (2016), 'Coercion in mental healthcare: time for a change in direction', *BJPsych Int*, 13(1): 1–3. Available at 10.1192/s2056474000000854.

psychiatric coercion reducing trust in services and breaking down the therapeutic relationship[7] and that its use defeats its purpose, resulting in repeated hospital admissions.[8] The UN also recognises that compulsive practices are contrary to a human rights-based approach,[9] and that they can cause trauma, 'enormous psychosocial pain and hopelessness'.[10] These negative impacts are diametrically opposed to the achievements sought under UN Sustainable Goal 3 (SDG3) which requires states to '[e]nsure healthy lives and promote well-being for all at all ages'.[11]

The biomedical model emanates from a skewed and outdated power dynamic with excessive deference offered to a medical profession unrealistically considered inviolable. The SR on health has described this unacceptable 'frozen status quo' as reinforcing 'a vicious cycle of discrimination, disempowerment, coercion, social exclusion and injustice'.[12] Other than for the treatment of psychosocial disability, compulsion is rarely directed at physical health issues (with the unprecedented quarantine and lockdown restrictions of the recent COVID-19 coronavirus pandemic a notorious exception).[13] Fourteen years have passed since the adoption of the

---

[7] Lamberti, J. S., Russ, A., Cerulli, C., et al. (2014), 'Patient experiences of autonomy and coercion while receiving legal leverage in forensic assertive community treatment', *Harv Rev Psychiatry*, 22(4): 222–230. Available at https://doi.org/10.1097/01.HRP.0000450448.48563.c1; Akhter, S. F., Molyneaux, E., Stuart, R., et al. (2019), 'Patients' experiences of assessment and detention under mental health legislation: systematic review and qualitative meta-synthesis', *BJPsych Open* 5, e37: 1–10. Available at https://doi.org/10.1192/bjo.2019.19.

[8] See, e.g., Swartz, M. S., Swanson, J. W., and Hannon, M. J. (2003), 'Does fear of coercion keep people away from mental health treatment? Evidence from a survey of persons with schizophrenia and mental health professionals', *Behav Sci Law*, 21(4): 459–472. Available at: https://doi.org/10.1016/S0140-6736(13)60107-5; Burns, T., Rugkåsa, J., Molodynski, A., et al. (2013), 'Community treatment orders for patients with psychosis (OCTET): a randomised controlled trial', *The Lancet*, 381(9878): 1627–1633. Available at https://doi.org/10.1016/S0140-6736(13)60107-5; Jaeger, S., Pfiffner, C., Weiser, P. et al. (2013), 'Long-term effects of involuntary hospitalisation on medication adherence, treatment engagement and perception of coercion', *Soc Psychiatry Psychiatr Epidemiol*, 48(11): 1787–1796. Available at https://doi.org/10.1007/s00127-013-0687-x;

[9] SR on health (2020), para. 19(d) and para. 64.

[10] GC1, para. 42; SR on health (2018), para. 19(d); Frueh, B. C., Knapp, R. G., Cusack K. J., et al. (2005), 'Patients' reports of traumatic or harmful experiences within the psychiatric setting', *Psychiatr Serv*, 56(9): 1123–1133. Available at https://doi.org/10.1176/appi.ps.56.9.1123; Paksarian, D., Mojtabai, R., Kotov, R., et al. (2014), 'Perceived trauma during hospitalisation and treatment participation amongst individuals with psychotic disorders', *Psychiatr Serv*, 65(2): 266–269. Available at https://doi.10.1176/appi.ps.201200556; Akhter, et al., 'Patients' experiences'; Broberg, E., Persson, A., Jacobson, A., and Engqvist, A., 'A human rights-based approach to psychiatry: is it possible?', *Harvard Health and Human Rights Journal*, June 2020, 22(1): 121–131, at 125. Available at www.hhrjournal.org/2020/06/a-human-rights-based-approach-to-psychiatry-is-it-possible/. See also Rose, D., Perry, E., Rae, S., and Good, N. (2017), 'Service user perspectives on coercion and restraint in mental health', *BJPsych International* 14(3): 59–61. Available at https://doi.org/10.1192/S2056474000001914.

[11] See www.un.org/sustainabledevelopment/health/.

[12] SR on health (2020), para. 82.

[13] For the preservation of the health of the nation. See, e.g., the UK's Health Protection (Coronavirus) Regulations 2020. Available at www.legislation.gov.uk/uksi/2020/129/contents/made. Another key exception is the provision of life-saving medical treatment to unconscious patients.

CRPD, yet even very recently drafted legislation fails to ban psychiatric coercion.[14] Further, in many low- and middle-income countries (LMICs) where no mental health legislation exists, force still takes place in psychiatric hospitals despite the absence of legal foundation and procedural protections.[15]

Although the wisdom and practicality of a complete ban on psychiatric coercion has been widely questioned,[16] this chapter assumes that the CRPD Committee's interpretations are accurate and valid. The CRPD forms part of the the cohort of international law and as involuntary psychiatric detention and enforced medical treatment are prima facie discriminatory, they are unlawful.[17] The chapter proposes

[14] C. Devandas-Aguilar, Report of the Special Rapporteur on the rights of persons with disabilities, UN Doc. A/HRC/37/56 (2017), para. 38. Available at https://undocs.org/en/A/HRC/37/56. See also Chapter 1 of this volume. For a critique of the compliance with the CRPD of recently passed and draft laws in China, England and Wales, Ontario (Canada) and Northern Ireland, see Dawson J. (2015), 'A realistic approach to assessing mental health laws' compliance with the UNCRPD', Int J Law Psychiatry 40: 70–79. Available at https://doi.org/10.1016/j.ijlp.2015.04.003.

[15] Almost a third of 111 countries reporting to the WHO in 2017 had no stand-alone mental health legislation whatsoever: WHO (2018), Mental Health Atlas 2017 (Geneva: World Health Organization), para. 2.2, pp. 18–21. Available at www.who.int/mental_health/evidence/atlas/mental_health_atlas_2017/en/. Mental health laws existed in only 36 per cent of low-income states: WHO (2014), Social Determinants of Mental Health (Geneva: World Health Organization). Available at www.who.int/mental_health/publications/gulbenkian_paper_social_determinants_of_mental_health/en/.

[16] See, e.g., Bach, M. and Kerzner, L. (2010), 'A new paradigm for protecting autonomy and the right to legal capacity: advancing substantive equality for persons with disabilities through law, policy and practice', commissioned by the Law Commission of Ontario, October 2010. Available at www.lco-cdo.org/wp-content/uploads/2010/11/disabilities-commissioned-paper-bach-kerzner.pdf; Dute, J. (2015), 'Should substituted decision-making be abolished?', European Journal of Health Law, 22(4): 315–320. Available at https://doi.org/10.1163/15718093-12341371; Freeman, M. C. et al. (2015), 'Reversing hard won victories in the name of human rights: a critique of the General Comment on Article 12 of the UN Convention on the Rights of Persons with Disabilities', The Lancet Psychiatry, 2(9): 844–850. Available at https://doi.org/10.1016/S2215-0366(15)00218-7; Davidson, L. (2017), 'Capacity to consent to or refuse psychiatric treatment: an analysis of South African and British law', South African Journal on Human Rights, 11 January 2017, 32(3): 457–489, at 463. Available at http://dx.doi.org/10.1080/02587203.2016.1263417; Scholten, M. and Gather, J. (2018), 'Adverse consequences of article 12 of the UN Convention on the Rights of Persons with Disabilities for persons with mental disabilities and an alternative way forward', Journal of Medical Ethics, 44: 226–233. Available at https://jme.bmj.com/content/medethics/early/2017/10/25/medethics-2017-104414.full.pdf; Szmukler, G. (2019), '"Capacity", "best interests", "will and preferences" and the UN Convention on the Rights of Persons with Disabilities', World Psychiatry 18(1): 34–41. Available at http://doi.org/10.1002/wps.20584; Wilson, K. (2018), 'The call for the abolition of mental health law: the challenges of suicide, accidental death and the equal enjoyment of the right to life', Human Rights Law Review, 18(4): 651–688. Available at https://doi.org/10.1093/hrlr/ngy029.

[17] Some scholars disagree with the CRPD Committee's interpretation of 'discrimination', however; see, e.g., Gurbai, S. (2020), 'Beyond the pragmatic definition? The right to non-discrimination of persons with disabilities in the context of coercive interventions', Harvard Health and Human Rights Journal, June 2020, 22(1): 279–292, at 289. Available at www.hhrjournal.org/2020/05/beyond-the-pragmatic-definition-the-right-to-nondiscrimination-of-persons-with-disabilities-in-the-context-of-coercive-interventions/; Martin, W., and Gurbai, S. (2019), "Surveying the Geneva impasse: coercive care and human rights," Int J Law Psychiatry, 64 (2019): 117–129, at 125. Available at https://doi.org/10.1016/j.ijlp.2019.03.001; Dawson, 'A realistic approach', 71; Appelbaum, P. S. (2016), 'Protecting the rights of persons with disabilities: an international convention and its problems', Psychiatr Serv, 67: 366–368, at 367. Available at https://doi.org/10.1176/appi.ps.201600050; The UN Human Rights Committee has

a practical way out of the deadlock through stop-gap mental health legislation that continues to permit coercive practices in tightly circumscribed circumstances for a specified interim period only. With the aim of ending psychiatric compulsion by 2030 in alignment with the UN Sustainable Development Agenda, alternatives to institutional care must be expanded within the community. The CRPD Committee is urged to issue a general comment commending such an approach, thereby (no doubt begrudgingly) endorsing the 'progressive realisation' of Articles 12 and 14 of the CRPD.

PSYCHIATRIC COERCION IN THE CRPD ERA

The definition of disability in Article 1 of the CRPD includes those with 'long-term mental ... impairments'.[18] Signatory states agree to 'promote, protect and ensure the full and equal enjoyment of all human rights and fundamental freedoms by all persons with disabilities and to promote respect for their inherent dignity'. Article 12 of the CRPD requires appropriate support and 'reasonable accommodation' to be provided to those with psychosocial disabilities to enable them to make decisions about treatment and care 'on the basis of free and informed consent'.[19] The 'existence of a disability *shall in no case justify a deprivation of liberty*' according to Article 14.[20] The duty not to discriminate per se is enshrined in Article 28. Clearly, compulsory hospitalisation and enforced medical treatment practices violate the Convention.[21] This is reiterated in General Comment No. 1 on Article 12 (GC1)[22]

---

also stated that '[n]ot every differentiation of treatment will constitute discrimination, if the criteria for such differentiation are reasonable and objective and if the aim is to achieve a purpose which is legitimate under the Covenant' – see UN Doc. HRI\GEN\1\Rev.1 (1989), General Comment No. 18 (Non-discrimination) on the International Covenant on Civil and Political Rights, para. 13.

[18] The definition of 'long-term' with respect to mental impairments is unclear and open to interpretation, as is whether or not the CRPD would protect someone suffering from a drug-induced psychosis or from brief or occasional relapses.

[19] Human Rights Council, Mental health and human rights, UN Doc. A/HRC/36/L.25 (2017), para. 10. Available at https://undocs.org/en/A/HRC/36/L.25; GC1, para. 41; Article 2 CRPD states that '"Reasonable accommodation" means necessary and appropriate modification and adjustments not imposing a disproportionate or undue burden, where needed ... to ensure to persons with disabilities the enjoyment or exercise on an equal basis with others of all human rights and fundamental freedoms'.

[20] All emphases are added unless otherwise stated.

[21] Concluding Observations: Tunisia, UN Doc. CRPD/C/ TUN/CO/1 (2011). Available at https://undocs.org/CRPD/C/TUN/CO/1; Committee on the Rights of Persons with Disabilities, Concluding Observations: Spain, UN Doc. CRPD/C/ESP/CO/1 (2011). Available at https://undocs.org/en/CRPD/C/ESP/CO/1. See also GC1, para. 42; *Guidelines on article 14 of the Convention on the Rights of Persons with Disabilities: The right to liberty and security of persons with disabilities* (G14), Annexed to the Report of the Committee on the Rights of Persons with Disabilities (A/72/55), 14th session, September 2015, para. 3. Available at https://undocs.org/A/72/55; SR on health (2018), para. 49; C. Devandas-Aguilar, Report of the Special Rapporteur on the rights of persons with disabilities, UN Doc. A/73/161 (2018), para. 74(b). Available at www.ohchr.org/Documents/Issues/Disability/A_73_161_EN.pdf.

[22] GC1, paras. 18 and 42. Available at https://undocs.org/en/CRPD/C/GC/1.

and the CRPD's *Guidelines on Article 14 concerning the right to liberty* (G14).[23] Controversially, the CRPD Committee has interpreted Article 12 as requiring the complete prohibition of substitute decision-making – a view shared by some other UN bodies,[24] such as the UN Working Group on Arbitrary Detention,[25] and several Special Rapporteurs.[26] Unusually, not all treaty bodies agree. For example, in 2014 the Human Rights Council deemed certain safeguards sufficient protection for lawful coercive treatment based in part upon disability under the International Covenant of Civil and Political Rights (ICCPR).[27]

The CRPD Committee's interpretations have been doubted by academics, clinicians and others, who have highlighted a plethora of possible negative impacts arising from a complete ban on psychiatric coercion.[28] Even if the political will existed, immediate full CRPD compliance would compromise the right to the highest attainable standard of health which is protected under Article 25 of the Convention.[29] The right requires sufficient available, accessible, adequate and affordable alternatives to compulsory inpatient treatment within the community, and its global lack is a major reason for the current impasse.[30] Further, in many LMICs staffed residential placements and psychological services are non-existent, particularly at the primary care level. The creation of the necessary community-based infrastructure and the development of non-coercive interventions worldwide requires significantly more political and financial commitment.

---

[23] G14.

[24] Working Group on Arbitrary Detention, *UN Basic Principles and Guidelines on remedies and procedures on the right of anyone deprived of their liberty to bring proceedings before a court*, para. 126(a), para. 126(d)-(f)). Available at www.ohchr.org/Documents/Issues/Detention/DraftBasicPrinciples/BasicPrinciplesAndGuidelines.doc.

[25] Ibid. The Principles govern 'specific measures for persons with disabilities', and state that psychiatric hospitals should 'immediately cease any forced treatment' and release psychiatric patients; June 2015, Guideline 20, para. 123 and para. 126(d).

[26] SR on health (2015), para. 98; and HRC (2016); D. Pūras, Report of the Special Rapporteur on the right of everyone to the enjoyment of the highest attainable standard of physical and mental health, UN Doc. A/HRC/35/21 (2017), 5–6. Available at https://undocs.org/A/HRC/35/21; SR on health (2018); see also CRPD Committee's Statement on article 14 of the Convention on the Rights of Persons with Disabilities, CRPD/C/12/2, Annex IV, paras. 1–2. Available at https://undocs.org/CRPD/C/12/2; Report of the SR on disabilities (2018); SR on torture (2013).

[27] Human Rights Committee, General Comment No. 35 on Article 9 (Liberty and Security of Person), UN Doc. CCPR/C/GC/35 (2014) (GC35), para. 19. Available at https://undocs.org/CCPR/C/GC/35.

[28] See Footnote 15 above.

[29] The right to health, first articulated in Article 25 of the Universal Declaration on Human Rights (UDHR), has been recognised in international law for over fifty years. See also Knapp, M., Beecham, J., McDaid, D., et al. (2011), 'The economic consequences of deinstitutionalisation of mental health services: lessons from a systematic review of European experience', *Health and Social Care in the Community*, 19(2), 113–125. Available at https://doi.org/doi.10.1111/j.1365-2524.2010.00969.x.

[30] See Committee on Economic, Social and Cultural Rights, General Comment No. 14, The Right to the Highest Attainable Standard of Health, UN Doc. E/C.12/2000/4 (2000) (GC14), para. 12, which explains the need for availability, accessibility, acceptability, and quality of care within facilities, medicines, and health services. Available at https://undocs.org/E/C.12/2000/4.

Global Failure to Ban Psychiatric Coercion

In 2017, over thirty countries reported that they had recently updated legal capacity legislation.[31] The amendments, which mostly related to a new (and appropriate) emphasis on supported decision-making,[32] significantly did not include mental health legislation. Thus, seven years on from the publication of GC1, no country has fully complied with Articles 12 and 14 of the CRPD. Some have specifically rejected the CRPD Committee's interpretation that a ban on all psychiatric coercion is necessary. For example, following a full and independent review of the Mental Health Act 1983 in the UK, the review Chair stated, 'I don't agree with it, and I am far from sure that is what most service users want either, as well as many others'.[33] The final Report instead uses the UN Human Rights Council resolution of 28 September 2017 on human rights and mental health as its interpretive guidance on the CRPD.[34]

INTERIM LEGISLATION AS A STOP-GAP MEASURE

This stalemate enables continued discrimination against those with psychosocial disabilities worldwide, curtailing their rights to autonomy, self-determination and liberty. The practical solution contended for is the amendment of mental health legislation by all states (or if non-existent, its introduction) with three aims: (1) amplifying the rights of those with psychosocial disabilities; (2) radically reducing coercion;[35] (3) aiming for the elimination of psychiatric coercion altogether. Although stopgap mental health legislation would fail to comply fully with the CPRD, it would break the impasse and foster the necessary mindset change to end the biomedical model's dominance in psychiatric care.

Progressive Realisation

However, such a proposal leads to a legal conundrum. Interim legislation would be a form of 'progressive realisation' only permitted with respect to social, cultural and

---

[31] C. Devandas-Aguilar, Report of Special Rapporteur on the rights of persons with disabilities, UN Doc. A/HRC/37/56, 12 December 2017, para. 38. Available at https://ap.ohchr.org/documents/dpage_e.aspx?si=A/HRC/37/56.

[32] See, e.g., the Mental Capacity Act (NI) 2016, which came into force in 2019. The Mental Health (NI) Order 1986 still applies to those with psychosocial disabilities, but will be repealed for those over age sixteen on full commencement. Impaired decision-making capacity permits non-consensual interventions, but it remains discriminatory since it impacts more on those with psychosocial disabilities.

[33] Final report of the Independent Review of the Mental Health Act 1983, 'Modernising the Mental Health Act: increasing choice, reducing compulsion', 14, 61–62. Available at https://www.gov.uk/government/publications/modernising-the-mental-health-act-final-report-from-the-independent-review See also Freeman et al., 'Reversing hard won victories'.

[34] Ibid., at 13–14 – although the Chair misinterprets the CRPD Committee's pronouncements, as it did not call for 'the abolition of all mental health legislation'.

[35] The SR on health has called for a radical reduction in medical coercion and institutionalisation in several of his reports – see SR on health (2017), paras. 65–66; SR on health (2018), para. 51 and para. 98(d).

economic rights like the right to health, and not civil and political rights such as the right to liberty. Furthermore, it does not apply to discrimination, as GC1 highlights.[36] Progressive realisation requires 'deliberate, concrete and targeted' steps to be taken to protect rights as swiftly and effectively as possible within the confines of a state's finite resources.[37] Despite its insistence on 'immediate realization', the CRPD Committee's contradictory language at times lends itself to pragmatic, gradual measures to eliminate coercion. Thus, states must take 'deliberate, well-planned' actions, and consult with and ensure the 'meaningful participation of people with disabilities and their organizations'.[38] Similarly, in its General Comment No. 5 on Article 19 (living independently and being included in the community (GC5)), published three years after GC1, the CRPD Committee urges states to '*take steps* to the maximum of their available resources' to meet Article 19, and to adopt '*strategies* for deinstitutionalization, with *specific time frames* and adequate budgets ... to eliminate all forms of isolation, segregation and institutionalization of persons with disabilities'.[39] These pragmatic 'concessions' may emanate from a resigned acceptance that an immediate ban on coercive psychiatric practices in the absence of sufficiently available and acceptable alternative community care and support would be liable to harm the rights holders whom the Convention is meant to protect. Improved protection, promotion and fulfilment of rights is preferable to the status quo.

Why Not Soft Law?

Updating 'soft law', such as rules, regulations or a code of practice, is cheaper and less time consuming than legislative amendment.[40] However, it would be insufficient in three key regards. First, it is more likely that source legislation will be respected and utilised than the soft law extrapolating it. Secondly, if a primary law permits significant restrictions on liberty, where there is disparity, healthcare staff are likely to favour it. Accordingly, coercion may fail to be reduced, particularly in LMICs where hard copies of legislative guidance tend to be less available within hospitals. Thirdly, archaic mental health legislation in many countries contains highly stigmatising language.[41] For example, Sierra Leone's Lunacy Act of

---

[36] See Article 4(2) CRPD.
[37] GC35, para. 19.
[38] GC1, para. 30.
[39] Committee on the Rights of Persons with Disabilities, General Comment No. 5 on Living Independently and Being Included in the Community, UN Doc. CRPD/C/GC/5 (2017), para. 97(g). See also SR on health (2018), paras. 24, 51, 98(d) and 99.
[40] 'Soft law' is not easily fully defined, but refers to necessary implementing frameworks surrounding primary legislation, delegated legislation and rules or regulations pursuant to statutes (which are binding and known as 'hard law'). See further, e.g., Cerone, J., 'A Taxonomy of Soft Law: Stipulating a Definition' in Lagoutte, S., et al. (eds.) (2016), *Tracing the Roles of Soft Law in Human Rights* (Oxford: Oxford University Press), 16–17. Available at https://doi.org/10.1093/acprof:oso/9780198791409.003.0002.
[41] In 2011 the WHO found that 15% of countries had mental health legislation enacted before 1970. See WHO (2011) *Mental Health Atlas 2011* (Geneva: World Health Organisation), para. 1.3, p. 22. Available at www.who.int/mental_health/publications/mental_health_atlas_2011/en/.

1902 permits the declaration of a person as a 'lunatic' where there is 'no reasonable doubt'.[42] The dehumanising terminology in Gambia's Lunatic Detention Act 1917 was held to violate the African Charter on Human and People's Rights.[43] Similarly, a domestic constitutional court declared the Zambian Mental Disorders Act 1951 unlawful partly due to its discriminatory language.[44] Such discriminatory relics emanate from an era when those with psychosocial disabilities were considered subhuman, dangerous or comical, requiring removal from society. Legislation containing an approach so fundamentally abhorrent and contrary to today's human rights standards requires urgent repeal, and would be fundamentally incompatible with extra-statutory guidance requiring the reduction of coercion and enhancement of autonomy. However, depending on the time taken for the passage of national legislation, more recent laws drafted or amended some years after GC1 was published – or, indeed, since normative change within international human rights standards – may require additional updating.

GUIDANCE ON LEGISLATIVE AMENDMENT

It is necessary for states to undertake comprehensive legislative reviews prior to legal reform in order to identify potential or actual violations of international human rights law.[45] Mental health issues are relevant to many different areas of law, including family, criminal, tort and contract law. Once all provisions pertaining to mental health have been identified, laws must be amended in accordance with updated policies that state the clear intention to ban psychiatric coercion (within a suggested timeframe of ten years).[46] The WHO's *Resource Book on Mental Health, Human Rights and Legislation* was previously widely utilised for drafting mental health laws, but it has been withdrawn for non-compliance with the CRPD, with no known publication date for its much anticipated replacement.[47] However, the WHO's QualityRights training and guidance materials are useful to inform policy

---

[42] Section 4. Even some regional treaties fall short, such as Art. 5(1)(e) of the European Convention on Human Rights (ECHR) which permits the detention of those of 'unsound mind' – an antiquated and offensive term.

[43] *Purohit and Moore v. Gambia*, Communication No. 241/2001 (2003).

[44] *Mwewa, Kasote and Katontoka v. The Attorney General and Zambia Agency for Persons with Disabilities* [2017] ZMHC 77, 9 October 2017, 2017/HP/204. Section 5 of the 1951 Act, containing the categories 'idiot', 'imbecile', and 'moral imbecile', was held incompatible with the Zambian Persons with Disabilities Act 2012.

[45] SR on disabilities (2018), para. 14 and para. 74(b).

[46] Notably, reduced coercion can also contribute to a better working environment for staff, with a recent study finding a decrease in sick leave and an increase in job loyalty; see Broberg et al., 'Human rights-based approach', 125.

[47] WHO (2005), *Resource Book on Mental Health, Human Rights, and Legislation* (Geneva: World Health Organisation). Available at www.paho.org/hr-ecourse-e/assets/_pdf/Module1/Lesson2/M1_L2_23.pdf. See also WHO (1996), 'Mental health care law: ten basic principles' (Geneva: World Health Organization). Available at https://apps.who.int/iris/handle/10665/63624.

decision-making.[48] The provision of a complete guide to all necessary principles governing internationally compliant mental health legislation is beyond the scope of this chapter, but the substantive and procedural protections of 'the old paradigm' remain crucial as a foundation for the next decade of change.[49] Legislative provisions towards full CRPD compliance should focus on four essential aims: (1) building upon extant procedural and substantive protections; (2) reducing coercion and unnecessary interferences with liberty and bodily integrity; (3) non-discrimination and empowerment; and (4) target setting to reduce and eventually eliminate coercion within a reasonable specified period.[50]

(1) Building on Extant Procedural and Substantive Protections

Mental health legislation is a paradox, permitting, governing and circumscribing the contexts in which psychiatric coercion, including seclusion and restraint, may take place.[51] Although rights activists object to the law's legitimisation of coercion on the basis of disability, mental health legislation simultaneously protects human rights, both substantively and procedurally.[52] Accordingly, it can be a powerful transformative and protective tool. Legally permitted rights interference necessitates significant procedural checks and balances, along with provisions safeguarding negative rights (including legal enforcement mechanisms). All current provisions enhancing disability rights must be maintained in mental health legislation,[53] within an overarching 'harm-reduction' framework.[54] More recently drafted legislation has often sought

---

[48] Available at www.who.int/publications/i/item/who-qualityrights-guidance-and-training-tools. See further Funk, M., and Drew, N. (2020), 'WHO's QualityRights initiative: transforming services and promoting rights in mental health', *Harvard Health and Human Rights Journal*, June 2020, 22(1): 69–75. Available at www.hhrjournal.org/2020/06/perspective-whos-qualityrights-initiative-transforming-services-and-promoting-rights-in-mental-health/. See also Chapter 20.

[49] Bartlett, P. (2019), 'Mental disability, the European Convention on Human Rights and Fundamental Rights and Freedoms, and the Sustainable Development Goals', in L. Davidson, (ed.) *The Routledge Handbook of International Development, Mental Health and Wellbeing* (London: Routledge), 273–290, at 283.

[50] SR on disabilities (2018), para. 74(b).

[51] For procedural protections usually included in mental health legislation, see Davidson, L. (2020), 'A key, not a straitjacket: the case for interim mental health legislation pending complete prohibition of psychiatric coercion in accordance with the Convention on the Rights of Persons with Disabilities', *Harvard Health and Human Rights Journal*, June 2020, 22(1): 163–178, at 168–169. Available at www.hhrjournal.org/2020/06/a-key-not-a-straitjacket-the-case-for-interim-mental-health-legislation-pending-complete-prohibition-of-psychiatric-coercion-in-accordance-with-the-convention-on-the-rights-of-persons-with-disabilit/.

[52] See, e.g., Drew, N., Funk, M., Tang, S., et al. (2011), 'Human rights violations of people with mental and psychosocial disabilities: an unresolved global crisis', *The Lancet*, 378(9803): 1664–1675. Available at https://doi.org/10.1016/S0140-6736(11)61458-X; Martin, and Gurbai, S., 'Surveying the Geneva impasse'; Sashidharan, S. P., Mezzina, R., and Pūras, D. (2019), 'Reducing coercion in mental healthcare', *Epidemiology and Psychiatric Sciences*, 28(6): 605–612, at 610. Available at https://doi.org/10.1017/S2045796019000350.

[53] See also WHO, *Mental Health Atlas 2017*, para. 2.2, p. 20.

[54] SR on health (2020), para. 62.

the integration of mental health into primary healthcare, demanding community rehabilitation options for those with psychosocial disabilities – an important step in the deinstitutionalisation process. Innovation is essential to account for normative change. For example, the frequently criticised lack of parity between physical and mental health requires policy and legislative focus.[55] A positive statutory right to mental health services that have parity with physical health (in other words, that are equally available, accessible, adequate and affordable) would be a watershed, with an integral universal health coverage surety. Similarly, legislation could outlaw discriminatory health insurance practices that exclude mental health conditions.[56]

(2) Reducing Coercion and Unnecessary Interferences with Liberty and Bodily Integrity

Restricting Hospitalisation

Until the abolition of psychiatric coercion, mental health legislation remains the basis for psychiatric admission and enforced treatment. Traditionally, the right to liberty has been subject to exceptions based on criminality, dangerousness (to self or others, necessarily judged subjectively) or necessity.[57] However, as the Special Rapporteur on persons with disabilities, Catalina Devandas-Aguilar (SR on disabilities), has pointed out, coercion is impermissible 'even if additional factors or criteria are used to justify them'.[58] The Human Rights Committee's General Comment No. 35 on Article 9 (Liberty and Security of Person) (GC35) suggests that 'any deprivation of liberty must be necessary and proportionate, for the purpose of protecting the individual in question from serious harm or preventing injury to others'.[59] These 'broad and subjective grounds' have been criticised by the SR on health.[60] In some countries, compulsory hospitalisation is extremely arbitrary or blatantly discriminatory, being founded purely on disability. For example, in Malawi – which ratified the CPRD in 2009 – hospital orders are based on 'unsoundness of mind', with need for neither severity nor medical diagnosis.[61] What is certain is that states must reduce

---

[55] Bhugra, D., Campion, J, Ventriglio, A., et al. (2015), 'The right to mental health and parity', *Indian J Psychiat*, 57(2), 117–121. Available at https://doi.org/10.4103/0019-5545.158130.

[56] See, e.g., ibid; Patel, V., and Saxena, S. (2019), 'Achieving universal health coverage for mental disorders', *BMJ* 366(l4516): 1–3. Available at https://doi.org/10.1136/bmj.l4516.

[57] Szmukler, G. (2015), UN CRPD: equal recognition before the law, *The Lancet Psychiatry*, 2(11): e29, 232–233. Available at: https://doi.org/10.1016/S2215-0366(15)00369-7. See also European Union Agency for Fundamental Rights (2012), *Involuntary placement and involuntary treatment of persons with mental health problems* (Luxembourg: Publications Office of the European Union). Available at https://doi.org/10.2811/87077.

[58] SR on disabilities (2018), para. 14 and para. 74(b).

[59] GC35, para. 19.

[60] SR on health (2018), para. 85.

[61] Laws of Malawi Chapter 34.02, Mental Treatment Act 2005, s. 11. The petition may be based on the opinion of a 'relative, partner or assistant' of the person with disabilities.

institutionalised services,[62] and any continuing legislative justifications for psychiatric coercion must be further constrained, based on objective criteria, and contain strong procedural and substantive protections.[63] This is the preferred approach of the Council of Europe, which adopted a resolution in June 2019 seeking the end of mental health coercion, with a consultation between July and December 2020 on good practices in mental health care to promote voluntary care and treatment.[64]

Reducing Seclusion and Restraint

Along with 'all forced and non-consensual medical interventions ... including the non-consensual administration of psychosurgery, electroshock and mind-altering drugs', the SR on torture has advocated for the elimination of seclusion and physical and/or chemical restraint.[65] Resort to these draconian coercive hospital practices is often too rapid, with utilisation frequently for staff convenience or to control or punish.[66] Restraint has no therapeutic justification and may cause significant harm or even death – a fact brought into sharp focus by the tragic demise of George Floyd during arrest in the United States in May 2020. Recent research by Chieze et al. estimated a 25 to 47 per cent incidence of post-traumatic stress disorder following such interventions.[67]

---

[62] D. Pūras, Report of the Special Rapporteur on the right of everyone to the enjoyment of the highest attainable standard of physical and mental health on his visit to Paraguay, UN Doc. A/HRC/32/32/Add. 1 (2016).

[63] See, e.g., Fistein, E. C., Holland, A. J., Clare, I. C. H, et al. (2009), 'A comparison of mental health legislation from diverse Commonwealth jurisdictions', *Int J Law Psychiatry*, 32(3): 147–155. Available at https://doi.org/10.1016/j.ijlp.2009.02.006. See also WHO, Resource Book on Mental Health, Human Rights and Legislation, which sets out key principles previously accepted as good practice when legislating.

[64] Council of Europe Resolution 2291 (2019), 'Ending coercion in mental health: the need for a human rights-based approach', was adopted by the Assembly on 26 June 2019. Available at http://assembly.coe.int/nw/xml/XRef/Xref-XML2HTML-en.asp?fileid=28038&lang=en. The Council's Committee on Bioethics (DH-BIO) is drafting a 'Compendium of good practices in mental health care – how to promote voluntary care and treatment practices' within the framework of its Strategic Action Plan on Human Rights and Technologies in Biomedicine (2020–2025), which should be available from 2021.

[65] SR on torture (2013), para. 63. See also, e.g., P. Lehmann (2019), 'Paradigm shift: treatment alternatives to psychiatric drugs, with particular reference to low- and middle-income countries', in Davidson, *International Development, Mental Health and Wellbeing*, 251–269, at 263–267; United Nations Human Rights Council, Report of the Special Rapporteur on torture and other cruel, inhuman or degrading treatment or punishment, Juan E Méndez, A/HRC/22/53 (1 February 2013) p. 15. Available at www.ohchr.org/Documents/HRBodies/HRCouncil/RegularSession/Session22/A.HRC.22.53_English.pdf; United Nations Human Rights Council, Report of the Special Rapporteur on torture and other cruel, inhuman or degrading treatment or punishment, Juan E Méndez, A/HRC/22/53 (1 February 2013) p. 15. Available at www.ohchr.org/Documents/HRBodies/HRCouncil/RegularSession/Session22/A.HRC.22.53_English.pdf.

[66] Richter, D., 'How to De-Escalate a Risk Situation to Avoid the Use of Coercion', in T. W. Kallert, J. E. Mezzich, and Monahan, J. (eds.) (2011) *Coercive Treatment in Psychiatry: Clinical, Legal and Ethical Aspects* (Oxford: Wiley Blackwell), 57–79. Available at https://doi.org/10.1002/9780470978573.ch5.

[67] Chieze, M. Hurst, S., Kaiser, S., et al. (2019), 'Effects of seclusion and restraint in adult psychiatry: a systematic review', *Front. Psychiatry* 10: 491. Available at https://doi.org/10.3389/fpsyt.2019.00491. See also Broberg, et al., 'Human rights-based approach', 125.

Although some contend for the impracticality of their universal application,[68] de-escalation techniques can prove equally effective.[69] A substantial diminution of psychiatric coercion is entirely possible with concerted effort.[70] For example, a two-year pilot study applying a human rights-based approach in Gothenburg, Sweden, reduced an average of four 'belt' restraints per month to the same amount annually. The research revealed that coercion often resulted from behaviour arising from escalating frustration about petty rules involving 'seemingly small interventions in a person's life'. Their elimination appreciably improved patient autonomy and sense of dignity.[71] This successful human rights-based approach resulted in a strategic human rights action plan which incorporates a 'zero vision' goal with the aim of the complete abolition of coercion.[72] In Australia, user-led research seeking to reduce seclusion rates led to incidence rates falling from 6.9 per cent in 2008–2009 to less than 1 per cent in 2010–2011.[73]

If not banned immediately, restraint must be severely curtailed in law, and permissible only in an emergency for the shortest period of time commensurate with any objectively assessed risk. Its use must be strongly discouraged and staff accountability increased through training and onerous procedural protections. For example, legislation should specify the swift and regular review of restraint and seclusion after commencement, demand careful records and ensure that its use always triggers an independent review.

Availability of Community Options

Arguably, the principles of least restriction and detention as a last resort[74] are now binding as part of customary international law.[75] Further, Article 19 of the CRPD

---

[68] Knox, D. K, and Holloman Jr., G. H. (2012), 'Use and avoidance of seclusion and restraint: consensus statement of the American Association for Emergency Psychiatry Project BETA Seclusion and Restraint', *Workgroup West J Emerg Med*, 13(1): 35–40. Available at https://dx.doi.org/10.5811%2Fwestjem.2011.9.6867.

[69] Primor, S., and Virtzberg, D. (2019), 'Breaking the restraints. Civil Society's struggle to abolish human rights violations in Israel's psychiatric system', in Davidson, *International Development, Mental Health and Wellbeing*, 385–395.

[70] See Sashidharan et al, 'Reducing coercion', 610.

[71] Broberg, et al., 'Human rights-based approach', 125.

[72] Ibid., 128–129.

[73] Foxlewin, B. (2012), *What Is Happening at the Seclusion Review that Makes a Difference?: A Consumer Led Research Study* (ACT Mental Health Consumer Network), p. 11.

[74] See, e.g., Mental Welfare Commission Scotland (2016), 'Seeking your views consultation: Capacity, Detention, Supported Decision Making and Mental Ill Health'. Available at www.mwcscot.org.uk/sites/default/files/2019-06/capacity__detention__supported_decision_making_and_mental_ill_health.pdf; Mental Health Alliance (2017), 'A Mental Health Act fit for tomorrow: an agenda for reform' (Rethink Mental Illness), June 2017; A. Plumb, 'UN Convention on the Rights of Persons with Disabilities: out of the frying pan into the fire? Mental health service users and survivors aligning with the disability movement', in Spandler, H., Anderson, J., and Sapey, B. (eds.) (2015), *Madness, Distress and the Politics of Disablement* (Bristol: Policy Press), 183–198.

[75] The Statute of the International Court of Justice defines customary international law in Art.38(1)(b) as 'a general practice accepted as law'.

provides for the right to live independently and the right to community inclusion. The need for less restrictive alternatives to coercive care is emphasised in both GC1 and GC35.[76] Article 26 of the CRPD requires signatory states to 'organize, strengthen and extend comprehensive habilitation and rehabilitation services and programmes' to ensure the full inclusion of those with disability. Strong community mental health services must be embedded in law.[77] Research on non-institutionalised treatment reports better continuity of care, increased adherence to treatment and greater user-satisfaction due to minimal interruption to family relationships, friendships and employment.[78] The creation of community-based support requires strategic change in policy priorities, including mainstreaming mental health into primary care to enable local accessibility and reduce stigma.[79] There are clear multifaceted benefits to non-coercive models of community care,[80] and thus curfews, tagging and other community practices based on force should be eliminated from practice and legislation, as advocated for by the SR on disabilities.[81]

Due to the vast cultural and resource differences worldwide, no single global model of community care is viable.[82] The SR on health recently called for 'non-violent, peer-led, trauma-informed, community-led programmes, healing and cultural practices preferred by local groups of persons with psychosocial disabilities'.[83] Many successful evidence-based models exist worldwide already. To complement its QualityRights training and guidance modules, human rights-based practice guidance is expected from the WHO in June of 2021. This will provide comprehensive examples of community mental health services that uphold autonomy, emphasise community inclusion and involve those with lived experience of psychosocial disability at all levels. The SR on health has commended the 'quiet revolution' globally in 'alternative practices with transformative potential', rooted in human rights, dignity and non-coercive practices. People-centred services include peer-respite centres, medication-free wards, recovery communities and community

---

[76] GC1, para. 44; GC35, para. 19.
[77] GC35.
[78] See, e.g., Rossi, A. F, Bisoffi, G., Ruggeri, M., et al. (2002), 'Dropping out of care: inappropriate termination of contact with community-based psychiatric services', Br J Psychiatry, 181(4): 331–338. Available at https://doi.org/10.1192/bjp.181.4.331.
[79] SR on disabilities (2018), para. 66.
[80] Sashidharan, S. P., Mezzina, R., and Pūras, D. (2019), 'Reducing coercion in mental healthcare', Epidemiology and Psychiatric Sciences, 28(6), p. 610. See also SR on health (2018), para. 52; Lehmann, 'Paradigm Shift'.
[81] SR on disabilities (2018), para. 39. See also Molodynsky, A., Rugkåsa, J., and Burns, T. (2016), Coercion in Community Mental Health Care: International Perspectives (Oxford: Oxford University Press).
[82] See, e.g., European Union Agency for Fundamental Rights (FRA) & Finnish League for Human Rights (November 2017), Summary overview of types and characteristics of institutions and community-based services for persons with disabilities available across the EU. Available at https://fra.europa.eu/sites/default/files/fra_uploads/2017-10-independent-living-mapping-paper_en.pdf; Knapp et al. (2011) 'Economic Consequences of Deinstitutionalisation', in G. Thornicroft, M. Semrau, A. Alem, et al., Global Mental Health: Putting Community Care into Practice (London: Wiley-Blackwell).
[83] SR on health (2020), para. 12. See also para. 62.

development models.[84] Finland's open dialogue model and Sweden's personal ombudsman approach have both shown promise.[85] The 'Soteria paradigm' first developed in the United States utilises lay support and social networks within small, community-based therapeutic environments aimed at enhancing autonomy for those with schizophrenic spectrum disorders.[86] Trieste in Italy pioneered a move away from 'hospitalisation to hospitality' fifty years ago. Ever since, a holistic approach involving participatory healthcare at community centres with limited beds for 'guests' instead of patients has been cultivated to good effect.[87] Due to reduced funding in many LMICs, resort to psychiatric coercion may happen more frequently than in higher-income countries. However, some innovative programmes exist, such as Seher Urban Community Mental Health and Inclusion Program in Pune, India.[88] For over a decade its holistic community approach to mental health has provided care, peer support and counselling to those with psychosocial disabilities in severe emotional distress. Volunteers discuss the causes of the person's distress with them as an equal partner, along with their family members. The NGO also assists with access to social support systems to ensure basic needs are met.[89] Each country must develop its own accessible and culturally adapted needs-based community psychosocial interventions,[90] 'attentive to the movement of non-medical alternatives and progressive community support worldwide'.[91]

Ringfencing Community Care Budgets

The abolition of psychiatric coercion will require careful planning and budgeting to prevent a reduction in quality of life and morbidity, or indeed the violation of the right to life.[92] For example, in South Africa at least a hundred patients discharged

---

[84] SR on health (2020), para. 54.
[85] See Sugiura, K., Mahomed, F., Saxena, S. and Patel, V. (2020), 'An end to coercion: rights and decision-making in mental health care', *Bull World Health Organization*, 98(1): 52–58, Box 2, p. 55. Available at https://dx.doi.org/10.2471/BLT.19.234906.
[86] See, e.g., Calton, T., Ferriter, M., Huband, N., et al. (2008), 'A systematic review of the Soteria paradigm for the treatment of people diagnosed with schizophrenia', *Schizophr Bull* 34(1): 181–192. Available at https://dx.doi.org/10.1093%2Fschbul%2Fsbm047. See also Dhanda, A. (2019), 'Legislating on Mental Health in India to Achieve SDG3', in Davidson, *International Development, Mental Health and Wellbeing*, 373–384, at 380.
[87] Mezzina, R. (2014) 'Community mental health care in Trieste and beyond: an "Open Door–No Restraint" system of care for recovery and citizenship', *The Journal of Nervous and Mental Disease*, 202: 440–445. Available at https://doi.org/10.1097/nmd.0000000000000142. On Trieste, see also Gooding, P., McSherry, B., Roper, C., et al. (2018), *Alternatives to Coercion in Mental Health Settings: A Literature Review* (Melbourne: Melbourne Social Equity Institute, University of Melbourne), Section 2.2. On non-coercive approaches generally, see Broberg, et al., 'Human rights-based approach', 126–127.
[88] See Chapter 20.
[89] Lehmann, 'Paradigm Shift', 266.
[90] SR on health (2015), para. 84.
[91] SR on health (2020), para. 12. See also para. 62.
[92] See, e.g., Prins, S. J. (2011), 'Does transinstitutionalization explain the overrepresentation of people with serious mental illnesses in the criminal justice system?', *Community Ment Health J*, 47: 716–722; Fakhoury W. and Priebe, S. (2007), 'Deinstitutionalization and reinstitutionalization: major changes

from psychiatric hospitals in Gauteng province to poorly monitored and inadequate community care died within a year.[93] Nonetheless, whilst community rehabilitation programmes require an inevitable initial outlay, responsible hospital bed reduction has not been found to increase cost compared to community care which simultaneously and significantly improves quality of life.[94] In terms of affordable financial outlay, pragmatic innovations in LMICs like 'task-shifting' through the utilisation of lay workers 'with a rich understanding of the socio-cultural context'[95] have been found to be cost-effective interventions.[96]

However, as Patel and Farmer have stated, '[t]he aspiration of universal health coverage cannot be met solely through considerations of what constitutes good value for money, but what is good value for humanity'.[97] The lack of parity between physical and mental health worldwide is acutely evident when considering the woeful global median spend on the latter (approximately 2 per cent of total government health spending), with expenditure per head only USD $2.50 in eighty countries.[98] Diminutive mental health budgets in LMICs, where the stigma

---

in the provision of mental healthcare', *Psychiatry*, 6(8): 313–316. Available at https://doi.10.1016/j.mppsy.2007.05.008; Samartzis, L. and Talia, M. A. (2020), 'Assessing and Improving the Quality in Mental Health Services', *Int J Environ Res Public Health*, 7(1): 249–279, at para. 3.1.1. Available at https://doi.org/10.3390/ijerph17010249; Winkler, P., Barrett, B., McCrone, P., et al. (2016), 'Deinstitutionalised patients, homelessness and imprisonment: systematic review', *Br J Psychiatry*, 208(5): 421–428. Available at https://doi.10.1192/bjp.bp.114.161943.

[93] See, e.g., South African Human Rights Commission, 'Report of the national investigative hearing into the status of mental health care in South Africa', 14–15 November 2017. Available at www.sahrc.org.za/home/21/files/SAHRC%20Mental%20Health%20Report%20Final%2025032019.pdf.

[94] Thornicroft, G., Deb, T., and Henderson, C. (2016), 'Community mental health care worldwide: Current status and further developments', *World Psychiatry*, 15(3), 276–286, at 282. Available at https://doi.org/10.1002/wps.20349.

[95] See, e.g., Ebenezer, J. A. and Drake, R. E. (2018), 'Community mental health in rural India: the Shifa project in Padhar Hospital, Madhya Pradesh', BJPsych Int, 15(2): 38–40. Available at https://dx.doi.org/10.1192%2Fbji.2017.8; Chatterjee, S., Pillai, A., Jain, S., et al. (2009), 'Outcomes of people with psychotic disorders in a community-based rehabilitation programme in rural India', *Br J Psychiatry*, 195(5): 433–439. Available at https://doi.org/10.1192/bjp.bp.108.057596; Araya, R., Rojas, G., Fritsch, R., et al. (2003), 'Treating depression in primary care in low-income women in Santiago, Chile: a randomised controlled trial', *The Lancet*, 361(9362): 995–1000. Available at 10.1016/S0140-6736(03)12825-5; McPake B. and Mensah K. (2008), 'Task shifting in health care in resource-poor countries', *The Lancet*, 372: 870–871. See also Thornicroft, et al. 'Community mental health care worldwide', Table 1, 280–281, for a summary of challenges, lessons learned and solutions in implementing community-oriented mental health care.

[96] Petersen, I., Evans-Lacko, S., Semrau, M., et al. (2016), 'Promotion, prevention and protection: interventions at the population- and community-levels for mental, neurological and substance use disorders in low- and middle-income countries', *Int J Ment Health Syst*, 10: 30. Available at: https://doi.org/10.1186/s13033-016-0060-z; Roberts, E., Cumming, J., and Nelson, K. (2005), 'A review of economic evaluations of community mental health care', *Journal Indexing and Metrics*, 62(5): 503–543. Available at: https://doi.org/10.1177/1077558705279307. See also Knapp et al., 'Economic consequences of deinstitutionalisation'.

[97] Patel, V. and Farmer, P. E. (2020), 'The moral case for global mental health delivery', *The Lancet*, 395 (10218): 108–109, at 109.

[98] WHO, *Mental Health Atlas 2017*, para. 3.1, p. 26. For a recent exploration of the current landscape of mental health financing, see Mahomed, F. (2020), 'Addressing the problem of severe

attached to mental health tends to be severe,[99] are spent mainly on inpatient care.[100] In view of the current disease burden and the likely imminent spike in anxiety, depression and trauma in the wake of the novel coronavirus pandemic,[101] governments have an imperative to increase financial pledges and ringfence mental health budgets. The health parity gap could be narrowed by a concrete CRPD Committee recommendation on the budgetary proportion considered adequate to fulfil state responsibilities under Article 25 of the Convention. Even a modest 25 per cent of health spend would be a vast improvement on the status quo, albeit far lower than the disease burden warrants.[102] The incorporation of such pledges into both policy and legislation is essential to hold states accountable.

(3) Non-discrimination and Empowerment

Those with psychosocial disabilities have the same decision-making rights as others, including deciding whether or not to accept treatment, and if so, where. Respect for autonomy has been evidenced to improve health outcomes, with empowerment a basic precondition for recovery.[103] Sugiura et al. provide a useful list of mental health laws passed between 2011 and 2017 with ground-breaking autonomy enhancing provisions based on the biopsychosocial model of care, including relationships of therapeutic reciprocity.[104] As the SR for health has emphasised, 'inherent power asymmetries in policy and clinical practice ... actively undermine users of services as passive recipients of care instead of the active rights holders they are'.[105] Creating subtle mindset shifts in mental health care is possible through simple language change. For example, swopping the term 'patient' for 'service user' alters the perspective from someone viewed as ill and helpless to a recipient of services with rightful expectations of good standards. During one successful pilot study on

---

underinvestment in mental health and well-being from a human rights perspective', *Harvard Health and Human Rights Journal*, June 2020, 22(1): 163–178, at 35–50. Available at www.hhrjournal.org/2020/06/addressing-the-problem-of-severe-underinvestment-in-mental-health-and-well-being-from-a-human-rights-perspective/.

[99] Knapp et al., 'Economic consequences of deinstitutionalisation'.
[100] SR on disabilities (2018), para. 29 and para. 66. See also WHO, *Mental Health Atlas 2017*, para. 3.1, 26–27; Thornicroft et al, 'Community mental health care worldwide', Figure 2, p. 278.
[101] WHO, *Mental Health Atlas 2017*, para. 3.1, p. 26; WHO, *Mental Health Atlas 2011*, para. 2.1, pp. 26–27.
[102] See, e.g., WHO, *Mental Health Atlas 2017*; Vigo, D. V., Kestel, D., and Pendakur, K., et al. (2019), 'Disease burden and government spending on mental, neurological, and substance use disorders, and self-harm: cross-sectional, ecological study of health system response in the Americas', *Lancet Public Health*, 4: e89–96. Available at https://dx.doi.org/10.1016/S2468-2667(18)30203-2.
[103] SR on health (2018), para. 52. See also Mezzina, 'Community mental health care in Trieste and beyond'; WHO (2010) 'User empowerment in mental health – a statement by the WHO Regional Office for Europe' (Geneva: World Health Organization). Available at www.euro.who.int/__data/assets/pdf_file/0020/113834/E93430.pdf.
[104] Sugiura et al, 'An end to coercion', Box 1, 54.
[105] SR on health (2020), para. 59 and para. 14.

coercion reduction in Sweden, rights holders identified their preferred terms of address, such as a 'self-specialist' and 'experience expert', rather than 'patient'.[106] Such terminology can be incorporated easily into laws, and have meaningful impact.

Service-user Involvement

Article 4(3) of the CRPD requires states to 'consult with and actively involve persons with disabilities, including children with disabilities, through their representative organizations'. This applies both to strategic planning, and the development and implementation of legislation and policies.[107] Any new mental health law should incorporate such rights, and persons with psychosocial disabilities must be appointed to monitoring bodies. For example, in the UK those with lived experience of psychosocial disability ought to be permitted to apply for appointment as lay members (traditionally, social workers) of first-tier tribunals which review compulsory detention, providing invaluable insight and balance within the power dynamic.

Respecting Will and Preferences

The right to the highest attainable standard of health enshrined in Article 25 of the CRPD requires 'free and informed consent' to be given *prior* to any treatment.[108] Those with psychosocial disabilities are often forced to accept treatment following a professional and inherently subjective assessment. A finding that a person lacks capacity to provide consent to (or, more usually, to refuse) treatment is generally based on an alleged inability either to understand, weigh up and/or retain relevant information, or (less commonly) to communicate a decision. For others, the threat of coercive detention and treatment frequently negates supposed consent, with the result that decisions made to accept hospital stays and/or medication are not truly 'free'. Where mental capacity is thought lacking, the prevalent treatment model is founded on substitute decision-making. The wishes of persons with psychosocial disabilities are often overridden and usually replaced by a decision-maker's interpretation of their 'best interests'. Depending on domestic law, the decision-maker may be an individual (such as a relative, carer, clinician, state-appointed advocate or support worker, guardian or judge), or a group of individuals forming a board, panel or tribunal. Some regimes allow family members to insist on hospitalisation or to provide treatment consent contrary to the wishes of a person with psychosocial disability.[109] Even where decision-makers are required to be neutral and independent and to consider all relevant circumstances (such as under section 4 of the UK's

---

[106] Broberg, et al., 'Human rights-based approach', 126–127.
[107] See GC1, para. 50(c).
[108] Ibid., para. 41.
[109] SR on health (2018), para. 50.

Mental Capacity Act 2005), substituting someone's personal decision about what happens to their body for that of someone else 'contradicts respect for the will and preference of individuals'.[110] Furthermore, Article 25 of the CRPD demands respect for the decision-making capacity of those with disability 'at all times, *including in crisis situations*'.[111] Similarly, those with psychosocial disabilities 'enjoy legal capacity on an equal basis with others in all aspects of life' under Article 12(2).[112] Although 'legal capacity' is not defined (or differentiated from 'mental capacity', which does not appear at all within the CRPD text) in GC1, the CRPD Committee insists that the two terms are equivalent and without properly explaining their elision.[113] In any event, it has called for the replacement of provisions permitting substitute decision-making by supported decision-making regimes. States are encouraged 'to develop effective mechanisms to combat both formal and informal substitute decision-making'.[114] Additionally, the CRPD Committee has decreed that where it is 'not practicable' to determine will and preferences despite 'significant efforts', the 'best interpretation of will and preferences' must replace 'best interests' determinations.[115]

Paragraph 29 of GC1 sets out nine (non-exhaustive) 'key provisions to ensure compliance with article 12 of the Convention' which should be included in policy and mental health legislation (see Figure 5.1). To date, the majority of efforts towards introducing supported decision-making regimes maintain elements of substitute decision-making and/or coexist with such regimes.[116] Non-discriminatory models may take some time to elaborate, although Peru recently abolished substitute decision-making through a bill drafted by multi-stakeholder commissions.[117] During the global phase-out, and in accordance with the principle of empowerment, mental health legislation should ensure that supported decision-making is the rule, rather than the exception. Onerous safeguards, including the requirement for careful, complete records, should encourage the reduction of substitute decision-making and dissuade staff from failing to respect a person's choices. Regular reviews of substitute decisions will be vital to ensure they are just and appropriate, and comply with domestic law. Any departure from a person's wishes must always be explained to them in a communication mode and form they understand, as well as to other care staff.

'Support' is a broad term which must be personalised in form and intensity;[118] there is no 'one size fits all'.[119] The SR on disabilities has listed various possible types of

[110] SR on disabilities (2017), para. 48.
[111] GC1, para. 18.
[112] Ibid., para. 42 and para. 50(a).
[113] For a critique of the CRPD Committee's view that legal and mental capacity are in essence the same thing (see GC1, para.14) see Davidson, 'Capacity to consent', 463–464.
[114] GC1, para.21.
[115] Ibid., para. 20.
[116] Ibid., para. 48 and para. 64.
[117] Legislative Decree No. 1384. Available at www.mindbank.info/item/6782.
[118] GC1, para. 17.
[119] SR on disabilities (2017), para. 55

GC1, para. 29

Support for decision-making must:

(1) be provided where necessary
(2) be free or inexpensive
(3) be tailored to a person's mode of communication
(4) not limit fundamental rights
(5) be based on non-discriminatory indicators when legal capacity is exercised (rather than on mental capacity - no examples provided)
(6) be based on will and preferences (not 'best interests')
(7) be protected through safeguards ensuring respect for will and preferences
(8) respect a person's right to refuse or terminate support, and to change the support person
(9) be challengeable if will and preferences are not respected, and enable access to legal support

FIGURE 5.1 Key provisions to ensure legal compliance with Article 12 CPRD. Source: GC1, para. 29.

useful support that might be relevant and/or necessary.[120] Guidance in the form of examples can be incorporated into a code of practice or regulations. To protect against inadvertent or intentional undue influence – or outright exploitation – by decision-making supporters, onerous safeguards must be integrated into any new systems, practices and legislation, 'premised on respect for the rights, will and preferences of persons with disabilities'.[121] Sugiura et al. have conveniently highlighted global examples of context-appropriate approaches to supported decision-making in mental health care.[122] These include formal and informal networks, support agreements, independent advocates to represent and defend the individual's 'wishes and interests', advance directives, legal capacity assistance from a trusted person of the individual's choice, and peer support.[123] A 2018 Kenyan study explored the impact of various organised and informal peer support practices on the exercise of legal capacity and the reduction of coercive interventions (see Figure 5.2). Garnering the expertise of peers with lived experience was found to be highly beneficial, and in the global move towards a complete ban on coercion, it accords with Article 4(3) of the CRPD.

---

[120] Ibid.
[121] GC1, para. 29 and para. 50(b).
[122] See, e.g., Sugiura et al, 'An end to coercion'.
[123] GC35. The SR on disabilities has made a specific call for the integration of peer support into legislative frameworks; SR on disabilities (2017), para. 54.

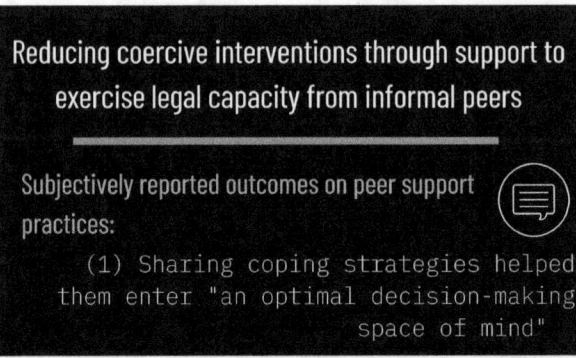
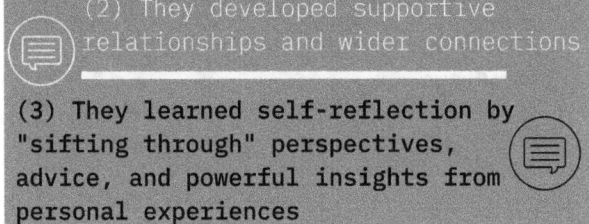

FIGURE 5.2 Study of the impact of various organised and informal peer support practices on the exercise of legal capacity and the reduction of coercive practices. [124]

Guardianship

Guardianship and trusteeship provisions which give third parties control over the place of residence and/or treatment of a person assessed as lacking mental capacity are contrary to Article 12 of the CRPD.[125] The CRPD Committee has repeatedly exhorted states to 'develop laws and policies to replace [such] regimes' through supported decision-making'.[126] Peru and Costa Rica were amongst the first nations to respond to the call of the SR on health for the immediate abolition of guardianship.[127] However, in the event

[124] Users and Survivors of Psychiatry – Kenya (April 2018), 'The role of peer support in exercising legal capacity in Kenya', Section 4 (Decision-making with support). Available at www.uspkenya.org/wp-content/uploads/2018/01/Role-of-Peer-Support-in-Exercising-Legal-Capacity.pdf. See also GC1, para. 50(c).
[125] See also SR on disabilities (2017), para. 51.
[126] GC1, para. 26
[127] SR on health (2018), para. 50; see Peru's Legislative Decree No. 1384. Available at www.mindbank.info/item/6782; Costa Rica's 2016 Law No. 9379 has replaced guardianship with the legal figure of 'guarantor of equality before the law of persons with disabilities'.

of its continued use prior to the global ban on psychiatric coercion, states should bolster current procedural protections. Guardianship should always be a last resort, periodically reviewed, and involve a guardian of the person's own choice. The law must also enable the guardian's removal, and permit appeals against their decisions.[128]

Advance Planning

Advance planning provides legal recognition for decisions made in advance by anyone who might not be able to make a decision during an emergency or when physically unable to do so. For example, advance decisions may apply to particular medical treatment or request the withdrawal of life-sustaining treatment measures in certain future health scenarios. Although those with psychosocial disabilities have a right to make decisions even if objectively unwise – just like others – advance decisions can be useful in preserving the autonomy of those who struggle to make clear decisions during acute episodes of ill-health. In the UK, joint crisis plans containing elements of advanced directives have improved therapeutic relationships through shared decision-making between service-users and professionals.[129] Advance planning fits with an empowerment approach and should be included in mental health laws.[130] However, most such provisions permit the overriding of decisions in various circumstances. For example, Section 25 of the UK's Mental Capacity Act 2005 permits challenge to the validity and applicability of 'advance directives' made pursuant to Section 24 on less - than rigorous subjective grounds.[131] Proposed new UK mental health legislation is also expected to allow advance directives to be ignored for 'compelling reasons'.[132] Prior to a full ban on psychiatric coercion, legislation must tighten criteria to allow for departure from an advance decision about hospital admission and treatment only in highly circumscribed circumstances. The person to whom the advance directive pertains must control the time the advance directive enters into force and when it ceases to have effect.

---

[128] However, all such reforms 'fall short in respecting the rights of persons with disabilities' (GC1, para. 50).

[129] Henderson, C., Flood, C., Leese, M., et al. (2004), 'Effect of joint crisis plans on use of compulsory treatment in psychiatry: single blind randomised controlled trial', *BMJ*, 329(7458): 136. Available at https://doi.org/10.1136/bmj.38155.585046.63. However, cf. Thornicroft, G., Farrelly, S., Szmukler, G., et al. (2013), 'Clinical outcomes of Joint Crisis Plans to reduce compulsory treatment for people with psychosis: a randomised controlled trial', *The Lancet*, 381: 1634–1641. Available at https://doi.org/10.1016/S0140-6736(13)60105-1.

[130] SR Report on health (2018), para. 66 and para. 50.

[131] Section 25(2)(c) of the Mental Capacity Act 2005 states that '[a]n advance decision is not valid if P . . . has done anything else clearly inconsistent with the advance decision remaining his fixed decision'. Section 25(4)(c) states that '[a]n advance decision is not applicable to the treatment in question if . . . there are reasonable grounds for believing that circumstances exist which P did not anticipate at the time of the advance decision and which would have affected his decision had he anticipated them'. The application of both of these subsections is necessarily subjective.

[132] Final Report of the Independent Review of the Mental Health Act 1983, 'Modernising the Mental Health Act'.

Furthermore, the CRPD Committee has stated that its applicability 'should not be based on an assessment that the person lacks mental capacity'.[133] Once psychiatric compulsion is outlawed, advance decisions will need to be respected even if contrary to clinical opinion.

(4) Target-setting to Reduce and Eliminate Coercion Within a Specific and Reasonable Period

Conscientious implementation of the CRPD is vital and requires timebound targets. Policy and legislation must insist upon community rehabilitation options. Supervisory bodies must be created and empowered to ensure that policy and legislative targets are met, including through legal challenge of government failure to end psychiatric coercion within the specified timeframe where necessary. High-income countries have approximately two hundred times more financial resources available for mental health services than low-income counterparts,[134] and already possess significant community care infrastructure. Thus, they have little justification for delaying the implementation of necessary measures to prioritise community care and enable the abolition of psychiatric coercion. Whilst each state must set its own goals and targets within the strictures of its particular context and resources, an outer time limit for abolition set by the CRPD Committee would greatly assist in preventing drift. Until then, a decade is suggested as a reasonable timeframe for all signatory states.

ADDITIONAL BENEFITS OF INTERIM MENTAL HEALTH LAW AMENDMENT

Improving Care Standards and Reducing Stigma

Mental health legislation also has 'an important symbolic as well as functional role, and can progress a moral imperative for improved mental health systems', as Liebling and Davidson, et al. have observed.[135] This oft-undervalued benefit has subtle, unmeasurable impact. Public dissemination of the content of legislation and the basis for it (including information on human rights) can cause gradual and positive change in the understanding and values of the general public and healthcare staff alike, helping dismantle discriminatory beliefs. Training on the need to maximise autonomy and for genuine partnerships between clinicians and service-users will slowly alter attitudes about coercion, thereby reducing the stigma

---

[133] GC1, para. 17.
[134] WHO, *Mental Health Atlas 2017*.
[135] Liebling, H., and Davidson, L., et al., (2016) 'The experiences of survivors and trauma counselling service providers in northern Uganda: implications for mental health policy and legislation', *Int J Law Psychiatry*, Part A, November–December 2016, 49: 84–92, at 88. Available at https://doi.org/10.1016/j.ijlp.2016.06.012.

surrounding psychosocial disability.[136] Professional development and training components should include education on legal rights and obligations for all clinical and social care staff, ensuring reconsideration of the levels of acceptable risk to others. Indeed a Swedish study found that, for staff,

> [c]onnecting ... daily work to UN covenants made their work [feel] more valuable and increased the importance of executing it as well as possible. This ... created a sense of pride for duty bearers in tasks that would previously have been viewed as trivial or mundane.[137]

The research also concluded that relationships between care providers and rights holders had improved. Language can also have a profound effect on stigma. For example, the SR on health recently noted that labelling innovations in community health as 'alternatives' 'paradoxically renders them easier to ignore as not a part of mainstream efforts to transform mental health'.[138] Utilising instead the proffered phrase, 'rights-based supports', within mental health policy and legislation can potentially break down discriminatory beliefs and bolster a human rights-based care approach. A shift in terminology can thus gradually reduce pervading and long-held paternalistic views and prejudices.

CONCLUSION

The CRPD and its Committee's interpretations have challenged the very fundamentals of psychiatry and medical paternalism. In addition, the special focus given to mental health by Dainius Pūras in his mandate as UN Special Rapporteur on health, and his support for the CRPD Committee's pronouncements, has chipped away at psychiatric complacency, confronting long-held and discriminatory practices. There may be divided opinion on the appropriateness and viability of ending all coercive psychiatric practices, but the uneasy dialectic that has been engendered is liable to result in significantly reduced coercion globally in the not-too-distant future. Now that Pūras has completed his second and final term as SR on health, it is essential that the new incumbent Tlaleng Mofokeng continues his legacy in what could be a watershed moment for the recognition of mental health rights.

This chapter has argued that mental health legislation must continue to protect the international human rights of those with psychosocial disabilities. Whilst to date such laws have legitimised psychiatric compulsion, they remain a tool through which coercion may be considerably reduced and eventually eliminated. The current inexcusable inertia on the elimination of psychiatric compulsion can be

---

[136] The WHO's fifteen QualityRights guidance and training tools can be utilised in this process. Available at www.who.int/publications/i/item/who-qualityrights-guidance-and-training-tools. See further Funk, M., and Drew, N. (2017), WHO Qualityrights: transforming mental health services, *The Lancet Psychiatry*, 4: 826–827.
[137] Broberg, et al., 'Human rights-based approach', 126.
[138] SR on health (2020), para. 55.

ended by a global commitment to improved and strengthened interim legislation as a precursor to a complete ban. All states have a duty to mobilise the necessary resources, which includes providing, seeking and accepting international cooperation where necessary under UN Sustainable Development Goal 17.[139] Stringent substantive and procedural protections and empowering provisions which enhance the right to autonomy and enshrine the principles of least restriction and last resort within national legislation globally could herald an end to the current stalemate. Taking more palatable steps towards the ultimate goal, legislation has the ability to demand improved compliance with international human rights and good practice standards. The quality of mental health care can be driven up, protections bolstered, and prejudice and stigma reduced through new or improved laws. Those with psychosocial disabilities must be consulted about and involved in all modernising processes in accordance with Article 4(3) of the CRPD. However, realistically, transmuting the former paternalistic paradigm will take time. The CRPD Committee is urged to take a more pragmatic approach, and to end the current stasis by issuing a general comment which provides the necessary 'reluctant permission' for the progressive realisation of respect for Articles 12 and 14 of the CRPD. It should set a specific and realistic target date for full compliance (such as within a decade), with earlier fulfilment where possible. During the transformation process and to fulfil Article 25 of the CRPD, a staunch recommendation for the ringfencing of budgets for mental health is required – including, it is suggested, allocation of at least 25 per cent of the total health budget spend. Such commitment is all the more vital given the immensely increased mental health burden resulting from the COVID-19 pandemic. Only with the CRPD Committee's acquiescence in pragmatic progressive realisation can the global elimination of psychiatric coercion transmogrify from pipe dream to reality.

---

[139] See also SR on disabilities (2018), para. 65.

6

The 'Fusion Law' Proposals and the CRPD

John Dawson and George Szmukler

Abstract

This chapter: (i) provides a succinct statement of our proposal for the 'fusion' of mental health and capacity legislation into a single legal regime governing the provision of all healthcare without consent, and the reasons behind this proposal; (ii) argues that a carefully designed scheme of this kind would be consistent with the Convention on the Rights of Persons with Disabilities (CRPD); (iii) responds to the contrary arguments about the CRPD's interpretation made by the UN Committee on the Rights of Persons with Disabilities, in its General Comment No 1 (2014); and (iv) considers the extent to which the Mental Capacity Act (Northern Ireland) 2016 is consistent with the 'fusion' approach, and whether this Act ultimately complies with the CRPD.

1 INTRODUCTION

We have advocated an approach to reform of mental health law that involves the 'fusion' of the two main legal schemes used in most jurisdictions to regulate involuntary treatment – mental health legislation governing the civil commitment process, and general capacity (or competency) legislation, governing proxy decision-making for adults who lack the 'capacity' to make decisions on their own behalf about their care or property (Dawson and Szmukler, 2006; Szmukler, Daw & Dawson, 2010). We propose that these two legal schemes be fused into one. The primary legal standard for intervention used would be lack of 'capacity' to make the relevant decisions, with capacity defined in 'functional' terms: that is, by reference to a person's ability to perform the functions (mainly mental functions, such as understanding relevant information) that are vital to autonomous decision-making in that zone.

We argue that such 'fusion' legislation would not discriminate on the ground of disability per se, because the functional approach to capacity assessment upon which it is based would be of universal application: every adult within the jurisdiction would need to meet the capacity test established for their decisions about treatment to be considered legally valid. Nor would this legislation be inconsistent with the CRPD – despite arguments to the contrary made by Committee on the

Rights of Persons with Disabilities (the CRPD Committee), particularly in its General Comment No 1 on equal recognition before the law (2014) (hereafter GC1). Here, we present an alternative interpretation under which the fusion proposals would be Convention compliant. We note that the Mental Capacity Act 2016 of Northern Ireland incorporates many elements of our preferred legal scheme.

2 THE TWO LEGAL SCHEMES TO BE 'FUSED'

Currently, most Western legal systems operate two distinct legal schemes regulating involuntary treatment. First, a civil commitment scheme, usually termed a Mental Health Act (MHA), authorising involuntary psychiatric treatment and hospital placement of people with a 'mental disorder' (in some statutory sense) who pose a serious 'danger' (or 'risk') to themselves or others. Second, a scheme centred on the decision-making capacity of adults, especially capacity to make decisions about personal care, residence and finances.

This second scheme establishes a legal standard of capacity (or competence),[1] which, if not met, permits a proxy (or substitute) decision-maker to be appointed to make specified decisions on another's behalf. It requires certain principles to be followed, such as considering carefully the known, prior views of the person for whom the proxy acts. Plus, independent review is available, permitting the proxy's appointment and decisions to be subject to scrutiny before a court or tribunal.

In such a capacity scheme, there is no need to refer to the concept of 'mental disorder' in the legal standards. A purely functional definition of capacity is sufficient, referring, for instance, to a person's ability to understand and recall information relevant to a particular decision; to use and weigh that information in reaching a decision; and to communicate a decision – functions widely recognised as preconditions of autonomous decision-making. The law need not refer to any particular diagnosis or health condition as the cause of the impaired mental functioning. It is the fact of its impairment that is critical. To this extent, the legal criteria can be considered 'disability-neutral'; they are not based on disability per se, but on the performance of specific mental functions underpinning the recognition of any adult's legal capacity.

So, for instance, if a person were unable – by any means – to communicate their views about a decision they needed to make, that could constitute incapacity due to inability to perform that function of communicating a decision, regardless of the cause and whether it was the result of a 'physical' or a 'mental' health condition. Similarly, a person could be considered to lack capacity to make a treatment decision who was otherwise fit but suffered a serious head injury in a traffic accident, and then, in an impaired state of consciousness, insisted they needed no medical

---

[1] In this field, these two concepts generally have the same meaning, the former being used in Europe, the latter in North America.

intervention. Or a person could be considered to lack capacity who was previously well, but now has impaired consciousness or confusion as a result of a chest or urinary tract infection, or due to an adverse reaction to prescribed medication for a significant but non-disabling medical condition. In all these situations, the lack of capacity can be viewed as due to an inability to perform the relevant mental functions, not due to any particular disabling condition.

3. THE 'FUSION' PROPOSAL

The central idea of the 'fusion' proposal, then, is that the civil commitment and general capacity schemes would be merged. The resulting legislation would not use mental disorder and risk of harm as the basis for intervention. It would use incapacity to make relevant decisions, and it would be immaterial whether the cause of the incapacity was a 'mental' or a 'physical' disorder. Thus, it would be immaterial whether a person's inability to process the necessary information was caused by delirium, or gross intoxication, or traumatic brain injury, or a neurological or psychiatric condition: the question in each case would be whether in fact they lacked the ability to perform the functions required for autonomous decision-making in the relevant zone.

Nevertheless, this new law would not abolish all elements of a civil commitment scheme. Instead, it would incorporate the usual powers, procedures and protections for compulsory patients, including powers of emergency intervention, detention, compulsory assessment and treatment. The law would permit the exercise of emergency powers when there were 'reasonable grounds to believe' the person lacked capacity to decide on their need for an urgent intervention, when no opportunity had existed for a full assessment. Following such an emergency, the full capacity test would apply, and appropriate treatment arrangements made if justified.

Other usual requirements of civil commitment would also continue to apply, including: formal assessment by independent, qualified clinicians; investigation of the person's social circumstances; mandatory consultation with family, carers or nominated persons; appointment of a responsible clinician; advocacy; second opinions on particularly intrusive treatments; and speedy and effective access to a court or tribunal to determine whether the grounds for compulsion continue to exist.

Within a few weeks, a person subject to this regime would come before a court (or tribunal) for their position to be reviewed. Further decisions could then be made, based on a well-developed treatment plan: about the nature and place of their care, and whether their detention was necessary to receive it. The court could make a treatment order – of defined length. That order would have flexible, individualised content. The person's ongoing treatment could be authorised for a mental or physical health condition, on an in-patient or community basis. Appropriate accountability mechanisms would apply, such as mandatory peer review and continuing access to judicial or tribunal oversight.

In addition, this 'fusion' law would incorporate the usual elements of a decision-making capacity scheme – the appointment of proxy decision-makers, execution of enduring (or lasting) powers of attorney and orders to be made by a court or tribunal concerning a person's care or property. This regime would apply only where reasonable attempts at supported decision-making were insufficient to secure an autonomous expression of the person's views. But where it did apply, the person might be deprived of their liberty when they lacked the capacity to decide their own care arrangements, detention was necessary in their 'best interests'[2] and there was no less restrictive means of managing the situation. Where they did not object to their detention via a proxy's decision, only limited procedural protections might apply. Where they did object, more extensive procedural protections would operate, akin to those provided by an MHA.

In this manner, the civil commitment and the general decision-making capacity schemes could be 'fused' into a single, generic regime.[3]

3 ADVANTAGES OF THE FUSION PROPOSAL

The effect of these proposals would be to abolish specific mental health laws. Instead, all involuntary, health-related interventions would be based on capacity principles – especially any intervention to which the person objected, or that involved detention – whether the lack of capacity was due to a 'physical' or 'mental' disorder.

The primary aim would be to eliminate discrimination against people with mental health disabilities by applying the same capacity principles to all forms of healthcare. This would acknowledge the problematic character of the distinction between 'mental' and 'physical' illness. It would confirm that a diagnosis of mental disorder is not invariably associated with loss of decision-making capacity. It would recognise that many general medical patients also lack capacity and refuse care, with equally, or more, serious consequences than refusal of psychiatric care – and yet, in such situations, the law does not permit their involuntary treatment unless they lack capacity in the matter. Thus, the law does not permit an adult Jehovah's Witness, with capacity to refuse, to be given a blood transfusion to which they object, even if their death would follow. To achieve such consistency, the new law would not expose people who *retain* their decision-making capacity – but are said to be 'mentally disordered' – to detention or compulsory treatment on the basis of

---

[2] Public health interests (for example, preventing the spread of infectious disease) that might lead to a person's detention despite their retaining capacity would be covered by separate public health legislation. Public safety interests (or potential harm to others) would be addressed primarily through the criminal law, *except* in the common situation where it *would be* in the best interests of a person who lacked capacity to be detained under the fusion legislation (see Szmukler, 2020 for a fuller discussion). See also *supra* note 1.

[3] In those jurisdictions where aspects of forensic mental health care are covered by the MHA, it would also be possible, with imagination, to devise a capacity-based forensic scheme (Szmukler, 2020).

perceived 'danger' or 'risk' to others, when those *not* said to be 'mentally disordered' can usually be placed under compulsion only when the relevant 'risk' has manifested itself in a breach of the criminal law.

In addition, the 'fusion' model would offer the practical advantage that the (often uncertain) boundaries between the spheres of operation of the civil commitment and incapacity schemes would no longer need to be defined, as they would fall under the same scheme.

But would these proposals be consistent with the CRPD?

4 THE VIEWS OF THE UN COMMITTEE ON THE RIGHTS OF PERSONS WITH DISABILITIES

Under the CRPD Committee's interpretation of the CRPD, particularly that in GC1, these fusion proposals would clearly be *inconsistent* with the CRPD; the Committee considers any legislation non-compliant that is based on a mental capacity test (even one using the 'functional' approach) (Series and Nilsson, 2018).

The Committee would say the fusion model involves 'discrimination on the basis of disability', contrary to article 5 of the Convention, if mental capacity – a concept commonly associated with mental disability – were the basis for denying a person the right to make their own decisions.

It would also say the fusion model denies people 'recognition . . . as persons before the law', contrary to article 12(1). A person could be denied the right to make certain decisions (or be denied certain forms of 'legal agency') when considered to lack the ability to perform the mental functions required. To the Committee, such denial violates the principle of 'universal legal capacity', and automatically denies the individual recognition as a person before the law. For similar reasons, the Committee would consider the fusion model fails to ensure 'persons with disabilities enjoy legal capacity on an equal basis with others *in all aspects of life*' – contrary to article 12(2).

Further, the Committee would oppose the fusion model because it does not fully realise the supported decision-making approach the Committee says is necessary to comply with articles 12(3) and 12(4). Instead, it would permit proxy (or substitute) decision-making, as a last resort, when 'supported decision-making' could not secure an autonomous expression of the person's views (for example, based on their deep beliefs and values, strongly held commitments or personal conception of the good) – which the Committee says is forbidden.

Finally, the Committee would consider article 14(1)(b) violated, regarding deprivation of liberty, if placement under compulsory hospitalisation were based on assessment of capacity. The Committee would say this authorised 'deprivation of liberty' based on 'the existence of a disability'.

For these reasons, the Committee has demanded the removal of mental capacity assessment from the law, and abolition of all proxy decision-making schemes, such as the 'fusion' proposals. Ultimately, says the Committee, giving effect to the Convention requires acceptance of the idea that every adult enjoys full legal capacity, at all times, in every sphere of life, without exception: that is, acceptance of 'universal legal capacity' – even if the person is unable to perform the mental functions essential to autonomous decision-making.

What response can we make, then, to these views?

5 AN ALTERNATIVE INTERPRETATION OF THE CONVENTION

Responses in Principle

The most telling response to the Committee's views is the argument that to abolish the use of capacity tests and abandon proxy decision-making would undermine the main purposes and principles of the CRPD (Freeman et al, 2015). In particular, the radical legal changes suggested by the Committee would not always 'promote respect' for 'the inherent dignity' of all persons with disabilities (articles 1, 3(a)), especially 'those who require more intensive support' (preamble (j)). So, it may not promote such respect to permit a person, who lacks understanding of the consequences, to refuse all offers of adequate housing or social support.

Nor may it invariably promote a person's 'full and effective participation in society' (article 3(c)), or enjoyment of other positive rights under the Convention, such as rights to life (article 10) or health (article 25) – to permit their withdrawal from participation in society or their withdrawal from treatment, for instance, where they lack sufficient understanding of the opportunities they would forego.

It could prevent measures being taken to restore a person's autonomy and their ability to give informed consent, following treatment, if their capacity to refuse treatment were simply assumed, without assessment. It could prevent proper realisation of their 'will' (or their long-term, deeply-held beliefs and values), when that is contradicted by their currently expressed wishes or 'preferences', especially where their will was expressed in an advance statement or directive, and their current preferences must be given priority – when their prior views more accurately indicate their deeply held beliefs, values, commitments or conception of the 'good' (Szmukler, 2017).[4]

The Committee's position ignores the fact that in virtually all contemporary legal systems, for all persons, capacity is a pre-condition of valid (or effective) legal agency, because it is viewed as an essential foundation of personal autonomy (Dawson, 2015;

---

[4] 'Capacity' and 'best interests' can be reformulated to be consistent with the primacy given in the CRPD to a person's 'will and preferences'. Decision-making capacity is undermined when a person's 'preference', expressed in the moment, substantially contradicts their relatively stable, deeply held beliefs, values or commitments – that is, their 'will'. Acting in the person's 'best interests' means ensuring that effect is given to the person's 'will'. The graver the consequences of the inconsistency between the 'preference' and the person's deeply held beliefs and values (the 'will'), the stronger is the case for an intervention.

Freeman et al, 2015). Under this more orthodox approach, when a person's legal agency is impaired due to incapacity, a proxy decision-maker must be appointed to permit legally effective decisions to be taken on their behalf.

Moreover, legal arrangements based on capacity principles have other major advantages. They can prevent the unnecessary prosecution, criminalisation and longer-term deprivation of liberty of a person who, lacking capacity, breaks the criminal law and may be imprisoned, with greater restrictions imposed on their rights and poorer treatment options. Such arrangements may prevent the stigma that can be associated with untreated mental illness. They can mitigate the problem of undue influence that can arise when one person claims to be merely supporting another to make their own decision (despite the latter's incapacity). Formal mechanisms for appointing a proxy also clarify the lines of responsibility for decisions made: responsibility is placed *on the proxy*, who can therefore be called to account (Scholten et al, 2020).

We accept that the starting point should be the presumption that all adults have capacity in all matters. A proxy's appointment should be surrounded by adequate legal safeguards, including swift and effective access to a court or tribunal to challenge the appointment, if the person objects, and a proxy's appointment should only cover decisions in those areas in which the person's incapacity has been assessed. Such an appointment should only occur when supported decision-making cannot secure an autonomous expression of the person's views (or 'will'); it should last for the shortest possible time; the proxy should give effect to the 'will and preferences' (or best interpretation thereof) of the person for whom they act; and the proxy's appointment and decisions should be readily open to independent review, at the instigation of a range of parties. But abandoning the concept of capacity or proxy decision-making entirely would not further the main purposes of the CRPD – promoting the dignity, autonomy and equality of persons with disabilities, on all occasions.

6 AN ALTERNATIVE INTERPRETATION OF THE CONVENTION'S TEXT

We therefore support a different reading of the Convention's text than that offered by the Committee and suggest that certain 'justified limitations' can be placed on the Convention's statement of rights (in a manner consistent with international human rights law). The UN Human Rights Committee, for instance, that is responsible for interpretation of the ICCPR,[5] takes the view, in its General Comment 35 (GC35),[6] that 'necessary and proportionate' limits can be placed on the right to liberty of persons with a disability, as a last resort, when subject to appropriate legal

---

[5] UN General Assembly, International Covenant on Civil and Political Rights, 16 December 1966, United Nations, Treaty Series, vol. 999, p. 171.
[6] UN Human Rights Committee (2014), General Comment No 35, article 9 (liberty and security of person), CCPR/C/GC/35.

safeguards – a position incompatible with the view that the CRPD's rights are absolute (Martin and Gurbai, 2019).

So, what is our alternative interpretation?

6.1 Discrimination

Article 5(2) of the CRPD says 'State Parties shall prohibit all discrimination on the basis of disability' and article 2 defines 'discrimination on the basis of disability' as:

> any distinction, exclusion or restriction on the basis of disability which has the purpose or effect of impairing or nullifying the recognition, enjoyment or exercise, on an equal basis with others of all human rights and fundamental freedoms ...

For several reasons, we argue it is *not* discrimination in this sense for the law to employ capacity criteria or proxy decision-making arrangements. First, such a scheme, used properly, does not have the purpose or effect of 'impairing or nullifying' the enjoyment of a person's rights on an equal basis with others (or, to put it another way, it does not confer a disadvantage on the person concerned). Instead, it facilitates the exercise of rights – by permitting a person who lacks capacity in a matter to benefit from decisions made on their behalf by a proxy (preferably one whom they have appointed in advance), and from decisions that reflect their 'will' (or deeply held beliefs and values). They can thus enjoy other Convention rights, consistent with their values, whose benefits they otherwise might forgo. In short, it permits *all rights* guaranteed by the CRPD to be taken into account.

Second, it does not constitute direct discrimination 'on the basis of disability' to assess a person as lacking capacity on the basis of their ability to perform mental functions vital to a particular task. This assessment is not based on 'disability' per se. Instead, it is based on a test that any adult, with or without a disability, must meet in order to be recognised as an effective legal agent in that zone.

Third, even if such arrangements have a disproportionate effect (as is likely) on persons with disabilities, they can still be justified under the usual calculus of justification in international human rights law; and, if so, no 'indirect discrimination' under the Convention occurs. The UN Human Rights Committee, for instance, declared in its General Comment on Non-Discrimination (1994), that (para. 8) 'the enjoyment of rights and freedoms on an equal basis with others does not mean identical treatment in every instance', and (para. 13):

> not every differentiation of treatment will constitute discrimination if the criteria for such differentiation are reasonable and objective and if the aim is to achieve a purpose which is legitimate [under international human rights law].

The 'differentiation' with which we are concerned – in the use of capacity tests and appointment of proxies – can therefore be considered 'legitimate' (or justified) if the criteria used are 'reasonable' and 'objective' and promote the purposes of the CRPD.

To be 'reasonable', the legal arrangements must meet the test of 'proportionality' under human rights law. That is, they must advance the aims of the Convention; the means used must be properly related to those aims; there must be no less restrictive means of achieving them; and, overall, the right balance must be struck between the importance of the aims pursued and the limits placed on rights (Clayton and Tomlinson, 2009). To be 'objective' requires a sufficiently rigorous assessment of the person's performance of the relevant mental functions, which is open to challenge through a fair and independent process. A legal scheme satisfying those requirements would not 'discriminate', contrary to the Convention.

The European Court of Human Rights reached just such a conclusion, in *A M-V v Finland*[7] (a decision reached *after* release of the UN Committee's GC1). The Court held it was not a breach of either the ECHR or the CRPD to appoint a 'mentor' under Finnish law to make care and residence decisions on behalf of a man with an intellectual disability when he lacked the capacity to make those decisions. The Court found explicitly that appointing a mentor in that situation 'was not based on the qualification of the applicant as a person with a disability', when:

> Instead, the decision was based on the finding that, in this particular case, the disability was of a kind that, in terms of its effects on the applicant's cognitive skills, rendered the applicant unable to adequately understand the significance and the implications of the specific decision he wished to take, and that therefore, the applicant's well-being and interests required that the mentor arrangements be maintained.[8]

On this approach, the Court concluded that employing 'functional' capacity tests and properly appointed proxies does not constitute 'discrimination on the basis of disability' under the CRPD.

6.2 Equal Recognition before the Law

Article 12(1) CRPD declares: 'persons with disabilities have the right to recognition everywhere as persons before the law'. The Committee says this means that *any* denial of legal capacity to a person with a disability – even denial of specific legal capacities, in the circumstances contemplated by the ECtHR above – *automatically* denies a person recognition before the law.[9]

The Committee says the concept of legal capacity has two main elements and denial of either is denial of recognition as a person before the law. First is the ability of a person 'to hold rights and duties (legal standing)'; second is the ability 'to exercise those rights and duties (legal agency)'.[10]

---

[7] [2017] ECHR 273.
[8] At para. 89.
[9] GC1, at para. 9.
[10] GC1, at para 13.

We agree that denying a person either element of legal capacity *unnecessarily* could constitute denial of recognition as a person before the law. But is such recognition denied where only specific aspects of a person's legal capacity are suspended, based on a proper assessment of their mental functioning in relation to the particular task? In most legal systems, a person's legal capacity is not assessed in general, but in relation to particular contexts or tasks: it is assessed in relation to consent to treatment, entering a contract, making a will, instructing defence counsel and so on. It is a task-specific matter. What, then, if a person's capacity is limited only in discrete areas, based on criteria that go to their ability to perform the functions necessary to complete that task, following a fair process?

'The right to recognition everywhere as a person before the law' was originally affirmed in article 6 of the 1948 Universal Declaration of Human Rights (UDHR).[11] It was included mainly to counteract the principle found in some legal systems in the past that members of certain groups – such as slaves, married women, colonised peoples or convicts – did not count as persons before the law, so could not enjoy the same rights or privileges as others, or could not bring proceedings to assert their rights (Bogdan, 1992). The UDHR rebuts that idea, and article 12(1) CRPD repeats that rebuttal with respect to persons with disabilities.

Thus, the right to recognition before the law is an indelible human right. But it does not follow that denial of specific legal capacities, based on inability to perform relevant mental functions and subject to proper safeguards, contravenes that right. Any person may be denied a certain capacity under relevant legal standards – to personally make a will, sell a house or drive a car, for instance – without that denying their recognition generally as a person before the law, or denying recognition of their other legal capacities. They remain an effective legal agent for other purposes. And, where specifically their legal capacity is not recognised, based on proper evidence, their will and preferences can still be asserted – and 'respected' – through a proxy. Indeed, it may be only through a proxy that rights can be asserted effectively on their behalf: by the proxy bringing litigation, for instance, to protect their rights. Moreover, a person deprived of specific capacities retains all other rights and privileges recognised within the legal order: it would still be a crime or a civil wrong (the tort of trespass to the person, for instance), to violate their rights, in many other respects.

The Committee therefore overstates the case when it says denial of specific legal capacities automatically constitutes denial of recognition as a person before the law.

6.3 *Enjoying Legal Capacity 'on an Equal Basis with Others'*

Article 12 (2) declares: 'State Parties shall recognize that persons with disabilities enjoy legal capacity on an equal basis with others in all aspects of life'. The

---

[11] Universal Declaration of Human Rights GA Res 217A (1948). This right is also affirmed in article 16 of the International Covenant on Civil and Political Rights 999 UNTS 171 (opened for signature 16 December 1966, entered into force 23 March 1976).

Committee considers this clause supports the notion of 'universal legal capacity' – though that phrase does not appear in the Convention (the actual phrase used is enjoyment of legal capacity 'on an equal basis with others').

In our view, capacity laws do not deny persons with disabilities the enjoyment of legal capacity 'on an equal basis with others', when every adult in the jurisdiction is subject to the same capacity requirements. Capacity tests are universally applicable: every adult must meet the relevant tests of mental function to be recognised as capable of making legally effective decisions in the relevant zone. So, every adult must be able to understand the character of the proposed medical treatment and its likely consequences in order to have the capacity to give their consent; every adult must understand, broadly, the scope of their property in order to have the capacity to dispose of it by will; and so on. These are general requirements of the legal system. Moreover, if such requirements have a 'disproportionate effect' on persons with disabilities, this may still be justified, under the 'reasonable', 'objective' and 'legitimate purpose' tests set, for example, by the UN Human Rights Committee.

6.4 Only 'Supported Decision-Making' Is Authorised

The Committee claims, based on its interpretation of articles 12(3) and (4), that only supported, and not substitute, decision-making is permitted by the Convention (with a possible exception where a proxy has been appointed by the person and acts in accordance with their 'will and preferences').

Article 12(3) says: 'States parties shall take appropriate measures to provide access by persons with disabilities to the support they may require in exercising their legal capacity', and article 12(4) adds that all such 'measures that relate to the exercise of legal capacity' must 'provide for appropriate and effective safeguards to prevent abuse'. These 'safeguards' must include 'respect' for the 'rights, will and preferences of the person'. The measures must be 'free of conflict of interest and undue influence', apply for the shortest possible time and be subject to regular, independent review. And – significantly – these safeguards must 'be proportional to the degree to which such measures affect the person's rights and interests'.

Thus the Convention clearly contemplates that such support 'measures' could 'affect the person's rights and interests', and that the 'safeguards' required around these measures include those typical of proxy decision-making schemes – especially that any measure be 'proportional' and open to review. Moreover, the clause says these measures must 'respect' the person's 'rights, will and preferences' – respect all three of them – and all three should, we can fairly assume, have a distinct meaning. Thus, respecting a person's 'rights' and 'will' may not be the same as respecting their current 'preferences' when decisions are made. Instead, a choice may have to be made between respecting their 'rights' and 'will' and respecting their current 'preferences'.

The Committee says *only* 'supported decision-making' is to be included in the range of 'appropriate measures' to provide persons with disabilities with 'the support they may require in exercising their legal capacity'. In our view, the more accurate interpretation is that these clauses permit *a range* of 'appropriate measures' to be used. Supported decision-making, whereby a person is supported to – ultimately – make their own decision, should be the first preference. But 'support' via a proxy is also permissible where, despite all supportive efforts, the person is incapable of reaching their own decision. There, it may be 'appropriate' to give effect to the person's legal agency via a proxy, with all the 'safeguards' in article 12(4). A number of States Parties, when ratifying the CRPD, declared this was their understanding.

The Federal Constitutional Court of Germany reached a similar conclusion concerning the duty of the state to provide medical care to a person who lacked the capacity to decide on their own need for treatment (Federal Constitutional Court, 2016). It held that article 12 CRPD did not prohibit such measures – even provision of treatment contrary to the current preferences *(natürlichen Willen)* of the person concerned – when the person's 'capacity of self-determination' *(freien Willen)* was 'limited due to illness' (para. 88).

This is the more convincing interpretation.

6.5 Other Rights are Denied

Finally, there is the question of breach of other Convention rights, when a person is detained in hospital, for instance, or subject to involuntary treatment on the basis of a capacity assessment. Some rights affirmed in bold terms by the Convention clearly would be limited in such circumstances, including the right to enjoy liberty and security of person (article 14(1)(a)), and choosing one's residence (article 19(a)). The Convention says that persons with disabilities enjoy these rights 'on an equal basis with others'.

Such rights are not, however, absolute. They may also be subject to 'justified' limits prescribed by law that are acceptable in a free and democratic society (Clayton and Tomlinson, 2009). Some international human rights are absolute, such as the right not to be tortured, but the rights above are not of that kind. The UN Human Rights Committee makes this clear in GC35, regarding the right to liberty. These rights may therefore be subject to justified limitations, provided the calculus of 'proportionality' is satisfied.

We propose that the limits on rights contemplated here can be justified, where: the person lacks the capacity to make the relevant decision; the intervention would be in their 'best interests' because it would respect their deeply-held 'will and preferences'; significant harm would be avoided; there is no less restrictive way to achieve the relevant aims (for example, respect for the person's inherent dignity and autonomy); and a fair process exists, before a court or tribunal, to review the limits on rights.

7 THE NORTHERN IRELAND LEGISLATION

The Mental Capacity Act 2016 of Northern Ireland (the NI Act) comes close to enacting the 'fusion' model. When fully in force, it will repeal separate mental health legislation and merge aspects of that legislation into a single legal scheme based on capacity principles. In particular, non-consensual *treatment* – for a 'mental' or 'physical' condition – will be based squarely on incapacity to consent and on the person's 'best interests', not on 'mental disorder' and 'risk'. Certain steps would have to be taken to 'support' a person to reach their own decision before they could be found to lack capacity in this matter, including providing adequate information, in the right environment, and ensuring the right persons were present (ss. 1(4), 5).

A special regime is provided for forensic patients. They can be directed into care from the criminal justice system (Part 10), and be *detained* on the basis of 'mental impairment' and 'risk' to others – an exception to pure capacity principles. But, even then, forensic patients' *treatment* is 'to be determined in the same way as if the person were not so detained' (s. 171(1)(c)): that is, capacity principles apply.

Under the civil (or non-forensic) aspects of the legislation, intervention is based on a functional capacity test (ss. 1, 4, 5), and the application of that test, says the Act (s. 1(3)):

> is not to be determined merely on the basis of any condition that the person has, or any other characteristic of the person which might lead others to make unjustified assumptions about his or her ability to make a decision.

The Northern Ireland legislature presumably takes the view that, where those requirements are met, it would not be 'discrimination on the basis of disability' to employ a functional capacity test.

Any intervention must generally be in the 'best interests' of the person concerned (s. 2), and certain principles and consultation requirements must be followed when determining their 'best interests' (s. 7). Their wishes, feelings, beliefs and values 'that would be likely to influence' their decision on the matter if they 'had capacity' must be taken into account (s. 7(6)(b)). Information on their wishes and values must be gathered from many 'relevant people' (s. 7(7)). Consideration must be given to less restrictive ways to handle the situation (s. 7(8)). And, where the person has issued an advance directive refusing the proposed treatment, that will generally be binding. Special procedures apply to deprivations of liberty; mandatory second opinions are required to administer certain intrusive forms of treatment; and regular access is available to a tribunal for review of compulsory status. Subject to those requirements, however, the Act will permit emergency intervention, detention, restraint, involuntary treatment and 'community residence requirements' when the person concerned lacks the capacity to make the relevant decisions about their care.

The NI Act therefore cleaves quite closely to the 'fusion' model. It is an important new development in health law.

8 CONCLUSION

The case for a 'fusion law' – a generic law applicable to all persons who are unable to make a serious decision, regardless of the cause – is presented. Its aim of eliminating discrimination against persons with a mental health disability, and promoting their dignity, is shared with the CRPD. We argue that an appropriate 'capacity' criterion is not discriminatory in international law if certain strict conditions are met. Indeed, through the agency of an appropriate proxy, it may respect the person's 'will and preferences' and protect important rights.

REFERENCES

Bogdan, M (1992). Article 6. In Eide, Asbjørn et al. (eds.) *The Universal Declaration of Human Rights: A Commentary*. Oslo: Scandinavian University Press, 111–113.

Clayton, R and Tomlinson, H (2009). *The Law of Human Rights* (2nd ed.). Oxford: Oxford University Press.

Dawson, J, and Szmukler, G (2006). Fusion of mental health and incapacity legislation. *British Journal of Psychiatry*, 188, 504–509.

Dawson, J (2015). A realistic approach to assessing mental health laws' compliance with the UN Convention on the Rights of Persons with Disabilities, *International Journal of Law and Psychiatry*, 40, 70–79.

Federal Constitutional Court of Germany, BVerfG, Order of the First Senate of 26 July 2016 – 1 BvL 8/15.

Freeman, M et al. (2015). Reversing hard won victories in the name of human rights: a critique of the General Comment on Article 12 of the UN Convention on the Rights of Persons with Disabilities, *Lancet Psychiatry*, 2, 844–850.

Martin, W and Gurbai, S (2019). Surveying the Geneva impasse: coercive care and human rights. *International Journal of Law and Psychiatry*, 64, 117–128.

Scholten, M, Gather, J and Vollman, J (2021). Equality in the informed consent process: competence to consent, substitute decision-making, and discrimination of persons with mental disorders. *Journal of Medicine and Philosophy*, 46(1), 108–136.

Series, L and Nilsson, A (2018). Article 12 CRPD: Equal Recognition before the Law. In Bantekas, I, Stein, MA and Anastasiou D (eds.) *The UN Convention on the Rights of Persons with Disabilities*. Oxford: Oxford University Press, 339–382.

Szmukler, G, Daw, R, and Dawson, J (2010). A model law fusing incapacity and mental health legislation. *Journal of Mental Health Law*, Special Issue, 11–24 and 101–128.

Szmukler, G (2017). The UN Convention on the Rights of Persons with Disabilities: "rights, will and preferences" in relation to mental health disabilities. *International Journal of Law and Psychiatry*, 54, 90–97.

Szmukler, G (2020). Offenders with a mental impairment under a fusion law. *International Journal of Mental Health and Capacity Law* 26, 35–51.

United Nations Committee on the Rights of Persons with Disabilities (2014). General Comment No 1: Article 12: Equal Recognition before the Law. CRPD/C/GC/1, 19 May 2014.

United Nations Committee on the Rights of Persons with Disabilities (2018). General Comment No. 6 on Equality and Non-Discrimination, CRPD/C/GC/6.

United Nations Human Rights Committee (1994). General Comment 18, Non-Discrimination, U.N. Doc. HRI/GEN/1/Rev.1 at 26.

7

Contextualising Legal Capacity and Supported Decision Making in the Global South: Experiences of Homeless Women with Mental Health Issues from Chennai, India

Mrinalini Ravi, Barbara Regeer, Archana Padmakar, Vandana Gopikumar, and Joske Bunders

Abstract

Persons with mental health issues are among the most under-represented populations in rights discourse, and more so those from the Global South, who have been further subjugated by the intersections of poverty, patriarchy, and systemic isolation wrought by colonial and outmoded psychiatric treatments. The issue is worse still for women with mental illness in the Global South, many of whom are driven to the extreme margins, including but not limited to chronic homelessness. Through an enquiry into the lives of these women, and their experiences of exclusion, homelessness, and involuntary commitment, this chapter aims to deconstruct traditionally accepted notions of human rights and recalibrate a service paradigm that can mould itself to fit the diverse needs of an ultra-vulnerable population over a strong foundation of liberty, access to choice, and commitment to diversity. The study is set in The Banyan, a Chennai (India)-based not-for-profit organisation, focussed on humanitarian, equity, and justice-centric responses to the needs of homeless women with mental health issues.

INTRODUCTION

The voices of persons with mental illnesses are often silenced under the weight of stigma, societal apathy, and insensitive healthcare systems preoccupied with the illness and not the individual. However, through the efforts of human rights scholars and advocates, service users, and responsive care providers, the rights and preferences of persons with mental health issues in treatment and rehabilitation decisions have taken centre stage in global service discourse over the past forty years. There has, for instance, been a significant turn towards the ethics of procedural justice, which emphasises the participation of an individual in decisions made about them, especially in decisions involving involuntary commitment and substituted decision making.

Editing support from Rachel Brenner, Vishalinee Barendra, and Divya Nadkarni.

The United Nations Convention for the Rights of Persons with Disabilities (UNCRPD) emerged in 2006 as a result of these discourses [5]. The UNCRPD creates a template steeped in dignity for persons with mental health issues not just by promoting access to care, but by making the need to live in the community a fundamental right for individuals with mental health issues, thereby promoting equal access to civil and political life and enriching individual capabilities [1][16].

Article 12 of the UNCRPD has, however, come under scrutiny for creating a distinction between care and choice, by abolishing all forms of substituted decision making and conferring legal capacity upon individuals with disabilities at all times, irrespective of mental state [20]. By driving a wedge between two components that otherwise work in tandem to facilitate individual well-being and flourishing, it also contravenes with the rest of the treaty, including Articles 16, 17, and 25, which focus respectively on the right to be protected from exploitation, violence, and abuse; the right to access; and the right to physical and mental integrity and access to the highest attainable standards of care [6]. If Article 12 is interpreted wrongly (e.g., with broad exceptions), then existing practices that violate human rights will continue, especially for scores of individuals facing extreme vulnerabilities, such as the homeless mentally ill, who may have had no prior access to supported decision-making assistance from care providers. The General Comment on Article 12 has, in addition, been critiqued for not taking into consideration voices of user-survivors and caregivers from the Global South, or those from a multitude of cultural milieus who face the additional challenges of a sizeable care gap, socioeconomic stressors that further exacerbate ill health, high prevalence of homelessness, and lack of state support to meet economic and other rehabilitation needs [6][25].

This chapter presents the case of The Banyan, a mental health service provider from Chennai, India that began as an empathetic response to homeless women with mental health issues. The Banyan has, since its establishment, developed several learning algorithms to navigate dilemmas related to involuntary admissions and inpatient treatment for acutely ill individuals, the chief of which was creating feedback loops and user audits that place clients at the centre of the discourse.

HOMELESSNESS AND MENTAL ILLNESS

Homeless persons with mental health issues are among the most vulnerable populations in the world, subjected to various forms of (structural) abuse. Not only are they vulnerable to a host of physical health problems and have a markedly increased death rate from a variety of causes (such as poor diet, cardiovascular disease, HIV/AIDS, pneumonia, smoking-related fatal disease, liver disease, and suicide [2]), persons with mental health issues are at a significantly higher risk of being robbed, beaten, injured, or assaulted [2][7][13][14][19]. In India, homeless women report habitual rape and other forms of violence at the hands of partners and strangers, as well as blackmail, property destruction, and abuse of their children [4]. Moreover, the experience of homelessness interplays with pre-existing psychiatric conditions which have not received concerted clinical attention. Conceptualisation of illnesses such as PTSD among homeless women have, in fact, been found to include and go beyond DSM notions [9][23][24].

INVOLUNTARY COMMITMENT IN PSYCHIATRIC CARE

Numerous civil commitment laws have created an expansive definition of involuntary commitment, wherein a state can invoke inpatient admission for a person with mental health issues, who is gravely disabled, deemed unable to make a decision for themselves, or is suicidal. The state is obligated to make a decision in the best interest of the individual that most clearly reflects the choice of the individual when they were 'competent' [26].

Criteria for admissions have, however, been vulnerable to exploitative practices by governments that seek to silence the voices of dissidents by classifying them as 'clinically insane' and relegating them to prolonged institutionalisation. This has also held true for homeless mentally ill people, who are incarcerated just to be 'cleared off the streets'. This is especially problematic in states and countries where homelessness is considered a crime. The lack of intent on the part of governments and public health systems to offer assistance or alleviate distress often results in poorly executed involuntary admissions, carried out in ways that negate human rights covenants and individual dignity. These methods include public humiliation, coercion, and brute force which at times results in injuries so severe so as to lead to permanent impairment or death [18].

Article 12(4) of the UNCRPD mandates that state parties ensure all measures that relate to the exercise of legal capacity provide for appropriate safeguards which respect the rights, will, and preferences of the person. Szmukler considers 'will' as founded on a person's deeply held, reasonably stable and coherent personal values. These are not the same as a desire or currently held preference, even a strongly expressed one [22]. Flynn and Arstein-Kerslake illustrate the example of self-harm, where an individual may not 'prefer' help, but have the 'will' to live, thereby justifying intervention. However, the General Comment in Article 12 acknowledges that it is not always possible to discern these, in which case the best interpretation of will and preferences should replace 'best interest' determinations [6][8].

INDIAN SCENARIO

India is legally bound by the UNCRPD (ratified in 2007) and the Mental Health Care Act (since 2017), both of which allow for involuntary commitment of homeless individuals by organisations recognised by the government to provide psychiatric care. In the case of individuals who are not homeless, the jurisdictional police officer is expected to get a court order stating that the individual needs care, and take the responsibility of admitting the individual to a nearby government-appointed mental health facility. According to the Act, the mental health facility is required to submit a progress report to the State Mental Health Authority within thirty days of admission, and request an extension of ninety days to offer further support to the individual.

Involuntary admissions of this nature have received a mixed response from service users. On the one hand, many believe that their treatment was justified; that it benefited them and prevented self-harm. Alan Stone refers to this as the 'thank you' test. On the other hand, poorly executed admissions and lack of 'procedural justice' have resulted in individuals being mistrustful of mental health services, to the extent of withholding relevant clinical information for fear of being reincarcerated or treated against their will [12].

Further understanding of substituted decision-making processes in times of extreme distress is required to align this process to promote individual rights and supported decision making as articulated by the UNCRPD, so as to do away with the false dichotomy that has now emerged in the service discourse between access to care and access to choice.

Through an analysis of Banyan's care structures, this chapter aims to substantiate a more nuanced approach to human rights, and a responsive framework that reinforces dignity, personal recovery, and social inclusion.

METHODS

The Banyan was founded in 1993, and has since grown to offer end-to-end inpatient, outpatient and long-term care through Emergency Care and Recovery Centres (ECRCs), mental health and social care clinics, and inclusive housing with graded support services in three states in India [17].

Entry as an inpatient into ECRC takes place through critical time interventions (CTIs), or 'rescues',[1] facilitated by The Banyan team, the general public, or the police, or by family members in cases of non-homeless individuals. Clients who participated in this enquiry had been admitted into the facility when the Mental Health Act of 1987 was still in effect. Staff participants that have been performing CTIs have been trained in procedures per both legislations.

This study aggregates and analyses data that has been generated since The Banyan's inception. The study selected forty clients through purposive sampling who accessed the ECRC from Year 1 to Year 20 for a structured interview. Out of the forty clients, two did not respond and one had passed away. Thirty-seven interviews were conducted in order to generate quantitative and qualitative data about clients' experiences with care through involuntary admissions. In order to validate the

---

[1] The previously used word 'rescue' is a legacy of The Banyan's founding principles, which aimed to prevent harm from befalling a homeless mentally ill woman experiencing several dangers and insecurities.

results and gain further insight, two focus group discussions (FGDs) were conducted, with three and eight clients, respectively.

To elicit staff experiences, five staff members were interviewed about their experiences in carrying out CTIs. This includes the co-founder, one of the first employees of The Banyan, two social workers, and the overall head of the ECRC programme. Moreover, three of the five authors in the study have been engaged in direct service provision for between ten and thirty years, and engaged in service audits, participant observations, and autoethnographies of their work.

This enquiry was approved by The Banyan Academy of Leadership's Internal Review Board. Informed consent was received from all participants in writing. All names have been initialised to preserve the anonymity of the individual.

RESULTS

The seeds of The Banyan's founding philosophy to prohibit harm and promote individual capabilities were planted through the founders' encounter with a frail, terrified woman wandering alone outside their college, talking to herself [10]. She was not much older than them, but they lived in different worlds; theirs abounded with ontological security, social networks, and monetary comfort enabling them to explore capabilities and pursue aspirations; hers was a lonely place with erratic access to food and water, where bodily integrity and trustworthy human contact was a distant dream, and surviving through the night the only conceivable aspiration.

The only option the founders had at the time to ensure her health and safety was to go to the government mental hospital, which could not accommodate her; so she was taken to an old-age home, where she would at least gain access to food, clothing, and shelter. Finding the setting unsuitable for her needs, she left in a week. The Banyan began six months later in a facility similar to a crisis home, with women from circumstances similar to hers; however, she was nowhere to be found.

While the organisation was not explicitly founded within a particular human rights framework, the service blueprint was drawn up to accord every respect, equal treatment, dignity, freedom, and fairness in all aspects of outreach and care.

> [Rescuers] went with the idea of protection and safety from the distress ... I didn't have the feeling of 'Okay is it human rights or not?' Of course, at that point it seemed like it was a right, the human right [for our clients] to live like I was living (Dr V).

Individuals, especially those admitted from the streets, come into the facility under extremely distressing circumstances – inadequately or barely clothed, battered physically and sexually, with multiple fractures, pregnant or with children, presenting with serious health issues and skin disorders, and – in some cases – with maggots. In such circumstances, it is often incumbent upon the organisation to take decisions on the individual's behalf, when substituted decision making is the only choice, albeit with access to information and respect for agency in other aspects of outreach, so a person feels validated even when a difficult decision has to be made.

> One of the worst rescues we ever did was Ms T's. We rushed to the spot when we got the call from a volunteer, to find her consuming her own faeces, with a heap of clothes and garbage beside her. We tried to offer food and water, talked to her, but nothing worked. We couldn't bear seeing her in that state anymore, so we had to force her into the auto with us, kicking and screaming. She is of course, happy now, still with us, twenty-five years later, and we are a family, but I've always wondered if there was anything we could have done differently to reflect the respect we had even then for her, but could not express clearly. It could have perhaps built a relationship of trust from the get-go. (Dr V)

However, at times it was difficult to strike a balance between the values of client-centric care within the facility, and the frequently dire circumstances of rescue and admission. The absence of perceived fairness and respect for agency during the time of 'rescue' began to feature as a domain for improvement, as expressed during service audits and case management sessions. The team's focus and a sense of urgency in moving an individual from the streets were also influenced by incidents of delayed responses by The Banyan and civil society overall costing a person's life.

> I am still haunted by the memory of my first rescue call. It was from the police, about a woman in a bus stop who was creating nuisance in the area for over a week. We were working in a clinic not too far, and reached there in an hour, only to realise she had passed away by then. She possibly suffered electrolyte disturbances and brain damage, and we were too late in reaching her. It was maybe not the one hour that impacted her life, but the one week it took for us to know she even existed. She died alone, without support and respect. I dreamt about her for weeks after that, and have since ensured that there will be no delays in responding to an individual in dire and desperate need. (Dr A)

The next section elucidates clients' specific feedback from the survey, which facilitates a recognition and reconciliation of the cracks between individual choice and the need for care.

OVERALL EXPERIENCES

Ninety-five per cent of clients responded positively when asked if they were happy to have been admitted and provided with treatment. They felt relief and calm in moving to a place of safety.

> While I was scared of the other patients on my first night, I also felt a little happy that an orphan like me found a new home (Devi).

However, many clients on the first few nights reported apprehension and disorientation about the nature of the place and the reason they were being asked to stay.

> In the night I thought the place was a railway station, so I kept walking up and down. When no trains arrived, I stopped. I was also scared because it was a new place (Ms JJ).

Clients' thoughts on the components of the rescue process, dialogue prior to leaving their current place of stay, and experience of interactions and affiliations at their residence have helped build protocols focussed on procedural justice and an environment of mutual respect and trust.

NEED FOR PROCEDURAL JUSTICE

Procedural justice constitutes subjective perceptions of having a voice and being heard and respectfully considered by decision makers and figures of authority, and is key to creating a mutually trustworthy therapeutic relationship [16].

I RESPECT AND CONCERN DURING ADMISSION PROCESS

Majority of the clients were satisfied with the rescue, describing the staff to be caring. Two clients, however, felt that they were forced by The Banyan team to leave the streets. Eight said they were given food and water prior to the rescue, which they felt was crucial to being made comfortable. Twelve weren't offered anything, and two could not recall.

> I was brought to The Banyan from the railway station. A member of the rescue team told me this is a good place to live in, and people will speak well to me. She bought me *dosa* [food similar to savoury pancakes] and coffee before coming (Ms G).

Eleven clients said they were offered an explanation as to where they were being taken; four were not offered any; and five could not recall what was said to them, if anything. Predominant explanations that were given included 'being taken to the doctor or hospital', 'being taken home or to hometown', or 'being taken to a place of safety and shelter'. They also expressed disappointment at this not being the case, upon reaching the facility.

> I felt sad because I didn't know if I was going to be taken to my hometown, which is what was told to me when I was being brought here (Ms VR).

II ACCESS TO INFORMATION AND SHARED DECISION MAKING AFTER ADMISSION

There was a mixed reaction among participants when they first saw the place. Nine participants felt positively. They said they felt happy, safe, and comfortable. They also spoke of help sought from other residents, who made them feel safe in a new place. Other participants recalled feeling lonely, scared of the building and the residents, and disoriented.

> I didn't understand why I was kept there, since they spoke between themselves in English. I was very scared of some of the other residents, some of whom were violent. (Ms VR)

> I felt a little scared in the night but MS spoke to me which gave me strength (Ms DP).

Fifteen participants said that the staff explained why they were there, and what the place was. Eighteen said no explanation was provided, and four could not recall. One client was oriented to services by others, through whom she felt reassurance and support.

> It was the evening when I came and no one acknowledged me. The first night I was very confused about what was happening and was put in the acute ward. Only the next day someone spoke to me and explained where I was (Ms RJ).

> I came here in the night and I was scared. The staff explained to me that I am unwell and they will send me back home once I get better (Ms LP).

Thirteen participants felt that they were coerced into doing things they didn't want to do. Coercion was applied the most to taking a bath (six participants), changing clothes (one), and participants having their head shaved their head or hair cut (five).[2] One felt she was coerced into taking medicines. One was coerced into waking up early.

III ACKNOWLEDGING INDIVIDUAL READINESS FOR DISCHARGE AND PROMOTING DIGNITY OF RISK

In keeping with the principle of 'dignity of risk', The Banyan, from its inception, has created provisions for clients to exit the institution when they see fit. 'Dignity of risk' refers to the concept of affording a person the right (or dignity) to take reasonable risks, which, when impeded, suffocates personal growth, self-esteem, and overall quality of life [11]. This component of the service was also disseminated to clients as soon as they began treatment. However, in several cases, discharge was contingent upon the client's physical and mental state, as in cases of severe cognitive impairment, relapse into a severely psychotic state, or presence of intellectual disability. Returning to a state of homelessness for individuals who may not be in a position to mobilise resources for their safety and subsistence was not conducive to their survival. In these instances, individuals were deterred from leaving the institution and exhorted to continue with care until they could be agents of their security on the streets.

---

[2] In some cases, a haircut may be unavoidable – for example, if clients present with maggots, skin infections, or excessive lice and nits.

Eighteen out of thirty-seven participants were aware of this option and given a choice to leave the institution at any time. Fifteen were not. One person tried to leave over a disagreement with a staff member; she was asked to remain by another member whom she trusted, and she did so. One participant could not recall whether this was communicated; one participant did not understand the question; and two did not respond.

Many clients, however, availed of the option to leave, against the recommendation of the care team.

> When G decided to leave prematurely, we tried negotiating with her to stay and complete her treatment. Her acquiescence only lasted for a few weeks, and the lack of autonomy for a fiercely independent individual like her was more painful than the burden of the illness itself. This became apparent to us and we took a joint call that she should leave. G moved back to Delhi in a few days and stayed in touch on and off. We tried looking for her in Delhi as part of our aftercare process; she was not to be found, but members of the general public in the temple she stays in [religious sites often used as safe spaces/havens for homeless persons] assured us that she was indeed alive and well. This may well not be the case, and they could have referred to somebody else, but it was not up to us or anyone to override G's autonomy and happiness for extrinsically mandated standards of safety and well-being (Dr V).

Treatment as a Basic Right

Clients reinforced the need for responsive mental health care as a civic duty for an organisation and governments to preserve the safety and dignity of citizens, and adopt a wider framework on what constitutes rights to place equal value to the well-being and quality of life of every individual, irrespective of their affliction or ability to articulate their needs.

> I can see why I had to be admitted. I was unwell, without a normal life (and money), and needed treatment. When people are out on the street, they are deprived of food, shelter and protection which are basic rights. When they harm themselves, it is imperative for a healthy society to intervene. There are too many people with mental illness not being cared. (Ms M)

One of The Banyan's first clients, now accessing supported housing and leading the rural mental health program's vocational training unit, emphasised the benefits of treatment that fulfils an individual's deeper will to remain well and partake in wider society.

> How can someone who is unwell decide their course of treatment? No one can say they don't want to be treated. If this person is stubborn and opts out of treatment, someone who knows her should secretly check on her every day. We cannot allow an unwell woman commit suicide or die alone. (Ms AN)

The next section expands on The Banyan's response to assuring procedural justice in the treatment process.

Restoring Procedural Justice

This section reflects the protocolisation of The Banyan's rescue process (see Table 1) in line with client preferences expressed during one-on-one sessions, through grievance redress platforms and this enquiry.

CTI Protocols

The Banyan's experience clearly points to the criticality of procedural justice whilst approaching the client on the streets and admitting them to the institution. To this end, the team conducting the CTI has been curated to include staff members who play unique roles to respond to the multiple needs of stakeholders present with the client on the streets. The team undergoes several dry runs to prepare for a host of situations to facilitate a smooth transition from the streets. The language employed by them is choice-centric, and encourages the client to make a considered decision.

> In cases where the individual is severely psychotic and unable to respond or give consent, it becomes all the more critical for the team to take their time demonstrating positive intent, and help keep the general public and the law at bay, so they can take their time to build trust, at least to the extent that they're convinced that no harm will befall them by the care team (Ms P).

The following case study from one of the authors of this chapter offers an example of a nuanced CTI undertaken by The Banyan team.

> S was referred to us by the police. She was living by the market close to a bus stand, which attracts thousands of people every day. She was visually impaired and screaming at the police and the general public. She was completely disinterested in engaging with the CTI team, threw things at them and yelled at them to leave her presence. The team waited for four hours, engaging in conversations on and off with her, and helping her with food and water. To the social worker with whom she began to develop a rapport after the commotion quietened down through the evening, she confided that she's been fielding unwanted approaches by a man who had just the previous night raped her. The social worker stayed with her through the night, and the CTI took nine hours to complete. By this time, the police were alerted to her experience of assault, which helped them develop a sense of empathy which they could not muster previously. They assured her safety against any form of assault, accorded her the respect she deserved, and politely requested her to move to a place of safety where she would receive healthcare, shelter and positive human contact. Genuine intent and concern for her well-being by people who several hours ago just wanted to be rid of her, helped her build faith that she was indeed moving to a safer space, and left with the CTI team.

TABLE 7.1 *Procedures for CTIs (Adapted from The Banyan's structure and process document)*

Stages of engagement	Steps to be followed	Values to be espoused
CTI	• Trained team with social worker, primary care worker, driver, and peer worker following a predetermined script • Rescue kits – food, water, first aid items, change of clothes • Information brochures on the organisation and referral services • Avoid rescues at night unless it's an emergency	• Open communication • Empathetic listening • Validation of distress • Upholding individual dignity • Cultural humility • Personal recovery • Promotion of individual capabilities
First few nights in the facility	• Welcome kit with new clothes, toiletries, snacks, and drinks (fruit juice, coconut water) • Space for grooming in line with their cultural affiliations • Walkabout and orientation to services and individual rights • Safe space for rest personalised with preferred religious entity; interactions with peer worker • Icebreaker sessions with other clients • Options for skills development and vocational training • Orientation to Mental Healthcare Act (MHCA 2017) with details on reasons and duration of involuntary commitment	
Exiting the institution	• Advance directives for all clients with preferences on nominated representative, treating team and location, information sharing with next of kin • Evaluation of client's mental health status thirty days after admission (per MHCA 2017). The care provider carries out an assessment towards discharge or extended stay in the facility (ninety days), and submits it to the mental health review board • If no exit options to families of origin or independent living are available, refer client to long-term, community-based care options, such as The Banyan's Home Again model, where clients identify a group of friends from the institution with whom they can set up an independent home, and seek further assistance with mental health and social care, rental and personal assistance	

This anecdote reflects the dynamic of any decision-making process, which – especially in collectivist societies – involves multiple players. In creating a platform for the individual to express their will and preferences in a safe space and feel heard by other stakeholders (which is the cornerstone of supported decision making), procedural justice is achieved.

Promoting Supported Decision Making

One of the key components in supported decision making is the creation of advance directives for clients accessing mental health treatment, to help them retain agency and individual preference even during times of extreme mental ill health and incapacitation [21]. In line with the MHCA and UNCRPD, every client accessing inpatient and long-term care at The Banyan submits an advance directive.

Another strategy is peer-promoted care. Integrating persons with lived experience as health workers and/or case managers as a practice has been adopted by The Banyan since its inception and strengthened in the past ten years, in keeping with global trends in promoting evidence-based practice. Persons with lived experience now make up 20 per cent of The Banyan's treatment team. Peer providers, by sharing personal experiences that very often mirror what the client is undergoing, have proven to be an invaluable resource during CTIs for building trust and lending credibility to the treatment team. Their role extends to other aspects of service provision as well.

Discussion

This inquiry can be credited to be the first of its kind in studying involuntary commitment and procedural justice as perceived by homeless women with mental health issues accessing care at a not-for-profit organisation in a developing country. Voices from the Global South, and those of homeless individuals, are conspicuous in their absence from several international human rights discourses, including the General Comment of Article 12 of UNCRPD.

Access to care and procedural justice have emerged as basic rights for women who have experienced homelessness and mental health issues, as illustrated in this enquiry. Procedural justice through all phases of care has been reinforced time and again by patients as key to building a trustworthy therapeutic relationship, where transparency and the values of client-centric care are ensured by providers. Procedural justice is even more critical during involuntary commitment, when decisions are made on behalf of the individual. In a study in Sweden, eighteen patients who were committed involuntarily in an institution were asked to speak about their experiences [18]. One of the key themes that emerged was 'not feeling like a human being' throughout the time of their stay, induced by not having a say in their own care, not being listened to, not receiving information and knowledge, not getting a response to their queries and not understanding the treatment. These components corroborate some of the clients' experience of their commitment to an ECRC without being consulted on their needs and preferences at the time. In the Swedish study, patients attributed good care to the responsiveness of staff and their proximity to staff members. This feedback is once again corroborated by clients at The Banyan, who spoke about staff members who carried out the rescue and others who spent time with them through the first night and week, responding to their queries and concerns.

Article 12 restricts itself by promoting only one form of decision making in psychiatric treatment – that is, supported decision making. This approach paints an individual as somewhat unilateral in their thinking, and assumes consistency in choices, ethos and behaviour, which is never the case, irrespective of whether or not they are afflicted with a mental health issue or developmental disability. The aforementioned study reaffirms this, and reiterates the need for an approach that integrates multiple decision-making paradigms at different stages of care. *Facilitated* decision making, as described by Bach and Krezner, emphasises that a person who is unable to express their will and preferences clearly requires a facilitator who responds in their best interests [3]. This is especially critical in the case of homeless persons with mental health issues, most of whom may not have (access to) advance directives. In such cases, understanding the will and preferences of the individual and abiding by basic human rights covenants of doing no harm and protecting the dignity of the individual is the service algorithm to which the treatment team should adhere, and to which they must be held legally accountable. As illustrated above, The Banyan's outreach has, over the past three decades, aimed to adhere to these covenants using a combination of facilitated and supported decision making in instances where clients found themselves indisposed and unable to clearly express their will and preferences.

Conclusion

This enquiry reflects the perceptions of a single organisation, albeit with vast and diverse experience in mental health care for poor and homeless persons in India. Further study is required from other geopolitical settings working with vulnerable populations to better understand the nuances of rights-centric care provision.

The element of universal legal capacity for persons with mental health issues tends to contradict those other articles of the UNCRPD related to the right to life, protection from harm, access to healthcare, and the right to live in the community. For a document that is extremely futuristic and representative of the needs of persons with disabilities, the General Comment on Article 12 is not robust in terms of representation from ultra-vulnerable populations and or those from the Global South. This leads to a silencing or abstraction of practical issues faced by the aforementioned population and treatment responses of those states that have ratified it.

Flourishing, as articulated by Alasdair McIntyre, requires virtues that enable us to function as independent and accountable, practical reasoners who acknowledge the nature and extent of our dependence on others [15]. We are always going to depend on one another. How we choose to respond to each other needs to be embedded within a framework of dignity, inclusion, and oneness.

REFERENCES

1. Alexander, J. M. (2008). *Capabilities and Social Justice: The Political Philosophy of Amartya Sen and Martha Nussbaum*. Ashgate Publishing, Ltd.
2. Babidge, N. C., Buhrich, N., & Butler, T. (2001). Mortality among homeless people with schizophrenia in Sydney, Australia: a 10-year follow-up. *Acta Psychiatrica Scandinavica*, 103(2), 105–110.
3. Bach, M., & Kerzner, L. (2014). *A New Paradigm for Protecting Autonomy and the Right to Legal Capacity*. Law Commission of Ontario.
4. Chaudry, S., Joseph, A., & Prakash Singh, I. (2014). *Violence and Violations: The Reality of Homeless Women in India*. Retrieved from http://hlrn.org.in/documents/Violence_and_Violations_Homeless_Women_in_India_2014.pdf.
5. Convention on the Rights of Persons with Disabilities (CRPD) (2016). Retrieved from www.un.org/development/desa/disabilities/convention-on-the-rights-of-persons-with-disabilities.html.
6. de Bhailís, C., & Flynn, E. (2017). Recognising legal capacity: commentary and analysis of Article 12 CRPD. *International Journal of Law in Context*, 13(1), 6–21. https://doi.org/10.1017/S1744552316000046X.
7. Fischer, P. J. (1992). Criminal Behavior and Victimization among Homeless People. In R. I. Jahiel (ed.), *Homelessness: A Prevention-Oriented Approach*. Johns Hopkins University Press, 87–112.
8. Flynn, E., & Arstein-Kerslake, A. (2014). Legislating personhood: realising the right to support in exercising legal capacity. *International Journal of Law in Context*, 10(1), 81–104. https://doi.org/10.1017/S1744552213000384.
9. Gilmoor, A. R., Vallath, S., Regeer, B. et al. (2020). 'If somebody could just understand what I am going through, it would make all the difference': conceptualizations of trauma in homeless populations experiencing severe mental illness. *Transcultural Psychiatry*, 57(3), 455–467. https://doi.org/10.1177/1363461520909613.
10. Gopikumar, V., Easwaran, K., Ravi, M. et al. (2015). Mimicking family like attributes to enable a state of personal recovery for persons with mental illness in institutional care settings. *International Journal of Mental Health Systems*, 9(1), 30.
11. Ibrahim, J. E., & Davis, M. C. (2013). Impediments to applying the 'dignity of risk' principle in residential aged care services. *Australasian Journal on Ageing*, 32(3), 188–193. https://doi.org/10.1111/ajag.12014.
12. Katsakou, C., Rose, D., Amos, T. et al. (2012). Psychiatric patients' views on why their involuntary hospitalisation was right or wrong: a qualitative study. *Social Psychiatry and Psychiatric Epidemiology*, 47(7), 1169–1179. https://doi.org/10.1007/s00127-011-0427-z.

13. Kushel, M. B., Evans, J. L., Perry, S. et al. (2003). No door to lock: victimization among homeless and marginally housed persons. *Archives of Internal Medicine*, 163(20), 2492–2499. https://doi.org/10.1001/archinte.163.20.2492.
14. Lam, J. A., & Rosenheck, R. (1998). The effect of victimization on clinical outcomes of homeless persons with serious mental illness. *Psychiatric Services (Washington, D.C.)*, 49 (5), 678–683. https://doi.org/10.1176/ps.49.5.678.
15. MacIntyre, A. C. (1999). *Dependent Rational Animals: Why Human Beings Need the Virtues*. Open Court Publishing
16. Molas, A. (2016) Defending the CRPD: dignity, flourishing, and the universal right to mental health, *The International Journal of Human Rights*, 20:8, 1264–1276, https://doi.org/10.1080/13642987.2016.1213720.
17. Narasimhan, L., Gopikumar, V., Jayakumar, V. et al. (2019). Responsive mental health systems to address the poverty, homelessness and mental illness nexus: The Banyan experience from India. *International Journal of Mental Health Systems*, 13, 54. https://doi.org/10.1186/s13033-019-0313-8.
18. Olofsson, B., & Jacobsson, L. (2001). A plea for respect: involuntarily hospitalized psychiatric patients' narratives about being subjected to coercion. *Journal of Psychiatric and Mental Health Nursing*, 8(4), 357–366. https://doi.org/10.1046/j.1365-2850.2001.00404.x.
19. Padgett, D. K. & Struening, E. L. (1992). Victimization and traumatic injuries among the homeless: associations with alcohol, drug, and mental problems. *American Journal of Orthopsychiatry* 62, 525–534.
20. Series, L., & Nilsson, A. (2018). Article 12 CRPD: Equal Recognition before the Law. In I. Bantekas, M. A. Stein, and D. Anastasiou (eds.), *The UN Convention on the Rights of Persons with Disabilities: A Commentary*. Oxford University Press.
21. Stacey, G., Felton, A., Morgan, A. et al. (2016). A critical narrative analysis of shared decision-making in acute inpatient mental health care. *Journal of Interprofessional Care*, 30(1), 35–41. https://doi.org/10.3109/13561820.2015.1064878.
22. Szmukler G. (2017). The UN Convention on the Rights of Persons with Disabilities: 'rights, will and preferences' in relation to mental health disabilities. *International Journal of Law and Psychiatry*, 54, 90–97. https://doi.org/10.1016/j.ijlp.2017.06.003.
23. Vallath, S., Luhrmann, T., Bunders, J. et al. (2018). Reliving, replaying lived experiences through auditory verbal hallucinations: implications on theories and management. *Frontiers in Psychiatry*, 9, 528. https://doi.org/10.3389/fpsyt.2018.00528.
24. Vallath, S., Ravikanth, L., Regeer, B. et al. (2020). Traumatic loss and psychosis – reconceptualising the role of trauma in psychosis. *European Journal of Psychotraumatology*, 11(1), https://doi.org/10.1080/20008198.2020.1725322.
25. Stein, M. A., & Lord, J. E. (2010). Monitoring the Convention on the Rights of Persons with Disabilities: innovations, lost opportunities, and future potential. *Human Rights Quarterly*, 32, 689–728. At 709 and 711.
27. Substance Abuse and Mental Health Services Administration. (2019). *Civil Commitment and the Mental Health Care Continuum: Historical Trends and Principles for Law and Practice: Substance Abuse and Mental Health Services Administration*. Office of the Chief Medical Officer, Substance Abuse and Mental Health Services Administration. www.samhsa.gov/sites/default/files/civil-commitment-continuum-of-care.pdf.

8

The Potential of the Legal Capacity Law Reform in Peru to Transform Mental Health Provision

Alberto Vásquez Encalada

Abstract

In 2018, Peru achieved a milestone reform in the recognition of the right to legal capacity of persons with disabilities. As a result, the Peruvian legal system abolished disability-related guardianship and restrictions to the legal capacity of persons with disabilities, and introduced different regimes for supported decision-making. Following this reform, Peru adopted in 2019 a new Mental Health Act aimed to strengthen the mental health care reform in progress and to ensure a rights-based approach in mental health provision. Against this background, this chapter explores the impact of Peruvian legal capacity law reform on the new regulatory and policy framework concerning mental health and its potential to end all forms of coercion. In particular, the chapter identifies the legal capacity reform as a key precursor to the rights-based approach to disability in mental health provision and highlights the role of the disability rights movement and civil society in driving forward these unprecedented advances.

INTRODUCTION

In 2018, Peru achieved a landmark reform on the recognition of the right to legal capacity of persons with disabilities. As a result, the Peruvian legal system abolished disability-related guardianship and other restrictions to the legal capacity of persons with disabilities, and now recognizes the full legal capacity of all persons with disabilities, accompanied by different regimes for supported decision-making.[1] This reform was welcomed internationally and is considered to be the best example of implementation of Article 12 of the UN Convention on the Rights of Persons with Disabilities (CRPD).[2] The UN Special Rapporteur on the rights of persons with

---

[1] Legislative Decree No. 1384, published on September 4, 2018. Translated into English by SODIS at http://sodisperu.org/wp-content/uploads/2019/08/Legislative-Decree-No-1384-Peruvian-legal-capacity-reform-2.pdf.

[2] Office of the United Nations High Commissioner for Human Rights (OHCHR) (September 4, 2018), Peru: milestone disability reforms lead the way for other States, says UN expert. OHCHR. www.ohchr.org/en/NewsEvents/Pages/DisplayNews.aspx?NewsID=23501&LangID=E; Inter-American Commission on Human Rights (October 2, 2018), IACHR welcomes measures recognizing the legal capacity of people

disabilities called it a "milestone" in the recognition of the full citizenship of persons with disabilities.[3]

Following this reform, Peru adopted its first Mental Health Act aimed to strengthen ongoing mental health care reform and ensure a rights-based approach in mental health provision. While the new mental health legislation did not directly address the legal capacity of people with disabilities, and in some places may seem to contradict the advances achieved, its accompanying regulations have allowed a coherent reading of both regulatory frameworks that enhances respect for legal capacity and supported decision-making in the field of mental health.

Against this background, the chapter will explore the impact of the Peruvian legal capacity law reform on the new regulatory and policy framework concerning mental health and its potential to end all forms of coercion. In particular, the chapter identifies the legal capacity reform as a key precursor to the rights-based approach to disability in mental health provision and highlights the role of the disability rights movement and civil society in driving forward these unprecedented advances.

THE LEGAL CAPACITY REFORM

In January 2008, Peru ratified the CRPD and its Optional Protocol.[4] According to the Peruvian constitutional system, ratified human rights treaties are part of national legislation and hold a constitutional status, prevailing over ordinary laws.[5]

Up until the time of ratification, articles 43 and 44 of the Civil Code authorised the restriction or denial of legal capacity of a range of people, including minors, people with disabilities, drug users, "prodigals" and "bad administrators," and people with criminal convictions.[6] A judge could declare them legally incompetent, restrict their legal capacity in one or more areas of life, and appoint a guardian to represent and substitute them in the exercise of their rights. Although incapacity had

---

with Disabilities in Peru. OAS. www.oas.org/en/iachr/media_center/PReleases/2018/216.asp; OHCHR (September 12, 2018), Perú: ONU Derechos Humanos celebra reformas legislativas en materia de discapacidad y desaparición forzada. https://acnudh.org/peru-onu-derechos-humanos-celebra-reformas-legislativas-en-materia-de-discapacidad-y-desaparicion-forzada/; Ríos, C. (October 1, 2018). Peru's groundbreaking legislation gives equality of choices to people with disabilities. *Human Rights Watch*. www.hrw.org/news/2018/10/01/perus-groundbreaking-legislation-gives-equality-choices-people-disabilities.

[3] Devandas, C., UN Special Rapporteur on the rights of persons with disabilities (September 4, 2018); OHCHR. Peru: milestone disability reforms.
[4] The Convention was ratified without any reservation or declaration by Supreme Decree No. 073–2007-RE and published on December 31, 2007; the formal deposit of the ratification document was on January 30, 2008.
[5] Political Constitution of Peru, article 55 and Fourth Final and Transitory Provision. See Constitutional Court, Case No. 0047–2004-AI/TC, April 24, 2006.
[6] Persons who "lack discernment," persons who "could not express their will in an undoubtable manner," "mentally retarded persons," persons who "suffer from mental deterioration that prevents them from expressing their will," "prodigals," "bad administrators," "habitual drunkards," "drug addicts," and those whose penalties carry with civil interdiction.

to be judicially declared, a general presumption of lack of capacity prevailed; in practice, people with disabilities could not carry out legal transactions or access certain services or benefits without a guardian.[7] In addition, further restrictions to specific rights of persons with disabilities were permitted without being declared legally incompetent, such as the right to marry, vote, or make a will.[8]

Following CRPD ratification, the Peruvian disability movement – together with civil society allies – drafted and submitted a citizen's initiative for a new legal framework on disability.[9] This resulted in the adoption of the General Law on Persons with Disabilities, Law No. 29973, on December 13, 2012. This omnibus law introduced a veritable shift in approach to the rights of people with disabilities based on the standards enshrined in the CRPD.[10] Acknowledging the challenges of reforming the Civil Code as it related to legal capacity, the civil society proposal deferred the legal capacity reform to a second stage. Hence, besides article 9 of Law No. 29973 stating that persons with disabilities enjoy legal capacity in all aspects of life on an equal basis with others, its final provision mandated the creation of a Special Committee for the reform of the Civil Code concerning the legal capacity of persons with disabilities. Notwithstanding, the General Law advanced the repeal of article 43(3) of the Civil Code, which was commonly used to restrict the legal capacity of deaf, blind, and deafblind people.[11]

The Special Committee for the reform of the Civil Code (CEDIS) began its activities in March 2014, composed of representatives of three branches of government, the Office of the Ombudsperson, academia and civil society. In February 2015, CEDIS approved a draft reform of the Civil Code amending more than 80 provisions in line with civil society proposals.[12] However, with the arrival of the new government in July 2016, this bill was regretfully archived. A revisited multiparty bill, supported by a broader civil society coalition, was eventually presented in January 2017.[13] Following a delay in Congress, the

---

[7] See Confederación Nacional de Personas con Discapacidad del Perú, Asociación de Sordos del Perú, Federación Nacional de Mujeres con Discapacidad, SODIS (February 11, 2013). Report to the Human Rights Committee on the civil and political rights of persons with disabilities. OHCHR. https://tbinternet.ohchr.org/_layouts/15/treatybodyexternal/Download.aspx?symbolno=INT%2fCCPR%2fNGO%2fPER%2f14428&Lang=en

[8] Civil Code, articles 45, 241, 274, 687, 693, and 694.

[9] Bill No. 04707/2010-IC. For more on the process of advocacy leading to the adoption of this law, see Vásquez Encalada, A. (2019). Transforming disability law and policy in Peru: The role of civil society. In K. Soldatic & K. Johnson (eds.), *Global Perspectives on Disability Activism and Advocacy: Our Way*. 232–244.

[10] English translation of the law available at www.internationaldisabilityalliance.org/es/resources/peru-ley-general-de-la-persona-con-discapacidad-ley-no-29973 (accessed May 13, 2020).

[11] General Law on Persons with Disabilities, Sole Complementary Derogatory Provision.

[12] Bill No. 04601/2014-CR.

[13] Bill No. 00872/2016-CR.

Executive requested legislative powers[14] and adopted the reform as Legislative Decree No. 1384, published on September 4, 2018.

Legislative Decree No. 1384, which holds the same status as a law, amends the Civil Code, the Civil Procedural Code, and the Notary Act concerning the legal capacity of persons with disabilities. It recognises the full legal capacity of all persons with disabilities, abolishes disability-related guardianship and other restrictions to their legal capacity, and introduces a range of regimes for supported decision-making. It also recognizes the right to reasonable and procedural accommodations in courts and notary offices.

Recognition of Full Legal Capacity in All Aspects of Life

The amended Civil Code expressly recognizes the legal capacity of persons with disabilities on equal basis with others (art. 3). It clarifies that adults with disabilities have full capacity to act in all aspects of life, regardless of whether they require reasonable accommodation or support to express their will (art. 42). The legislative decree further abolished provisions that provided for the legal incapacitation of various groups of persons with disabilities (arts. 43(2), 44(2), 44(3)), as well as restrictions to their right to marry, parental rights, and the right to make a will (arts. 241, 274, 466, 687, 693, 694, and 697). In addition, the reform expunged from the Civil Code the possibility for a guardian to admit an incapacitated person into an institution (art. 578).

Despite these advances, provisions of curatorship and guardianship were preserved for a limited group of people: "habitual drunkards," "drug addicts," "prodigals,"[15] "bad administrators,"[16] criminally convicted people, and people in a coma who have not previously designated a support.[17] While civil society fell short of its objective to abolish all forms of substitute decision-making, the remaining forms of curatorship were formerly rarely ever used.[18]

Right to Reasonable Accommodation in the Exercise of Legal Capacity

The amended Civil Code recognizes the right to reasonable accommodation in the exercise of legal capacity (art. 45). Its regulations[19] define reasonable accommodation as "necessary and appropriate modifications and adjustments needed in a particular case,

---

[14] The legislative powers were granted by the Congress by Law No. 30823, published on July 20, 2018.
[15] A person who has a spouse or forced heirs (a common feature of civil-law legal systems) and dispenses their assets beyond the limit of the discretionary portion (Civil Code, article 584).
[16] A person who has a spouse or forced heirs and has lost more than half of their assets due to their own bad administration (Civil Code, article 585).
[17] While people in a coma could be incapacitated, the judge will appoint a support measure (Civil Code, article 45-B).
[18] Persons with addictions were not usually put under guardianship because, prior to the 2018 Mental Health Act, legislation permitted their involuntary treatment and institutionalization without the need of a guardian. "Bad administration" and "prodigality" are archaic legal provisions, not linked to mental capacity assessments.
[19] Adopted by Supreme Decree No. 016-2019-MIMP, published on August 29, 2019.

not imposing a disproportionate or undue burden, which serve to guarantee the enjoyment and exercise of the legal capacity of the person with disabilities, on equal terms with others, of all human rights and fundamental freedoms" (art. 2(1)). They include measures of accessibility relating to the environment, communications or information, the use of informal supports, and other adaptations required for exercising legal capacity. In accordance with the CRPD, denial of these accommodations constitutes an act of disability-based discrimination, unless such measures impose a disproportionate or undue burden (art. 5(1)). Hence, public and private actors are only permitted to refuse carrying out legal transactions for a person with disability where the necessary reasonable adjustments impose a disproportionate or undue burden.

Supported Decision-Making

Legislative Decree No. 1384 introduced supported decision-making into the Civil Code. Supports are defined as forms of assistance to facilitate the exercise of legal capacity, including support in communication, support to understand legal acts and their consequences, and support in the expression and interpretation of will (art. 659-B). Support measures are voluntary ("freely chosen"), can be accessed by any person of legal age, and are not limited to persons with disabilities. Each individual determines the type, scope, and duration of their own support measures, and designates the identity and number of their supporters (art. 659-B), which can comprise one or more natural persons, public institutions, or non-profit organizations. The person benefitting from support maintains responsibility for their own decisions, including those made with such support, and has the right to recourse against the supporters for damages and losses generated for faulty support (art. 1976-A). Finally, representation powers, or powers of attorney, are not included in the support measure unless expressly stated (art. 659-B).

Three types of support regimes are foreseen. First, an individual can designate their supporter(s) and have this filed in court or notarized (art. 659-D). This designation is made directly by the individual and does not in any case imply a renunciation of their legal capacity. Second, the right to make advance decisions in anticipation of requiring future assistance for the exercise of their legal capacity (art. 659-F); a person with or without disabilities can foresee how and who will provide support, should it become necessary. This is recorded in a notarized document and must state the moment or circumstances in which the designation of future support becomes effective. Third, in exceptional cases in which the individual cannot express their will by any means and thus cannot designate supporter(s) on their own, the court can appoint support measures (art. 659-E).[20] In implementing these exceptional support measures, the

---

[20] This measure is justified only after having made real, considerable, and pertinent efforts to obtain an expression of will from the person, and having provided them with measures of accessibility and reasonable accommodations, and when the designation of supports is necessary for the exercise and protection of their rights. Civil Code, article 659-E.

TABLE 8.1 *Support in the Peruvian legal system*

	Individual designation of support	Individual designation of support for the future	Exceptional judicial appointment of support for the individual
Beneficiary	Any person over eighteen	Any person over eighteen	Persons in a coma or persons with disabilities who cannot express their will by any means
Supporters	One or more individuals or non-profit organizations	One or more individuals or non-profit organizations	One or more individuals, public institutions, or non-profit organizations. The judge considers relationships of cohabitation, trust, friendship, care, and/or kinship. Prohibition of appointing a support person with a criminal record of domestic or sexual violence
Procedure	Notarial or judicial	Notarial. Person indicates when it comes into effect	Judicial
Representation powers (powers of attorney)	No representation powers except where expressly established	Public deed expressly establishes representation powers for specified acts	The judge must evaluate the necessity and apply the best interpretation of will and preferences of the individual.

Source: Author's analysis based on Legislative Decree No. 1384 and its regulations

judge and the designated supporter(s) will carry out the best possible interpretation of the will and preferences of the individual, considering their life trajectory.[21]

Safeguards

Legislative Decree No. 1384 introduced a flexible system of safeguards which seeks to guarantee respect for the rights, will, and preferences of the person, and prevent abuse and undue influence (art. 659–G). The beneficiary establishes the safeguards

---

[21] The criterion of the best interpretation of will implies taking into account the life trajectory of the person, including previous expressions of will in similar contexts, information provided by trusted people of the assisted person, consideration of their preferences, and any other consideration relevant to the specific case. Civil Code, article 659-B.

that they deem appropriate, indicating, as a minimum, the deadlines for the review of supports. The judge makes decisions on safeguards only in the case of exceptional appointment of support. The related regulations establish an open list of possible safeguards which people can elect, including reporting, audits, periodic supervision, unannounced visits, interviews, and information requests (art. 21(3)).

Accessibility and Accommodations

The Civil Procedural Code and the Notary Act were also amended to ensure respect of the legal capacity of persons with disabilities in judicial and notarial proceedings. Limitations to the participation of persons with disabilities in judicial proceedings were abolished from the Civil Procedural Code (arts. 61, 66, 207), and their right to have procedural accommodations in all judicial proceedings expressly recognized (art. 119-A). Furthermore, court decisions related to the designation or appointment of support should be written in easy-to-read formats (art. 847). The Notary Act was also amended to include the obligation to provide accessibility measures, reasonable accommodation, and safeguards (art. 16).

Implementation

The implementation of this paradigmatic reform has been disorderly and uneven. Despite its significance and complexity, Legislative Decree No. 1384 did not foresee a period of time to prepare for its implementation. Hence, the amended provisions entered into force the day after their publication, which – in addition to legislative inconsistencies – left legal operators (e.g. judges, notaries, lawyers, and health authorities), people with disabilities, and their families unprepared and taken unawares.[22] Moreover, provisions related to the restoration of the legal capacity of those under guardianship were not clear, generating confusion and – to some extent – resistance from public officials.[23]

Notwithstanding these limitations, since the reform, the judiciary together with the Office of the Ombudsperson and non-governmental organizations have carried out various training courses on the legal capacity innovations.[24] Likewise, civil society has

---

[22] See Espinoza Espinoza, J. (2018). Las nuevas coordenadas impuestas en el Código Civil en materia de capacidad (... o el problema de la "falta de discernimiento" en una reforma legislativa inconsulta y apresurada). *Gaceta Civil & Procesal Civil*, 64, 13–25; Vega Mere, Y. (2018). La reforma del régimen legal de los sujetos débiles made by Mary Shelley: notas al margen de una novela que no pudo tener peor final. *Gaceta Civil & Procesal Civil*, 64, 27–45.

[23] The Judiciary clarified the transition process by Administrative Resolution No. 046-2019-CE-PJ, published on February 13, 2019. Problems in implementation led to many people with intellectual and psychosocial disabilities not being able to vote in the 2020 elections. See Human Rights Watch (January 20, 2020). Peru: many with disability left off voting lists. www.hrw.org/news/2020/01/20/Peru: many with disability left off voting lists.

[24] Comisión Permanente de Acceso a la Justicia de Personas en condición de Vulnerabilidad y Justicia en tu Comunidad (February 5, 2019). Comisión de Acceso a la Justicia del PJ coordina el inicio de

been raising awareness and providing training to other actors, including notaries and families. According to the Peruvian National Public Registry,[25] the number of registered guardianships fell from 818 new cases in 2017 to 223 new cases in 2019,[26] and up until January 2020, 608 new support measures were registered.

THE MENTAL HEALTH REFORM

Along with the legal capacity reform, the mental health system in Peru has been undergoing a major transformation over the last five years. Led by the Ministry of Health, the aim is to implement a community mental health model[27] through four pillars: i) the reorganization of mental health services in primary and secondary care; ii) the creation of new community-based mental health services; iii) the expansion of mental health insurance coverage; and iv) the availability of psychiatric medication at the first level of care.[28] The National Plan for the Strengthening of Community Mental Health 2018–2021[29] and other Ministry of Health directives are guiding the scaling-up of the mental health reform across the country.[30]

While the seeds of this process date back more than a decade, to the reports of the Ombudsperson denouncing the situation of mental health in Peru, the turning point was the adoption of Law No. 29889 in 2012.[31] Considered to be landmark legislation,[32] this law amended the General Health Act with the objective of restoring the full exercise of the rights of users of mental health services and people with psychosocial disabilities. Law No. 29889 repealed Law No. 29737, which regulated involuntary hospitalization and treatment, and ordered the Executive Branch to adopt specific measures to transform the mental health system into a community-based healthcare model.[33]

---

actividades de capacitación sobre D.L. 1384. *Poder Judicial del Perú*. www.pj.gob.pe/wps/wcm/connect/ajpvyjc/s_ajpvcyjc/as_noticia/cs_n_sodis-05-02-2019.

[25] Request for public information, Letter No. 021-2020-SUNARP/OGA of January 28, 2020.

[26] The information provided does not disaggregate the data by type of guardianship, so it is impossible to know whether those 223 cases involve persons with disabilities. As the regulations were not adopted until August 2019, guardianship sentences may have continued to be recorded despite the reform.

[27] See World Bank (2018). *Healing Minds, Changing Lives: A Movement for Community-Based Mental Health Care in Peru – Delivery Innovations in a Low-Income Community, 2013–2016*. Global Mental Health Initiative. http://documents.worldbank.org/curated/en/407921523031016762/Healing-minds-changing-lives-a-movement-for-community-based-mental-health-care-in-Peru-delivery-innovations-in-a-low-income-community-2013-2016.

[28] See Toyama, M., Castillo, H., Galea, J., et al. (2017). Peruvian mental health reform: a framework for scaling-up mental health services. *International Journal of Health Policy and Management*, 6(9), 501–508. https://doi.org/10.15171/ijhpm.2017.07

[29] Ministry of Health, Plan Nacional de Fortalecimiento de Servicios de Salud Mental Comunitaria 2017–2021, available at http://bvs.minsa.gob.pe/local/MINSA/4422.pdf

[30] See Orellano, C. &Macavilca, M. (2019). New guidelines on mental health in Peru. *Lancet Psychiatry*, 6(3), 201–202.

[31] Law No. 29889, Law that modifies Article 11 of Law 26842, the General Health Law, and guarantees the rights of people with mental health problems, published June 24, 2012.

[32] Toyama, et al. Peruvian mental Health Reform.

[33] Law No. 29889, First Complementary and Final Provision

These reform efforts were accompanied by new financial resources. In 2014, a results-based budgeting program, entitled "0131: Control and Prevention in Mental Health," established a ten-year financing framework for mental health action, which has allowed a sustained increase in the resources available for mental healthcare reform activities. For example, the national budget for the fiscal year 2020 allocated PEN 350 million (approximately USD 103 million) to mental health, an increase of PEN 70 million from 2019 (USD 20.5 million).[34]

As a result, a network of 151 community mental health centres have been created across the country, and fifty more are expected in 2020.[35] Staffed by interdisciplinary teams, these centres bring service provision out of psychiatric hospitals into the communities; carry out technical assistance, supervision, and training to primary care providers; and coordinate actions with community actors for the promotion of mental health. In addition, sixteen halfway houses were established, managed by the Ministry of Health, to provide temporary residential services to people with psychosocial disabilities with weak family support networks. The 2020 target is to have forty halfway houses in operation.[36] In parallel, the process of reforming and, in some cases, closing specialized psychiatric hospitals has begun in different regions of the country, albeit more slowly.[37]

New Mental Health Act

In 2019, upon the initiative of several parliamentary groups, a new Mental Health Act (MHA), Law No. 30947, was adopted.[38] Replacing Law No. 29889, it regulates the framework for guaranteeing access to services, promotion, prevention, treatment, and rehabilitation in mental health, and establishes a community-based model of mental healthcare.[39] The law proposal had the support of the Ministry of Health and other sectors; however, civil society was not formally consulted.[40] Nevertheless, thanks to their advocacy and engagement with parliamentarians,

---

[34] Andina (November 20, 2019). Minsa: Presupuesto 2020 destina 350 millones de soles para salud mental. https://andina.pe/agencia/noticia-minsa-presupuesto-2020-destina-350-millones-soles-para-salud-mental-775724.aspx

[35] Andina (February 14, 2020). Minsa atendió más de un 1.2 millones de casos de salud mental durante 2019. https://andina.pe/agencia/noticia-minsa-atendio-mas-un-12-millones-casos-salud-mental-durante-2019-785099.aspx

[36] Ibid.

[37] PAHO (December 12, 2015). OPS felicitó al Minsaporcierreemblemático del CREMI en Iquitos. www.paho.org/per/index.php?option=com_content&view=article&id=3183:ops-felicito-al-minsa-por-cierre-emblematico-del-cremi-en-iquitos&Itemid=900.

[38] Law No. 30947, Mental Health Act, published May 24, 2019.

[39] Mental Health Act, article 1.

[40] See Peruvian Congress, Committee on Health and Population, Opinion No. 07-2018-2019/CSP-CR of December 4, 2018. www.leyes.congreso.gob.pe/Documentos/2016_2021/Dictamenes/Proyectos_de_Ley/00138DC21MAY20181204.pdf.

representatives of civil society managed to remove some provisions from the text openly contradicting the progress achieved by the legal capacity reform.[41]

As a result, the MHA neither refers to involuntary hospitalization and treatment, nor seclusion and restraints. Mental health care must be provided on a voluntary basis and, preferably, in a community setting (arts. 8 and 9). Hospitalization is considered an "exceptional therapeutic resource," periodically reviewable, and which can only be considered when it provides greater therapeutic benefits for the individual compared to other possible interventions (art. 27.1). Further, the MHA abolished the involuntary commitment of drug users, which had been previously permitted.[42]

The MHA maintains the rule that informed consent is not necessary in case of "psychiatric emergencies" (art. 20(2)). This is consistent with the General Health Act, Law No. 26842, which exempts medical emergencies from the requirement of informed consent (art. 4).[43] According to Ministry directives, a medical emergency is "any sudden and unexpected condition that requires immediate attention as it imminently endangers life, health or that may leave disabling consequences for the patient."[44] To distinguish it from "hospitalization," which always requires informed consent, the MHA labels as "internment" the proceeding by which a person is admitted to a health facility in a psychiatric emergency for up to twelve hours, renewable to a maximum of seventy-two hours.[45]

Civil society has expressed various concerns with the MHA. Despite its community-based discourse, it is argued that the law maintains a biomedical approach to mental health, giving priority to the administration of medication and failing to address the social determinants of health.[46] In addition, although the law avoids making reference to involuntary hospitalization and treatment, people can be "interned" during psychiatric emergencies without their consent.[47] Similarly, those detained or imprisoned within criminal proceedings can be hospitalized by court order.[48] Furthermore, the MHA does not include any mechanism for

[41] See, for example, the differences between the version of the Opinion No. 07-2018-2019/CSP-CR and the final text adopted.
[42] Law No. 29889, which amended article 11 of the General Health Act, permitted the involuntary hospitalization and treatment of "persons with addictions."
[43] Tina Minkowitz and other legal experts from the survivor community have argued that the concept of "emergency" needs to be reconsidered in the mental health context and reframed as psychosocial crisis. See Minkowitz, T. (October 19, 2018). Peruvian legal capacity reform – celebration and analysis, *Mad in America*. www.madinamerica.com/2018/10/peruvian-legal-capacity-reform-celebration-and-analysis/
[44] Supreme Decree No. 016-2002-SA, article 3(5).
[45] The MHA regulations establish that an internment order last twelve hours but could be renovated up to seventy-two hours. Supreme Decree No. 007-2020-SA, article 27(7).
[46] Smith, P. (July 3, 2019). La nueva ley de salud mental: ¿Un cambio de paradigma? *IUS360*. https://ius360.com/sin-categoria/la-nueva-ley-de-salud-mental-un-cambio-de-paradigma/
[47] General Health Act, article 11(e), amended by the Mental Health Act.
[48] Mental Health Act, article 29.

supported decision-making nor does it make any reference to the new framework established by Legislative Decree No. 1384.

BRIDGING TWO FRAMEWORKS

The CRPD recognizes that all persons with disabilities, including those with psychosocial disabilities, enjoy all human rights and fundamental freedoms on an equal basis with others.[49] Its article 12 states that persons with disabilities enjoy legal capacity on an equal basis with others in all aspects of life. Article 14 prohibits the unlawful or arbitrary deprivation of liberty of persons with disabilities and states that the existence of a disability cannot justify a deprivation of liberty. Article 25 highlights the obligation of States to provide healthcare on the basis of free and informed consent.

Based on these standards, the CRPD Committee has systematically raised the obligation to end all forms of coercion in mental health services. In particular, the CRPD Committee's jurisprudence on article 14 calls for the absolute prohibition of detention based on disability, including through mental health legislation that authorizes involuntary commitment based on risk to self or others.[50] Other UN agencies, global and regional human rights mechanisms have echoed this position by developing standards and guidelines for its implementation.[51] Advance planning, supported decision-making, and the best interpretation of will and preferences have been proposed as possible ways to deal with crisis situations.[52]

The Peruvian Constitutional Court has recently commented on this matter.[53] In an appeal on a case involving an individual with disabilities deprived of their liberty at home, the court concluded that while deprivation of liberty "solely" based on disability is prohibited, international human rights law does not

---

[49] CRPD, article 1.
[50] See CRPD Committee, Guidelines on article 14 of the CRPD: the right to liberty and security of persons with disabilities, A/72/55, 2015.
[51] OHCHR, A/HRC/10/48, A/HRC/34/32, A/HRC/36/28, and A/HRC/39/36; WHO, QualityRights guidance and training tools, available at www.who.int/mental_health/policy/quality_rights/en; Working Group on Arbitrary Detention, UN Basic Principles and Guidelines on Remedies and Procedures on the Right of Anyone Deprived of Their Liberty to Bring Proceedings Before a Court, 2015; Devandas, C., Special Rapporteur on the rights of persons with disabilities (2019). Deprivation of liberty of persons with disabilities, A/HRC/40/54; Puras, D., Special Rapporteur on the right of everyone to the enjoyment of the highest attainable standard of physical and mental health (2017). The right to mental health, A/HRC/35/21; Parliamentary Assembly of the Council of Europe (2019), Resolution 2291 & Recommendation 2158 (2019); Commissioner for Human Rights of Council of Europe (June 26, 2019). It is time to end coercion in mental health. www.coe.int/en/web/commissioner/-/it-is-time-to-end-coercion-in-mental-health
[52] See Devandas, C., Special Rapporteur on the rights of persons with disabilities (2019). Deprivation of liberty of persons with disabilities, A/HRC/40/54; Zinkler, M. & von Peter, S. (2019). End coercion in mental health services – toward a system based on support only. *Laws*, 8(3), 19. https://doi.org/10.3390/laws8030019; Minkowitz, T. (2017). CRPD and transformative equality, *International Journal of Law in Context*, 13(1), 77–86.
[53] Constitutional Court, Case 00194-2014-HC, April 30, 2019.

prohibit the exceptional deprivation of liberty of a person in order to guarantee their safety or that of others, as long as adequate procedural and substantive guarantees are established. While this interpretation does not follow the absolute prohibition position of the CRPD Committee, it is significant that the Constitutional Court acknowledged that such an exceptional scenario is "in clear decline," stressing that the State must undertake a process to achieve its "absolute disappearance" through the concrete and effective implementation of a community mental health care model.

Together the legal capacity and the mental health reforms in Peru carry the potential to end mental health coercion. By recognising that persons with disabilities enjoy full legal capacity on an equal basis with others in all aspects of life, the Peruvian legal capacity reform challenged legislation and practices restricting personal decision-making on account of a psychiatric diagnosis or subjective distress, including decisions about medical treatment. The flexibility of the support measures introduced in the Civil Code also opened up the possibility for their implementation in the context of mental health provision. However, Legislative Decree No. 1384 did not define to what extent the legal capacity reform applies in the field of mental health, nor did the Mental Health Act include measures related to legal capacity.

The need to bridge these two frameworks was finally addressed by the regulations of the MHA adopted in March 2020. Drawing heavily on the contributions of civil society, the new regulations include a series of provisions that recognise the legal capacity of service users and the role of supported decision-making in the context of the mental health provision. Furthermore, these regulations significantly reframe the case of "internment" for a psychiatric emergency, bringing the Peruvian system closer to the standards established by the CRPD Committee.

Informed Consent

While the MHA recognizes the right to informed consent prior to treatment and hospitalization, the new regulations acknowledge that, for people with disabilities to express their informed consent, it is necessary to ensure "real and effective access to information" (art. (3(1)(12)). For this purpose, they consider the provision of accessibility measures and reasonable accommodation, including the participation of informal supporters ("trusted persons").

The MHA regulations further clarify informed consent for the administration of psychotropic drugs (art. 17(4)). Accordingly, medical professionals now have an obligation to inform users of the possible risks and adverse effects associated with medication in the short, medium, and long term; and users have a right to be supported in discontinuing psychiatric medication.

Advance Planning and Supported Decision-Making

The MHA regulations mandate the development of advance planning mechanisms. Expressly referring to the legal capacity reform, the Supreme Decree adopting the MHA regulations orders the Ministry of Health to develop protocols and measures aimed at providing mental health service users access to advance planning tools for mental healthcare decisions (Fourth Final Supplementary Provision).

Moreover, the MHA regulations recognize supported decision-making in mental health services. Mental health service users have the right to have one or more persons for decision-making support at any time, assisting them to "evaluate and weigh the therapeutic alternatives for their personalized and autonomous recovery" (art. 17(11)).

Prohibition of Coercive Measures

While the MHA does not refer to coercive measures, its regulations expressly prohibit measures that "violate the rights of persons such as isolation, the application of psychotropic drugs or electroconvulsive therapy without informed consent, as well as procedures that affect the dignity of persons, even if in the community" (art. 17(6)). Additionally, the regulations order psychiatric and general hospitals to eradicate "isolation rooms, electroconvulsive therapy or pharmacological interventions without informed consent," among other "practices that violate the human rights of mental health service users" (art. 20(2)).

The MHA regulations further establish that hospitalization environments must not contain security mechanisms that violate the rights of mental health service users, "including the right to free transit, privacy and all those considered in the CRPD" (art. 27(14)). The regulations prohibit the existence of rooms and wards locked by a key or closed with bars (art. 27(14)). Despite these provisions, it is worth noting that there is a stark absence of references to restraints.

Respecting Will and Preferences in Psychiatric Emergencies

While the MHA permits "internment" without informed consent in psychiatric emergencies, the regulations significantly reframe the context for their application. First, the definition of "psychiatric emergency" follows the general understanding of medical emergency: "any sudden and unexpected condition, associated with a mental health problem, that requires immediate attention as it imminently endangers life, health or that can leave disabling consequences for the user."[54] This definition leaves out the notion of "danger to others," reversing previous regulations,[55] making it no longer

---

[54] Supreme Decree No. 007-2020-SA, article 3(1)(5).
[55] Article 3(5) of the Supreme Decree No. 033-2015-SA defined "psychiatric emergency" as a "mental alteration which puts the integrity of the patient at risk and/or third parties, determined by the evaluating doctor".

permissible to intern someone deemed to pose a "risk to others." An individual who has actually committed an offence should have the opportunity to access justice on an equal basis with others and be provided with procedural accommodations and support.[56]

Second, psychiatric emergencies must be handled by the staff of health facilities "without stigmatization or discrimination, and within the framework of the community mental healthcare model, based on human rights and the recovery approach" (art. 21(1)). Third, the regulations call for interdisciplinary responses, including emotional support and strategies to reverse conflict escalation (art. 21(3)).

Significantly, the regulations acknowledge that people may be in position to consent to or refuse treatment during psychiatric emergencies, as in any medical emergency. Therefore, they provide for the implementation of "real, considerable and relevant efforts to obtain the manifestation of the will of the person, including the provision of decision-making support" (art. 26(4)). Only if an individual is unable to express their consent by all means, a previously designated supporter or a supporter appointed by a judge can authorize the internment. The appointment of the supporter must be carried out in accordance with Legislative Decree No. 1384 and its regulations (art. 26(4)), hence it should be based on the best interpretation of the will and preferences of the individual. As such, the regulations significantly shift the traditional approach of the MHA toward the support paradigm of the CRPD. However, concerns remain on the practical implementation of this innovative solution, given the significant delays in the administration of justice.[57]

Deinstitutionalization

Finally, the MHA regulations order all mental health facilities to initiate the process of deinstitutionalization of long-term hospitalized patients, "guaranteeing the exercise of their autonomy, independent living, and respecting their personal dignity and human rights" (arts. 31). Mental health facilities must create standing committees with the participation of service user organizations (art. 32). Discharged patients are expected to return home or benefit from the new halfway houses.

CONCLUSIONS

The CRPD and CRPD Committee's jurisprudence have been received with incredulity and contempt from part of the psychiatric community.[58] The CRPD has undoubtedly made it possible to problematize normalized medical practice,

---

[56] Devandas, C., Special Rapporteur on the rights of persons with disabilities (2019). Deprivation of liberty of persons with disabilities, A/HRC/40/54, para. 14.

[57] Gaceta Jurídica (2015). Informe la Justicia en el Perú. Cinco grandes problemas. 34. www.gacetajuridica.com.pe/laley-adjuntos/INFORME-LA-JUSTICIA-EN-EL-PERU.pdf

[58] Appelbaum, P. S. (2019). Saving the UN Convention on the Rights of Persons with Disabilities – from itself. *World Psychiatry*, 18(1), 1–2. https://doi.org/10.1002/wps.20583; Freeman, M. C., Kolappa, K., de Almeida, J. M., et al. (2015). Reversing hard won victories in the name of human rights: a critique of

such as involuntary hospitalization, forced medication, isolation, and restraints. There are an increasing number of agencies and experts calling to prevent and end all forms of coercion in mental health services, which is consistent with rising evidence showing that community-based crisis services can deliver the desired outcomes in assisting people during crisis situations.[59] Moreover, contrary to initial skepticism, many countries are carrying out important efforts to end guardianship and other forms of substitute decision-making,[60] and – as this chapter demonstrates – some have taken significant steps to end coercive practices in mental health.

The reforms on legal capacity and mental health discussed in this chapter reflect a clear adherence by Peru to the standards of the CRPD and the interpretation advanced by the CRPD Committee.[61] This commitment was reaffirmed in the course of the COVID-19 crisis in which the Ministry of Health recommended to "increase efforts to deinstitutionalize persons with severe mental disorders and/or psychosocial disabilities."[62] Furthermore, responding to civil society demands, it called on services to stop all coercive measures, stressing that "no one shall be forced to remain hospitalised against their will, where they are at increased risk of infection and more severe symptoms."[63]

Against this background, the Peruvian process is promising. It aims to recognize the equal rights of service users, including persons with psychosocial and intellectual disabilities; to guarantee informed consent and facilitate supported decision-making in mental healthcare; to promote the shift to a human rights and recovery-based approach; and to provide community-based services. By attaining the legal capacity and mental health reforms, Peru has a unique opportunity to end all forms of coercion in mental health services. However, this requires determined action by the Ministry of Health to translate these national standards into practice, including by engaging in awareness raising, training, monitoring,[64] and providing more

the General Comment on Article 12 of the UN Convention on the Rights of Persons with Disabilities. *Lancet Psychiatry*, 2(9), 844–850.

[59] Gooding, P., McSherry, B., Roper, C. et al. (2018). *Alternatives to Coercion in Mental Health Settings: A Literature Review*. University of Melbourne. https://socialequity.unimelb.edu.au/news/latest/alternatives-to-coercion

[60] Apart from Peru, Costa Rica and Colombia have eradicated guardianship from their legal frameworks. See Devandas, C., Special Rapporteur on the rights of persons with disabilities (2017). Legal capacity and supported decision-making, A/HRC/37/56.

[61] In 2012, the CRPD Committee recommended Peru amend the Civil Code to abolish guardianship and replace regimes of substitute decision-making by supported decision-making. See CRPD Committee (May 16, 2012). Concluding observations on the initial report of Peru, CRPD/C/PER/CO/1. Paras. 24–27.

[62] Ministry of Health of Peru (April 20, 2020). Ministerial Resolution No. 186-2020-MINSA, GuíaTécnica para el cuidado de la Salud Mental en el contexto del COVID-19. www.gob.pe/institucion/minsa/normas-legales/473416-186-2020-minsa

[63] Ibid.

[64] There is a need for better data about coercive practices in mental health facilities. In 2018, the Office of the Ombudsperson was only able to identify eighty-three people involuntarily hospitalized across the country. See, Office of the Ombudsperson (2018), Report No. 180. www.defensoria.gob.pe/categorias_informes/informe-defensorial/

technical and practical guidance to mental health providers. In this regard, the government should seriously consider the implementation of the WHO QualityRights initiative.[65]

The reforms achieved in Peru illustrate the transformative nature of the CRPD, revealing its call to challenge longstanding norms which have resulted in long-lived exclusion. While it is undeniable that these reforms have made waves to the entrenched status quo, time will tell whether they were successful in turning the tide.

---

[65] Funk, M. & Drew, N. (2017). WHO QualityRights: transforming mental health services. *Lancet Psychiatry*, 4(11), 826–827.

Conflict of interest declaration: as President of the Peruvian NGO Society and Disability (SODIS), Alberto Vásquez participated in the Peruvian Congress' Special Committee for the reform of the Civil Code (CEDIS), and was actively involved in the drafting and advocacy related to the legal capacity reform.

9

Advancing Disability Equality Through Supported Decision-Making: The CRPD and the Canadian Constitution

*Faisal Bhabha**

Abstract

Canada is known around the world for being a leader in disability rights and a champion of the Convention on the Rights of Persons with Disabilities (CRPD). Notwithstanding this reputation, Canada has failed to fully embrace Article 12, the right to equal protection under the law. Canada has given only a qualified endorsement of supported decision-making, which empowers individuals with mental disabilities to exercise the right to legal capacity by making and communicating decisions for themselves. Canadian law preserves substitute decision-making regimes, which can arbitrarily strip persons with mental disabilities of their decision-making authority. This chapter looks at Canadian federalism (division of powers) as an obstacle to Canada's effort to implement its international human rights obligations. Taking a fresh approach, the author argues that the federal government could be constitutionally permitted to legislatively redesign legal capacity in a way that enhances the dignity and autonomy interests of people with mental disabilities by ensuring comprehensive Article 12 compliance. This, it is argued, can be done with constitutional authority never before acknowledged but demonstrably defensible on the basis of promoting the full and equal inclusion of persons with mental disabilities in Canadian society as a matter of national concern.

I INTRODUCTION

Although Canada has ratified the United Nations Convention on the Rights of Persons with Disabilities ([CRPD], 2006) and its Optional Protocol, Canadian law fails to guarantee people with mental disabilities (including intellectual, cognitive and psychosocial disabilities) the right to exercise legal capacity without discrimination on the basis of disability. Notwithstanding the fact that the Supreme Court of Canada has been viewed as a world leader in developing the constitutional right to equality (Groppi, 2007 at 347, 351) and the fact that Canadian disability activists were

---

* The author is indebted to Lauren D'Angelo and Faraz Kourangi for their invaluable research assistance. He thanks Brendon Pooran, Michael Bach, Lana Kerzner, Ruby Dhand, Kerri Joffe and Sarah Mason-Case for helpful conversations. Any errors are the author's alone.

instrumental in ensuring the inclusion of robust disability rights in the CRPD (see, e.g., Council of Canadians with Disabilities, 2012), Canadian domestic law remains non-compliant with the Article 12 duty to take "appropriate measures" to ensure access to supports for persons with disabilities to exercise their legal capacity. The main obstacle to implementing Article 12 is the inconsistent recognition of "supported decision-making" in provincial, territorial and federal legislation.[1] This reality persists notwithstanding the fact that both Article 12 of the CRPD and section 15 of the Canadian Charter of Rights and Freedoms ([Charter], 1982) guarantee equality for persons with physical and mental disabilities.

The number of people with mental disabilities is increasing in Canada, at least in part due to the country's ageing population (Public Health Agency of Canada, 2014). Evidence suggests that by 2031 there will be nearly one million Canadians experiencing cognitive decline as a result of dementia (Alzheimer Society of Canada, 2016). Supported decision-making preserves the individual's ability to exercise legal capacity by broadening the scope for how a person is understood to exercise personal decision-making. It legally recognises different modes of communication and decision-making in a way which carefully advances individual autonomy, freedom and dignity. For these reasons, disability advocates view supported decision-making as the best alternative to legal guardianship regimes.

Provincial and federal legislatures have failed to ensure that supported decision-making is consistently provided or permitted as an option for exercising legal capacity in Canada. The legal recognition of supported decision-making varies from province to province. This grounds the argument that the federal government has failed to set a national standard or direction on how this international human right is to be enforced across the country (Bach & Kerzner, 2010 at 18–20). Numerous federal laws do not include a definition of "capacity" for the purposes of exercising statutory rights, instead referring to the provincial laws in effect. As a result, in some provinces, people with mental disabilities are effectively barred from exercising legal capacity under federal laws, creating significant obstacles to their accessing benefits and entitlements on account of their disability. Such individuals have no access to a legal remedy and there is no clear pathway to compel a constitutional fix.[2]

As an international treaty, the CRPD is not domestically enforceable in Canada until it has been incorporated into legislation. At first glance, the role and power to amend relevant mental health laws to provide for supported decision-making appear to fall primarily within provincial constitutional jurisdiction. While the federal government's spending power has given it authority to influence social policy, the design and delivery of social policy has been assumed to be strictly within the provincial domain, though some scholars have challenged this assumption (Choudhry, 2002, at 164). The challenge comes

---

[1] Alberta, British Columbia, Manitoba and the Yukon are the only jurisdictions that specifically recognise in their legislation supporters or representatives to assist a person in decision-making.
[2] In the absence of clear government action or under-inclusive legislation, it is difficult to establish a case that a Charter right was breached.

down to priorities and coordination: provincial governments may not have sufficient interest in law reform to implement international law; and the desire to maintain federal-provincial balance may chill the federal will to lead a law reform initiative in the face of the risk of a vires challenge by one or more of the provinces.

Despite challenges, there remains a plausible if not compelling argument that in light of the Charter's guarantee of equality and non-discrimination for persons with a mental disability, there must be a way of interpreting Canadian federalism in a way that does not prevent a federal government from aligning Canadian constitutional rights and freedoms with international human rights. This chapter confronts this unique constitutional obstacle and argues that federalism, though a hurdle, is not insurmountable. It posits that the modern approach to the division of powers under the Constitution of Canada readily supports positive federal legislative action to implement Article 12 of the CRPD, even though such action may affect provincial legislative powers. This chapter begins by highlighting the need for supportive decision-making as a matter of protecting equality; it then outlines a constitutional approach the Parliament of Canada could adopt to navigate the division of powers.

II LEGAL CAPACITY AND SUPPORTED DECISION-MAKING

Legal capacity refers to a person's recognised authority under the law to make specific decisions, such as the decision to own property, to consent to medical treatment, to enter into a contract, to open a bank account, to get married and so on. Legal capacity is commonly equated with mental capacity, which requires that a person have: (1) the ability to understand the information relevant to making a particular decision; and (2) the ability to appreciate the reasonably foreseeable consequences of the decision or lack of decision (see e.g. Substitute Decisions Act [SDA], 1999 at §§6, 45).

The test for whether one possesses legal capacity depends on the nature of the decision at hand; the time at which the decision is sought to be made; and the laws of the governing jurisdiction. Both the common law and provincial statutes recognise that a person may be incapable with respect to some decisions while capable with respect to others. Each province in Canada has established its own laws pertaining to legal capacity, and these laws are all slightly different from one another. As a result, a person may be considered to have the legal capacity to make certain decisions in some provinces but not in others. Only some provinces recognise the exercise of legal capacity through supported decision-making.

Canadian disability groups insisted on including Article 12 in the CRPD to ensure the development of alternatives to guardianship laws (Bach & Kerzner, 2010 at 33–34). Under Canadian law, persons under guardianship are stripped of their right to make decisions (Salami & Lashewicz, 2015 at 91–113). Yielding decision-making authority over one's own life, even "voluntarily," can have a profound impact on one's sense of identity, self-worth and independence. The power of decision is an essential aspect of having control over one's life. Even where the decision being made is not necessarily the correct decision, or the best among possible options, there may still be value in being free to make "bad" decisions. Indeed, there is freedom in directing one's life and there is value in having the opportunity to learn from experience.

There is also value in mitigating the potential harmful effects of making decisions entirely on one's own. Supported decision-making refers to the arrangement where an adult who may not otherwise be found "capable" of making decisions is assisted by a trusted person or network of persons (typically family and friends) to make decisions without having to give up decision-making authority (Bach & Kerzner, 2010). The trusted person – often referred to as the "supporter" or "representative" – helps the adult to understand and appreciate the information and consequences relevant to a decision, and to communicate his or her choice in light of that understanding and appreciation.

Supported decision-making emanates from the same social theory of disability that casts away paternalism in favour of individual rights and empowerment for persons with disabilities (Kaiser, 2009 at 143–155). The CRPD embraces the social theory of disability. It seeks to end guardianship and ensure the availability of supported decision-making.[3] Where permitted by law, supported decision-making arrangements can be formalised in written agreements, similar to powers of attorney. The agreement signifies to others that the person presenting the agreement is able to exercise legal capacity with the assistance of the supporter(s). An example is found in the province of Alberta's Adult Guardianship and Trusteeship Act ([AGTA], 2008), which allows for the execution of "supported decision-making authorizations" (art. 12(1), (2)).

The purpose of supported decision-making is to protect legal personhood. It does so by providing a mechanism to provide supports for making and/or communicating one's will and preferences. Supports allow people with mental disabilities to make, direct and act on their personal decisions through alternative means, such as interpreter assistance or facilitated communication (Bach & Kerzner, 2010 at 73–74, 77–78). Similar to how a ramp for a mobility device can remove physical accessibility barriers for people with physical disabilities, supported decision-making can remove cognitive and communication barriers for people with mental disabilities.

Where a legal regime does not recognise supported decision-making, individuals can be subjected to the stigmatising process of a capacity assessment, potentially being labelled as "legally incapable," and left with no option but to surrender decision-making authority to a substitute. By enabling the right to exercise legal

---

[3] Thus far, guardianship regimes remain intact in most countries. Notably, in September 2018, Peru adopted Legislative Decree No. 1384, which grants full legal capacity to all persons with disabilities, abolishes guardianship in almost all instances and introduces a framework for supported decision-making.

capacity to the greatest extent possible, supported decision-making can enhance the dignity and autonomy of individuals with mental disabilities.

III CRPD AND THE CANADIAN CONSTITUTION

In 2006, the United Nations General Assembly adopted the CRPD, the world's latest UN human rights convention. The CRPD requires states to take necessary action to advance disability human rights, including legislative action, to implement the rights recognised in the treaty and to modify or eliminate discriminatory laws, regulations, customs and practices (art. 4(1a), (1b)). Under Article 12, states are required to ensure equality in decision-making by providing supports, where appropriate, to enable the exercise of legal capacity.

Canada ratified the CRPD in March 2010, but issued the following Declaration and Reservation:

> Canada recognises that persons with disabilities are presumed to have legal capacity on an equal basis with others in all aspects of their lives. Canada declares its understanding that Article 12 permits supported and substitute decision-making arrangements in appropriate circumstances and in accordance with the law. *To the extent Article 12 may be interpreted as requiring the elimination of all substitute decision-making arrangements, Canada reserves the right to continue their use in appropriate circumstances and subject to appropriate and effective safeguards.*[4]

Despite Canada's refusal to abolish guardianship entirely, the affirmation of equality in legal capacity and the endorsement of supported decision-making led Canadian disability rights defenders, including the Canadian Association for Community Living and the Council of Canadians with Disabilities, to celebrate the ratification of the Convention (Kaiser, 2009 at 161–162). The CRPD specifically addresses the challenge of federalism: "The provisions of the present Convention shall extend to all parts of federal States without any limitations or exceptions" (art. 4(5)). This means that both federal and provincial governments are bound by the CRPD notwithstanding that the federal executive has the constitutional authority to negotiate, sign and ratify international treaties. Even in the absence of positive incorporation, the treaty remains legally binding, if not enforceable. The Vienna Convention on the Law of Treaties (1969) provides that: "Every treaty in force is binding upon the parties to it and must be performed by them in good faith" (art. 26). As a signatory to the CRPD, Canada is under a legal obligation to fulfil its obligations in good faith.

Since the Charter came into effect, the relationship between Canada's international human rights obligations and its domestic constitutional law has not been well developed. Text that is "not law" in the eyes of Canadian courts cannot ground a court-ordered remedy, even if what is sought is reasonable and necessary according

---

[4] *Status of Ratification*, United Nations Office of the High Commissioner for Human Rights, online: https://indicators.ohchr.org/ [emphasis added].

to an international human rights convention that Canada has signed and ratified. While unincorporated treaties are not cognisable as "law," they do have some interpretive influence. The Supreme Court has stated that international law may help inform the statutory interpretation of domestic law and, insofar as possible, interpretations that reflect the values and principles contained in international instruments should be preferred (Baker, 1999 at paras. 70–71).

In the absence of domestic implementation, and notwithstanding the role for international law in statutory interpretation, Canadian courts have not made much use of the CRPD. Courts and tribunals have been inconsistent, at best, in determining a role for the CRPD in legal interpretation. For example, in *Cole v. Cole (Litigation Guardian of)* (2011), the Ontario Superior Court of Justice preferred federal legislation (the Divorce Act) over the CRPD in an instance of clear conflict. Similarly, in *S. (B.) Re* (2011), the Ontario Consent and Capacity Board expressed uncertainty about the application of the CRPD in the absence of its incorporation into Canadian law. In *Nova Scotia (Minister of Community Services) v. Z. (C.K.)* (2016), the Nova Scotia Court of Appeal noted the lack of guidance regarding the effect of the CRPD on child protection legislation. Without legislation incorporating CRPD obligations into domestic law, Canadian courts will not view themselves as competent to treat the CRPD as justiciable or enforceable. The result will be disappointing for Canadian disability rights advocates, who no doubt hoped their efforts to secure the adoption of the CRPD would have translated into enforceable action and meaningful change.

IV INCONSISTENT LEGAL RECOGNITION OF SUPPORTED DECISION-MAKING

In Canada, at both provincial and federal levels, supported decision-making is not consistently available as an option for exercising legal capacity. It is possible to make decisions using supported decision-making under some provincial and federal statutes but not others. The availability of support arrangements depends on the specific wording in the particular statute. For example, under Ontario's Substitute Decisions Act, the court may not appoint a guardian for property for a person if it is satisfied that "the need for decisions to be made will be met by an alternative course of action that, (a) does not require the court to find the person to be incapable of managing property; and (b) is less restrictive of the person's decision-making rights than the appointment of a guardian" (§22(3)). While this provision does not appear to be at odds with the use of supported decision-making, it nevertheless fails to mandate, guide or facilitate supported decision-making in circumstances where it could be effectively used to exercise legal capacity. In the absence of mandated availability, it remains likely that it will be under-utilised even where it could operate as a better alternative to guardianship.

In some Canadian jurisdictions, the law explicitly provides for supported decision-making. Alberta's AGTA allows adults to make "supported decision-making authorisations" to enable "supporters" to assist them with decision-making in respect of "personal matters" (§4). Under British Columbia's Representation Agreement Act ([RAA], 1996) an adult can make a "representation agreement" to authorise a representative to help make decisions about the adult's personal care, routine management of adult's financial affairs, major and minor health care concerns, obtaining legal services and instructing legal counsel (§7). Furthermore, the RAA promotes the use of representation agreements by limiting the liability of representatives for injury to or death of the adult or for loss or damage arising from the routine management of the adult's financial affairs, insofar as representatives comply with their statutory duties (§23).

As with provincial guardianship schemes, inconsistencies in the legal recognition of supported decision-making can also be found at the federal level. For example, the Criminal Code (1985) contains special provisions dealing with physician-assisted death. If a person has difficulty communicating, a medical practitioner or nurse practitioner must "take all necessary measures to provide a reliable means by which the person may understand the information that is provided to them and communicate their decision" (§241.2(3)(i)). While this provision has not yet been interpreted judicially, it does not on its face prohibit access to supported decision-making in end-of-life decisions. The language of "all necessary measures" creates the widest possible discretion to allow for individual tailoring in communications and decision-making.

Unlike the Criminal Code provisions, other federal laws defer to the old rules applying to legal capacity contained in provincial laws. Indeed, numerous federal laws deny benefits to, or impose burdens on, individuals who are deemed to not meet existing standards of legal capacity set by provincial legislation. In such cases, individuals are compelled either to relinquish personal decision-making authority to a substitute decision maker, or to forego altogether statutory entitlements or opportunities that are available to others who meet the test for legal capacity. Regardless of whether such individuals are in fact capable of making decisions with supports, most existing legal capacity regimes do not offer an alternative option for people who cannot meet the capacity test.

For example, in order to personally enter into a Registered Disability Savings Plan (RDSP) or to regain control over an RDSP opened on one's behalf under the Income Tax Act ([ITA], 1985), an individual must be the age of majority and have "contractual competence to enter into a disability savings plan," as determined under the laws of a province or in the opinion of an RDSP issuer after "reasonable inquiry" (ITA, 1985 at §146.4). "Reasonable inquiry" is not a defined term in the ITA and offers no assurance that the issuer will consider the use of supports when assessing an individual's capacity. What is needed is explicit language requiring a "reasonable inquiry" to examine the feasibility of supported decision-making to satisfy the capacity requirement. Without the explicit recognition of supported decision-making under the ITA, or under provincial law, the ITA effectively signals to issuers to refuse to provide RDSPs to individuals who do not meet the traditional definition of "capable". This exclusion of supported decision-making from the equation for establishing legal capacity to enter into an RDSP is precisely the kind of discrimination that Article 12 is designed to prevent.

The problem of exclusion from supported decision-making is not consistent across the country. Each jurisdiction determines its own laws. A person with a disability may have the right to enter into an RDSP through supported decision-making in one province, but be denied this right in another province, instead having to submit to legal guardianship to achieve the same result. The federal government has described this problem in the following terms:

> In many provinces and territories, the only way that an RDSP can be opened... is for the individual to be declared legally incompetent by a court or tribunal and have someone named as their legal guardian – a process that can involve a considerable amount of time and expense and may have significant repercussions for the individual (RDSP, 2018).

A similar result flows from the operation of a variety of other federal statutes and regulations, which are contingent on the individual having traditional "capacity," with no provision for supported decision-making. For example, the Canada Pension Plan Regulations provide that a person must be "capable of managing the person's own affairs" in order to personally apply for a benefit, for a division of unadjusted pensionable earnings, or for an assignment of a portion of a retirement pension (§44(1)), or to personally receive benefits (§55(1)). The Immigration and Refugee Protection Act (2001) and the Regulations thereunder provide that, in order to pay for certain deposits or to post certain guarantees, a person must have the "capacity to contract in the province where the deposit is paid or the guarantee is posted" (Immigration and Refugee Protections Regulations, 2002 at §47(1)). Finally, under the Bank Act (1991) and numerous other federal corporate statutes,[5] if a person is deemed to be "without capacity to act by reason of... incompetence," the person's "fiduciary" becomes the "appropriate person" and takes over some of the person's decision-making authority, such as the ability to endorse securities (Bank Act, 1991 at §110(1)(d)).

The legal capacity required to make decisions under these and other federal laws is determined with reference to provincial substitute decision-making regimes, which do not uniformly recognise that legal capacity may be exercised through supported decision-making. By denying the right to use supports in decision-making,

---

[5] See e.g. Canada Business Corporations Act, R.S.C. 1985, c. C-44 (Can.); Canada Not-for-profit Corporations Act, S.C. 2009, c. 23 (Can.); Insurance Companies Act, S.C. 1991, c. 47 (Can.); Trust and Loan Companies Act, S.C. 1991, c. 45 (Can.); Cooperative Credit Associations Act, S.C. 1991, c. 48 (Can.).

the impugned laws prevent people with mental disabilities in some provinces from enjoying legal capacity on an equal basis with their fellow citizens in other provinces. It effectively produces a form of second-class citizenship for some people with mental disabilities, depending on where in the country they reside.

VI CONSTITUTIONAL GROUNDS FOR FEDERAL LEGISLATIVE ACTION

Historically, legal capacity was viewed as a private law matter which fell under a provincial head of power. Over the years, both levels of government have enacted legislation addressing the legal capacity required for various kinds of decisions. For example, provincial governments have passed laws addressing the legal capacity to appoint powers of attorney for the management of property and personal care,[6] and to consent to medical treatment,[7] pursuant to their jurisdiction over "property and civil rights in the province" and "generally all matters of a merely local or private nature in the province" (Constitution Act, 1867 at §92(16)). In contrast, the federal government has legislated the legal capacity to consent to medical assistance in dying (Criminal Code, 1985 at §241.2(3)(i)), to consent to sexual activity (Criminal Code, 1985 at §150.1), and to testify in criminal and civil proceedings under federal jurisdiction (Canada Evidence Act, 1985 at §16), pursuant to its criminal law jurisdiction (Constitution Act, 1867 at §91(27)). The federal government has also adopted legislation dealing with the legal capacity to enter into a marriage contract (Civil Marriage Act, 2005 at §§2.1–2.3), pursuant to its power over "marriage and divorce" (Constitution Act, 1867 at §91(26)).

Section 91 of the Constitution Act, 1867 creates a residual power reserved for Parliament to "make laws for the peace, order and good government of Canada in relation to all matters not coming within the classes of subjects by this Act assigned exclusively to legislatures of the provinces". The Supreme Court of Canada has characterized the "peace, order and good government" (POGG) power as having three branches: (1) national emergencies; (2) filling gaps in the Constitution; and (3) areas of national concern. No court has yet ruled that implementation of international human rights treaties meets the criteria of being an "area of national concern," but there is no reason to assume that argument could never succeed. In recent times, the courts have interpreted POGG expansively in ways never imagined by the drafters of the Constitution Act, 1867. For example, in 1992, the Court categorised environmental protection as a matter of national concern (Friends of the Oldman River Society v. Canada (Minister of Transport), 1992).

Legal capacity is no longer strictly a matter of private law with limited national interest. Disability human rights have become both a national and global priority over the last 40 years, culminating in the adoption of the CRPD. During that same

---

[6] See e.g. SDA (1999, Can. Ont.); Power of Attorney Act, R.S.B.C. 1996, c. 370 (Can. B.C.).
[7] See e.g. Health Care Consent Act, 1996, S.O. 1996, c. 2, Sched. A (Can. Ont.); Health Care (Consent) and Care Facility (Admission) Act, R.S.B.C. 1996, c. 181 (Can. B.C.).

time period, Canada patriated its Constitution with an entrenched bill of rights which includes a strong disability equality right. The priorities of the CRPD and the Charter align. The issue of legal capacity now implicates core constitutional values: those of liberty, equality, freedom, autonomy and dignity. It makes sense to develop a uniform, national approach to legal capacity which recognises supported decision-making. While this would ideally be accomplished through political negotiation and cooperation between the federal and provincial governments, in the absence of a collective will or coordinated action, there may be a way for the federal government to lead the implementation of Article 12 with legislation ensuring the availability of supported decision-making where a province or territory fails to do so. This is the national benchmark/provincial backstop approach to statutory design. Climate action offers one example of flexing the bounds of Canadian federalism to enable federal leadership to meet pressing needs and global standards.

The signing of the Paris Agreement in December 2015 brought hope that greenhouse gas emissions would be reduced through collective global action.[8] Although the Agreement does not prescribe methods, the use of a carbon tax is widely viewed as an effective means of reducing emissions and slowing environmental degradation. In April 2019, Canada's Greenhouse Gas Pollution Pricing Act (GHGPPA) went into force.[9] It established minimum national standards for greenhouse gas pricing in order to meet the Paris Agreement emission reduction targets. Under the law, provincial and territorial governments may implement their own carbon pricing legislation to meet the global target within the particular needs and requirements of the jurisdiction. However, where a province or territory fails to adopt an appropriate carbon pricing system, the federal government will implement its own carbon tax and levy a fee on the province or territory. Revenues generated from the operation of the Act are redistributed to the provinces in the form of tax credits to offset individual and business losses caused by the higher consumer prices.

Four provinces challenged the constitutionality of the GHGPPA. Relying on the division of powers as established in the Canadian Constitution, objecting provinces argued that the Act oversteps the federal government's power to legislate in areas of provincial jurisdiction. In May 2019, the Court of Appeal for Saskatchewan upheld the federal legislation by a margin of 3–2 in an advisory opinion.[10] Writing for the majority, the Chief Justice wrote that establishing minimum national standards for a price on greenhouse gas emissions falls under federal jurisdiction. One month later, Ontario's Court of Appeal delivered a similar advisory opinion in which it found that the federal carbon tax does not improperly encroach on provincial

---

[8] United Nations C.N.735.2016.TREATIES-XXVII.7.d
[9] Greenhouse Gas Pollution Pricing Act, SC 2018, c. 12.
[10] *Reference re Greenhouse Gas Pollution Pricing Act*, 2019 SKCA 40.

jurisdiction.[11] The 4–1 opinion confirmed that fighting climate change is a matter of "national concern," grounding the federal government's authority in its residual POGG power. In April 2020, the Alberta Court of Appeal went the other way, releasing a 4–1 opinion concluding that the federal legislation is unconstitutional.[12] The advisory opinion emphasised provincial competence to legislate in several important areas, such as healthcare and justice, and observed that the national importance of these areas does not in and of itself justify federal intrusions on the basis of "national concern." All three appellate decisions were appealed.

On March 25, 2021, as this Chapter was being finalised, the question of the constitutionality of Canada's federal carbon tax legislation was decided by the Supreme Court of Canada.[13] Splitting 6 to 3,[14] a majority of the Court upheld the federal carbon tax legislative scheme under the national concern branch of the POGG power. Though not directly determinative of the issue of legal capacity, the Court's judgment bolsters the argument for federal authority to legislate equality in legal capacity across the country under a national concern justification. Indeed, a Supreme Court affirmation of a benchmark/backstop model for meeting climate action goals may also bolster arguments calling for federal initiatives to fulfil an array of international human rights obligations for which there is demonstrable national concern.

There is little by way of domestic precedence on which to base proposed language legislating a federal benchmark and provincial backstop pertaining to legal capacity. Some provinces have legislated to permit supported decision-making arrangements, such as British Columbia's Representation Agreement Act (RAA, 1996). The following text represents a first attempt to propose what kind of federal legislation might achieve the goal of creating the desired benchmark and backstop. These draft provisions outline: (1) a statement of statutory purpose; (2) a definition of capacity; and (3) a regulatory offence.

Purpose of this Act
1 The purpose of this Act is

    (a) To establish a new definition of legal capacity under Canadian law; and
    (b) To encourage the Provincial and Territorial governments to establish a legal mechanism
        i. to allow adults to arrange in advance how, when and by whom, decisions about their health care or personal care, the routine

---

[11] *Reference re Greenhouse Gas Pollution Pricing Act*, 2019 ONCA 544.
[12] *Reference re Greenhouse Gas Pollution Pricing Act*, 2020 ABCA 74.
[13] *Reference re Greenhouse Gas Pollution Pricing Act*, 2021 SCC 11 (*Greenhouse*).
[14] Côté, Brown and Rowe JJ wrote three separate dissenting judgments.

management of their financial affairs, property, or other matters will be made if they become incapable of making decisions independently; and
ii. to avoid the need for the court to appoint someone to help adults make decisions, or someone to make decisions for adults, when they are incapable of making decisions independently.

Legal Capacity

3 (1) Legal capacity is defined as the demonstrated ability
   (a) to exercise independent decision making; or
   (b) to make one's will and preferences cognisable to a representative or representatives.
 (2) All adult persons are presumed to possess legal capacity, the exercise of which shall only be constrained or removed on lawful authority and not unnecessarily.

Prohibition

18 (1) No person shall seek to constrain or remove another person's legal capacity by any means for an improper purpose and without lawful authority.
 (2) Every person who contravenes section 18(1) is guilty of an offence and on conviction is liable to a fine of,
   (a) not more than $25,000 for a first offence; and
   (b) not more than $50,000 for each subsequent offence.

The power to implement the CRPD in this manner is not a given. It would certainly face significant resistance. Some provinces would likely view such action as trampling on provincial rights. Yet, the pith and substance of the proposed CRPD legislation could be characterised explicitly as implementing, at the national level, a unified approach to legal capacity that is consistent with international human rights law. Or, it could be characterised more narrowly as ensuring the countrywide availability of supported decision-making as an alternative to guardianship in all aspects of life. The justification for this legislation would be to promote individual human dignity and to remove barriers preventing people with disabilities from enjoying full inclusion under Canadian law. In other words, the purpose would be to create a nationwide legal capacity framework which recognises that legal capacity may be exercised through supported decision-making. As a federal benchmark and backstop for the provinces, the legal effect of the legislation would be to require that all Canadian laws imposing standards of legal capacity be interpreted or amended to allow those standards to be met through supported decision-making, where such laws do not already do so. The practical effect of the legislation would be to ensure that people with mental disabilities enjoy legal capacity on an equal basis with others, regardless of their province of residence, thereby decreasing the number of Canadians requiring legal guardianship.

The pith and substance of the proposed CRPD legislation framed in this manner – namely, to ensure uniform access to supported decision-making – could fall within the "national concern" branch of the federal government's POGG power. In *Greenhouse*, the Court revisited the former leading case on national concern, R. v. Crown Zellerbach Canada Ltd. (1988). The Court began by emphasising that the recognition of a matter of national concern must be based on evidence. If the federal government wishes to spearhead a legislative effort in an area of potentially overlapping jurisdiction, it bears the onus to justify its assertion of jurisdiction.

Wagner CJ, writing for the majority, laid out a three-step analysis to determine whether a matter constitutes a national concern. First, as a threshold question, the assertion of federal authority must be justified on the basis that the matter is of sufficient concern to the country as a whole. Secondly, the matter must have the qualities of singleness, distinctiveness and indivisibility. Thirdly, the federal government must show that the proposed exercise of power has a scale of impact on provincial jurisdiction that is reconcilable with the division of powers.

The purpose of the national concern analysis is to identify matters of "inherent national concern;" that is, issues which, by their nature, transcend provincial and territorial boundaries. As described above, it is necessary to have national coordination in order to ensure the availability of supported decision-making across the country, which only Parliament can do. Without a uniform approach to legal capacity that allows legal capacity to be exercised through supported decision-making anywhere in the country, the right to the equal enjoyment of legal capacity would be difficult to consistently protect. Provinces are unable to address the national dimensions of the denial of legal capacity within their borders. A failure by one province to recognise supported decision-making as a valid exercise of legal capacity will harm Canadians with mental disabilities who visit or move to that province from other regions. It could also damage Canada's international relations and impede Canada's ability to meet its obligations under the CRPD. Meanwhile, recognising the regulation of legal capacity in all aspects of life as a matter of national concern has a scale of impact on provincial jurisdiction that would not compromise the fundamental division of legislative power.

VII CONCLUSION

The Supreme Court has consistently held that the Constitution must be interpreted flexibly over time to meet new social, political and historic realities.[15] At present, the reality in Canada is that the substantive rights of people with mental disabilities vary from province to province due to inconsistencies in provincial approaches to legal capacity. This has problematic implications for persons seeking access to federal statutory benefits, which are meant to be equally accessible across the country. In

---

[15] See e.g. Ward v Canada (Attorney General), 2002 SCC 17 at para 30, [2002] 1 SCR 569.

some provinces, individuals may enter into RDSPs through support arrangements for decision-making, whereas in others, they are prevented from doing so unless they waive their right to legal capacity and submit to legal guardianship. This violates their equality rights under Article 12 of the CRPD as well under as the Charter.

This chapter has surveyed the extent to which fundamental Canadian constitutional principles support federal legislative action to fully implement Article 12 of the CRPD and, more specifically, to recognise the right to exercise legal capacity through supported decision-making. For decades, the Supreme Court of Canada has endorsed an idea of "co-operative federalism," which accommodates overlapping jurisdiction, encourages coordination between levels of government and responds to changing social circumstances. This chapter has posited that the national concern doctrine under the residual POGG power retains authority for federal legislators to pass legislation necessary to address pressing human rights priorities. This argument, which flows from "national concern," builds on the recent Supreme Court holding in *Greenhouse* that POGG can be used to justify Parliamentary action to fight climate change, notwithstanding overlapping federal-provincial jurisdiction. By incorporating Article 12 of the CRPD into federal legislation as a benchmark and provincial backstop, Parliament could safeguard the dignity, autonomy and self-respect of Canadians with mental disabilities. In doing so, it could also better serve the interests of a growing and vulnerable community, while preserving Canada's reputation as a global leader in disability rights.

REFERENCES

Adult Guardianship and Trusteeship Act, S.A. 2008, c. A-4.2 (Can. Alb.).

Alzheimer Society of Canada. (2016). Prevalence and Monetary Costs of Dementia in Canada (2016): A Report by the Alzheimer Society of Canada. *Health Promotion and Chronic Disease Prevention in Canada*, 36(10), 231-232. Retrieved from https://doi.org/10.24095/hpcdp.36.10.04.

Bach, M., & Kerzner, L. (2010). *A New Paradigm for Protecting Autonomy and the Right to Legal Capacity*. Law Commission of Ontario. Retrieved from https://collections.ola.org/mon/24011/306184.pdf.

Baker v. Canada (Minister of Citizenship & Immigration), 1999 S.C.C. 699, [1999] 2 S.C.R. 817 (Can.).

Bank Act, S.C. 1991, c. 46 (Can.).

Canada Business Corporations Act, R.S.C. 1985, c. C-44 (Can.).

Canada Evidence Act, R.S.C. 1985, c. C-5 (Can.).

Canada Not-for-profit Corporations Act, S.C. 2009, c. 23 (Can.).

Canada Pension Plan Regulations, C.R.C., c. 385 (Can.).

Canadian Charter of Rights and Freedoms, Part I of the Constitution Act, 1982, being Schedule B to the Canada Act 1982 (U.K.), 1982, c. 11.

Choudhry, S (2002). Recasting Social Canada: A Reconsideration of Federal Jurisdiction Over Social Policy, *U Toronto LJ* (52) 163.

Civil Marriage Act, S.C. 2005, c. 33 (Can.).
Cole v. Cole (Litigation Guardian of), 2011 O.N.S.C. 4090, [2011] W.D.F.L. 4812 (Can.).
Convention on the Rights of Persons with Disabilities, 13 December 2006, U.N.T.S. vol. 2515 (entered into force 3 May 2008, accession by Canada 11 March 2010).
Cooperative Credit Associations Act, S.C. 1991, c. 48 (Can.).
Council of Canadians with Disabilities. (2012). *Renewed Political Commitment and Leadership: An Imperative for the Realization of the Human Rights of Canadians with Disabilities: Submission to the United Nations Human Rights Council Universal Periodic Review of May 2013*. Council of Canadians with Disabilities. Retrieved from www.ccdonline.ca/en/international/un/canada/upr-2012.
Criminal Code, R.S.C. 1985, c. C-46, (Can.).
Employment and Social Development Canada, (2018). Registered Disability Savings Plan. Retrieved from www.canada.ca/en/employment-social-development/programs/disability/savings/issuers/user-guide/section2.html
Friends of the Oldman River Society v. Canada (Minister of Transport), [1992] 1 S.C.R. 3, [1992] S.C.J. No. 1 (Can.).
Groppi, T. (2007). A User-Friendly Court: The Influence of Supreme Court of Canada Decisions Since 1982 on Court Decisions in Other Liberal Democracies. *The Supreme Court Law Review* 36(2), 337
Health Care (Consent) and Care Facility (Admission) Act, R.S.B.C. 1996, c. 181 (Can. B.C.).
Health Care Consent Act, 1996, S.O. 1996, c. 2, Sched. A (Can. Ont.).
Immigration and Refugee Protection Act, S.C. 2001, c. 27 (Can.).
Immigration and Refugee Protection Regulations, S.O.R./2002–227 (Can.).
Income Tax Act, R.S.C. 1985, c. 1 (5th Supp.) (Can.).
Insurance Companies Act, S.C. 1991, c. 47 (Can.).
Kaiser, H.A. (2009). Canadian Mental Health Law: The Slow Process of Redirecting the Ship of State, *Health L. J.* (17) 139
Nova Scotia (Minister of Community Services) v Z. (C.K.), 2016 N.S.C.A. 61, [2016] W.D.F.L. 4826 (Can.).
Power of Attorney Act, R.S.B.C. 1996, c. 370 (Can. B.C.).
Public Health Agency of Canada. (2014). *Mapping Connections: An Understanding of Neurological Conditions in Canada – The National Population Health Study of Neurological Conditions*. Retrieved from www.mybrainmatters.ca/wp-content/uploads/Mapping_Connections.pdf
R. v. Crown Zellerbach Canada Ltd., [1988] 1 S.C.R. 401 (Can.).
Representation Agreement Act, R.S.B.C. 1996, c. 405 (Can. B.C.).
Salami, E. & Lashewicz, B. (2015). More than Meets the Eye: Relational Autonomy and Decision Making by Adults with Developmental Disabilities. *Windsor Yearbook of Access to Justice* (32) 89-110.
S. (B.) Re, 2011 Can LII 26315 (O.N. C.C.B.) (Can. Ont.).
Substitute Decisions Act, 1992, S.O. 1992, c. 30 (Can.).
Trust and Loan Companies Act, S.C. 1991, c. 45 (Can.).
Vienna Convention on the Laws of Treaties, May 23, 1969, 1155 U.N.T.S. 331 (entered into force Jan. 27, 1980, accession by Canada Oct. 14, 1970).
Ward v. Canada (Attorney General), 2002 S.C.C. 17, [2002] 1 S.C.R. 569 (Can.).

10

Decisional Autonomy and India's Mental Healthcare Act, 2017: A Comment on Emerging Jurisprudence

Soumitra Pathare and Arjun Kapoor

Abstract

The Mental Healthcare Act, 2017 was enacted in pursuance of India's obligations under the United Nations Convention on the Rights of Persons with Disabilities. The Act seeks to regulate mental health care and treatment through a rights-based approach while protecting decisional autonomy. It brings forth a significant shift in the law on decisional capacity for persons with mental illness with respect to: (i) admissions in mental health establishments; (ii) access to support for exercising decisional capacity for mental health care and treatment decisions; and (iii) providing informed consent for treatment and care options in accordance with one's will and preferences. Additionally, emerging constitutional jurisprudence on decisional autonomy and privacy in India has significant implications for enabling the decisional capacity of persons with mental illness under the Act. In this light, this chapter will examine how the Act's provisions and emerging rights jurisprudence seek to protect decisional autonomy as a fundamental right under India's Constitution.

INTRODUCTION

The Mental Healthcare Act, 2017 (MHCA) was enacted in pursuance of India's obligations under the United Nations Convention on the Rights of Persons with Disabilities (CRPD). India ratified the CRPD in October 2007 and was therefore obligated to reform its mental health legislation in compliance with the Convention. The MHCA was enacted in compliance with this obligation through a legislative process which began in 2010 and lasted nearly seven years, before the President of India gave his assent to the new law on 7 April 2017. It was subsequently brought into force a year later on 29 May 2018, following a government notification. The MHCA repeals the erstwhile Mental Health Act, 1987 (MHA) which was not only poorly implemented but failed to protect persons with mental illness from human rights violations (Narayan & Shikha, 2013).

The MHCA seeks to regulate mental healthcare and treatment by adopting a rights-based and CRPD-compliant approach. Some of the salient features of the legislation include: (i) obligations on the Central and State Governments to ensure the right to access mental health care and treatment for all persons; (ii) protecting the rights of persons with mental illness; (iii) supported decision-making measures such as advance directives and nominated representatives; (iv) regulatory and adjudicatory mechanisms for reviewing rights violations; and (v) anti-discriminatory and parity provisions to eliminate discrimination against persons with mental illness.

The MHCA also brings forth a significant shift in the law on decisional capacity for mental healthcare and treatment by foregrounding 'decisional capacity' as the prevailing principle for assessing a person's capacity to make mental health care and treatment decisions. The MHCA recognises that persons with mental impairments can exercise decisional capacity with varying levels of support for making mental health care and treatment decisions. Thus, a person's decisional capacity should be determined by a combination of factors which include: (i) mental/cognitive abilities to make decisions (impaired or otherwise); (ii) varying levels of support; and (iii) reasonable accommodation (Bach & Kerzner, 2010). We believe this approach is in consonance with Article 12 of the CRPD, which facilitates legal capacity through supported decision-making for all persons with disabilities. Further, as we argue in this chapter, it also seeks to protect decisional autonomy, the right to privacy and the right to health, which have been recognised as fundamental rights under India's Constitution.

Consequently, in this chapter we will examine the MHCA's capacity provisions and their implications for persons with mental illness with respect to three specific aspects of mental health care and treatment: (i) voluntary and involuntary admissions in mental health establishments; (ii) access to support for exercising legal capacity with respect to mental healthcare and treatment decisions; and (iii) providing informed consent for treatment and care options in accordance with one's will and preferences.

The MHCA has been critiqued on grounds that it authorises involuntary admissions and substituted decision-making on the basis of capacity assessments (Davar, 2012). These critiques rely on General Comment 1 of the CRPD Committee which rejects 'mental capacity' as an assessment criterion for facilitating substituted decision-making even in extraordinary situations (Committee on the Rights of Persons with Disabilities, 2014; Kelly, 2016).

We believe such an 'absolutist' approach fails to account for pragmatic concerns in real-world settings across countries, especially in lower- and middle-income countries which are resource constrained and have complex socio-

> Decisional Capacity = Mental Abilities (with impairments) + Support Measures + Reasonable Accommodation

FIGURE 10.1 Elements of decisional capacity
Source: Bach & Kerzner, 2010

economic realities (Pathare & Kapoor, 2020). For instance, India is estimated to have over 150 million persons who have mental health problems, and between 70–92 per cent of these persons do not have access to any form of mental health care and treatment (Gururaj et al, 2016). India also spends a miniscule 1 per cent of its total health budget on mental health (Gururaj et al, 2016). Consequently, wide disparities in human resources and community rehabilitation services compound the barriers to providing persons with high support needs access to support mechanisms across resource-constrained settings. Further, in India's context, stigma around mental illness (and high economic costs for treatment) often compel families to abandon persons with mental illness in mental health establishments. In the absence of adequate community rehabilitation services, clinicians are confronted with ethical dilemmas, such as whether to extend involuntary admissions of persons with severe mental illnesses. To adopt the CRPD Committee's absolutist approach in such situations would be tantamount to denying persons with severe mental illness access to mental health care, eventually leading to poorer health outcomes. It would also compound the emotional and economic cost for many financially constrained families (particularly in rural areas) by prohibiting substituted decision-making in extraordinary situations as a means to facilitate mental health care and treatment for their family members.

Moreover, we believe that an absolutist approach is impractical and potentially harmful in extraordinary situations – for instance, in extremely severe cases wherein persons with mental illness may require substituted decision-making since they are unable to exercise decisional capacity even after exhausting all support mechanisms (what the CRPD Committee prefers to call 'best interpretation of will and preferences', thus indirectly acknowledging someone other than the person is making the decision). Thus, it would be simply implausible to adopt an absolutist approach without denying mental health care and causing considerable harm to persons with severe mental illness in such situations. It is also significant to highlight that the CRPD Committee's absolutist interpretation is at odds with States Parties' interpretations of Article 12 of the CRPD. For instance, countries such Germany, France and Norway have in their comments on draft General Comment 1 challenged the CRPD Committee's absolutist stand. The States Parties have argued that the CRPD does not exclude substituted decision-making in exceptional situations, wherein persons with disabilities are unable to make decisions even with the best support available or their will and preferences cannot be ascertained due to their severe conditions. However, it is noteworthy that the final version of General Comment 1 does not address any of the criticisms raised by the States Parties.

Consequently, we propose an alternative approach, which we term 'normative pragmatism', to interpret the CRPD's provisions in alignment with India's socio-economic context and address practical clinical dilemmas while providing mental health care and treatment. This approach seeks to enable legal capacity as normatively envisioned in Article 12 in consonance with India's evolving constitutional jurisprudence while addressing legitimate (and often conflicting) interests, such as the harm principle and socio-economic barriers, to balance autonomy considerations while ensuring better health outcomes. Such an approach is in consonance with rights jurisprudence emerging from liberal democracies such as India, which seeks to protect individual rights while ensuring any restrictions on such rights pass the test of constitutionality (Khaitan, 2008). In this light, we will examine how the MHCA's provisions and emerging rights jurisprudence seek to protect decisional autonomy as a fundamental right under India's Constitution.

DECISIONAL CAPACITY UNDER THE MHCA

The MHCA does not define capacity explicitly. However, Section 4 (9) states that every person (including a person with mental illness) shall be deemed to have capacity to make decisions regarding their mental healthcare and treatment, if such person has the ability to:

(a) Understand the information that is relevant to make a decision on one's treatment, admission or personal assistance.
   * Such information should be provided to the person in simple language, sign language, visual aids or any other means such that the person understands the information.
(b) Appreciate any reasonable foreseeable consequence of a decision or lack of decision on one's treatment, admission or personal assistance.
(c) Communicate one's decision by means of (i) speech (ii) expression (iii) gesture or any other means.

The Act's provisions on capacity are limited to mental health care and treatment decisions. Thus, for purposes of this legislation, clinicians are prohibited from assessing capacity for decisions which are not related to mental health care and treatment. Section 4 (1) lays down three criteria for determining whether a person has capacity to make mental health care and treatment decisions. This is a significant departure from the erstwhile MHA, which presumed lack of capacity if a person with mental illness was not 'willing' to be admitted voluntarily in a mental health establishment. Section 4 (1) does not stipulate a one-time capacity assessment before providing mental health care and treatment. In fact, a plain reading of this provision suggests that a person's capacity should be assessed for each mental health care and treatment decision (or at regular intervals in cases of supported admission). This is significant since decisional capacity may vary with time, the nature and severity of the condition, or the complexity of a decision. Thus, the Act recognises the dynamic and temporal nature of capacity rather than the false presumption that capacity (or lack of it) remains static and does not change.

The MHCA in its various provisions recognises that persons with mental illness may exercise decisional capacity with or without support. For instance, Section 14 (1) states that 'all persons with mental illness have capacity to make mental healthcare and treatment decisions but may require varying levels of support from their nominated representatives to make decisions'. Reading Section 4 (1) with Section 14 (9) leads to the logical conclusion that a person's decision-making abilities may hinge on access to appropriate mental health services *and* acceptable support measures for making decisions. Thus, we posit the following principle: persons with mental impairments or impaired decision-making abilities can make mental health care and treatment decisions with adequate and appropriate support. In other words, a person can exercise decisional capacity under Section 4 (1) if they are provided adequate support to overcome impairments while making decisions.

It is entirely plausible that persons with mental illness may be wrongly assessed as having impaired decision-making abilities because of the subjective bias of the clinicians assessing capacity (Banner, 2012). In this regard, Section 4 (3) makes it clear that if a person makes a decision which is perceived as wrong by others, this does not mean that the person 'lacks' capacity so long as the person satisfies the three criteria mentioned in Section 4 (1). The underlying principle of this provision is that capacity assessments should not be conflated with normative considerations or value judgments associated with decisions (Banner, 2012). In fact, decisions are very often guided by considerations which are not rational (Glad & Simon, 1984; Quinn, 2010). Consequently, it is completely natural for all persons (irrespective of mental illness) to make decisions which are perceived by others as irrational, unreasonable, emotional or wrong. Thus, through Section 4 (3) the law eschews a 'status' and 'outcomes' approach to assessing capacity (by rendering the propriety or 'subjectivity' of a decision irrelevant), so long as the person is able to make decisions with or without support. We believe that capacity assessments must adhere to this principle by ensuring that findings of decisional incapacity are limited to exceptional cases where the level of support required by the person is so high that it amounts to substituted decision-making or the will and preferences of the person cannot be ascertained at all.

PRESUMPTION OF CAPACITY

The MHCA eschews a 'status' approach to decisional capacity by creating a 'presumption of capacity' in favour of persons with mental illness. The Act presumes that all persons with mental illness have the capacity to make mental health care and treatment decisions but also recognises that they may require 'varying levels of support' from their nominated representatives to make decisions (Section 14 (9)). Thus, mental illness and capacity are to be dealt with as two mutually exclusive concepts. A determination of mental illness does not by itself imply impaired decision-making abilities or lack of decisional capacity, while lack of

Mental Impairments ≠ Impaired Decision-Making Ability ≠ Lack of Decisional Capacity

FIGURE 10.2 Presumption of decisional capacity
Source: Adapted from Bach & Kerzner, 2010

decisional capacity does not imply determination of a mental illness (Figure 10.2). This is reflected in the admissions procedures, wherein a determination of both – a severe mental illness and decisional capacity (or very high support) are preconditions for admitting a person with mental illness. Thus, if the clinician believes that a person with mental illness lacks decisional capacity, then the former must prove it by conducting a capacity assessment and documenting it in medical records. Section 81 mandates that capacity assessments must be carried out in accordance with guidelines issued by an expert committee appointed by the Central Mental Health Authority (CMHA). Thus, a person cannot be denied capacity solely on a determination of mental illness. This is significant, since by creating a 'presumption of capacity' in favour of the person with mental illness, the law ensures that the burden of proof does not lie on the person to prove their capacity, but on the clinician to prove that the person lacks capacity. This can be gleaned from the MHCA's provisions on admissions and treatment, which mandate medical personnel to conduct a capacity assessment while examining a person for admission in a mental health establishment.

SUPPORTED DECISION-MAKING UNDER THE MHCA

Supported decision-making is integral to the exercise of decisional capacity for persons with mental illness. As discussed above, the MHCA recognises that persons with mental illness require 'varying levels of support' for exercising their decisional capacity. The Act gives effect to the right to supported decision-making by providing for support measures such as advance directives and nominated representatives. These forms of support enable persons with mental illness to express their will and preferences while undergoing mental health care and treatment.

Advance Directives

An advance directive is a document for advance planning in cases when a person may not be able to communicate their will and preferences. General Comment 1 of the CRPD Committee recognises advance planning as a form of supported decision-making for persons with disabilities to exercise legal capacity. The MHCA allows any person to write an advance directive expressing their will and preferences for if they have a mental illness in the future and are unable to exercise decisional capacity. A person can specify in their advance directive how they wish to be cared for and treated (or not) for such situations. Advance directives can also be used to appoint one's nominated representative. To be valid, an advance directive must be registered before a Mental Health Review Board (MHRB) which is a district-level quasi-judicial body for monitoring implementation of the MHCA. Clinicians are obligated to provide treatment according to a valid advance directive, provided the person or the nominated representative gives them a copy before treatment begins. Advance directives are not applicable if the person regains decisional capacity. In case of multiple advance directives, only the latest advance directive can be considered as valid and representative of the person's latest will and preferences.

Advance directives are not absolute or beyond legal review. They can be challenged by a mental health professional, caregiver or relative before a MHRB on grounds that: (i) the advance directive was not made by the person out of their own free will; (ii) the circumstances have changed from that to which the person intended to apply the advance directive; (iii) the person was not sufficiently well informed to make a decision; (iv) the person lacked decisional capacity to take mental health care and treatment decisions while preparing the advance directive; or (v) the advance directive is contrary to the law or constitutional provisions. Consequently, advance directives can be altered, modified or cancelled as per the MHRB's findings based on the criteria mentioned above.

Nominated Representatives

Persons with mental illness have the right to appoint any person of choice as their nominated representative. The nominated representative has a duty to provide support while the person undergoes mental health care and treatment. The MHCA permits every adult to appoint their own nominated representative so long as the person being appointed as the nominated representative is an adult, is competent to discharge duties and consents in writing. Thus, the MHCA provides persons with mental illness the autonomy to choose a nominated representative whom they trust will provide support and take decisions on their behalf in accordance with their will and preferences. These provisions also provide safe alternatives for persons who experience violence at the behest of their families (Chakravarty, 2020).

The nominated representative is bound by specific statutory functions to provide support and facilitate decisional capacity for the person with mental illness. This specifically extends to providing support in making treatment decisions; applying for supported admissions and discharge; seeking information about the person's diagnosis and treatment; and applying to the MHRB against rights violations, among others. However, nominated representatives may be required to be a substituted decision-maker for persons who lack decisional capacity and are being treated in supported admission (see below).

Mostly significantly, the MHCA deviates from the CRPD by allowing both the 'will and preferences' and 'best interests' determination while providing support to persons with mental illness. Thus, as per the law, the nominated representative may consider (but is not obligated to follow) the current and past wishes, life history, values, cultural background *and* best interests of the person with mental illness while providing support. Notwithstanding, we believe that clinicians and nominated representatives are always obligated to take all reasonable efforts to ascertain the will and preferences of a person before every mental health care or treatment decision. However, there may be extraordinary situations in which it may not be possible to ascertain the same or, to use the CRPD Committee's phrase, arrive at the 'best interpretation of will and preferences'. For instance, while providing treatment to persons experiencing extreme psychic states, delirium, substance intoxication/withdrawal or unconsciousness, it may not be possible to ascertain their will and preferences. Additionally, in situations where such persons have been abandoned or their family members or caregivers cannot be traced, it may not be possible to arrive at a 'best interpretation of will and preferences'. In such situations, it may be necessary for the nominated representative to make a 'best interests' determination on behalf of the person. Here it is relevant to point out that in situations where a person has not appointed a nominated representative, the MHCA provides for a default list of persons whom clinicians may consider as the nominated representative until the person has appointed one of their own accord. This list includes, in the order of precedence: (i) a person appointed in the advance directive; (ii) a relative; (iii) a caregiver; (iv) a suitable person appointed by the MHRB; (v) the Director or designated representative of the Department of Social Welfare; or in the absence of any of the above, any person representing a civil society organisation working for persons with mental illness till the MHRB appoints a nominated representative (Section 14 (4)).

CAPACITY ASSESSMENT FOR ADMISSIONS AND TREATMENT

The MHCA allows two categories of admissions based on the severity of mental illness, decisional capacity and level of support required: (i) independent admission refers to the admission of a person who has capacity to take mental health care and treatment decisions or requires 'minimal support' in making decisions; and (ii) supported admission refers to the admission of a person who lacks decisional capacity or requires 'very high support' in making decisions. The law does not provide an objective standard for assessing 'minimal support' or 'very high support', which desirably leaves room for evolving judicial interpretations on a case-wise basis as and when legal challenges are made before adjudicatory bodies. Additionally, supported admission further requires satisfaction of any one of three conditions based on the principle of bodily harm to self, harm to other and inability to care for self.

Independent Admission

During independent admissions, medical personnel must first be satisfied that the person applying for admission has the capacity to make decisions regarding their own admission and treatment 'without support' or with 'minimal support' (Section 86 (2) (c)). Additionally, they must ensure that: (i) the person understands the nature and purpose of admission to the mental health establishment; and (ii) the request for admission has been made of their own free will without any duress or undue influence. Thus, 'capacity ... without support' or 'minimal support in making decisions' and 'free will' are the preconditions for authorising an independent admission. If the person is unable to understand the (i) purpose, (ii) nature, (iii) likely effects and (iv) probable result of not accepting treatment, or requires a very high level of support (approaching 100 per cent) in making decisions, the person will be deemed to not understand the purpose of admission and consequently be denied independent admission. Treatment cannot be administered to an independent patient without their informed consent.

Supported Admission

Supported admissions must be initiated on an application by the nominated representative. While conducting an independent examination, medical personnel should be satisfied that the person with mental illness is unable to make mental health care and treatment decisions 'independently' and needs 'very high support' from the nominated representative (Section 89 (1) (c)). However, lack of decisional capacity alone is not sufficient to authorise a supported admission. Supported admission must be the *least restrictive option* and can be authorised only if any one of the following additional conditions are fulfilled (Section 89 (1) (a)):

(i) *Bodily harm to self*: person has recently threatened or attempted or is threatening or attempting to cause bodily harm to self.
(ii) *Harm to other*: person has recently behaved or is behaving violently towards another person or is causing another person to fear bodily harm.
(iii) *Inability to care for self*: person has recently shown or is showing inability to care for themself to the degree that the person is a risk to their own self.

It is important to note that the above conditions are not based on an 'assessment of risk' or a 'presumption of risk'. On the contrary, legal provisions require that risk has been demonstrated. Further, the law uses the phrases 'threatened/attempted', 'threatening/attempting' or 'behaved/behaving'. The law therefore does not permit 'preventive detention' of persons on a presumption that they may be at risk or may pose a risk to themselves or others in the future.

During supported admissions, clinicians are supposed to provide treatment in accordance with the person's will and preferences. Thus, the person's informed consent should be taken with support of the nominated representative before administering any treatment plan (Section 89 (6)). However, if the person does not have decisional capacity but has an advance directive, clinicians should provide treatment in accordance with same. Further, if the person requires nearly 100 per cent support, the Act permits substituted decision-making and the nominated representative can 'temporarily' consent on behalf of the person (Section 89 (7)), subject to the person's decisional capacity being reviewed every seven days (or every fourteen days if the person is admitted beyond thirty days). Consequently, if during review the person is assessed as having capacity to make certain decisions, then informed consent should be taken from the person instead of the nominated representative. Thus, the law recognises that a person in supported admission can exercise decisional capacity (with support from the nominated representative) to make mental health care and treatment decisions when the person does not require 100 per cent support (Mandarelli et al., 2018).

Emergency Treatment

Section 94 of the MHCA permits emergency treatment for a maximum period of seventy-two hours in the community or any health establishment by any medical practitioner and without the person's consent. Emergency treatment can be provided only in situations to prevent: (i) death or irreversible harm to the person; (ii) the person inflicting serious harm to others or their own self; or (iii) serious damage to property belonging to the person or others due to the person's behaviour flowing from their mental illness. Emergency treatment does not require the nominated representative's consent, unless they are available at the time of treatment. The MHCA's emergency provisions are a limited departure from the supported decision-making framework to address practical constraints in receiving timely mental healthcare. For instance, in geographical areas where mental health services may not be available for long distances, persons with mental illness may require emergency treatment while they are being transferred to the nearest mental health establishment. However, the time limit and conditions ensure that these provisions are not applied indiscriminately and indefinitely.

The preceding discussion explicates the MHCA's statutory framework for enabling decisional capacity in the context of mental healthcare and treatment. In the next section we shall examine emerging rights jurisprudence on decisional autonomy and privacy in India, which has significant implications for enabling decisional capacity of persons with mental illness under the MHCA.

EMERGENT JURISPRUDENCE ON DECISIONAL CAPACITY

Right to Privacy and Decisional Autonomy

The Supreme Court of India in its recent landmark judgment *Justice K S Puttaswamy (Retd) v. Union of India* recognised the 'right to privacy' as a constitutionally protected right under the Constitution of India (Puttaswamy, 2017). A unanimous verdict by a nine-judge bench held that privacy is an inalienable natural and constitutionally protected right emerging from guarantee of life and personal liberty in Article 21 of the Constitution. In *Puttaswamy*, the Court recognises privacy as a concept founded on individual autonomy. The Court, while drawing an inextricable link between the right to privacy and the ability of a person to make choices about their life, observes:

> Privacy represents the core of the human personality and recognizes the ability of each individual to make choices and to take decisions governing matters intimate and personal ... (Puttaswamy, 2017)

The judgment, while examining various taxonomies of privacy, identifies decisional autonomy (making personal decisions) as an integral facet of privacy. Drawing upon various theoretical perspectives, the Court highlights 'decisional autonomy' as the right (or the ability) of citizens to make intimate personal decisions consisting one's sexual nature, reproductive rights or intimate relations. Consequently, the right to privacy implies a concomitant right to exercise decisional autonomy which is intrinsic to personal liberty and individual autonomy under Article 21, and the exercise of other fundamental rights under the Constitution.

Decisional Autonomy and Right to Access Mental Health Care and Treatment

The enjoyment of decisional autonomy is predicated on exercising decisional capacity. This raises significant questions: does the State have a duty to enable decisional capacity for persons with mental illness? If yes, what is the scope of these duties in the context of mental health care and treatment decisions? What is the duty of other parties who are providing mental healthcare and treatment to persons with mental illness?

It is a settled principle of rights jurisprudence that every right entails a corresponding duty on the State to actualise the right (Dworkin, 1977; Puttaswamy, 2017). The right to privacy entails two correlative connotations: (i) negative, which protects the person from intrusion of privacy; and (ii) positive, which obligates the State to adopt proactive measures to protect and enable privacy. Thus, the State has a duty not only to prevent intrusions in decisional autonomy, but to take proactive measures to ensure that persons with mental illness are enabled to exercise the same.

We believe the principle of decisional autonomy extends to all kinds of decisions which impact a person's life. These include decisions related to legal relationships, bodily privacy, intimate relations, reproductive rights and healthcare. Decisional autonomy is also directly linked to realising the 'right to health' which the Supreme Court in a litany of decisions has recognised as a constitutional right flowing from the right to life under Article 21 of the Constitution (Kapoor & Pathare, 2018). It follows that to protect and enable decisional capacity (and consequently decisional autonomy), the State has a two-fold duty: (i) to implement sufficient safeguards to protect a person's right to decisional capacity through regulatory and adjudicatory mechanisms; and (ii) to actively provide mental healthcare services *and* supported decision-making measures to enable decisional capacity (Figure 10.3).

This is significant for mental health care and treatment, since in the absence of rights-based mental health services and supported decision-making measures, decisional autonomy is an empty right. The MHCA plays a crucial role in this respect, since Section 18 guarantees all persons the right to access mental health care and treatment by placing a range of obligations on the Central and State Governments to provide affordable, accessible, available, quality and acceptable mental health services. The MHCA also addresses the privacy and information concerns of persons with mental illness. Section 23 ensures the 'right to confidentiality' in respect of a person's mental health, mental health care, treatment and physical healthcare. Further, the Supreme Court has in two landmark decisions adjudicated on issues relating to decisional autonomy in the context of sexual orientation and passive euthanasia relying on the MHCA's provisions. In *Navtej Singh Johar and Others v. Union of India*, the Court held that Section 377 of the Indian Penal Code, 1890 in so far as it criminalised consensual sexual acts between two consenting adults, was unconstitutional since it discriminated against LGBTQIA+ persons (Navtej Johar, 2018). In its reasoning, the Court relied on the anti-discriminatory provisions of the MHCA (Section 3, Section 18 (1) and (2) & Section 21 (1) (a)) to observe that homosexuality is not a mental illness or mental disorder, and that LGBTQIA+ persons cannot be discriminated against on the basis of their sexual orientation (Kapoor & Pathare, 2019). In *Common Cause (A Registered Society) v. Union of India and another* the Court upheld the constitutionality of passive euthanasia or the withdrawal of life-saving treatment for a patient suffering from a terminal disease with no possibility of recovery (Common Cause, 2018). For cases where such person does not have decisional capacity to take an informed decision, the Court relied on the MHCA's provisions on advance directives to hold that it is permissible to execute a valid medical advance directive directing withdrawal of life-support treatment, and further developed guidelines for making advance directives based on the MHCA's provisions. The Court's jurisprudence is thus notably evolving towards safeguarding and enabling decisional autonomy for persons with disabilities by authorising the use of supported decision-making measures such as advance directives to express their will and preferences.

Supported Decision-Making → Decisional Autonomy (Privacy) → Right to Life & Right to Health (Article 21 of the Constitution)

FIGURE 10.3 Decisional capacity and right to health
Source: Authors' original work

Challenges to Decisional Autonomy and Decisional Capacity

At this stage, we would like to highlight two specific challenges to decisional autonomy of persons with mental illness. Fundamental rights are not absolute in India's constitutional jurisprudence and may be subject to reasonable restrictions. This also applies to the right to privacy, which is subject to reasonable restrictions which adhere to the conditions of legality, legitimate state interest and proportionality (Puttaswamy, 2017). Consequently, the right to make decisions about one's mental healthcare and treatment can be subject to certain qualifications as well. As discussed, the MHCA authorises substituted decision-making in exceptional circumstances, based on the rationale of preventing bodily harm to self, harm to others and inability to take care of the self. These conditions are shaped by practical limitations such as unavailability of community and home-based treatment, lack of support measures, inadequate legal resources and economic constraints which, in the absence of accessible lesser restrictive alternatives, may necessitate substituted decision-making (Pathare & Kapoor, 2020; Pathare & Shields, 2012). However, we strongly believe that substituted decision-making must be exercised as an exception rather than the norm to prevent dilution of the MHCA's objectives of protecting decisional autonomy.

Second, clinicians in India are pre-disposed to perceive persons with mental illness as lacking capacity to make mental healthcare and treatment decisions (Math et al., 2019). This position is based on a false equivalence between lack of insight (propriety of decisions) and lack of decisional capacity (ability to make decisions), which is not only unscientific but also based on subjective value judgments rather than a mature understanding of the workings of the human psyche (Ali, Gajera, Gowda, Srinivasa, & Gowda, 2019; Allen, 2009). Contrary to this, research in India has demonstrated that patients who have a severe mental illness with active symptoms can still exercise decisional capacity to write and execute advance directives (Kumar et al., 2013). Additionally, clinicians also harbour the notion that the MHCA is a Western import and its emphasis on individual autonomy threatens the family's role as the primary caregiver (Math et al., 2019). However, this position is untenable since facilitating decisional autonomy is unlikely to decentre the family as the primary support unit in most situations, given India's socio-cultural realities. On the contrary, the challenge is to educate families about patient rights and encourage a shift in attitudes to adopt supported decision-making practices. Nonetheless, this conservative position is likely to influence how clinicians assess capacity, specifically for patients who express choices which conflict with the family's decisions.

Fortunately, the MHCA ensures adequate safeguards for persons with mental illness or caregivers to challenge rights violations, supported admissions or clinical decisions by approaching the MHRBs (and subsequently higher courts) to redress their complaints and seek relief (Section 77). However, the real challenge to protecting decisional autonomy lies in changing the attitudes and practices of clinicians to use these provisions sparingly, in exceptional situations, and with due deference to the person's will and preferences. Since the MHCA's implementation is still at a very nascent stage, it remains to be seen how existing practices and jurisprudence will evolve around these concerns on a case-by-case basis in the future.

CONCLUSION

India, in the coming decades, is faced with a monumental challenge to ensure rights-based mental health care for a burgeoning population (Pathare & Kapoor, 2020). The MHCA provides a coherent statutory framework to ensure the right to access mental health care and treatment and facilitate decisional autonomy for persons with mental illness. However, India is unlikely to make progress until implementation of this legislation is prioritised among all stakeholders led by the Government and mental health professionals. Two years since its enforcement, there is little progress in implementing the MHCA despite the Supreme Court's being actively seized of the matter (Pathare & Kapoor, 2020). Most States have still not established the MHRBs that are responsible for monitoring implementation and compliance of the law. In the absence of an actively functioning governance mechanism, it is unlikely that duty bearers such as mental health professionals and establishments will initiate the necessary changes in their clinical practice. For instance, even though the MHCA prohibits magisterial orders for authorising admissions, mental health hospitals continue to admit or deny admission, based on magistrates' orders, in contravention to the Act (Section 101). To leave the question of implementation to the Governments alone would be missing the wood for the trees. For instance, the Karnataka High Court recently intervened and issued directions to the Government of Karnataka to constitute the State Mental Health Authority and MHRBs for implementing the Act, based on a public interest litigation filed by a citizen of the state. In states such as Tamil Nadu and Kerala, civil society organisations have been actively pursuing the implementation of the MHCA. In the state of Chhattisgarh, committed bureaucratic officials have been proactively spurring onwards the implementation of the MHCA by ensuring regular meetings of the SMHA, drafting State Rules and minimum standards for mental health establishments. Thus, fast-tracking the MHCA's implementation will be possible only if all stakeholders – including civil society, the judiciary and a committed bureaucracy – make concerted efforts as has been evidenced in these states. However, we feel it is equally important to ensure that these implementation measures are guided by constitutional principles through an approach of normative pragmatism that balances decisional autonomy with barriers to ensuring better health outcomes in India's socio-economic context. The MHCA has been perceived as an exemplar of a CRPD-compliant legislation and a model law for countries across the world (Duffy & Kelly, 2019). It seeks to implement the CRPD's principles of autonomy and non-discrimination while eschewing the CRPD Committee's absolutist approach in favour of a pragmatic approach to address real-world constraints to mental health care and treatment in India's resource-constrained settings. Thus, the MHCA foregrounds a supported decision-making approach to protect decisional autonomy while recognising the need for substituted decision-making in exceptional situations to facilitate access to mental health care and other legitimate concerns. We believe this is a practical approach to enable a progressive transformation in the attitudes and practices of all stakeholders, specifically mental health professionals and family members, to protect the right to decisional autonomy of all persons with mental illness.

REFERENCES

Ali, F., Gajera, G., Gowda, G., et al (2019). Consent in current psychiatric practice and research: An Indian perspective. *Indian Journal of Psychiatry*, 61(10), 667–675. https://doi.org/10.4103/psychiatry.IndianJPsychiatry_163_19

Allen, N. (2009). Is capacity "in sight"? *Journal of Mental Health Law*, 165–170.

Bach, M., & Kerzner, L. (2010). *A New Paradigm for Protecting Autonomy and the Right to Legal Capacity*. Law Commission of Ontario. www.lco-cdo.org/wp-content/uploads/2010/11/disabilities-commissioned-paper-bach-kerzner.pdf

Banner, N. F. (2012). Unreasonable reasons: normative judgements in the assessment of mental capacity. *Journal of Evaluation in Clinical Practice*, 18(5), 1038–1044. https://doi.org/10.1111/j.1365-2753.2012.01914.x

Chakravarty, S. (2020). 'Nominated representative' and queer lives. *Research Journal of Humanities and Social Sciences*, 11(4), 371–373. https://doi.org/10.5958/2321-5828.2020.00059.5

Committee on the Rights of Persons with Disabilities. (2014). General Comment 1: Article 12 Equal recognition before the law.

Common Cause (A Registered Society) v. Union of India and another. (2018) 5 SCC 1. https://indiankanoon.org/doc/184449972/.

Davar, B. (June 2012). Legal frameworks for and against people with psychosocial disabilities. *Economic and Political Weekly*, 47(52). www.epw.in/journal/2012/52/special-articles/legal-frameworks-and-against-people-psychosocial-disabilities.html

Duffy, R. M., & Kelly, B. D. (2019). India's Mental Healthcare Act, 2017: content, context, controversy. *International Journal of Law and Psychiatry*. https://doi.org/10.1016/j.ijlp.2018.08.002

Dworkin, R. (1977). *Taking Rights Seriously*. Duckworth.

Glad, B., & Simon, H. A. (1984). Reason in human affairs. *Political Science Quarterly*, 99(1), 132–133. https://doi.org/10.2307/2150290

Gururaj G, Varghese M, Benegal V, et al. (2016). *National Mental Health Survey of India, 2015–16: Mental Health Systems*. National Institute of Mental Health and Neuro Sciences. http://indianmhs.nimhans.ac.in/Docs/Report1.pdf

Kapoor, A., & Pathare, S. (2018). Radicalising public mental healthcare in India. *Seminar*, 714. www.india-seminar.com/2019/714/714_arjun_soumitra.htm

Kapoor, A., & Pathare, S. (2019). Section 377 and The Mental Healthcare Act, 2017: breaking barriers. *Indian Journal of Medical Ethics*, 4(2), 111–114. https://doi.org/10.20529/IJME.2018.095

Kelly, B. (2016). Mental and human rights in India and elsewhere: what are we aiming for? *Indian Journal of Psychiatry*, 58(6), 168–174. https://doi.org/10.4103/0019-5545.196822

Khaitan, T. (2008). Beyond reasonableness – a rigorous standard of review for Article 15 infringement. *Journal of the Indian Law Institute*, 50(2), 177–208.

Kumar, T. C. R., John, S., Gopal, S. et al. (2013). Psychiatric advance statements: an Indian experience. *International Journal of Social Psychiatry*, 59(6), 531–534. https://doi.org/10.1177/0020764012443756

Mandarelli, G., Carabellese, F., Parmigiani, G. et al. (2018). Treatment decision-making capacity in non-consensual psychiatric treatment: a multicentre study. *Epidemiology and Psychiatric Sciences*, 27(5), 492–499. https://doi.org/10.1017/S2045796017000063

Math, S., Basavaraju, V., Harihara, S., et al. (2019). Mental Healthcare Act 2017 – aspiration to action. *Indian Journal of Psychiatry*, 61(10), 660–666. https://doi.org/10.4103/psychiatry.IndianJPsychiatry_91_19

Narayan, C. L., & Shikha, D. (2013). Indian legal system and mental health. *Indian Journal of Psychiatry*. 55(6), 177–181. https://doi.org/10.4103/0019-5545.105521

Navtej Singh Johar and Others v. Union of India. (2018) 10 SCC 1. https://indiankanoon.org/doc/168671544/.

Pathare, S., & Kapoor, A. (2020). Implementation Update on Mental Healthcare Act, 2017. In R. Duffy & B. Kelly, *India's Mental Healthcare Act, 2017: Building Laws, Protecting Rights*. Springer. 251–265.

Pathare, S., & Shields, L. S. (2012). Supported decision-making for persons with mental illness: a review. *Public Health Reviews*, 34, 15. https://doi.org/10.1007/bf03391683

Justice K S Puttaswamy (Retd) v. Union of India. (2017) 10 SCC 1. https://scobserver-production.s3.amazonaws.com/uploads/case_document/document_upload/624/Right_to_Privacy__Puttaswamy_Judgment_.pdf.

Quinn, G. (2010). Personhood and legal capacity: perspectives on the paradigm shift of Article 12 CRPD. www.anjalimhro.org/wp-content/uploads/2020/03/Legal_Capacity.pdf

11

Towards Resolving Damaging Uncertainties: Progress in the United Kingdom and Elsewhere

Adrian D. Ward

A common theme internationally is that uncertainty has been caused by all the discussion and debate about the meaning of international human rights principles, and how laws and procedures should be applied in ways consistent with them. That uncertainty is to the detriment of prompt and effective care and treatment, and is largely unnecessary. The discussion and debate can be esoterically distant not only from practical realities, but from what international human rights instruments actually say and were intended to say, as opposed to the varying views that have been expressed as to what they could or should have said.

That is true above all of the United Nations Convention on the Rights of Persons with Disabilities (CRPD). Talk of 'paradigm shift' is helpful if it spurs the accelerating trends towards doing things better, which trends were already in evidence before the promulgation of the CRPD. It is unhelpful to the extent that practitioners, in the course of their daily work, are made to feel propelled from old certainties into a morass of new uncertainties. Sadly, to a significant extent the uncertainties are a result of myths, misinformation and misinterpretation.

Following a real-life example of potentially fatal uncertainty, this chapter, in successive sections, considers basic concepts of 'capacity'; of 'decision-making' and the significantly broader concept, in the CRPD, of 'exercise of legal capacity'; the requirement of the CRPD for respect for rights, will and preferences; whether a person's will can be overridden without violating human rights norms; situations of urgency and necessity; and the significance of the recurring reference in CRPD to 'on an equal basis with others', including the question of restriction of rights for the protection of others. While this chapter seeks to address worldwide issues, it draws on examples from the United Kingdom, including Scottish experience as well as that of England and Wales, and one from Germany.

LETHAL UNCERTAINTIES

'Mrs H' was the person at the centre of a hearing in the Court of Protection (England and Wales) on 14 January 2020.[1] She had squamous cell carcinoma, manifested on her left cheek. Her bipolar affective disorder had previously led to compulsory hospital admission. It was determined that she did not have capacity to make decisions in relation to her medical treatment. There had been over seven months' delay in treating her carcinoma. Mr Justice Hayden was forthright: 'It is self-evident and, indeed, striking, that time here was of the essence and delay was likely to be inimical to Mrs H's welfare. Not only inimical but as it has transpired, potentially fatal.' He held further that the delay in treating Mrs H occurred because clinicians were 'perplexed' by uncertainties as to whether it was appropriate, and if so in what circumstances, 'for Mrs H effectively to be forced, physically and by coercion if necessary, to attend for her treatment.' During the delay the carcinoma progressed seriously and potentially fatally. The uncertainties, and resulting perplexities, can be reduced by addressing some of the myths, misinformation and misinterpretations.

'CAPACITY'

The term 'capacity', at least in the English-language version of the CRPD, has caused confusion. Put simply, it can mean the ability to hold rights, the ability to exercise them or both.[2] In the CRPD it refers to the ability to hold rights, hence the distinction between 'enjoy[ing] legal capacity' in Article 12.2 and the references to 'exercising... legal capacity' and 'the exercise of legal capacity' in Articles 12.3 and 12.4. People with disabilities hold the same rights as everyone else, however impaired might be their ability to exercise some or all of those rights (Article 12.2). Where they can exercise them with appropriate support, that support must be provided (Article 12.3). Where 'measures' are necessary to ensure the exercise of their capacity, 'appropriate and effective safeguards' must be applied (Article 12.4). This reflects the reality of a gradation in capabilities, and what may be required to ensure exercise of capacity, in this first sense of the word, by or on behalf of all people with relevant disabilities, while complying with the requirements of Article 12. What is clearly and correctly forbidden by the CRPD is 'incapacitation' in the sense of removing, judicially or in practice, any person's capacity in the first sense of holding the same rights as everyone else; and holding them subject to such limitations, qualifications and corresponding duties as everyone else.

In Scots law, and often in general use worldwide, 'capacity' has only the second meaning, namely the ability to exercise legal capacity. Scots law emphasises this by defining 'incapable' and then providing that '"incapacity" shall be construed

---

[1] *Sherwood Forest Hospitals NHS Foundation Trust and another v H*, [2020] EWCOP 5. See also *London Borough of Southwark v NP & Ors*, [2019] EWCOP 48.
[2] See for example the entry for 'capacity' in D M Walker (ed.) *The Oxford Companion to Law*, (OUP, 1980).

accordingly'.[3] The CRPD itself does not promote the myth that everyone has unimpaired capacity in that sense, despite any theoretical attractions of that proposition. People whose ability to exercise legal capacity is impaired must be central to the consideration of relevant issues, and not discriminatorily marginalised (sometimes as 'hard cases') or even ignored. They are the people whose protection is addressed by Article 12.4 CRPD. Moreover, they can only be protected in a human rights-compliant way if, in each case, the degree and extent of any such capabilities is understood.[4] Antiquated binary concepts of complete capability or complete incapability unfortunately sometimes persist.

'DECISION-MAKING'

The CRPD does not refer to so-called 'substitute decision-making', nor to so-called 'supported decision-making'. In particular, the CRPD does not call for the abolition of so-called 'substitute decision-making'. The intention of the wording adopted in Article 12, according to the formal record of the public sessions of the Drafting Committee (the travaux préparatoires), was that it should be silent on that issue 'by neither prohibiting nor endorsing substitutive[5] decision making'. Throughout the extensive discussions of the Drafting Committee, no state representative explicitly asserted that 'substitute decision-making' should be abolished. The wording that now appears in Article 12 of the CRPD was contained in a compromise proposal from Canada, which was adopted. The travaux préparatoires record that, upon introducing this proposal: 'Canada clarified that its proposal was not a prohibition of substitute decision-making, but an encouragement of supported decision-making'. The International Disability Caucus (IDC) stated that this was 'an approach that the IDC can accept'.[6] The UN Committee on the Rights of Persons with Disabilities (UN Committee) has until recently[7] consistently adhered to the view that 'substitute decision-making regimes such as guardianship, conservatorship and mental health laws that permit forced treatment' must be abolished.[8] That is a view expressed by the UN Committee, but such views of treaty bodies 'are to be accorded considerable importance... [but] they are not in themselves formally binding interpretations of the treaty'.[9] In this matter, the views of the UN Committee reflect neither the terms nor the intention of the CRPD.

[3] Adults with Incapacity (Scotland) Act 2000, section 1(6).
[4] Thus the outcome achieved in the case of AB, described later in this chapter.
[5] In this context, 'substitutive', 'substituted' and 'substitute' appear as synonyms.
[6] The relevant travaux préparatoires can be accessed at www.un.org./esa/socdev/enable/rights/adhoccom.htm.
[7] But see footnote 32.
[8] See for example para. 7 of the General Comment.
[9] See for example International Law Association: Committee on International Human Rights Law and Practice 'Final report on the impact of findings of the United Nations Human Rights Treaty Bodies' (London, 2004), para. 16.

Also, Article 12 does not follow the unhelpfully narrow approach of some national legal systems in referring only to 'decision-making'. Article 12.3 refers to support 'for the exercise of legal capacity', which encompasses any act or decision intended to have legal effect, that is to say taking any juridical act.[10]

The requirements of the CRPD itself (and not necessarily assertions about it) should certainly be followed in the methodology to be adopted by anyone implementing 'measures that relate to the exercise of legal capacity', as they are described in Article 12.4. That is addressed in this and the next section. Implementation of the CRPD, and in particular of the safeguards in Article 12.4, requires rejection of a traditional 'best-interests' methodology. The UN Committee was correct in General Comment No 1 (2014) (the General Comment)[11] to assert: 'The "will and preferences" paradigm must replace the "best interests" paradigm to ensure that persons with disabilities enjoy the right to legal capacity on an equal basis with others'.[12] That rejection should not cause alarm that it represents a 'new paradigm', as some would assert, because it does not. For example, a 'best-interests' approach was explicitly rejected for the purposes of the Adults with Incapacity (Scotland) Act 2000. The reasons are given in the relevant 1995 Report:

> "best interests" does not give due weight to the views of the adult, particularly to wishes and feelings which he or she had expressed while capable of doing so. The concept of best interests was developed in the context of child law . . . We think it is wrong to equate such adults with children, and for that reason would avoid extending child law concepts to them.[13]

By the time that the CRPD was promulgated, practical experience of operating regimes based on rejection of a best-interests test had already been gained, and methodologies derived from such experience had already been developed. Thus in Scotland application of the principles-based system, established as an alternative to a best-interests approach, has proved consistently helpful in resolving many practical situations, as well as providing a guide to proper interpretation of the legislation. It has enabled development of practical methodologies[14] which complied with the subsequently enunciated principles of the CRPD, and with recommendations such as that in paragraph 21 of the General Comment: 'Where, after significant efforts have been made, it is not practicable to determine the will and preferences of an individual, the "best interpretation of will and preferences" must replace the "best interests" determination'.

---

[10] An example of the contrast within the United Kingdom is the limitation in the Mental Capacity Act 2005 (applicable to England and Wales) to decision-making, and the broader approach of the Adults with Incapacity (Scotland) Act 2000, under which the definition of 'incapable' covers both acting and decision-making.

[11] Entitled 'Article 12: equal recognition before the law'.

[12] Paragraph 21 of the General Comment.

[13] Scottish Law Commission 'Report on Incapable Adults' (September 1995), Report No 151, para. 2.50.

[14] See for example Ward, A Adult Incapacity, (W. Green, 2003), at Chapter 15, 'Constructing Decisions'.

Even in jurisdictions that formally adopted a 'best-interests' approach, there has been a move away from any paternalistic use of that term, towards a clearly person-centred approach: an example was given by the President of the United Kingdom Supreme Court, Lady Hale, in *Aintree University Hospital NHS Foundation Trust v James*,[15] where she held that the purpose of the best-interests test in English legislation is 'to consider matters from [the patient's] point of view'; and that:

> Insofar as it is possible to ascertain [the patient's] wishes and feelings, his beliefs and values or the things which were important to him, it is those which should be taken into account because they are a component in making the choice which is right for him as an individual human being.

The prime responsibility of anyone who has a role in taking action or making a decision, with legal effect, on behalf of a person whose ability to take that action or make that decision is impaired, is to apply the requirement in Article 12.4 for respect for the full range of the rights, will and preferences of the person with a relevant disability, whether the role arises from authorisation or obligation. The Essex Autonomy Project Three Jurisdictions Report recommended a presumption, rebuttable only if stringent criteria are met, that effect should be given to the person's reasonably ascertainable will and preferences, subject to the constraints of possibility and non-criminality.[16] That presumption should be rebuttable only if stringent criteria are satisfied. 'Action which contravenes the person's known will and preferences should only be permissible if it is shown to be a proportional and necessary means of effectively protecting the full range of the person's rights, freedoms and interests.

Further uncertainty surrounds the requirement in Article 12.4 to 'respect the rights, will and preferences of the person'.

'RESPECT' FOR 'RIGHTS, WILL AND PREFERENCES'

'Respect' does not mean in all circumstances 'comply with', and certainly not to comply with any one or two of the elements of 'rights, will and preferences' in isolation. Those elements are often in conflict, and require to be balanced in the circumstances of each individual case. Likewise, the various provisions of the CRPD as a whole can often be in conflict with each other. That is sometimes portrayed as a defect in the CRPD. That is incorrect. It is also incorrect to treat any one provision as taking precedence over all others. Any principles-based legislation or international instrument sets out principles that must be identified and taken into account in any individual factual situation. To disregard any relevant principle is

---

[15] [2013] 3 WLR 1299, [2013] COPLR 492.
[16] Martin, W, Michalowski, S, Stavert, J et al. Three Jurisdictions Report: Towards Compliance with CRPD Art. 12 in Capacity/Incapacity Legislation across the UK, (Essex Autonomy Project, 6 June 2016), accessible at: http://autonomy.essex.ac.uk/eap-three-jurisdictions-report (Recommendation 1).

wrong. To balance principles against each other in the context of an individual factual situation is often essential. The challenge is to achieve that balance in a way that best achieves the overall purpose of the instrument or legislation in question when applied to particular facts and circumstances, and minimises the extent to which any principle is overridden by application of another.

Even before 'rights' are considered in any such balancing exercise, there can be uncertainty about what is 'will', what are 'preferences', and how to balance those two elements. The issues can be exemplified by two examples from real life.[17]

Firstly, a young man with considerable learning disabilities, and no verbal communication, started behaving unusually. Staff who knew him well noticed that he was very protective of his face. He absolutely wanted no-one to come close to it, never mind touch it. Staff surmised that he was suffering from toothache. His immediate reaction was to prevent any contact with his mouth, and certainly any examination of it. But without doubt he wanted the toothache to cease, and he had a right to receive appropriate healthcare treatment. That case was subsequently debated by a campaigning group of people with learning disabilities,[18] all completely committed to the requirement for respect for the will and preferences of persons with disabilities. Their conclusion was that his 'overriding will' was for the pain to cease, and he should be treated, if necessary using sedation or other means to ensure it, if persuasion was unsuccessful. Some experts assert that every effort should have been made to persuade the man to accept dental examination and treatment, but if he was not persuaded then he would have to continue to endure the pain. Practical experience indicates that he might then start clawing at his face to try to remove the pain, possibly causing significant injury.

Secondly, an elderly lady was adamant that she wished to remain in her own home. Article 19 of the CRPD safeguards that right, with right to receive necessary services there. However, she was convinced that she required no assistance, and refused to admit carers whose services were in fact essential if residence in her own home were to be sustained. Her son applied to be appointed her guardian with powers to ensure that her carers had access. She opposed: she loved her son and appreciated his help, but asserted that she did not need a guardian. Upon reasoning not dissimilar to that suggested in the first example, he was appointed.

In such situations, what is will and what are preferences? This author, as lawyer, and a psychologist colleague have offered the following analysis.[19] At any one time there can only be one expression of will, but that expression, even though based on the same considerations, may change. Conflicts such as those described in the above

---

[17] The first is from this author's experience as Chairman of NHS Trusts providing relevant services; the second from an unreported case in which a professional colleague acted.
[18] People First (Scotland), Law and Human Rights Group.
[19] Ward, A and Curk, P and People First, Scotland, Respecting 'will': Viscount Stair and online shopping. SLT News (2018). 123; also published in German translation in *Betreuungsrechtliche Praxis* (2019). 54.

two examples can be viewed as conflicts between different preferences, resulting at any one time in an expression of 'will'. Preferences are themselves underpinned by various considerations, motivations and factors, perhaps requiring a concept of 'preferences' extended to a wide range of values, identities, attachments, risks, fears, responsibilities, resources and so forth. The person may not always be aware of all of these factors, nor the complex relationships between them, nor of how a person arrives at a particular expression of 'will'. They are not limited to positive and rational considerations. Some may be in conflict not only with each other, but with what is realistically possible. Any significant decision will often, and perhaps always, require balancing of such preferences.

The group of people with learning disabilities referred to above[20] discussed with this author the concept of a single expression of 'will' that might vary over time. Broadly they agreed, and gave personal examples of when 'will' had altered prior to the final stage of commitment.[21] One wanted to move to other accommodation, but at the point of committing to that he changed his mind and chose to stay where he was. Another wanted to spend his savings on a particular appliance. His support worker persuaded him to think of the impact upon his budgeting, and eventually he decided not to. They were all nevertheless adamant that once they reached the point of commitment to acting in accordance with their will, their will should be decisive, not merely 'respected'.

However, they were asked to imagine the situation of a less able friend, governed solely by immediate impulse, and not able to review and reconsider. Suppose that the friend wanted to spend all his money this week, leaving nothing even for food next week. After anxious discussion, they concluded that the overriding will of such a friend would be not to go hungry next week, that such predictable 'future will' should override the 'present will' this week, and that he should be prevented from spending his money that way. That was perhaps a novel way of resolving the tension between autonomy and protection. It shows that those most adamantly committed to the principle of 'respect for will and preferences' (even with 'rights' set aside) would consider it appropriate and necessary to override a person's present expression of will in some circumstances. That leads to the general question that introduces the next section.

CAN A PERSON'S 'WILL' BE OVERRIDDEN WITHOUT VIOLATING HUMAN RIGHTS NORMS?

Moving from theorising to the need to find human rights-compliant ways to deal appropriately with real-life situations, courts in various jurisdictions have concluded that there are circumstances where overriding an expression of will is not only consistent with relevant human rights norms, but is necessary in order to comply

---

[20] See footnote 20.
[21] See Stair, J D Viscount of, *Institutions of the Law of Scotland* 1,10,2 (1681). Stair identified three stages in the engagement of the will, namely 'desire, resolution and engagement'.

with them. Two cases, one decided in Germany in 2016 and the other in Scotland in October 2019, illustrate this point.

The German case was a decision of the German Federal Constitutional Court dated 26 July 2016.[22] A preliminary explanation of the concepts of 'free will' and 'natural will' in German law may assist some readers. Put simply, 'free will' is understood to mean a competent formation and expression of will, sufficient for a valid juridical act; and 'natural will' means any wish or will that is consciously and wilfully expressed or made known to others, notwithstanding that it might lack legal validity because it was not capably formulated and communicated.[23] This case concerned a woman who was described as suffering from a 'schizoaffective psychosis'. A *'Betreuer'* (guardian) had been appointed to her in April 2014. In September 2014 she was briefly admitted to a care facility. While there, she declined to take medications prescribed to treat an auto-immune disorder. She refused to eat. She expressed the intent to commit suicide. In accordance with various orders of the court, she was transferred to a closed dementia unit at a clinic, and treated with medication 'through coercive medical measures'. Further examination showed that the woman also suffered from breast cancer. She refused treatment for the cancer. The court held that she was not capable of forming a 'free will'. Her 'natural will' was to refuse treatment. German legislation did not permit her 'natural will' to be overridden in such circumstances, but to exclude her from necessary medical treatment would conflict with the general duty of the state under constitutional law to protect its citizens. 'The state community cannot simply abandon helpless persons to their own devices'. In the context of the requirement of Article 12(4) of the CRPD that safeguards must 'respect the rights, will and preferences of the person', the court introduced the concept of the 'when-necessary-supported-will of the person with a disability'. The free will of the person should be respected even if it can only be determined by reference to previously expressed views of the person, or based on the quality of the natural will. The court explained that: 'This can, inter alia, require differentiation as to how much weight should be given to the natural will of the person, depending on how close it comes to the person's free (or presumed free) will after providing due support'.

The route towards this outcome may have been more sophisticated than that adopted by the group with learning disabilities as described at the end of the preceding section, but the outcome itself was the same. It can be not only permissible but necessary, having regard to relevant human rights principles, in some circumstances that a person's 'will' be overridden.

The Scottish case is *Scottish Borders Council v AB*[24] decided by Sheriff Janys M Scott QC at Jedburgh on 23 October 2019. 'AB' had recently reached the age of 18.

---

[22] Bundesverfassungsgericht, Beschluss (des ersten Senats) vom 26. Juli 2016 – 1 BvL 8/15.
[23] These are understood to be the core meanings, well established in German law, though there is some marginal ambiguity and scope for debate.
[24] 2020 SLT (Sh Ct) 41; see also case commentary at 2020 SLT (News) 44.

Prior to that, she had lived alone in a flat in 'Town X'. Men who frequented her flat had subjected her to physical, sexual and financial abuse. They had plied her with alcohol and injected her with drugs. They had obstructed contact between her and the social worker allocated to support her, and had destroyed the mobile telephone given to her for use in emergencies. Her social worker had had to resort to standing by the ATM machine to which he knew that one of the abusing males would bring her, in order to encash her benefit payments, with the intention of confiscating them.[25]

Under an order by a Children's Hearing, she was placed under supervision in 'Town Y'. That order fell away when she reached the age of 18. The Council sought a guardianship order with extensive powers. AB opposed the application. In particular, her settled will was to return to Town X. A Scottish guardianship application can only proceed further if it is demonstrated that, by reason of a 'mental disorder', the adult in question is 'incapable' in accordance with a statutory definition.[26] The Council submitted that AB was 'incapable of acting' in accordance with that definition. The sheriff disagreed. She held that the adult was capable of making decisions and communicating decisions, but that 'the problem is that she cannot understand the consequences of her decisions'. The sheriff emphasised that the finding of incapacity did not of itself justify overriding the expressed wishes of the adult.

The reporting mental health officer[27] described the powers sought in the application as 'protective, rather than a deprivation of liberty' in terms of Article 5 of the European Convention on Human Rights (ECHR).[28] The sheriff disagreed. She held that to grant powers to keep AB where she had been placed in Town Y, and to deny her wish to return to Town X, would amount to a deprivation of liberty in terms of Article 5 ECHR. The sheriff referred to interpretations supporting that view.[29]

Conflicting rights under the CRPD required to be balanced against each other. On the one hand, AB had the right under Article 19 CRPD to choose her place of residence, and where and with whom she should live, on an equal basis with others, and not to be obliged to live in a particular living arrangement. That right would be infringed by the proposed guardianship order, as would other provisions of the CRPD all assuring to people with disabilities the same rights as people with no relevant disabilities, including to autonomy and self-determination, and to

---

[25] While this might have been an extreme case, such abuse of persons with relevant intellectual disabilities is not uncommon, nor confined to younger women. The case of *West Lothian Council in respect of the adult KB*, [2019] SC Liv 62, concerned an abusive and exploitative relationship with one male. Mental Welfare Commission for Scotland, 'A Summary of our Investigation into the Care and Treatment of Ms A', (April 2008) concerned a 67 year-old victim of such abuse.
[26] In section 1(6) of the Adults with Incapacity (Scotland) Act 2000.
[27] A mental health officer is a specially trained social worker. Every guardianship application in which welfare powers are sought must be accompanied by such a report.
[28] The terms of which are legally binding on public authorities under Scots law.
[29] See paragraph [12] of her Judgment.

non-discrimination. On the other hand, AB's situation also engaged her right to protection from abuse under Article 16, and potentially her right to life under Article 10 because she had been free from injection of drugs for six months, and her tolerance of those drugs had thus reduced. If she returned to her abusers and they resumed injecting her at previous levels, the consequences could have been fatal. The imperative to respect those rights nevertheless engaged the requirement of Article 12.4 that measures relating to the exercise of legal capacity should be 'proportional and tailored to the person's circumstances, apply for the shortest time possible and [be] subject to regular review by a competent, independent and impartial authority or judicial body'.

Could AB's welfare be adequately safeguarded or promoted by means other than a guardianship order? Relevant provisions of Scots law prefer removing risk from an adult, rather than removing the adult from risk.[30] However, even if sanctions were imposed on past abusers, there was a significant risk that others would prey upon AB in similar fashion. The sheriff concluded that a guardianship order was necessary. In proceeding to grant it, the sheriff considered rigorously all of the powers sought and rejected most of them as being unnecessary. It had been shown that AB suffered from post-traumatic stress disorder (PTSD) as a result of past abuse. However, her PTSD was potentially treatable, and successful treatment might enable her to regain insight into the consequences of her decisions. The sheriff determined that the order should be limited to a period of six months. The sheriff made it clear that she expected that AB would receive treatment for her PTSD during that period. In the event that renewal were sought, review of the deprivation of liberty would be ensured.

Thus, the question posed at the beginning of this section was again answered to the effect that in exceptional circumstances, and subject to rigorous controls, a person's 'will' can be overridden without violating human rights norms.[31] Indeed, on a proper consideration and balancing of those norms, AB's rights would have been violated by not overriding her expressed will, provided that relevant human rights principles were rigorously applied in formulating the measures applied. It must always be recognised that the starting point should be that rights of autonomy and self-determination are of primary importance, and should only be restricted where: (a) all other options have been fully considered; (b) other fundamental rights can only be safeguarded if autonomy is restricted; (c) on balance, those other rights should be given precedence; (d) the extent to which autonomy is restricted should be the minimum necessary to achieve that balance; and (e) all necessary safeguards, including those in Article 12.4 CRPD quoted above, are applied.

---

[30] See the Adult Support and Protection (Scotland) Act 2007.
[31] The UN Committee appears to be moving cautiously towards acceptance of this: see Ruck Keene, A, The CRPD Committee and legal capacity – a step forwards? *Mental Capacity Law and Policy* (14 October 2019). Available at www.mentalcapacitylawandpolicy.org.uk/the-crpd-committee-and-legal-capacity-a-step-forwards/?/.

URGENCY AND NECESSITY

Situations addressed by mental health professionals can be too urgent to permit resolution by court procedure and careful consideration by a court. The decision may be whether immediately to override the express will of a patient in accordance with emergency statutory procedures, or to resort to the principle – available in many legal systems by one name or another – of necessity.[32] In making and implementing such decisions, healthcare professionals should take account of the relevant human rights principles referred to in this chapter. They should balance them and then apply them to the implementation of decisions made. The same methodology should be applied if more extended statutory procedures are engaged, following upon initial emergency decisions.

There is however one remaining issue that currently, in at least many jurisdictions, is specific to people diagnosed with mental ill-health. They can be deprived of their liberty, and subjected to other substantial limitations, not upon proper application of human rights principles to *them*, but for the protection of others.

'ON AN EQUAL BASIS WITH OTHERS'

Article 14 CRPD ('Liberty and security of person') requires States Parties to ensure that persons with disabilities should, on an equal basis with others, enjoy the right to liberty and security of person and are not deprived of their liberty unlawfully or arbitrarily. Any deprivation of liberty must be in conformity with the law. The existence of a disability never justifies a deprivation of liberty. Where persons with disabilities are deprived of their liberty through any process, they must be treated in compliance with the objectives and principles of the CRPD, including by provision of reasonable accommodation.

For Europeans, there is a question of incompatibility between this and Article 5 ECHR.[33] What is relevant here is that in terms of Article 14, persons with 'mental disabilities' (as they are characterised in CRPD)[34] may be susceptible to deprivation of their liberty, but not on grounds of existence of the disability, nor in any way that is not 'on an equal basis with others', nor on the basis that their disability differentiates them in the application of any rights within the description in Article 14.2. Their

---

[32] For general provision of medical treatment to people not capable of validly consenting to it, Scots law provides a procedure for authorisation by medical certification under section 47 of the Adults with Incapacity (Scotland) Act 2000, which however 'does not affect any authority conferred by any other enactment or rule of law' (section 47(2A)).

[33] Article 5 of ECHR provides inter alia that: 'No one shall be deprived of his liberty save in the following cases and in accordance with a procedure prescribed by law: ... (e) the lawful detention ... of persons of unsound mind'. In other words, the exception to Article 5 of ECHR under which detention of people with mental disabilities can be permissible is contradicted by the requirements of Article 14.1 (b) quoted above.

[34] CRPD Article 1: 'Persons with disabilities include those who have long-term physical, mental, intellectual or sensory impairments'.

treatment must be 'in compliance with the objectives and principles of the present Convention', which clearly includes that they be treated 'on an equal basis with others', and expressly includes an obligation to meet needs by reasonable accommodation.

In the United Kingdom, particularly in the period from December 2019 to February 2020, much public concern was expressed in relation to situations with the following pattern:[35] persons convicted of terrorist offences reach the end of their sentences and are released, or maybe released earlier under provisions and procedures for early release. They are known to be likely to commit further serious offences following release. They do so. In at least one case, the person in question was known to be so potentially dangerous that he was constantly shadowed by anti-terrorism officers. He nevertheless committed a random act of murder too quickly for them to intervene before they shot him dead.

Under English law, only persons with mental disorders may be detained, and continue to be detained, solely on grounds of the danger that they pose to others. Persons so detained could have grounds for submitting a complaint to the UN Committee,[36] citing the comparator of persons who have been convicted of terrorism offences and who have been assessed as continuing to pose significant danger to the general public. It could be argued that persons assessed as dangerous because of a mental disorder can be properly detained not primarily on grounds of that dangerousness, but because if their judgement was not significantly impaired by the mental disorder, they would not commit dangerous and criminal acts, nor would they wish to be tainted with having done so. It is difficult, however, to apply speculative reasoning to justify differentiation compared with persons convicted of terrorist offences.

Such discrimination against persons with mental disabilities could be avoided by adopting uniform criteria (firstly) for releasing dangerous people subject to monitoring, and (secondly) for detaining them (or continuing to detain them) on grounds of dangerousness.

A different example of affording protection to third parties, or to the general public, can be found in rules governing the practising of certain professions. In Scotland, for example, the practising certificate of a solicitor ceases to have effect upon detention in hospital under mental health legislation or granting of a guardianship order under incapacity legislation. That applies regardless of whether the solicitor's ability to practise safely and competently is impaired by reason of the 'mental disability' giving rise to the detention or guardianship.[37] That is not relevant

---

[35] See for example, 'Usman Khan was freed. Then he went on a killing spree. How did this happen?' *The Guardian* (1 December 2019); 'London stabbing prompts questions on policies for terrorism convictions' *The Times* (3 February 2020); and, 'Six terrorists convicted of further terror act after release, data shows' *The Guardian* (12 February 2020).

[36] Protocol 1 to the CRPD, ratified by the United Kingdom.

[37] Solicitors (Scotland) Act 1980 section 18(1).

to the position of such a person as patient, but is indicative of other essentially discriminatory practices.

For clinicians, concerns arising from Article 14 CRPD would not appear to apply where potential danger to third parties is not by itself the decisive reason for detention of a patient, or where such detention can reasonably be justified upon a balance of relevant human rights principles. Clinicians must make decisions which are as human rights compliant as can be achieved within the legal environment in which they work. Achievement of outcomes which best balance relevant human rights principles, where they may be in conflict, should not be inhibited by considerations that the broader legal context, provided by legislators, is open to criticism by reference to any human rights principles.

CONCLUSION

Human rights principles, properly interpreted and applied, can be supportive of prompt, effective and appropriate care and treatment. Crucially, that will often require anticipatory measures, such as powers of attorney and advance directives,[38] and carefully prepared anticipatory care plans which are readily available to clinicians.[39] The proper application of relevant human rights principles, particularly when they are in conflict, may require care. Relevant human rights instruments themselves are capable of being understood and applied by clinicians, including in the mental health sphere. A working knowledge of relevant instruments and their proper application should form part of the education of clinicians. Unhelpful uncertainties can be created when discussion and debate stray from what relevant human rights instruments actually provide, and were intended to provide, and from the interpretation and application of them authoritatively adopted by courts.[40]

---

[38] 'Enabling citizens to plan for incapacity: Report on a review of follow-up action taken by member states of the Council of Europe to Recommendation CM/Rec(2009)11 on principles concerning continuing powers of attorney and advance directives for incapacity; Report prepared by Mr Adrian D Ward on behalf of the European Committee on Legal Co-operation (CDCJ)', June 2018, published in English and French at www.coe.int/en/web/cdcj/activities/powers-attorney-advance-directives-incapacity.

[39] In the United Kingdom, at time of writing the importance of all such measures is being stressed to the general public in the context of COVID-19.

[40] It could reasonably be argued that widespread judicial consistency in interpretation of how the CRPD should be applied could establish a 'subsequent practice' in terms of Article 31 ('General Rule of Interpretation') of the Vienna Convention on The Law of Treaties, which includes '31.3 There shall be taken into account, together with the context: ... (b) any subsequent practice in the application of the Treaty which establishes the agreement of the parties regarding its interpretation'.

12

'The Revolution Will Not Be Televised': Recent Developments in Mental Health Law Reform in Zambia and Ghana

Heléne Combrinck and Enoch Chilemba

Abstract

Since the adoption of the Convention on the Rights of Persons with Disabilities (CRPD) in 2006, several African countries have undertaken reform of their mental health legislation. This chapter examines mental health laws introduced in recent years in two African countries, Zambia and Ghana, to establish whether these legislative measures comply with CRPD standards in respect of the recognition of legal capacity. To examine this question, we first provide a brief overview of Article 12 and General Comment No 1 issued by the Committee on the Rights of persons with Disabilities, briefly noting the controversy that has arisen in respect of the Committee's interpretation of this Article. We also consider the African Charter on Human and Peoples' Rights. The chapter then measures the Zambian Mental Health Act of 2019 as well as the Mental Health Act, 2012, of Ghana against the international and regional norms on legal capacity. In this process, we also consider the difficult question of whether the approach which holds that involuntarily psychiatric interventions can never be compatible with the CRPD is feasible in African contexts with limited resources. We finally look at the lessons that may be drawn from the legislative processes in these countries.

1 INTRODUCTION

The adoption of the Convention on the Rights of Persons with Disabilities[1] (CRPD or Convention) in 2006 lent significant impetus to the reconsideration of mental health legislation already in progress at the time.[2] The need for such reassessment arises from Article 12 of the CRPD,[3] which embodies a clear commitment by States parties to recognise the legal capacity of persons with disabilities on an equal basis with others. Further, States parties are enjoined by the general obligations in Article

---

[1] GA Res A/RES/61/06, adopted on 13 December 2006, entered into force on 3 May 2008.
[2] See e.g. R M Duffy & B D Kelly 'Rights, Laws and Tensions: A Comparative Analysis of the Convention on the Rights of Persons with Disabilities and the WHO Resource Book on Mental Health, Human Rights and Legislation' *International Journal of Law and Psychiatry* (2017) 26-27.
[3] Art 12(2) CRPD.

4 of the CRPD to take measures to (amongst others) modify or abolish existing laws amounting to discrimination against persons with disabilities.[4]

It was clear from the outset that mental health law reform pursuant to the CRPD would be disputed terrain – as became apparent almost immediately from the reservations and interpretive declarations made in respect of Article 12.[5] In fact, fervent disagreement about the meaning of 'legal capacity' pervaded the negotiation of the treaty, although a number of delicate concessions by negotiating parties ultimately allowed for the conclusion of the drafting process.[6] It is not surprising that this contestation has extended to the domestic implementation of the Convention by States parties.

In recent years, a number of African countries have, following their ratification of the CRPD, embarked on a review of their legal frameworks pertaining to mental health.[7] Mental health law reform in Africa compels interest for a number of reasons. Notably, the significant existing body of literature on mental health law has to date predominantly focussed on the economically advantaged Global North.[8] Bartlett convincingly argues that mental health legislation in these countries is firmly rooted in a particular legal culture (with an emphasis on established individual rights) and a socio-economic context which supports well-resourced service provision and increasingly active service user groups, and also sustains the development of community-based support programmes.[9] This stands in stark contrast with the Global South, which mostly includes middle- to lower-income countries – and with much smaller government spending in the mental health sector.[10] An analysis of mental health law reform in the African region therefore offers opportunities to consider the implementation of the CRPD in low-resource settings. A further consideration is the recent adoption by the African Union of the Protocol to the African Charter on Human and Peoples' Rights on the Rights of Persons with Disabilities in Africa (African Disability Protocol), which includes provisions on legal capacity and harmful practices perpetrated against persons with disabilities.[11]

---

[4] See art 4(1)(a) & (b) CRPD.
[5] See e.g. the declarations and/or reservations by Australia, the Netherlands, Canada and Ireland relating to Article 12. https://treaties.un.org/Pages/ViewDetails.aspx?src=TREATY&mtdsg_no=IV-15&chapter=4&clang=_en.
[6] For an extensive account of these events see A Dhanda 'Legal Capacity in the Disability Rights Convention: Stranglehold of the Past or Lodestar for the Future?' *Syracuse Journal of International Law and Commerce* (2006–2007) 438–456.
[7] Examples include: the Mental Health Act of 2008 (United Republic of Tanzania); the Mental Health Act of 2012 (Ghana); the Mental Health Act of 2019 (Zambia).
[8] P Bartlett 'Thinking about the Rest of the World: Mental Health and Rights Outside the "First World"' in B McSherry & P Weller (eds.) *Rethinking Rights-Based Mental Health Laws* (Bloomsbury, 2010) 397.
[9] Ibid. 397–398.
[10] See UNDP *Human Development Report 2019* (UNDP, 2019) 300–303.
[11] Adopted on 30 January 2018, not yet in force at the time of writing. See discussion in Section 3.2 below.

Ibrahim recounts that responses to psychosocial disability in Africa still strongly bear the mark of colonialism: in the majority of countries, mental health laws can be traced back to pre-independence (colonial) regimes.[12] Despite the fact that such legislation has unsurprisingly led to serious violations of the rights of persons with psychosocial disabilities, there are only a few African countries that have embarked on 'meaningful legal reforms [to] rid themselves of this legacy'.[13]

In this chapter, we inspect mental health law reform in two of these countries (i.e. Zambia and Ghana) in order to establish whether these newly minted legislative schemes in Africa are in fact in line with the Convention with regards to the legal capacity of persons with psychosocial disabilities. The inquiry starts with a brief overview of mental health legislation in African contexts. We then examine the standards set by Article 12 of the CRPD as well as selected African regional human rights instruments regarding legal capacity, and proceed to assess the mental health legislation adopted by Zambia and Ghana respectively against these norms.[14] This is followed by an evaluation of our findings and consideration of proposals flowing from these legislative reform processes.

It should be noted that our focus here is on mental health legislation, and so we do not provide a comprehensive analysis of constitutional provisions and related legislative and policy frameworks (although we do point out one or two aspects of these where particularly relevant).

2 OVERVIEW: MENTAL HEALTH LEGISLATION IN AFRICA

The low priority accorded to mental health services by the majority of African governments results in minimal levels of service provision,[15] which nevertheless strongly relies on the biomedical model of treatment. This situation is characterised by a lack of medical professionals (such as psychiatrists, psychologists and psychiatric nurses), poor institutional standards and an almost universal absence of community-based programmes.[16] Most persons with disabilities live with their families and rely on them as their main form of support, financial and otherwise.[17] In general, African countries have seen

---

[12] See M Ibrahim 'Mental Health in Africa: Human Rights Approaches to Decolonization' in M Morrow & LH Malcoe (eds.) *Critical Inquiries for Social Justice in Mental Health* (University of Toronto Press, 2017) 113; A Osei, *et al* 'The New Ghana Mental Health Bill' *International Psychiatry* (2011) 8.

[13] Ibrahim, 'Mental Health in Africa' 113.

[14] This part of the chapter is in part based on an unpublished submission to the parliament of Zambia on the draft Mental Health Bill of 2019 prepared by the first author in March 2019.

[15] Bartlett, 'Thinking about the Rest of the World' 406.

[16] Ibid. 406–407.

[17] E Kamundia 'Choice, Support and Inclusion: Implementing Article 19 of the Convention on the Rights of Persons with Disabilities in Kenya' *African Disability Rights Yearbook* 62.

relatively low rates of institutionalisation of persons with psychosocial disabilities.[18] Family environments are however not always benevolent and may contribute to the strong prejudice and stigma experienced by persons with psychosocial disabilities.[19]

The complexity of the African environment is deepened by a strong reliance on traditional and religious healers, who often afford the only treatment option available to persons with psychosocial disabilities.[20] Although treatment and care options provided by traditional and religious healers, usually community based, may offer advantages (for example, an understanding of unique cultural situations),[21] harmful practices have also been documented in this sphere, for example, in the case of 'prayer camps' in Ghana.[22]

As indicated, this chapter focusses on Zambia and Ghana due to their relatively recent mental health law reform processes. The legal systems of both countries originated from the English common law tradition, as is the case for most former British colonies in Africa (and elsewhere). Historical developments have resulted in hybrid legal systems in both jurisdictions consisting of common law and customary law, in each case bound together under a dispensation of constitutional supremacy.[23] Both countries have enacted general disability legislation as well as 'stand-alone' mental health legislation.

The constitution of each country includes an extensive Bill of Rights. Notably, the right to personal liberty entrenched in both constitutions is still circumscribed by the inclusion, among the permissible deprivations of liberty, of situations where a person is of 'unsound mind' and such deprivation is aimed at the provision of care or treatment or protection of the community.[24]

---

[18] See generally P Bartlett, et al. 'Mental Health Law in the Community: Thinking about Africa' *International Journal of Mental Health Systems* (2011) 1–7; Ibrahim, 'Mental Health in Africa' 113–137.
[19] Kamundia, 'Choice, Support and Inclusion' 62; Bartlett, 'Thinking about the Rest of the World' 407.
[20] Bartlett 'Thinking about the Rest of the World' 407–408.
[21] Ibid. 408.
[22] These camps are private Christian religious institutions usually managed by self-proclaimed prophets alleging the ability to heal various conditions, including cancer, infertility and physical or psychosocial disabilities through a combination of Christian and traditional religious beliefs and practices. Rampant human rights abuses have been observed in the prayer camps of Ghana, including forced starvation, poor hygiene and restraining practices such as shackling persons with psychosocial disabilities to trees or logs out of doors – see J Edwards 'Ghana's Mental Health Patients Confined to Prayer Camps' *The Lancet* (2014) 15–26; Human Rights Watch '"Like A Death Sentence": Abuses against Persons with Mental Disabilities in Ghana' (2012) 31.
[23] See art 1(1) of the Constitution of Zambia (as amended in 2016); art 1(2) of the Constitution of Ghana (as amended in 1996).
[24] Art 13(1)(h) of the Zambian Constitution; art 14(1)(d) of the Constitution of Ghana.

3 LEGAL CAPACITY IN SELECTED INTERNATIONAL AND AFRICAN REGIONAL HUMAN RIGHTS INSTRUMENTS

3.1 Article 12 of the CRPD

The changes to mental health laws resulting from the CRPD have been described as an 'evolving revolution',[25] with Article 12 of the CRPD at its heart.[26] The interpretation of this article has already generated extensive scholarly analysis, reflected in the diverse contributions to this book. It is however helpful to briefly examine the interpretive guidelines provided by the Committee on the Rights of Persons with Disabilities (CRPD Committee) in the form of General Comment No 1,[27] which to a large extent provides the criteria for measuring mental health legislation against the Convention.[28]

In this General Comment, the CRPD Committee firmly validates the principle of 'universal legal capacity'.[29] This point of departure first and foremost implies that denials of legal capacity which amount to disability-based discrimination are disallowed.[30] In addition, it entails that 'legal capacity' should be disentangled from 'mental capacity' in the sense that limitations in mental capacity cannot be utilised as the motivation for removing a person's legal capacity.[31] States parties are instead required to make the support required to exercise legal capacity available to persons with disabilities.[32]

The CRPD Committee spells out that the obligation to provide support encapsulated in Article 12(3) should effectively mark the end of so-called substituted decision-making systems such as guardianship: these regimes must now make way for models of supported decision-making.[33] As a consequence, practices such as involuntary treatment of persons with psychosocial disabilities or involuntary detention in institutions constitute violations of Article 12 as read with various other rights

---

[25] S Callaghan & C Ryan 'An Evolving Revolution: Evaluating Australia's Compliance with the Convention on the Rights of Persons with Disabilities in Mental Health Law' *University of New South Wales Law Journal* (2016) 596. The notion of an 'evolving revolution' inspired the title of this chapter: the (somewhat overused) phrase 'the revolution will not be televised' is the title of a poem/song by artist Gil Scott-Heron dating from the 1970s, often seen as a call for action against racial injustice.

[26] G Quinn 'Resisting the "Temptation of Elegance": Can the Convention on the Rights of Persons with Disabilities Socialise States to Right Behaviour?' in O Arnardóttir & G Quinn (eds.) *United Nations Convention on the Rights of Persons with Disabilities: European and Scandinavian Perspectives* (BRILL, 2009) 256.

[27] CRPD Committee General Comment No 1 (Art 12: Equal Recognition Before the Law) UN Doc CRPD/C/GC/1 (19 May 2014) (General Comment No 1).

[28] L Series, et al. 'Legal Capacity: A Global Analysis of Reform Trends' in P Blanck & E Flynn (eds.) *Routledge Handbook of Disability Law and Human Rights* (Routledge, 2017) 138.

[29] General Comment No 1 para 8.

[30] Ibid. para 25.

[31] Ibid. paras 13, 15.

[32] Art 12 (3) CRPD as discussed in General Comment No 1 paras 16–19.

[33] General Comment No 1 paras 3, 17, 26–27.

guaranteed in the CRPD,[34] including the right to liberty and security of the person (Article 14).[35]

The position adopted by the CRPD Committee has sparked considerable controversy. One group of commentators agrees with the CRPD Committee that substituted decision-making (including decisions regarding treatment) can never be consistent with the CRPD.[36] Others, however, decry the CRPD Committee's 'absolutist' viewpoint as unrealistic and argue for some exceptions where substituted decision-making may be permitted. These troubled waters were muddied further when the Human Rights Committee issued a general comment on the right to liberty,[37] shortly after the adoption of the CRPD Committee's General Comment No 1, which does permit involuntary detention of persons with psychosocial disabilities 'for the purpose of protecting the individual in question from serious harm or preventing injury to others.'[38] Martin and Gurbai aptly refer to this disagreement among key UN treaty monitoring bodies as 'the Geneva impasse'.[39]

The CRPD Committee's views on these principles, accepted as correct for the purposes of this chapter, of course shape the standards against which mental health legislation is measured.[40] It will therefore be assumed here that in order to be compliant with the CRPD, such legislation must incorporate at minimum an acknowledgement of universal legal capacity with support as well as a prohibition of substituted decision-making,[41] including decisions regarding admission and treatment of persons with psychosocial disabilities.

3.2 The African Charter and the African Disability Protocol

The foundational instrument in the African regional human rights system, the African Charter on Human and Peoples' Rights[42] (the African Charter), contains

---

[34] See General Comment No 1 paras 40–42.
[35] See also Committee on the Rights of Persons with Disabilities, Guidelines on Article 14 of the Convention on the Rights of Persons with Disabilities: The Right to Liberty and Security of Persons with Disabilities (2015) para 6.
[36] See e.g. literature cited in K E Wilson 'The Abolition or Reform of Mental Health Law: How Should the Law Recognise and Respond to the Vulnerability of Persons with Mental Impairment?' *Medical Law Review* (2019) footnote 6.
[37] Article 9 of the International Covenant on Civil and Political Rights (adopted 16 December 1977, entered into force 23 March 1976).
[38] Human Rights Committee General Comment No 35 on Article 9 (Liberty and Security of the Person) UN Doc CCPR/C/GC/35 (dated 16 December 2014) para 19.
[39] W Martin & S Gurbai 'Surveying the Geneva Impasse: Coercive Care and Human Rights' *International Journal on Law and Psychiatry* (2019) 117.
[40] A Dhanda 'From Duality to Indivisibility: Mental Health Care and Human Rights' *South African Journal on Human Rights* (2016) 442.
[41] See also the four criteria proposed by Davidson et al. for analysis of mental health law frameworks: G Davidson, et al. 'An International Comparison of Legal Frameworks for Supported and Substitute Decision-Making in Mental Health Services' *International Journal of Law and Psychiatry* (2016) 32.
[42] Adopted on 27 June 1981, entered into force 21 October 1986.

a very limited provision on persons with disabilities.[43] However, many other rights guaranteed in the Charter are of particular importance to persons with disabilities. This was illustrated in the communication brought before the African Commission on Human and Peoples' Rights (the African Commission) in the matter of *Purohit and Moore v The Gambia*,[44] where various provisions of the Gambian Lunatics Detention Act of 1917 were challenged for violation of the Charter. The complainants argued that this outdated legislation infringed (among others) the equality guarantees,[45] the right to dignity[46] and the right to personal liberty[47] of persons detained under this legislation.

The African Commission concurred with the complainants and found that the Act indeed constituted a violation of a number of Charter rights.[48] Although the African Commission's views have been subjected to some critique,[49] this pre-CRPD opinion is an important early endorsement of especially the right to dignity of persons with psychosocial disabilities in Africa, as well as state obligations to ensure the protection of these rights.

As mentioned, the African Union adopted the African Disability Protocol in 2018.[50] The question of legal capacity is dealt with in Article 7 of the Protocol, which to a large extent mirrors Article 12 of the CRPD. Article 7(2)(f) does elaborate on state obligations by affirming that persons with disabilities have an equal right to hold documents of identity and other documents that may enable them to exercise their right to legal capacity – of specific importance in the African context.[51]

Two other provisions of the Protocol are notable here: first, the inclusion of the state obligation to eliminate 'harmful practices'[52] perpetrated against persons with disabilities.[53] Second, under the non-discrimination provision, States parties have an obligation to protect parents, spouses and other family members closely related to

---

[43] Art 18(4) of the Charter. For a discussion of this provision, see S A D Kamga 'A Call for a Protocol to the African Charter on Human and Peoples' Rights on the Rights of Persons with Disabilities in Africa' *African Journal of International and Comparative Law* (2013) 213–249.
[44] Communication No 241/2001, Sixteenth Activity Report 2002–2003.
[45] Articles 2 and 3 of the Charter.
[46] Ibid. Art 5.
[47] Ibid. Art 6.
[48] The African Commission, Para 85.
[49] See L S Enonchong 'Mental Disability and the Rights to Personal Liberty in Africa' *International Journal of Human Rights* (2017) 1357–1358.
[50] For background on the development of the Protocol, see L Mute & E Kalekye 'An Appraisal of the Draft Protocol to the African Charter on Human and Peoples' Rights on the Rights of Persons with Disabilities in Africa' *East African Law Journal* (2016) 68–90.
[51] See e.g. Series et al., 'Legal Capacity' 141.
[52] 'Harmful practices' include attitudes and practices based on (amongst others) tradition, culture, religion or superstition which negatively affect the human rights of persons with disabilities – art 1 of the Protocol.
[53] Art 11(1).

persons with disabilities from discrimination on the basis of their association with persons with disabilities.[54]

Given the close congruence between Article 7 of the African Protocol and Article 12 of the CRPD, it is unlikely that the former will assist in resolving the 'Geneva impasse'. The Disability Protocol may nevertheless, once in operation, open up new prospects for the consolidation of human rights norms at the African regional level.

4 MENTAL HEALTH LAW REFORM IN ZAMBIA

4.1 Developing New Mental Health Legislation

The Persons with Disabilities Act (PDA), enacted in 2012, to a large extent incorporates the provisions of the CRPD into Zambian law.[55] Notably, section 8(1) of the Act provides that a person with a disability 'shall enjoy legal capacity on an equal basis with others in all aspects of life'.

Zambia enacted the Mental Health Act in 2019;[56] this Act was preceded by the Mental Disorders Act dating from 1949.[57] Over time, it became apparent that the 1949 Act had become outdated and that its implementation held deleterious consequences for persons with psychosocial disabilities.[58] As a result, a consultative process aimed at developing new mental health legislation that would be compliant with international standards was initiated. This was welcomed by the disability sector; however, this process appeared to stall after a promising start.[59]

In 2017, three disability rights activists, assisted by the Southern African Litigation Centre, launched a challenge to the Mental Disorders Act in the Zambian High Court.[60] They averred that the Mental Disorders Act unjustifiably violated a number of their constitutional rights and inter alia sought a declaration that the Act was unconstitutional.[61]

The High Court agreed that the definitions in section 5 of the Mental Disorders Act were derogatory and discriminatory and that they 'have no place in a modern

---

[54] Art 5(2)(c).
[55] Sec 12 (read with the definition of 'domestication' in sec 2) of the Ratification of International Agreements Act 34 of 2016 (Zambia); arts 75(1) & (2) of the Constitution of Ghana.
[56] Act No 6 of 2019.
[57] Chapter 305 of the Laws of Zambia.
[58] See e.g. generally Mental Disability Advocacy Center (MDAC) & Mental Health Users Network of Zambia (MHUNZA) *Human Rights and Mental Health in Zambia* (2014); A Raw 'You Only Have Rights if You are a Person: How Zambia is Legislating Away the Rights of Persons with Psychosocial Disabilities' (2019) https://africanlii.org/article/20190620/you-only-have-rights-if-you-are-person-how-zambia-legislating-away-rights-persons.
[59] Raw 'You Only Have Rights if You are a Person'.
[60] *Mwewa and Others v Attorney General and Another* (Case Number 2017/HP/204) judgment dated 9 October 2017. The three petitioners were persons with psychosocial disabilities who had experienced involuntary detention and/or treatment under the provisions of the Mental Disorders Act.
[61] See *Mwewa* judgment 3.

society'.[62] This provision, held to constitute a violation of Article 23(1)[63] of the Zambian Constitution, was accordingly declared null and void.[64] The other provisions[65] of the Mental Disorders Act impugned by the petitioners were held to be constitutionally sound.[66]

In February 2019, when a draft Mental Health Bill was eventually published, disability rights activists were dismayed to note that the contents of the Bill widely diverged from consensus reached during previous consultative processes. While ostensibly aimed at aligning policy and practice with CRPD standards, the Bill held the potential to undermine the human rights gains encapsulated in the Persons with Disabilities Act, especially the acknowledgement of universal legal capacity in section 8. The Bill also disconcertingly permitted 'special treatments' such as seclusion and restraint,[67] despite the absolute ban on such practices proposed by the UN Special Rapporteur on torture.[68]

Civil society organisations were given a very brief opportunity to comment on the proposed Bill.[69] A number of submissions were heard by the relevant parliamentary committee, with many stakeholders calling for the extensive revision of the Bill. Section 4, the key provision relating to legal capacity, came under particular scrutiny.[70] The committee's recommendations appeared to embrace many of the concerns and recommendations from civil society, and when the Bill was referred back for redrafting, hopes were raised that improvements were imminent.[71] However, the Bill soon reappeared for a final reading without any significant changes and it was this version which was enacted in April 2019.

4.2 Legal Capacity and Related Issues in the Mental Health Act of 2019

Section 4 of the Mental Health Act must be read with a number of other sections to gain a full picture of what the legislature envisaged. Subsection 4(1) affirms that

---

[62] *Mwewa* judgment 27.
[63] This article sets out the right to protection against discrimination.
[64] *Mwewa* judgment 28.
[65] Sections 6, 8, 9, 30 and 31 of the Mental Disorders Act.
[66] For a helpful discussion of the judgment, see F K Kalunga & C M Nkhata 'Protection of the Rights of Persons with Mental Disabilities to Liberty and Informed Consent to Treatment: A Critique of Gordon Maddox Mwewa & Others v Attorney-General & Another' *African Disability Rights Yearbook* (2018) 62–67, 75–80.
[67] Clause 27(2) of the Mental Health Bill, 2019; included as section 27(2) in final version.
[68] J E Méndez Report of the Special Rapporteur on torture and other cruel, inhuman or degrading treatment or punishment UN Doc A/HRC/22/53 (1 February 2013) para 63.
[69] See Raw 'You Only Have Rights if You are a Person' for an account of this process.
[70] Report of the Committee on Health, Community Development and Social Services on the Mental Health Bill NAB No 1 of 2019 for the Third Session of the Twelfth National Assembly (2019) (Committee Report).
[71] Raw 'You Only Have Rights if You are a Person'.

'mental patients'[72] 'shall enjoy legal capacity'. However, subsection 4(2) further provides that where the nature of the patient's mental disability or mental illness results in the absence of mental capacity, the person will not enjoy legal capacity and is 'legally disqualified from performing a function that requires legal capacity.'[73]

Subsection 4(3) provides that a 'supporter'[74] may be appointed by the court where a 'mental patient' lacks legal capacity.[75] Where a court declares that a 'mental patient' does not have legal capacity, that person is 'legally disqualified'.[76] (Here one assumes that the court would determine whether the person concerned lacks legal capacity.)

Section 23(1) allows for 'proxy consent' to treatment: where a 'mental patient' is unable to consent to treatment, such consent may instead be given by a supporter. The combined effect of these clauses is to put in place a system where a supporter has the power to make decisions (including treatment decisions) on behalf of a 'mental patient' perceived to lack decision-making capacity. This is borne out by section 22(1)(a), which confirms that a supporter may consent to the admission and treatment of a 'mental patient'.

Although section 25 proclaims that voluntary admission or treatment should be the preferred practice, this is qualified in that involuntary interventions '*shall* be provided' where these are necessary for the health and safety of the patient.[77] The Act further directs mental health practitioners to conduct involuntary admissions in emergency situations where it is not 'possible or reasonable' to comply with voluntary admission and treatment.[78] The criterion of 'reasonableness' introduces a significant degree of subjectivity on the part of the health practitioner.

5 MENTAL HEALTH LAW REFORM IN GHANA

5.1 *Outline of Constitutional and Legislative Framework*

Article 29 of the Constitution of Ghana addresses certain aspects of the rights of persons with disabilities.[79] On the positive side, this article guarantees persons with disabilities protection against exploitation and treatment of a discriminatory, abusive

---

[72] While the term 'mental patient' as employed in the Mental Health Act may be objectionable, it is used in this part of the chapter for purposes of correspondence with the legislation.
[73] Mental capacity is defined as 'the capability to make independent informed decisions and to act on that decision and understand the consequences of the decision made and action taken' – sec 2 of the Act.
[74] The term 'supporter' means a person who represents a mental health service user or mental patient's rights or interests – sec 2 of the Act.
[75] Subsec 4(4) deals with the appointment, through advance instructions, of a supporter by a legal patient *with* legal capacity.
[76] Sec 4(5) of the Mental Health Act.
[77] Sec 25(1)(c). Emphasis added.
[78] Sec 26.
[79] See art 29, which has eight separate sub-articles.

or degrading nature.[80] However, it also envisages the stay of persons with disabilities in a 'specialised establishment' if such stay is indispensable – which may pave the road for condonation of involuntary institutionalisation on account of psychosocial disability.[81]

The Persons with Disabilities Act, enacted in 2006,[82] includes a prohibition of discrimination against persons with disabilities;[83] this is important in the light of the omission of disability as a 'prohibited' ground of discrimination from the Constitution.[84] However, the Act makes no provision for the recognition of equal legal capacity for person with disabilities – unsurprisingly, given the date of its adoption. (The Ghanaian government, in its 2018 initial country report to the CRPD Committee, conceded that the Persons with Disabilities Act is deficient in its omission of the right to equal protection before the law.)[85] For guidance on legal capacity, resort must therefore be had to the Mental Health Act of Ghana of 2012,[86] which is discussed below.

4.2 Legal Capacity in the Mental Health Act of 2012

The Act envisages that all persons have capacity 'until reliably proven otherwise'[87] and makes provision for certain situations where such capacity may be lacking. For example, section 68 calls for the protection of persons with mental disorders who are unable to manage their personal affairs, including finance, business, marriage and the right to choice in treatment.[88] This section accordingly allows the appointment of a guardian under certain circumstances, on application to court.[89] The Act requires consultation as far as possible by the guardian with the 'incapacitated person'; however, decisions are made on behalf of the person under guardianship 'using a high standard of substituted judgement'.[90] The qualifier 'as far as possible' introduces an element of subjective judgement on the part of the guardian. Safeguards are admittedly included (for example, an affirmation of the right of the person concerned to contest the appointment of a guardian).[91]

The Mental Health Act also makes arrangements for a 'personal representative', defined as a family member or friend – whether appointed by the court or not – who

---

[80] Art 29(4).
[81] Art 29(3).
[82] Act 715 of 2006.
[83] Art 4(1).
[84] See art 7(2) of the Constitution of Ghana.
[85] Initial Report Submitted by Ghana (2018) UN Doc CRPD/C/GHA/1 (8 March 2019) paras 186, 189. The report currently awaits review by the CRPD Committee.
[86] Act 846 of 2012.
[87] Sec 79.
[88] Sec 68(1).
[89] Sec 68(2)-(4).
[90] Sec 68(6).
[91] Sec 68(5).

represents the interests of a person with a 'mental disorder'.[92] This personal representative may play a role by, for example, consenting to certain medical procedures (including sterilisation) if the person with a psychosocial disability is incapable of giving consent.[93] Involuntary interventions are permitted in terms of the Act, albeit with some procedural safeguards in place.

It is important to note that the full implementation of the Mental Health Act is dependent on the introduction, by legislative instrument, of regulations dealing with key aspects such as the provision of community health services.[94] The government of Ghana has received significant reproach from a range of bodies, including civil society organisations in Ghana and the UN Universal Peer Review process, for its ongoing failure to enact this pivotal legislative instrument.[95]

6 EVALUATION

6.1 Comparison of Mental Health Legislation in Zambia and Ghana

It is clear from the discussion above that the systems contemplated in the mental health legislation of both Zambia and Ghana amount to *substituted*[96] rather than *supported* decision-making (despite the use of the term 'supporter'). Although subsection 16(1) of the Zambian Act states that the rights of mental patients include '*supported decision-making* regarding treatment'[97], this term is not defined in the Mental Health Act and one therefore has to assume that it comports with the definition of 'supporter' as set out in section 2. This implies that the concept is similarly limited to substituted rather than supported decision-making.[98] Its Ghanaian counterpart, in section 68, explicitly states that a guardian must make decisions according to the principles of substituted decision-making.

It has been argued that persons with psychosocial disabilities in Zambia are potentially in a worse position under the new Act than would be the case under the common law position – despite the fact that the latter is not aligned with the

---

[92] As defined in sec 97.
[93] Sec 71(2).
[94] Sec 96(1)(f).
[95] A Osei 'The Mental Health Act 846, Six Years On' *Graphic Online* (28 Mar 2018) www.graphic.com.gh/news/health/the-mental-health-act-846-six-years-on.html; Human Rights Council 'Report of the Working Group on the Universal Periodic Review: Ghana' UN Doc A/HRC/37/7 (26 December 2017) paras 146.106–146.107.
[96] See description of 'substitute decision-making' provided by the CRPD Committee in General Comment No 1 para 27.
[97] Emphasis added.
[98] General Comment No 1 para 29.

CRPD requirements either.[99] This is clearly not an instance where 'bad law is better than no law at all'.[100]

Both pieces of legislation admittedly contain a number of advances. In the case of the Zambian Act these improvements include, for example, the option of advance directives[101] and the introduction of a statutory foundation for service standards.[102] However, the adoption of the Act in its current form, over the objections and concerns noted by a range of stakeholders, is disconcerting: it suggests a disregard of the obligation under the CRPD of close consultation with persons with disabilities in the development and application of legislation and policies.[103] At the time of writing, a constitutional petition challenging section 4 of the Mental Health Act is pending in the Zambian High Court and the outcome is eagerly awaited.[104]

For its part, the Ghanaian Mental Health Act is noteworthy for its clear articulation of the rights of persons with psychosocial disabilities[105] and its specific attention to vulnerable groups of persons with psychosocial disabilities (for example, women and children).[106] The Act has been hailed by commentators as 'a major milestone in addressing mental health as a public health issue'[107] and the process of consultation preceding the enactment has also met with approval.[108] Unfortunately, the potential impact of the Act is still subdued by the failure of the government to finalise the legislative instrument required for comprehensive implementation.[109] Authors such as Mfoafo-M'Carthy and Grishow have further emphasised, with reference to the questions of substituted decision-making and involuntary interventions, that the Act 'clearly contravenes the spirit and intention of the CRPD'.[110]

---

[99] MHUNZA and Disability Rights Watch 'Policy Brief: An Urgent Call to Amend Section 4 of the 2019 Mental Health Act' (June 2019) 9, 11.
[100] This phrase derives from the comment by Deng Xiaoping that it is better to have some laws than none, even if these laws may initially be imperfect – see Deng Xiaoping, *Selected Works* Vol 2 (1975–1982) (Foreign Language Press, 1995) 112.
[101] Sec 4 of the Mental Health Act. See also General Comment No 1 para 17 regarding the right of persons with disabilities to engage in advance planning.
[102] Part VI of the Act.
[103] Art 4(3) CRPD.
[104] Email communication dated 15 July 2020 from Wamundila Waliuya, director of Disability Rights Watch and one of the two petitioners in the matter – on file with authors. The Act is currently awaiting enactment of the Regulations required for its full implementation.
[105] Secs 54–56.
[106] See secs 64–66.
[107] V C Doku, et al. 'Implementing the Mental Health Act in Ghana: Any Challenges Ahead?' *Ghana Medical Journal* (2012) 241. See also G H Walker & A Osei 'Mental Health Law in Ghana' *BJ Psych International* (2017) 39.
[108] Doku et al. 'Implementing the Mental Health Act in Ghana' 241–242.
[109] As authorised under sec 96(1) of the Mental Health Act.
[110] See M Mfoafo-M'Carthy & JD Grishow 'Mental Illness, Stigma and Disability Rights in Ghana' *African Disability Rights Yearbook* (2017) 97.

6.2 Possible Solutions: What Then Is to Be Done?

It may become tempting to pose the question of whether the 'principled'[111] approach adopted by the CRPD Committee in respect of involuntary interventions is a feasible one in the case of lower-income countries in the Global South, where the development of alternatives to coercive practices may be greatly hampered by a lack of resources. However, this enquiry, taken to its extreme, may result in a form of 'human rights relativism'. In this regard, Bartlett cautions against departures from 'universal' human rights standards, meant to apply to everyone everywhere: such a selective approach would run the risk of eroding the recognition, hard-won by persons with disabilities, that all persons are worthy of human rights protection.[112] As noted above, the pervasive differences between the cultural, socio-economic and legal environments in the Global South and those in the Global North imply that mental health law reform initiatives may also at present require approaches that are dissimilar.

A number of proposals have been put forward aimed at resolving the so-called 'Geneva impasse'. For example, Davidson allows that the community-based alternatives with individualised support which are required to eliminate involuntary interventions are likely out of reach in lower- and middle-income countries.[113] This implies that even if a full ban of coercion were to be enacted, implementation in practice would be impossible. (It should be noted here that significantly more evidence is required before one would be able to identify 'best' support practices which are appropriate in all contexts – if that is possible at all.) Davidson accordingly proposes the introduction of 'stop-gap' legislative measures aimed at significantly reducing involuntary interventions while moving towards eventual full compliance with the CRPD.[114] At the same time, alternatives to involuntary interventions should be strengthened.[115] She accepts that such legislation effectively amount to 'progressive realisation', which would ordinarily not be applicable to the rights concerned,[116] and further that governments may well have qualms about recurrent legislative changes. At the same time, she pragmatically argues that an incremental approach, initiated by interim 'holding' legislation, may be more palatable to public sentiment and may serve to address stigma while also raising standards for human rights

---

[111] See O Lewis & A Campbell 'Violence and Abuse against People with Disabilities: A Comparison of the Approaches of the European Court of Human Rights and the United Nations Committee on the Rights of Persons with Disabilities' *International Journal of Law and Psychiatry* (2017) 56.
[112] Bartlett 'Thinking about the Rest of the World' 400.
[113] L Davidson 'A Key, Not a Straightjacket: The Case for Interim Mental Health Legislation Pending Complete Prohibition of Psychiatric Coercion in Accordance with the Convention on the Rights of Persons with Disabilities' *Health and Human Rights Journal* (2020) 166.
[114] Ibid. 167.
[115] Ibid.
[116] These rights include the right to equal recognition before the law, non-discrimination and the right to liberty. The CRPD Committee has expressly stated that 'progressive realisation' is not applicable to Article 12 – see General Comment No 1 (above) para 30.

protection (see also Chapter 5 by Laura Davidson in this volume). She accordingly calls on the CRPD Committee to issue a general comment authorising such measures.[117]

7 CONCLUDING OBSERVATIONS

[W]e should view the Convention less as a means for coercing States and more as a powerful tool for enabling its revolutionary insights to percolate into the political process...[118]

At the beginning of this chapter, the question was posed whether recent initiatives to reform mental health law in certain African jurisdictions can be seen as compliant with the CRPD in respect of universal legal capacity. The shortcomings we have observed above could lead one to answer in the negative. However, there are some positive aspects as well: the enactment of mental health legislation which expressly protects the rights of persons with psychosocial disabilities indicates (at least) a degree of political will on the part of the Zambian and Ghanaian governments. The court challenges of outdated legislation brought by persons with psychosocial disabilities in Zambia are also encouraging. Despite the lack of meaningful consultation with persons with psychosocial disabilities in the Zambian legislative process, and the long-standing hesitancy of the Ghanaian government to enact the required legislative instrument, it can be said that these two countries have taken steps in the right direction. Nonetheless, if we may ponder: is the current legislation perhaps the type of 'holding' law which Davidson envisages?

Realistically, States parties to the CRPD will be grappling with the implications of legal capacity and Article 12 for some time yet. It is becoming apparent that lawmakers will have to engage with the CRPD in a holistic sense, recognising the interconnectedness and indivisibility of rights. One also hopes that as implementation of the Convention at national level matures over time, it will be possible to provide more tangible guidelines on compliance with Article 12 to States parties (for example, in the form of replicable practices that have proven successful).[119] The revolution is not yet complete.

---

[117] Davidson 'A Key, Not a Straightjacket' 174. See also Martin and Gurbai 'Surveying the Geneva Impasse' 126–127; Martin and Gurbai similarly call for a general comment by the CRPD Committee, but in this instance aimed at clarifying the right to freedom from torture (art 15 of the CRPD) in the context of psychiatric practices.

[118] Quinn 'Resisting the "Temptation of Elegance"' 256.

[119] See generally E Flynn, et al. (eds) *Global Perspectives on Legal Capacity Reform* (Taylor & Francis, 2019).

13

Supported Decision-Making and Legal Capacity in Kenya

Elizabeth Kamundia and Ilze Grobbelaar-du Plessis

Abstract

The chapter reviews the mental health law reform relating to legal capacity and the involuntary treatment of persons with psychosocial disabilities in Kenya in response to the concluding observations of the Committee on the Rights of Persons with Disabilities in 2015 to reform mental health law. The chapter demonstrates that despite the progressive provisions of the Convention on the Rights of Persons with Disabilities and public participation in the legislative process of Civil Society Organisations (CSOs), including those of persons with disabilities (DPOs) and Kenya's national human rights institution (NHRI) on supported decision-making of persons with psychosocial disabilities in the Mental Health (Amendment) Bill of 2018, prevailing views of contemporary Kenyan society still conceptualise persons with psychosocial disabilities to be dependent on relatives and other third parties in decision-making processes. The socio-cultural perception of psychosocial disability in Kenya outlines the cultural and social underpinnings of decision-making, which inform and influence parliamentarians during the law reform process. The chapter considers alternative strategies to influence the law reform process, including the need to raise awareness among parliamentarians about the human rights, dignity and autonomy of persons with psychosocial disabilities, and the development of practical alternatives to the medical model of mental health care.

1 INTRODUCTION

All persons with disabilities, including those with psychosocial disabilities, are entitled to enjoy legal capacity on an equal basis with others in all aspects of life,[1] including in healthcare treatment decision-making.[2] In this regard, the UN

---

[1] Article 12(2) of the Convention on the Rights of Persons with Disabilities (CRPD) and its Optional Protocol (UN Doc A/RES/61/106), adopted by the General Assembly of the United Nations (UN) on 13 December 2006. See Dhanda, A. (2006–2007) Legal capacity in the disability rights convention: stranglehold of the past or lodestar for the future? *Syracuse Journal of International Law & Commerce*, 34(429), 442 for arguments raised during the negotiations of the CRPD.

[2] Series, L. and Nilsson, A. (2018). Article 12 CRPD Equal recognition before the law. In I. Bantekas, M. A. Stein and D. Anastasiou (eds.) *The UN Convention on the Rights of Persons with Disabilities, a Commentary* (366). Oxford University Press.

Committee on the Rights of Persons with Disabilities (CRPD Committee)[3] recommended in their 2015 concluding observations to Kenya's initial State party report that Kenya[4] should abolish its existing mental health laws (which authorise involuntary treatment and detention), and replace them with a regime of supported decision-making.[5] In 2018 Kenya's Senate[6] tabled the Mental Health (Amendment) Bill, which provides for the advancement of the rights of persons with disabilities in Kenya.

This chapter examines the law reform process in Kenya by briefly analysing the current Mental Health Act of 1989,[7] the report of the Kenyan Senate Standing Committee on Health that deliberated on the Mental Health (Amendment) Bill, as well as memoranda submitted by CSOs including those of persons with disabilities (DPOs) and Kenya's NHRI on the Mental Health (Amendment) Bill. The chapter demonstrates that although NHRIs and DPOs may make progressive submissions on amendments required to ensure a rights-based mental health law, parliamentarians – who hold the power to amend and repeal laws – may not easily accept the proposals for law reform. The chapter argues that while it is important for NHRIs and DPOs to participate in the law reform processes, other strategies should be considered to influence lawmakers to create legislation on mental health consistent with the CRPD. These include awareness raising about the human rights, dignity and autonomy of persons with psychosocial disabilities among lawmakers and the development of practical alternatives to the medical model of mental health care.

2 LAWS REGULATING HEALTHCARE IN KENYA

Kenyan law provides for different categories of public health and welfare laws,[8] one of which is to establish the right to the highest attainable standard of healthcare,[9] and

---

[3] Article 33 CRPD.
[4] The CRPD was signed on 30 March 2007 and ratified on 19 May 2008.
[5] Concluding observations on the initial report of Kenya, UN Doc CRPD/C/KEN/CO/1 (30 September 2015) paras 5, 23, 24, 28(a), 46.
[6] Article 93 of the 2010 Constitution of Kenya provides for Parliament to consist of the National Assembly and the Senate.
[7] Act 10 of 1989.
[8] The first category includes laws establishing the right to the highest attainable standard of health care. The second category provides for legislation aimed at regulating health system input, including medical education (Nurses Act 3 of 1983; Kenya Medical Training College Act 14 of 1990; and the Science, Technology and Innovation Act 28 of 2013). The third category includes laws that set up a legal framework for health insurance (National Social Security Fund Act 45 of 2013). The fourth category secures and maintains health, and protects against harmful substances (Public Health Act 38 of 1921; Radiation Protection Act 20 of 1982; Malaria Prevention Act 19 of 1929; Use of Poisonous Substances Act 23 of 1957; and Food, Drugs and Chemical Substances Act 8 of 1965). The fifth category is the Mental Health Act 10 of 1989.
[9] Article 2(5) and 2(6) of the 2010 Constitution of Kenya provides for international human rights instruments to form part of the Kenyan law. These include: International Covenant on Economic, Social and Cultural Rights (ICESCR), 6 ILM 368 (1967); CRPD, UN Doc A/61/611 (2006); and the African Charter on Human and Peoples' Rights (ACHPR), 21 ILM 58 (1982).

another of which is the Mental Health Act,[10] which provides for the 'care of persons who are suffering from mental disorder',[11] and the management of the estates of such persons.[12]

Article 43(1)(a) of the 2010 Constitution of Kenya protects every person's right to the highest attainable standard of health and by way of constitutional injunction in article 2(6) of the Constitution,[13] several international[14] and regional instruments[15] are part of Kenya's mental health law. Kenya's Mental Health Act[16] provides for voluntary, involuntary and emergency treatment decisions on behalf of persons with psychosocial disabilities, which will be assessed against the CRPD in the paragraphs that follow.

2.1 Assessing the Mental Health Act against the Backdrop of Article 12 of the CRPD

Contrary to the obligation imposed by article 12 of the CRPD,[17] the current Mental Health Act[18] expressly provides for guardianship of persons to whom the Act applies, as well as the management of the person's estate by another person on account of disability.[19] The medical model of disability is embedded in the Act, in prescribing that 'disability must be cured or managed with the assistance of medical practitioners and rehabilitation specialists'.[20] Further evidence of the model in the Act is provisions that legitimise the detention of persons with disabilities in institutions

---

[10] Act 10 of 1989.
[11] Preamble, Act 10 of 1989.
[12] Part XII, Act 10 of 1989, 'Judicial power over persons and estates of persons suffering from mental disorder.'
[13] The monist approach established in articles 2(5) and 2(6) of the 2010 Constitution of Kenya provides for 'general rules of international law' to 'form part of the law of Kenya'. See *Karen Njeri Kandie v Alssane & another* (CA, 13 February 2015); *R v Permanent Secretary Office of the President Ministry of Internal Security & another Ex-Parte Nassir Mwandihi* (HC, 3 April 2014) and *Re Zipporah Wangui Mathara* (HC, 24 September 2010).
[14] Article 12 ICESCR 6 ILM 368 (1967); Article 25 CRPD and its Optional Protocol, UN Doc A/RES/61/106; Article 5(e)(iv) International Convention on the Elimination of All Forms of Racial Discrimination, 660 UNTS 195; Articles 11.1 (f) and 12 Convention on the Elimination of All Forms of Discrimination against Women, 19 ILM 33 (1980); Article 24 of the Convention on the Rights of the Child, 28 ILM 1456 (1989).
[15] Article 16 ACHPR, 21 ILM 58 (1982); Article 14 of the Protocol to the African Charter on Human and Peoples' Rights on the Rights of Women in Africa OAU, Doc CAB/LEG/66.6 (13 September 2000); Article 14 of the African Charter on the Rights and Welfare of the Child, OAU Doc CAB/LEG/24.9/49 (1990).
[16] Act 10 of 1989.
[17] General Comment No. 1 (2014) Article 12: equal recognition before the law UN Doc CRPD/C/GC/1 paras 7; 26 and 27.
[18] Act 10 of 1989.
[19] Section 26(1), Act 10 of 1989.
[20] Grobbelaar-du Plessis, I., & Reenen, T. (2011). Introduction to Aspects of Disability Law in Africa. In Grobbelaar-du Plessis. , I & Reenen, T (Eds.). *Aspects of Disability Law in Africa*, xv, xxiii. Pretoria, Pretoria: Pretoria University Law Press.

against their will (either without their consent or with the consent of a substitute decision-maker).²¹

The Act provides for substituted decision-making²² when the individual becomes 'incapable of expressing himself as willing or unwilling to receive treatment',²³ as well as becoming 'incapable of managing his affairs'.²⁴ Under these provisions, the right to legal capacity of persons with psychosocial disabilities to make decisions in respect of mental health treatment is expressly limited.

No guidelines regarding decision-making are provided in the Act, when making decisions on behalf of the person concerned.²⁵ This means that the Act does not provide for any safeguards against exploitation and/or abuse by substitute decision-makers when making decisions regarding admission/treatment on behalf of the person with a psychosocial disability. In addition to the absence of safeguards, the Act does not provide for any requirements regarding record keeping surrounding the circumstances of the emergency treatment of the individual; neither does the Act provide for an appeals procedure.

The Act provides for the 'best interest' standard²⁶ with regard to admission and/or treatment of person with a psychosocial disability, rather than a standard based on the 'will and preference'²⁷ of the individual admitted. Very limited consideration is paid to patient autonomy during the admission and treatment process.²⁸ The will and preference of the person is not taken into consideration, which means that the individual is regarded as an object of treatment and not a subject of rights.²⁹ Finally, the Act does not provide for any assistance and/or support in communication during the admission and/or treatment process, and neither does the Act provide for a supported decision-making process.

However, it is important to note that Kenya's Mental Health Policy includes, as one of its strategies, the review and revision of Kenya's mental health legislation.³⁰ More specifically, the policy provides for law reform and to align mental health laws with constitutional requirements.³¹ Before addressing the ongoing process to amend

---

[21] Part VI (on involuntary treatment) and part VII (on emergency treatment) of Act 10 of 1989.
[22] Sections 10(3), 14(2) and 16(2), Act 10 of 1989.
[23] Section 14(1), Act 10 of 1989.
[24] Section 26, Act 10 of 1989.
[25] Kamundia, E. (30 October 2018). *Supported Decision-Making as a Human Rights Principle in Mental Health Care: An International and Comparative Analysis* (Doctoral dissertation, University of Pretoria).
[26] Section 14(1), Act 10 of 1989.
[27] Article 12(4) CRPD.
[28] Donnelly, M. (2010). *Healthcare Decision-Making and the Law: Autonomy, Capacity and the Limits of Liberalism* Cambridge University Press, 226.
[29] UN Division for Social Policy and Development. Convention on the Rights of Persons with Disabilities. Retrieved from www.un.org/development/desa/disabilities/convention-on-the-rights-of-persons-with-disabilities.html.
[30] Section 2.2, Kenya Mental Health Policy 2015–2030.
[31] Ibid., section 2.3.1.

the Kenyan Mental Health Act,[32] it is important to understand the prevailing views of contemporary Kenyan society regarding the socio-cultural constructs of psychosocial disability.

3 CONTEXTUALISING KENYAN SOCIETY AND MENTAL HEALTH LAW REFORM

Two important factors that influence the mental health law reform process in the Kenyan context, and subsequently had an impact on the Mental Health (Amendment) Bill of 2018, are Kenyan society's acceptance of substituted decision-making practices and family care dependency of persons with psychosocial disabilities.

Informal substituted decision-making practices that inevitably violate the right to legal capacity of persons with disabilities – and more specifically persons with psychosocial disabilities – are prevalent and embedded in the social mores, customs and practices of Kenyan society.[33] Decision-making on behalf of persons with disabilities, even when that person is not legally under guardianship, is made by family members and/or other third parties. They take decisions on behalf of the person with a disability, as if the person were formally placed under guardianship by a court.[34] The current Mental Health Act[35] provides for substitute decision-making in mental health treatment in accordance with and against the backdrop of these accepted Kenyan cultural and social norms and practices. It is therefore not surprising that the Mental Health (Amendment) Bill of 2018 maintains substitute decision-making practices, consistent with the current socio-cultural construct of psychosocial disability in Kenya.

Secondly, it is worth noting that a significant number of persons with psychosocial disabilities live with their families without individualised state-funded support services.[36] Importantly, unemployment and poverty among persons with psychosocial disabilities contribute to dependency on family members. The care dependency on family members contributes to decisions being made on their behalf and further undermines the exercise of legal capacity across many spheres of life.[37] Concurrently, with the concept of *Ubuntu* that underlies many African societies, the importance of the individual as a member of the community is recognised,[38]

---

[32] Act 10 of 1989.
[33] Users and Survivors of Psychiatry – Kenya (USPKenya). (2017). The role of peer support in exercising legal capacity. Retrieved from www.uspkenya.org/reports/.
[34] USPKenya, The role of peer support; Concluding observations on the initial report of Kenya, UN Doc CRPD/C/KEN/CO/1 (30 September 2015) paras 23–24.
[35] Act 10 of 1989.
[36] Kamundia, E. (2013). Choice, support and inclusion: implementing article 19 of the CRPD in Kenya. *African Disability Rights Yearbook* 1, 49.
[37] USPKenya, The role of peer support, 7.
[38] Howell, C., Lorenzo, T., & Sompeta-Gcaza, S. (2019) Reimagining personal and collective experiences of disability in Africa. *Disability and the Global South* 6(2) 1719–1735.

which may account for disability being a shared experience and responsibility of the family. Given the Kenyan context and the central role that families play in the lives of persons with psychosocial disabilities, it is not surprising that the Mental Health (Amendment) Bill of 2018 provides for a 'representative' who is (for the most part) a relative of the person, and who may make decisions on behalf of the person with a mental illness.[39] Kenyan mental health law reform takes place against the backdrop of these cultural and social underpinnings.

4 LAW REFORM: THE MENTAL HEALTH (AMENDMENT) BILL OF 2018

On 5 December 2018 the Mental Health (Amendment) Bill[40] underwent its first reading in Senate and was subsequently submitted to the Senate Standing Committee on Health.[41] In terms of articles 10 and 118(1)(b) of the 2010 Constitution of Kenya on public participation, the Committee received submissions from a variety of stakeholders, including Kenya's NHRI,[42] the Kenya National Commission on Human Rights (KNCHR or the Commission) and CSOs.[43] The KNCHR and CSOs' submissions to the Standing Committee on Health will be highlighted below.

4.1 Public Participation on the Mental Health (Amendment) Bill: KNCHR

The Commission is an independent national human rights institution established in terms of article 59 of the Constitution of Kenya and the Kenya National Commission on Human Rights Act.[44] The Commission has a broad mandate to promote the respect of human rights in the Republic of Kenya. The Commission's functions are guided by the 1993 UN Principles relating to the Status of National Institutions (Paris Principles),[45] and is accredited as an 'A' status institution for its

---

[39] Clause 3 Mental Health (Amendment) Bill, 2018.
[40] Kenya Gazette Supplement No. 136 (1 November 2018).
[41] Kenyan Parliament's Senate Standing Committee on Health (2019). Report of the Committee on the Mental Health (Amendment) Bill, Senate Bill No. 32 of 2018. 12th Parliament, 3rd Session (Report of Senate Standing Committee on Health), 6–7.
[42] Global Alliance of National Human Rights Institutions. Retrieved from https://ganhri.org/.
[43] The following stakeholders participated: Nursing Staff – Mathari National Teaching and Referral Hospital; Calmind Foundation; Kenya Psychiatrists Association; Validity Foundation; International Institute on Legislative Affairs; Ministry of Health; Kenya Progressive Nurses Association; Health Rights Advocacy Forum; Moi Teaching & Referral Hospital; KNCHR; True North; Kenya Private Schools Association; Chiromo Lane Medical Centre; USPKenya; Independent Medico Legal Unit; Befrienders; Headspace; Tom Osanjo; Mental360; Tinada Youth Organisation; and Kenya Nutrition and Dieticians Institute. Kenyan Parliament's Senate Standing Committee on Health (2019). Report of the Committee on the Mental Health (Amendment) Bill, Senate Bill No. 32 of 2018. 12th Parliament, 3rd Session (Report of Senate Standing Committee on Health) 20.
[44] Act 14 of 2011 (as amended 2012).
[45] Principles relating to the Status of National Institutions (The Paris Principles), adopted by the UN General Assembly resolution 48/134 of 20 December 1993.

compliance with the Paris Principles by the Global Alliance of National Human Rights Institutions.[46] The Commission also enjoys Affiliate Status before the African Commission on Human and Peoples' Rights.

The importance of NHRIs in implementation of the CRPD is recognised under article 33(2) of the CRPD,[47] which requires state parties to maintain, strengthen, designate or establish within the state party one or more independent mechanism(s) to promote, protect and monitor implementation of the Convention. The State party may choose to appoint an existing body or bodies and empower them with the mandate to promote, protect and monitor the implementation of rights contained in the Convention.[48] For purposes of this chapter it is important to note that the KNCHR has a specific mandate to monitor the implementation of the CRPD in terms of article 33(2), and is compliant with the Paris Principles as an independent body.[49]

Due to the monitoring obligations of the Commission, the Commission serves as the convener of the CSOs stakeholders' forum on Mental Health, which includes DPOs. The CSOs stakeholders' forum holds quarterly meetings, during which a variety of issues are discussed.[50] One recurrent theme on the stakeholders' forum is the proposed amendments to the current Mental Health Act, that have to be incorporated through the proposed Mental Health (Amendment) Bill of 2018. In this regard, Sections 5.1 and 6.1 of the chapter will focus on specific proposals made by the Commission and CSOs to the Senate Standing Committee on Health regarding the Mental Health (Amendment) Bill of 2018 relating to the right to exercise legal capacity on an equal basis with others, and the Committee's response thereto.

4.2 Public Participation on the Mental Health (Amendment) Bill: Perspectives from CSOs

CSOs that participated in the Mental Health (Amendment) Bill review process can be placed into three categories: organisations of persons with disabilities/DPOs,

---

[46] Global Alliance of National Human Rights Institutions. (October 2019). Report and recommendations of the session of the Sub-Committee on Accreditation. Retrieved from https://nhri.ohchr.org/EN/AboutUs/GANHRIAccreditation/Documents/SCA%20Report%20October%202019%20English.pdf?Mobile=1.

[47] Beco, G. D. (2011). Article 33(2) of the United Nations Convention on the Rights of Persons with Disabilities: another role for national human rights institutions. *Netherlands Quarterly of Human Rights* 29(3).

[48] Ibid.

[49] Ibid.

[50] Including key amendments to the Mental Health Act of 1989 and ways of engaging with the Mental Health Taskforce set up in December 2019 to assess mental health systems and mental well-being of Kenyans: Ministry of Health. (11 December 2019). Retrieved from www.health.go.ke/taskforce-formed-to-assess-mental-health-issues-of-kenyans/. The CSOs stakeholders' forum was instrumental to developing a mental health handbook: *The Many Faces of Mental Health in Kenya*. (2019). Retrieved from http://ilakenya.org/wp-content/uploads/2019/10/The-Many-Faces-of-Mental-Health-in-Kenya.pdf.

organisations for persons with disabilities and human rights-based CSOs that work to advance the rights of persons with psychosocial disabilities (among others).

There are many organisations of persons with disabilities/DPOs in Kenya that fully participate in the implementation of the CRPD. These organisations take part in and are involved in the monitoring process consistent with the CRPD.[51] However, mental health has historically been approached as a health and not a disability-related matter. Consequently only a few DPOs focus on the rights of persons with psychosocial disabilities in Kenya. Among the DPOs, Only USPKenya,[52] Calmind Foundation,[53] Headspace254[54] and Mental360[55] specifically focus on persons with psychosocial disabilities and their rights. True to the spirit of the rallying call 'nothing about us, without us' that was central in the process of drafting the CRPD,[56] all of the mentioned DPOs made submissions to the Senate Standing Committee on Health on the Mental Health (Amendment) Bill of 2018. However, DPOs that do not focus on the rights of persons with psychosocial disabilities did not participate in the process.

Organisations of persons with disabilities were joined by organisations for persons with disabilities in making submissions to the Senate Standing Committee on Health, including Basic Rights Basic Needs – Kenya,[57] True North,[58] Validity Foundation[59] and Befrienders.[60] Other CSOs that also focus on specific aspects pertaining to persons with psychosocial disabilities include the International Institute on Legislative Affairs,[61] Health Rights Advocacy Forum,[62] Independent Medico Legal Unit[63] and Tinada Youth Organisation.[64] These CSOs joined in the public participation process and also made submissions to the Senate Standing Committee on Health regarding the proposed Mental Health (Amendment) Bill of 2018.[65] Additionally, most of the aforenamed organisations (including the identified DPOs) are part of the CSOs stakeholder's forum convened by the KNCHR,[66]

---

[51] Art 33(3) CRPD; Kamundia, E. (2014). Kenya. *African Disability Rights Yearbook* 2, 198.
[52] USPKenya. Retrieved from www.uspkenya.org/about-us/.
[53] Calmind Foundation. Retrieved from http://calmindfoundation.org/.
[54] Headspace254. Retrieved from https://web.facebook.com/Headspace254/?_rdc=1&_rdr.
[55] Mental360. Retrieved from https://mental360.or.ke/.
[56] United Nations Department of Economic and Social Affairs (3 December 2004) Retrieved from www.un.org/development/desa/disabilities/international-day-of-persons-with-disabilities-3-december/international-day-of-disabled-persons-2004-nothing-about-us-without-us.html.
[57] Basic Rights Basic Needs – Kenya. Retrieved from www.basicneeds.org/where-we-work/kenya/.
[58] True North. Retrieved from https://fundrazr.com/71Lxm8?ref=ab_5RuqN2NzCTa5RuqN2NzCTa.
[59] Validity Foundation is an international non-governmental organisation. Retrieved from https://validity.ngo/.
[60] Befrienders Kenya. Retrieved from www.befrienderskenya.org/.
[61] International Institute on Legislative Affairs. Retrieved from https://ilakenya.org/.
[62] Health Rights Advocacy Forum. Retrieved from https://heraf.or.ke/.
[63] Independent Medico Legal Unit. Retrieved from www.imlu.org/.
[64] Tinada Youth Organisation. Retrieved from www.mhinnovation.net/organisations/tinada-youth-organization-tiyo.
[65] Report of Senate Standing Committee on Health, 20.
[66] Except True North, Independent Medico Legal Unit and Tinada Youth Organisation.

which took part in the public participation process on a range of issues including legal capacity, the appointment of a representative and involuntary admission.

5 LEGAL CAPACITY AND APPOINTMENT OF A REPRESENTATIVE

Clause 3 K of the Mental Health (Amendment) Bill 2018 provides for the right to equal recognition before the law for users of mental health services in all aspects of their life. However, the clause further provides that courts can determine whether a person has legal capacity,[67] and where the court finds that a person lacks legal capacity, appoint a representative to manage the person's affairs. Clause 3 of the Bill defines a 'representative' to mean the spouse, parent, guardian, next of kin or a court-appointed representative of the person suffering from mental illness. The representative has the legal capacity to make decisions on behalf of the person with mental illness. Clause 3J of the Bill provides for the right of a user of mental health services to choose and appoint a representative. However, the Bill also provides that a representative will be appointed on behalf of a person who is unable to appoint a representative for him or herself.[68]

Numerous other clauses make reference to 'representative', including clauses on consent to treatment; legal capacity; seclusion and restraint; and conditions for emergency admission and treatment. These clauses limit and/or restrict the rights of users of mental health care services, and more specifically their legal capacity, since legal capacity is to be determined by a court. In addition, the Bill empowers the court to remove legal capacity from an individual on the basis of a mental illness.[69]

5.1 Responses by the KNCHR and DPOs on Legal Capacity in the Mental Health (Amendment) Bill, 2018

In its memorandum to the Senate Standing Committee on Health, the Commission proposed that clause 3K be revised to provide for the right to legal capacity. This should be done with no restrictions and/or exclusions and support should be provided for the exercise of legal capacity where necessary.[70] The Commission recommended that where significant efforts were made to determine what the will and preferences of an individual is, and despite the efforts it was difficult to determine, the 'best interpretation' thereof should be followed.[71] The best interpretation of will and preference should be followed with due regard to certain safeguards.

---

[67] Clause 3K(2) and (3) Mental Health (Amendment) Bill, 2018.
[68] Ibid., Clause 3J(2).
[69] Ibid., clause 3K(2).
[70] KNCHR. (8 March 2019). Advisory on the Mental Health (Amendment) Bill, 2018. [Memorandum] KNCHR, 12.
[71] UN Doc CRPD/C/GC/1 (11 April 2014).

These include paying attention to the person's long-lasting or more general beliefs, values and desires[72] and having regard to an interpretation that upholds all rights under the Constitution and international law. The person(s) interpreting the individual's will and preferences should also not have a conflict of interest in relation to the decision that has to be made. The Commission also called for the deletion of clause 3J(2) where there is an inference that a representative can be appointed on behalf of a user of mental health services against his/her will.[73]

One DPO, USPKenya, took a similar position as the Commission on the issue of legal capacity. In its submission, USPKenya noted:

> If persons with psychosocial disabilities can exercise their rights on an equal basis with others, we cannot go on and say that a court may determine whether they can exercise the said rights, because the right is inherent by virtue of the fact that they are human beings. This means that section 3 K(2) is limiting the right to legal capacity which ought not to be limited according to Article 12 of the United Nations Convention on the Rights of Persons with Disabilities.[74]

The Senate Standing Committee on Health's report evaluating the views received from public participation, noted that '[a]n amendment is required to provide for supportive decision making in order to conform to the requirements on the Convention on the Rights of Persons with Disabilities'.[75] The Committee emphasised that the proposed clauses 3K(2) and (3) are in conflict with the CRPD.[76] According to the Committee, supported decision-making 'promotes respect for the will and preferences of persons with mental illness'.[77] However, the Committee maintained 'there is still a need for "representatives" as defined under the Bill where a supporter has not been appointed by the person with mental illness'.[78]

6 INVOLUNTARY ADMISSION

Clause 22 of the Mental Health (Amendment) Bill of 2018 proposes amendments to section 14 of the Mental Health Act,[79] which provides for instances where a mental health facility may admit a person to a mental health facility involuntarily. Clause 22 proposes that a person may be admitted involuntarily if a qualified medical practitioner is of the opinion that the person poses imminent harm to him/herself or others

---

[72] Skowron, P. (2019). Giving substance to 'the best interpretation of will and preferences'. *International Journal of Law and Psychiatry*, 62, https://doi.org/10.1016/j.ijlp.2018.12.001.
[73] KNCHR. (8 March 2019). Advisory on the Mental Health (Amendment) Bill, 2018. [Memorandum] KNCHR, 14.
[74] USPKenya. (8 March 2019). *Comments on the Mental Health (Amendment) Bill, 2018.* [Memorandum].
[75] Report of Senate Standing Committee on Health, 35.
[76] Ibid., 36.
[77] Ibid., 66.
[78] Ibid.
[79] Act 10 of 1989.

due to mental illness;[80] if the failure to admit the person will lead to serious deterioration in the condition of the person;[81] or if failure to admit will hinder the provision of appropriate treatment which can only be given through the admission of the person to a mental health facility.[82] Clause 22(b)(1D) authorises the person in charge of the facility to 'detain the person for the duration necessary to stabilize the person with mental illness and provide mental health care services to the person'. Involuntary admission is permitted for a period not exceeding six months.

6.1 Responses by the KNCHR and CSOs on Involuntary Admission in the Mental Health (Amendment) Bill of 2018

In its submission to the Senate Standing Committee on Health, the Commission recommended the deletion of clause 22 of the Mental Health (Amendment) Bill and referred to article 14 of the CRPD,[83] which determines that persons with disabilities are not deprived of their liberty unlawfully of arbitrary.[84] Furthermore, the Commission highlighted that the CRPD Committee in its review of Kenya's state report in 2015 expressed concern that 'persons with disabilities can be detained on the basis of actual or perceived impairment (existence of mental illness); the alleged danger of persons to themselves or to others and the alleged need of care and treatment which is incompatible with the Convention.'[85] In this regard, the CRPD Committee called on Kenya to amend its legislation especially the Mental Health Act to prohibit involuntary placement.[86]

Validity Foundation, an international non-governmental organisation operating in Kenya, referred to both the UN Special Rapporteur on the right to health, Dainius Pūras,[87] as well as the UN Special Rapporteur on torture and other cruel, inhuman or degrading treatment or punishment, Juan E Méndez,[88] who both denounced the practice of involuntary treatment and other forced psychiatric interventions as contraventions of the CRPD.[89] Validity Foundation noted that Pūras argues that forced treatment is ineffective and 'perpetuates power imbalances in care

---

[80] Clause 14 (1) (a) Mental Health (Amendment) Bill, 2018.
[81] Ibid., clause 14(1)(b).
[82] Ibid., clause 14(1)(c).
[83] Committee on the Rights of Persons with Disabilities' Guidelines on the right to liberty and security of persons with disabilities, UN Doc. A/72/55 (17 August 2015–4 September 2015).
[84] KNCHR. (8 March 2019). Advisory on the Mental Health (Amendment) Bill, 2018. [Memorandum] KNCHR. 21–22.
[85] UN Doc CRPD/C/KEN/CO/1 (30 September 2015), para 27.
[86] Ibid., para 28(a).
[87] Human Rights Council, Report of the Special Rapporteur on the right of everyone to the enjoyment of the highest attainable standard of physical and mental health, Dainius Pūras, (2017) A/HRC/35/21.
[88] Human Rights Council, Report of the Special Rapporteur on torture and other cruel, inhuman or degrading treatment or punishment, Juan E. Méndez, (2013) A/HRC/22/53.
[89] Validity. (2019). Submissions by Validity NGO on the Mental Health (Amendment) Bill, 2018. [Memorandum].

relationships, causes mistrust, exacerbates stigma and discrimination and has made many turn away, fearful of seeking help within mainstream mental health services'.[90] Validity Foundation also highlighted that involuntary hospitalisation has been associated with increased risk of suicide both during the time of hospitalisation,[91] and after hospitalisation.[92]

In its response to the submissions, the Committee declined to remove the provisions on involuntary admission. However, the Committee noted that safeguards should be built into the Bill to protect individuals against violation of rights during involuntary placement. The Committee further noted the importance of amending the provision to conform to the CRPD, and to provide for supported decision-making.[93]

7 OTHER ISSUES RAISED BY ORGANISATIONS OF AND FOR PERSONS WITH DISABILITIES ON THE MENTAL HEALTH (AMENDMENT) BILL OF 2018

Other issues that were raised by organisations of and for persons with disabilities include use of dignifying language in referring to people with psychosocial disabilities;[94] the need to include persons with psychosocial disabilities and their caregivers in county mental health councils and as county executive committee members;[95] and provision of legal representation for persons with psychosocial disabilities.[96] Organisations also called for the establishment of a mental health service response to national disasters;[97] express provisions for vulnerable groups such as women, children,[98] prisoners and people emerging from conflict or disasters;[99] and the integration of traditional and alternative medicine practitioners into the mental health care and support system.[100]

---

[90] Ibid.
[91] Daniel, C., Christopher, R. & Mathew L. (2016). Commentary: adverse experiences in psychiatric hospitals might be the cause of some post discharge suicides. *Bulletin of the Menninger Clinic* 80(4), 371–375.
[92] Jordan, J. T., & McNeil, D. E. (2019). Perceived coercion during admission into psychiatric hospitalization increases risk of suicide attempts after discharge. *Suicide and Life-Threatening Behavior*, 50(1), 180–188. https://doi/10.1111/sltb.12560.
[93] Report of Senate Standing Committee on Health, 54, 67.
[94] USPKenya. (2019). Comments on the Mental Health (Amendment) Bill, 2018. [Memorandum].
[95] Validity, Submissions.
[96] Health Rights Advocacy Forum (2019). Comments on the Mental Health (Amendment) Bill, 2018. [Memorandum].
[97] Ibid.
[98] Calmind Foundation (2019) Comments on the Mental Health (Amendment) Bill, 2018. [Memorandum].
[99] Health Rights Advocacy Forum, Comments.
[100] Ibid.

8 CONCLUSION

The chapter reviewed current mental health care law reform in Kenya with a specific focus on persons with psychosocial disabilities and their right to exercise legal capacity in healthcare decision-making. It is evident from the review than Kenya is lagging behind in the full realisation of legal capacity of persons with psychosocial disabilities in healthcare decision-making. In order to advance mental health law reform consistent with the provisions of article 12 of the CRPD, certain recommendations can be made.

Firstly, in order for persons with psychosocial disabilities to exercise legal capacity in treatment decision-making, law reform is needed with regard to legislative provisions that permit forced interventions in the provision of mental health care. To ensure that the right to legal capacity is protected, persons with psychosocial disabilities, their representative organisations and partners (including the Kenyan NHRI) must remain vigilant during the mental health law reform process and take part in all the legislative processes.

Secondly, the chapter highlights the importance of awareness raising throughout Kenyan society to foster respect for the rights, dignity, autonomy and needs of persons with psychosocial disabilities in order to combat harmful practices relating to mental health treatment decision-making. Without a clear understanding through awareness raising of the right to legal capacity of persons with psychosocial disabilities by the Kenyan NHRI (in collaboration with persons with psychosocial disabilities and their representative organisations), lawmakers will not likely be receptive towards law reform processes consistent with article 12 of the CRPD. Some of the pushback from lawmakers discussed in this chapter related to practical aspects regarding the exercise of legal capacity and how to protect all the rights of persons with psychosocial disabilities during crisis situations. In this regard it is recommended to develop practical alternatives to the medical model of mental health care, such as the peer-support model.[101] This model is one of the viable support options currently available and funded on a small scale by the government.[102]

While various stakeholders await mental health law reform and the passing of the Mental Health (Amendment) Bill, awareness should be raised among persons with psychosocial disabilities and healthcare professionals regarding progressive provisions in the current Health Act.[103] These provisions provide for directives in mental health care and treatment which could possibly advance the exercise of the right to legal capacity in Kenya.[104]

---

[101] KNCHR. (2013). *How to Implement Article 12 of the Convention on the Rights of Persons with Disabilities Regarding Legal Capacity in Kenya: A Briefing Paper*. KNCHR. 117.

[102] Human Rights Council 'Report of the Special Rapporteur on the Rights of Persons with Disabilities, Catalina Devandas' UN Doc A/HRC/34/58 (2016) para 64.

[103] Act 21 of 2017.

[104] Ibid., Section 9(a).

Finally, the effectiveness of the implementation of the Mental Health (Amendment) Bill depends on the budgetary allocation at all spheres of government. Resources should also be allocated to a wide range of community-based services that respond to the needs of persons with disabilities and respect their autonomy. This includes the human resources needed for state-appointed supporters. These supporters should be appropriately trained to advance the human rights of persons with disabilities, and in communication skills and skills related to advocating for persons with psychosocial disabilities.

14

Seher's "Circle of Care" Model in Advancing Supported Decision Making in India

Bhargavi V. Davar, Kavita Pillai, and Kimberly LaCroix

Abstract

The Convention on the Rights of Persons with Disabilities (CRPD) is seen by the disability movement as the foundation for inclusion and for enabling independent living for persons with psychosocial disabilities. Acknowledging the need for legal reforms to realize supported decision making (SDM), this paper focuses more on the role of communities for supporting a person with psychosocial disabilities in decision making about various aspects of life. The chapter describes the design of Seher, working in low-income communities of Pune, India, as a model in the practice of inclusive community mental health. The "Circle of Care" practice within Seher is provided as illustrative of developing community support networks based on a person's will and preference to foster inclusive actions in the community and to support the person in decision making. SDM however is not an all encompassing, or the one and only solution in terms of full human rights realization. All articles of the CRPD are relevant.

INTRODUCTION

It has been stated that the Convention on Rights of Persons with Disabilities (CRPD) has provided for a paradigm shift from the "medical model" of disability to the "social model"[1] (Cote, 2018; Harpur, 2012; Kamundia, 2013; Minkowitz, 2017; Series, 2015). Article 19, on the right to living independently and being included in communities, is seen by the disability movement as the foundation for inclusion (Kamundia, 2013). The right to life in the community presumes the realization of the right to liberty (Article 14) and having the right to full legal capacity (Article 12). Debates continue on having a "balanced view" of involuntary treatment within the mental health sector (Szmukler, 2020; Wigand, Orzechowski, Nowak et al. 2020).

---

[1] There is a misconception that denial of the "medical model" means the denial of healthcare. It is the master narrative of medication and the force associated with it that is concerning. People may in general seek healthcare, including psychiatric care, of their choice.

However, human rights reports by various Special Rapporteurs serving at the Office of the High Commission for Human Rights (OHCHR) have noted that coercion, stigma and discrimination against persons with disabilities are due to practices existing within the field of mental health, particularly the denial of legal capacity (Devandas, 2018, 2020; Puras, 2017, 2020). Recognition and respect for full legal capacity (Article 12) includes the obligation to provide support to exercise that right.

While supported decision making (SDM) has engendered legal reform and creation of new legal applications, this paper focuses more on the role of communities in supporting persons with psychosocial disabilities, including in decision making about various aspects of life. This paper is based on the reasoning that, while the right to legal capacity requires a state obligation to support with appropriate legal and policy remedies, the actual practice of fulfilling that obligation happens closer to people's homes and lives. Elaborating on the application of such community transformation, Devandas (2018) writes that pilots, schemes and community models could include "formal and informal networks, support agreements, independent advocates, peer support, advance directives and personal assistance." Support areas could include access to information, support for communication, empowerment, building self-confidence, relationship building, personal planning, independent living assistance and administrative support. Robust community-based integrated development programs, working cross-sectorally and engaging deeply with neighborhoods, would offer choice and flexibility for customizing support systems. The access, availability and affordability of such programs would make SDM a reality in the lives of persons with disabilities. Thus, a program design for preparing inclusive communities, robust program strategies and involvement of a whole range of social networks, service providers and formal and nonformal partnerships can provide a psychosocially conducive human habitat for everyone (Inclusion International, 2012). This chapter describes the Seher community mental health and inclusion program (located in Pune, India) as illustrative of such an approach.

The Seher program works in about 30 percent of the city's low-income *bastis* (communities), with the vision of creating inclusive communities. Working from a disability inclusion perspective, rather than a "mental health" perspective, Seher started in 2009 with the aim of being a model program to fulfill the standards set by the CRPD on "zero coercion." Over the past decade, Seher developed several strategies and field micro-actions to fulfill this purpose. The program has four key strategies for community engagement: (1) peer support (individual and groups); (2) a system for dialogue and negotiation with families and communities; (3) crisis response and support; and (4) linkages with various development-linked schemes and programs, both government and non-government. The bulk of service providers are from the communities themselves, many of them being persons with mental health issues and psychosocial disabilities. The program works intensively with individual persons with psychosocial disabilities, as well as with families and neighborhoods. Of particular interest to Seher was the notion of SDM, achieved by respecting the voices of persons with psychosocial disabilities without exception. In this paper, the concept and use of "Circle of Care" is described, in regard to how this improves personal autonomy and independent decision making by persons with psychosocial disabilities, within an environment where development-linked services and community support systems are available.[2]

This chapter provides an illustration and a reasoning that SDM is only one outcome, among others, of a program that enables inclusive communities. SDM, if practiced in compliance with the CRPD, will allow for the practice of independent (as opposed to lonely) living for all people in the neighborhoods and communities, as they will have a social support system. An inclusive community is not a special place created only for persons with psychosocial disabilities, but intended for all persons in it.

MOVING TOWARDS ZERO COERCION IN MENTAL HEALTH

If community support systems provide an enabling environment for SDM, coercion in mental health care compromises life, liberty and self-determination. SDM is not achievable within a coercive environment. Article 19 directs that persons with disabilities exercise choice on their place of residence, not being compelled to live in any particular living arrangement, specifically prohibiting seclusion and segregation. Additional to Article 14 and its prohibition on detention on the basis of disability, a number of guidelines, concluding observations and UN Special Procedures reports have viewed solitary confinement and coercion as torture and cruel, inhuman and degrading treatment (Melzer, 2019, 2020). An increasing number of writers have also challenged the fine line between "torture" and "cruel, inhuman, degrading treatment" (e.g., De vos, 2007). Recently, Patel and Farmer (2020) have expressed moral indignation at "the lethal consequences of coercion, social isolation and exclusion." However, coercion, in its gross and subtle forms, is a colonial practice of "withdrawing justice to deliver care," deeply embedded within mental health care (Davar & Ravindran, 2015). A General Comment (No. 5)[3] from the CRPD Committee has elaborated the difference between "communities" and "institutions," – in particular, that an institution should not be considered as a "place of residence." Coercion includes a custodial mentality, and not just a physical infrastructure – for example, in the regimented schedules and surveillance over

---

[2] In the selection of *bastis* to begin work, Seher team makes an initial assessment about the availability of services: civic amenities, institutions offering education, vocational training, employment, sports and recreation, healthcare services and nongovernmental organizations, etc. The team also verifies the interest of local authorities working in the area.
[3] CRPD/C/GC/5 General comment No. 5 (2017) on living independently and being included in the community.

residents in a community group home; or social services that enforce medication compliance to access insurance, employment, housing and social protection, etc.

Describing the ways in which social determinants cause or accelerate the experience of mental health problems and psychosocial disabilities, Puras (2020) challenges the policy of medicalization of social problems. Noticing the routine escalation of such practices within mental health care to the colonial framework of forced seclusion, he condemns the medicalization of coercion. Drawing from the Bali Declaration (TCI 2018), he strongly argues for two other entry points: inclusion in development and policies that will ensure the full realization of all human rights. Distinctively, this report starts with the stated premise: 'There is no mental health without human rights." Patel and Farmer (2020) also challenge the "need to find evidence" when we already know about "positive impacts on life expectancy of freedom, social networks, dignified work and decent housing." Taking a Capability Approach (Burchardt, 2004) and highlighting the interaction between internal and external factors determining agency, Gupta (2020) argues for personal support services for persons with disabilities.

Gooding et al. (2018) compiled projects moving in the direction of zero coercion in the Global North, but such documentation does not exist for the Global South. While Puras (2020) amply cautioned about transferring Western models to other regions of the world, critiques have emerged of globalizing psychiatry, the disregard for the social, economic, intersectional contexts for psychosocial distress, disturbance and disability; and the erasure of local support practices (Das & Rao, 2012; Davar, 2014; Jadhav & Jain, 2016; Mills & Fernando, 2014). Definitions of "recovery" have also been critiqued as Anglo-Saxon and culturally doubtful (Bayetti, Jadhav & Jain, 2016). Arguing for paying attention "to the movement of non-medical alternatives and progressive community support worldwide", the "focus should be on developing and strengthening existing movements for the non-violent, peer-led, trauma-informed, community-led programmes, healing and cultural practices preferred by local groups of persons with psychosocial disabilities" (Puras, 2020). The Seher program has also been enlisted herein, as a good practice example from the Global South.

SEHER URBAN COMMUNITY MENTAL HEALTH AND INCLUSION PROGRAM – ENABLING CHOICE[4]

Seher adapted community development concepts such as "Social Capital" (McKenzie, Whitley & Weich, 2002; McKenzie & Harpham, 2006), "Social Prescribing" (Aggar et al., 2020) and "Community Based Inclusive Development" (Carroll et al., 2016), more widely used in the disability sector. The "Circle of Care"

---

[4] The program is running to scale, covering approximately thirty low-income communities and 800,000 population, with over seventy staff members and several dozens of community volunteers, partner organizations and key resource people.

is a central part of field interventions; however, it is conducted within the context of the whole program. This section presents the framework, actions and actors of this program.

1 The Multidimensional Framework of Mental Health

Seher uses a multidimensional concept of mental health, inclusive of wellbeing, stress, distress and disability. In the early stages of the program, the terminology of "severe mental disorders" and "common mental disorders" was used. However, this did not reflect the full diversity of human experiences of psychosocial distress, disturbance and disability. It did not give an indication of the levels of social and other barriers faced by a person or the restriction of their participation in society. Further, this nomenclature did not match peoples' own cultural expressions of the disability. Finally, the expected outcome of the program was inclusion and not treatment, so the program needed different concepts and tools. Over the years, the Seher team arrived at the "Mental Health Spectrum." (See Fig. 14.1 below) The "low support needs" and "high support needs" concepts brought in a more disability-sensitive language, to an extent matching the disability definition found in the Convention.

To offer choice in support, the program must have robust assessments of psychosocial and inclusion needs along the entire spectrum. The team arrives at an assessment of social, economic, family and psychosocial needs by delivering a batch of assessment questionnaires, other than extensive field inquiry. In the *bastis*, people express a range of *"traas"* ("problems") with culturally grounded expression of distress (Davar & Lohokare, 2009). Using qualitative ethnographic methods, the program developed a glossary of items, selected five of the most frequently occurring items and added them to the twenty-item WHO Self Reporting Questionnaire (Beusenberg, Orley & WHO, 1994).[5] The most frequently occurring cultural items included lower back pain, being possessed, being a victim of black magic, feeling pressure on the chest and feeling a burning sensation. In the decade of Seher's work, the SRQ has proven most useful for making an initial assessment of a person's needs, and for identifying people with stress and distress below disability and illness levels. As necessary, depending on the SRQ and field inquiry, other tools are also used, such as the WHO Quality of Life (QOL), the Simple *Manosik Arogya* [mental health survey] Survey tool (S-MAS), the Inclusion survey, the Family Support tool and the Nutrition assessment. Sometimes a diagnostic tool such as the Brief Psychiatric Rating Scale or the Depression and Anxiety Assessment Scale or projective tools such as House Tree Person or Mandala assessment may be used. When Seher refers people to other general services and healthcare, service providers often add their own evaluations, especially if it involves obtaining a disability certificate. The Seher team is involved in

---

[5] The WHO Self reporting questionnaire has been used widely in the Asian region, including in Sri Lanka, Nepal, Pakistan, Malaysia, Philippines, Hong Kong, Vietnam and India.

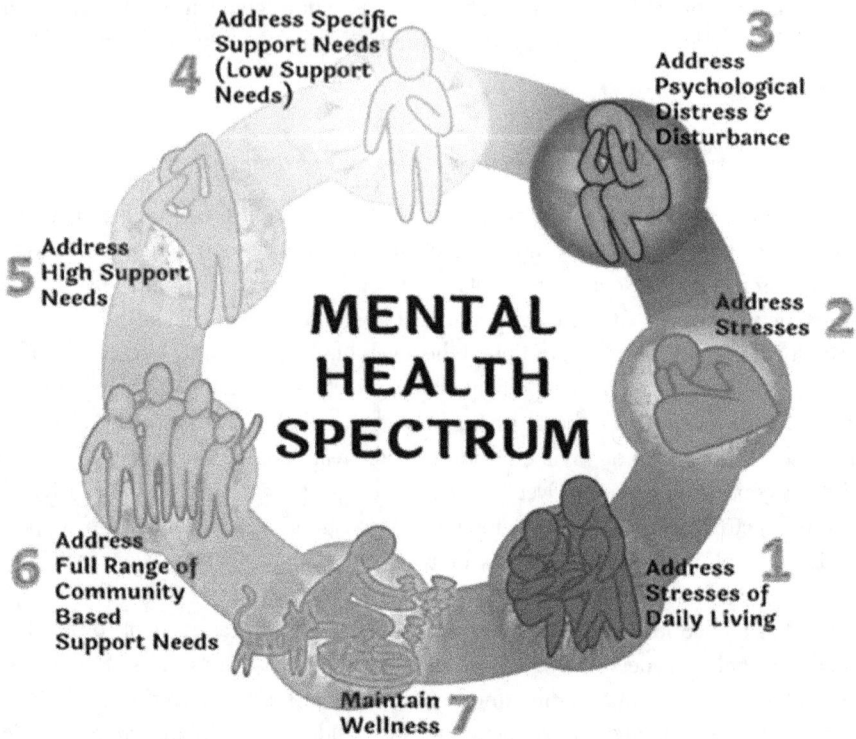

FIGURE 14.1 The Mental Health Spectrum
Source: Bapu Trust for Research on Mind & Discourse

all those external assessments for supporting the person with information, communication, personal assistance where needed and decision making.

To assess the support system a person enjoys, a "Circle of Care" tool is used.[6] Comprising nested circles and straight lines, the tool allows someone to mark how close a particular person is as a support person (see Figure 14.4 below). The categories of support may range from nonformal (family, friend, neighbor, etc.) to formal (service providers of different kinds) to community networks. The team is also able to identify the most trusted person ("primary care giver") or persons who can be mobilized for support. This support group may or may not include family members. Especially in the case of persons with high support needs, family members are often perpetrators of abuse. However, the Seher team mobilizes neighbors, extended family or friends into the circle based on the person's expressed preference. The tool also helps the person identify the kind of social and other services or support groups or recreational, sporting or spiritual groups they may be a part of. The tool

---

[6] At Seher assessment team may comprise a project leader, counsellor, arts-based therapist, senior field counsellors and grassroots peer supporters.

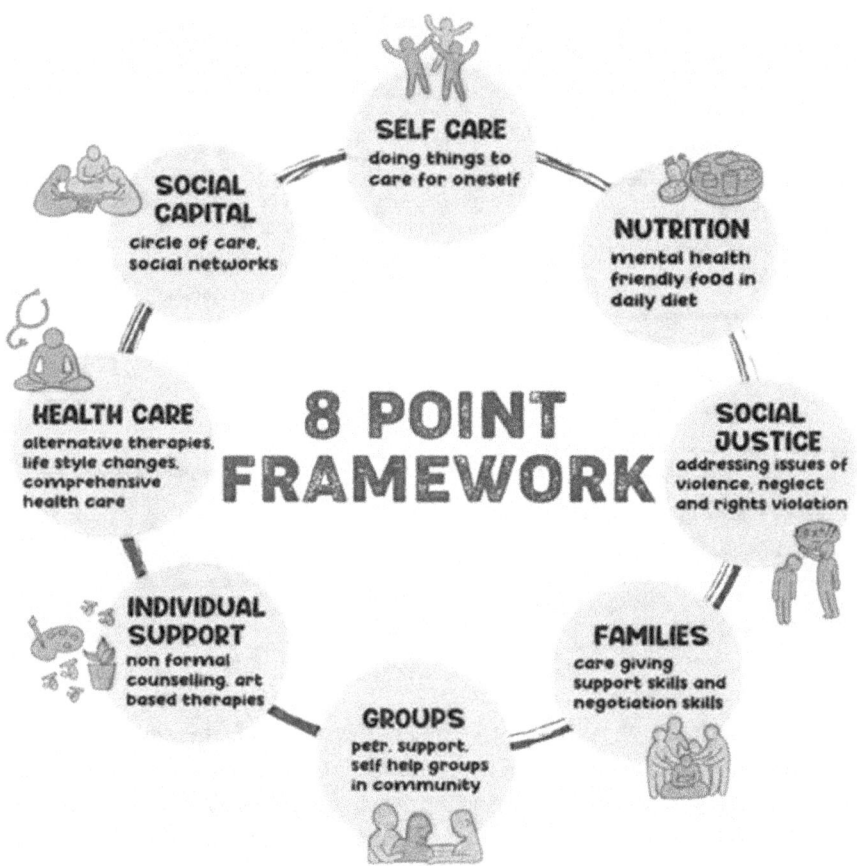

FIGURE 14.2 The Eight-point Framework
Source: Bapu Trust for Research on Mind & Discourse

offers this variety of social opportunities for the person to enhance their social capital and on which they can depend for support during critical times.

2 The Seher Framework of Goals and Actions

With the many provisions on civil, political, socioeconomic and cultural rights in the CRPD, service providers are obliged to think about offering not just *consent*, but *choice* to those who seek their services. While "consent" is best described in Article 26 (Right to Health), Article 19b on support services is broader, including several kinds of general and specific services and rights. Choice implies the exercise of control by the person over his or her own life; whereas consent is derived on the part of the service provider, typically to cover for or comply with service conditions. Of special interest to persons with psychosocial disabilities are the availability of choice in housing,

What is the eight-point framework?

SELF-CARE	Self concept; self value; self confidence; doing things to care for oneself; self connect; integration of experiences
NUTRITION	Including mental health-friendly foods into one's daily diet; addressing malnutrition
SOCIAL JUSTICE	Addressing issues of violence, stigma, neglect, seclusion and rights violations
FAMILIES	Working with families on their care-giving and support skills; negotiation and arbitration; linked to social justice
GROUPS	Peer groups; support groups; self help; volunteers; other available options in communities
INDIVIDUAL SUPPORT	Befriending; home visitors; peer support; non-formal counselling; arts-based therapies
HEALTHCARE	Comprehensive healthcare; homeopathy; Yoga; breath practices; exercise; lifestyle changes
SOCIAL CAPITAL	Circle of Care: friendships; neighbours; social networks; systems; people in social services

FIGURE 14.3 What is the Eight-Point Framework?
Source: Bapu Trust for Research on Mind & Discourse

employment, livelihoods, social protection, privacy, family life, friendships, relationships, support systems and inclusion in various schemes on an equal basis with others.

Once the assessment is complete, a support plan is made using a framework developed over the years called the Eight-Point Recovery Framework (EPRF) See Fig. 14.2, 14.3 above. The EPRF matches the mental health needs spectrum in offering a choice of solutions. Recovery focuses on a personal meaning-making process of "selfing" and change as defined by oneself. This may also include support in making decisions about various daily matters of life. Members from the Circle of Care remain close to the individual while the process plays itself out. Decisions may range from personal grooming and daily scheduling, to work, participation in various social events, recreation, relationships and food. In terms of SDM in the context of their mental wellbeing, a person may decide from among a wide range of recovery opportunities starting from "coping" and extending to "wellbeing."

Psychiatric solutions are one part of the range of solutions offered within comprehensive healthcare, and only if a person prefers this option (as is the case with everything else). [7] Seher also supports with withdrawing safely from psychiatric drugs, if a person asks for this. The exhaustive list of field actions under EPRF divide into eight different

---

[7] Experiences of psychiatry is variable in the communities where Seher works, with a few people having their own doctors while others are afraid of that system of care due to intractable iatrogenic damage. Seher does not interfere in decisions about medication. However, Seher also supports with withdrawing from psychiatric drugs if a person so chooses.

FIGURE 14.4 Circle of Care
Source: Bapu Trust for Research on Mind & Discourse

domain areas, as a way of simplifying and specifying the intervention plan for each person with a psychosocial need. Work, livelihoods, vocational training, social protection and healthcare referrals are high priority in the social inclusion actions. Daily self-care and nutrition for enhancing mental health are critical for enabling fitness and resilience. Different options are usually devised in each domain, so that the person may pick and choose what works for them. For example, in the "Self-Care" domain, there are over 100 activities in which grassroots field workers are trained to address daily self-care needs, which enhance the experience of mental health and wellbeing. A person with *"dhad dhad'"* (a fast beating heart, usually interpreted as anxiety) may be offered two or three kinds of breathing practices along with a body relaxation activity. Someone with racing thoughts and a sad mood may be supported by basic integrated arts-based therapy practices, such as automatic writing, doodling, forceful or "console" breathing, body scanning and calming mindfulness practices.[8]

---

[8] There are over 600 integrated arts-based therapy practitioners in India alone. The innovation of this form of arts therapy is that it mobilizes communities around cultural ways of being and expression; it also stimulates the sensory faculties (touch, smell, vision, hearing, taste and intuition), bypassing the

3 Circle of Care: Actors and Strategies

Recovery, even in the comprehensive way Seher has defined it, is driven by a service protocol. It has elements of service provider structure, but also hidden bias and control; whereas inclusion actions have elements of flexibility, community negotiation, communitarian sentiments and the local strengths of available social capital (Kamundia, 2013). Learning from Seher's experience that recovery actions may not always lead to social inclusion (Rankin, 2005), and that the program must go beyond an individual and engage neighborhoods, Seher adopted "care" as the basic ingredient for inclusion. "Care" includes those "small micro-affirmations of helpful professionals" (Topor, Bøe & Larsen, 2018) that may go beyond a role definition. While care actions are closely monitored for boundary and privacy violations, they are difficult to typify and standardize as their terms are not set by service providers alone. They are spontaneous, "in the moment," affirmative, altruistic, "heartfelt" responses to what the person needs. Such actions, with positive sentiments drawn from the local culture, populate the "Circle of Care." For example, a "care" issue may be articulated as a moral or a value issue and negotiated in the community, such as the lack of a decent place for the person to sleep in the household or denial of food. Teams talk about "putting moral pressure" on the family typically when a care issue is involved, evoking community justice and bystander ethics, as in the case of domestic violence. Often, team members step in with basic needs such as food, which are care actions. Senior managers are involved in every step of crisis resolutions at the community level.

To realize the full potential of the Circle of Care model of community support, thought must be given to the team and other animators of the model at different levels. Several of the field staff and program leaders are persons with lived experiences of psychosocial disability, particularly living with long-term trauma. Many also have formal training in social work, clinical psychology, counselling or arts-based therapy; while new field staff recruited from the communities take intensive training in formal care, with modules on peer support, cultural and group support, social work and development practice.[9] Recruitment into the field staff position – which is the lowest paid in the functional hierarchy – is in fact the toughest, with lively group exchanges, roleplays and interviews by seasoned field officers. Other partners enlisted into the program range from development NGOs, a range of public health service providers, general healthcare practitioners, psychiatrists and AYUSH (Ayurveda, Yoga, Unani, Siddha and Homeopathy) practitioners. Article 19b of the CRPD provides for services to be available near the residence of a person with a disability. At any time, there may be

---

cognitive realm. The modality has a legacy in the Indian mind traditions, neuroscientific studies on healing from trauma and psychologies of body intelligence. See https:/bt-abt.in.

[9] Training in nonformal care is usually on-the-job training, along with Friday learning sessions on mental health spectrum, the eight-point framework, befriending, peer and support counselling, conducting awareness programs, and learning the self-care and nutrition modules. Several field staff complete undergraduate courses in social work or counselling along with their in-house training.

up to over 100 live partnerships for provision of these services to a person or their families. In an earlier phase, a referral was made without further follow up of outcomes. However, since this did not result in inclusion, the program now monitors outcomes of referrals and independently cultivates a number of nongovernment and government partners. Spatially, Seher has six nodal centers in the inner-city areas of Pune; however, the team works deep within the communities, using community centers and primary schools, for example, to reach closer to people's homes. The program is running to scale, covering about thirty low-income community pockets in the inner-city areas of Pune (See Fig. 14.5 below).

In terms of refusals, a person may refuse a support action while still allowing a care action. Even when refusing a specific intervention, a staff member may be allowed to visit and express care. This is a culturally acceptable and "decent" thing to do as a member of the same community. For example, when a person does not engage, staff may be on a simple befriending protocol, standing by without intrusion, negotiating basic needs and protection from neglect and violence with the family or community. The situations under which a person may not take up an offer for support varies according to time factors (e.g. being too busy working), remission of the problem or family pressure not to take "mental health" support (especially if the person is an unmarried woman). Occasionally, there may be a vested interest (e.g. usurping a house or a pension) to maintain the status quo. Addiction is a major reason why a person may refuse Seher services, where the team, which was mostly women, experienced frustration: "He is not listening to us!!" [To support the men with substance abuse issues, Seher started hiring more men into the field team, and cultivated local 'Alcoholics Anonymous' groups to encourage the men to think about de-addiction].

Support by Seher is not an enduring activity, and the support provider may come and go as needed by the person; when and how often is a matter to be determined individually, in order to comply with the CRPD's mandate. "Negotiation," "partnership," "person's choice," "independence," "confrontation (with family or community)," "contracting" and "letting go" are key words used by the field team in the context of negotiating the scope and duration of support. The Seher team has to innovate to find spaces and times, for ensuring privacy and confidentiality, which may mean many more visits to field areas than planned and sensitive exchanges with the person. This may also involve several field staff, each having a different role to play.

A "crisis" is a situation where an event transpires requiring immediate intervention by the team. The program defines "crisis" as a "high restriction of participation," when custodial mentality and control practices start to take over and then overwhelm the person with a disability. A crisis could include violence against the person; deprivation of food; the person being led through continuous provocations and conflicts to a point of suicide; being driven away from the household; inhuman, degrading or forced treatment; and institutionalization and a "peak" in the denial of

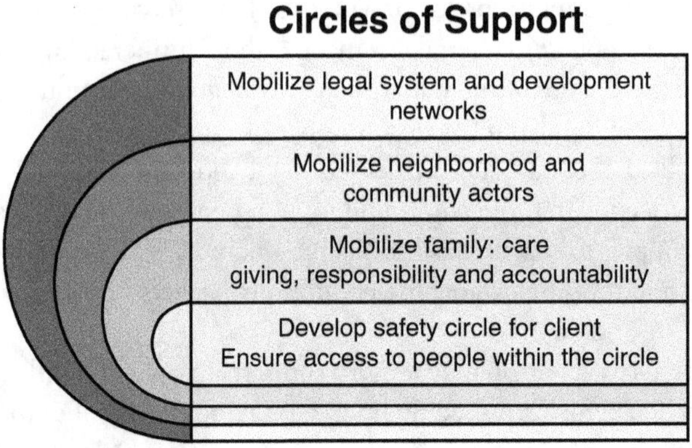

Circles of Support

- Mobilize legal system and development networks
- Mobilize neighborhood and community actors
- Mobilize family: care giving, responsibility and accountability
- Develop safety circle for client. Ensure access to people within the circle

FIGURE 14.5 Circles of Support
Source: Bapu Trust for Research on Mind & Discourse

living life on one's own terms. It is a situation which is created by the interaction of a number of actors, situations and systems.

While the conventional mental health care systems cut back on social support, using isolation and segregation methods during crisis, Seher does the opposite. It mobilizes the Circle of Care to the maximum extent possible. In a crisis, an "escalation protocol" for reporting is mounted within the program hierarchy, as a person at this time may need more people in a support role, and a wider, more diverse range of program and community supports and basic care. Sometimes, the Seher team is challenged to offer what the person needs at that time, especially if there is total social withdrawal or overstimulation or sensory overload with hearing voices. Senior field staff with skills to connect with the person and mobilize community support are highly respected by their coworkers. For example, a person who is hearing voices and left stranded on the street may be audience to one or several Seher staff walking past them waving or smiling, sitting next to them briefly, or leaving a food packet for them, for days. Usually the person would eventually smile back, ask for a name, yell, throw something at the staff or ask for food. This does not mean that the person has been "cured" of hearing voices, but that communication has been possible and that it is not the hearing of voices that is a barrier. That is a good starting point for learning what the person needs. Seher draws from various nonverbal and arts based communication modalities to engage persons with psychosocial disabilities in such situations.

A CIRCLE OF CARE CASE STUDY

Thirty-two-year-old "Meera,"[10] from "K N" *basti*, Pune, lives in a small house with her mother, brother and his family. Her mother sought Seher services, sharing that

---

[10] Name and other identity markers changed.

Meera was not sleeping well and that she was mostly irritable (*chid chid*), wandering away through the day. During our field inquiry visits, we found Meera had a mental disability as well as epilepsy. Her psychosocial distress also was evident, to warrant a finding of multiple disabilities and the imperative to provide a full range of services suitable for any person facing a high restriction to community participation and with high support needs.

Meera could understand all that we were asking or saying, but had difficulty in verbally responding. She would do so nonverbally or in monosyllables, taking time to respond. Meera's mother was her strongest support person who, however, at times spoke for her. In the initial visits, the team took the time it needed to explain about the services and the supports Seher could offer. When she (and not her mother) gave consent to work with her, she was registered into the program and invited for an assessment[11].

At her assessment, Meera shared that, while her desire was to play with the children in her neighborhood, they teased her a lot, including name calling ("*vedi*", meaning "mad" etc.). The frequent name calling would anger her and she would run after them to deter them. The children's parents would respond by quarrelling with Meera. This would upset her further. It was a vicious cycle of stigma in her neighborhood.

Working on the eight-point framework, the service team began supporting Meera by addressing her overall health care (epilepsy diagnosis and treatment); nutrition (ensuring a balanced diet and helping her and her family in the months when there was not enough food in the household); arranging social protection (registration under the disability pension scheme and ensuring she got a monthly pension); and offering training and livelihood opportunities to support her independent living. Seher also offered her specific psychosocial support services (e.g., improving assertiveness and self-confidence using nonverbal creative techniques), being attentive to her preferences and not judging her behaviors (e.g. wandering).

Inclusion actions taken helped in improving acceptance within the neighborhood and the capacity of neighbors to support her as needed. To give a specific example relevant to this paper, on one occasion, the familiar neighborhood game with the children took an ugly turn. A policeman from the community's outpost (*thana*), seeing Meera running after a child, beat her up with his "*danda*" (wooden baton). Meera stopped in her tracks and went back home. At night when the pain was unbearable, she complained to her mother, the first time she shared with anyone what had happened. Her mother requested Seher support. As part of the protocol, the field team visited and heard the story directly from Meera. Meera had marks on her body, inflamed bruises on her chest, thighs and stomach. Needing immediate medical help, she went with the team to the hospital. Upon inquiry, the hospital also created a report on the injury caused by the beating.

---

[11] In Seher, an "invitation" for assessment involves discussions and sharing of information.

The following day, the team informed Meera about her right to file a complaint against the policeman. Meera was uncertain. Through dialogue, awareness was also raised among her support system (especially her primary caregiver, the mother) on the thin line between "supporting" Meera and "acting on her behalf." Having the confidence of her family's and Seher's support,[12] Meera decided to go to the police station. There Meera was given the space to voice her complaint. She showed the police inspector the marks on her body. Protecting their own, the police refused to file her complaint.

This rejection not being just, the team proposed escalating the complaint to the area police station and/or filing a complaint with the Police Commissioner's office. This generated a sense of threat and fear of backlash within the family, who were justifiably wary of escalating a complaint about the authorities to the *same* authorities. Meera's brother strongly opposed the proposal. Her mother too was unsure about the action. As customary, the team raised the proposal with Meera.

To assist Meera in her decision, the team wrote down the series of events that had transpired. They read out the narration to her. The Seher proposal was that this content could make up a complaint letter. Meera took a few days to reflect and the Seher team asked her if she wanted to make any changes. She came back with requests to change some content, to reflect exactly what she would like to communicate. A neighborhood support system was established to support Meera and her family in case of threat or intimidation.[13] (Already the neighborhood had been primed about her disability status and need for support because of Seher awareness raising regarding the rough games played with the children).

The following day Meera decided she would like to file the complaint at the area police station. Her mother decided to accompany her daughter. To support her and her family, a Seher team accompanied the family to the station.

This support instance is particular to a legal decision. Supported decision making was enabled at each interaction with Meera, including registering into the program, taking an assessment and thereafter making decisions about a range of actions forming the recovery plan. Meera was also supported with other decisions, such as attending a medical consultation for epilepsy; registering under the disability pension scheme; accepting support for food and nutrition; and giving permission for us to work with children, their parents and her neighbors in order to decrease instances of taunting and name calling.

---

[12] Where the family is the perpetrator, the Seher team will mobilize the neighborhood and key resource persons in the community for support.

[13] Called a "Neighbourhood Alert," this is a system where extensive awareness activities are conducted in the neighboring area of a Seher client, and the Seher team, together with neighbors and supportive others, create strategies for safeguarding the client's interests if and when this is requested. Sometimes, such a system is created for persons who are in crisis and who need their basic needs addressed, particularly food. Sometimes a foster care system is also informally established, especially for those who are wandering in the neighborhood.

CONCLUSION

Having worked on the full range of the mental health spectrum, from wellbeing to psychosocial disability, Seher's learning is that the expression of a need for support is possible for *every* person on that spectrum. While it is necessary to expand the scope of support actions, it is important to abstain from rash intervention actions which lead to substituted decision making or coercion. There is no aspect of the mental health experience that warrants a speed of action likely to take away a person's right to full legal capacity. Having a range of skills for communicating with the person (i.e., going beyond the linguistic and cognitive) is important. More important is faith in the claim that coercion is not necessary at all: Seher has never restrained or incarcerated anyone. Seher has intervened in several instances of forced incarceration, and worked with families and the neighborhood to have relatives amicably received back into their homes. Seher's wide matrix of field actions is a supportive safety net for people to continue to negotiate their circumstances, make choices and gain control over their lives. The program also works on family counseling and empowerment, as the problems of the individual mirror problems in the household and the wider community.

This paper has described community processes that may be put in place, through community development and inclusion programs, along with law reform for SDM. Hitherto, the lives of persons with psychosocial disabilities have been under an implacable medicolegal regime, preventing any possibility of a full community life. SDM will be meaningful only if the larger universe of human rights, as embodied in the CRPD and various other human rights treaties, are fulfilled. In achieving this outcome, however, all stakeholders have to be involved, fully respecting the will and preferences of the person with a disability.

REFERENCES

Aggar, C., Thomas, T., Gordon, C. et al. (2020). Social prescribing for individuals living with mental illness in an Australian community setting: A pilot study. *Community Mental Health Journal*, 57, 189–195. https://doi.org/10.1007/s10597-020-00631-6

Anthony, W. A. (1993). Recovery from mental illness: The guiding vision of the mental health service system in the 1990s. *Psychosocial Rehabilitation Journal*, 16(4), 11–23.

Bayetti, C., Jadhav, S. & Jain, S. (2016). The re-covering self: A critique of the recovery-based approach in India's mental health care. *Disability and the Global South*, 3(1), 889–909.

Beusenberg, M., Orley, John, H. & World Health Organization. Division of Mental Health. (1994). *A User's Guide to the Self Reporting Questionnaire*. Geneva: World Health Organization.

Bracken, P. Thomas, P., Timimi, S. et al. (2012). Psychiatry beyond the current paradigm. *The British Journal of Psychiatry* 201, 430–434. https://doi.org/10.1192/bjp.bp.112.109447

Burchardt, T. (2004). Capabilities and disability: The capabilities framework and the social model of disability. *Disability & Society* 19(7), 735–751. https://doi.org/10.1080/0968759042000284213.

Das, A. & Rao, M. (2012). Universal mental health: Re-evaluating the call for global mental health. *Critical Public Health*, 22(4), 383–389. https://doi.org/10.1080/09581596.2012.700393

Davar, B. V. & Lohokare, M. (2009).Recovering from psychosocial traumas: The place of dargahs in Maharashtra. *Economic & Political Weekly*, 44(16), 60–67.

Davar, B. V. (2014). Globalizing psychiatry and the case of 'vanishing' alternatives in a neo-colonial state. *Disability and the Global South*, 1(2), 266–284.

Davar, B. V. (2015). Delivering Justice, Withdrawing Care. In B. V. Davar & S. Ravindran, eds. *Gendering Mental Health: Knowledges, Identities, Institutions*. New Delhi: Oxford University Press.

De Vos, C. M. (2007). Mind the gap: Purpose, pain, and the difference between torture and inhuman treatment. *Human Rights Brief*, 14(2), (2007): 4–10.

Devandas, C. (2018). Report of the Special Rapporteur on the rights of persons with disabilities – Legal capacity. A/HRC/37/56 adopted in the 37th Session of the Human Rights Council, Geneva, 2018.

Gooding, P., Mc Sherry, B., Roper, C. & Grey, F. (2018) *Alternatives to Coercion in Mental Health Settings: A Literature Review*. Melbourne: Melbourne Social Equity Institute, University of Melbourne.

Gupta, S., de Witte, L. P. & Meershoek, A. (2020). Dimensions of invisibility: insights into the daily realities of persons with disabilities living in rural communities in India. *Disability & Society*. https://doi.org/10.1080/09687599.2020.1788509

Harpur, P. (2012). Embracing the new disability rights paradigm: The importance of the Convention on the Rights of Persons with Disabilities. *Disability & Society*, 27(1), 1–14. https://10.1080/09687599.2012.631794

Inclusion International (2012). *Inclusive Communities = Stronger Communities. Global report on Article 19: The Right to Live and Be Included in the Communities*. London: Inclusion International.

Jain, S. & Jadhav, S. (2009). Pills that swallow policy: Clinical ethnography of a Community Mental Health Program in northern India. *Transcultural Psychiatry*, 46(1), 60–85.

Kamundia, E. (2013). Choice, support and inclusion: Implementing Article 19 of the Convention on the Rights of persons with disabilities in Kenya. *African Disability Rights Yearbook*, Pretoria University Law Press, 1, 49–72.

McKenzie, K. & Harpham, T. (2006). *Social Capital and Mental Health*. London: Jessica Kingsley Publishers.

McKenzie, K., Whitley, R. & Weich, S. (2002). Social capital and mental health. *British Journal of Psychiatry*, 181(4), 280–3. https://doi.org/10.1192/bjp.181.4.280

Melzer, N. (2019). Torture and other cruel, inhuman or degrading treatment or punishment. Report of the UN Special Rapporteur on Torture. Geneva. Adopted in the 40th Session of the Human Rights Council. A/HRC/40/59.

Melzer, N. (2020). Torture and other cruel, inhuman or degrading treatment or punishment. Report of the UN Special Rapporteur on Torture. Geneva. Adopted in the 43rd Session of the Human Rights Council. A/HRC/43/49.

Mills, C. & Fernando, S. (2014). Globalising mental health or pathologising the Global South? Mapping the ethics, theory and practice of global mental health. *Disability and the Global South*, 1(2), 188–202.

Minkowitz, T. (2017). CRPD and transformative equality. *International Journal of Law in Context*. 13, 77–86. https://doi.org/10.1017/S1744552316000483.

Patel, V. & Farmer, P. (2020). The art of medicine. The moral case for global mental health delivery. *The Lancet*, 395, 108–9.

Puras, D. (2020). 'Report of the Special Rapporteur on the right of everyone to the enjoyment of the highest attainable standard of physical and mental health', adopted in the 44th Session of the Human Rights Council, Geneva, 2020. A/HRC/44/48

Puras, D. (2017). 'Report of the Special Rapporteur on the right of everyone to the enjoyment of the highest attainable standard of physical and mental health', adopted in the 35th Session of the Human Rights Council, Geneva, 2017. A/HRC/35/21

Series, L. (2015). The development of disability rights under international law: From charity to human rights. *Disability & Society*, 30(10), 1590–1593. https://doi.org./10.1080/09687599.2015.1066975

Szmukler, G. (2020). Involuntary detention and treatment: Are we edging toward a "paradigm shift"? *Schizophrenia bulletin*, 46(2). https://doi.org/10.1093/schbul/sbz115.

TCI (2018). The Bali Declaration. Transforming Communities for Inclusion of persons with psychosocial disabilities – Asia Pacific. Pune, India. Accessed at www.tci-asia.org/bali-declaration/.

Topor, A., Bøe, T. D. & Larsen, I.B. (2018). Small things, micro-affirmations and helpful professionals: Everyday recovery-orientated practices according to persons with mental health problems. *Community Mental Health Journal*, 54, 1212–1220. https://doi-org.ezproxy.library.ubc.ca/10.1007/s10597-018-0245-9

Wigand, M., Orzechowski, M., Nowak, M. et al. (2020). Schizophrenia, human rights and access to health care: A systematic search and review of judgments by the European Court of Human Rights. *International Journal of Social Psychiatry*. https://doi.org/0020764020942797.10.1177/0020764020942797

15

The Swedish Personal Ombudsman: Support in Decision-Making and Accessing Human Rights

Ulrika Järkestig Berggren

Abstract

De-institutionalisation of people with mental health conditions brought about the need to develop community-based support. In response to a request from user organisations, the Personal Ombudsman was implemented. This service provides professional support on behalf of the person seeking help to obtain his or her citizen rights in society. The personal ombudsman occupies a freestanding position, independent of authorities, and reports recurring social issues affecting persons with psychosocial disabilities directly to the national agency for healthcare and social services. In 2001, this service was permanently implemented and is provided free of charge for persons with psychosocial disabilities. Personal ombudsmen are to act only on the behalf of their clients, often concerning issues of daily provision, homelessness, medical treatment and improper reception from professionals in medical and social services. The first step in the relationship between the personal ombudsman and the client is to help the client formulate his own decisions on how he wants to proceed with the present problem. The second step is often aiding the client by advocating his perspective in decision-making with professionals responsible for his rights. This chapter illustrates the working relationship between the personal ombudsmen and their clients and the decision-making process therein.

INTRODUCTION

The human right to enjoy the same legal capacity as others has been an issue for persons with psychosocial disabilities (PSD) due to the politics surrounding the coercive practice of institutionalisation, a major criticism being the abuse of the human right to decide over one's own life (Goffman, 1991). The social justice movement of the 1960s and 1970s and the more recent focus on consumer choice have brought about a shift in politics, now emphasising active user involvement, where service users have rights, but also duties, in the decisions concerning their care and support (Grim, 2019). The United Nations Convention on the Rights of Persons with Disabilities (CRPD) article 12 demands a shift in the responsibility of society to secure the right for and aid persons with disabilities to make decisions concerning their lives. Simultaneously, the convention demands that the disabled person actively exerts the right, which at times may be perceived as challenging, due to a discriminatory society.

This change in social policy brought about the need to establish new forms of community-based services that aid persons with disabilities in voicing their wishes and knowledge. Case management is a response to this challenge (Zwarenstein, Stephenson and Johnston, 2008).

In this chapter, I describe the method of the case manager role, the Personal Ombudsman (PO), developed in Sweden as a community-based support, detailing how the PO supports decision-making for persons with PSD and what is helpful about this assistance. Also, I discuss a theoretical model of *modes of actions* assumed by POs, together with empirical examples. The data presented are derived from the author's study of interviews with twenty-five POs, as well as twenty-three interviews with clients and a study of documents from between 1995 and 2020.

MENTAL HEALTH REFORM AND THE NEW PERSONAL OMBUDSMAN

The psychiatric investigation in 1992 (SOU, 1992) criticised the lack of municipal support services in Sweden, which resulted in poor living conditions for persons with psychosocial disabilities. The investigation was inspired by case management models in the USA and the UK, which provided service in the community. The subsequent mental health reform of 1995 closed all mental institutions, announcing that persons with psychosocial disabilities were to live in society exercising their citizen rights like everyone else. The reform also suggested a case manager to help obtain and coordinate support for persons with psychosocial disabilities; however, no specific management model was chosen, and therefore the Swedish PO was defined during its process of implementation (Järkestig Berggren, 2010). By way of comparison with existing models of case management, the Strengths model as described by Rapp and Goscha (2006) in the USA shares many of the values and characteristics that have developed in the PO model. The Strengths model builds on the principles that support should focus on the person's strengths rather than deficits; society provides the resources to be used by the person; and the person directs the support process. In addition, the Strengths model is described as contributing to the recovery and empowering of persons with PSD.

Starting in 1995, ten pilot trials as variants of the PO service were conducted and evaluated for efficacy (Björkman, Hansson and Sandlund, 2002), with the finding that service users in contact with a PO decreased their use of inpatient care and suggesting that the PO pilot service met some demands concerning coordination of support and service. During the implementation period of 2000 to 2005, the focus was less on efficacy and more on supporting the person with PSD in decision-making. Client organisations emphasised that the PO was to act on behalf of the client, which was also stated as the core aim in the first PO guidelines (NBHW, 2000). These values are in line with the CRPD (2007), which was signed during the same era.

THE PERSONAL OMBUDSMAN

As one part of the national reform agenda, the PO was implemented by the National Board of Health and Welfare (NBHW), which is the nationally responsible agent for providing education for all personal ombudsmen employed locally. Still today, the NBHW provides a couple of days' training for new POs that covers the core assignment, work methods and dilemmas that POs frequently face in their daily practice. The vocational backgrounds among POs are diverse; however, most POs have some education in pedagogy, social work or health and medical care. Most POs also have previous work experience in healthcare or community care in different positions (Järkestig Berggren, 2010).

Some POs are recruited from user organisations for their personal experience of PSD. Today there are POs in 253 of the 290 municipalities in Sweden (NBHW, 2018). Each municipality receives funding for POs based on the population at large. Municipalities are not required to offer the PO service, and therefore there is considerable variability among municipalities in the accessibility to a PO and in the ratio of clients to each PO. PO services operate Monday to Friday during office hours and do not offer 24-hour support officially, although some clients and POs comment that they have an arrangement for telephone support outside office hours.

The organisational context differs regionally. POs are most commonly employed by social services. Client organisations also act as employers for POs, and there is a plethora of organisational collaborations among municipalities that together offer support from POs. Nevertheless, the PO is to retain a 'freestanding position' to secure service users' assistance in accessing support.

In addition to assisting clients in claiming their rights to welfare services, the PO also fulfils the duties of reporting recurring societal problems and counteracting discrimination. Therefore all PO organisations are to interact with important collaborative partners, by having a board consisting of local managers from social services, healthcare, the Social Insurance Agency and the Public Employment Service. Furthermore, the assignment states that the PO will:

- together with the client identify and formulate his or her needs for care, support, service, rehabilitation and occupation;
- together with the client make sure that all support and service are planned, coordinated and carried through by the responsible authorities;
- aid the client in the contact with authorities;

- make sure that the client receives care, support and service, rehabilitation and an occupation according to the client's wishes, needs and legal rights; and
- work towards the client getting access to rehabilitation and an occupation and/or employment (NBHW, 2011).

This assignment is shared in part with welfare services and healthcare, and therefore coordinating support is often the responsibility of the PO in collaboration with other actors and authorities. In one respect, the PO role is unique in identifying recurring societal problems that persons with PSD encounter. These issues are reported by POs to their board and, once a year, directly to the NBHW. In 2018, lack of housing was reported along with a lack of psychiatrists, which caused long waiting times for assessment and treatment, leading to an unstable livelihood due to the difficulty in getting a doctor's certificate for sick payments. Also noted were an insufficient number of legal guardians and problems related to the digitisation of society, which excludes persons who do not have access to digital media (NBHW, 2018).

That the education of new POs is the responsibility of the NBHW creates a significant connection with the national government agency under the Ministry of Health and Social Affairs responsible for healthcare and social services nationally.

Having presented the organisation and assignment of the PO service, we will turn to the persons seeking help from a PO. Who is eligible for the support?

TARGET GROUP

Initially, PO support was mostly directed towards persons with severe PSD who previously had been living in institutions. From 2001 to 2020, the target group has expanded to cover younger persons with PSD, persons with addictions and PSD, and persons with neuropsychological impairments (NBHW, 2014). A person seeks support from a PO mainly for help contacting authorities, or because of difficulties in accessing support and vulnerability to homelessness (NBHW, 2014).

'Client' is the concept used by POs for the persons whom they help, implying a professional relationship in which a PO takes the side of the person being supported and protects the interests of that person. A PO is assigned to assist adult persons free of charge. According to the NBHW definition, the target group consists of persons who:

- have significant and substantial difficulties in carrying out activities in important areas of life, and these restrictions have been consistent or are likely to continue. The difficulties are a consequence of (severe) psychiatric ill health ... [and where]
- the target group has complex and extensive needs for care, support, services, rehabilitation and occupation and requires prolonged contact with social

services, primary healthcare and/or specialist psychiatric services (without the requirement of a medical diagnosis) and other authorities (NBHW, 2011).

PO support is not on condition of a doctor's certificate of a medical diagnosis; instead the eligibility is based upon self-identification. Moreover, POs are easy to contact directly without any need of referral, and they do not keep files on their clients. Therefore, POs are often the first to be contacted by persons who lack any kind of support and network. Hence, this can be viewed as inconsistent with the target group identified above and the design of the PO service. The target group described has extensive needs for basic amenities, such as housing, daily provision and medical care, while the PO as a service in itself does not provide any of these resources, but rather has the agency to mobilise other authorities who manage the assistance needed. It does mean that the person seeking the help of a PO still needs further referral to other services.

A PROFESSIONAL RELATIONSHIP BUILT ON TRUST AND MUTUALITY: CLIENTS' VOICES

The official description (NBHW, 2011) of a PO is a case manager working on behalf of clients according to their wishes and needs. Interviews with twenty-three clients reveal that clients call the relationship with a PO a 'professional friendship' built on trust and reciprocity (Järkestig Berggren & Gunnarsson, 2010). Clients describe their PO in terms of an official, professional assignment to coordinate and aid contacts with authorities, while also relating to a mutual relationship, like a friend whom you can trust and call at any time. Sometimes the professional role and the friendly aspect interact in a safe, relaxed relationship in which clients can talk about their distress over issues in their lives. The relationship is built on trust. Klockmo, Marnetoft and Nordenmark (2012) found that often the PO's work facilitates the client's recovery process. This is illustrated by Ann, who tells about her PO Ingrid.

> We talk when we clean the kitchen. Ingrid has been, she has been a therapist and a doctor and everything in one, and a friend. Like the therapist I went to, we did not get anywhere during all that time. But Ingrid and I we moved on... like when we went to fix the coffeemaker that was broken, we like talked in the car, sort of killing two birds with one stone. (Järkestig Berggren & Gunnarsson, 2010)

In clients' narratives about their POs, they emphasise that their discussions help them make up their minds about important decisions in their lives, foremost by identifying the problem and finding information about possible ways to solve it. The PO assists with questions of how to get access to community support, contact healthcare providers and obtain everyday provisions by applying for benefits. POs also assist by conversing about their psychosocial problems. Clients narrate that in conversations with POs, they identify their wishes about how and what they want to do in their lives.

As a client example, Johan narrates that he felt very alone at home all day, not having any friends or family. He talked to his PO about his loneliness, his wishes to have some activities with other people, and his fear of not coping in new situations. His PO told him about activities in the community, and he found interest in one of them. He visited the daily activity group a couple of times with his PO, until gradually he felt safe enough to go there by himself.

The official assignment of the PO is to be short-term support (less than six months) for persons with PSD. However, clients say that they value having contact over time, emphasising that their issues can recur, and new problems need to be discussed to find advice. Knowing the PO exists as a back-up is reassuring; this in itself helps them to solve matters on their own at times. Jonna talks about her relationship with Pia, her PO, saying she occasionally meets her or calls for advice on important matters:

> We did have a closing talk, but I know I will be in touch with her and it is OK that we meet, that I call her and she calls me. It happens less often now and that is because I feel better. I have become stronger. I can take being on my own.

The assignments of POs are in practice translated into many different duties. POs often perform practical tasks, frequently related to lack of daily necessities, income or housing. However, it is also common for the PO to act as a mentor in everyday matters (Klockmo, 2013). Furthermore, POs are sometimes present as informal support in court trials and lawyer meetings, and as support or a representative in meetings with welfare services or healthcare professionals in dire situations. In situations when a caregiver and the PO disagree on the interpretation of the client's wishes and needs, the PO may decide, if the client agrees, to go further with the discussion to the PO board of managers for the caregiver and consequently take the client's needs to the manager's level.

CLIENTS' DECISION-MAKING TOGETHER WITH A PO

POs are to work in the interest of their clients. How do POs describe their work model and strategies? Table 1 below shows the PO modes of action theoretically, using ideal types (Swedberg, 2018) as an analytical tool to highlight differences across the work of POs. In reality, with the same client, the four types may overlap each other or occur at different times. The table derives from twenty-five PO interviews with stories of interactions with a total of 125 clients.

The model shows that clients can take different positions in their relationship with their PO. In choosing to be active in discussing their issues with their PO, clients assume a subjective position in the relationship. Other clients, who may be very ill and request the PO to step in and speak on their behalf as a representative with a letter of attorney, take on a passive role. In some cases, the client will be given

TABLE 15.1 *POs: four modes of action*

	Model of disability	
Client's relation to the PO	Individualisation; medical model	Citizenship; social model
Subjective and mutual	**Case work and/or rehabilitation** The client decides the pace. The PO assesses and sets a goal, but adjusts to the client and awaits the client to move forward. The PO takes on a role as a *supporting memory, lifeline* or *mentor*.	**Empowerment** The client decides what the mission is. The PO adjusts to the wishes of the client and works according to the mission plan. The PO takes on a role as a *witness, negotiator* and guide in welfare rights.
Passive and/or objective	**Paternalism** The client's wishes and description becomes irrelevant. The PO acts on his own judgement. The PO takes on a role as an *authority*.	**Advocacy** The PO acts as a representative for the client. The PO applies and appeals for support services. The PO takes on a role as a *representative* and *actor for social change*.

a passive, objective role due to an issue identified by the PO that leads to the PO acting in opposition to the client's wishes.

Another differing factor is related to the model of disability. A PO may interpret a present issue as an individualised problem due to a medical condition, such as mental illness. Strategies to improve the situation involve rehabilitation, psychiatric care and aiding recovery from the disabling symptoms. Other problems the PO can define as socially constructed, rooted in society due to disabling barriers in attitudes and absent support from an insufficient welfare system. Here strategies for improvement involve further efforts to coordinate welfare support systems and raise awareness about missing support.

Rehabilitation

The mode of action based upon rehabilitation emphasises the ultimate goal: aiding the client in the recovery process.

The client takes an active part in the relationship with the PO, describing and discussing his or her own wishes and needs. The PO supports the client in taking decisions and respects the wishes of the client, but the PO also assesses what would be important for the client's recovery. The PO adapts to the client's pace, but moves the client toward recovery. The PO describes motivational strategies – this mode of action also being connected to case work. The PO acts as a mentor or a teacher, guiding how to cope with problems, and sometimes as a lifeline in acute situations. In meetings, the PO functions like a supporting memory for the client, so that afterwards the PO can fill in memory gaps that the client may have of the discussions.

Case

Magnus has been very ill physically and has been treated for a long time for depression. He has led an independent life with full-time work up until he became ill. He has instructed his PO clearly to help with contacts with the Swedish Insurance Agency in applying for a disability pension. The PO also notices many other needs, such as engaging in physical activity and finding new ways and places to meet and interact with other people. 'I continue to support him and motivate him; we have worked for a year ... I will continue meeting him. I have to wait and see'.

Empowerment

Working in the empowerment mode of action means the PO helps the client to formulate his or her wishes, and then acts on these with the client taking an active part. The PO functions as a discussion partner, helping the client to find arguments for or against specific actions, or to find ways to solve problems. Thus, the client finds alternatives and assesses consequences. In meetings with professionals in healthcare or social care services about access to support, the client uses the PO as a back-up, but speaks for him- or herself. Issues they solve together often concern poor treatment, discrimination and rejected applications for welfare services. In this mode of action, the PO acts as a guide to citizen rights and advisor about the welfare system, and at times, the PO steps in as a negotiator for the client's right to support. This mode of action, most commonly described by the PO, could also be understood as an SDM method. POs work with their clients to help them formulate their needs and wishes and find arguments to present to caregivers; for example, they sometimes help their clients to prepare for a meeting with a psychiatrist or a social worker. Also, they could accompany the client to a shared decision meeting, then acting as reinforcement of the client's view.

Case

Jonas told his PO Anders that he had a severe gambling addiction that he was ashamed of. He had lost his own money on gambling and also embezzled money from family and friends. This problem weighed on Jonas, and he wanted help. Not knowing where to turn, he asked Anders for advice. Together Jonas and Anders searched for professional gambling treatment. Jonas contacted a specialised psychiatric ward they found, but he felt insulted in the contact with the therapist and discussed with Anders what had happened. They talked it through, considering whether Anders or Jonas should go back to the therapist and confront him. Together they made a list of what Jonas could tell the therapist. Then Jonas went alone, and the therapist apologised for his behaviour.

Paternalism

The paternalistic mode of action contradicts the assignment of the PO in that the client's voice and wishes are treated as irrelevant and the PO acts according to his or her professional judgement. The PO uses this mode in specific circumstances related to professional ethical values: 1) when the PO files a child protection report if the client has children perceived to be at risk; and 2) when the PO's professional judgement deems the client's life is at serious risk due to psychosocial illness or addiction.

In this mode of action, the PO is caught in the conflict of caring professions that have to walk the line between violation of self-determination and negligence of human needs. Paternalism by definition means to impose professional actions upon a person with the argument that it is in his or her best interest. Paternalism has been a trait of social case work and psychiatric treatment (Dominelli, 2002) that has affected living conditions for persons with physical or psychosocial disabilities. Hence, this mode of action poses a dilemma for the PO, who is explicitly assigned to work on behalf of clients.

Case

Esther, working as a PO, had contact with Diana, a client with severe depression and anxiety. She helped Diana get in touch with healthcare and find a therapist. In meeting Diana at home, she found the circumstances for her two young children were unsafe, with no food in the refrigerator and very unsanitary conditions. Concerned, Esther discussed the situation of the children with her manager. They decided Esther should tell Diana that a report to child protection services had to be filed. Esther told Diana that her children were at risk in this situation and that she would contact child protection services. Once this agency was informed, Diana ended her contact with Esther since she felt she could no longer trust her.

Advocacy

In the advocacy mode of action, the PO becomes a representative on behalf of the client, who often chooses not to be actively involved. The two agree on the issue and the strategies, but the PO often proceeds with a letter of attorney to speak for the client. At times, the PO represents the target group as a whole by helping an individual client to apply for support that is not currently provided by the municipality. Subsequently, the PO helps the client to appeal, demonstrating that this specific intervention must be implemented. Reporting recurring problems, such as lack of housing, to the board and to the NBHW is also advocating for the target group, in that the PO acts as a representative and strives for social change against discrimination (Payne, 2002).

Case

Mats, a PO, tells of a client who was treated at a psychiatric ward for a long time. She had severe PSD as well as physical disabilities. When she was discharged from the psychiatric ward, she needed a new home which provided care around the clock. Mats helped her apply for an apartment and support from a mobile team. The municipality rejected the application, arguing that mobile teams for persons with PSD could not be provided. The PO, acting as a representative, helped appeal the decision.

Summary

In summarising the modes of actions for the PO, the modes of empowerment and advocacy are specific traits of POs that distinguish them from most other professions in the field of psychosocial disability. The focus of POs is first and foremost to help their clients to articulate their needs and wishes from the client's point of view, in order to voice their right to support from society in their current situation. On the other hand, healthcare as well as community care often have the long-term, ultimate goal of the client's rehabilitation and recovery, which primarily involves a professional assessment of what is best for the client. The question then is, what knowledge do POs build upon in their work? The next section presents the knowledge base of the professional PO.

CLIENT KNOWLEDGE AS THE OCCUPATIONAL BASIS FOR THE PO

From the modes of PO actions above, it is clear that their work is defined in close interaction with their clients. POs do not often take a standpoint of their own. The case examples highlight that the client contributes knowledge which becomes the basis for the PO's work. In this sense, the PO strengthens the voice of the person with PSD – for instance, in meetings with psychiatric care. The PO can take the initiative for shared decision-making directly between the client and the professional caregiver or can act as the representative for the client.

Client organisations have long advocated for working on behalf of the client during the implementation process of community-based support. This is a core value of the assignment even today. In terms of gaining employment as a PO, client organisations have emphasised the importance of competence and knowledge in how to build relationships with clients where the clients are supported in their decision-making processes (Klockmo, 2013). Professional knowledge from academic studies, however, has been questioned by client organisations as a basis for the PO's qualification, referring to a risk that professionals may form opinions based on their own judgements.

In summary, the legitimacy of a PO's work depends on a knowledge base built upon the client's understanding in terms of identifying the problem, expressing the client's view and determining a solution. Hence, this PO trait of building on the clients' knowledge is a 'user-mandated professionalism' which defines and distinguishes this occupation (Järkestig Berggren, 2015).

Evidence of this user-mandated professionalism lies in the creating of relationships with clients based on trust and the exercising of discretion on how to act and with which questions to assist. To help a client, both parties need to trust the other to achieve any change for the client (Grimen, 2009). Moreover, the PO assignment has wide boundaries, being a freestanding position, and each PO applies professional discretion in what kinds of issues to work with and which work methods and actions to use. Combining this discretional, freestanding position with a trust-based relationship provides the PO with the means to aid clients with most issues in their lives.

WIDE DISCRETION AND LACK OF TRANSPARENCY – A RISK?

From the description above, the PO does exercise some power and a wide discretion to be used for the client's benefit; but since power and discretion may also be misused, are there any means for transparency? Are there any risks for persons who seek a PO's assistance?

POs are not under the scrutiny on the system surrounding social workers and healthcare professionals in Sweden, which means that few external parties have an insight in the work of the PO. This poses a risk for vulnerable persons who choose to seek PO assistance. The understanding of a PO, expressed by many clients as a 'professional friend', suggests that there is some closeness in this relationship that can be misused.

Also, the main requirement of a PO seems to be having had experience of working with persons who have PSD, and academic education in this regard is not as important. However, POs do face many difficult problems that can accompany PSD; consequences of poverty and risks for children involved are only a few of the most common issues. This means that in order to help a person, the PO needs knowledge from a wide area around PSD, as well as rights and duties related to citizenship and societal support. This competence is necessary to be able offer helpful support, but if lacking there is a risk that the person with PSD will receive bad advice or inaccurate information. In such cases, would then have been better to seek social services or healthcare support directly.

There are some means to create transparency in the PO work role. The Board of the Personal Ombudsman works with POs in some matters and is thereby able to provide advice to POs about dilemmas or issues involving their clients. The Professional Organisation of Personal Ombudsmen has set up professional ethical guidelines (YPOS, 2016) for POs to follow. Finally, reports to the NBHW are a follow-up of the evolving PO assignment (Järkestig Berggren, 2015) at a statistical level. Hence, there is still a need for a system of professional monitoring at the individual level that will help to secure the safety of the clients.

CONCLUDING REMARKS

The PO has been established in Sweden since 2001 in response to user organisations. According to research (Järkestig Berggren, 2010, 2015; Klockmo, 2013) and evaluations (NBHW, 2005, 2014), the PO has evolved into valued support for persons with PSD, characterised by being directed by the client and in the interests of the client. With their assignment to help clients obtain their legal rights to care, support and treatment, POs have built this occupation from clients' input of their knowledge.

POs do not personally provide any benefits or assets for their clients. Their main assignment is to aid their clients in the decision-making process to exercise their citizen rights. First, POs help clients to identify their needs and find solutions, by creating a trustful relationship where the client's knowledge and the PO's knowledge interact. Second, the POs have a freestanding position and professional power exercised to help clients be heard and get access to legal rights.

Furthermore, the PO also holds professional power on a structural level, in reporting recurring societal problems to their local boards and to the NBHW. They act as a source of information for the government about the actual living conditions for persons with PSD and the issues faced as a group.

Returning to the CRPD mandate of equal legal recognition for persons with disabilities, the PO exemplifies supported decision-making, most obvious in what has been identified as an 'empowerment' mode of action. However, Grim (2019) found that methods for supported decision-making may fall short, due to a professional's mistrust in the ability, agency and insight of persons with psychosocial disabilities. This view corresponds to a logic of care where the professional knows what is best for the client (in this chapter denoted the 'paternalistic' mode of action).

Although the PO model was developed before the CRPD raised the demand of supported decision-making, the PO has established a work method proven to be a support in decision-making for their clients when they raise their voices to claim their legal rights. Possibly, the value of the PO in supporting decision-making is two-fold: the support is personal, offering empathy and security in the personal relationship; and POs have their vocational position, which they can use in helping clients to exert their rights. The power of a PO thus becomes an asset for the client to use in meetings with authorities and in negotiations about access to healthcare and welfare services. In conclusion, the PO model could be systematically developed and tested in any society as a means of strengthening supported decision-making for persons with PSD, with adjustments made according to the relevant societal prerequisites. Personal ombudsmen also act as support for relatives who are responsible for care and support for persons with PSD, in giving advice and some respite in terms of the responsibilities of coordinating treatment and care. This is a responsibility that is often given to family members in any society, regardless of national wealth or the existing support of the welfare state.

REFERENCES

Dominelli, L. (2002). *Antioppressive Social Work: Theory and Practice*. Basingstoke: Palgrave Macmillan.

Goffman, E. (1991). *Asylums: Essays on the Social Situation of Mental Patients and Other Inmates*. Harmondsworth: Penguin.

Björkman, T., Hansson, L., & Sandlund, M. (2002). Outcome of case management based on the strengths model compared to standard care. A randomised controlled trial. *Social Psychiatry and Psychiatric Epidemiology*, 37(4), 147–152.

Grim, K. (2019). *Legitimizing the knowledge of mental health service users in shared decision-making. Promoting participation through a web-based decision support tool*. Doctoral dissertation, School of Education, Health and Social Studies, Dalarna University.

Grimen, H. (2009). *Hva er tillit* [What is trust?]. Oslo: Universitetsforlaget.

Järkestig Berggren, U. (2015). Building on users' knowledge as a basis for professional expertise? An example from Swedish social care services. *European Journal of Social Work*, 18(5), 718–730.

Järkestig Berggren, U., & Gunnarsson, E. (2010). User-oriented mental health reform in Sweden: featuring 'professional friendship'. *Disability & Society*, 25(5), 565–577.

Järkestig Berggren, U. (2010). *Personligt ombud och förändringsprocesser på det socialpsykiatriska fältet* [Personal ombudsman and processes of change in the field of socialpsychiatry]. Doctoral dissertation, Department of Social Work, Linnaeus University.

Klockmo, C. (2013). *The role of personligt ombud in supporting the recovery process for people with psychiatric disabilities*. Doctoral dissertation, Department of Health Sciences, Mid Sweden University.

Klockmo, C., Marnetoft, S., & Nordenmark, M. (2012). Moving toward a recovery-oriented approach in the Swedish mental health system: an interview study of *Personligt Ombud* in Sweden. *Vulnerable Groups & Inclusion*, 3(1), 1–16.

National Board of Health and Welfare. (2018). *Lägesrapport om verksamheter med personligt ombud*. [Report on Personal ombudsman services] Stockholm: National Board of Health and Welfare.

National Board of Health and Welfare. (2014). *Personligt ombud för personer med psykisk funktionsnedsättning. Uppföljning av verksamheten med personligt ombud*. [Personal ombudsman for persons with serious psychiatric impairments. Evaluation.] Stockholm: National Board of Health and Welfare.

National Board of Health and Welfare. (2011). Meddelandeblad 5/2011. [Report 5/2011] Stockholm: National Board of Health and Welfare.

National Board of Health and Welfare. (2000). Meddelandeblad 14/2000. [Report 14/2000] Stockholm: National Board of Health and Welfare.

Rapp, C. A., & Goscha, R. J. (2006). *The Strengths Model: Case Management with People with Psychiatric Disabilities.* New York: Oxford University Press.

SOU (1992:73). *Psykiatriutredningens slutbetänkande* [Final report of the psychiatric government investigation]. Government report. 73. Stockholm: Fritze.

Swedberg, R. (2018). How to use Max Weber's ideal type in sociological analysis. *Journal of Classical Sociology*, 18(3), 181–196.

YPOS. (2016). Ethical guidelines, https://uploads.staticjw.com/yp/ypos/personliga-ombud-etikdokument-2016-slutver.pdf.

Zwarenstein, M., Stephenson, B., & Johnston, L. (2008). Case management: Effects on professional practice and health care outcomes. *Cochrane Database Systematic Reviews* 4.

16

Strategies to Achieve a Rights-Based Approach through WHO QualityRights

Michelle Funk, Natalie Drew Bold, Joana Ansong, Daniel Chisholm, Melita Murko, Joyce Nato, Sally-Ann Ohene, Jasmine Vergara and Edwina Zoghbi

Abstract

Numerous reports from countries, the UN, NGOs and the media underscore extensive human rights violations experienced by people with psychosocial disabilities, including the denial of the right to exercise their legal capacity. Within the mental health care context people report that services do not respond to their needs and fail to respect their will and preferences or to support community inclusion. This underscores the need to adopt a human rights approach in mental health and to radically shift the way services operate, towards care and support that is recovery and rights oriented and that ensures service users are the drivers of their own healthcare. WHO QualityRights, established in 2012, is an initiative to improve access to good-quality mental health and social services and to promote the rights of people with psychosocial disabilities worldwide in line with the CRPD. The initiative works in several areas: capacity building to combat stigma and discrimination and promote rights and recovery; creating community-based services that respect human rights and person-centered recovery approaches; supporting civil society movements and people with lived experience to conduct advocacy and influence policymaking; and reforming policy and law in line with the CRPD and other human rights standards.

INTRODUCTION

Over the last several years numerous reports from countries, the United Nations (UN), nongovernmental organizations (NGOs) and the media have highlighted that people with psychosocial disabilities experience extensive violations.[1] In the

---

[1] The term "psychosocial disability" is being used here to include people who have received a mental health-related diagnosis or who self-identify with this term. People with psychosocial disabilities include ex- and current users of mental health care services, as well as persons that identify as survivors of these services or with the psychosocial disability itself. The use of the term "disability" is important in this context because it highlights the significant barriers that hinder the full and effective participation in society of people with actual or perceived impairments and the fact that they are protected under the UN Convention on the Rights of Persons with Disabilities (CRPD).

community, people experience exclusion, marginalization and discrimination, in addition to denial of rights and opportunities to employment, education, healthcare, housing and social welfare, as well as restrictions in the exercise of civil and political rights. Many experience physical and sexual abuse and violence, arbitrary detention and financial exploitation.

People are also denied the right to exercise their legal capacity and to make decisions and choices for themselves. Decisions are instead made by family members, court-appointed guardians, government officials or service providers regarding important aspects of their lives, including where and with whom they should live, how their money, property and personal affairs should be managed, and other aspects of their lives. Decisions concerning healthcare are also often made by others, which in many cases results in people being detained in mental health facilities and treated against their will.[2]

Human rights abuses, coercion and violence are also endemic in many mental health services themselves, including in low-, middle- and high-income countries – although how these play out can differ according to the specific context (e.g., chains in low income contexts, and chemical restraints in high-income contexts).[3] Nevertheless there are more commonalities than differences across countries, including misconceptions around mental health, stigma and discrimination, chronic underfunding of mental health services, a lack of available options to respond to what might be perceived as disruptive behavior or emotional crisis and an acceptance of the use of coercion as a legitimate way to respond to people in crisis.

People also commonly report that mental health services fail to respond to their needs, to respect their will and preference or personhood or to support them to live the in the community. Instead, people's experiences leave them feeling dehumanized, hopeless and disempowered. As highlighted by the World Network of Users

---

[2] Drew N, Funk M, Tang S et al. (2011). Human rights violations of people with mental and psychosocial disabilities: an unresolved global crisis. *Lancet*; 378: 1664–75.
[3] Royal Commission into Victoria's Mental Health System (2019). *PP 87, Session 2018–2019 Interim Report*. https://s3.ap-southeast-2.amazonaws.com/hdp.au.prod.app.vic-rcvmhs.files/4215/8104/8017/Interim_Report__FINAL_.pdf. Human Rights Watch (2018). "They stay until they die" A lifetime of isolation and neglect in institutions for people with disabilities in Brazil. www.hrw.org/report/2018/05/23/they-stay-until-they-die/lifetime-isolation-and-neglect-institutions-people. Mental Health Europe (2017). *Mapping and Understanding Exclusion- Institutional, Coercive and Community Based Services and Practices across Europe*. https://mhe-sme.org/wp-content/uploads/2018/01/Mapping-and-Understanding-Exclusion-in-Europe.pdf. Human Rights Watch (2016). Living in hell. Abuses against people with psychosocial disabilities in Indonesia. www.hrw.org/report/2016/03/20/living-hell/abuses-against-people-psychosocial-disabilities-indonesia. Mental Disability Advocacy Centre (2014). *Psychiatric Hospitals in Uganda – A Human Rights Investigation*. www.mdac.org/en/resources/psychiatric-hospitals-uganda-human-rights-investigation. Parliamentary and Health Service Ombudsman (2018). NHS failing patients with mental health problems. www.ombudsman.org.uk/news-and-blog/news/nhs-failing-patients-mental-health-problems. Behrens R (2018). Failings in mental healthcare are violating basic human rights. *The Guardian*. www.theguardian.com/commentisfree/2018/mar/21/failing-mental-healthcare-violating-basic-human-rights.

and Survivors of Psychiatry (WNUSP), "stigma and discrimination have created a class of people who have been systematically disempowered and impoverished."[4]

These reports underscore the urgent need to prioritize a human rights approach in mental health. The UN Special Rapporteur on the right to health in his 2017 report asserted that a significant shift is needed to move away from a biomedical paradigm towards mental health systems that prioritize respect for human rights.[5]

This "paradigm shift" involves rethinking the way in which mental health and psychosocial issues are understood, and promoting mental health care and support based on informed consent and respecting people's will and preference. Approaches that focus solely on diagnosis, treatment, symptom reduction and containment fail to adequately address all important areas of a person's life – and must be replaced with person-centered recovery approaches that respect rights and ensure that people are the primary drivers of their own healthcare. Such an approach, while not ignoring clinical concerns, places importance on issues such as meanings, values, relationships, work, family and education.[6]

FRAMEWORKS FOR SUSTAINABLE CHANGE

The UN Convention on the Rights of Persons with Disabilities (CRPD) explicitly articulates the human rights of all people with disabilities, including people with psychosocial disabilities. It affirms and sets obligations on countries to take concrete measures to promote the rights of persons with disabilities and ensure that all services provided are aligned with its provisions.

The need for a new approach has recently been underscored by the UN Office of the High Commissioner for Human Rights, the UN Special Rapporteurs on the right to health and on the rights of persons with disabilities.[7] Three recent

---

[4] WNUSP (2001). Human rights position paper of the World Network of Users and Survivors of Psychiatry. http://wnusp.net/index.php/human-rights-position-paper-of-the-world-network-of-users-and-survivors-of-psychiatry.html.

[5] Mann S P, Bradley V J and Sahakian B J (2016). Human rights-based approaches to mental health: a review of programs. *Health and Human Rights Journal*; 18: 263–275. Pūras D (2017). UN Human Rights Council: Report of the Special Rapporteur on the right of everyone to the enjoyment of the highest attainable standard of physical and mental health, (A/HRC/35/21). https://socialprotection-humanrights.org/resource/report-special-rapporteur-right-everyone-enjoyment-highest-attainable-standard-physical-mental-health-dainius-puras-ahrc3521/. Pūras D (2019). The role of the determinants of health in advancing the right to mental health. (A/HRC/41/34).

[6] Slade M (2009). *Personal Recovery and Mental Illness: A Guide for Mental Health Professionals.* Cambridge: Cambridge University Press.

[7] Pūras D (2017). Special Rapporteur on the right to health. Pūras D (2019). The role of the determinants of health. UN Human Rights Council (2018). Peru: Milestone disability reforms lead the way for other States, says UN expert. www.ohchr.org/en/NewsEvents/Pages/DisplayNews.aspx?NewsID=23501&LangID=E. Devandas Aguilar C (2018). Report of the Special Rapporteur on the rights of persons with disabilities: right to health. (A/73/161). www.ohchr.org/Documents/Issues/Disability/A_73_161_EN.pdf. UN Human Rights Council (2017). Report of the United Nations High Commissioner for Human Rights: Mental health and human rights, 31 January 2017. A/HRC/34/32. UN Human Rights Council (2020). Report of the Special Rapporteur on torture and other cruel,

resolutions of the Human Rights Council have also called for a human rights approach to mental health.[8] These reports and resolutions have specifically called for World Health Organization (WHO) leadership in making this happen, through its QualityRights initiative.

WHO QUALITYRIGHTS

QualityRights is the WHO's global initiative to improve the quality of care in mental health and social care services and promote the rights of people with psychosocial, intellectual and cognitive disabilities across the world. Over the last several years, the initiative has specifically focused its efforts on identifying strategies and solutions to promote a human rights and recovery approach to mental health in line with the CRPD. This involves four core areas of work, outlined below.

Building Capacity to Combat Stigma and Discrimination and Promote Human Rights

Through systematic and sustained capacity-building efforts, the WHO is working to change attitudes and practices among national stakeholder groups – including policymakers, health and mental health professionals, social workers, people with lived experience, families, NGOs and organizations of persons with disabilities, the police, judges, schools and the wider community – in countries across all regions, to integrate human rights and recovery approaches in mental health.

As part of these efforts, the WHO developed the QualityRights training materials and tools, launched in November 2019.[9] These resources aim to transform health systems and services towards a person-centered, recovery-oriented and human rights-based approach in line with the CRPD. The materials comprise core and specialized training modules (see Table 16.1) and use exercises, debates, discussions, case studies and scenarios from countries around the world to engage people, on a personal and emotional level, with the concepts of human rights and recovery.

In addition, in order to maximize reach, WHO has also developed the QualityRights fifteen-hour multi-module QualityRights e-training platform on

---

inhuman or degrading treatment of punishment, 14 February 2020. A/HRC/43/49. www.ohchr.org/EN/HRBodies/HRC/RegularSessions/Session43/Pages/ListReports.aspx.

[8] UN Human Rights Council (2017). Resolution on Mental health and human rights. Adopted by the Human Rights Council on 26 September 2017. A/HRC/36/L.25. UN Human Rights Council (2016). Resolution on Mental health and human rights. Adopted by the Human Rights Council on 29 June 2016. A/HRC/32/L.26. UN Human Rights Council (2020). Resolution on Mental health and human rights. Adopted by the Human Rights Council on 20 March 2020. A/HRC/43/L.19. https://ap.ohchr.org/Documents/dpage_e.aspx?si=A/HRC/43/L.19.

[9] WHO (2019). QualityRights materials for training, guidance and transformation. www.who.int/publications-detail/who-qualityrights-guidance-and-training-tools.

TABLE 16.1 *WHO QualityRights training materials*

WHO QualityRights training materials	
Core training modules • Human rights • Mental health, disability and human rights • Legal capacity and the right to decide • Recovery and the right to health • Freedom from coercion, violence and abuse	**Specialized training modules** • Supported decision-making and advance planning • Recovery practices for mental health and well-being • Strategies to end seclusion and restraint

Source: WHO, QualityRights.

mental health, disability, human rights and recovery. The platform has the potential for reaching tens of thousands of stakeholders within and across countries.

Both the face-to-face training materials and the e-training explore critical issues related to equal recognition before the law and article 12 of the CRPD. They build knowledge and skills on how to end coercive practices such as seclusion and restraint, as well how to respect people's will and preferences in order to end forced admission and treatment. In relation to ending coercive practices, several strategies are introduced, such as: individualized plans to explore and respond to sensitivities and signs of distress before any potential crisis emerges; creating a "saying yes" and "can-do" culture to avoid frustrations from intensifying; supportive environments and the use of comfort rooms; de-escalation of tense and conflictual situations; and trained response teams that intervene during crises without force.

In relation to will and preference and ending forced admission and treatment, the training materials introduce supported decision-making processes – for example, actively identifying and bringing in a support network of the supported person's choosing; introducing advance plans in which a person specifies the treatments and support that they are willing or unwilling to receive; and other potentially therapeutic actions. The training materials also introduce the "Ulysses clause" as part of advance planning, which enables people to state that any objections they may express "in the moment" should be overruled in favor of the advance directive. This also allows options for people using services who report that they are in favor of involuntary treatment.[10]

---

[10] WHO (2019). Supported decision-making and advance planning. WHO QualityRights Specialized training. Course guide. https://apps.who.int/iris/bitstream/handle/10665/329609/9789241516761-eng.pdf. WHO (2019). Strategies to end seclusion and restraint. WHO QualityRights Specialized training. Course guide. https://apps.who.int/iris/bitstream/handle/10665/329605/9789241516754-eng.pdf. WHO (2019). Legal capacity and the right to decide. WHO QualityRights Core training: mental health and social services. Course guide. https://apps.who.int/iris/bitstream/handle/10665/329539/9789241516716-eng.pdf.

Experts from all regions and all stakeholder groups – including health professionals, people with lived experience, policymakers, researchers, academics and civil society actors – were involved in the development of the capacity-building materials to ensure that all training is relevant to different local contexts, is culturally appropriate, and is focused on elevating local good practice rather than prescribing an "outside" model. The materials encompass case studies and examples from countries in all regions in order to optimize relevance to local contexts.

In addition, for face-to-face training, local trainers are recruited and trained to ensure that the cultural, social and economic context and language is reflected in the training. For the e-training platform, local online coaches are recruited in order to mentor platform users from their own countries. The face-to-face training and e-training platform have been implemented in countries in all regions and translated into many languages.

A 2019 evaluation of attitude change conducted by the Institute of Mental Health, University of Nottingham,[11] specifically for participants completing the e-training course demonstrated important and positive attitudinal shifts towards a human rights-based approach and legal capacity specifically, with mainly moderate to large effect sizes (Table 16.2).

Approximately 83 percent of the 733 people completing (or partially completing) the pretraining questionnaire went on to complete the full e-training course. The majority of respondents completing the e-training identified as "female" at baseline (61.8 percent). Ages ranged from twenty to seventy-six, with the majority being between the ages of thirty to thirty-four (23 percent). Most respondents were either affiliated with their country's ministry of health (27.4 percent) or a service provider in mental health or related areas (23.6 percent). Other respondents were from academia, disabled people's organizations, NGOs, other government ministries, department or commissions, professional organizations or associations, general health service providers, people with lived experience and UN organizations and agencies, including the WHO. Ghana and Indonesia were the two countries in which the majority of respondents said they were currently residing (35.9 percent and 31.6 percent, respectively). Other respondents were spread across sixty-five other countries across all regions.

Seven hundred thirty-three respondents completed or partially completed the pretraining questionnaire. Upon successful completion, learners receive an automated request to complete the post-training questionnaire. Of these, 181 completed or partially completed the post-training questionnaire.[12] The pre- and post-training questionnaires included twenty-six statements in five-point Likert

---

[11] Authors of the QualityRights training evaluation Report: Harriet Dilks, Caitlin Hand, Deborah Oliveira and Martin Orrell.

[12] The numbers for the completion of the post-training questionnaire were low and participants advised that this was because they did not see the automated request to complete the follow-up questionnaire.

TABLE 16.2 *QualityRights e-training questionnaire*
Only people who had completed both a pre- and post-training questionnaire were included in this analysis.

Statement	Mean (before)	Mean (after)	Percent change	Direction of change	P value	Effect size (Cohen's d)
a. Knowledge and understanding of human rights can improve the quality of care in mental health-related services.[1]	4.77	4.78	0.2%	Positive	.916	0.011
b. There is a lot that mental health and other practitioners can do to promote the rights of people with mental health conditions.[1]	4.57	4.73	3.5%	Positive	.095	0.159
c. Persons with severe mental health conditions should consult their doctor before marrying.[2]	3.52	2.16	38.6%	Positive	.000	0.886
d. A lot can be improved within mental health services without additional resources.[2]	2.68	3.36	25.4%	Positive	.000	0.389
e. People with dementia should always live in group homes where staff can take care of them.[2]	2.77	1.67	39.7%	Positive	.000	0.845
f. People with psychosocial disabilities should not be hired in work requiring direct contact with the public.[3]	1.74	1.38	20.7%	Positive	.002	0.298
g. Mental health services should support and encourage people to access education and employment opportunities in the community.[3]	4.74	4.68	1.3%	Negative	.456	0.067
h. Medication is the most important factor to help people with mental health conditions get better.[3]	2.79	1.74	37.6%	Positive	.000	0.715
i. You can only inspire hope once a person has recovered.[4]	2.22	1.97	11.3%	Positive	.058	0.185
j. People using mental health services should be empowered to make their own decisions about their treatment.[4]	4.31	4.60	6.7%	Positive	.015	0.240
k. Following the advice of other people who have experienced mental health issues is too risky.[4]	2.07	1.73	16.4%	Positive	.001	0.326
l. It is important to appear tough with people using mental health services in order to avoid being manipulated.[5]	2.47	1.58	36.0%	Positive	.000	0.638
m. People with psychosocial disabilities need someone to plan activities for them.[5]	2.77	1.63	41.2%	Positive	.000	0.872
n. The opinions of a person with an intellectual disability about care and treatment should carry more weight than those of health practitioners.[6]	3.12	3.94	26.3%	Positive	.000	0.582
o. It is acceptable to pressure people using mental health services to take treatment that they don't want.[6]	2.00	1.34	33.0%	Positive	.000	0.571
p. Persons with mental health conditions should not be given important responsibilities.[6]	1.95	1.51	22.6%	Positive	.000	0.372

Statement						
q. When people are unable to communicate, you need to make decisions based on your ideas about what is best for them.[6]	2.83	1.86	34.3%	Positive	.000	0.656
r. Health practitioners are in the best position to know what people with dementia are capable of achieving in their lives.[7]	2.91	1.87	35.7%	Positive	.000	0.759
s. People with intellectual disabilities have the right to make their own decisions, even if I don't agree with them.[7]	3.92	4.43	13.0%	Positive	.000	0.417
t. Controlling people using mental health services is necessary to maintain order.[7]	2.72	1.54	43.4%	Positive	.000	0.824
u. The use of seclusion and restraint is needed if people using mental health services become threatening.[7]	2.83	1.76	37.8%	Positive	.000	0.683
v. Seclusion is not an appropriate way to manage a crisis.[7]	3.75	4.41	17.6%	Positive	.000	0.523
w. The use of seclusion and restraint negatively affects the therapeutic relationship between people using mental health services and staff.[8]	3.99	4.68	17.3%	Positive	.000	0.640
x. Locking people in a room is acceptable if they are at risk of harming themselves or others.[8]	3.00	1.91	36.3%	Positive	.000	0.727
y. Most people do not mind if they are sedated to de-escalate a tense situation.[8]	2.80	1.81	35.4%	Positive	.000	0.789
z. Involuntary admission does more harm than good.[8]	3.20	4.22	31.9%	Positive	.000	0.674

[1] n = 113
[2] n = 112
[3] n = 109
[4] n = 108
[5] n = 103
[6] n = 102
[7] n = 99
[8] n = 98

Source: Attitudinal change following QualityRights e-training

scales ("1 – strongly disagree" to "5 – strongly agree") to measure individuals' attitudes towards human rights in mental health. Paired t-tests were run on all the statements to see if there was a change in the responses from before the training to after training. Only those who had completed both a pre- and post-training questionnaire were included in this analysis.

The evaluation showed that for all but three of the statements, the responses showed a significant improvement in attitudes towards human rights after the training. The statement that had the largest improvement based on percentage change was "Controlling people using mental health services is necessary to maintain order," where the mean score was 2.72 at baseline and 1.54 at follow-up.

The qualitative data analysis indicated that the training was overwhelmingly well received. The most common impact highlighted was gaining general knowledge of human rights and recognizing that people with disabilities have the same rights to legal capacity as everybody else. Feedback comprised statements such as:

> "I now understand that people with psychosocial disabilities have rights just like anyone else and these rights have to be respected despite personal bias or perception of severity of the disability."

Participants also described how they would promote informed consent to treatment:

> "Informed consent is key in every treatment, and allowing patients to make their own treatment or recovery plan . . ."
>
> "In the event I need to deal with a family member with declining cognitive function, I understand the importance of adhering to their own wishes."

Many participants mentioned they will no longer use coercive practices such as seclusion, even in a crisis situation:

> "My attitude changed especially with respect to seclusion, before I thought it is appropriate to some extent."
>
> "Clients/patients choice first, not to use seclusion as a means of calming a disturbed patient."

Wide-scale implementation of the QualityRights e-training and face-to-face training is made possible through a comprehensive strategy involving the appointment of national champions and well-known personalities; social media and traditional media; integration into health professional development and quality assurance processes; and integration into university and college teaching and curriculums. Reaching all relevant stakeholder groups through the e-training is also critical in order to realize sustainable change at the societal level.

Creating Community-Based and Recovery-Oriented Services that Respect and Promote Human Rights.

Assessing and Improving Existing Services

The WHO also provides countries requesting support for service improvement with assistance to assess and transform their mental health services in order to align with human rights and recovery principles. Technical assistance includes support for the establishment and training of national multidisciplinary assessment teams on the standards and processes for assessment; support for reporting assessment findings; and capacity building on how to develop and implement improvement plans based on the assessment results.

A number of tools have been developed in order to conduct this work, including the WHO QualityRights assessment toolkit, which enables countries to assess their services against standards derived from the CRPD, covering issues related to legal capacity, informed consent to treatment, supported decision-making, advance directives and freedom from violence, coercion and abuse, as well as promoting community inclusion, among other areas.[13]

The recently published WHO QualityRights module on transforming services and promoting human rights provides guidance to address gaps and improve services in line with CRPD standards.[14] The module covers critical issues that are a prerequisite for transforming services sustainably, including exploring how to change the service culture and power dynamics in order to ensure that core values such as equality, respect and dignity are embedded in the service. It outlines how to define a shared vision reflecting the perspective of staff as well as people who use the service. Through a participatory approach, the module also provides guidance on how to work through the specific priorities identified during the service assessment, and develop an action plan to address these.

Assessments of one or more mental health services have been carried out in at least forty-seven countries (that the WHO is aware of) since the publication of the QualityRights tools and methodology in 2012, although this number is likely to be higher, as many countries and organizations use the tools without communication with the WHO.[15]

---

[13] WHO (2012). WHO QualityRights toolkit to assess and improve quality and human rights in mental health and social care facilities. https://www.who.int/mental_health/publications/QualityRights_toolkit/en/.

[14] WHO (2019). Transforming services and promoting human rights. WHO QualityRights training and guidance: mental health and social services. Course guide. https://apps.who.int/iris/bitstream/handle/10665/329611/9789241516815-eng.pdf.

[15] Examples of country experiences in undertaking QualityRights Assessments are available on the WHO Country Implementation Portal at https://qualityrights.org/in-countries/. See for example, the experiences of France, Chile, Ghana, Lebanon and several other countries.

The most comprehensive implementation of QualityRights service assessments is in the European region. As part of the WHO EURO project on adults with mental health conditions, psychosocial and intellectual disabilities living in institutions in the European Region, assessments were conducted in seventy-five facilities across twenty-four WHO Member States and Kosovo[16] throughout 2017. Some key findings confirmed that long-term institutional care in many European countries violates people's fundamental rights, including their legal capacity, autonomy, dignity, liberty and security of person, physical and mental integrity and freedom from torture and ill treatment and from exploitation, violence and abuse.[17] The next phase of the WHO EURO project has focused on providing key national actors from fifteen countries with QualityRights capacity building via face-to-face workshops and the QualityRights e-training in order to address the gaps identified during the assessment phase and promote quality and rights within services.

Establishing and Scaling-Up Innovative Services

As part of this area of work, QualityRights is developing a good-practice service document on community mental health services that promote rights and recovery, scheduled at time of writing to be published in early 2021.

The document describes innovative good-practice services and outlines how each service complies with criteria around respect for legal capacity, noncoercive responses, community inclusion, participation and the recovery approach. It provides evaluation and cost information for each service and discusses the applicability of services in different settings and contexts.

This document will complement several other QualityRights guidance documents, in particular two modules published in 2019 on setting up individualized peer-support services and on establishing peer-support groups within services and the community.[18]

Supporting Civil Society Movements to Conduct Advocacy and Influence Policymaking

Historically, people with psychosocial disabilities have been excluded from participating not only in decision-making regarding their own health and life choices, but

---

[16] In accordance with Security Council resolution 1244 (1999).
[17] Regional Office for Europe of the World Health Organization (2018). Mental health, human rights and standards of care. Assessment of the quality of institutional care for adults with psychosocial and intellectual disabilities in the WHO European Region. www.euro.who.int/__data/assets/pdf_file/0017/373202/mental-health-programme-eng.pdf?ua=1.
[18] WHO (2019). Peer support groups by and for people with lived experience. WHO QualityRights guidance module. https://apps.who.int/iris/bitstream/handle/10665/329594/9789241516778-eng.pdf. WHO (2019). One-to-one peer support by and for people with lived experience. WHO QualityRights guidance module. https://apps.who.int/iris/bitstream/handle/10665/329591/9789241516785-eng.pdf.

also from policymaking. This exclusion is further exacerbated by the lack of organizations for and by people with lived experience. Establishing or strengthening such organizations, overcoming barriers to their full and effective participation and building capacity to advocate for their interests are essential to ensuring that policies, laws, services and systems are responsive to people's needs and rights.

Through QualityRights, the WHO works to promote the full participation of people with psychosocial disabilities and their organizations in actions and decision-making processes. At the national level, an increasing number of people with lived experience and their organizations are being engaged to deliver QualityRights training and the pool of experts-by-experience will continue to grow as more countries embark on the initiative.

In line with QualityRights's methodology, national committees (set up to assess mental health services using WHO's QualityRights assessment toolkit) comprise people with lived experience; who are also actively involved in the development of service transformation plans.

At the international level, QualityRights systematically engages people with lived experience and their organizations in the development of all normative, guidance and training materials. Furthermore, in light of identified gaps, specific guidance modules were published in 2019 on strengthening civil society organizations and advocacy to promote human rights. These modules – developed with substantial input from people with lived experience – provide step-by-step guidance and case studies on how national civil society movements can take action to advocate for human rights approaches in the mental health and social sectors in order to achieve impactful and durable change.[19]

Reforming National Policies and Legislation in Line with the CRPD and Other International Human Rights Standards

Mental health, guardianship and other substitute decision-making laws in countries around the world violate people's rights and serve to legitimize restrictions in the exercise of legal capacity, severely curtailing people's right to make decisions on all aspects of their lives.[20] These laws also often authorize coercive practices such as involuntary admission and treatment and seclusion and restraint. In a similar way, many countries have outdated policies related to mental health that, although not mandating coercive practices or restrictions in legal capacity, nevertheless fail to put in place services, supports and processes that challenge and mitigate these practices. Countries have specific obligations to align their policies and laws with the CRPD and

---

[19] WHO (2019). Civil society organizations to promote human rights in mental health and related areas. WHO QualityRights guidance module. https://apps.who.int/iris/bitstream/handle/10665/329589/9789241516808-eng.pdf. WHO (2019). Advocacy for mental health, disability and human rights. WHO QualityRights guidance module. https://apps.who.int/iris/bitstream/handle/10665/329587/9789241516792-eng.pdf

[20] Bhugra D, Pathare S, Gosavi C et al. (2016) Mental illness and the right to vote: a review of legislation across the world. International Review of Psychiatry. 28(4): 395–9, 402–8.

other international human rights standards. To date, no countries have achieved complete compliance with the CRPD, although there are efforts in this direction. Peru, Colombia and Costa Rica, for example, have recently reformed their legislation to end guardianship and promote legal capacity and supported decision-making[21].

Many countries rely on WHO technical support to develop or reform their national laws and policies related to mental health. Previous WHO guidance in these areas were drafted prior to the coming into force of the CRPD, and thus does not comply fully with the standards set by the Convention. To address this gap, the WHO is currently in the process of developing new CRPD-compliant guidance in order to support countries in their efforts to put in place human rights-oriented policy and law, in line with their obligations under the Convention.

The WHO's new guidance will focus on providing holistic, person-centered care and recovery-oriented community services, promoting legal capacity and supported decision-making processes, strategies for ending coercive practices, community inclusion and participation of people with psychosocial disabilities and their organizations. Establishing legal provisions around supported decision-making and advance planning in particular will be critical to ensuring a definitive move away from substitute decision-making and towards frameworks that safeguard people's right to legal capacity on an equal basis with others.

WHO QualityRights – National Implementation

Uptake of WHO QualityRights has started to accelerate rapidly over the last two years. Implementation started several years ago with small pilot projects in different countries. Subsequently from 2014 to 2016 comprehensive statewide implementation of QualityRights was undertaken in the state of Gujarat in India.

Launched in July 2014 by the Ministry of Health and Family Welfare of Gujarat, the project focused on undertaking assessments of mental health services throughout the state and developing an individualized improvement plan for each of the services using the QualityRights tools and methodology.[22] Additionally, a comprehensive QualityRights capacity-building program was implemented to

---

[21] (Legislative Decree No. 1384). Decreto legislativo que reconoce y regula la capacidad jurídica de las personas con discapacidad en igualdad de condiciones. https://busquedas.elperuano.pe/normaslegales/decreto-legislativo-que-reconoce-y-regula-la-capacidad-jurid-decreto-legislativo-n-1384-1687393-2 (LEY N° 9379). Ley para Promoción de la Autonomía Personal de las Personas con Discapacidad. www.ilo.org/dyn/natlex/docs/ELECTRONIC/103229/125236/F1379760652/LEY%209379%20COSTA%20RICA.pdf.
Minkowitz T (2018). Peruvian Legal Capacity Reform – Celebration and Analysis. *Mad in America*. www.madinamerica.com/2018/10/peruvian-legal-capacity-reform-celebration-and-analysis/. United Nations (2019). UN expert welcomes legal capacity reform in Colombia to end guardianship regime. www.ohchr.org/EN/NewsEvents/Pages/DisplayNews.aspx?NewsID=24926&LangID=E.

[22] WHO (2012). WHO QualityRights toolkit to assess and improve quality and human rights in mental health and social care facilities. www.who.int/mental_health/publications/QualityRights_toolkit/en/. WHO (2019). QualityRights materials for training, guidance and transformation. www.who.int/publications-detail/who-qualityrights-guidance-and-training-tools.

train healthcare staff, people using services and families on mental health and human rights and the recovery approach.[23]

In addition, people with psychosocial disabilities were trained and recruited as peer support volunteers at each of the services to support service users. Their role was to ensure that people understood their rights and to help them develop recovery plans, including identifying their goals and wishes for treatment and recovery. Peer-support groups led by people with psychosocial disabilities (known as "*Maitri*") and peer-support groups led by families (known as "*Saathi*") were also established as part of QualityRights Gujarat.[24]

The project showed significant results and impact in services throughout Gujarat. Over a twelve-month period, the quality and human rights conditions in services receiving the intervention improved significantly, with important advancements noted on standards for all five themes assessed with the QualityRights assessment toolkit, including around legal capacity and informed consent. Staff in the services showed substantially improved attitudes towards people using services and service users reported feeling significantly more empowered and satisfied with the services offered.[25]

The QualityRights initiative is now entering a new phase of large-scale, country-wide implementation in regions across the world. Countries are putting in place multiple QualityRights strategies in efforts to improve quality of services and promote human rights on a wide scale.

In Lebanon, as part of a comprehensive mental health system reform outlined in a five-year strategy for 2015 to 2020, there is now a large pool of service assessors who have been through the QualityRights training program. These include mental health professionals, social workers, lawyers and people with psychosocial disabilities. Since 2017, five services have been assessed using the assessment toolkit. Certain facilities have gone on to develop and implement improvement plans using the QualityRights service transformation module and a number of people have also been trained through the QualityRights training materials highlighted above. By end of 2020 the Ministry of Health planned to have all services throughout the country assessed using the QualityRights tools and methodology. Additionally, a ministerial decision has mandated that all psychiatric hospitals and in-patient mental health wards within general hospitals be subject to an assessment concerning the quality of care and human rights using the WHO QualityRights framework.[26]

In 2019 the governments of both Ghana and of Kenya launched QualityRights initiatives. This involves nationwide capacity building among key stakeholders

---

[23] Ibid.
[24] Pathare, S., Funk, M., Drew Bold, N. et al. (2019). Systematic evaluation of the QualityRights programme in public mental health facilities in Gujarat, India. *The British Journal of Psychiatry*, 1-8. https://doi.org/10.1192/bjp.2019.138.
[25] Ibid.
[26] Ministry of Public Health, Lebanon, decision No. 270/1. www.moph.gov.lb/userfiles/files/Minister%20Decision-%20Concerning%20the%20Quality%20of%20Care%20and%20Human%20Rights%20in%20the%20Field%20of%20Mental%20Health.pdf.

based on the WHO QualityRights face-to-face and e-training program. Since the launch of QualityRights in Ghana in February 2019 until the time of writing, around 18,000 people enrolled and around 9,000 people completed the course and received a WHO certificate. In Kenya, which launched in November 2019, over 4000 people enrolled and around 860 received their certificates by time of writing. In addition, in 2020, both countries planned to undertake countrywide QualityRights assessment and transformation of services.

In 2019, Turkey, Estonia and Czechia translated and launched the QualityRights e-training program on mental health, disability, human rights and recovery in each of their respective countries and languages. This will enable the nationwide capacity building of thousands of health professionals and other stakeholders in each country. The e-training was made available in Bosnia and Herzegovina in the second half of 2020.

In the Western Pacific, the Philippines officially launched the QualityRights e-training in Filipino on World Mental Health Day, October 10, 2019, at the Third Public Health Summit of the Department of Health. The e-training will be one of the core interventions in the five-year Strategic Plan of the Philippine Council for Mental Health for the implementation of the Mental Health Act.

The creation of Spanish and French versions of the QualityRights e-training, currently underway, will further open up the possibility of large-scale uptake of QualityRights in French and Spanish-speaking countries throughout the world, notably throughout Latin America.

A WHO QualityRights country online portal has been created to enable countries to document their activities and share information, strategies, experiences and resources. It is hoped that the portal will also be a means of showcasing what can be achieved in countries with varying social and economic contexts in order to promote access to quality care and respect for human rights, thus inspiring other countries to take similar actions.

Conclusion

While the WHO QualityRights initiative has had some success in bringing about attitude and practice change on critical human rights issues, including the need to promote legal capacity and supported decision-making, these successes are tempered by the fact that legislative frameworks in most countries continue to uphold substitute decision-making systems and coercive practices such as involuntary admission and treatment, seclusion and restraint, among other coercive measures. Thus, substantial efforts are still needed in all countries to reform national mental health and capacity-related legislation in order to align with the requirements of the CRPD and Article 12.

At the same time, successful law reform depends on substantial attitude change and human rights literacy among all key actors, including policymakers, legislators, health professionals, civil society, people with lived experience, families and others. Despite early wins in bringing about such changes through QualityRights capacity-building efforts in some countries, resistance remains among many national stakeholders, particularly in the health field, including in relation to replacing involuntary admission and treatment and substitute decision-making mechanisms and practices in favor of those that promote legal capacity and supported decision-making. This indicates the need for ongoing and sustained capacity-building efforts over time, targeting wide-ranging stakeholders.

Many countries lack financial and human resources for mental health, which can make the implementation of certain QualityRights strategies more complex. Other challenges include the lack of employment, education, social welfare, housing and other services and supports required to enable people to live and be included in the community. No doubt much can be achieved through capacity building, investment in civil society and advocacy, and policy and law reform. However, significant sustained commitment from governments is required to align all actions with the CRPD.

17

The Clubhouse Model: A Framework for Naturally Occurring Supported Decision Making

Joel D. Corcoran, Cindy Hamersma, and Steven Manning

Abstract

This chapter provides an overview of the Clubhouse model of psychosocial rehabilitation, reviewing the basic components of the approach: building community, shared work, meaningful relationships, and a commitment to the rights and self-determination of participating individuals. As a recovery-oriented environment for people living with mental health challenges, supported decision making is a naturally occurring aspect of the Clubhouse model. In the context of the ongoing discussion regarding Article 12 of the Convention on the Rights of People with Disabilities (CRPD), this chapter considers the Clubhouse model as an example of a social support network that can help individuals make constructive decisions while at the same time maintaining their autonomy and living independently on an equal basis with others.

The Clubhouse model of psychosocial rehabilitation is an approach that promotes self-determination and empowerment for people living with mental illness. Built into the fabric of the model is a depth of support from staff and peers, helping each participant to create a satisfying life as a full citizen of the community. Although to date Clubhouse programs across the world have been largely uninvolved in the dialogue about Article 12 of the CPRD and supported decision making versus substitute decision making, the Clubhouse stands as a clear example of how individuals can benefit from an informal network of friends and colleagues while maintaining autonomy on their recovery journey. This chapter will provide an overview of the Clubhouse model and demonstrate how, as part of a community healthcare or social service system, it can play a significant role in providing access for people with mental illness to the support in decision making they may need.

One of the most devastating effects of mental illness for an individual can be the damaging impact of societal intolerance, prejudice, and discrimination. For many, the experience of being unwanted and unwelcome by others leads to social isolation, a loss of hope, and the perception that one is less than a full and empowered member of society. In addition to seeking help with the real and disruptive aspects of having a significant health issue, a person with mental illness often has to deal with the profoundly painful loss of equal status as a valued citizen in their community.

The Clubhouse model targets the issue of social isolation by creating intentional communities in which people living with mental illness can find a respectful and dignified path to recovery and a personally satisfying life. A Clubhouse is a community center; but it extends far beyond a building or an address, and cannot be fully understood when defined as only a mental health program. A Clubhouse is, primarily, a supportive community of people sharing work and purpose, and in so doing creating opportunities for individual growth and development. Participation at a Clubhouse creates a springboard for meaningful relationships, which are invaluable in managing the many challenges associated with mental health problems. The friendships and trust-based relationships developed through shared work become an important resource when individuals need assistance with important decisions, social services, medical care, living independently, or legal concerns. Naturally occurring member-to-member (or peer-to-peer) as well as staff-to-member support in decision making is common at a Clubhouse.

CLUBHOUSE

The descriptive name "Clubhouse" was taken from the original language that was used to communicate the work and vision of the first Clubhouse: Fountain House in New York City, started in 1948. As the first community of its kind, Fountain House has served as the initial model for the hundreds of subsequent Clubhouses that have developed around the world. Fountain House began when former patients of a psychiatric hospital began to meet together informally, as a kind of "club" (Anderson, 1998). It was organized to be a support group for ex-patients rather than as a service or treatment program. Over the years, communities that have replicated and enhanced the original model have embraced the term "Clubhouse," because it clearly communicates the message of membership and belonging.

VOLUNTARY MEMBERSHIP

A Clubhouse is a membership organization, and therefore the individuals who participate are referred to as "Members" The concept of membership is an empowering designation that gives an immediate sense of belonging to a vital community (Singer, 2002). Membership also acknowledges the voluntary participation of the individual, instead of the coerced or mandatory participation that can sometimes be associated with public mental health services. Membership is open to anyone who has a history of mental illness.

Membership is a fundamental Clubhouse concept; having membership means that an individual has shared ownership and responsibility for the success of the organization. To have membership somewhere means that you belong, you fit in, and you have a place where you are always welcome. This in itself can prove to be transformative.

Mental illness can be a great separator, inflicting terrible pain on people who have consistently found themselves excluded from the warmth of society. The Clubhouse works to completely change this experience (Beard, Propst, and Malamud, 1982). In a Clubhouse, a person with the lived experience of mental illness is first understood to be an individual who, by participating, will bring value to rest of the group. Each member is seen as a colleague and a contributor to the important daily work and the success of the whole community. The Clubhouse is designed to be a place where people with mental health problems are not separated or defined because of a label, a diagnosis, or an emphasis on what they cannot do. Instead, each person is embraced by the community and encouraged to join in. All contributions are valued and celebrated.

Members always choose how little or how much they will participate. The work is organized and carried out each day in a way that continuously delivers the message of welcome, inclusion, and self-determination; and that the member is a valued and needed contributor to the group. The contribution of talents, energy, and creative ideas are encouraged every day. While participation is always voluntary, attending members are consistently invited to be involved in the work. The ongoing work of a Clubhouse, engaging both staff and members, typically includes clerical work; reception; food service; transportation management; organizing and running meetings; outreach to absent members; building maintenance; managing the employment, education, and wellness programs; planning evening and weekend recreational activities; financial services; data collection; and much more.

This excerpt from a presentation by Cindy Hamersma, a member of Clubhouse De Waterheuvel in Amsterdam, demonstrates the impact of a Clubhouse community on a member's sense of value and dignity and how it can provide support with important decisions.

> Through a companion whom I had met at the psychiatric hospital center, I found my way to the Clubhouse. The formula of the Clubhouse was so different from my experience in the hospital, and it worked well for me. It allowed me to regain structure – and finally – I had real people around me, that I could connect with. The people at the Clubhouse did not see me as a "mental patient," but as a person. They encouraged me to use my abilities and other good qualities, which made me feel increasingly better. Over time I began to crawl out of my shell and regain control of my life.
>
> Even though I found that I was still bouncing back and forth between mania and depression, I now had my Clubhouse community, which made it possible so I didn't have to be committed to the hospital. The reason I always voluntarily returned to the Clubhouse was that they offered everything I needed to recover. Firstly, the Clubhouse offered a community of people – who actually cared about

me as a human being. The staff and other members had time for me and when I needed it, they took time to sit down and talk. They always looked at what I could do and did not pay much attention to what I could not. The members and staff at the Clubhouse actually seemed to like me, and to welcome me. They listened and showed understanding. They offered activities that built my self-image and self-esteem. You have no idea how important those simple things are for someone struggling with the devastation of a serious mental illness.

This was pretty much the total opposite of the way I had been treated in the hospital.

As I connected more and more to my Clubhouse community, my life began to become stable again. Through a paid job arranged by the Clubhouse, I started working part time. For the first time in ten years I did not feel like a patient, but like someone contributing fully in society. I grew more and more in my abilities until I was back at my old level.

In the hospital, my identity was "patient" – and often it was "bad patient," because I did not do a good job of following their rules. In the hospital, my opinion was never asked for or taken into consideration, even when it involved big decisions about my own life.

My experience of becoming a part of my Clubhouse community was a very stark contrast to that. At the Clubhouse, from my first visit, I was welcomed – as myself. At my Clubhouse, I have been appreciated, and listened to, and heard. The experience of knowing that, at last, I truly belonged and was being welcomed and heard, rather than judged, became the foundation of my recovery journey.

CLUBHOUSE VALUES

Clubhouse communities are built on the belief that every member can sufficiently recover from the effects of mental illness to lead a personally satisfying life. Clubhouses are communities of people dedicated to one another's success – no matter how long it takes or how difficult it is. A Clubhouse offers repeated opportunities for each member to succeed. The Clubhouse concept is organized around a belief in the potential for productive contributions from everyone, even the member struggling with the most severe effects of mental illness. Clubhouse communities hold the conviction that meaningful work, and work-mediated relationships, are restorative and provide a firm foundation for growth and important individual achievement (Beard, Propst, and Malamud, 1982).

This excerpt from a paper written by Robby Vorspan, a long-time Fountain House and Clubhouse International employee who also has a history of mental illness, describes why work is a highly valued component of the Clubhouse approach.

> It is not the illness itself that hurts the most. It is the effects of the illness, the panic at the thought of the future, the ever-widening chasm the person feels between him or

herself and everyone else, the dread of drowning in the intensity of one's own thoughts and fantasies. Once a person experiences the trauma of mental illness, he or she inevitably feels snapped off from the tree of normal everyday life. Social interactions become more and more difficult as the common realities you used to share with others slide away from you. It is not that people who are mentally unwell simply lose their ability to socialise, but that they lose their sense of connectedness with others in a very deep and frightening way. Becoming engaged in the valuable work of the community provides a re-entry point into the mainstream of life. It provides a sense of belonging, being valued and being needed. The work a person is engaged in also becomes a very basic starting off point in making conversations – something which can be very difficult for people who have become isolated in their illness.

Therefore, when we insist on a Clubhouse day that springs from real and meaningful work, we are not ignoring the profound reality of the pain of emotional illness. We are addressing it head-on. We are saying that work can become a potent tool in dealing with the deepest life issues for our members (Vorspan, 1992).

Meaningful Relationships

The Clubhouse environment and activities are formed in a way that maximizes the opportunities for human interaction, and where there is always more than enough work to do. Clubhouse staffing levels are purposely kept low to create a perpetual circumstance in which staff will genuinely need the help of members in order to accomplish their jobs. Members also need the help of staff and other members in order to complete the necessary work. It is these evolving, mutually interdependent relationships that become the key ingredient in the Clubhouse approach to promoting recovery (Vorspan, 1986).

Relationships between members and staff, and amongst the members, develop naturally as they work side-by-side carrying out daily duties. Clubhouse staff have generalist roles. They participate in all of the Clubhouse activities, including the daily work projects; the evening, weekend, and holiday social and recreational programs; the employment, education and wellness programs; reaching out to absent members; and helping individual members make decisions about and acquire any social or healthcare services they may need. Members and staff share the responsibility for the successful operation of the Clubhouse. Working closely together each day, members and staff learn of each other's strengths, talents, and abilities. Because the environment and activity in a Clubhouse is much like a typical workplace, relationships develop in much the same way.

Clubhouse staff have the additional role of helping members identify and address their individual community support needs, preferences, and personal goals. Members choose the staff with whom they work and how much, if any, assistance they want with their needs and goals. The Clubhouse staff role is not to educate or provide treatment for the members. The staff are there to engage with members as colleagues in important work, while being encouraging and providing support for people who might not yet believe in themselves. Clubhouse staff are charged with being coworkers, talent scouts, cheerleaders, and supportive friends.

Together the members and staff in a Clubhouse form a supportive network that is available to help each member as needed and requested through important events and decisions. Clubhouse members frequently bring personal needs to a Clubhouse meeting to ask for and receive help from their Clubhouse community of staff and fellow members.

Steven Manning, a Clubhouse member in Indiana, describes how his Clubhouse supported his recovery:

> One day I started feeling kind of strange. I felt tired and sluggish; my thoughts turned negative. This eventually became a severe and persistent depression. This feeling, which seemed to come out of nowhere, was joined by additional symptoms that bombarded me: insomnia, loss of appetite, and suicidal thoughts. It became an absolute nightmare. As the days, weeks, and months progressed, so did the illness. My suicidal ideation turned into actual suicide attempts. I ended up losing my job as the city's program director for the public access TV station, and due to poor decisions caused by my mental illness, I found myself homeless. At my worst, I was walking around our city with a green garbage bag filled with my clothes: nowhere to stay, nothing to eat, no money to buy food. I was hopeless and homeless.
>
> One day my case manager introduced me to a "Clubhouse" called Carriage House. I can't recall my initial thoughts and feelings about my first visit to that beautiful white house but I do know that my life has not been the same since I stepped through the door.
>
> In addition to doing a great job of welcoming its members, Clubhouses specialize in inviting members and staff to create working partnerships with each other. These partnerships allow us to have natural, real relationships. This also allows us to have something in common with one another, which places staff and members together on the same playing field. These healthy, collegial relationships are simple yet powerful components of the healing process that takes place every day in our Clubhouses.
>
> When I first became a member I was asked by staff if I wanted to do a task or two. I can recall turning them down multiple times. But as time passed and as I improved in my recovery, I began to volunteer to work a task. However, what really drew me in to become more involved at Carriage House was when we started our audiovisual department, which produced a daily Clubhouse news show that helped our Clubhouse community stay connected.
>
> Getting involved with the Carriage House Audiovisual unit has been a vital spoke in the wheel of my recovery. Not only did I benefit from this experience, but I've witnessed time and time again the wonderful impact it has had on many of our members and staff.

The Basic Components of a Clubhouse

1 A Workday

The daily activity of a Clubhouse is organized around a structured system known as the "work-ordered day." The work-ordered day is open for an eight-hour period, typically Monday through Friday, which parallels the business hours of the working community in which the Clubhouse is located. Members are free to join for any length of time, according to their own needs. Members and staff work side by side, as colleagues, to carry out the work that is important to their community. There are no clinical therapies or treatment-oriented programs in the Clubhouse. Members volunteer to participate as they feel ready, and according to their individual interests. They are never coerced or required to participate.

There are meetings held each day to organize the work. The meetings, typically referred to as "unit meetings," usually occur twice per day, once at the start of the day and again in the early afternoon. At unit meetings, members and staff identify the work that needs to be done and call for volunteers to complete the tasks involved. All members are encouraged to participate, and staff attempt to engage the members requiring the most support by inviting them to share work projects. The work is organized in a way that provides many opportunities for projects to be completed by two or more people working on the same task together. It is through this process of collaborating on meaningful work projects that members begin to regain a sense of their own value and strengths.

2 The Employment Programs

As a right of membership Clubhouses provide members with opportunities to engage in or return to paid employment in integrated community work settings through transitional, supported, and independent employment programs. Employment is a foundational part of the Clubhouse approach because it is an expressed goal of many members at every Clubhouse. Employment is often a critical component for members to experience themselves as being included in the larger community, and in reducing isolation and poverty. Therefore, every Clubhouse offers an array of employment programs and support. The Clubhouse staff and peers provide encouragement and advice about which employment strategy a member might choose to try.

3 The Evening, Weekend and Holiday Programs

In addition to the work opportunities, Clubhouses provide evening, weekend, and holiday social and recreational programming. Members and staff together choose and organize structured and nonstructured social activities. These activities are always scheduled outside the hours of the workday, as is the case with most working adults. Participation is always optional.

4 Community Support

Clubhouse members often require a variety of social and healthcare services. As part of the workday, members are given help accessing the best quality services in their community. Support is given to members to assist them to make decisions regarding acquiring affordable and dignified housing, good mental health and general medical services, government disability benefits and any other services they may need.

5 "Reach Out"

Part of the daily work of the Clubhouse involves keeping track of all of the active members. When a member does not attend the Clubhouse or is in the hospital, a "reach out" telephone call, text, social media contact, or visit is made to the absent member. Each member is reminded that he or she is missed, welcome and needed at the Clubhouse. This process not only encourages members to participate but can be an early warning system for members who are experiencing difficulties and may need extra assistance with decisions about getting help with needed services. Clubhouse staff and peers who know the absent member well are often able to identify potential issues and help organize support before larger problems arise.

6 Education

Often Clubhouse members have had their education plans interrupted by mental illness. Some have not finished secondary school and others had their university experience disrupted. Education is often a life goal for members and an important factor in gaining employment. Therefore, the Clubhouse offers educational opportunities and support for members wishing to restart their education.

7 Wellness

As people living with mental illness typically die ten to twenty years earlier than the general population (World Health Organization), the Clubhouse approach also prioritizes providing assistance, activities, and opportunities designed to help members develop and maintain healthy lifestyles (Clubhouse International, 2018). Clubhouses offer advice, health education, physical fitness opportunities, nutritious meals, and assistance with accessing and participating in preventative and treatment-oriented healthcare.

8 Housing

Safe, decent, dignified housing is a basic human right and therefore a priority in every Clubhouse. The Clubhouse helps members to choose, access and sustain quality housing.

9 Policy and Governance

Policymaking and governance are an important part of Clubhouse work. Members and staff meet in open forums to discuss and make decisions together about policy issues and future planning for the Clubhouse.

Clubhouses also have a board of directors or advisory board that provides oversight management, fundraising, public relations, and help with developing employment opportunities for members. Most Clubhouses include members on the board.

The Clubhouse approach is therapeutic and provides an array of restorative activities. Although it is not a healthcare program and does not provide clinical or treatment-oriented services, it is a sophisticated opportunity system in a safe and encouraging environment, drawing on a community of peers for assistance, encouragement, and support. A Clubhouse provides multiple avenues for reintegration and success in the larger community (McKay, 2017). It is adaptable to any geographic location or culture because it is community oriented and supportive, and respectful relationships are the core elements of the model. A Clubhouse can be an important component in a community in which there is a well-developed mental health system, as well as in a community that has no mental system at all.

The Clubhouse and Supported Decision Making

While the debate about implementation of CRPD Article 12 continues, and governments seek to transition to a better understanding of how supported decision making fits into their laws and mental health systems, Clubhouses have created an informal yet effective method for assisting people living with mental illness to create a social support network consisting of mental health workers and peers with lived experience. When assistance with important decisions is needed, a Clubhouse member can draw on these meaningful relationships, which develop over time, through the process of shared work.

In General Comment 1 on Article 12 the United Nations Committee on the Rights of Persons with Disabilities (CRPD Committee) refers to Article 19 of the CRPD and states:

> It is imperative that persons with disabilities have opportunities to develop and express their will and preferences, in order to exercise their legal capacity on an equal basis with others. This means that persons with disabilities must have the

opportunity to live independently in the community and to make choices and to have control over their everyday lives, on an equal basis with others.

The Committee also states:

> State parties must recognize that communities are assets and partners in the process of learning what types of support are needed in the exercise of legal capacity, including raising awareness about different support options. State parties must recognize the social networks and naturally occurring community supports (including friends, family and schools) of persons with disabilities as key to supported decision-making (CRPD Committee, 2014).

The Clubhouse model creates an intentional community of people uniquely positioned to provide the kinds of opportunities and naturally occurring supports described in these statements. Participation in a Clubhouse community gives an individual access to mental health workers and peers who understand the challenges of mental illness, and to a system of opportunities and choices organized to help rebuild their lives regardless of any disability.

An important aspect of a Clubhouse is the evolving collective knowledge about resources that exist in the community in which the Clubhouse is located. This is particularly important when it comes to assisting Clubhouse members with decisions about issues such as whether to change, reduce, or increase medications; asking for help when needed; which mental health clinic to use; how to navigate the government entitlement office; or whether to seek help from the university disability office.

The daily work at the Clubhouse is organized around providing support for individuals as they make choices about their futures, and creating ongoing opportunities for recovery. In an entirely natural way, Clubhouse members develop friendships and supportive relationships with the staff and members with whom they work each day. These relationships are similar to the relationships people without a disability develop with their friends and coworkers. But in a Clubhouse, these relationships are nurtured and prioritized as the key to Clubhouse rehabilitation.

Because of this, it is very natural for Clubhouse staff and members to intervene when potential problems begin to develop, and work together to find solutions. Examples of this might include helping someone make good decisions about keeping his or her housing, or ending an abusive relationship. The Clubhouse support network of peers and staff can often help members avoid the harmful consequences of psychosis by helping them seek help earlier than they would otherwise. Some Clubhouses develop expertise with advance directives, and assist members that choose to complete them. Additionally, the Clubhouse community is there to help members make decisions about returning to school or employment, and to support them through the process.

In a typical day, members come and participate in activities that interest them and contribute to the daily operations of the Clubhouse. Activities such as preparing the daily meal, managing the employment program, publishing a Clubhouse newsletter, managing the website, or helping other members with transportation or housing needs provide shared work and the opportunity for an individual to interact with others and develop friendships and collegial relationships. It is through these relationships that a Clubhouse members can find the support they may need in making decisions about both simple and more complicated important life decisions. For example, a Clubhouse member might seek advice from other members about the benefits and challenges of employment as it relates to his or her government disability income. Another example of supported decision making might be a conversation between a member and a trusted staff person over lunch or while working together at the reception desk about developing a plan to save for a new car or how to resolve a dispute with a neighbor.

Cindy and Steven's stories, recounted above, are strong examples of how Clubhouse supported decision making works in this approach. Both of these individuals found help from their colleagues in Clubhouses and changed the trajectory of their lives for the better. Not until they had a community of people that valued them as equals were they able to begin to rebuild their futures. Today Cindy and Steven both report experiencing recovery. Both are employed, and they continue to be members of their Clubhouses and give support to fellow members.

With the advent of Clubhouse International (the global coordinating center for advocacy, training, and quality assurance),[1] a small and loosely affiliated group of like-minded community mental health programs has grown into a formal association of 326 Clubhouse programs operating in accordance with a codified set of best-practice standards (Clubhouse International, 2018). Today about twelve new Clubhouses open each year. The Clubhouse approach has been adopted in more than thirty countries, spanning six continents, in a variety of social, economic, and cultural circumstances. Currently there are also more than fifty communities in fifteen separate countries with active grass-roots Clubhouse startup efforts. Clubhouse International envisions a time when everyone everywhere dealing with mental health issues will have access to the kinds of opportunities and support commonly found in Clubhouses.

There is a substantial and growing body of research providing evidence about the positive impact of Clubhouses. A few examples include articles on the following topics:

- A significant decrease in hospitalizations as a result of membership in a Clubhouse program (De Masso, Avi-Itzak, and Obler 2001).
- Reduced incarcerations, with criminal justice system involvement substantially diminished during and after Clubhouse psychosocial program membership (Johnson and Hickey, 1999).

[1] http://clubhouse-intl.org.

- Lower public mental health costs for Clubhouse members compared to a control group of local nonmembers of a similar age and diagnosis (Hwang, Woody, and Eaton, 2017).
- Improved wellbeing compared with individuals receiving psychiatric services without Clubhouse membership. Clubhouse members were significantly more likely to report that they had close friendships and someone they could rely on when they needed help (Warner, Huxley, and Berg, 1999).
- Families recognize positive changes in their family members who participate in Clubhouses and these changes align with areas of functional recovery (Chung, Pernice-Duca, Biegel, Norden, and Chang, 2016).
- Better physical and mental health. A recent study suggests that service systems like Clubhouses that offer ongoing social supports enhance mental and physical health by reducing disconnectedness (Leff, et al., 2004).

The Clubhouse model has been successfully operating in many communities for decades. There is ample evidence demonstrating the effectiveness of this approach in supporting people living with mental illness to live independently in the community. The positive impact of a mutually supportive environment stands as a clear example of how supported decision making can and does occur within a community mental health program and through meaningful trusted relationships in a personal network of friends and colleagues.

REFERENCES

Johnson, J. & Hickey, S. "Arrests and incarcerations after psychosocial program involvement: Clubhouse vs. jailhouse," *Psychiatric Rehabilitation Journal*, 1999, 23, 66–70.

Warner, R., Huxley, P., & Berg, T. "An evaluation of the impact of Clubhouse membership on quality of life and treatment utilization," *International Journal of Social Psychiatry*, 1999, 45(4), 310–320.

Masso J. D., Avi-Itzhak T., Obler D. R., "The Clubhouse model: An outcome study on attendance, work attainment and status, and hospitalization recidivism," *Work*, 2001, 17(1), 23–30.

Hwang, S., Woody, J., & Eaton, W. W., "Analysis of the association of Clubhouse membership with overall costs of care for mental health treatment," *Community Mental Health Journal*, 2017, 53(1), 102–106.

Leff, H. S., McPartland, J. C., Banks, S., et al. "Service quality as measured by service fit and mortality among public mental health system service recipients," *Mental Health Services Research*, 2004, 6, 93–107.

Anderson, S. B., *We Are Not Alone: Fountain House and the Development of the Clubhouse Culture*, New York, NY, Fountain House, 1998.

Singer, B., "The Clubhouse: Its structure, philosophy and values," *The Clubhouse Community Journal*, 2002, 4, 20–23.

Beard, J., Propst, R. N., and Malamud, T. J., "The Fountain House model of psychiatric rehabilitation," *Psychosocial Rehabilitation Journal*, 1982, 5(1), 56–68.

Clubhouse International, International Standards for Clubhouse Programs, 2018.

Vorspan, R., "Why work works," *Psychosocial Rehabilitation Journal*, 1992, 16(2).

Vorspan, R., "Attitudes and structure in the Clubhouse model," *The Fountain House Annual*, 1986, 4(1), 1–7. Based on an address given at the Vermont Conference on Community Rehabilitation, Stowe, VT.

World Health Organization, "Premature Death Among People with Severe Mental Disorders." Information sheet. www.who.int/mental_health/management/info_sheet.pdf.

Corcoran, J., "Clubhouses: Communities Creating Opportunities for People with Mental Illness," in *Clubhouse International New Clubhouse Development Training Manual*, 2019.

United Nations Convention on the Rights of People with Disabilities. 2007. General Assembly resolution 61/106 of 24 January 2007; United Nations Committee on Rights of Persons with Disabilities. General Comment No. 1: Article 12, Equal Recognition before the law. 11th session, March 31–April 11, 2014. https://digitallibrary.un.org/record/779679?ln=en.

McKay, C., (2017), Results from the 2016 Clubhouse Profile Questionnaire, *Clubhouse International World Seminar*, Detroit, Michigan, September 23–28, 2017. Conference presentation. www.umassmed.edu/globalassets/systems-and-psychosocial-advances-research-center/publications/presentations/pre2020/results-from-the-2016-clubhouse-profile-questionnaire.pdf.

McKay, C. (2017). Examining the difference in accredited and non-accredited Clubhouses, *Massachusetts Department of Mental Health Conference*, (2017). Conference presentation. www.umassmed.edu/globalassets/systems-and-psychosocial-advances-research-center/about-our-center/dmh-conference/examining-differences-in-accreditation-poster.pdf.

18

Mind the Gap: Researching 'Alternatives to Coercion' in Mental Health Care

Piers Gooding

Abstract

Globally, there is a surprisingly small amount of empirical research into efforts to reduce and prevent 'coercion' in mental health settings. Indeed, there is a paucity of empirical evaluation of coercion in mental healthcare more generally. These gaps hamper efforts to create rights-based models of support. This chapter considers the evidential issues around coercion in relation to major debates about legal capacity, mental health and the Convention on the Rights of Persons with Disabilities (CRPD). It examines the prevalent norms of knowledge concerning coercion, including underlying traditions and assumptions, and what is considered ethically desirable. The chapter concludes by recommending more research on reduction and prevention of coercion as a practical and unifying step, but with careful consideration of the epistemic and evidentiary cultures guiding the research.

INTRODUCTION

> The amount of research devoted to reducing recourse to involuntary detention has been lamentably small. (Szmukler, 2020, p. 233)

In 2018, the UN Special Rapporteur for the rights of persons with disabilities commissioned a systematic literature review of efforts to reduce, prevent and eliminate 'coercion' in mental healthcare (the Coercion Review). The Coercion Review, of which I was a contributing author, was published as a standalone report (Gooding et al., 2018) and a peer-reviewed summary (Gooding et al., 2020), and it appears to be the largest survey of its kind. The findings, perhaps surprisingly, were rather straightforward: various efforts have been made to prevent and reduce coercion worldwide and, for the most part, they seem effective.

The Coercion Review suggested that much could be achieved under current conditions, and – importantly for this Chapter – they could proceed despite the so-called 'Geneva Impasse'. The Geneva Impasse is a term used by Wayne Martin and Sándor Gurbai to describe the almost sclerotic debate about the legitimacy of involuntary mental health interventions under the Convention on the Rights of Persons with Disabilities (CRPD). In their terms:

> The watershed question might be posed as follows: Can coercive treatment ever comply with UN human rights standards? The answer from one part of the UN human rights system seems to be: "Yes, provided that certain conditions are met." But another part of the same system seems to be pointing towards an exceptionless "No". (Martin and Gurbai, 2019)

The authors of the Coercion Review posited that our findings could help act on several points of agreement across the impasse; namely, that many coercive practices are unacceptable, can cause serious harm (regardless of intent), and – even if it is accepted that coercion may be necessary in some circumstances – should generally be viewed as 'a system failure' (see eg, Bhugra et al., 2017, p. 793). We concluded that these concerns could be addressed to a large extent by implementing, and where necessary, testing, a broad suite of reduction and prevention initiatives that could be collated into a policy 'charter' or 'framework'.

A less encouraging finding, however, was that reduction and prevention measures had been seldom initiated. When steps had been taken, the measures were largely ad hoc. One particularly striking finding, which was noted only briefly toward the end of the study, was that there were only forty-two studies identified that explicitly aimed at preventing or reducing coercion in mental health settings (Gooding et al., 2020, p. 9). This may seem high by the standards of clinical meta-analyses, but it appeared – at least to the authors – to be low, if not extremely low, given the broad sampling frame used in the review. We had adopted an expansive definition of coercion and extended the search to over three decades of global, English-language scholarship.[1] The terms 'coercion' and 'coercive practices' were defined broadly to refer to forceful persuasion and/or the physical compulsion of a person due to an actual or perceived mental health condition (Gooding et al., 2020, p. 1). Hence, the studies encompassed initiatives as diverse as national policies to reduce seclusion and restraint, the use of advance crisis planning, the invalidation of powers under mental health legislation, the development of non-hospital crisis services, statutory taxation to increase service funding, community-based initiatives to reduce 'shackling' of individuals in a low-resource setting, and so on. Given this broad frame, the

---

[1] The scope entailed all studies within a selective sampling frame, including English-language studies published after 1990 and before September 2018, that answered the following research questions: What practices, policies and laws help to reduce and prevent coercive practices in mental health settings? What alternative strategies, laws, policies and/or practices exist which could be positioned as 'alternatives' to or replacements for coercive practices? (See Gooding et al., 2020, p. 2)

figure of forty-two, again, appears low – a view that was subsequently shared by others (see eg, Sashidharan et al., 2019; Szmukler, 2020) and conforms with broader concerns about the lack of empirical research on coercion in mental healthcare more generally (see eg, Molodynski, Khazaal, et al., 2016; Nilsson, 2014; Prinsen & van Delden, 2009).

This paucity of research into efforts to reduce and prevent coercion is the starting point for this chapter. The chapter will consider the evidential issues around coercion in light of major debates concerning legal capacity, mental health and the CRPD. This line of enquiry invites questions about the prevalent norms of knowledge concerning coercion, the traditions and assumptions that guide them, and ideas about what is considered ethically desirable. It is hoped that these questions will help draw out points of agreement across the Geneva Impasse, and move beyond theoretical dispute toward practical action to improve support for people in serious distress and mental health crises.

BACKGROUND: NAVIGATING THE GENEVA IMPASSE

The Geneva Impasse primarily concerns the conflicting interpretive guidance of two United Nations treaty bodies, the Committee on the Rights of Persons with Disabilities (CRPD Committee) (2014, paras 17, 26, 40) and the Human Rights Committee (HRC) (2014, p. 6 para 19). Their diverging views are set out in General Comments. In norms of human rights law, there is a broad global 'presumption in favour of [the] substantive correctness' of such views (Tomuschat, 2003, p. 220), which leaves governments and civil society to navigate the divergence of the HRC and the CRPD Committee. The discord has now been well covered and doesn't need to be repeated here (see eg, Arstein-Kerslake, 2017; Mahomed et al., 2018; Martin & Gurbai, 2019; Szmukler, 2019). This coverage builds on a large body of scholarship concerning Article 12 about which 'much ink has been spilled – or keyboard text manipulated', (Rosenbaum, 2019, p. 61) as one commentator put it (see eg, Callaghan & Ryan, 2016; Gooding, 2017; Mahomed et al., 2018; Zinkler & von Peter, 2019). Anna Arstein-Kerslake (2017, p. 15) has rejected the framing of this matter as an interpretive dispute and instead poses the rejection of the CRPD Committee's viewpoint on Article 12 as part of the 'palpable resistance' to the article itself.

The dynamic of resistance or interpretive debate, however framed, goes beyond the United Nations, and can be seen unfolding in legislatures, government agencies and civil society organizations worldwide. Debates have also occurred among service user advocates and persons with psychosocial disabilities (see eg, Plumb, 2015; Sunkel, 2019; cf Minkowitz, 2007), as well as among clinicians (see eg, Appelbaum, 2019; cf Zinkler & von Peter, 2019), and others (see eg, Committee on Bioethics (DH-BIO), 2015) – and have played out in prominent court decisions around the world (see eg, Freckelton, 2019; Müller, 2018). The seeds of this discontent were present early on in negotiations of the CRPD itself. As Sheila Wildeman (2013, p. 56) adroitly observed, issues of involuntary treatment were 'pressed to the point of negotiation impasse and then resolved by way of textual silence – leaving considerable scope for interpretive controversy in their wake' (see also Dhanda, 2006; Kämpf, 2010).

Despite this cleft, several scholars who have considered the controversy closely tend to conclude that the 'impasse' may be less intractable than first appears (Martin & Gurbai, 2019; Arstein-Kerslake, 2017; McSherry, 2014; Wildeman, 2013), though most of them come from the fields of law and ethics. Much of this optimism centres on shared agreement that the range of *voluntary* options for support should be expanded (Herrman, 2019; McSherry, 2014; Ruck Keene, 2019; Szmukler, 2019). Another point of consensus is the acknowledgement of the inherent harm in any deprivation of liberty, even as proponents of involuntary psychiatric intervention believe and assert that there are greater benefits – and duties – that outweigh this harm. The HRC (2014, p. 6 para 19), for example, even as it endorses the valid use of compulsory treatment and detention in circumstances of last resort, nevertheless emphasised the 'harm inherent in any deprivation of liberty' and the 'particular harms that may result in situations of involuntary hospitalization'. The HRC (2014, p. 6 para 19) further noted States' obligation to 'provide less restrictive alternatives'.

In appraising the impact of Article 12 of the CRPD, Lucy Series and Anna Nilsson argue that it has created 'a powerful platform for difficult conversations about the nature and effects of restrictions on legal capacity experienced by disabled people worldwide, challenging the status quo and forcing advocates of [such practices] to re-examine assumptions that have been taken for granted' (2018, p. 342). However, this elevation of *debate* is likely to be little consolation for those frustrated by the slow pace of action in mental health law, policy and practice (see Glen, 2018, pp. 36–37, n. 168), nor for those who reject aspirations of abolition of involuntary psychiatric intervention as a harmful and unrealistic diversion (see eg, Dawson, 2015).

MIND THE GAP: RESEARCH ON COERCION

The use of coercion, according to Andrew Molodynski et al. (2016), 'is one of the defining issues of mental health care and has been intensely controversial since the very earliest attempts to contain and treat the mentally ill'. Some may dispute this historical framing by pointing to a longstanding public mandate for compulsory interventions (see eg, Appelbaum, 2019). At the very least, coercion remains a defining feature of clinical mental health practice and, in public discourse if not in legislation, it has remained controversial throughout the post-war era. Coercion is also a practice that health practitioners often characterise as regrettable, even if it is viewed as necessary in certain circumstances (see eg, Burns, 2015). Certainly, there is a large international body of first-person accounts of traumatic coercive experiences, which has been growing for many decades, even as some of these accounts endorse its limited use. There also appears to be growing agreement within the mental health professions, at least among many prominent clinicians, that coercive practices are over-used, and that – even if it is accepted that some benefits and duties may compel its continued use – there are compelling concerns about the clinical validity of treatment involving coercion, which warrants critical attention (see eg, Bhugra et al., 2017; Herrman, 2019; Mahomed et al., 2018; Sugiura et al., 2020; Szmukler, 2018).

It is striking therefore, as George Szmukler (2020, p. 233) has noted, and as cited in the epigraph to this Chapter, that the amount of research dedicated to 'reducing recourse to involuntary detention [has been] lamentably small'. Szmukler's observation is strongly supported by the findings of the Coercion Review, to which he points as evidence of 'a number of leads not further evaluated' (p. 233). This concern also appears to be supported by a systematic review by Corrado Barbui et al. (2020). Others have argued that this gap extends to a lack of practical guidance as to how actors have successfully achieved change, the challenges they faced, how they managed those challenges, and what factors were crucial to their success (see eg, Stastny et al., 2020).

Interestingly, this research gap extends to empirical research into coercive psychiatric interventions *in general*. This is not to suggest a lack of scholarship on coercion in mental health settings per se (see eg, World Association of Social Psychiatry, 2017) but rather on its evaluative empirical basis. E. J. Prinsen and J. van Delden (2009, p. 69), for example, argued that there is a 'total lack of controlled trials about the beneficial effects of coercive measures in different populations'. This gap, they argue, undermines the justification for coercive measures (although they point to other ethical justifications, such as beneficence/non-maleficence, for its continued use). Molodynski et al. (2016) similarly note that 'robust evidence [on the use of coercion] is hard to come by' and argue that the limited evidence that does appear 'suggests that coercion in most definable and measurable forms is not associated with improved outcome and may negatively affect the individual'. In her legal analysis of the standards of relevance, necessity and proportionality to involuntary detention and treatment, Anna Nilsson (2014, p. 473) similarly commented that:

> our knowledge of whether or not civil commitment and compulsory clinical interventions do protect the health of those subjected to such practices is limited. Rather few studies have been carried out on the subject, and those that have been carried out indicate that a majority of those subjected to such practices experience health improvement on being discharged, but a significant number do not. The empirical evidence for long-term health benefits of compulsory interventions seems to be particularly weak.

These observations are perhaps unexpected given the longstanding legal standard of 'least possible restrictive' interventions during involuntary interventions.

The low numbers of coercion-reduction studies in the mental health context can be compared to major research efforts that are prioritised in contemporary mental health care. An obvious example is the vigorous scientific pursuit of the pathophysiology of mental disorder (Kleinman 2012, p. 421). Sarah Carr (2017, p. 740) has queried whether the continued pursuit of genetic, neuroscientific, and – more recently – digital technological research addresses what 'patients, service users, families, friends, communities, and societies want and need'. Taking the United States as an example, consider the following statement by Thomas Insel, former head of the US National Institute of Mental Health (NIMH), which is arguably the largest mental health research agency in the world:

> I spent 13 years at NIMH really pushing on the neuroscience and genetics of mental disorders, and when I look back on that I realize that while I think I succeeded at getting lots of really cool papers published by cool scientists at fairly large costs – I think $20 billion – I don't think we moved the needle in reducing suicide, reducing hospitalizations, improving recovery for the tens of millions of people who have mental illness. (Rogers, 2017)

It is noteworthy that in Barbui and colleagues' (2020) systematic review of interventions to reduce coercive treatment in mental health services, not a single empirical study that used randomised evidence appeared from the US during the time Insel describes. Indeed, the most recent US study they identified was from 1999 (Barbui et al., 2020, p. 5). The Coercion Review did identify two US studies that used randomised evidence after this time (Greenfield et al., 2008; Swanson et al., 2008), though Barbui et al. may have excluded them for other reasons. Regardless, the stark contrast of research priorities stands.

Notably, the coercion research gap also extends to other forms of longstanding state intervention into the lives of persons with other disabilities. For example, Nina Kohn et al. observe that there is 'surprisingly little evaluative empirical literature on guardianship' (Kohn et al., 2012, p. 1129, n. 75), which largely impacts persons with long-term cognitive or intellectual disabilities and Mary Donnelly (2009) highlighted a lack of research into the conceptual basis for the 'best interests' standard despite its widespread use in law, and in health and social service provision – and in ways that have an enormous impact on the lives of people with disabilities. The CRPD has arguably provided a 'common language' (Quinn, 2009, p. 7) to draw attention to these similarities in substituted decision-making systems and in societal responses to disability more broadly.

There are several possible explanations for the research gap in the mental health context. Szmukler (2020, p. 233) offers the following hypothesis from a clinical perspective:

> A reason, perhaps, for such little research interest is a sense that the process of involuntary detention is not part of the "real" treatment, but a prelude to it. This view is certainly not shared by patients; for many, it becomes their worst experience of mental health services. This has become clearer as the patient "voice" has grown louder in many places.

Other suggestions that may be gleaned from the literature include the view that questioning the validity of restrictions challenges the professional identities of the medical and legal professionals involved (Arstein-Kerslake, 2017, p. 221), or that health professions, more generally, have paid insufficient attention to power imbalances that suppress the patient's voice (Greenhalgh et al., 2015; Diana Rose et al., 2017), and that this power imbalance is exacerbated by lawful coercion in the mental health context (Roper, 2019; Russo & Beresford, 2015). Acute ethical challenges also arise, which may be prohibitive in establishing experimental research conditions in standard scientific research practices; for example, in randomised control trials where some people are subject to coercion and others are not, or in efforts to devise 'optimal' restrictive practices, such as working out the 'appropriate' max duration of prone restraint or the 'best' dose for rapid tranquilisation for the purpose of chemical restraint—each of these research scenarios would pose profound ethical (and in some cases, legal) challenges (McSherry & Maker, 2021).

Indeed, several methodological challenges are cited as contributing to the research gap (Gooding et al., 2020; Molodynski, Khazaal, et al., 2016). Many of the practices for preventing, ending or reducing coercive practices are complex social interventions. The complexity of these interventions can have an impact upon the effectiveness of quantitative methods, and particularly those at the top of traditional hierarchies of evidence, such as randomised control trials. There is great difficulty of randomisation in a prospective study, for example, and confounding factors make replication difficult. Further, many of the studies noted in the Coercion Review may suffer from selective sampling in a way that remains unacknowledged. Seclusion and restraint rates, for example, may be driven down by transferring certain individuals with severe impairments who are more likely to be subject to restraint to other facilities (see eg, Pollmächer & Steinert, 2016). Difficulties also arise with definitions of coercion, including whether the same intervention (for example, the hard-to-define notion of 'chemical restraint') is being recorded in the same way in different services, let alone jurisdictions. Certainly, the methodological challenges of researching coercion must partly explain the relatively small body of reduction and prevention research.

However, another way to view these concerns is a lop-sided preference in mental health research for the natural scientific method. The socio-political complexity of prominent reduction strategies challenges what is arguably an idealised conception of scientific research in the clinical mental health fields (Kleinman, 2012). This tendency may give rise to an unforgiving culture of research in which experimental designs are expected to be flawless or near-flawless and to achieve statistical significance (Peterson, 2016). Yet, most reduction strategies – such as advance planning, tightening of legal grounds for intervention, crisis respite services, trauma-informed approaches and family and social network responsiveness – are complex social interventions; each occurs in a complex web of formal and informal relationships. Multiple contested ideas and values are at play. Notably, humanities and social science disciplines were scant among the reduction studies identified in the Coercion Review. This seems regrettable, given these disciplines are primarily concerned with making sense of the interaction in social, cultural, environmental, economic and political contexts, including through modes of inquiry – often multi-method – that can capture the interactions between social structures and individual agency (see eg, Evans et al., 2012; Tew et al., 2012). 'Organisational culture', for example, was identified in the Coercion Review as an important site for addressing the use of coercion in several studies (Bowers et al., 2015; Fisher, 2003; Keski-Valkama et al., 2007). Yet social science and humanities disciplines that would be well equipped to address organisational culture and human behaviour, such as sociology, anthropology and psychology, were almost entirely absent among the studies. In addition to evaluating complex interventions, such disciplines can help guard against the broader risk that objectivity and reliability are fetishised in mental health research, such that value choices and politics are disguised with scientific methods and measurements of risk and benefit.

'A POWERFUL PLATFORM FOR DIFFICULT CONVERSATIONS'

Exacerbating the research gap further was the limited engagement of mental health professional associations with the CRPD in the years after it came into force. With very few exceptions, mental health professional associations did not publish materials on the CRPD in the ten years after its adoption, at least not in high-income, English-language countries. In examples where the CRPD was mentioned in such public materials, the CRPD was often noted briefly and in passing in documents such as policy submissions and individual member perspectives (Gooding, 2017, p. 228, fn. 50).[2] In the UK, Peter Bartlett points out that despite the Royal College of Psychiatrists strident criticism of the CRPD Committees General Comment 1 in the years after its publication, the College never responded to any consultation preceding the issuing of a General Comment by the CRPD Committee (Gosney & Bartlett, 2020, p. 299), and nor did any other professional mental health associations (see United Nations Office of the Human Rights Commissioner, 2014). This limited activity may speak to the tentative role of professional bodies in representing the views of a 'broad church' of members, but it nevertheless seems unfortunate, given the role of professional bodies in education and training and in setting and raising professional standards.

---

[2] These comments are confined to English-language countries. One exception here was the (British) Royal College of Psychiatry, which, by 2014, had produced a specific, albeit brief, three-page document discussing the implications of the CRPD to psychiatrists and mental health law, whilst also including a considerable number of materials on its website. See www.rcpsych.ac.uk/docs/default-source/about-us/who-we-are/schr-convention-on-the-rights-of-persons-with-disabilities-q-and-a.pdf?sfvrsn=c8d1db87_2.

There are signs, however, that this disengagement is at an end – and this new interest is being married to broader efforts to address the coercion research gap. Perhaps most prominently, the World Psychiatric Association (WPA) appointed a taskforce to work with the Royal Australian and New Zealand College of Psychiatrists in a joint project to develop a 'framework on minimizing coercion' (Herrman, 2019, p. 368). At the time of writing, the taskforce is garnering comments and discussion from Member Societies (national psychiatric professional associations) in order to prepare a 'position paper with recommendations for action and an optional protocol designed to support Member Societies to engage with this work in ways that suit their local circumstances' (Herrman, 2020, p. 256). Other examples of this rising engagement include the forty psychiatrist authors of the World Psychiatric Association-Lancet *Commission on the Future of Psychiatry*, who commented that the '[d]evelopment of alternatives to compulsion requires research, of which little has been done' (Bhugra et al., 2017). Similarly, the Council of Europe (COE) Committee on Bioethics (DH-BIO) (2015) have resolved, subject to funding, to carry out and publish a '[d]raft study on good practices in mental healthcare [concerning] how to promote voluntary measures'. The COE Committee on Social Affairs, Health and Sustainable Development (2019) have encouraged the DH-BIO to 'carry out such a study, while also proposing to prepare guidelines on ending coercion in mental health' – a comment that also hints at the unresolved matters of the Geneva Impasse that will colour any such efforts.[3] These developments are also reflected in the work of clinician scholars (Sugiura et al., 2020; Szmukler, 2020; Zinkler & von Peter, 2019). Notwithstanding differences in the way the Geneva Impasse is addressed in these initiatives, the movement suggests that a considerable body of evaluative empirical research into coercion is on the horizon, if it is not already underway.

EPISTEMIC AND EVIDENTIAL CULTURES OF COERCION

It is unclear which research methodologies are most appropriate in investigating these efforts. More work is needed. This is true both of jurisdictions in which CRPD-based legislative change is not going to occur in the short- or mid-term, as well as those in which such legal change has already happened or is underway, such as in Peru and Colombia (see Chapter 8 by Alberto Vásquez Encalada in this volume).

Another way of viewing this issue is to ask which 'evidential and epistemic cultures' of research are in operation. 'Evidential cultures' is a term coined by sociologist Harry Collins (2004) to refer to scientists' approach toward the use of evidence in general. 'Epistemic cultures', coined by Karin Knorr-Centina (1999),

---

[3] Indeed, the DH-BIO itself created additional protocol concerning involuntary psychiatric intervention to the 'Oviedo Convention' or the Convention for the Protection of the Human Rights and Dignity of the Human Being with regard to the Application of Biology and Medicine. DH-BIOs working draft endorses the use of coercion in alignment with the HRC position in the Geneva Impasse.

refers to experts' views about specific pieces of theory or data within whole sciences. It is not always clear what evidential and epistemic cultures are at play in research on coercion, but it would be helpful to draw them out into the open. Some efforts have been made to explore these matters in the mental health context in general. For example, Diana Rose, George Thornicroft and Mike Slade (2006, p. 109) have raised concerns about the way prevailing models of evidence-based medicine and evidence-based policy, which guide societal responses to mental health, 'usually stop short of considering who defines information as evidence, and in the case of differing views over the evidence-base, whose views should predominate' (see also Diana Rose, 2018; Diana Rose et al., 2017; N. Rose, 2018; Tew et al., 2012). This observation is certainly true of research into coercion in mental healthcare.

Multiple questions could be asked to bring these concerns to the surface. What evidential and epistemological cultures are desirable? Are some methodological frameworks mis-evaluating the problems? What type of research is at the top of the prevailing hierarchy of knowledge? How is analytic, quantitative knowledge, as opposed to situated and experiential knowledge, regarded in the hierarchy of evidence? How are experimental conditions to be governed, particularly those that carry a degree of risk? On which side of the Geneva Impasse, and in relation to what specific matter, is the research premised? If the work is premised on a rights-based approach and an interpretive silence is being maintained, on which points? Is there a conflict of interest that must be mitigated, in which researchers who evaluate coercive practices would be too close, organisationally or cognitively, to the institutions in which they participate to critically review practices? Are particular researchers or groups of researchers able to critically review particular practices, and produce negative or positive decisions about them? What role for the expertise of persons with psychosocial disability, and those who have come through experiences of profound distress or involuntary intervention, in shaping the future for psychosocial disability support? Are there features of the epistemic and evidentiary cultures that marginalise health and disability activists, even those that work to put their claims through in scientific terms?

Key questions about the evidential and epistemic cultures in mental health research have been addressed in different strains of scholarship, but the development of a research agenda concerning coercion in the post-CRPD era will benefit from confronting these questions head on (Roper, 2019). Understanding how these cultures work can improve the quality of research collaborations and outputs in an era in which scientific research of all kinds is increasingly interdisciplinary and collaborative (McLevey, 2020). Bringing key questions out into the open by clearly explaining differences in how expert communities create and evaluate knowledge will help to avoid instances in which participants in debates misunderstand one another and offer arguments that do not meet. In addition to avoiding confusion among relevant actors, the distinctions can assist to indicate when an analysis – and for the purposes of this research agenda, an analysis based in the CRPD – is good, or comparably better.

CONCLUSION

If appropriate services and supports are provided, the argument goes, compulsion will be no more necessary for people with mental disabilities than for anyone else ... And, if the state refuses to offer services that people do want to use, it is ethically dubious to force them to use services they do not want to use. (Bartlett, 2012, p. 834)

It is not clear what would happen if a single city, country, or region implemented the broad range of measures outlined in the Coercion Review and other measures that will be identified in similar reviews to come. Nor is it clear what will emerge when these surveys are extended to non-English language studies and initiatives. If responses to people experiencing profound distress and psychosocial disability are to move toward a system based squarely on voluntary support, not only is a greater focus required on removing coercion (and not just 'adding on' measures of supported decision-making) but so is a deeper exploration of epistemic and evidential cultures behind research to these ends. Presupposing that coercion is undesirable – even if some view it as necessary and wish to test that view – helps to refine the focus toward prevention, reduction and, if indeed it is possible, elimination. This course of action won't resolve all disagreements raised by Article 12, but it will agitate key assumptions on which many of them rest and may help to chart the path ahead.

REFERENCES

Appelbaum, P. S. (2019). Saving the UN Convention on the Rights of Persons with Disabilities – from itself. *World Psychiatry*, 18(1), 1–2. https://doi.org/10.1002/wps.20583

Arstein-Kerslake, A. (2017). *Restoring Voice to People with Cognitive Disabilities: Realizing the Right to Equal Recognition before the Law*. Cambridge Core. https://doi.org/10.1017/9781316493526

Barbui, C., Purgato, M., Abdulmalik, J., et al. (2020). Efficacy of interventions to reduce coercive treatment in mental health services: umbrella review of randomised evidence. *The British Journal of Psychiatry*, 1–11. https://doi.org/10.1192/bjp.2020.144

Bartlett, P. (2012). A mental disorder of a kind or degree warranting confinement: examining justifications for psychiatric detention. *The International Journal of Human Rights*, 16(6), 831–844. https://doi.org/10.1080/13642987.2012.706008

Bhugra, D., Tasman, A., Pathare, S., et al. (2017). The WPA-Lancet Psychiatry Commission on the Future of Psychiatry. *The Lancet Psychiatry*, 4(10), 775–818. https://doi.org/10.1016/S2215-0366(17)30333-4

Bowers, L., James, K., Quirk, A. et al. (2015). Reducing conflict and containment rates on acute psychiatric wards: the Safewards cluster randomised controlled trial. *International Journal of Nursing Studies*, 52(9), 1412–1422. https://doi.org/10.1016/j.ijnurstu.2015.05.001

Burns, T. (2015). *Our Necessary Shadow* (Reprint ed.). Pegasus Books.

Callaghan, S., & Ryan, C. J. (2016). An evolving revolution: evaluating Australia's compliance with the Convention on the Rights of Persons with Disabilities in Mental Health Law. *UNSW Law Journal*, 39(2), 596–624.

Carr, S. (2017). Renegotiating the contract. *The Lancet Psychiatry*, 4(10), 740–741. https://doi.org/10.1016/S2215-0366(17)30365-6

Cetina, K. K. (1999). *Epistemic Cultures: How the Sciences Make Knowledge*. Harvard University Press.

Collins, H. (2004). *Gravity's Shadow: The Search for Gravitational Waves*. (First ed.). University of Chicago Press.

Committee on Bioethics (DH-BIO). (2015). Additional Protocol on the protection of the human rights and dignity of persons with mental disorders with regard to involuntary placement and involuntary treatment: Compilation of comments received during the public consultation (DH-BIO/INF (2015) 20). Council of Europe. https://rm.coe.int/16805ab6fe

Committee on Social Affairs, Health and Sustainable Development. (2019). Ending coercion in mental health: The need for a human rights-based approach (Doc. 14895). Parliamentary Assembly for the Council of Europe. http://assembly.coe.int/nw/xml/XRef/Xref-XML2HTML-EN.asp?fileid=27701&lang=en

Committee on the Rights of Persons with Disabilities. (2014). General Comment No 1: Article 12 – Equal Recognition before the Law, 11th sess, UN Doc CRPD/C/GC/1.

Dawson, J. (2015). A realistic approach to assessing mental health laws' compliance with the UNCRPD. *Mental Capacities and Legal Responsibilities*, 40, 70–79. https://doi.org/10.1016/j.ijlp.2015.04.003

Donnelly, M. (2009). Best interests, patient participation and the Mental Capacity Act 2005. *Medical Law Review*, 17(1), 1–29. https://doi.org/10.1093/medlaw/fwn021

Evans, J., Rose, D., Flach, C., et al. (2012). VOICE: developing a new measure of service users' perceptions of inpatient care, using a participatory methodology. *Journal of Mental Health*, 21(1), 57–71. https://doi.org/10.3109/09638237.2011.629240

Fisher, W. A. (2003). Elements of successful restraint and seclusion reduction programs and their application in a large, urban, state psychiatric hospital. *Journal of Psychiatric Practice*, 9(1), 7–15.

Freckelton, I. (2019). Electroconvulsive therapy, law and human rights: *PBU & NJE v Mental Health Tribunal* [2018] VSC 564, Bell J. *Psychiatry, Psychology and Law*, 26(1), 1–20. https://doi.org/10.1080/13218719.2019.1604111

Glen, K. B. (2018). Introducing a 'new' human right: learning from others, bringing legal capacity home. *Columbia Human Rights Law Review*, 49(3), 1–98.

Gooding, P. (2017). *A New Era for Mental Health Law and Policy: Supported Decision-Making and the UN Convention on the Rights of Persons with Disabilities*. Cambridge University Press.

Gooding, P., McSherry, B., & Roper, C. (2020). Preventing and reducing 'coercion' in mental health services: an international scoping review of English-language studies. *Acta Psychiatrica Scandinavica*. https://doi.org/10.1111/acps.13152

Gooding, P., McSherry, B., Roper, C., & Grey, F. (2018). *Alternatives to Compulsory Detention and Treatment and Coercive Practices in Mental Health Settings*. Melbourne Social Equity Institute, University of Melbourne. https://socialequity.unimelb.edu.au/__data/assets/pdf_file/0012/2898525/Alternatives-to-Coercion-Literature-Review-Melbourne-Social-Equity-Institute.pdf

Gosney, P., & Bartlett, P. (2020). The UK Government should withdraw from the Convention on the Rights of Persons with Disabilities. *The British Journal of Psychiatry*, 216(6), 296–300. https://doi.org/10.1192/bjp.2019.182

Greenfield, T. K., Stoneking, B. C., Humphreys, K., Sundby, E., & Bond, J. (2008). A randomized trial of a mental health consumer-managed alternative to civil commitment for acute psychiatric crisis. *American Journal of Community Psychology*, 42(1–2), 135–144. Health & Medical Collection; Psychology Database. https://doi.org/10.1007/s10464-008-9180-1

Greenhalgh, T., Snow, R., Ryan, S., Rees, S., & Salisbury, H. (2015). Six 'biases' against patients and carers in evidence-based medicine. *BMC Medicine*, 13(1). https://doi.org/10.1186/s12916-015-0437-x

Herrman, H. (2019). Psychiatry, human rights and social development: progress on the WPA Action Plan 2017-2020. *World Psychiatry*, 18(3), 368–369. https://doi.org/10.1002/wps.20686

Herrman, H. (2020). The practice of psychiatry in health care and sustainable development: progress on the WPA Action Plan 2017-2020. *World Psychiatry*, 19(2), 256–257. https://doi.org/10.1002/wps.20750

Keski-Valkama, A., Sailas, E., Eronen, M. et al. (2007). A 15-year national follow-up: legislation is not enough to reduce the use of seclusion and restraint. *Social Psychiatry and Psychiatric Epidemiology*, 42(9), 747–752.

Kleinman, A. (2012). Rebalancing academic psychiatry: why it needs to happen – and soon. *The British Journal of Psychiatry*, 201(6), 421–422. https://doi.org/10.1192/bjp.bp.112.118695

Kohn, N. A., Blumenthal, J. A., & Campbell, A. T. (2012). Supported decision-making: a viable alternative to guardianship? *Penn State Law Review*, 117(4), 1111–1157. https://doi.org/10.2139/ssrn.2161115

Mahomed, F., Stein, M. A., & Patel, V. (2018). Involuntary mental health treatment in the era of the United Nations Convention on the Rights of Persons with Disabilities. *PLoS Medicine*, 15(10). https://doi.org/10.1371/journal.pmed.1002679

Martin, W., & Gurbai, S. (2019). Surveying the Geneva impasse: coercive care and human rights. *International Journal of Law and Psychiatry*, 64, 117–128. https://doi.org/10.1016/j.ijlp.2019.03.001

McLevey, J. (2020). Epistemic and Evidential Cultures. In P. A. Atkinson et al. *SAGE Research Methods Foundations*. SAGE Publications Ltd. https://doi.org/10.4135/9781526421036840315

McSherry, B. (2014). Mental health law: where to from here? *Monash University Law Review*, 40(1), 175–197.

McSherry, B., & Maker, Y. (2021). *Restrictive Practices in Health Care and Disability Settings: Legal, Policy and Practical Responses*. Routledge.

Minkowitz, T. (2007). The United Nations Convention of the Rights of Persons with Disabilities and the right to be free from nonconsensual psychiatric interventions. *Syracuse Journal of International Law and Commerce*, 34(2), 505–529.

Molodynski, A., Khazaal, Y., & Callard, F. (2016). Coercion in mental healthcare: time for a change in direction. *BJPsych International*, 13(1), 1–3.

Molodynski, A., Rugkåsa, J., & Burns, T. (2016). *Coercion in Community Mental Health Care: International Perspectives*. Oxford University Press.

Müller, S. (2018). Einfluss der UN-Behindertenrechtskonvention auf die deutsche Rechtsprechung und Gesetzgebung zu Zwangsmaßnahmen [The influence of the UN Convention on the Rights of Persons with Disabilities on the German jurisdiction and legalisation regarding compulsory measures]. *Fortschritte Der Neurologie-Psychiatrie*, 86(8), 485–492. https://doi.org/10.1055/a-0597-2031

Nilsson, A. (2014). Objective and reasonable? Scrutinising compulsory mental health interventions from a non-discrimination perspective. *Human Rights Law Review*, 14(3), 459–485. https://doi.org/10.1093/hrlr/ngu022

Peterson, D. (2016). The baby factory: difficult research objects, disciplinary standards, and the production of statistical significance. *Socius*, 2. https://doi.org/10.1177/2378023115625071

Plumb, A. (2015). UN Convention on the Rights of Persons with Disabilities: Out of the Frying Pan and into the Fire? Mental Health Service Users and Survivors Aligning with the Disability Movement. In H. Spandler, J. Anderson and B. Sapey (eds), *Madness, Distress and the Politics of Disablement*. Policy Press.

Pollmächer, T., & Steinert, T. (2016). Arbitrary classification of hospital policy regarding open and locked doors. *The Lancet Psychiatry*, 3(12), 1103. https://doi.org/10.1016/S2215-0366(16)30346-7

Prinsen, E. J. D., & van Delden, J. J. M. (2009). Can we justify eliminating coercive measures in psychiatry? *Journal of Medical Ethics*, 35(1), 69–73. https://doi.org/10.1136/jme.2007.022780

Rogers, A. (2017). Star Neuroscientist Tom Insel Leaves the Google-Spawned Verily for ... A Startup? *Wired*. www.wired.com/2017/05/star-neuroscientist-tom-insel-leaves-google-spawned-verily-startup/

Roper, C. (2019). Ethical peril, violence, and "dirty hands": ethical consequences of mental health laws. *Journal of Ethics in Mental Health*, 10. https://jemh.ca/issues/v9/documents/JEMH%20Inclusion%20vi.pdf

Rose, D., Thornicroft, G., & Slade, M. (2006). Who decides what evidence is? Developing a multiple perspectives paradigm in mental health. *Acta Psychiatrica Scandinavica. Supplementum*, 429, 109–114. https://doi.org/10.1111/j.1600-0447.2005.00727.x

Rose, Diana. (2018). Participatory research: real or imagined. *Social Psychiatry and Psychiatric Epidemiology*, 53(8), 765–771. https://doi.org/10.1007/s00127-018-1549-3

Rose, Diana, Perry, E., Rae, S., & Good, N. (2017). Service user perspectives on coercion and restraint in mental health. *BJPsych International*, 14(3), 59–61.

Rose, N. (2018). *Our Psychiatric Future*. John Wiley & Sons.

Rosenbaum, S. A. (2019). Restoring voice to people with cognitive disabilities: realizing the right to equal recognition before the law. *Journal of Legal Medicine*, 39(1), 61–74. https://doi.org/10.1080/01947648.2019.1587653

Ruck Keene, A. (2019). Disability rights, mental health treatment and the United Nations #RonR2019. *The Mental Elf Blog*. www.nationalelfservice.net/mental-health/disability-rights-mental-health-treatment-and-the-united-nations-ronr2019/

Russo, J., & Beresford, P. (2015). Between exclusion and colonisation: seeking a place for mad people's knowledge in academia. *Disability & Society*, 30(1), 153–157. https://doi.org/10.1080/09687599.2014.957925

Sashidharan, S. P., Mezzina, R., & Puras, D. (2019). Reducing coercion in mental healthcare. *Epidemiology and Psychiatric Sciences*, 28(6), 605–612. https://doi.org/10.1017/S2045796019000350

Series, L., & Nilsson, A. (2018). Article 12 CRPD: Equal Recognition Before the Law. In I. Bantekas et al. (eds.) *The UN Convention on the Rights of Persons with Disabilities, a Commentary*. Oxford University Press.

Stastny, P., Lovell, A. M., Hannah, J. (2020). Crisis response as a human rights flashpoint. *Health and Human Rights*, 22(1), 105–119.

Sugiura, K., Mahomed, F., Saxena, S., & Patel, V. (2020). An end to coercion: rights and decision-making in mental health care. *Bulletin of the World Health Organization*, 98(1), 52–58. https://doi.org/10.2471/BLT.19.234906

Sunkel, C. (2019). The UN Convention: a service user perspective. *World Psychiatry*, 18(1), 51–52. https://doi.org/10.1002/wps.20606

Swanson, J., Swartz, M., Elbogen, E., et al. (2008). Psychiatric advance directives and reduction of coercive crisis interventions. *Journal of Mental Health*, 17(3), 255–267.

Szmukler, G. (2018). *Men in White Coats: Treatment Under Coercion*. Oxford University Press.

Szmukler, G. (2019). 'Capacity', 'best interests', 'will and preferences' and the UN Convention on the Rights of Persons with Disabilities. *World Psychiatry*, 18(1), 34–41. https://doi.org/10.1002/wps.20584

Szmukler, G. (2020). Involuntary detention and treatment: are we edging toward a 'paradigm shift'? *Schizophrenia Bulletin*, 46(2). https://doi.org/10.1093/schbul/sbz115

Tew, J., Gould, N., Abankwa, D. et al. (2006). *Values and Methodologies for Social Research in Mental Health*. Social Perspectives Network. www.birmingham.ac.uk/Documents/college-social-sciences/social-policy/IASS/publications/social-research-mental-health.pdf

Tomuschat, C. (2003). *Human Rights: Between Idealism and Realism*. Oxford University Press.

United Nations Human Rights Committee. (2014). General Comment No. 35 – Article 9: Liberty and Security of Person [UN Doc CCPR/C/GC/35].

United Nations Office of the Human Rights Commissioner. (2014). OHCHR | Draft General Comments on Articles 12 and 9. https://www.ohchr.org/EN/HRBodies/CRPD/Pages/DGCArticles12And9.aspx

Wildeman, S. (2013). Protecting rights and building capacities: challenges to global mental health policy in light of the Convention on the Rights of Persons with Disabilities. *The Journal of Law, Medicine & Ethics*, 41(1), 48–73. https://doi.org/10.1111/jlme.12005

World Association of Social Psychiatry. (2017). Resources. *Coercion in Psychiatry*. https://coercioninpsychiatry.com/references/

Zinkler, M., & von Peter, S. (2019). End coercion in mental health services – toward a system based on support only. *Laws*, 8(3), 19. https://doi.org/10.3390/laws8030019

19

Psychiatric Advance Directives and Supported Decision-Making: Preliminary Developments and Pilot Studies in California

Christopher Schneiders, Elyn R. Saks, Jonathan Martinis, and Peter Blanck

Abstract

The Saks Institute for Mental Health Law, Policy, and Ethics at USC Gould School of Law is engaged in an innovation planning project in California to pilot programs and test the feasibility of using psychiatric advance directives (PADs) within the supported decision-making (SDM) paradigm. The project is supported by California's Mental Health Services Oversight and Accountability Commission. This chapter provides an overview of the preliminary developments and pilot studies in the California PADs/SDM project. The project is a first-of-its-kind effort to explore the efficacy of the PADs/SDM paradigm across behavioral health county systems in the State of California. This chapter presents an overview of the pilot project and describes its research questions and implications, and ways in which the project and SDM paradigm embodies the principles of the United Nations Convention on the Rights of Persons with Disabilities.

INTRODUCTION

The Saks Institute for Mental Health Law, Policy, and Ethics at USC Gould School of Law[1] is engaged in an innovation planning project in California to pilot programs and test the feasibility of using psychiatric advance directives (PADs) within the supported decision-making (SDM) paradigm. The project is supported by California's Mental Health Services Oversight and Accountability Commission (MHSOAC). It is to develop a county-level and longitudinal PADs/SDM project to improve community mental health services for people with psychiatric disabilities

---

[1] The Saks Institute was founded in 2010 by Professor Elyn Saks as a think-tank dedicated to research among scholars, professionals, consumers, and policymakers. The institute studies issues at the intersection of mental health law and policy with a primary focus on improved treatment of, and quality of life for, people with mental illness.

at risk of involuntary care, criminal justice involvement, and involuntary hospitalization.[2]

SDM is a relatively new paradigm in the American context, and prominently in the context of the principles of the United Nations Convention on the Rights of Persons with Disabilities (CRPD).[3] In particular, CRPD Article 12 affirms that persons with disabilities have the human right to recognition as persons before the law. States Parties to the CRPD must recognize that persons with disabilities enjoy legal capacity on an equal basis with others in all aspects of life. They must take appropriate measures to provide access by persons with disabilities to the supports they may require in exercising their legal capacity, such as through SDM. Under Article 12, States Parties are to enact measures that relate to the exercise of legal capacity in accordance with international human rights law. These safeguards are to ensure that the exercise of legal capacity respects the rights, will, and preferences of the person, and are tailored to the person's circumstances.

The California Behavioral Health Departments of Fresno and Orange Counties Saks Institute project uses SDM paradigm in employing PADs. The Saks Institute's collaborative team includes the Burton Blatt Institute (BBI) at Syracuse University, Laurie Hallmark of Texas Rio Grande Legal Aid (TRLA), and other organizations and subject matter experts. The Saks Institute's partnership with BBI includes development and implementation of a separate SDM pilot research study focused on people with psychiatric disabilities, specifically people with schizophrenia and bipolar disorder who have experienced psychosis.[4]

Professor Elyn Saks, Founder and Faculty Director of the Saks Institute, contributes as a person diagnosed with schizophrenia. Professor Saks' work has focused on autonomy and independent choice for persons with mental illness. Saks writes:

> Not being allowed to make decisions for oneself is very degrading, painful, and disempowering. Patient choice is important even if the patient is impaired. Or even if we think he or she is making an obviously wrong decision. We allow people to make foolish or unwise decisions all the time.
>
> Indeed, force is an unstable solution. If we encourage the patient to make her own decision, she is likely to be more committed going forward.[5]

This chapter provides an overview of the preliminary developments and pilot studies in the Saks/California PADs/SDM project. It is a first-of-its kind effort to explore the efficacy of the PADs/SDM paradigm across behavioral health county systems in the State of California. The next part, and thereafter the following part, present an

---

[2] Staff Analysis: Fresno County, Psychiatric Advance Directive Supportive Decision Making (2019, on file with first author).
[3] Blanck, P. & Martinis, J. (2015). "The right to make choices": National Resource Center for Supported Decision-Making, *Inclusion*, 3(1), 24–33.
[4] Schneiders, C. (2019). Supported decision-making and people with psychiatric disabilities: Pioneering research at California's Saks Institute. *Impact* 32(1), 40–41.
[5] Saks, E. R. (2019). The power of making decisions. *Impact* 32(1), 42.

overview of the project. The final part considers the pilot project's implications and next steps.

SAKS INSTITUTE/CALIFORNIA PADS/SDM PARADIGM AND PILOT PROJECTS

Historically, people with psychiatric disabilities and other cognitive conditions have been segregated from society and subjected to lesser services, supports, and opportunities than their neurotypical peers.[6] Because they also are often incorrectly viewed as "dangerous" or "less able," countless individuals are unjustifiably institutionalized, faced undeserved levels of scrutiny from law enforcement, have high rates of unemployment, incarceration, and homelessness, and suffer loss of legal rights and social opportunities through conservatorship or guardianship.[7] This situation has been the case both in the United States and globally, and it has been greatly exacerbated as a result of the COVID-19 pandemic.

The landmark Americans with Disabilities Act of 1990 (ADA) guarantees people with disabilities the "right to fully participate in all aspects of society."[8] A crucial component of the ADA, the "integration mandate," requires state and local governments to provide supports and services to people with disabilities in integrated, community-based settings.[9] As interpreted by the US Supreme Court in *Olmstead v. L.C.*,[10] the mandate "aims to end centuries of US government-approved and assisted segregation, whether in state-run institutions or state-sponsored programs."[11] The integration mandate also is consistent with the principles of the CRPD.

More than twenty years after *Olmstead*, and at the thirtieth anniversary of the ADA, significant numbers of people with psychiatric disabilities in California and across the United States – and globally – still have not received the social and economic opportunities promised by the ADA and other laws, and continue to cycle through hospitalization, criminal justice involvement, unemployment, and homelessness.[12] As mentioned, since enactment, the world has been watching the ADA. Other countries have been spurred on to follow its model, notably in the case of the CRPD as a seminal international initiative that reflects a new global era in

---

[6] See, e.g., Logue, L. M. & Blanck, P. (2018). *Heavy Laden: Union Veterans, Psychological Illness, and Suicide*, Cambridge University Press. Wood, E. (2005). History of Guardianship. In Quinn, M. J. *Guardianship of Adults: Achieving Justice, Autonomy, and Safety*. Springer Publishing Company.
[7] Blanck, P. (2020). *Disability Law and Policy*. Foundation Press. Hallmark, L. & Martinis, J. (2019). Psychiatric advanced directives: The TRLA model in Texas. *Impact* 32(1), 43–44.
[8] 42 U.S.C. § 12101(a)(1). Blanck, 2020.
[9] 28 C.F.R. § 35.130(d).
[10] *Olmstead v. L.C., ex rel. Zimring*, 527 U.S. 581 (1999).
[11] Blanck, 2020; Hallmark & Martinis, 2019, 43.
[12] Hallmark & Martinis, 2019; See, also, e.g., Fresno County Mental Health Plan, 2017–18. Available at: www.co.fresno.ca.us/home/showdocument?id=34653; Monterrey County Cultural Competency Plan Requirements, 2018/19 Update. Available at: www.co.monterey.ca.us/home/showdocument?id=84723.

disability human rights. The product of years of work by organizations of people with disabilities and disability experts from every continent, the CRPD was adopted by the United Nations General Assembly in 2006. It is an international treaty, protecting people with disabilities from discrimination. Like the ADA, the CRPD establishes a foundation for the protection and treatment of people with disabilities across a wide range of social and cultural activities. For instance, as mentioned, Article 12 is to ensure that States Parties enact measures that relate to the exercise of legal capacity by persons with disabilities.

In the spirit of the principles of the ADA and the CRPD, the Saks Institute project aims to create pilot programs among county-identified populations in the State of California to address and ameliorate these continuing disability rights problems. The objective is to enhance individual independence and self-determination for persons with psychiatric needs in areas such as education, housing, medical, employment, and financial empowerment. The aim is to understand and help implement ways for California counties, as models for others to follow, to improve access to personal, health, and daily life care, and improve the appropriateness and quality of care. It also aims to help in the preservation of each individual's life goals and preferences, and produce better self-determined outcomes for those with psychiatric disabilities who are at risk of involuntary commitment, homelessness, conservatorships, unnecessary hospitalizations, and involvement with the criminal justice systems at all stages of life.

Understandably, the COVID-19 pandemic has altered aspects of this project because county partners have refocused their primary efforts on the immediate threat from the virus to the disability and other vulnerable communities. Nevertheless, substantial progress is being made in collaboration with Fresno and Orange Counties, even during the difficult months of the pandemic.

In essence, the project is intended to model and assess strategies to use PADs under the SDM paradigm, to improve the effectiveness of community mental health services.[13] With PADs, people with psychiatric disabilities use the SDM paradigm to identify and document their preferences for treatment, communication, and other issues to help them (or responders) in a crisis situation. This aspect of self-determination, and the right to make life choices, are key elements of a meaningful and independent life. Yet people with psychiatric disabilities are often denied their right to make daily life choices about where they live and who they interact with, their finances, and their healthcare.[14]

One major objective of this project, in accord with the SDM paradigm and globally with the CRPD, is to empower individuals with mental health conditions to be more self-determined in all aspects of their lives. SDM is a paradigm in which people use trusted friends, family members, and professionals to help them

---

[13] Staff Analysis – Fresno County June 2019. Available from first author, or at: https://mhsoac.ca.gov/sites/default/files/Fresno%20County_Inn%20Staff%20Analysis_PAD_062419_FINAL_ADA.pdf.

[14] Blanck, & Martinis, 2015.

understand the situations and choices they face, including risks and benefits, so they may make their own decisions.[15] SDM is a means for increasing self-determination by encouraging and empowering people to make decisions about their lives to the maximum extent possible.[16]

PADs are a form of SDM and provide a means for documenting an individual's preferences in a legally recognized manner. The California project is among the first significant examinations as to the efficacy of PADs. PADs contain information as simple as medications or treatment modalities that have or have not worked, or as complex as specific steps that should be taken in a crisis. When the individuals choose, their PADs can be provided to law enforcement, crisis responders, medical personnel, and others so they are aware of the person's preferences.[17] "PADs can inform responders and medical personnel that a person reacts poorly to Haldol or well to Zyprexa; has an attorney or supporter who should be contacted as soon as possible; or is a survivor of sexual assault who should be approached by a woman; or is helped by eye contact, which facilitates communication, or threatened by it, which causes a defensive response."[18]

In using PADs, people with psychiatric disabilities also have the proactive opportunity to provide law enforcement, medical, and Crisis Intervention Team (CIT) personnel with information to help avoid or deescalate a potential crisis situation and provide informed better short-term treatment. This may lead CIT teams and other personnel to respond in a more positive and informed way, consistent with the person's preferences and experiences, while reducing the likelihood that interactions will result in criminal charges or long-term, involuntary hospitalization. In addition, nonviolent crisis engagement may encourage people with psychiatric disabilities to view law enforcement and medical personnel as a helpful resource.[19]

In the United States, there is growing support for the use of PADs to encourage people to participate in and determine their care, even during times of limited decision-making capacity.[20] They are a recognized strategy to improve the quality of the caregiver-client relationship and to improve healthcare outcomes.[21] More than half of US states have authorized some form of a PADs, and standard healthcare power of attorney statutes extend that authorization throughout the United States.[22]

---

[15] Ibid.
[16] Ibid. Shogren, K., Wehmeyer, M., Martinis, J., & Blanck, P. (2019). *Supported Decision-Making: Theory, Research, and Practice to Enhance Self-Determination and Quality of Life*, Cambridge University Press.
[17] Hallmark & Martinis, 2019.
[18] Ibid., 43.
[19] Ibid.
[20] Staff Analysis – Fresno County June 2019, 2.
[21] Swanson, J. W., Swartz, M. S., Elbogen, E. B., et al. (2006). Facilitated psychiatric advance directives: A randomized trial of an intervention to foster advance treatment planning among persons with severe mental illness. *American Journal of Psychiatry* 163(11), 1943–1951.
[22] Appelbaum, P. S. (2004). Law and psychiatry: Psychiatric Advance Directives and the treatment of committed patients. *Psychiatric Services* 55(7), 751–763. California Probate Code Section 4800. Link to California Probate Code Section 4800.

The Joint Commission on the Accreditation of Healthcare Organizations, a major accrediting organization, recognizes the value of PADs for treatment decisions when an individual is unable to make decisions for herself or himself.[23]

While PADs were first put into use in the United States in the 1990s, and have widespread support, research suggests their use is still limited by lack of awareness and significant challenges with implementation.[24] Some barriers involve working with individuals with persistent mental health needs to create the PADs, and sometimes the reluctance of clinicians to follow an advance directive.[25]

PADs can enable people with mental illness to provide treating physicians with critical information in writing, in advance, that they may not be able to communicate during a psychotic episode or at the time of hospitalization.[26] Consequently, PADs may improve medical care by reducing "coercive crisis intervention," facilitating doctor/patient communication and relationship development.[27]

SAKS INSTITUTE CALIFORNIA INNOVATION PROJECT OBJECTIVES

The project includes SDM as a strategy to support the creation and use of the PADs. SDM, as mentioned, is when people choose their supporters to help them understand the situations and choices they face to enhance their self-determination to the maximum extent possible.[28] Research finds that using SDM "may enhance feelings of self-empowerment and yield improved functional outcomes" for people with disabilities.[29] To that end, PADs and SDM are used to empower people with psychiatric and other disabilities to understand, make, and communicate decisions in all life spheres, including daily life, education, housing, medical treatment, employment, and financial empowerment.[30]

---

[23] JCAHO (2011). Revised Standard CTS.01.04.01. Care, Treatment, and Services. The Joint Commission, Behavioral Health Care Accreditation Program. Retrieved from: www.jointcommission.org/-/media/deprecated-unorganized/imported-assets/tjc/system-folders/topics-library/post_bhc_cts-chapter_20100630pdf.pdf?db=web&hash=199A99A175398868A527C942486EC96D.

[24] Staff Analysis – Fresno County June 2019, 2.

[25] SAMHSA (2019). Substance Abuse and Mental Health Services Administration: A Practical Guide to Psychiatric Advance Directives. Substance Abuse and Mental Health Services Administration. Retrieved from: www.samhsa.gov/sites/default/files/a_practical_guide_to_psychiatric_advance_directives.pdf.

[26] Hallmark & Martinis, 2019, 43.

[27] Swanson, J. W., Swartz, M. S., Elbogen, E. B., et al. (2008). Psychiatric advance directives and reduction of coercive crisis interventions. *Journal of Mental Health*, 17(3), 255–267.

[28] Blanck & Martinis, 2015.

[29] Jeste, Eglit, Palmer, Martinis, Blanck, & Saks, 2018, 36.

[30] Hallmark & Martinis, 2019; Stoeltje, M. (2019). People with mental illness can get a say in their own treatment. *San Antonio Express-News*. Retrieved from: www.expressnews.com/news/local/article/People-with-mental-illness-can-get-a-say-in-their-13747403.php; Belluck, Pam (2018). Now mental health patients can specify their care before hallucinations or voices overwhelm them. *New York Times*. Retrieved from: www.nytimes.com/2018/12/03/health/psychiatric-advanced-directives.html. Swanson et al., 2008.

The Saks Institute and its project partners outside of California have considerable experience designing, leading, implementing, and evaluating the impact of projects that empower people with disabilities to use PADs and SDM paradigm. Saks partner Laurie Hallmark, Special Projects Director at TRLA,[31] is leading a project in Texas to empower people with psychiatric disabilities to create PADs that identify and state their preferences for treatment, communication, and other elements in a crisis situation.[32] In this project, people with psychiatric disabilities use SDM to draft individualized PADs to create a sustainable process for life and treatment decisions.[33] Project participants are encouraged and supported to identify their preferred treatments, support methods, supporters, medication, and providers. Once completed, the PADs are provided to law enforcement, crisis responders, medical personnel, and others so that they are aware of the person's preferences.[34]

The predicted outcome of the Texas project is for PADs to enable participants to create their own legally recognized "rights document" with information critical to de-escalation and treatment. This is to help crisis personnel respond in a way consistent with the person's preferences and experiences – for example, in terms of medication usage and hospitalization choices and locations. PADs may include other critical information such as physical medical conditions, a statement of individual mental health care instructions and informed consent, medications for routine psychiatric treatment, preferences for emergency treatment, and powers of attorney for healthcare choices. The objective is to reduce the likelihood that interactions will result in criminal charges or long-term, involuntary hospitalization. In addition, nonviolent crisis engagement may encourage people with psychiatric disabilities to view law enforcement and medical personnel as a helpful resource.[35]

The PADs may also enable increased collaboration and communication between people with psychiatric disabilities and their healthcare professionals and providers. Through their PADs, individuals with psychiatric disabilities "provide treating physicians with critical information in writing, in advance, that they may not be able to communicate at the time of hospitalization."[36] When implemented, the PADs help build relationships and trust between people with psychiatric disabilities and healthcare professionals.[37] Research shows that such enhanced relationships and communication leads to better health outcomes, more consistent medication management, and enhanced plan

---

[31] www.trla.org.
[32] Hallmark & Martinis, 2019, 43.
[33] Ibid., 44.
[34] Ibid., 43.
[35] Ibid.
[36] Ibid.
[37] See, e.g., Swanson et al., 2008.

effectiveness and compliance, as well as increased job satisfaction and decreased burnout for healthcare professionals.[38]

Beginning in 2016, the Saks Institute and its partner the BBI developed and is implementing a multisite pilot research project designed to examine the ways in which participants with diagnosed psychiatric disabilities, and in other studies persons with intellectual and developmental disabilities, use SDM to make decisions in multiple life areas; for example, in the areas of medical care and financial determinations, and to study the impact of SDM on their quality of life.[39] At three university sites in California and one in New York, the research team is partnering with people with psychiatric disabilities to educate them on the creation of SDM plans, "identifying areas in their life where they want support making decisions, the type of support they want, who will provide it, and how."[40]

Through their personal life plans, for instance in accord with the self-determination and legal capacity principles of the ADA and CRPD, project participants use SDM in areas including daily living, healthcare, employment, and financial management. As the participants implement their SDM plans, the Saks team is examining the impact SDM has on quality of life, including community integration and life satisfaction.[41] The main prediction is that SDM usage will significantly increase participants' self-determination and enhance their life outcomes, including their ability to access and use community-based resources and services.

The Saks Institute's core project partner, BBI, is a cross-disability institute that has designed, implemented, and evaluated SDM programs in several states. BBI's projects are funded by national governmental agencies and designed to help people with intellectual and developmental disabilities link to, plan for, and implement SDM in daily life, education, housing, medical, employment, financial empowerment, and other life spheres. For example, in the "Successful Transition Program," BBI worked with students with disabilities, their families, and the state vocational rehabilitation agency and service providers to enhance student services and increase coordination and collaboration among the parties through the SDM paradigm.[42]

BBI currently is undertaking a first-of-its-kind randomized control trial (RCT) experiment to test the efficacy of SDM over time for a large cohort of persons with intellectual and developmental disabilities. In that study, the "treatment" condition involves strategies for enhanced usage and training on SDM. The predicted outcome is that individuals in the experimental treatment condition, as compared to controls who received no enhanced training on SDM, over time will report greater

---

[38] See, e.g., Berg, S. (2017). Better communication with patients linked to less burnout. *American Medical Association*. Retrieved from: www.ama-assn.org/practice-management/physician-health/better-communication-patients-linked-less-burnout.

[39] Schneiders, 2019, 40–41.

[40] Ibid., 41.

[41] Ibid.

[42] Martinis, J., Cassidy, K., Gustin, J., Nadeau, J., & Robinson, D. (2019). Creating a culture of coordinated support: Vermont's successful transition program. *Impact*, 32(1), 19–21.

self-determination and autonomy in daily life, and show a higher tendency to make decisions about their own lives with the support of others. As part of its projects, BBI and its partners have developed the Supported Decision-Making Inventory (SDMI). The SDMI is a validated survey instrument to assess the environment in which individuals make decisions. To date, the SDMI has been used with persons with intellectual and developmental disabilities, and in the future will be used in the Saks Institute projects with people with serious psychiatric disabilities.[43] The SDMI is not a mental or legal capacity instrument, but rather a means for an individual to assess his or her supports in the natural living environment.

The Saks Institute project partners also recognized that many state and local agencies serving people with disabilities often operate in "silos," in which they typically are not aware of, or are not working collaboratively with, individuals and their providers of services.[44] To address this issue, and based on BBI's prior studies, the Saks Institute focuses on educating individuals and service agencies to use SDM to develop individualized support plans that have cross-service provider system goals and supports based on the person's abilities and interests.[45]

CALIFORNIA COUNTY PARTNERS ENGAGEMENT AND DEVELOPMENT OF THE PILOT PROJECTS

The Saks Institute's project team's direction and experience in creating, implementing, and analyzing programs using PADs and other forms of SDM, such as powers of attorney and forms of advanced directives, is consistent with the values and ongoing efforts of several California counties, including the Fresno County Adult System of Care Division, and the Monterrey County Behavioral Health Board.[46] Like those programs, and others, the pilot project stresses self-determination by individuals with psychiatric disabilities and encourages coordination and collaboration among people, professionals, and service providers.

Fresno County, a county in central California, has been approved by MHSOAC as the lead county for a three-year project to pilot and implement the PAD/SDM innovation programs, with the Saks Institute project partners providing technical assistance and support. Orange County, near Los Angeles, has also committed to the innovation project. Modoc, which is a small county in northeastern California, has also expressed interest in joining the project.

---

[43] Shogren, K., Rifenbark, G., Wehmeyer, M., et al. (2020). Refining the Supported Decision Making Inventory, *Journal of Policy and Practice in Intellectual Disabilities*, https://doi.org/10.1111/jppi.12335.
[44] Martinis et al., 2019, 19.
[45] Ibid.
[46] See, e.g., Fresno County Mental Health Plan, Outcomes Report, 2017-2018. Retrieved from: www.co.fresno.ca.us/home/showdocument?id=34653; Monterrey County Behavioral Health Board, FY 2018/2019 Update: Monterey County Cultural Competency Plan Requirements. Retrieved from: www.co.monterey.ca.us/home/showdocument?id=84723.

For its part, Fresno County's project focuses on wellness and recovery throughout their county mental health system. The county trains in and uses the client-driven process of creating a Wellness Recovery Action Plan (WRAP) as part of crisis planning. WRAPs include aspects of SDM principles, such as the use of supporters to enhance self-determination. However, WRAPs lack legal standing with regard to the crisis system of care. Fresno County is proposing to deploy PADs to strengthen its commitment to client-driven planning and care provision, and to enhance the recovery focus of the county mental health system. The county's objective is to develop a legal process for the design, deployment, and recognition of PADs to normalize formal recognition of a client's preferences and wishes during a mental health crisis.[47]

The Saks Institute team has convened in-person and virtual meetings with the California counties to discuss potential activities and pilot programs, and to brainstorm new approaches. In Fresno County, for instance, one first topic discussed potential target groups of people with psychiatric disabilities to consider as the focus for Innovation Projects. The counties identified potential target groups, including individuals who are in or at risk of conservatorship, involuntary hospitalization, homelessness, and incarceration, as well as transition-aged foster youth who have been cycling into and out of hospitals. The COVID-19 pandemic response has necessarily taken priority for Fresno's Behavioral Health department activities in Central California. As a result, the size and scope of initial PAD/SDM pilot projects are being adjusted, beginning with a pilot program for individuals with psychiatric illness and who are currently homeless in the county.

The Saks Institute project team members have also held substantive virtual meetings with key personnel of Orange County's Behavioral Health department, as well as convening their community mental health stakeholders. The goals discussed included identifying barriers and challenges and legal implications. In addition, the goals are focused to evaluate the impact on participants and outcomes, and to understand use across participating counties and different target populations. Among the potential populations, as mentioned, the county recognized individuals living with serious psychiatric disabilities who are at risk of needing involuntary care, criminal justice involvement and involuntary hospitalization, and engagement with the Transitional Age Youth-Program of Assertive Community Treatment and Health Care Agency Correctional Health Services.

The California counties also examined with Saks Institute partners discussed how they may conduct education and outreach to the target groups about PADs/SDM. This discussion centered around the common and logical "entry points" for the PAD/SDM process in the county service systems, such as the peer-to-peer and legal services, hospitals, schools, law enforcement, and the criminal justice and conservatorship systems. The counties discussed when and how PADs/SDM may be introduced in

---

[47] Staff Analysis – Fresno County June 2019, 3.

those systems. They also identified critical junctures – intake, discharge planning, transition planning for Special Education, peer-to-peer and legal services, and when conducting outreach to people who are homeless – when it will be most effective to introduce PAD/SDM processes and encourage target group members to take part.

The California counties additionally examined ways that service systems may use SDM to create individualized PADs. The counties agreed that this process should include agencies and providers engaging in a person-centered process, that people may create and implement PADs based on their individual abilities, needs, interests, and informed choice. The Saks Institute project team members are collaborating with participating counties to schedule and conduct on-site and virtual technical assistance and training to help each county to develop policies and procedures that ensure their PAD process is the product of SDM and person-centered thinking. An essential element of this process will be cross-county collaboration in the development of their projects.

The counties further discussed ways to ensure that people are recognized as having PADs. For example, individuals in crisis may not be able to inform first responders that they have PADs. In those and other cases, county providers and responders will need mechanisms to make them aware the person has a PAD and ways to meaningfully review and follow it. This will help ensure effective, personalized care and build trusting relationships between people with psychiatric disabilities and their healthcare and other providers.

Throughout the collaborative discussions, it was acknowledged that the core issue of PAD recognition and use will be among the project's greatest challenges. During the project, we are developing processes and technologies to enhance acceptance of PADs by key stakeholders and providers, and most importantly by the individuals with psychiatric disabilities. To this end, the project team plans to enlist leading members from the technology arm of Painted Brain, which is a California-based mental health arts and tech organization that uses a peer model focused on recovery.[48] The Saks Institute and partners' "tech brainstorm" with Painted Brain's leadership, all of whom are individuals with psychiatric disabilities, was highly productive and planning is underway for collaboration on a consumer-driven model to enhance PAD recognition and use.

CALIFORNIA COUNTY PADS PILOT PROJECT ADVANCEMENTS AND BARRIERS

From meetings with the counties, initial ideas for advancement of the PADs project and next steps also included possible identification bracelets that people may wear voluntarily, alerting providers and responders they have a PAD (e.g., similar to the ROAD ID bracelets used by runners, bicyclists, and motorcyclists).[49] Other ideas for

---

[48] https://paintedbrain.org/about/the-peer-run-business-model/.
[49] www.roadid.com/.

advancement included a secure online cloud-based or blockchain-type repository where people may voluntarily store copies of their PADs, and choose to allow providers and responders to access them as needed. In addition, the partners are discussing secure Quick Response (QR) codes that link to a person's PAD, which may be scanned to provide the information, while also encouraging people to keep physical and/or digital copies of their PADs on their person.

In project interviews, as mentioned, the counties reported that one barrier to adoption of PADs/SDM was the "silo" nature of service systems and providers. In such siloed systems, public and private providers often do not communicate or collaborate most effectively in the "voice" (will and preferences) of the individual. Consequently, each provider may have operating policies and procedures that conflict in practice with those of other providers. In such systems, PADs typically are of limited use because providers and first responders may not have (or may have conflicting) policies or practices to encourage people to create them, or mechanisms to recognize and respect them.

Accordingly, in the project the counties agreed that they would actively collaborate with the Saks Institute team partners and others to coordinate with public and private agencies and providers to work within existing systems. They also agreed to develop new, collaborative approaches that may empower people to create PADs, increase awareness when people have PADs, and enhance respect for the terms of people's PADs.

As the Saks Institute project progresses, next steps include working closely with each county to identify a roster of potential partners to target for outreach, training, and participation in this project. While the counties discussed the need to create unified, cross-system policies and procedures that encourage, empower, and respect PADs/SDM, it will be important to incorporate their service system policies and procedures, rather than only requiring partners to create new discrete policies and procedures.

After identifying potential public and private partners, the counties further brainstormed about ways to conduct outreach to other potential partners to provide important information about PADs/SDM and this project, and to encourage them to participate. The methods discussed included targeted educational and training material (that may be provided in-person, remotely, in writing, or online), and providing information on the research foundation and documented benefits. This also includes how PADs/SDM may be used as an alternative to conservatorship and guardianship, commitment, and involuntary treatment and as ways to reduce incarceration, homelessness, underemployment, and hospitalization. It also includes best practices, and development of case studies in accessible formats, in working with people to create and implement PADs through SDM, located on an accessible website hosted by the Saks Institute.

Finally, the counties discussed how they and the Saks Institute research team will evaluate and measure the efficacy of their Innovation Projects. As BBI is currently conducting in projects across the country, it will be necessary to determine whether

PADs/SDM have a positive and meaningful impact on reduced interactions with the criminal justice system, quality of life (using quantitative and qualitative measures) of target groups, and the quality of services and supports provided by and in the county. These issues also may be comparable across counties, and scaled across smaller and larger counties.

NEXT STEPS AND RESEARCH QUESTIONS TO EXAMINE

The Saks Institute project team in partnership with the California counties are currently identifying and examining potential quantitative and qualitative evaluative metrics, some previously validated by BBI, such as the SDMI, and others to be validated and tested. These measures include evaluations during crisis and other situations of the degree to which the PAD was effectively accessible, accessed, and used by the person, the provider (e.g., first responder, hospital, or doctor), or others such as family members or friends. Additionally, in what ways did use of the PAD increase the amount and quality of communication and collaboration between the person and his or her service providers.

It also will be necessary to examine the degree to which use of PADs/SDM increase the project participants' engagement with county supports and services, in areas such as housing, social services, supported employment, special education, adult education, and child welfare programs. Moreover, examination will occur as to the degree to which use of PADs/SDM increase participants' engagement in county supports and services. In addition, the project will consider whether use of PADs facilitates involvement and follow-through in their support plans.

Other research questions to examine include ways in which use of PADs/SDM enhance positive life and programmatic outcomes (community integration, housing stability, program completion, employment). In addition, the project will examine the degree to which use of PADs/SDM reduce people with psychiatric disabilities' criminal justice system involvement and recidivism; rates and length of hospitalization; or use and length of conservatorship. The rate and length of involuntary commitment and homelessness are important issues that the Saks Institute partners will explore in the future.

CONCLUSION: MENTAL HEALTH AND DECISION MAKING, THE ADA AND THE CRPD

As the Saks Institute project team and its partners in California continue this project with the support of MHSOAC, the efforts are proceeding cautiously, but with optimism. In accord with the guiding principles of the ADA and the CRPD, the longer-term objective is to enhance and extend human rights to all people with disabilities. The CRPD is spurring such change in domestic laws to address equal treatment of people with psychiatric disabilities. Like the ADA, the CRPD is a milestone in the advancement of the disability rights and inclusive principles to foster individual agency and self-determination in accord with the SDM paradigm.

The overarching objective of the Saks Institute portfolio of projects, in accordance with the principles of SDM and self-determination in the ADA and CRPD, is that these programs may lead to greater autonomy and reduced harm for individuals living with psychiatric disabilities. There currently is some uncertainty around the real-life use of PADs. However, the present project is one among many innovation projects supported by California's Mental Health Services Act with the goal of increasing the quality of mental health services in the state through self-determination principles.[50] Despite the challenges in this undertaking, including the current COVID-19 pandemic, progress is being in the United States and globally made to enhance the quality of life for people living with psychiatric disabilities.

The leadership of the California Fresno and Orange counties, in partnership with the Saks project team, is helping to better understand how development and implementation of PADs and the SDM paradigm can result in a more informed, person-centered approach to crisis situations. The belief is that this effort will lead to improved quality of life for those with psychiatric disabilities as active and self-determined individuals throughout their daily lives. The Saks Institute's efforts are meant to further such positive outcomes in California, nationally, and globally, towards the self-determination of persons with psychiatric disabilities in all aspects of life.

---

[50] MHSA'S Innovation Projects. www.mhsoac.ca.gov/sites/default/files/documents/2018-06/MHSOAC-IncubatorStakeholderHandout.pdf.

20

Community-Based Mental Health Care Delivery with Partners In Health: A Framework for Putting the CRPD into Practice

Stephanie L. Smith

Abstract

For people with psychosocial disabilities living in poverty, the effective protection of human rights outlined in the CRPD requires attention to social and economic inequities, including the promotion of the right to health. The starting point for CRPD adherence in resource-limited settings should be the adequate provision of rights-based support which optimizes individuals' functioning and helps them achieve effective recovery and rehabilitation, alongside full inclusion and participation in their communities. Strategies to build systems which can provide this support should be of interest to multiple stakeholders including service users, clinicians, health system planners, NGOs, and CRPD duty bearers such as states.

This chapter describes the mental health system development efforts of Partners In Health (PIH), a non-profit organization operating in ten countries. Our implementation framework has focused on the spread and scale of decentralized, voluntary mental health care delivered primarily by lay and other non-specialist providers in communities and local health facilities. In our experience, there is insufficient implementation guidance to build the health system and community-based environments in which the practical realization of the CRPD can be achieved. The chapter also discusses how our mental health care delivery framework could be used to implement interventions specifically designed to support decision-making.

INTRODUCTION

The Convention on the Rights of Persons with Disabilities (CRPD) has been hailed as a "paradigm shift" through its adoption of a model of disability which regards social and environmental barriers to be the disabler of individuals, rather than individual problems to be corrected (Mittler, 2015). The CRPD's use of a socio-ecologic model of disability lays bare the indivisibility of socioeconomic, civil, and political rights, highlighting the imperative for states, including their health systems and civil society members, to provide whatever support is required for people with psychosocial disabilities to achieve equal enjoyment of all rights. This includes equal recognition before the law, articulated in Article 12 of the CRPD, which rejects involuntary treatment and substituted decision-making in mental health care, instead recognizing the right of all individuals to make their own treatment decisions, with adequate support if needed (Arstein-Kerslake and Flynn, 2016). Together with the growing documentation of widespread human rights abuses occurring within psychiatric institutions worldwide, the CRPD has the potential to galvanize a global dismantling of coercive mental health care practices and to reimagine a rights-based approach to mental health care. The CRPD challenges mental health programs to engage with people with mental health conditions as rights bearers, rather than passive recipients of care. Adherence to the CRPD requires an additional paradigm shift for mental health service planners and implementers, who must shift from services focused on diagnosis and homogenous grouping of individuals to instead focus on optimizing whatever supports an individual needs to be successful in their daily context and typical environments.

Achieving CRPD compliance presents significant practical challenges across much of the globe. The indivisibility of rights codified by the CRPD means that those seeking to implement its mandates must spend at least as much time considering how to uphold the right to health through the creation of effective community-based services for people living with mental and psychosocial disabilities, as they do so considering how to ensure the abolition of substituted decision-making and involuntary treatment outlined in Article 12. The majority of the world's population living with mental health conditions and psychosocial disabilities cannot currently access effective support or care that promotes recovery and meaningful participation in their communities. Human resources for mental health care in low- and middle-income countries (LMICs) are severely limited; a World Health Organization (WHO) survey of the mental health workforce globally (including nurses, psychologists, social workers, psychiatrists, occupational therapists, and other paid mental health workers) found an average of 6.2 mental health workers per 100,000 population in lower middle-income countries, and just 1.6 per 100,000 in low-income countries (WHO, 2018). In many LMICs, particularly in rural areas, there is an almost complete absence of psychosocial interventions, rehabilitation programs, or formal peer- or other support mechanisms that could contribute to the well-being of individuals with disabilities and create the conditions necessary to promote and protect the rights of those individuals (Eaton et al., 2011). Without the effective optimization of support for all individuals with psychosocial disabilities to succeed in their own communities, efforts to ensure freedom from coercion or substituted decision-making will be significantly impaired. An additional challenge is the lack of development assistance focused on person- and rights-based approaches to mental health care and psychosocial support. Legislation which promotes rights-based services and support, where it exists, often is incompletely implemented, especially in rural areas of LMICs (Bartlett et al., 2011). For people living with the most disabling mental health conditions, this lack of effective programs or support puts them at high risk of additional human rights abuses such as chaining or other stigmatizing practices within communities.

Some progress has been made in articulating specific community-based interventions which could help to prevent coercion and move towards person- and rights-centered interventions, even in resource-limited settings. For example, peer support models, as well as specific psychological care and support provided by community health workers within a task-sharing model, have been articulated (Davidson et al., 2012; Raviola et al., 2019). These interventions could theoretically be expanded on and made more widely available across LMICs, even as the evidence base for effective support mechanisms for the promotion of civil rights, including supported decision-making, continues to grow. Yet in most places the implementation is still entirely aspirational, let alone the spread or scale-up of care and support for people with mental health conditions and psychosocial disabilities. To begin to approach CRPD compliance in spirit or in letter, effective strategies that account for the planning, implementation and sustained supply of comprehensive interventions designed to optimize functioning for individuals within their own communities are still needed.

This chapter describes key elements of our approach to comprehensive community-based mental health system development at PIH over the past ten years. Founded in the 1980s, PIH collaborates with local sister organizations in the ten countries where it works to build community-based, clinic-supported, hospital-linked healthcare continuums capable of delivering high-quality services in rural areas, simultaneously addressing the social and economic injustices contributing to health inequities (Farmer et al., 2001, 2006). From the beginning, the incorporation of mental health care into the systems strengthening efforts of PIH has leveraged its accompaniment model – providing quality care with robust, concurrent social supports – to ensure the building of decentralized, voluntary, community-based care and support for people living with mental health conditions and psychosocial disabilities across the PIH catchment areas. Our approach has focused on managing the challenges of the *spread* and *scale* of a variety of interventions addressing the multiple and varied needs of people with mental health conditions, delivered in community and local health facilities in Haiti, Rwanda, Liberia, Sierra Leone, Malawi, Lesotho, Peru, and Chiapas, Mexico. Our implementation strategies have included: value-based systems design; task sharing including community health workers (CHWs) and peers; workforce development including training, supervision, and management; quality improvement measures; effective partnerships; and material investment which addresses the social and economic problems that reinforce vulnerability to human rights violations. These key building blocks can be leveraged to transform systems to build effective, scalable, rights-based support of people living with mental health conditions and psychosocial disabilities. They can also be used to facilitate the implementation of coordinated interventions designed to eliminate coercion and involuntary treatment, and advance supported decision-making across LMICs. Our approach is adaptable to different community and health system contexts, and could support a wide range of localized innovations that adhere to human rights law, while offering workable alternatives to a coercive mental health system.

VALUE-BASED SYSTEMS DESIGN

Establishing the effective delivery of interventions which can provide care and needed support to individuals living with mental health conditions and psychosocial disabilities is complex. Delivery platforms through which interventions can be successfully implemented, and coordination among those platforms, is imperative if the goal is to provide a range of supports designed to reduce distress, improve functioning, maintain personal autonomy, and promote the equality of opportunity, full participation, independent living, and economic self-sufficiency of service users. For example, someone with a severe mental health condition may require a set of interventions and supports which assist that person with alleviation of symptoms, livelihood engagement, and skill development for effective community participation – all of which are essential prerequisites for optimizing that person's ability to express their will and preferences for important decisions. Such care and support must flow effectively through delivery platforms, and activities must be coordinated in order to optimize outcomes for service users – particularly if care and support is to be personalized to bridge the specific gap between the demands of the person's environment and their ability to meet those demands. A shared service delivery infrastructure is also essential so that personnel are used wisely toward an optimization of economies of scale (Kim et al., 2013). In practice, this means the more that care and support for a variety of mental health conditions and psychosocial disabilities is effectively coordinated across interventions and platforms, the more that the human and financial resources required for the delivery of that care and support are optimized, rendering the potential for scale-up of services more feasible.

To approach this design for mental health care delivery, the PIH mental health program has iteratively developed a *mental health care delivery value chain*. Care delivery value chains offer a framework for understanding, improving, and integrating the set of activities involved in the full cycle of care for any health-related condition. The value chain framework conceives of care delivery as an overall system, not a collection of discrete interventions, and each individual activity is interrelated with other activities to produce improved outcomes (value) for service users (Rhatigan et al., 2009). Our mental health care delivery value chain was iteratively developed with teams from all PIH local sites using a Theory of Change (ToC) process, through which we identified long-term goals for community mental health care and worked backward to identify all the conditions (outcomes) that must be in place (and their causal relationships) to achieve those goals (Raviola et al., 2020). Aligned with CRPD aspirations, the starting point for the ToC process was the development of decentralized, voluntary, recovery-oriented, and community-based mental health services integrated into the continuum of care delivery platforms supported by PIH. The ToC process has guided the systems planning across all PIH sites as each site continuously develops and refines its specific program goals across the value chain. Taken together with the critical components needed to build and sustain the value chain within context, these elements constitute PIH's Mental Health Service Delivery Planning Matrix to Achieve Universal Health Coverage (Figure 20.1).

Our PIH mental health value chain describes the essential service activities for quality mental health care across communities and health system platforms, including health centers and hospitals, which enable people with psychosocial disabilities to live independently in their communities. Although our value chain focuses on health-related activities delivered in community settings and health facilities, many components could potentially be delivered from platforms outside of the health system, such as schools. Primary activities described in the value chain include self-care, psychosocial support, including psychoeducation by peers and other non-specialist providers, peer support groups, psychotherapy, livelihood support, social support interventions, and many other activities that comprise a mental health service delivery plan focused on health equity and inclusion, and which effectively integrates contemporary, evidence-based biopsychosocial approaches, strong traditional perceptions and beliefs, and religious influences of value to communities (Raviola et al., 2019, 2013). The value chain focuses on achieving outcomes of value *for service users* across a wide variety of mental health conditions and psychosocial disabilities. Each local site team uses the value chain to articulate local service delivery priorities to drive management decision-making, organization of care processes, and system change to focus on achieving those outcomes of value for individuals receiving services and support for mental health conditions.

TASK SHARING IN MENTAL HEALTH INTERVENTION DELIVERY

Since its inception, PIH has used lay providers and community members to link communities and the health system in order to address individuals' clinical and psychosocial needs, called "task-sharing" (Franke et al., 2013; Palazuelos et al., 2018). Activities across our mental health care delivery value-chain also employ task sharing, wherein lay and other non-specialist providers, including peers, are capacitated to provide aspects of care, including the delivery of a range of interventions specific to mental health and well-being such as skills building, problem solving, and low-intensity psychological treatments (Chatterjee et al., 2009; Hoeft et al., 2018; Singla et al., 2017). Strategies like task sharing have been shown to be effective to improve distress and functioning for people with a range of mental health conditions

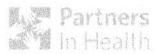

FIGURE 20.1 Partners In Health mental health service delivery planning matrix to achieve universal health coverage Source: Partners in Health, 2020.

and disabilities (Patel et al., 2016; van Ginneken et al., 2013), and urge the possibility of sharing tasks among available health workers as an alternative to specialist-focused care when addressing mental health and psychosocial disabilities.

At PIH, our approach to task sharing in mental health care and support has focused on several key elements increasingly recognized to ensure optimal functioning of a task-shared mental health care system (Ballard et al., 2017):

1) defining the skills/core competencies required for successful participation in care activities as defined by the value chain;
2) ensuring continuous training and in-service learning for lay and non-specialist providers of those core competencies;

3) ensuring support from a dedicated supervisor; and
4) ensuring integration and coordination of non-specialist delivered activities into and across platforms, especially through effective human resource management and quality improvement practices.

These key elements have enabled us to implement and strengthen sensible, ethical, comprehensive and rights-based interventions to support people living with mental health conditions, adapted for local contexts (Raviola et al., 2020).

For example, in Rwanda, initial steps taken to build task sharing into mental health care delivered across rural district health system platforms included defining the skills and competencies needed to provide care and support for people with severe mental health conditions and significant functional impairments in multiple domains. Specific tasks were then assigned to various providers in the system based on those defined skills and competencies. Next, training plans tailored to each cadre of provider were developed and implemented, with a focus on frontline nurses at health centers and CHWs in the community. A structured supervisory process was established, focusing on ensuring that basic standards of care for the assigned tasks were encouraged, taught, mentored and delivered by non-specialist providers (S. Smith et al., 2017; S. L. Smith et al., 2017).

Peer support groups and peer-to-peer support for people living with mental health conditions and psychosocial disabilities have also increasingly been incorporated into the task-sharing model across PIH sites. In Rwanda, peer self-help groups were initiated alongside the integration of mental health into health centers, with a focus initially on stigma reduction and building social connections. Some groups have evolved to include peer-led agriculture cooperatives which include livelihood skills building and rotating credit to facilitate group members' economic empowerment. In Liberia, youth using substances have self-organized to support each other using principles of harm reduction. Service users across multiple PIH sites have facilitated community education, stigma reduction activities, and informal peer-support mechanisms through direct outreach and engagement with CHWs (Partners In Health, 2020, 2014).

Training, and in particular supervision, has required significant attention for the successful implementation of task sharing across community and health facilities, and has comprised some of the greatest cost burdens across PIH global sites. Task sharing in community settings has demanded the initiation of services and interventions which generally did not previously exist, as countries have slowly decentralized mental health services from centralized facilities over the past decade. Distributing tasks among a multitude of non-specialist providers has required significant supervisory commitments in order to sustain basic care delivery, particularly the specifics of good psychosocial and psychotherapeutic (nonpharmacologic) care within recovery-oriented models (Chatterjee et al., 2009). Supervision is especially critical as care is scaled and providers, including community health workers and peers, are taking on more and unfamiliar tasks (Dlamini-Simelane and Moyer, 2017; Verdeli et al., 2016). The iterative development of achievable standards and competencies as tasks are shared with non-specialist providers, adapted over time as the task-shared mental health system matures, may be the most appropriate process to ensure basic quality of care. This is especially important as care delivery continues to expand to include complex interventions which can provide the care and support required for all people with mental health conditions and psychosocial disabilities to achieve full and effective inclusion, participation, recovery, and rehabilitation.

CONTINUOUS QUALITY IMPROVEMENT

The use of quality improvement (QI) methods have also been critical to PIH's development of sustained services and support for persons with mental health conditions and psychosocial disabilities. Consistent with the principles of nondiscrimination and equality, programs and systems of mental health care and psychosocial support must meet the quality standards for general health care and other types of support and hold reasonable promise for improved well-being and recovery (Stastny et al., 2020). Use of the mental health care delivery value chain has been particularly helpful when designing processes to evaluate the quality of care and support provided, and in developing QI practices, including measurement-based QI projects specifically designed to reduce coercion and involuntary treatment. Our QI practices are characterized by continuous, ongoing hypothesis testing to address health system challenges including the implementation and evaluation of small-scale care improvement demonstrations, and improvement of communication with and engagement of all participants in the health system (Leatherman et al., 2010). These practices have been coupled by outcomes measurement (including monitoring and evaluation), and the use of routine data to drive performance improvement (Raviola et al., 2020; Smith et al., 2020).

Across PIH sites, some key quality-of-care indicators have included: number of frontline health providers trained in provision of care and support across the value chain; number of primary care health centers offering basic care and support, clinical supervision checklist completion; and service user and community perspectives on mental health care delivery. Other care-quality indicators have focused specifically on indicators of noncoercive practices, such as the number of transfers to centralized locked facilities outside the PIH catchment areas. Each site chooses relevant quality indicators and use local data sources for measurement and evaluation of quality improvement measures. For example, in rural Maryland County, Liberia, the team established a care intervention in which lay health workers provided social assistance and assistance with practical problem solving to improve the daily functioning of persons with severe mental health conditions living on the streets (Cyrus et al., 2020). The success of the intervention was measured by the number of individuals able to engage in income-generating activities. To date, the intervention has led to over 100 people more stably housed and engaging in economic empowerment activities, while continuing to receive support at the community level. Alongside adequate program and human resource management practices, quality improvement has allowed frontline teams to face and resolve 'real-world' implementation challenges as they are occurring in sustained delivery across platforms.

AUGMENTING MATERIAL SUPPORTS

A core component of PIH's health systems-strengthening approach is to meet people where they are with whatever means necessary, until outcomes are equitable for all (Palazuelos et al., 2018). People with psychosocial disabilities are often marginalized and constitute a disproportionately impoverished population. Concrete material investment is required to address the social and economic problems that may worsen mental health and psychosocial disabilities. For example, in resource-limited settings, individuals often have limited access to clean water, safe housing, reliable food supplies, or transportation. Addressing these barriers are understood as part of the mental health care delivery value chain, not outside of it, and the mental health care value chain recognizes that other care and support for mental health conditions cannot occur without first addressing these barriers (Rhatigan et al., 2009). For example, social support for individuals is included across all PIH mental health programs. Direct cash transfers are used to address transportation challenges, insurance payments, and food insecurity, alongside in-kind support such as food packages. Specific actions and interventions focused on income generation, education and livelihoods are also undertaken as a critical feature of the value chain, and as a crucial component of realizing the right to health for individuals living with mental and psychosocial disabilities. In 2019, as part of the community-based delivery platform, 2,061 individuals participated in peer-led self-help and livelihood groups in Rwanda, including independent farming projects and animal husbandry (Partners In Health, 2020).

EFFECTIVE PARTNERSHIPS

A primary function of PIH globally as a healthcare delivery organization is to work with communities, governments, and other partners committed locally to supporting the strengthening of the public health system. As the public sector is the ultimate rights guarantor for its citizens, PIH works directly with local and national government partners to build scalable models of care for long-term implementation, in order to operationalize the right to health in the countries where it works. Our mental health programs have directly innovated and iterated all of its service delivery and care activities in partnership with the public sector. Care and support across the sites is provided primarily by government health providers, and particular effort is paid not to create parallel structures of support and care in mental health. Partnering with non-public sector actors such as advocacy organizations for mental health, academic institutions and individual content experts (clinical, educational, and scientific), transnational global health initiatives, multilateral donor organizations, and private philanthropy have also provided opportunities to coinvest and build capacity in our innovative, locally designed care and support – which, if successful, can be scaled up to the national level.

IMPLEMENTING THE CRPD

The elements we have described frame the critical aspects of the strategic planning and large-scale implementation of mental health services and support within community settings across ten diverse PIH global sites. Our programs offer individualized support and care to almost 11,000 individuals annually across our sites, including 55,800 visits in community-based health centers (Partners In Health, 2020). Many more receive support and outreach within communities via CHW and peer networks. Our programs have contributed to significant improvements in distress levels and improving functioning for individuals living with mental health conditions and psychosocial disabilities. Individuals supported by our work have also demonstrated increased engagement with community activities and meaningful work, alongside individual and family improvements in economic status (Smith et al., 2020).

Fulfillment of the right to health is a fundamental component of the CRPD, and is inextricably linked to the freedom from coercion and involuntary treatment outlined in Article 12. Our implementation framework describes key strategies for coordinating and scaling multiple interventions across platforms that focus on providing the support needed for people receiving mental health services to optimize their functional status and achieve the right to the highest attainable level of health. The iteratively developed value chain offers a mutual approach to shared objectives in mental health care delivery across the ten global sites supported by PIH, including an explicit focus on the decentralization of care away from locked facilities towards voluntary services delivered in communities and at health facilities through task sharing (Smith et al., 2015). As mental health programs and policymakers seek to adhere to CRPD standards, our implementation framework could support that shift towards shared rights objectives – for example, the effective implementation of a variety of person-centered interventions which emphasize a person's strengths and abilities and full and equitable participation in all aspects of life. Adherence to CRPD mandates are more likely to be achieved within a framework which can support the complex, multifaceted cross-platform interventions needed to ensure the promotion and protection of all rights outlined in the CRPD, including the right to health, as well as interventions supporting civil rights such as freedom from coercion and the abolishment of substituted decision-making articulated in Article 12. These interventions should go hand-in-hand with community engagement and education on mental health and human rights, and include opportunities for ongoing involvement with other persons with lived experience of mental health conditions and psychosocial disabilities.

The planning and implementation framework we have described can be linked to the dissemination of rights-based mental health care and supports, as we have done across multiple health system platforms and community settings. It also could be used to implement new practices designed specifically to promote and uphold Article 12 of the CRPD as they emerge, including interventions focused on supported decision-making. Supported decision-making requires that people are supported effectively, regardless of disability, to make life decisions for themselves. While our mental health care delivery value chain begins with the service user as rights-bearer, including the right to self-determination, further research is needed to describe the essential factors related to decision-making – particularly in rural, resource-limited settings – including the specific supports needed to enable people to fully engage in decision-making processes, as well as interventions that can promote knowledge and skills pertaining to decision-making, in order to realize the goal that people with psychosocial disabilities are fully supported to make their own decisions (Shogren and Wehmeyer, 2015). Drawing on the agency of service users in LMICs to understand best approaches to the development of interventions designed to support decision-making in local contexts will be essential. Explicitly linking local efforts to uphold the CRPD with their global contexts may also be helpful.

Although interventions for supporting decision-making, particularly in LMICs, are still nascent, the components of our PIH mental health care delivery framework could be used to enable the implementation of supported decision-making interventions as they reach across multiple platforms and settings, including intersectoral work. It is likely that the unique types and amount of support for decision-making needed for each individual will require a range of health system and intersectoral interventions, and implementing those interventions would require considerable human interaction with paid human resources. Task sharing could potentially provide the requisite human interaction, although supervision and support for non-specialist and lay providers engaging with supported decision-making will need to be built into all interventions from the beginning.

A robust human rights accountability framework should also accompany any new rights-based interventions incorporated into mental health system platforms, including those designed to facilitate supported decision-making, taking into account local law and practices. The upholding of CRPD standards, including Article 12, could be incorporated into continuous QI and monitoring and evaluation frameworks like those we have described. Accountability frameworks should also incorporate tools such as the WHO QualityRights toolkit, designed for assessing and improving human rights standards in mental health care delivery (WHO, 2012). The meaningful and routine inclusion of service users within quality improvement teams that can evaluate, monitor, and report on service implementation and human rights outcomes is also an important part of ensuring accountability (Stastny, 2020).

CONCLUSION

The CRPD offers an opportunity to reimagine mental health care across the globe, particularly in countries where the integration of mental health care into health system platforms is nascent. Models of mental health care embedded within communities are easier to access, promote greater integration of traditional perceptions within system building efforts, reduce stigma, and can better protect against coercion through engagement with service users directly in system building. Community mental health system development must be coordinated among health system and community-based platforms, including attention to training, supervision, management, care quality, and – perhaps most important – addressing the social and economic determinants of wellness and mental health. In this chapter, we have offered our strategic design and implementation building blocks iteratively developed with PIH teams and public health systems across ten countries, designed to achieve the highest attainable standard of health for those living with mental health conditions and psychosocial disabilities. Although our system-building efforts continue to be refined, we offer human rights-driven implementation strategies that can function to incorporate noncoercive interventions focused on inclusion and empowerment, including those which promote supported decision-making. In order to advance the paradigm shift highlighted in the CRPD, health systems and programs need concrete and pragmatic, usable strategies which can help to leave behind the legacy of human rights violations in mental health services, and provide a framework for the full realization of all rights for people living with mental health conditions and psychosocial disabilities around the globe.

REFERENCES

Arstein-Kerslake, A., Flynn, E., 2016. The General Comment on Article 12 of the Convention on the Rights of Persons with Disabilities: A roadmap for equality before the law. *Int. J. Hum. Rights* 20, 471–490. https://doi.org/10.1080/13642987.2015.1107052

Ballard, M., Schwartz, R., Johnson, A., et al., 2017. Practitioner expertise to optimize community health systems: Harnessing operational insight.

Bartlett, P., Jenkins, R., Kiima, D., 2011. Mental health law in the community: Thinking about Africa. *Int. J. Ment. Health Syst.* 5(21). https://doi.org/10.1186/1752-4458-5-21

Chatterjee, S., Pillai, A., Jain, S., Cohen, A., Patel, V., 2009. Outcomes of people with psychotic disorders in a community-based rehabilitation programme in rural India. *Br. J. Psychiatry* 195, 433–439. https://doi.org/10.1192/bjp.bp.108.057596

Cyrus, G., Lusaka, J., Yansine, W. A., et al., 2020. Care and community reintegration of homeless people living with severe mental disorders: A community-based mental health programme in Maryland County, Liberia. *Lancet Glob. Health, Consortium of Universities for Global Health Abstracts* 4. https://www.thelancet.com/journals/langlo/article/PIIS2214-109X(20)30145-5/fulltext

Davidson, L., Bellamy, C. B., Guy, K., Miller, R., 2012. Peer support among persons with severe mental illnesses: A review of evidence and experience. *World Psychiatry* 11, 123–128. https://doi.org/10.1016/j.wpsyc.2012.05.009

Dlamini-Simelane, T., Moyer, E., 2017. Task shifting or shifting care practices? The impact of task shifting on patients' experiences and health care arrangements in Swaziland. *BMC Health Serv. Res.* 17. https://doi.org/10.1186/s12913-016-1960-y

Eaton, J., McCay, L., Semrau, M., et al., 2011. Scale up of services for mental health in low-income and middle-income countries. *The Lancet* 378, 1592–1603. https://doi.org/10.1016/S0140-6736(11)60891-X

Farmer, P., Léandre, F., Mukherjee, J., et al., 2001. Community-based treatment of advanced HIV disease: introducing DOT-HAART (directly observed therapy with highly active antiretroviral therapy). *Bull. World Health Organ.* 79, 1145–1151.

Farmer, P. E., Nizeye, B., Stulac, S., Keshavjee, S., 2006. Structural Violence and Clinical Medicine. *PLoS Med.* 3, e449. https://doi.org/10.1371/journal.pmed.0030449

Franke, M. F., Kaigamba, F., Socci, A. R., et al., 2013. Improved retention associated with community-based accompaniment for antiretroviral therapy delivery in rural Rwanda. *Clin. Infect. Dis.* 56, 1319–1326. https://doi.org/10.1093/cid/cis1193

Hoeft, T. J., Fortney, J. C., Patel, V., Unützer, J., 2018. Task-sharing approaches to improve mental health care in rural and other low-resource settings: A systematic review: Task-sharing rural mental health. *J. Rural Health* 34, 48–62. https://doi.org/10.1111/jrh.12229

Kim, J. Y., Farmer, P., Porter, M. E., 2013. Redefining global health-care delivery. *The Lancet* 382, 1060–1069. https://doi.org/10.1016/S0140-6736(13)61047-8

Leatherman, S., Ferris, T. G., Berwick, D., Omaswa, F., Crisp, N., 2010. The role of quality improvement in strengthening health systems in developing countries. *Int. J. Qual. Health Care* 22, 237–243. https://doi.org/10.1093/intqhc/mzq028

Legha, R., Eustache, E., Therosme, T., et al., 2015. Taskshifting: Translating theory into practice to build a community based mental health care system in rural Haiti. *Intervention* 13, 248–267. https://doi.org/10.1097/WTF.0000000000000099

Mittler, P., 2015. The UN Convention on the Rights of Persons with Disabilities: Implementing a paradigm shift: UN Disability Convention and Millennium Development Goals. *J. Policy Pract. Intellect. Disabil.* 12, 79–89. https://doi.org/10.1111/jppi.12118

Palazuelos, D., Farmer, P. E., Mukherjee, J., 2018. Community health and equity of outcomes: The Partners In Health experience. *Lancet Glob. Health* 6, e491–e493. https://doi.org/10.1016/S2214-109X(18)30073-1

Partners In Health, 2020. Story map: mental health at Partners In Health. https://storymaps.arcgis.com/stories/8dca051575aa4dd983e9fe1e21bcff6b

Partners In Health, 2014. 'I'm not afraid anymore': A young man recovers from a mental illness. www.pih.org/article/im-not-afraid-anymore-a-young-man-recovers-from-mental-illness

Patel, V., Chisholm, D., Parikh, R., et al., 2016. Addressing the burden of mental, neurological, and substance use disorders: Key messages from Disease Control Priorities, 3rd edition. *The Lancet* 387, 1672–1685. https://doi.org/10.1016/S0140-6736(15)00390-6

Raviola, G., Naslund, J. A., Smith, S. L., Patel, V., 2019. Innovative models in mental health delivery systems: Task sharing care with non-specialist providers to close the mental health treatment gap. *Curr. Psychiatry Rep.* 21, 44. https://doi.org/10.1007/s11920-019-1028-x

Raviola, G., Rose, A., Fils-Aimé, J. R., et al., 2020. Development of a comprehensive, sustained community mental health system in post-earthquake Haiti, 2010–2019. *Glob. Ment. Health* 7, e6. https://doi.org/10.1017/gmh.2019.33

Raviola, G., Severe, J., Therosme, T., et al., 2013. The 2010 Haiti earthquake response. *Psychiatr. Clin. North Am.* 36, 431–450. https://doi.org/10.1016/j.psc.2013.05.006

Rhatigan, J., Jain, S., Mukherjee, J., Porter, M.l, 2009. Applying the Care Delivery Value Chain: HIV/AIDS Care in Resource Poor Settings (Working Paper No. 09–093). Harvard Business School.

Shogren, K. A., Wehmeyer, M. L., 2015. A framework for research and intervention design in supported decision-making. *Inclusion* 3, 17–23. https://doi.org/10.1352/2326-6988-3.1.17

Singla, D. R., Kohrt, B. A., Murray, L. K., et al., 2017. Psychological treatments for the world: Lessons from low- and middle-income countries. *Annu. Rev. Clin. Psychol.* 13, 149–181. https://doi.org/10.1146/annurev-clinpsy-032816-045217

Smith, S., Kayiteshonga, Y., Misago, C. N., et al., 2017. Integrating mental health care into primary care: The case of one rural district in Rwanda. *Intervention* 15, 136–150.

Smith, S. L., Franke, M. F., Rusangwa, C., et al., 2020. Outcomes of a primary care mental health implementation program in rural Rwanda: A quasi-experimental implementation-effectiveness study. *PLOS ONE* 15, e0228854. https://doi.org/10.1371/journal.pone.0228854

Smith, S. L., Grelotti, D. J., Fils-Aime, R., et al., 2015. Catatonia in resource-limited settings: A case series and treatment protocol. *Gen. Hosp. Psychiatry* 37, 89–93. https://doi.org/10.1016/j.genhosppsych.2014.10.009

Smith, S. L., Misago, C. N., Osrow, R. A., et al., 2017. Evaluating process and clinical outcomes of a primary care mental health integration project in rural Rwanda: A prospective mixed-methods protocol. *BMJ Open* 7, e014067. https://doi.org/10.1136/bmjopen-2016-014067

Stastny, P., Lovell, A., Hannah, J., et al., 2020. Crisis response as a human rights flashpoint: Critical elements of community support for individuals experiencing significant emotional distress. *Health Hum. Rights J.* 22, 105–120.

United Nations General Assembly, 2007. Convention on the Rights of Persons with Disabilities: Resolution/Adopted by the General Assembly (No. A/RES/61/106). United Nations General Assembly.

van Ginneken, N., Tharyan, P., Lewin, S., et al., 2013. Non-specialist Health Worker Interventions for the Care of Mental, Neurological and Substance-Abuse Disorders in Low- and Middle-Income Countries, in The Cochrane Collaboration (ed.), *Cochrane Database of Systematic Reviews*. John Wiley & Sons, Ltd, Chichester, UK.

Verdeli, H., Therosme, T., Eustache, E., et al., 2016. Community norms and human rights: supervising Haitian colleagues on Interpersonal Psychotherapy (IPT) with a depressed and abused pregnant woman. *J. Clin. Psychol.* 72, 847–855. https://doi.org/10.1002/jclp.22366

WHO, 2018. Mental Health Atlas 2017. WHO, Geneva.

WHO, 2012. Who QualityRights tool kit: Assessing and Improving Quality and Human Rights in Mental Health and Social Care Facilities. WHO, Geneva.

21

Lived Experience Perspectives from Australia, Canada, Kenya, Cameroon and South Africa – Conceptualising the Realities

Charlene Sunkel, Andrew Turtle, Sylvio A. Gravel, Iregi Mwenja and Marie Angele Abanga

Abstract

The Global Mental Health Peer Network (GMHPN) is an international lived experience organisation, constituted by a diverse group of people with lived experience of a mental health condition. The expertise by experience within the GMHPN provides valuable insights into the realities of navigating both health and societal systems to obtain services and interventions to discover a means for recovery, while at the same time respect and protect human rights. In this chapter, we as lived experience advocates from the GMHPN provides perspectives from Canada, Kenya, Australia, Cameroon and South Africa, and share the realities of what is experienced by persons with lived experience within these country contexts and share our perspectives on the domestication of the CRPD in relation to mental health, human rights and legal capacity. We further share insights into our own lived experience journeys that give substance to the conceptualisation of the debate around mental health, human rights and coercion in view of the CRPD.

INTRODUCTION

The Global Mental Health Peer Network (GMHPN) was established to create an extensive, globally diverse mental health community and cadre of leadership among persons with lived experience of mental health conditions in order to enhance the value of sharing initiatives, perspectives and the realities that the lived experience community face.[1] The GMHPN believes in a human rights-based approach within an operating framework focused on empowerment, recovery and peer support – placing an emphasis on the critical element of lived experience being authentically involved in transformation, destigmatisation, quality of life, equality and equity. The GMHPN further strongly supports and advocates for a person-centred and recovery-based approach to mental health care and services as a human right. It is challenging the paradigm of medical traditions and institutional care models that have subjected

[1] www.gmhpn.org/.

individuals with lived experience of mental health conditions to severe human rights violations, developed structures of societal segregation, and denied the inherent human dignity and voice of this community.

Coercion is among the most prevalent of human rights abuses that is not an isolated practice in terms of receiving mental health care or treatment – the definition is understood as the 'practice of persuading someone to do something by using force or threats' – thus is when someone else forces their values on others.[2] By this definition and in relation to actual experiences of persons with lived experience of mental health conditions, this may include being forced to terminate studies, live in a certain dwelling or hand over finances to a relative or administrator – and of course, being forced into undesirable health or mental health treatment options – because of the presumption or false perception that the person with lived experience of a mental health condition is automatically unable to manage aspects of their own lives or future. Paternalism has been historically a 'culture' where others adopted the belief that they know what's in the 'best interest' of that person and feel compelled to make decisions for that person to 'protect' them from making wrong decisions. Doesn't everyone at times make wrong decisions – isn't that what makes everyone human? The real question however is to what extent have countries domesticated the Convention on the Rights of Persons with Disabilities (CRPD) within countries, and whether this transition has afforded persons with lived experience with mental health conditions inherent worth as a person.

In this chapter we, through our own lived experiences, recovery journeys and advocacy work, give perspectives on the realities experienced by persons with lived experience in relation to mental health, human rights and legal capacity in the contexts of Australia, Canada, Kenya, Cameroon and South Africa.

CHANGING PARADIGMS IN LEGAL CAPACITY IN AUSTRALIA: A STORY OUT OF EXPERIENCE

Andrew Turtle

In Australia, there is a rich history of mental health legislation within state governments around legal capacity. Laws of involuntary hospitalisation and treatment in relation to the capacity of adults are often associated with informed consent to psychiatric treatment, seclusion and restraint. Each state and territory has its own Mental Health Act that governs the legal capacity an individual has during 'involuntary' detainment into psychiatric hospitals.[3]

---

[2] Lexico Dictionaries (2020). Meaning of Coercion by Lexico. Retrieved 7 May 2020, from www.lexico.com/definition/coercion.

[3] Office of the Public Advocate [Victoria, Australia]. (2020). The illusion of 'choice and control': the difficulties for people with complex and challenging support needs to obtain adequate supports under the NDIS. Retrieved 7 May 2020, from www.publicadvocate.vic.gov.au/resources/research-reports/519-the-illusion-of-choice-and-control?path=.

In November 2019 I was given access to the records of my third and longest time I was 'scheduled' to a psychiatric hospital in New South Wales, Australia. Being 'scheduled' meant being detained involuntarily in a psychiatric hospital based on the fact that I 'required psychiatric treatment' and was 'at harm to myself and/or others'.[4] I was involuntary detained in a mental health facility under a Community Treatment Order as it was deemed that I was legally incapable of making decisions for myself.[5] On my first and second admission to hospital I was released into my parents' care; however, as I had turned eighteen by my third admission, under law, my parents did not have power to act on my behalf based on being a 'near relative'.[6] Under the Mental Health Act of 1990, neither myself, my parents nor my treating psychiatrist or psychologist had control over my treatments; instead, my care was placed into the hands of the hospital's psychiatrist and nursing staff, who unsuccessfully trialled me on a new medication and had no understanding of what I was like when I was well. My experience related to legal capacity and involuntary treatment was no doubt quite traumatic.

In September 2004, I was 'scheduled' under the Mental Health Act 1990 into the Pialla Psychiatric Ward in Penrith Hospital, New South Wales. I had been brought to this 'public' hospital as a result of delusional behaviour, being 'unresponsive verbally when questioned', 'demonstrating persecutory and grandiose delusions', as well as 'relaying persistent paranoid statements'. I was scheduled under the Act for 47 days in the Pialla Psychiatric Ward prior to being admitted into the 'private' Northside West program for three weeks.

The difference I perceived between private and public hospitals was enormous. I perceived that the 'public' hospital provided 'care', focused on reactive, short-term, drug-related treatments aiming to suppress symptoms, whereas the 'private' hospital delivered a proactive program in which therapeutic options were provided, including daily mindfulness walks, gym access and even laughter therapy. In the 'public' system, by contrast, I felt like I was maintained in a 'zombie-like' medicated trance, with my paranoia, delusions and lack of insight being preyed upon by other 'scheduled' patients. In a place where I was constantly bored due to the rare involvement in any activity or recreational outlet, it took seventeen days for an occupational therapist to determine that I had 'strengths' and that I was not always paranoid, irritable, insightless and delusional. Within my first four days of admission I was given eight different medications, and I would go on to take fifteen different medications throughout my time in the public hospital system, without any consultation with my external treating professionals. At one point a nurse expressed to my parents that the best form of treatment was to 'keep their minds blank'. At another time the staff declined an opportunity for me to do music and other forms of exercise

---

[4] Bird, S. (2011). Capacity to consent to treatment. *Australian Family Physician* 40(4).
[5] NSW Mental Health Act 2007 No 8. Retrieved 7 May 2020, from www.legislation.nsw.gov.au/#/view/act/2007/8.
[6] Bird. Capacity to consent to treatment.

that had been keeping me well in the community, due to my requiring monitoring within close confines of the observatory realms of the hospital ward.

Since my hospitalisation in 2004 there has been a change to the law in mental health services in New South Wales,[7] as well as a paradigm shift into legal capacity in Australia in light of the CRPD.[8] When Australia ratified the CRPD on the 17 July 2008, this declaration initiated a commitment towards a 'supported decision-making' model in contrast to the 'substituted decision-making' framework that had been so evident in my hospital stay.[9] This change in perspective ensured that persons with disability receive the support they need to exercise their legal capacity on an equal basis with others, in all aspects of their lives. Supported decision-making ensures that the person receiving care is given help to make decisions when exercising legal capacity, and ensures that family members or nominated support persons can make decisions based on a person's known preferences.[10] As a local area coordinator working in partnership with the National Disability Insurance Scheme (NDIS), for example, I conduct planning meetings that allow participants and their informal supports to collaborate in determining their goals and to give them choice and control over the types of support they require for their recovery.

Born out of the conceptual frameworks of the CRPD, NDIS has created a new generation of legislation around legal capacity in Australia.[11] Advance care directives also provide a relatively new way to give guidance to healthcare professionals and healthcare providers about how people want to be treated if they lose capacity. Advance care directories provide information about where one wishes or does not wish to be cared for, and by whom, and what treatment one does or does not want to be carried out.[12] An advance statement may set out a person's preferences about electroconvulsive treatment, for example. While advance care directives have no legal force in New South Wales, they clearly resonate with the principles embodied in the CRPD and should be incorporated into the mental health legislation in New South Wales to give people more legal capacity in making decisions about their own care.[13] Perhaps, however,

---

[7] United Nations. Convention the Rights of Persons with Disabilities and Optional Protocol (CRPD) (2007). Geneva. Retrieved 7 May 2020, from www.un.org/disabilities/documents/convention/convopt prot-e.pdf.

[8] McSherry, B. and Wilson, K. (2005). The concept of capacity in Australian mental health law reform: going in the wrong direction? *International Journal of Law and Psychiatry*.

[9] Mental Health Coordinating Council (2015). Chapter 5 Section F: Advanced Care Directives in *Mental Health Rights Manual*. Retrieved 8 May 2020, from https://mhrm.mhcc.org.au/chapters/5-substitute-decision-making-and-capacity/chapter-5-section-f-advance-care-directives/

[10] Warr, D. et al (2017). *Choice, Control and the NDIS: Service Users' Perspectives on Having Choice and Control in the New National Disability Insurance Scheme*. The University of Melbourne.

[11] NDIS (n.d.). Snapshot 4 – Functional Capacity and Mental Health. Retrieved 8 May 2020, from www.ndis.gov.au/understanding/how-ndis-works/mental-health-and-ndis.

[12] Mental Health Coordinating Council. Advance Care Directives.

[13] Government of Canada. (2020). Rights of people with disabilities. Retrieved 7 May 2020, from www.canada.ca/en/canadian-heritage/services/rights-people-disabilities.html.

treating professionals are not quite ready to actualise these models, which yet show so much promise.

It is hoped that this new model of supported decision-making will be incorporated into mental health legislation in Australia rather than a model of compulsory care and treatment. I would like to think that with this paradigm shift, myself and those whom I prefer to act on my behalf (i.e., my parents and my private mental health treating team), would have more legal capacity to intervene in my care if I were scheduled into a psychiatric hospital in Australia today, where they would be acting in a supported decision-making capacity to enable me to make empowered decisions about my rehabilitation, recovery and ongoing journey in the real world. In the wake of the CRPD, and its emphasis on non-coercive treatment and care, mental health laws should allow for people to have the capacity to consent to or refuse treatment, even under involuntary care, providing a more proactive therapeutic approach rather than the reactive, sedative-based control methods that set the tone of care I was provided more than fifteen years ago.

CANADIAN LIVED EXPERIENCE PERSPECTIVE – RIGHTS, FREEDOMS AND PEER SUPPORT

Sylvio Gravel

Canada ratified the CRPD on 11 March 2010.[14] This was done in consultation with the ten provinces and three territories, Aboriginal Self-Government and Canadians – particularly those from the disability community. That being claimed, its implementation is perhaps hindered most by Canada's reservations to Article 12 of the CRPD on legal capacity for persons with lived experience of mental health conditions.

The overseeing CRPD Committee has stated that Article 12 only permits 'supported decision-making' regimes, yet most Canadian provinces maintain their 'substitute decision-making' regimes. This means that many Canadians with lived experience with mental health conditions continue to be denied legal capacity to make decisions related to their healthcare, housing, legal affairs and finances.[15] But changes are afoot, as new legislation has been introduced in different provinces across the country, and recent court decisions have started to push policymakers in this direction. For example, while supported decision-making regimes are not yet ubiquitous throughout Canada, some academics look to British Columbia's Representation Agreement Act as a model that has received praise from the disability

---

[14] Hoffman, S., Sritharan, L., & Tejpar, A. (2016). Is the UN Convention on the Rights of Persons with Disabilities impacting mental health laws and policies in high-income countries? A case study of implementation in Canada. *BMC International Health and Human Rights*, 16(1). https://doi.org/10.1186/s12914-016-0103-1

[15] Hoffman, S. & Laguwaran, L. & Tejpar, A. (2016). The UN Convention on the Rights of Persons with Disabilities and its Impact on Mental Health Law and Policy in Canada. In J. A. Chandler, C. M. Flood (eds). *Law and Mind: Mental Health Law and Policy in Canada*.

community. Under this Act, a person with a lived experience of a mental health condition can communicate an intention to select a trusted representative who will provide support in managing the person's healthcare, personal care, finances and legal affairs. British Columbia's decision-making regime is also heralded for safeguarding against abuse of the system; a person with a lived experience of a mental health condition must select someone to monitor their trusted representative to ensure he or she is not abusing his or her responsibilities.

While this system is more closely aligned with the intentions of Article 12 of the CRPD, it is still probably not fully compliant, in that the trusted representative is granted the authority to 'substitute' decisions for the person with lived experience of mental health conditions under the qualification that they comply with the individual's wishes if found to be 'reasonable'.[16] Two obligations to the CRPD are to ensure access to justice on an equal basis with others (Article 13), and making sure that persons with disabilities enjoy the right to liberty and security and are not deprived of their liberty unlawfully or arbitrarily (Article 14).[17]

The Canadian Charter of Rights and Freedoms is a part of the Canadian Constitution, but is not yet necessarily aligned with CRPD, as mentioned earlier – especially not Article 12.[18] The Charter is a set of laws containing the basic rules about how the country operates. Section 15 of the Charter makes it clear that every individual in Canada – regardless of race, religion, national or ethnic origin, colour, gender, age or physical or mental disability – is to be considered equal. This means that governments must not discriminate on any of these grounds in its laws or programs. At the same time as it protects equality, the Charter also allows for certain laws or programs aimed at improving the situation of disadvantaged individuals or groups. The Charter is divided into seven categories and includes fundamental freedoms, democratic rights, language rights, mobility rights, minority language educational rights, legal rights and equality rights. Such a Charter should mean more than words, and should involve an investment in the infrastructure required to support such an obligation and an alignment with the CRPD in all articles. Such infrastructure should involve adequate monitoring and accountability mechanisms to track concrete changes in how these rights have been implemented and where implementation is still lacking; these mechanisms should have diverse representation involved – for example, persons with lived experience of mental health conditions providing perspective from mental health-related rights.

During my earlier career as a police officer it often frustrated me that I, as a law enforcement officer tasked with maintaining the peace, was the only resource available to someone dealing with a mental health problem, especially if there was a situation where laws were in conflict with their behaviour or situation. They

---

[16] CRPD.
[17] Constitution Acts, 1867 to 1982. Retrieved 7 May 2020, from https://laws-lois.justice.gc.ca/eng/const/page-15.html.
[18] World Health Organization. (2020). WHO MiNDbank: Mental Health Act – British Columbia. Retrieved 7 May 2020, from www.mindbank.info/item/1034.

needed more than what the justice system was built to handle and more than the resources available to me (as a law enforcement officer). Incarceration in detention centres was often the only option available in trying to help ensure the safety of persons who were in emotional or mental distress and seen to be in conflict with the law. Far too many people with lived experience of mental health conditions are still to this day temporarily incarcerated in detention centres due to the lack of availability of the proper community-based mental health resources and services that speak to their unique needs and based on how they define their own needs.

In British Columbia, the Mental Health Act of 2011 allows for persons with lived experience of mental health conditions to draw up an Advance Directive, declaring their will and preferences in terms of mental health care and services should they find themselves in crisis. With safeguards in place, such as periodical reviews, the Act does however allow for a psychiatrist to order an involuntary admission should they deem it necessary.[19]

There is, however, hope, for people who are seen as criminal offenders whilst they are in reality struggling with mental health problems; the province of Newfoundland and Labrador have revived a court program that offers an alternative, focusing on treatment instead of time behind bars. This focus on treatment, however, is in conflict with the CRPD, since treatment would not be presented as a choice, but rather in terms of an ultimatum to choose between treatment or a judicial sentence.

The Court is designed to provide an increased level of support, both medical and community based, to accused persons appearing before it. The Mental Health Court is based on the recognition that certain offenders who live with a mental health condition may commit offences as a consequence of symptoms of a mental health condition or due to lifestyle issues related to such a condition.[20] In the context of a person with lived experience of a mental health condition, the Court recognises that inadequate or inappropriate housing, unemployment, lack of support, non-compliance with medications and inappropriate self-medication with alcohol or drugs may be contributing factors to committing a criminal offense. One of the goals is to provide effective treatment options instead of, or in addition to, criminal sanctions crafted to reflect the needs of the offender and the community. Interventions are developed in collaboration with key community partners, who provide community-based support and medical support to these individuals. In the past two years, more than 130 criminal cases have gone before Saint John's revived Mental Health Court. At this point in time there is no evidence to offer yet as to the positive outcomes of this new court, but it could produce qualitative data in the near future.

---

[19] Atlantic. (2020). Success of Saint John Mental Health Court has advocates calling for expansion in N. B. Retrieved 7 May 2020, from https://atlantic.ctvnews.ca/success-of-saint-john-mental-health-court-has-advocates-calling-for-expansion-in-n-b-1.4689070.

[20] World Health Organization. (2020). About WHO QualityRights. Retrieved 7 May 2020, from https://qualityrights.org/resources/about-qualityrights/.

Structured peer support should be a part of the resources called upon to help transform the mental health system to align with international human rights instruments such as the CRPD. Peer support is extremely important in advancing the right to participation, and can be defined as the foundation through which persons with lived experience connect with empathy towards those who have been traumatised and who find themselves in emotional or mental distress – it is through our peers that many of us survived. Peer support is a healing process and source of reassurance and guidance, and can be seen as a facilitator to help a person identify what services they may find beneficial – be it medical, psychological or other forms of psychosocial support. Peers receiving support from peers are under no obligation to continue the support that has been offered, allowing them to make the choice based on their will and preference and self-identified needs.

It is important to acknowledge that no single mental health service on its own can provide everything that a person needs; therefore a comprehensive and recovery-based approach is key to allowing the person to build a service and support package that is based on what they require to recover. All services and support, however, need to work as one to ensure maximum impact for the benefit of the person.

In my view Canada would go a long way in ensuring coercion in mental health is eliminated by investing in mental health resources at the social level and empowering peer-support infrastructures, instead of imposing and using enforcement agencies, who are not trained or equipped to work as if they were highly trained social workers. For them, it is just one more thing they have to do as law enforcement officers amongst everything else they 'enforce', and it makes no sense at all to deploy them as the first, and sometimes only, point of contact.

THE RIGHT TO LEGAL CAPACITY FOR PEOPLE WITH LIVED EXPERIENCE IN KENYA

Iregi Mwenja

There is a commonly held, yet false, assumption that people with lived experience of mental health conditions lack the capacity to assume responsibility, manage their affairs and make decisions about their lives. These misconceptions contribute to their ongoing marginalisation, disenfranchisement and invisibility within communities.[21]

Kenya has made steps to promote legal capacity in its 2010 Constitution and through the CRPD, which was ratified in 2008. The CRPD now forms part of the laws of Kenya after Article 2(5)1 and 2(6) of the Kenyan Constitution incorporated all treaties and conventions ratified by Kenya.[22]

---

[21] Ndetei, D., Muthike, J. & Nandoya, E., 2017. Kenya's mental health law. *BJPsych. International*, 14(4), 96–97.

[22] KNCHR. (2016). *A Briefing Paper on Implementing Article 12 of the Convention on the Rights of Persons with Disabilities Regarding Legal Capacity in Kenya*. KNCHR. Retrieved from www.knchr.org/Portals/0/Disability%20Publications/Implementing%20Article%2012%20of%20the%20CRPD_Legal%20Capacity.pdf?ver=2018-06-03-174713-957

Conversely, Kenya's policymakers and implementers have not understood the full implications of Article 12 of the CRPD.[23] Even the existing laws like the 1989 Mental Health Act (amended in 1991) has provisions that are outdated, at odds with Kenya's Constitution and incompatible with present international standards, and which fail to address the patient's right to information, consent to treatment, confidentiality and conditions in mental health facilities.[24] In addition, Section 26 of the Mental Health Act allow for the deprivation or restriction of legal capacity by courts and directors of psychiatric hospitals.[25]

Similarly, the Kenyan judicial process for determination of an adult's legal capacity fails to place any emphasis on their choices, will or preferences. Instead, laws are premised on an assumption of the adult's incapacity, contrary to provisions of Article 12 of the CRPD.[26]

To address these challenges, the mental health community in Kenya pushed through the process of amending the Mental Health Act. A nominated member of the Senate of Kenya's bicameral parliament, Senator Sylvia Kasanga became the face of the review process; however, this was resisted by various government departments and stakeholders who were unwilling to change the attitudes and practices that the law review sought to change.

The Mental Health Amendment Bill 2018 that was passed by the Senate in July 2019 was forwarded to the National Assembly for debate in Kenya's bicameral parliament, but sadly the Bill still allowed the provision for involuntary hospital admission.[27]

The principle of 'Nothing About Us Without Us' was, however, grossly violated in the review process. There was generally no deliberate effort to involve or consult people with lived experience of mental health conditions, even during the mandatory public participation forums.

On the positive side, the Bill has provisions for reducing stigma, improving mental health services delivery, increasing government funding and improving the welfare of people with lived experience of mental health conditions. The Bill also tries to increase compliance with international standards, including the CRPD, even though Sections touching on legal capacity and decision-making do not fully meet the threshold set on Article 12. Section 2B(2) and 3C(2) of the Bill retained substituted decision-making clauses and failed to include appropriate and effective

---

[23] Ndetei, D., Muthike, J. & Nandoya, E., 2017. Kenya's mental health law. *BJPsych. International*, 14(4), 96–97.
[24] Muga, F., & Jenkins, R. (2010). Health care models guiding mental health policy in Kenya 1965–1997. *International Journal of Mental Health Systems*, 4(1), 9. https://doi.org/10.1186/1752-4458-4-9
[25] MDAC. (2014). *The Right to Legal Capacity in Kenya*. MDAC. 6–8. Retrieved from https://tbinternet.ohchr.org/Treaties/CRPD/Shared%20Documents/KEN/INT_CRPD_ICO_KEN_19784_E.pdf
[26] Ibid.
[27] Ndetei, D., Muthike, J. & Nandoya, E., 2017. Kenya's mental health law. BJPsych. International, 14(4), 96–97

safeguards to prevent abuse. Supported decision-making and advance directives are not explicitly sanctioned in the Bill.

Sustained advocacy efforts by mental health groups and unprecedented reporting of mental health cases by the Kenyan media saw the President direct the formation a task force in November 2019. Its mandate was to assess Kenya's mental health systems, including the legal, policy and administrative environment, to identify areas that may benefit from reform.[28]

The same year, the WHO launched the QualityRights Initiative, to unite and empower people to improve the quality of care in mental health services and to promote the rights of people with lived experience of mental health conditions and intellectual and cognitive disabilities.[29] Ghana and Kenya became the first two African countries to implement this initiative.

What we need in Kenya is express recognition of legal capacity for people with lived experience with mental health conditions in Kenya, which does not exist.[30] There is need to adopt and enforce measures to protect the legal capacity and recognition before the law of persons with disabilities. These should be measures that can be invoked before courts and for which victims receive appropriate redress.[31]

Currently, legal capacity is a legal question and institutions in Kenya can only rely on the Court's interpretation. This means that the justice, health and financial sectors and county government structures have to rely on various formal and informal guardianship mechanisms to determine legal capacity for persons with lived experience of mental health conditions and other forms of disabilities.[32]

In spite of the few gains registered, it is important that a review of all laws that touch on legal capacity or equal recognition before the law be done to check for language and compliance with Article 27 of the Kenyan Constitution and Article 12 of the CRPD.[33]

There is also need to adopt and implement a policy, legislative and administrative framework replacing all forms of substituted decision-making regimes or other deprivation of legal capacity on the basis of impairment with an appropriate system of supported decision-making.[34]

Following the devolution of health services in 2013 under the 2010 Constitution of Kenya, when counties became responsible to taking over health-related functions from the national structure, the counties were ill prepared to fulfil this role; none of

---

[28] World Health Organization, About QualityRights.
[29] KNCHR, *A Briefing Paper*.
[30] Ibid.
[31] Ibid.
[32] Ibid.
[33] National Action Plan. (2016). *National Action Plan on implementation of recommendations made by the Committee on the Rights of Persons with Disabilities in relation to the initial report of the Republic of Kenya, September 2015–June 2022*. Nairobi: State Department for Social Protection. 9–31.
[34] Treaty Bodies Treaties. (n.d.). Treaty Body Internet – Home. Retrieved 7 May 2020, from https://tbinternet.ohchr.org/_layouts/15/TreatyBodyExternal/Treaty.aspx?CountryID=30&Lang=EN.

the counties have enacted mental health policies and legislation to guide the allocation of resources and delivery of services. Effective legal instruments are necessary to ensure adequate resource allocation and protect these resources from reallocation to other 'appealing' departments of health.

A VIEW OF CAMEROON AND THE RIGHTS OF ITS LIVED EXPERIENCE COMMUNITY

Marie Abanga

Cameroon signed the CRPD in 2008, but has not ratified it.[35] With no mental health policy in place as yet, Cameroon has lagged behind in domesticating the CRPD by ensuring that the rights of persons with lived experience of mental health conditions are protected as outlined in the CRPD. The CRPD is an extraordinary instrument which was long overdue, a wake-up call and motivating instrument for further advocacy and action. As a country, we cannot continue to lag behind as far as mental health is concerned, because there is no health without mental health. Human capital is short-changed if a percentage of the population cannot be productive to their optimum because of the individual, social and economic impact of mental health conditions. In Cameroon it is still largely taboo to talk about mental health and mental illness, and even about the different options (although insufficient) available to help someone in distress. Mental health conditions as 'invisible disabilities' were for some time not included in the disability sector and therefore further marginalised. Some persons with lived experience of mental health conditions, like myself, are stepping up and advocating through sharing our stories and those of others, for a national policy on mental health to be adopted that aligns with the provisions of the CRPD. When we look at what has been achieved in other countries with similar settings in developing their mental health policies and laws, we remain hopeful in our country.

Cameroon has a population of over 25 million people who face several challenges, including a lack of resources in the education system, a poor healthcare system and poverty.[36] Furthermore, the civil crisis that has been going on in the country for more than three years has added strain on the mental health and wellbeing of the people of Cameroon. Such factors have implications in terms of the human rights of people in Cameroon where the right to health and mental health is jeopardised.

It is in the above context that there has been recorded a steep increase in the number of people struggling with mental health problems, and with very few options available for support, care or treatment. In an article on depression becoming

---

[35] United Nations Development Programme. (2019). *Human Development Report*. United Nations Development Programme. Retrieved 7 May 2020, from http://hdr.undp.org/sites/default/files/hdr2019.pdf.
[36] Cameroon Postline. (2020). Depression, serious health concern in Cameroon. Retrieved 7 May 2020, from http://cameroonpostline.com/depression-serious-health-concern-in-cameroon.

a serious health concern in Cameroon, Leocadia Bongben said that the WHO representative in Cameroon was very concerned with the situation, and that the WHO urged 'governments to allocate more human and financial resources to support mental health programs to respond to the growing burden'.[37] Bongben further noted that 'governments also need to include mental health on national agenda in line with the Brazzaville Declaration on Non-Communicable Diseases outlining the steps on how to achieve this'.

Having said the above, where does that leave those of us battling with mental health problems? What is the treatment some of us get either from the hospital or society, or both? How do our families support us? Do we have any say at all with regards to our treatment protocol or any opinion with regards to the projected mental health policy yet to be adopted in our country? Are our human rights respected when we face serious mental health crises? Today, I will honestly say that there is so much to be desired. Ours is a culture of silence concerning mental health conditions and the first point of help for anyone who presents with symptoms of a mental health condition is the native healer or spiritualist. Many are coerced in taking traditional medicines, some are chained up and even subjected to unorthodox procedures such as blood sacrifice to be 'purged of these evil spirits' through the blood they will lose.

In 2014 I was diagnosed with post-traumatic stress disorder with severe anxiety, panic attacks and disturbing effects on my mood and behaviour, resulting from a traumatic childhood of physical and emotional abuse that extended into adult relationships. Fearing to be exposed to traditional and outdated approaches, often harmful and coercive, that are yet to acknowledge a recovery- and human rights-based approach to mental health in Cameroon, I turned to online resources and specialists outside of my own country for help, where I discovered peer support. Today, through help that was offered to me, I am in a better space. I might not be completely recovered or ever say that I will never experience a relapse again (which has happened before), but I am now empowered to identify and act on my triggers and stressors and control anxious thoughts, while knowing I have my peers to turn to, should I find myself in crises. My own lived experience with a mental health condition and recovery journey has given me the opportunity to establish an organisation called the Association Hope for the Abused and Battered, to help my peers and to share our lived experience and plight in order to transform mental health on social media platforms. Through sharing our realities, we are able to inform policymakers of the critical gaps in mental health care services and emphasise that we are equally entitled and deserving of human rights and decision-making on what we need to heal, emotionally and socially, and reach our potential in life.

One of my organisation's clients was a patient in a psychiatric hospital section reserved for 'dangerous patients' called the '*cabano*'. During a visit he shared his desperate story with me, one that is a typical situation for many in Cameroon who are struggling with

---

[37] Ibid.

mental health problems. The client was diagnosed with schizophrenia when he was thirteen years old and was immediately withdrawn from school and sent to live with a native healer for one year, far away from his family home, in a very cold area of the country. It was held that such cold weather and native treatment was conducive to 'heal' him. He was kept in chains and administered traditional medicines. At some point it was alleged that family witches were after him. He became suicidal and soon began a downward spiral which lasted over twenty-five years. During this part of his journey, he was in and out of psychiatric hospital while being given medications which he had not consented to. His family had all but given up on him, and he said that he felt worthless and abandoned. This is but one story of the complete denial of a person with lived experience of a mental health condition's legal capacity, along with a number of other human rights violations involving harmful practices and failure to offer supported decision-making. Since the onset, he had been denied the opportunity to make decisions about his education, where and with whom he lived and what health and mental health care needs he had as an individual. It is these stories that call for action to place the mental health of people in Cameroon on the general health and human rights agenda.

Transforming the mental health system in Cameroon through adopting a mental health policy within a human rights framework will start giving effect to the domestication of the CRPD. Critically, policy and strategic plans should not only address the high levels of stigma, but afford people with lived experience of mental health conditions a range of treatment and care options that are community based. We, as a country, can then start moving away from institutional care and harmful practices that infringe on human rights rather than provide services that respect and protect dignity and choice in what the individual requires to be set on their recovery journey.

SOUTH AFRICAN PERSPECTIVE OF COERCION IN MENTAL HEALTH

Charlene Sunkel

South Africa became a State Party of the CRPD in November 2007. Following the initial country report (CRPD/C/ZAF/1 and Corr. 1) submission, the CRPD Committee adopted the concluding observations at its 413th meeting in September 2018. The CRPD Committee raised several concerns and recommendations, and specifically related to legal capacity noted that 'the current guardianship and mental health laws, which maintain a substitute decision-making regime, and the absence of legislation and supported decision-making mechanisms for persons with disabilities that uphold the autonomy, rights, will and preferences of persons with disabilities in all areas of life' and recommended to 'repeal all legislation that allows for substitute decision-making, and adopt legislation on supported decision-making and measures'.[38]

---

[38] United Nations. (2018). Committee on the Rights of Persons with Disabilities: Concluding observations on the initial report of South Africa. Retrieved 25 June 2020, from https://tbinternet.ohchr.org/_layouts/15/treatybodyexternal/Download.aspx?symbolno=CRPD%2fC%2fZAF%2fCO%2f1&Lang=en

The South African Mental Health Care Act of 2002, however, continues to legislate involuntary treatment and hospitalisation, which has remained unchanged despite the CRPD Committee's recommendations to 'repeal all legislation that authorizes forced institutionalization and repeal all laws that allow for deprivation of liberty on the basis of impairment'.[39]

The South African government has taken some positive actions in terms of involving persons with lived experience of mental health conditions in policy, through:

1) the establishment of the Presidential Working Group on Disability, mainly mandated to advise on the implementation of the White Paper on the Rights of Persons with Disabilities which emerged as an instrument to domesticate the CRPD;[40] and
2) the Ministerial Advisory Committee on Mental Health, who are mandated to advise on the implementation of the Mental Health Policy and Strategic Plan 2013–2020.[41]

On both these structures, persons with lived experience with mental health conditions are represented. In my view, and despite this involvement of representation, very little progress has been seen in terms of implementation, nor in addressing the concerns and recommendations proposed by the CRPD Committee regarding coercion and legal capacity. I believe that the government should make a better effort in strengthening its relationship with the disability sector and recognise persons with all types of disabilities as key partners who contribute valuable expertise that would not otherwise be obtained elsewhere. Only then can we effectively domesticate the CRPD and explore and implement evidence-based alternatives to coercive practices.

Describing my own lived experience gives some context to a South African perspective of coercion and failure of being awarded the right to decision-making or supported decision-making.

Sometime after I received a diagnosis of schizophrenia it was communicated to me, or rather decided for me, based on my diagnosis (not on who I was as an individual irrespective of a diagnosis) that I will never be able to work, live on my own, be independent or make my own decisions, and will never be able to 'live a normal life'. Over a space of several years I had numerous hospital admissions on the 'presumption' of being a danger to myself and/or others and in need of medical treatment. Although most hospital admissions were classified as 'voluntary', it was,

---

[39] Ibid.
[40] Government Gazette. South African Government. (2016). White Paper on the Rights of Persons with Disabilities. Retrieved 25 June 2020, from www.gov.za/sites/default/files/gcis_document/201603/39792gon230.pdf
[41] Department of Health. South African Government (n.d.). National Mental Health Policy Framework 2013–2020. Retrieved on 1 March 2021, from www.health.gov.za/wp-content/uploads/2020/11/National-Mental-Health-Policy-Framework-and-Strategic-Plan-2013-2020.pdf.

however, threatened that should I refuse to be admitted voluntarily, I would be admitted as an involuntary patient. As a voluntary admission I could refuse treatment, and had attempted to do so on several occasions, only to be threatened again with having my voluntary status changed to involuntary, which would not have allowed me to leave the hospital until the medical team decided to discharge me. Either way I was deprived of decision-making and not afforded consideration for my will and preferences. The main reason why I so often expressed my unwillingness to be admitted to a psychiatric hospital – although it made no difference in the decisions the medical team took on my behalf – was the fact that the psychiatric hospital setting presented more as a prison (both the physical and attitudinal environments), than a place of care, compassion and recovery. Even though at the time I did acknowledge the need for treatment and care to help set me off on a recovery path, I just could not see that being obtained in an environment that was not dignified or accepting of me as a human being and holder of rights.

In my view, the mental health system in South Africa has made some degree of progress towards a more human rights-based framework of service delivery and policy, but has some shortcomings that could be improved upon to make a significant stride towards eliminating coercion and ensure compliance with the CRPD. This includes, but is not restricted to:

1) providing a person-centred care package that first and foremost considers and respects all the rights of the person, and ensures that treatment and recovery is guided by the individual without any power imbalances;
2) improving both physical and attitudinal environments at psychiatric hospitals and community-based clinic services to create a space that is conducive for recovery and ensures that people feel safe, cared for and respected; and
3) introducing peer-to-peer support as a fundamental component of a person-centred care package.

On the latter (peer support), South Africa lags somewhat behind in recognition of peer-to-peer support work forming part of service delivery, despite evidence indicating its value in advancing recovery and potential to reduce coercion.

In a literature review on alternatives to coercion in mental health settings, Gooding and colleagues described a number of examples of peer-led initiatives that lead to a range of positive health and mental health outcomes of individuals receiving peer support and noted a reduction in coercive practices.[42] Peer support provides for a unique opportunity to focus mental health care and services on the overall real-life experiences of the individual, placing the person at the centre of

---

[42] Gooding, P., McSherry, B., & Roper, C. (2018). Alternatives to coercion in mental health settings: a literature review. Retrieved 1 July 2020, from https://socialequity.unimelb.edu.au/__data/assets/pdf_file/0012/2898525/Alternatives-to-Coercion-Literature-Review-Melbourne-Social-Equity-Institute.pdf.

decision-making in policy and practice. Peer support promotes choice, shared decision-making, empowerment and care that is tailored to the individual's unique set of needs, interests, will and preferences.

CONCLUSION

The extent to which countries have adopted their commitments in terms of domestication of the CRPD no doubt varies and many have (often with good intention) made efforts to align policies and laws to incorporate the rights of persons with all disabilities as outlined in the CRPD. The variation within countries is often related to involuntary treatment and coercion in mental health, where many countries still legislate substitute decision-making as opposed to supported decision-making regimes.

We do acknowledge that at times we, as persons with a lived experience of a mental health condition, may lose capacity as a result of momentary impairment caused by mental health problems, and may find it particularly difficult to make informed decisions about important aspects of our lives. Respectfully, there are however different and often opposing views on instances where people with lived experience of mental health conditions may lose capacity; our views on this matter are coherent with the views and experiences of members of the GMHPN, who are and have been users of mental health care services. We acknowledge that in such instances we may need support to express the choices that are aligned with our own values and principles, where 'support' is the operative term. Substitute decision-making and paternalism however has been a 'symptom' of our diagnoses for decades, which far too often have led to coercion, lost dignity and disempowerment, and even abuse.

We believe it is critical for much more demographically diverse voices of people with lived experience of mental health conditions to join this global debate and become instrumental in finding context-specific alternatives to coercion and practices that pose harm to our mental health and overall wellbeing. To truly uphold our rights, specifically in regards to legal capacity, our realities and lived experiences must be central to policy and practice, which must also consider the contexts in which we live and in which we need to thrive.

Finally, the value and benefits of peer support (peer support groups and peer-to-peer support) cannot be underestimated, nor the evidence be denied as a cost-effective and human rights-orientated alternative approach in efforts to eliminate coercion and promote legal capacity (decision-making and supported decision-making) of individuals with lived experience of mental health conditions.

22

In the Pursuit of Justice: Advocacy by and for Hyper-marginalized People with Psychosocial Disabilities through the Law and Beyond

Lydia X. Z. Brown and Shain M. Neumeier

Abstract

Disabled advocates' work has resulted in many domestic and international laws enshrining equal rights to access, opportunity, and inclusion, yet implementation lags far behind. Even where disability rights laws carry force, disabled people at the margins of the margins face appalling human rights violations, many deriving from social and legal structures designed to enact harm on marginalized, exploited, and targeted communities. Yet even laws meant to protect disabled people in theory often enable abuse and harm in reality, such as guardianship and involuntary commitment laws that may contravene the Convention on the Rights of Persons with Disabilities. Additionally, ableist oppression does not impact all disabled people equally, both across different disabilities, and among disabled people differentiated by race, gender, class, sexuality, language, or nation.

In this chapter, we provide an overview of existing U.S. and international legal frameworks governing rights, freedoms, and legal capacity for people with psychosocial disabilities, and then discuss applications of those laws and policies in current contexts. In both sections, we describe harms disabled people experience in the United States, ways in which legal structures enable or fail to prevent those harms, and potential avenues for legal and nonlegal advocacy. We highlight ways in which current law fails to adequately recognize people with psychosocial disabilities as full persons with autonomy and dignity.

1 INTRODUCTION

Disabled advocates' work over many decades to advance civil and human rights frameworks for disability has resulted in many domestic and international laws enshrining equal rights to access, opportunity, and inclusion, yet implementation lags far behind. Even where disability rights laws carry force, disabled people at the margins of the margins face appalling human rights violations, many deriving from social and legal structures designed to enact harm on marginalized, exploited, and targeted communities. Yet even laws meant to protect disabled people in theory often enable abuse and harm in reality, such as guardianship and involuntary commitment laws that may contravene Article 12 protections in the Convention on the Rights of Persons with Disabilities.

Many disabled advocates, including both of the authors, also discuss disability hierarchies in advocacy – the belief that while some disabilities are acceptable, others are uncomfortable, scary, or ugly. That hierarchy often leaves people with intellectual and psychosocial disabilities at the bottom. In other words, ableist oppression does not impact all disabled people equally, both across different types of disabilities, and among disabled people differentiated by race, gender, class, sexuality, language, or nation. Here, we seek to address particular challenges and harms facing people with psychosocial disabilities in particular, and how human rights and social justice advocacy might intervene.

In this chapter, we first provide an overview of existing U.S. and international legal frameworks governing rights, freedoms, and legal capacity for people with psychosocial disabilities, and then discuss applications of those laws and policies in current contexts. In both of these sections, we will describe harms disabled people experience in the United States, ways in which legal structures enable or fail to prevent those harms, and potential avenues for legal and nonlegal advocacy against them. In particular, we will highlight the ways in which current law fails to adequately recognize people with psychosocial disabilities as full persons with autonomy and dignity.

2 LEGAL AND POLICY OVERVIEW

2.1 *General Disability Rights Law under U.S. and International Frameworks*

Many countries across the world have sought to address the lasting legacies of historical injustices against people with psychosocial and other disabilities by enacting laws prohibiting discrimination in various forms and contexts on the basis of disability. In the United States, the primary federal disability rights laws are the Rehabilitation Act and the Americans with Disabilities Act of 1990 (ADA), which prohibit disability discrimination in access to programs and services in different but overlapping contexts (Americans with Disabilities Act of 1990; Rehabilitation Act of 1973). Both laws require covered entities to provide reasonable accommodations that would allow people with disabilities to access their facilities, programs and services to the same extent as nondisabled people (Americans with Disabilities Act of 1990; Existing facilities, 2003). Because the legal definition of disability encompasses nearly all physical and mental impairments that substantially limit a major life activity, the statutes impose a duty to provide an equally wide range of accommodations (Americans with Disabilities Act of 1990; Definition of "disability," 2016; Rehabilitation Act of 1973). The U.S. Supreme Court has ruled that the ADA in particular includes a community integration mandate that prohibits states from segregating disabled people in institutional settings (Olmstead v. L.C. ex rel. Zimring, 1999).

International law protects the human rights of people with disabilities through various United Nations treaties and conventions. In particular, the Convention on the Rights of Persons with Disabilities (CRPD) guarantees the rights of people with disabilities to physical and mental integrity and prohibits sterilization on the basis of disability (The United Nations, 2006, art. 17, 23(1)(c)). Among the most radical sections of the CRPD is Article 12, which establishes people with disabilities' rights to equal recognition before the law and legal capacity in all areas of life (The United Nations, 2006, art. 12(1, 2)). Under Article 12, not only would States parties have to put in place significant legal safeguards against the unnecessary loss of rights, but they would also have to provide access to supports that would enable people with disabilities to exercise their legal capacity (The United Nations, 2006, art. 12(3, 4)). These protections require States parties to make significant changes to if not abolish the institution of guardianship, which takes away a person's legal capacity on the basis of disability. The United States, however, has failed to ratify the CRPD, much less come into compliance with it (U.S. National Council on Disability, 2016).

2.2 Involuntary Inpatient and Outpatient Commitment

Neither state nor federal disability rights law in the United States meaningfully protects people from involuntary confinement and treatment on the basis of psychosocial disability. All fifty states still allow for detention and forced treatment in mental health facilities under certain circumstances (Treatment Advocacy Center, 2018). These laws contain provisions for both short-term hospitalization without a hearing as well as longer periods of court-ordered civil commitment (Treatment Advocacy Center, 2011; Treatment Advocacy Center, 2018). Some states have also established drug courts that can order people to participate in inpatient or outpatient addiction treatment based on a process that mirrors the civil commitment process (Gray, 2016). Meanwhile, many state laws effectively allow indefinite detention of at least a subset of people, particularly those who have committed acts of sexual violence (Hamilton-Smith, 2018). The Supreme Court of the United States has held that this does not violate a person's constitutional due process rights, even if psychiatric confinement begins after that person has already served a criminal sentence for the same conduct (Kansas v. Hendricks, 1997).

States can generally commit someone involuntarily to a mental health facility if, because of a mental health condition, a person poses a direct risk of harm to themselves or others (Treatment Advocacy Center, 2018). Many state laws also allow commitment if a person is so gravely disabled that they cannot care for or protect themselves in the community (Treatment Advocacy Center, 2018). Various states have, either through statute or case law, imposed a requirement that there be no less restrictive setting in which a person could be kept safe (Treatment Advocacy Center, 2018). Although a few states' laws require proof beyond a reasonable doubt for inpatient commitment as in a criminal case, the U.S. Constitution only requires "clear and convincing evidence" that a person meets the standard for civil commitment (Addington v. Texas, 1979; Conservatorship of Davis, 1981; Superintendent of Worcester State Hosp. v. Hagberg, 1978). Courts have ruled in favor of commitment for reasons that go beyond a person's own conduct, including their homelessness or vulnerability to violence and exploitation (In re Det. of R.H., 2014; In re J.C., 2001).

Outpatient providers in all but three states can use the courts to require people to undergo specific forms of treatment, such as medication or electroconvulsive therapy (Treatment Advocacy Center, 2018). There is no consistency in the legal standard in outpatient commitment hearings (Ridgely, Borum, & Petrila, 2001; Treatment Advocacy Center, 2018). Perhaps most significantly, not all states have established a right of access to court-mandated treatment (Ridgely, Borum, & Petrila, 2001). While this enables many people to avoid effective enforcement of unwanted treatment orders, it has made it impossible for others to comply with treatment orders because of medication costs, long waitlists, and similar barriers (Ridgely, Borum, & Petrila, 2001). Furthermore, states that have established a right to mental health treatment along with a court-ordered duty have done so at the expense of people who voluntarily seek it out (New York Lawyers for the Public Interest, 2005; Ridgely, Borum, & Petrila, 2001). Under New York's involuntary outpatient commitment law in particular, there have been marked racial disparities in who the courts will require to undergo treatment (New York Lawyers for the Public Interest, 2005). Compared to white people, Black people were almost three times as likely to be subject to an involuntary outpatient commitment order and Latinx people were twice as likely to be under one (New York Lawyers for the Public Interest, 2005).

If the United States ratified the CRPD, it may be bound to abolish involuntary mental health treatment. The CRPD guarantees people with disabilities the right to liberty and security of the person, and states that "the existence of a disability shall in no case justify a deprivation of liberty" (The United Nations, 2006, art. 14(1)). Likewise, it protects people with disabilities' right to physical and mental integrity on par with that of nondisabled people (The United Nations, 2006, art. 17). Finally, given the severe side effects and significant level of uncertainty in how an individual will respond to antipsychotic medications, which are perhaps the foremost form of coercive treatment, the CRPD's protection against involuntary medical experimentation may also preclude coercive treatment (Muench & Hammer, 2010; The United Nations, 2006, art. 15(1)).

2.3 Guardianship and Conservatorship

Laws across the United States also allow states to directly and intentionally take away a person's rights and autonomy on the basis of a psychosocial or other mental disability through adult guardianship proceedings, ostensibly for their own protection (American Bar Association on Law and Aging, 2018a; American Bar Association Commission on Law and Aging, 2018b; U.S. National Council on Disability, 2018). A court that finds a person to be incapacitated may delegate any number of these rights (such as making medical decisions or choosing where to live) to another person, who is usually a family member or a professional guardian (U.S. National Council on Disability, 2018). Other rights, such as voting and marriage, may be lost entirely (U.S. National Council on Disability, 2018).

As with commitment, guardianship laws and procedures vary widely across the United States. The state laws with the strongest due process protections require a formal hearing where the allegedly incapacitated person has the right to counsel (American Bar Association Commission on Law and Aging, 2018b; American Bar Association Commission on Law and Aging, 2018c). Other states allow a court to impose a guardianship in absentia with no right to counsel (American Bar Association Commission on Law and Aging, 2018b; U.S. National Council on Disability, 2018). Laws also differ in terms of how much responsibility they impose on states to review the ongoing need for guardianship (American Bar Association Commission on Law and Aging, 2019).

Despite the growing consensus of the international community that guardianship should be limited if not abolished, as represented by Article 12 of the CRPD, most states nonetheless allow for plenary guardianship, which takes away most or all of the rights that come with legal adulthood regardless of a person's actual abilities or needs (American Bar Association Commission on Law and Aging, 2018b; U.S. National Council on Disability, 2018). Though a number of states now require judges to consider alternatives to guardianship and allow people under guardianship to retain rights they are capable of exercising, courts in these states still routinely grant plenary guardianships (U.S. National Council on Disability, 2018). So far, no laws have replaced guardianship altogether in favor of less restrictive alternatives such as supported decision-making (U.S. National Council on Disability, 2018).

2.4 Criminalization

Disability – particularly psychosocial disability – and criminality are intricately interlinked in U.S. jurisprudence and juridical history (Ben-Moshe, 2020; Lewis, 2019; Annamma, 2017; Price, 2011; Schweik, 2009). It is impossible to divorce definitions of crime from societal impulses to control and contain undesirable behavior, traits, or people. Crime is not synonymous with harm, even in codified criminal law, but is instead legislated into existence by criminalizing certain actions or omissions. Historical legacies of criminalized blackness, queerness, impoverishment, and femininity still linger today.

Helping Educate to Advance the Rights of Deaf Communities has estimated that as many as 80 percent of people killed by police or incarcerated are disabled, and, due to trauma-related disabilities, 100 percent of people sentenced to capital punishment are disabled (Lewis, 2020; American Civil Liberties Union, 2015).[1] According to the Department of Education's Civil Rights Data Collection (2014),[2] disabled Black and Latinx students face restraint, seclusion, suspensions, expulsions, and arrests at significantly higher rates than other groups (Landberg & Ciolfi, 2016). In the context of involuntary commitments, which frequently involve police taking people to hospitals in handcuffs, more Black people appear in psychiatric wards and involuntary outpatient programs than any other group (New York Lawyers for the Public Interest, 2005; Albiges, 2019; Boatner, 2019). Under racial capitalism, Black and Native disabled people comprise the largest group targeted for criminalization and incarceration – and as disabled people of color continually experience, police, prosecutors, and prisons flagrantly disregard the ADA's protections against discrimination (Seevers, 2016; Morgan, 2017; Ben-Moshe, 2020; Lewis, n.d.).

People who are or are assumed to be homeless, using substances, or doing sex work also face dual effects of psychiatrization and criminalization – impoverishment, substance use, or sex work can become bases for civil commitment regardless of legal standards, and involvement with the psychiatric or criminal legal systems often result in greater surveillance and further criminalization (Foscarinis, 1996; Amster, 2003; Chisholm, G. D., 2013; Meronek & Meiners, 2018; Wiltz, 2019). Public policy response has transitioned from launching a War on Drugs defined by lengthy prison sentences for drug use, possession, or small-time sales that targeted and devastated Black communities, to addressing an opioid epidemic as a public health issue for impoverished white people (Steiner & Argothy, 2001; Alexander, 2010; Netherland & Hansen, 2017). Beginning in 1989, courts instituted drug court programs – where people have regular sessions in court with the judge, prosecutor, and defense attorney acting as part of a team to oversee substance use treatment – either as diversion to avoid records or alternative sentencing instead of jail, under the theory that people using drugs needed help rather than punishment (Lurijio, 2008). While well-intentioned, the shift from a punitive approach to a treatment-based approach never changed the carceral nature of the judicial system; it only shifted the approach from jails and prisons to long-term residential treatment and institutionalization – and can still lead to jail (Fluellen & Trone, 2000).

---

[1] Exact numbers are difficult to determine, because of both inadvertent and intentional omissions and exclusions – as well as inconsistent definitions – whenever researchers, government agencies, or others attempt to collect statistics on disabilities. Nonetheless, all available reports indicate significant overrepresentation of disabled people targeted by police violence or incarceration, when compared to the overall population.

[2] This is the most recent available data as of May 2020.

2.5 Gun Ownership, Gun Control, and Gun Violence

The Constitution's Second Amendment recognizes the right of the people "to keep and bear arms." Although some advocates argue that it only establishes that right for an established militia and not an individual, the Supreme Court recognized an individual right to bear arms in District of Columbia v. Heller (2008). Nonetheless, the Brady Handgun Violence Prevention Act defines classes of people banned from possessing or receiving firearms, including people who have been convicted of any felony, are subject to civil protection or restraining orders, have been convicted of any domestic violence-related crime, use or have addictions to any criminalized substances, or have "been adjudicated as a mental defective or committed to a mental institution." (18 U.S.C.A. §§ 921–922.) In *Heller*, the Supreme Court noted that the right to bear firearms is not unlimited, and that their decision "should not be taken to cast doubt on longstanding prohibitions on the possession of firearms by felons and the mentally ill." (District of Columbia v. Heller, 2008). Later court decisions considered whether people barred from possessing firearms had actually been adjudicated as mentally ill or committed to an institution *ever*, or alternately, whether they had demonstrated sufficient time or rehabilitation *since* the commitment (U.S. v. Rehlander, 2012; Tyler v. Hillsdale County Sheriff's Dept., 2016; Beers v. Attorney General, 2019; Mai v. U.S., 2020).[3] In one telling opinion, the Third Circuit wrote that because "judicial officials were authorized to 'lock up' so-called 'lunatics' or other individuals with dangerous mental impairments," laws barring people with psychosocial disabilities from possessing firearms had been unnecessary earlier, since confiscating someone's weapon due to lack of capacity would be less intrusive than outright imprisoning them (Beers v. Attorney General, 2019).

Contemporary demands for gun control in response to mass shootings – largely attributable to white men with histories of misogyny, white supremacist ideology, or both – originated with white conservative backlash to Black Panther Party members exercising legal open-carry in self and community defense (Cottrol & Diamond, 1991; Cramer, 1995; Morgan, 2018). That backlash in turn stems from Reconstruction-era fear of white slaveholders that formerly enslaved, freed Black people would threaten white people's power (Cottrol & Diamond, 1991). The ensuing legal matrix to both disproportionately target Black people for diagnoses like schizophrenia and for criminalization has ensured that those most likely to be able to legally access firearms remain nondisabled white people (Metzl, 2010; Pickens, 2019). Simultaneously, these matrices systematically deprive marginalized communities of access to firearms often based on imputed disability or criminality, that is, through enacting psychiatric stigma and eroding legal capacity.

---

[3] The most damaging language in *Beers v. Attorney General* (2019) is no longer legally binding, because the Supreme Court vacated the opinion and judgment as moot. (Beers v. Barr, 2020). Note also that among only two decisions that resulted in successful restoration of rights, the petitioners were working as prison guards in Pennsylvania; others who had ever been committed in the past tended to be unsuccessful. (Franklin v. Sessions, 2017; Keyes v. Sessions, 2017).

2.6 Reproductive Freedom

Both United States and international law protect the right to make reproductive decisions. The U.S. Supreme Court has held that procreation is a fundamental right protected by the Constitution (Skinner v. State of Okl. ex rel. Williamson, 1942). Americans with disabilities have not consistently enjoyed the benefits of reproductive rights under domestic law. In particular, the Supreme Court's infamous decision in *Buck v. Bell* declaring forced sterilization on the basis of disability to be constitutional on the grounds that "[t]hree generations of imbeciles are enough" has never been overruled (Buck v. Bell, 1927). State sterilization laws as such have been repealed or fallen out of favor in recent decades, but guardianship statutes that allow for involuntary sterilization remain in effect, and United States courts have yet to definitively decide whether disabled people are fully entitled to the (otherwise) fundamental right to procreation (Cohen, 2016; Ditkowsky, 2019; U.S. National Council on Disability, 2018).

Meanwhile, the Convention on the Rights of Persons with Disabilities protects against forced sterilization, explicitly and implicitly (The United Nations, 2006, arts. 17, 23(1)). The prohibition on forced sterilization arguably rises to the level of being an international norm for the purposes of binding the United States, regardless of its willingness to ratify any such instruments; but even then its protection would remain theoretical without the will or ability to enforce it (International Justice Resource Center, 2019).

3 APPLICATION IN CURRENT CONTEXTS

3.1 *Extremism*

Ever since the 1999 mass shooting at Columbine, a particular genre of journalism has emerged examining underlying causes and buildup for shootings. In many stories, journalists describe each aspect of a shooter's life that could possibly derive from psychosocial or developmental disability – sensory aversions, social difficulties, perceived aloofness, emotional outbursts, depression, or suicidality (Price, 2011). Regardless of political ideology or personal background, the most common response is to presume psychosocial or developmental disability as the primary cause. Similar reporting depicts potential or actual ISIS/Daesh recruits as socially isolated, bullied, awkward loners, using coded language to imply – or occasionally explicitly state – that those most likely to join are people with psychosocial or developmental disabilities (Doward, 2008; Pishko, 2016; Allely, 2017; Dearden, 2018).

As a result, policymakers are quick to propose increased funding for involuntary outpatient commitment and long-term inpatient treatment (Rogers & Rosenthal, 2013; Autistic Self Advocacy Network, 2016). At the same time, they seek decreased funding for community-based, peer-led treatment and services, as well as protection and advocacy programs that investigate and advocate against institutional abuse (Rogers & Rosenthal, 2013; Autistic Self Advocacy Network, 2016). Likewise, police and nondisabled people clamor for police funding for mental health training and partnerships with psychiatrists, schools, and universities to predict which people pose highest risks of future violence and stage interventions focused on increasing surveillance and decreasing freedom (Kaba, 2014; Moore, 2016; Barnes, 2019; Lewis, 2019).

Current legal mechanisms do not protect disabled people from harmful effects of widespread ableism in media coverage and policy proposals responding to mass violence and terrorism. While public entities including schools, police, hospitals, jails, and prisons are barred from discriminating based on mental disability, the law does not prevent state actors from either inadvertently or willfully disregarding rights – irreversible damage is done, even if judges later take the disabled person's side (Patrick v. Success Academy Charter Schools, 2018; Bristol Township School District v. Z.B., 2016). The state cannot dictate beliefs that appear in the press. When a person faces coercive treatment ordered by courts, probation offices, or threat assessment teams, they have little recourse under law, and few avenues for advocacy within existing institutions. Possible legal claims or basis for court orders in a person's favor could depend on proving specific discriminatory intent and impact, which can be nearly impossible. Claims could also depend on access to opaque algorithms analyzing people's digital footprints for information that correlates to race, class, gender, and disability-related characteristics and experiences caused by systemic discrimination (K.W. ex re. D.W. v. Armstrong, 2015; Benjamin, 2019; Bloch-Wehba, 2020). No possible litigation, however, can stop the existence or spread of ableist beliefs about disabled people's supposed proclivities for violence, or prevent deployment of legal mechanisms to restrict rights.

At the same time, most arguments against involving mental illness in gun violence prevention policies fail to address underlying issues. Those arguments usually state that because people with psychosocial disabilities are both less likely to commit violence and more likely to be victimized by violence, gun violence prevention efforts should not mention mental illness. But those arguments are not relevant or helpful in understanding how existing legal frameworks systematically undermine all rights of people with psychosocial disabilities whenever any right defined as fundamental (regardless of whether it should be) is placed at risk based on (putative or actual) disability. Gun ownership and mass gun violence may be largely U.S. issues, but they have implications for state violence against people with psychosocial disabilities globally. Because the prevailing view is that we are necessarily more dangerous than nondisabled people, any policies increasing surveillance, decreasing civil liberties, or expanding imprisonment (for psychiatric, penal, or national security reasons) will cause vastly more harm for multiply marginalized disabled people in any nation implementing them (Altiraifi & Novack, 2019).

3.2 Socioeconomic and Social Welfare Issues through the Presumptions of Incompetence and Criminality

Legal structures tend to frame socioeconomic and social welfare issues impacting people with (actual, perceived, or presumed) psychosocial disabilities in terms of burden/charity, danger/control, or protection/help.

Disability is not a neutral, objective category, but one shaped largely by sociocultural values and political need (Lewis, 2019; Withers, 2012). The United States' political economy relies on neoliberal and capitalist approaches to resource distribution and production, which translate into both valuing people on means, frequency, and output of production, and imputing disability as a natural cause and moralized consequence of impoverishment and deprivation. Through this logic, people who are homeless or hungry are at fault because of supposed laziness, irresponsibility, or lack of intelligence – a presumption that frequently leads to petitions for involuntary commitment or guardianship for impoverished people with psychosocial disabilities (Wright, 1993; Yusuf, 2017; Turner, Funge, & Gabbard, 2018; Ellen, 2015). Sometimes, this logic explicitly names mental illness as the cause of impoverishment and homelessness, instead of recognizing that under capitalism, impoverishment is a cause and a consequence of disability (Bowman, 2019; Vallas & Fremstad, 2014). Ableism and capitalism create self-perpetuating cycles that both inflict deprivation (and trauma-related disabilities, and environmental racism-induced disabilities) and blame those it impoverishes. This perpetuates eugenicist "burden" rhetoric and neoliberal charity responses, with the state privileging a nonprofit industry through tax-exemption, while simultaneously trapping disabled people receiving public assistance with income and asset caps, intensified surveillance, and decreased recognition of legal capacity, along with victim blaming for continued impoverishment.

Likewise, in a carceral state, policing justifies itself through self-perpetuating predictive tools or preventative policies like "broken windows" policing strategies that target so-called low-level crime – often caused by impoverishment and deprivation – in attempts to forecast and preempt violence (Richardson, Schultz, & Crawford, 2019; Heatherton & Camp, 2016). Incarceration justifies itself through engendering high recidivism rates and appealing to white nondisabled people's "safety," while suppressing alternate responses to harm. Pretrial imprisonment justifies itself through increasingly automated risk assessments purporting to neutrally analyze people's "dangerousness," but instead relying on proxies for race, class, gender, and disability (Benjamin, 2019; Angwin et al., 2016; Hill, 2021). U.S. immigration laws likewise rely on ableist and racist dynamics by imposing education and work requirements for visas, and barring immigration by people deemed insufficiently productive. Those rules, amended under the Trump administration to apply retroactively to people already in the United States, derive from public charge statutes originally designed to entrap, criminalize, and incarcerate

Black people freed from enslavement, and enslaved Black people hoping for manumission – in part by defining Black people as uniquely threatening (84 FR 41292; Lewis, 2019). Similarly, racialized ableism traces its roots from depictions of Native peoples as uncivilized and violent, Latinx (particularly Mestizx and Afro-Latinx) peoples as criminal and promiscuous, and Southwest, South, East, and Southeast Asian peoples as dirty, contaminated, and dangerous (Chen, 2012; Ware, Ruzsa, & Dias, 2014; Erevelles, 2014; Smith, 2017; Stern et al., 2017).

Further, disability law upholds the notion of the state and private actors as disabled people's protectors, while positioning us as permanently incompetent. While institutionalization and guardianship may seem separate from enforced impoverishment or mass criminalization, they are deeply interrelated. Ableism frames disability as both dangerous and scary, and as innocent and needing protection. People with psychosocial disabilities thus face increasing erosion of freedoms and rights in the name of both protecting society from us and protecting us from ourselves. The reality is that coercive treatment, civil commitment, and institutionalization operate to exert control over disabled people in the same ways as incarceration, criminalization, impoverishment, and deprivation. Thus, diversionary programs like drug, mental health, veterans, or homeless court not only replicate carceral systems, but actually lead both to increased incarceration and increased acceptance for institutionalization. Instead of pushing for reforms that legitimize existing systems, advocates must focus on decarceration through abolishing jails, prisons, and institutions; defunding coercive and involuntary treatment and policing; and promoting peer support for crisis intervention without police; peer-led hotlines and warmlines (for support other than during a crisis); autonomy-focused short-term and long-term treatment; and development of local capacity for transformative justice processes to achieve accountability and address conditions that engender harm.

3.3 Reproductive Rights

Although some states now afford various forms of protection against forced sterilization, many allow it to varying degrees in the context of adult guardianship (Ditkowsky, 2019; U.S. National Council on Disability, 2018). As recently as 2012, a Massachusetts probate granted a petition by the parents of a pregnant woman with schizophrenia to declare her incompetent and order her to have an abortion over her religious objections, because the pregnancy would require her to stop taking her psychotropic medications (In re Guardianship of Moe, 2012). The judge in fact went beyond the scope of the petition to order that the woman be forcibly sterilized to prevent further pregnancies and thus further abortions (In re Guardianship of Moe, 2012). The woman was only able to avoid undergoing both procedures because the state Court of Appeals reversed the decision on the basis that it had violated her due process rights (In re Guardianship of Moe, 2012).

Because the United States has refused to ratify the Convention on the Rights of Persons with Disabilities, it is not bound by its prohibition of disability-based sterilization (The United Nations, 2006, art. 23(1)). The best legal avenue for challenging these remaining vestiges of the eugenics movement is therefore through domestic courts, particularly in the context of adult guardianship proceedings. An allegedly incapacitated person facing the possibility of sterilization could argue that a court-ordered sterilization violates their due process rights, drawing on constitutional case law that has developed since the decision in *Buck v. Bell* (Skinner v. State of Okl. ex rel. Williamson, 1942). The law allowing for forced sterilization also likely violates Title II of the ADA because it allows the state, through court-appointed guardians, to infringe upon reproductive rights based on disability (Salzman, 2011). However, this will almost certainly have to occur on a state-by-state basis, challenging individual laws based on their specific statutory provisions. It will also have to overcome existing case law establishing standards that allegedly protect a person's rights while nonetheless still allowing for forced sterilization in some cases (In re Grady, 1981; In re Hayes, 1980).

4 CONCLUSION

Despite domestic and international law protecting the civil and human rights of people with disabilities, ableist oppression remains severe, widespread, and legal. Policymakers and judges often enact or uphold such rights violations to address larger social problems, real or imagined, on a surface level without making fundamental changes to society or its institutions. Disabled people, therefore, bear the brunt both of problems that we are not responsible for causing, and of the supposed solutions.

Disability justice advocates can sometimes make use of legal protections to avoid such outcomes. However, even when there are both favorable laws and the political will to enforce and abide by them, advocacy within a system based on the same underlying beliefs that allow for the aforementioned structural problems is insufficient to solve them. Both people with disabilities and (arguably, to a greater extent) those without must shift the general public's attention toward these problems and build up the collective will to directly address them. Meanwhile, where certain institutions will by their nature inevitably harm or unjustly restrict disabled people, we must be core participants in efforts to create and perfect replacements – formal or otherwise – that will treat each one of us as inherently valuable and indispensable.

REFERENCES

Addington v. Texas, 441 U.S. 418 (1979).
Albiges, M. (May 17, 2019). Thousands in mental health crisis are handcuffed by police. The state wants to cut that number. *The Virginian-Pilot.* www.pilotonline.com/government'/virginia/article_c728d742-78ab-11e9-a85c-a733fb0ae39a.html.

Alexander, M. (2010). *The New Jim Crow: Mass Incarceration in the Age of Colorblindness*. New York: The New Press.
Alley, C. (June 22, 2017). Are autistic people at greater risk of being radicalised? *The Conversation*. https://theconversation.com/are-autistic-people-at-greater-risk-of-being-radicalised-76726.
Altiraifi, A. & Novack, V. (February 20, 2019). Efforts to address gun violence should not include increased surveillance. *Center for American Progress*. www.americanprogress.org/issues/disability/news/2019/02/20/466468/efforts-address-gun-violence-not-include-increased-surveillance/.
American Bar Association Commission on Law and Aging (2018). Capacity Definition & Initiation of Guardianship Proceedings (Statutory revisions as of December 31, 2018). www.americanbar.org/content/dam/aba/administrative/law_aging/chartcapacityandinitiation.pdf.
American Bar Association Commission on Law and Aging (2018). Conduct and Findings of Guardianship Proceedings (Statutory revisions as of December 31, 2018). www.americanbar.org/content/dam/aba/administrative/law_aging/chartconduct.pdf.
American Bar Association Commission on Law and Aging (2018). Monitoring Following Guardianship Proceedings (Statutory revisions as of December 31, 2019). www.americanbar.org/content/dam/aba/administrative/law_aging/chartmonitoring.pdf.
American Bar Association Commission on Law and Aging (2018). Representation and Investigation in Guardianship Proceedings (Statutory revisions as of December 31, 2018). www.americanbar.org/content/dam/aba/administrative/law_aging/chartrepresentationandinvestigation.pdf.
Americans with Disabilities Act of 1990, 42 U.S.C.A. § 12101. (2009).
Amster, R. (2003). Patterns of exclusion: Sanitizing space, criminalizing homelessness. *Social Justice*, 30(1), 195–221.
Angwin, J., Larson, J., Mattu, S., & Kirchner, L. (May 23, 2016). Machine bias. *ProPublica*. www.propublica.org/article/machine-bias-risk-assessments-in-criminal-sentencing.
Autistic Self Advocacy Network. (March 9, 2016). ASAN joins letter opposing harmful mental health bill. https://autisticadvocacy.org/2016/03/asan-joins-letter-opposing-harmful-mental-health-bill/.
Barnes, B. (August 29, 2019). Targeted: A family and the quest to stop the next school shooter. *The Oregonian*. www.oregonlive.com/news/erry-2018/06/75f0f464cb3367/targeted_a_family_and_the_ques.html.
Beers v. Attorney General United States, 927 F.3d 150 (3rd Cir. 2019).
Beers v. Barr, Attorney General, et al., 2020 WL 2515441 (Mem) (2020).
Benjamin, R. (2019). *Race after Technology: Abolitionist Tools for the New Jim Code*. New York: Polity.
Ben-Moshe, L. (2020). *Decarcerating Disability: Deinstitutionalization and Prison Abolition*. Minneapolis: University of Minnesota Press.
Boatner, C. (October 15, 2019). 'They probably thought I was a criminal': Baker Acted students say wearing handcuffs worsens their experience. *University Press*. www.upressonline.com/2019/10/they-probably-thought-i-was-a-criminal-baker-acted-students-say-wearing-handcuffs-worsens-their-experience/.
Bowman, S. (November 25, 2019). Mental health and homelessness: An update. *Resources to Recover*. www.rtor.org/2019/11/25/mental-health-and-homelessness/.
Bloch-Wehba, H. (2020). Access to algorithms. *Fordham Law Review*, 88, 1265–1314. https://poseidon01.ssrn.com/delivery.php?ID=620116007095115074111071070067127067035074090016037034077025122100120000078005083068098110016004116055039006060

1912603110700007409802502908403911001808602700201812209105601600100701512308903109906908710701312309600709406412202512210010808 3068072087125031&EXT=pdf.
Brady Handgun Violence Prevention Act, 18 U.S.C.A. §§ 921–922.
Brief for the American Civil Liberties Union et al. as Amicus Curiae, City and County of San Francisco v. Sheehan, 575 U.S. __ (2015), www.thearc.org/file/public-policy-document/Sheehan-Amicus-Brief.pdf.
Bristol Township School District v. Z.B., 2016 WL 161600 (E.D. Pa. 2016).
Chen, M. Y. (2012). Queer Animality. In M. Y. Chen, *Animacies: Biopolitics, Racial Mattering, and Queer Affect*. Durham, North Carolina: Duke University Press. 89–126.
Chisholm, G. D. (2013). A yawning black abyss: Section 35 and the equal protection of women in the Commonwealth of Massachusetts. *Suffolk University Law Review*, 46(4), 1033–1065. https://pdfs.semanticscholar.org/fdaf/917076ae8bb148a35e83e6c34d682f27df85.pdf.
Cohen, A. (2016). *Imbeciles: The Supreme Court, American Eugenics, and the Sterilization of Carrie Buck*. New York: Penguin Press. 318–319.
Conservatorship of Davis, 124 Cal. App. 3d 313 (1981).
Cottrol, R. J. & Diamond, R. T. (1991). The second amendment: Toward an Afro-Americanist reconsideration. *Georgetown Law Journal*, 80, 309–361. https://digitalcommons.law.lsu.edu/cgi/viewcontent.cgi?article=1283&context=faculty_scholarship.
Cramer, C. E. (1995). The racist roots of gun control. *Kansas Journal of Law and Public Policy*, 4(17). https://heinonline.org/HOL/LandingPage?handle=hein.journals/kjpp4&div=22&id=&page=.
Dearden, L. (March 2, 2018). Autistic teenager who planned Isis-inspired terror attack in Cardiff jailed for life. *The Independent*. www.independent.co.uk/news/uk/crime/isis-attack-plot-cardiff-justin-bieber-concert-lloyd-gunton-wales-online-radicalisation-a8237366.html.
Definition of "disability," 28 C.F.R. § 35.108 (2016).
District of Columbia v. Heller, 554 US 570 (2008).
Ditkowsky, M. (2019). Choice at risk: The threat of adult guardianship to substantive and procedural due process rights in reproductive health. *National Lawyers Guild Review*. www.nlg.org/nlg-review/article/choice-at-risk-the-threat-of-adult-guardianship-to-substantive-and-procedural-due-process-rights-in-reproductive-health/.
Doward, J. (May 25, 2008). Inside bizarre world of the Big Friendly Giant. *The Guardian*. www.theguardian.com/uk/2008/may/25/uksecurity.terrorism.
Ellen, B. (November 29, 2015). Austerity, not ignorance or laziness, lies at the heart of eating problems in the young. *The Guardian*. www.theguardian.com/commentisfree/2015/nov/29/kis-junk-food-dont-blame-parents.
Erevelles, N. (2014). Crippin' Jim Crow: Disability, Dis-location, and the School-to-Prison Pipeline. In L. Ben-Moshe, C. Chapman & A. C. Carey, *Disability Incarcerated: Imprisonment and Disability in the United States and Canada* New York: Palgrave MacMillan. 81–99.
Existing facilities, 28 C.F.R. § 42.521 (2003).
Fluellen, R. & Trone, J. (2000). State sentencing and corrections program issues in brief: Do drug courts save jail and prison beds? *Vera Institute of Justice*. www.prisonpolicy.org/scans/vera/drugcourts.pdf.
Foscarinis, M. (1996). Downward spiral: Homelessness and its criminalization. *Yale Law & Policy Review*, 14(1), 1–63. https://digitalcommons.law.yale.edu/cgi/viewcontent.cgi?referer=https://scholar.google.com/&httpsredir=1&article=1288&context=ylpr.
Franklin v. Sessions, 291 F.Supp.3d 705 (W.D. Pa., 2017).

Gray, H. (2016). State laws related to involuntary commitment of individuals with substance use disorder and alcoholism – part 2 of 2. *National Alliance for Model State Drug Laws. NAMSDL News: Subject Matter Analysis.* https://namsdl.org/wp-content/uploads/NAMSDL-News-October-19-2016.pdf.

Hamilton-Smith, G. (September 4, 2018). The endless punishment of civil commitment. *The Appeal.* https://theappeal.org/the-endless-punishment-of-civil-commitment/.

Heatherton, C. & Camp, J. T. (October 28, 2016). Broken windows policing and institutionalised racism: An extract from 'Policing the planet: Why the policing crisis led to #BlackLivesMatter.' *The Institute of Contemporary Arts.* https://archive.ica.art/bulletin/broken-windows-policing-and-institutionalised-racism.

Hill, S. A. (2021). Bail reform and the (false) racial promise of algorithmic risk assessment. *UCLA Law Review* 68 (in press).

Inadmissibility on Public Charge Grounds, 84 FR 41292.

International Justice Resource Center (2019). Forced sterilization: Developments in international human rights law 2016–2018. http://ijrcenter.org/wp-content/uploads/2019/04/FS-IHRL-Developments-Summary-w-links.pdf.

In re Det. of R.H., 178 Wash. App. 941 (2014).

In re Grady, 426, A.2d 467 (N.J. 1981).

In re Hayes, 608 P.2d 635 (Wash. 1980).

In re J.C., 803 So. 2d 38 (La. 2001).

In re Guardianship of Moe, 81 Mass. App. Ct. 136 (2012).

Johnson, M. & Strauss, V. (April 25, 2017). Why are we criminalizing behavior of children with disabilities? *The Washington Post.* www.washingtonpost.com/news/answer-sheet/wp/2017/04/25/why-are-we-criminalizing-behavior-of-children-with-disabilities/.

Kaba, M. (December 7, 2014). Police "reforms" you should always oppose. *TruthOut.* https://truthout.org/articles/police-reforms-you-should-always-oppose/.

Kansas v. Hendricks, 521 U.S. 346 (1997).

Keyes v. Sessions, 282 F.Supp.3d 858 (M.D. Pa., 2017).

K.W. ex re. D.W. v. Armstrong (D. Idaho 2016; 9th Cir. 2015).

Landberg, J. & Ciolfi, A. (May 2016). Suspended progress report. *Legal Aid Justice Center, JustChildren Program.* www.justice4all.org/wp-content/uploads/2016/05/Suspended-Progress-Report.pdf.

Lewis, T. A. (June 2019). Concerns re disability/deaf rights communities' responses to policing systems' violence. http://bit.ly/policeviolencePWDresponse.

Lewis, T. A. (January 2020). Creating disability justice: Understanding the fullness of Deaf/Disabled communities. Session presented at the National LGBTQ Task Force's Creating Change conference, Dallas, TX.

Lewis, T. A. (n.d.). Perspectives in belonging: Talila Lewis. Othering & Belonging Institute We Too Belong Report. https://belonging.berkeley.edu/perspectives-belonging-talila-lewis.

Lewis, T. A. (August 27, 2019). Trump's rule attacking disabled and low-income migrants has violent history. *TruthOut.* https://truthout.org/articles/trumps-rule-attacking-disabled-and-low-income-migrants-has-violent-history/.

Lurijio, A. J. (2008). The first 20 years of drug treatment courts: A brief description of their history and impact. *Federal Probation Journal,* 72(1). www.uscourts.gov/sites/default/files/72_1_2_0.pdf.

Mai v. United States, 952 F.3d 1106 (9th Cir. 2019).

Meronek, T. & Meiners, E. (May 31, 2018). The prison-like public hospital systems disproportionately packed with gay men. *The Advocate.* www.advocate.com/current-issue/2018/5/23/prison-federal-hospital-system-disproportionately-packed-gay-men.

Metzl, J. M. (2010). *The Protest Psychosis: How Schizophrenia became a Black disease*. Boston, Massachusetts: Beacon Press.
Mont. Code Ann. § 53-21-126 (2005).
Moore, L. (March 28, 2016). Mother/activist, Kerima Çevik, tells why police crisis/disability training is not the answer. *POOR Magazine*. https://poormagazine.org/node/5510.
Morgan, J. (January 2017). Caged in: The devastating harms of solitary confinement on prisoners with physical disabilities. *American Civil Liberties Foundation*. www.aclu.org/sites/default/files/field_document/010916-aclu-solitarydisabilityreport-single.pdf.
Morgan, T. (August 30, 2018). The NRA supported gun control when the Black Panthers had the weapons. *History Stories*. www.history.com/news/black-panthers-gun-control-nra-support-mulford-act.
Muench, J. & Hammer, A. M. (March 1, 2010). Adverse effects of antipsychotic medications. *American Family Physician*, 81, 617–622. www.aafp.org/afp/2010/0301/p617.pdf.
Netherland J. & Hansen, H. (2017). White opioids: Pharmaceutical race and the war on drugs that wasn't. *Biosocieties*, 12(2), 217–238. www.ncbi.nlm.nih.gov/pmc/articles/PMC5501419/.
Olmstead v. L.C. ex rel. Zimring, 527 U.S. 581 (1999).
New York Lawyers for the Public Interest, Inc., (2005.) Implementation of "Kendra's Law" is severely biased. www.prisonpolicy.org/scans/Kendras_Law_04-07-05.pdf.
Patrick v. Success Academy Charter Schools, 354 F.Supp.3d 185 (E.D. NY 2018).
Pickens, T. A. (2019). *Black Madness: Mad Blackness*. Durham, North Carolina: Duke University Press.
Pishko, J. (September 8, 2016). The FBI accused him of terrorism. He couldn't tie his shoes. *Esquire*. www.esquire.com/news-politics/a47390/alabama-isis-peyton-pruitt/.
Price, M. (2011). Assaults on the Ivory tower: Representations of Madness in the Discourse of U.S. School Shootings. In M. Price, *Mad at School: Rhetorics of Mental Disability and Academic Life*. Ann Arbor, Michigan: The University of Michigan Press. 141–175.
Rehabilitation Act of 1973, 29 U.S.C.A. § 701. (2014).
Richardson, R., Schultz, J., & Crawford, K. (February 13, 2019). Dirty data, bad predictions: How civil rights violations impact police data, predictive policing systems, and justice. *New York University Law Review Online*, 24, 192–234.
Ridgely, M.S., Borum, R., & Petrila, J. (2001). The effectiveness of involuntary outpatient treatment: empirical evidence and the experience of eight states. *Rand Institute for Civil Justice*. http://psychrights.org/Research/Digest/OutPtCmmtmnt/RandOutPtCommitmentEffectiveness.pdf.
Rogers, S. & Rosenthal, H. (December 12, 2013). Mental health advocates blast Rep. Tim Murphy's bill as a costly step backward, to the days when a mental illness diagnosis was a life sentence. *National Coalition for Mental Health Recovery, National Disability Rights Network, Bazelon Center for Mental Health Law*. www.prnewswire.com/news-releases/mental-health-advocates-blast-rep-tim-murphys-bill-as-a-costly-step-backward-to-the-days-when-a-mental-illness-diagnosis-was-a-life-sentence-235602341.html.
Salzman, L. (2011). Guardianship for persons with mental illness – a legal and appropriate alternative? *Saint Louis University Journal of Health Law & Policy*, 4(249), 314–327. http://supporteddecisionmaking.org/sites/default/files/guardianship_for_persons_with_mi.pdf.
Schweik, S. M. (2009). Race, Segregation, and the Ugly Law. In S. M. Schweik, *The Ugly Laws: Disability in Public*. New York: New York University Press.
Seevers, R. (June 16, 2016). Making hard time harder: Programmatic accommodations for inmates with disabilities under the Americans with Disabilities Act. *Disability Rights*

Washington, AVID Prison Project. http://avidprisonproject.org/Making-Hard-Time-Harder/assets/making-hard-time-harder–pdf-version.pdf.

Skinner v. State of Okl. ex rel. Williamson, 316 U.S. 535 (1942).

Smith, s. e. (February 1, 2017). 'When you try to stop it, nothing happens': A Q&A on the history of coerced sterilization in California. *Rewire*. https://rewire.news/article/2017/02/01/try-stop-nothing-happens-qa-history-coerced-sterilization-california/.

Steiner, B. D. & Argothy, V. (2001). White addiction: Racial inequality, racial ideology, and the war on drugs. *Temple Political and Civil Rights Law Review*, 10, 443.

Stern, A. M., Novak, N. L., Lira, N., O'Connor, K., Harlow, S. & Kardia, S. (2017). California's sterilization survivors: An estimate and call for redress. *American Journal of Public Health*, 107(1), 50–54. https://ajph.aphapublications.org/doi/10.2105/AJPH.2016.303489.

Superintendent of Worcester State Hosp. v. Hagberg, 374 Mass. 271 (1978).

Treatment Advocacy Center. (2011). Emergency hospitalization for evaluation: Assisted psychiatric treatment standards by state. www.treatmentadvocacycenter.org/storage/documents/Emergency_Hospitalization_for_Evaluation.pdf.

Treatment Advocacy Center. (2018). State standards for civil commitment. www.treatmentadvocacycenter.org/storage/documents/state-standards/state-standards-for-civil-commitment.pdf.

Turner, M. M, Funge, S. P. & Gabbard, W. J. (2018). Victimization of the homeless: Perceptions, policies, and implications for social work practice. *Journal of Social Work in the Global Community*, 3(1), 1–12. https://scholarworks.waldenu.edu/cgi/viewcontent.cgi?article=1010&context=jswgc.

Tyler v. Hillsdale County Sheriff's Department, 837 F.3d 678 (6th Cir. 2016).

The United Nations. (2006). Convention on the Rights of Persons with Disabilities. Treaty Series, 2515, 3.

U.S. Department of Education. (March 2014). Civil Rights Data Collection: Data snapshot: School discipline. https://www2.ed.gov/about/offices/list/ocr/docs/crdc-discipline-snapshot.pdf.

U.S. National Council on Disability. (2016). CRPD. https://ncd.gov/policy/crpd.

U.S. v. Rehlander, 666 F.3d 45 (1st Cir. 2012).

Vallas, R. & Fremstad, S. (September 19, 2014). Disability is a cause and consequence of poverty. *Talk Poverty*. https://talkpoverty.org/2014/09/19/disability-cause-consequence-poverty/.

Ware, S., Ruzsa, J & Dias, G. (2014). It Can't be Fixed because It's Not Broken: Racism and Disability in the Prison Industrial Complex. In L. Ben-Moshe, C. Chapman & A. C. Carey, *Disability Incarcerated: Imprisonment and Disability in the United States and Canada*. New York: Palgrave MacMillan. 163–184.

Wiltz, T. (September 11, 2019). 'Gravely disabled' homeless forced into mental health care in more states. *Pew Trusts*. www.pewtrusts.org/en/research-and-analysis/blogs/stateline/2019/09/11/gravely-disabled-homeless-forced-into-mental-health-care-in-more-states.

Withers, A. J. (2012). *Disability Politics and Theory*. Black Point, Nova Scotia: Fernwood Publishing.

Wright, S. E. (1993). Blaming the victim, blaming society or blaming the discipline: Fixing responsibility for poverty and homelessness. *The Sociological Quarterly*, 34(1), 1–16.

Yusuf, T. (May 24, 2017). A close call with homelessness shatters victim-blaming myths. *The Seattle Globalist*. www.seattleglobalist.com/2017/05/24/a-close-call-with-homelessness-shatters-victim-blaming-myths/65337.

23

The Danish Experience of Transforming Decision-Making Models

Dorrit Cato Christensen

Abstract

In this chapter, I share my impressions of how far the Danish psychiatric treatment system has come in implementing the Convention on Rights for Persons with Disabilities (CRPD), specifically Article 12 paragraphs 1 and 2. I have chosen to describe how human rights are respected in relation to people who are diagnosed with severe mental health problems, as in my opinion this group is given far too little attention. My insight into how psychiatry is practised was developed through my advocacy for my daughter Luise, who was diagnosed with severe mental health problems. As chairman of the association Death in Psychiatry, I have confirmed that my experience with Luise's treatment was typical. In this chapter, I identify reasons why the human rights of people with mental health problems are not respected enough, and I conclude that there needs to be a paradigm shift in the professionals' and the public's view of mental disability. I have great confidence that the Safewards and Recovery treatment models, which are being employed more and more in Danish psychiatry, are steps in the right direction.

1 INTRODUCTION

This chapter presents my analysis of Danish experiences of transforming decision-making models as part of Denmark's implementation of the Convention on Rights for Persons with Disabilities (CRPD) and its Article 12 mandate for equal recognition before the law, recognition as persons before the law, and legal capacity.[1] I have chosen to describe how the CRPD is engaged in the Danish psychiatric treatment system, with a particular focus on how it works in relation to the group of persons labelled as having severe mental health problems. The analysis describes, inter alia, the Safewards model[2]

---

[1] Convention on Rights for Persons with Disabilities (CRPD) Article 12. Retrieved from www.un.org/development/desa/disabilities/convention-on-the-rights-of-persons-with-disabilities/article-12-equal-recognition-before-the-law.html.

[2] Bowers, Len (n.d.). Safewards: a new model of conflict and containment on psychiatric wards. Retrieved from www.safewards.net/images/pdf/Safewards%20model.pdf.

and the Recovery model.[3] The Danish Regions – the authority responsible for mental health issue in hospitals and for psychiatry in Denmark – inform me that these two treatment models are practised with success in some psychiatric wards in Denmark. I am also informed that the two models provide a sound basis for decision-making for people in the treatment system.

I have obtained critical and detailed insight into how psychiatric treatment in Denmark is practised through my advocacy for my daughter Luise. She was in psychiatric treatment for thirteen years, diagnosed with severe mental health problems. There I saw for myself how and why – in my opinion – the CRPD's requirements are not well complied with for people like my daughter. I also include a summary of what I have heard from different people, be it users or their friends or relatives, about this subject during my eleven-year presidency of the association Death in Psychiatry (DiP).[4] Most people who have contacted me are people who have had more or less the same experiences of psychiatry as I have.

I strongly believe that particular focus should be placed on persons labelled as having severe mental health problems. This is because, in my opinion, they are often sentenced to treatment that is a violation of their human rights, in that they are heavily medicated with psychotropics without their consent. This medication tends to keep them in the treatment system for far too many years. A report from Danish Regions entitled 'Mental health – better treatment for people with severe mental health problems'[5] provides figures that give me good justification for my statement above: 'New estimates show that a small group of people with severe mental illness and complex courses of treatment consisting of approximately 7,400 patients – equivalent to 5 per cent of all persons who seek help in psychiatry – account for almost 50 per cent of the total treatment costs in psychiatry. These patients are to a large extent also the citizens who receive social support and training from the municipality [e.g. in living a normal life]'.[6] This group so far gets too little attention. It seems as if the specialists are uncritical and maintain previously prescribed treatment courses without considering whether they are adequate. For example, they don't question why a person in treatment gets huge doses of medication and doesn't get any better. The Danish psychiatrist Birgit Petersson, who writes

---

[3] Lyon, Sarah (2020). The Recovery model. Retrieved from www.verywellmind.com/what-is-the-recovery-model-2509979.
[4] DiP, founded in 2009, has tried to contribute to a more nuanced discussion about psychiatric treatment. The association is considered a watchdog that seeks to influence psychiatric treatment to make it less dangerous. This is effected through collaboration with the treatment system, meetings with treatment personnel, different activities on psychiatry, and participation in conferences on CRPD Article 12. In addition, DiP has given lectures on the same and holds an annual memorial service where we commemorate our deceased family members. See http://doedipsykiatrien.dk.
[5] All quotes from Danish journals, publications and newspapers etc. are translations by the author.
[6] Danish Regions, (2018). Mental health – better treatment for people with severe mental health problems. P. 4. Retrieved from www.regioner.dk/media/9762/mental-sundhed-bedre-behandling-til-mennesker-med-svaer-psykisk-sygdom.pdf.

about medical science, medicalisation, and ethics, puts it this way: 'Taking care of the chronically ill and the old gives no prestige'.[7]

This chapter is organised as follows: Sections 1 to 5 describe the status of co-decision-making in psychiatry in Denmark. Sections 6 and 7 describe the human rights aspects of co-determination. Section 8 deals with decision-making models. Section 9 states that an ongoing debate is crucial. Finally, Section 10 concludes with some thoughts about the future of the Danish healthcare system.

2 NOT ALL PSYCHIATRIC PATIENTS ARE ALIKE

When talking about how human rights and legal capacity are respected for people diagnosed with mental health problems, it is crucial to bear in mind that not all such persons are alike. Therefore, one cannot refer to them as one homogeneous group. You find people with psychiatric diagnoses who can live a healthy life, with family, work and friends et cetera. Then, at the other end of the scale, you find people with severe mental health problems and complex courses of treatment. These persons have a difficult life, both because of their psychoses and because many of them are treated with large doses of psychotropics. The result is that they lose all energy and ability to think or react normally. Some are so affected by the medication that the specialists describe them as 'mentally retarded'. A terrible example of this phenomenon was found on my daughter Luise's death certificate. It said, 'death from unknown causes', and as a contributory cause of death it had 'epilepsy and mental retardation'.[8] But Luise was an intelligent young woman who only seemed 'mentally retarded' due to high doses of psychotropics.

Many of the people with severe mental health problems and complex courses of treatment are being coerced, as many of them have a court order for mental health treatment. They have 'no voice' and, as far as I can see, nobody seems to care whether their human rights are respected. In my opinion, they are often left to themselves and without much attention from healthcare professionals, caseworkers, or local or national politicians. Politicians do often speak out when a story about a disaster in psychiatry comes up in the media – for example, a sudden and unexpected death. But the problem is that it is just words, not action. When Luise died from overmedication, many politicians, mostly local, spoke out. The office manager of the Danish Board of Health Anne Mette Dons was quoted in *Today's Medicine* as saying: 'The psychiatrists must follow the guidelines for medication with psychotropic drugs – meaning they must not exceed the recommended dose of psychotropics ... If they do not follow the guidelines they will be held accountable for their action. For example, the doctor may receive criticism from the Patient Complaint Board or alternatively a case in the courts'.[9] Strong

---

[7] Petersson, Birgit (1991), *De falske guder*. København: Munksgaard. P. 30–32.
[8] Christensen, Dorrit Cato (2012), *Dear Luise – a Story of Power and Powerlessness in Denmark's Psychiatric Care System*, Portland, Oregon: Jorvik Press. P. 209.
[9] Albinus, Niels Bjørn (26 January 2006). Dødsfald i psykiatrien udløser domino-effect [Deaths in psychiatry trigger domino-effect]. *Today's Medicine*. P. 8. https://dagensmedicin.dk/dodsfald-i-psykiatrien-udloser-domino-effekt/

words, but nothing changed – rather the opposite. Numbers show that more psychotropics are used today than when Luise was alive. People with mental health problems get a lot of negative publicity in the media if they commit a criminal act, such as a serious assault or a murder. However, one seldom hears about crimes committed against people with mental health problems; nevertheless, in fact, it happens very often. It occurs in the streets and unfortunately also in psychiatric wards, in prisons and in their homes. This group should be subject to more considerable attention, and proper research should be done on how human rights and legal capacity applies to that group.

3 A DANISH EXPERT'S VIEW ON DECISION-MAKING MODELS IN DENMARK

I wanted to hear an expert's view upon the Danish experience of transforming decision-making models. Consultant Psychiatrist Torsten Bjørn Jacobsen (TBJ)[10] agreed to talk to me on 5 February 2020. Introducing myself, I stated that in my opinion, basically, far too little attention is paid to the group of people labelled as having severe mental health problems and that I feared that the human rights of this group are not adequately protected.

TBJ gave a minor introduction to the living conditions for people in this group. He told me how 'severe mental illness' often affects their emotional life, and why it is difficult for many of them to make quick decisions. I wanted to know if that meant that the staff sometimes have to make decisions for them. To that, TBJ answered: 'We try our best, and the Safewards model which we have implemented in our treatment helps a lot as the patients and the staff via this model learn to know each other on equal terms and so get more comfortable with each other.' He furthermore told me, that out of the ten Safewards interventions, his wards specifically focus on three of them, those being 'Say NO', 'Know each other' and 'Clear mutual expectations'. The overall treatment concept is: 'give room and understand'. Then, of course, in each ward they have 'the big tree' in the hall where people can write their ideas – for example, suggestions for improvements, complaints, or just something they want to say.

TBJ found that the Safewards model had been a significant step forward as a concept of treatment, as well as in terms of self-determination for people undergoing treatment. Another interviewee, Maria, aged seventy and diagnosed with bipolar disorder, experienced how Safewards changed the treatment culture on the psychiatric ward she was normally admitted to. She told me:

> I was surprised by the major changes that had happened since I was last admitted to this ward. The physical framework had changed. The rooms had been beautifully decorated and I could relax in a sensory room or in a relaxation room if I was uneasy. But most importantly, the staff spoke to me on an equal footing.

[10] TBJ works as Consultant psychiatrist at Psychiatric Center Copenhagen – The Capital Region of Psychiatry.

I myself experienced the changes when visiting her at the ward, and especially when I assisted her during a medical consultation.

TBJ took the view that people with severe mental health problems should be supported in their self-determination. He further suggested that such people should receive extensive additional care, which in his opinion means that they need intensive support in social issues and specifically in decision-making.

TBJ also emphasised that things have in many ways worsened for people with 'serious mental illness'. In the report 'Enhanced efforts for people with mental disorders',[11] the National Board of Health has focused on strengthening the rights of such people by equating them with people with somatic diseases. It means that today all those in need of treatment are offered a 'treatment package' which describes the procedure from day one to the moment of healing. In this way, the therapy system should have become more efficient and results oriented. But, as TBJ explained, this is not necessarily an improvement for people with severe mental health problems.

The 'treatment package' is meant to be a reinforcement of the rights of people with a mental health problems. However, TBJ said that in his opinion most people with 'severe mental health illness' do not fit into the pattern of a 'treatment package', as some people from that group have difficulty in managing their time. Simple propositions like going to a meeting at a specific time on a particular date pose insurmountable difficulties for many. And if the person does not show up, then the treatment offer is removed. Likewise, if individuals cannot make a quick decision on what type of treatment and possible medication they want, it will be decided for them (i.e., substitute decision-making). So extended support in the decision-making process is indispensable.

4 THE 2015 REPORT ON TREATMENT OF PSYCHIATRIC PATIENTS

Someone I know well once told me:

> When I got into psychiatric treatment, which I was in for more than ten years, I was forced to take a lot of psychotropics in such high doses that I was unable to think or feel myself. That's why I didn't care if my human rights were respected. I just accepted the medical treatment as I didn't have the energy to resist. Nothing mattered.

This person, who wants to be anonymous, is now a psychologist. Her luck was that somebody she trusted helped to wean her off of psychotropics. Many people like her are far too heavily medicated, and they don't benefit from it; on the contrary, they are usually worse off.

---

[11] The National Board of Health (2018). *Styrket indsats for mennesker med psykiske lidelser*. P. 13. Retrieved from www.sst.dk/-/media/Udgivelser/2018/Styrket-indsats-for-mennesker-med-psykiske-lidelser,-d-,-Fagligt-oplæg.ashx.

The Danish National Board of Health published a report in 2015,[12] the *National Clinical Guideline for the Treatment of Patients with Schizophrenia and Complex Treatment Programs*. The report tries seriously to describe the difficulties of treating the group of patients who do not benefit from medical treatment. It also seeks to come up with solutions to that problem. A large number of people with severe mental health problems will possibly not benefit from medical treatment. My daughter Luise was certainly one of them. She did, I noticed, become more and more psychotic the more psychotropics she was prescribed. People have contacted me telling stories equivalent to Luise's story, about forced treatment and overmedication, often resulting in their symptoms becoming worse.

I include a few important viewpoints from the 2015 report. In the introduction it states:

> Patients with schizophrenia may have very different disease pathways in terms of the nature and extent of symptoms as well as their temporal course. In some patients with schizophrenia, the course of the disease may be further complicated by the fact that they do not respond satisfactorily to the pharmacological treatment or that they have an inadequate connection with the established treatment system. The presence of concurrent abuse can also complicate treatment.[13]

Later, the report states: 'In the absence of response to several different antipsychotic drugs in adequate dosage and duration, including clozapine, it will be good practice to try gradual dose reduction and, if necessary, cessation of treatment.'[14]

To the best of my knowledge, the guidelines mentioned above for good practice are not sufficiently adhered to in Danish psychiatry – at least, not for people with severe mental health problems. This may in part be due to the fact that the biological view of psychiatric disorders is widespread in Danish psychiatry. From the biological point of view, a mental health disorder is a disease in the brain and may thus be compared to (for example) diabetes, which consequently implies that it can be treated with medication.

5 THE CONSEQUENCES OF LACK OF CO-DETERMINATION FOR THE PEOPLE IN THERAPY

No person may be deprived of the right to self-determination. But if you have a mental health problem and you are in treatment in the psychiatric treatment system, you may easily lose that ability, for a number of reasons. Basically, everything is decided for you; the staff enters your room, often without knocking; the doctors and the staff always know how you feel, whether you actually feel that way or not;

---

[12] The National Board of Health, (2015). *National Klinisk Retningslinje for Behandling af Patienter med Skizofreni og Komplekse Behandlingsforløb*. Retrieved from www.sst.dk/-/media/Udgivelser/2015/NKR-Kompliceret-skizofreni/NKR_skizofreni-og-komplekse-behandlingsforløb_ENDELIG.ashx.
[13] Ibid., p. 9.
[14] Ibid., p. 7.

they know better than you which medication is appropriate for you; they decide whether a visit from friends or relatives is right for you; and so forth. If a person complains about having unpleasant side effects from the psychotropics, a prompt answer from the therapist may often be: 'We can see that the medication helps you.' A complaint about some physical pain will often be met with the answer: 'You must relax. Nothing is wrong. It is just your imagination.' Implied: 'It is part of your disorder.' Who would be able to live a normal life with normal everyday demands after many years under such circumstances?

People with severe mental health problems are often deprived of their self-determination. It may be about fundamental matters concerning their treatment, or whether they want medicine or not, and possibly how much. Having taken too many psychotropics, those people often suffer from lack of energy – they may be too exhausted to care, or they may lack the ability to think or react normally. Also, the unequal power dynamics between clinicians and mental health service users may come into play. Many people who have been in the treatment system for several years may have given up the fight against medical treatment. Experience has taught them who makes the decisions.

Patient consent is essential before treatment can begin. In my opinion, such consent is often given indirectly – in other words, by substitute decision-making. It happens because the person in treatment will eventually accept the proposed treatment plan, as he or she knows that the staff will continue to ask until consent is given. My daughter Luise quickly gave up fighting against the psychiatrists' decisions about how much psychotropic medication she needed. The following account, drawing from her medical record, is very telling:

> On October 19, 1992, she was transferred again to St Hans Hospital. Right away, she said NO to psychotropics because it made her sick; and for a good reason: Three months earlier she almost died because of a malignant neuroleptic syndrome caused by psychotropics. Shortly after, the mandated medication began – administered by syringe – along with periodic use of belt restraints; after 12 days – on November 11, 1992 – she was broken: "Today, the patient shows no physical resistance, but is anxious about being medicated, and afterwards, she is somewhat tearful."[15]

Bent's story offers another real-life illustration of this crisis. Bent was a healthy young man who had just started an education to be a journalist. Aged twenty-two, he had anxiety attacks. Bent consulted a psychiatrist, who gave him some medication for his problems. Bent didn't tolerate the medicine; he felt exhausted and hallucinated. Telling the psychiatrist about his miserable condition resulted in him getting more and stronger medication, now in a psychiatric ward. Bent was now forced to take medicine and thus deprived of his human rights. This horrible scenario went on for years. At a certain point, Bent's life had become so chaotic that he agreed to move into a social institution, with psychiatric treatment offered on a consultation basis.

[15] Christensen, *Dear Luise*, p. 125.

Twenty-five years passed. Over the years, Bent continuously received different psychotropics in large doses and often by covert coercion. Bent was indirectly forced to take medicine because the psychiatrists told him that if he didn't, he would not be able to stay at his place of residence. In the meantime, Bent had become so ill from the massive doses of psychotropics that he did not dare to move to an apartment of his own.

A psychologist from the institution started talking with Bent and realised that the diagnosis and the treatment was wrong. A second opinion on Bent's psychiatric disorder showed that he had anxiety attacks and that, instead of psychotropics, he should be treated for anxiety only. Therefore, he now could move to a regular flat and live a normal life. Bent is now out of the institution, living in his own flat. He finds it extremely difficult. He describes it as like being thrown out of an aeroplane without a parachute. He has suddenly realised how difficult it is to live alone, having lived all his adult life in an institution. For twenty-five years, he had hardly made his own decisions; he had not cooked nor bought his own food or made any other purchases. But altogether, of course, he is happy with his new situation.

DANISH LEGISLATION

The following legislation deals with compulsory treatment of mental health patients in Denmark.

Sundhedsloven – The Danish Health Act, 2007

In dealing with patients' involvement in decisions, §15 asserts that 'no treatment should be initiated or continued without the patient's informed consent, unless otherwise provided by law or regulations provided by law or by §§17–19'.

Psykiatriloven – The Psychiatry Act, 1989

The Psychiatric Act determines under which circumstances compulsory hospitalisation and detention can take place in the psychiatric ward, as well as the conditions for other compulsions to be exercised such as restraint, belt fixation and forced treatment.

...

§5. Detention
Compulsory hospitalisation, cf. sections 6-9, or compulsory detention, cf. section 10, may only take place if the patient is mentally ill or in a state which must be equated with it, and it would be unjustifiable not to deprive the person concerned for the purpose of treatment because:

1) the prospect of healing or a significant and decisive improvement in the condition would otherwise be significantly impaired...

6 HUMAN RIGHTS AND DANISH LEGISLATION

Forced treatment means, to a great extent, a violation of CRPD Article 12 paragraphs 1 and 2, referring to decision-making rights for people with mental health problems. Official figures from the Danish Institute for Human Rights (DIHR) 2019 report 'Forensic psychiatry in a human rights perspective' states that circumstances for these people are largely getting worse: '4,000 forensic psychiatric patients have been sentenced to placement or treatment'.[16] I have been closely involved with this practice through my advocacy for my daughter Luise.[17]

The Danish Board of Health together with the Danish Regions decided in 2014 that coercion in psychiatry must be reduced by 50 per cent by 2020.[18] The impact was subsequently monitored in 2016.[19] The result was disappointing, as it was evident that the planned outcome would not be achieved. The monitoring was repeated in 2018, and from then on, progress has been monitored every half a year. The annual report for 2018 states that overall use of force has not been reduced and that restraint has been altered to other kinds of coercion.[20] This might include to ban the person from smoking a cigarette if he or she doesn't do as told. A harsher method could be that one or two of the staff together try to calm the person by holding him or her in an unfriendly and harsh manner.

The DIHR operates with what they call a 'disability barometer'. The disability barometer compares the living conditions of people with mental health problems to the rest of the population. The trend in recent years points in the wrong direction. This is evident from the fact that five out of six indicators show a deterioration in the situation of people with disabilities compared to the rest of the population from 2012 to 2016 in respect of freedom and personal integrity, accessibility, and education.[21] Further, a sample survey conducted by the Danish police shows a significant increase in police actions against the mentally ill compared to the population as a whole (see Figure 23.1).

---

[16] DIHR, (2019). Forensic psychiatry in a human rights perspective. P. 4. Retrieved from https://menneskeret.dk/sites/menneskeret.dk/files/media/dokumenter/udgivelser/ligebehandling_2019/forensic_psychiatry_summary.pdf.

[17] Christensen, *Dear Luise*, p. 125. 'The mandated medication began – administered by syringe – along with periodic use of belt restraint.'

[18] The National Board of Health, (2018). Monitorering af tvang i psykiatrien, Opgørelse for perioden July 1, 2017–June 30, 2018. P. 4. Retrieved from www.sst.dk/da/sygdom-og-behandling/psykisk-sygdom/~/media/9756456420DC4720 A03C2FEEE735923E.ashx.

[19] The National Board of Health, (2016). Monitorering af tvang i psykiatrien opgørelse for perioden July 1, 2015–June 30, 2016. P. 39. Retrieved from www.sst.dk/da/sygdom-og-behandling/psykisk-sygdom/~/media/841322FA069544B6834B6CE18B51A59A.ashx

[20] The National Board of Health, (2018). Monitorering af tvang i psykiatrien, p. 6.

[21] DIHR, Report to the UN Committee on the Rights of Persons with Disabilities Prior to Adoption of List of Issues. P. 10. Retrieved from https://menneskeret.dk/sites/menneskeret.dk/files/02_februar_19/report_to_the_un_committee_on_the_rights_of_persons_with_disabilities_prior_to_adoption_of_list_of_issues.pdf.

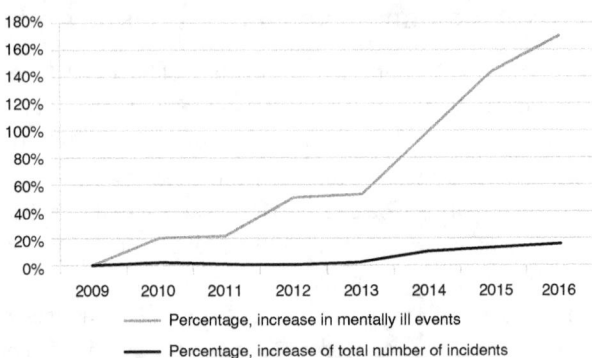

FIGURE 23.1 Police actions against the mentally ill, Denmark
Source: Rigspolitiet – National Beredskabsafdeling[22]

Significant questions[22] remain about how the provisions of Article 12 of the CRPD can be implemented in day-to-day clinical practice and in legislation, policies, and protocols. These questions remain largely unresolved. In 2014, the DIHR recommended that substituted decision-making be replaced by supported decision-making, including with regard to consent for medical treatment, access to justice, voting, marriage, and work.[23]

7 FORCIBLE DETENTION

Forcible detention of persons convicted of a criminal offence is a deprivation of human rights. People with mental health problems are not punishable according to the Danish Criminal Code, so they are exempted from punishment through fines or imprisonment.[24] However, instead of punishment, mentally ill offenders can be sentenced to forced admission – that is, they are subjected to compulsory placement or treatment at a psychiatric ward or in another institution, and often for a very long time. Such compulsory placement always results in deprivation of civil rights. Other measures can include outpatient treatment with supervision by the Danish Prison and Probation Service.[25] The purpose of the said Criminal Code is that people with mental health problems find it difficult to cope with a prison stay, which is why they will be sentenced to a softer kind of punishment. But to be sentenced to psychiatric

---

[22] Rigspolitiet – National Beredskabsafdeling (August 2018). *Beredskabets arbejde med personer med psykiske lidelser* https://politi.dk/-/media/mediefiler/landsdaekkende-dokumenter/nyheder/temaanalyse-om-beredskabets-arbejde-med-psykisk-syge-personer.pdf.
[23] Ibid., p. 13.
[24] DIHR, Forensic psychiatry in human rights perspective, p. 4.
[25] Region Midtjylland Psykiatri og Social i samarbejde med Kriminalforsorgen, (n.d.). Information til personer, der dømmes til psykiatrisk behandling. Retrieved from www.psykiatrien.rm.dk/siteassets/afdelinger/auh-risskov/afdeling-r/hvem-behandler-vi/72008-information-til-personer-der-idommes-til-psykiatisk-behandling-1-01_web-3.pdf

treatment is often a far harsher punishment than a regular prison sentence for at least two reasons: a psychiatric sentence will almost always be of significantly longer duration than a typical prison sentence, and – most important – it involves a deprivation of the convicted person's human rights.

The following excerpt from 'Information for persons sentenced to psychiatric treatment' reveals how a convicted person in a psychiatric ward is deprived of his or her civil rights: 'It is expected that you follow the treatment plan that has been prepared in collaboration with you. This – among other things – concerns: regular conversations; medical treatment; treatment for addiction.'[26] The DIHR likewise states that it is a major problem that so many people with mental health problems are criminalised; they write: 'The amendment should aim to ensure that psychiatric measures are only used in cases concerning crimes that would lead to imprisonment in the ordinary penal system.'[27] The DIHR further notes that 'the regulations in the Danish Criminal Code with regard to psychiatric measures should generally be revised so that Danish law better reflects international standards for equal treatment of people with disabilities and standards for respecting basic freedoms'.[28] The report furthermore states: 'Almost all sentences to psychiatric measures issued in 2017 include an option for compulsory admission (97%), while a considerable percentage are of indeterminate duration (40%).'[29] Also, the report highlights the problem of discrimination against people with long-term mental illness: 'The problem – that people with long-term mental illness receive longer sentences – is even more pressing today. It is a massive human rights challenge for Denmark, because disproportionately long-term measures may constitute discrimination against people with long-term mental illness.'[30]

Sadly, more and more people are being subjected to forced admissions. Figures from the police report 'Emergency preparedness for work with people with mental disorders' show that in the period from 2009 to 2016, there was an increase of approximately 45 per cent in the number of forced admissions (see Figure 23.2).

One reason for the increase could be that 'minor incidents' in psychiatry are reported as violence. This is emphasised by what the Danish union for social assistants working in psychiatry (FOA) state on their report on violence in psychiatry: 'Threatening or aggressive behaviour [against health care workers] is reported to the police almost as routine, as we would like to send a signal that such behaviour is not acceptable.'[31]

In the context of coercion in psychiatry, it is also important to mention covert, coercive medication. It is rarely reported, but it happens all the time. The risk of covert, coercive medication is particularly high in forensic psychiatry. A possible explanation could be that the convicted person feels forced to follow the therapist's

---

[26] Ibid.
[27] DIHE., Forensic psychiatry in a human rights perspective, p. 8.
[28] Ibid.
[29] Ibid., p. 5.
[30] Ibid.
[31] FOA. (2015). Vold i psykiatrien. P. 7. Retrieved from www.foa.dk/~/media/faelles/pdf/rapporter-undersoegelser/2015/vold%20i%20psykiatrien%20pdf.pdf.

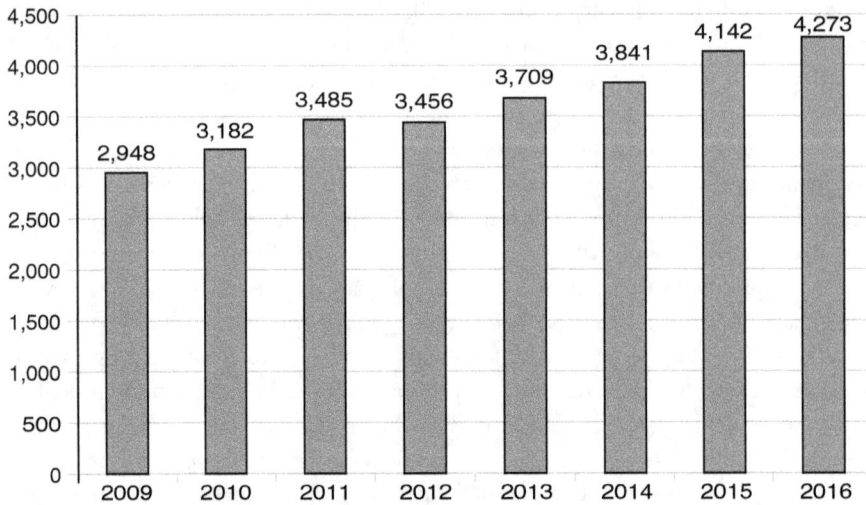

FIGURE 23.2 Forced admissions, Denmark, 2009–16
Source: Rigspolitiet – National Beredskabsafdeling[32]

instruction about medical treatment to avoid spending a long time in detention or to get permission to smoke a cigarette, etc. It must nevertheless be regarded as a violation of Article 12 of the CRPD.

8 DECISION-MAKING MODELS: THE SAFEWARDS MODEL AND THE RECOVERY MODEL

The Safewards model is an evidence-based conflict-resolution model.[33] Conflict often occurs in the interaction between staff and patients. If the communication with the patients is negative and authoritarian, it can lead to aggressive situations. Conflict can also occur as a result of situations where staff restrict the patient's freedom, prevent activities the patient is fond of, or verbally impose restrictions. When staff know these flashpoints, staff can influence the extent of conflicts and the management of those in the section. There are ten Safewards interventions. They are:

1. Clear mutual expectations – staff and patients agree on expectations of each other and put a laminated poster on the notice board; this is about acceptable and unacceptable behaviour.
2. Positive words – staff to acknowledge the positive during handovers.

---

[32] Rigspolitiet, Beredskabets arbejde med personer med psykiske lidelser.
[33] Bowers, Safewards.

3. Soft words – message on office message boards to remind staff about how to communicate in helpful ways.
4. Mutual help meetings – staff and patients meet at set times to share news, say thank you, come up with suggestions, make requests, or make offers to help.
5. Bad news mitigation – put staff in the shoes of patients to think how they convey difficult messages and what support is needed.
6. Talk down – talk and act in a way to decrease the tension.
7. Calm down – to make use of various methods to calm down (e.g. music, stress balls, etc.).
8. Know each other – patients and staff can share non-personal information such as hobbies; sports teams can be formed to connect with each other by talking about shared interests.
9. Reassurance – staff to support patients at times when they are stressed or if something of concern has happened and they are worried.
10. Discharge messages – patients who leave may want to write a message which can be displayed on the notice board and shared with new patients to give them hope.

Psykiatrisk Center Ballerup, one of the five centres in the Copenhagen region, successfully introduced Safewards in January 2017. As a result, the psychiatric centre was free from the use of mechanical restraint for at least the following 100 days, without having increased the use of medication.[34] Most sections of the psychiatric centre still have very few restraints. This is in stark contrast to other psychiatric centres, where the discussion is about reducing the number of belt fixings above 48 hours.

The Recovery model emphasises that co-determination, respect, dialogue, equality, and several other social skills are essential.[35] It is a completely different and more respectful way of looking at people with mental illness, giving them courage in life and engaging them with their own opinions and perceptions of illness. One of the major strengths of the recovery model is that it focuses on individual strengths and abilities rather than on deficits and pathologies.

9 AN ONGOING DEBATE IS CRUCIAL

Reactions to Article 12 range from unqualified enthusiasm to strong disapproval. Some theorists tend to see the article as the key to considerable improvement in respect of human rights compliance for people with mental health problems. On the other side, you find psychiatrists who have voiced the opinion that its provisions will

---

[34] Region Hovedstaden, Safewards er landet på PC Ballerup. Retrieved from www.psykiatri-regionh.dk/centre-og-social-tilbud/Psykiatriske-centre/Psykiatrisk%20Center%20Ballerup/Om-centret/Vil-du-have-et-spaendende-job-i-psykiatrien/Saerligt-for-Yngre-Laeger-paa-Psykiatrisk-Center-Ballerup/Sider/Arbejdsmiljø.aspx

[35] Lyon, The Recovery model.

make many persons with mental disabilities worse off. A third position is expressed as moderate criticism of Article 12 or attempts to limit how its provisions can be implemented in their local treatment system. The fronts in the debate on psychiatric treatment in Denmark seem to have become increasingly sharp.

On 1 May 2019, columnists in the Danish newspaper *Jyllands-Posten* stated: 'We need a national council for psychiatry. It is obvious to ask whether there is a more fundamental problem behind the visible issues, a "design flaw" in psychiatry that creates and maintains the apparent problems.'[36] Under this heading, it was stated that Danish psychiatrists are concerned about what they call a crisis in Danish psychiatry. That is the angle under which they contribute to the debate. They are worried that too much force is used in treatment, and that far too many do not get better from the therapy. On 16 June 2016, the newspaper *Information* featured an interview with the Danish chief psychiatrist Hans Henrik Ockelmann under the heading, 'We still suffer from the scourge of antipsychiatry'.[37] Ockelmann criticised the rigid procedures in psychiatric treatment: 'In some situations, it is necessary to violate a person's autonomy to give them a chance to try what it means not to be insane so that they have the option to opt in or out. But the choice should be delayed, so we act first.' And also: 'I talk first and foremost about medical treatment... But if it were up to me, I would also like to see electroshock not having a special position.' Many specialists agree with this point of view. On 24 April 2019, the newspaper *Politiken* reported: 'Startling report from the Forensic Psychiatric Clinic shows that multiple killings and attempted killings could have been avoided if treatment had been sufficient.'[38]

Ultimately, a constructive debate is required that eventually – and hopefully – will lead to a paradigm shift. UN's Special Rapporteur on the right to health, Dainius Pūras, stated in a report from 6 June 2017:

> We need little short of a revolution in mental health care to end decades of neglect, abuse and violence... Mental health is grossly neglected within health systems around the world. Where mental health systems exist, they are segregated from other healthcare and based on outdated practices that violate human rights. I am calling on States to move away from traditional practices and thinking, and enable a long overdue shift to a rights-based approach. The status quo is simply unacceptable.[39]

---

[36] Vestergaard, Per and Kristensen, Knud (1 May 2019). We need a national council for psychiatry. *Jyllands-Posten*. Retrieved from https://jyllands-posten.dk/debat/kronik/ECE9544310/vi-har-brug-for-et-nationalt-raad-for-psykiatri/

[37] Toft, Soren Bergreen (10 June 2016). Interview. *Information*. Retrieved from www.information.dk/debat/2016/06/lider-stadig-antipsykiatriens-svoebe.

[38] Schmidt, Anders Legarth and Rasmussen, Lars Igum (24 April 2019). Opsigtsvækkende rapport: Flere drab og drabsforsøg begået af psykisk syge kunne muligvis være undgået. Behandlingen var utilstrækkelig. *Politiken*. Retrieved from https://politiken.dk/forbrugogliv/sundhedogmotion/art7157494/Flere-drab-og-drabsforsøg-begået-af-psykisk-syge-kunne-muligvis-være-undgået.-Behandlingen-var-utilstrækkelig.

[39] OHCHR report (6 June 2017), Dainius Pūras. World needs "revolution" in mental health care. Retrieved from www.ohchr.org/EN/NewsEvents/Pages/DisplayNews.aspx?NewsID=21689

Obviously, there are different points of view. The ambiguities should not impede solving the treatment problem, though. They should instead lead to a more varied discussion where opinions from a variety of interest groups could be canvassed.

10 CONCLUSION

The Danish health care system still has a long way to go, though actions have been taken to pave the way for better conditions. I truly believe that the Safewards model and the Recovery model are steps in the right direction. Still, people with mental health problems are not afforded the same opportunities to make decisions on a par with others in society in accordance with Article 12 of the CRPD. Despite the good intentions and extensive debate on the subject, things have not improved sufficiently. In 2014, the Committee on the Rights of Persons with Disabilities recommended that substituted decision-making be replace by supported decision-making. To my knowledge, this has not happened.[40]

According to the DIHR, the number of people receiving court-ordered psychiatric treatment increasing, either as a new sentence or as an extension of an existing sentence. Also, the Danish Board of Health reports that force in psychiatric treatment has increased. This is partly due to a widespread perspective in relation to mental health problems. They are seen as diseases, like diabetes (i.e., the biological approach). This, in turn, means that people with psychiatric diagnoses can only be treated with medication – often for their entire life. I do not agree that mental health problems can be viewed that way. A person can have a mental health problem for a period, but it must not be considered a lifelong disease, as is often the case.

So, I agree with the United Nations Special Rapporteur on the right to health Dainius Pūras's words as stated above.[41] In my opinion, the treatment culture should focus on people's resources instead of treating them as 'deficient'. Therefore, the discussion must be more nuanced. We must have in mind who we are talking about, and what their individual needs are. Why don't we ask the users?

[40] CRPD.
[41] Pūras, World needs "revolution" in mental health care.

24

The Use of Patient Advocates in Supporting People with Psychosocial Disabilities

Aikaterini Nomidou

Abstract

It is now well documented that support is an essential ingredient of the Convention on the Rights of Persons with Disabilities' (CRPD) paradigm shift for the exercise of legal capacity, and that patient advocacy has the potential to promote the CRPD's values. What remains less documented is the support sought by and given to persons with psychosocial disabilities by family members and representative psychosocial disability organizations, consisting of persons with psychosocial disabilities and family members, and group advocacy undertaken by the latter. This chapter uses the personal story of a family member of a person with psychosocial disability to lay out some of the key issues relating to exercising legal capacity, including legal and practical barriers and obstacles, enabling factors, and supports that foster autonomy through honoring interdependence with family and friends, and the pivotal role of mixed groups of persons with psychosocial disabilities and family members in working to promote and ensure the right of persons of psychosocial disabilities to be consulted and to express their own views.

INTRODUCTION

One of the overriding messages of the CRPD is the idea that persons with disabilities may require support in the exercise of legal capacity. Patient advocacy is intended to be a means of promoting and safeguarding the CRPD values; however, the absence of consensus as to its meaning has prompted an explosion of different types of advocacy and advocates. This chapter will refer to the Greek context as I have experienced it; firstly the support given to persons with psychosocial disabilities by family members and representative psychosocial disability organizations, and secondly group advocacy undertaken by psychosocial disability organizations consisting of persons with psychosocial disabilities and family members. In both cases the aim is to enable persons with psychosocial disabilities to realize their own human potential. I will share my personal story of living with and providing spontaneous support to my brother, who has schizophrenia, and who relies on family connectedness and supports to chart his own life course and get as much fulfillment as he can. My intention is to use this story to lay out some of the key issues it highlights about exercising legal capacity, including legal and practical barriers, enabling factors and supports that foster autonomy through honoring interdependence with family and friends, and the pivotal role of mixed groups of persons with psychosocial disabilities and family members in working to promote and ensure the right of persons with psychosocial disabilities to be consulted and to express their own views.

LIKE A BOLT FROM THE BLUE

I never dreamed of becoming a patient advocate or felt it as a calling or career prospect. I grew up in a middle-class Greek family in a provincial Greek town in an agricultural area close to the Bulgarian border. It is a quiet town where people seem to live uneventful lives. Languages were my passion, and my dream was to work with words, as a translator. However, needs led me down another road, and this is a road about which I am still learning after forty years.

When I was fourteen, it became more than obvious that my sixteen-year-old brother's behavior represented something more than typical teenage issues. I remember my father telling my brother that he would send him to "Leros" and me searching in the encyclopedias to find out what "Leros" was. Years later I read that it was "Europe's guilty secret" (Merrit, 1989, pp. 1,7), "a cemetery of souls," and "a colony of psychopaths" (Gabriel, 1990). I remember hiding my brother from my father and hiding myself from my brother. I remember the smell of blood, the pain, the fear, the shame, and the agonizing question of who was to blame. I remember my family spending so much time striving to disguise vulnerability in order to appear normal.

My brother is one of the most extraordinary persons I've ever met. I have always admired his sharp mind, his goodness, his vast interests, and his gift for being good in so many fields I could only dream about: a mathematician, a snake whisperer, a fish charmer, a chess player, a skier, a passionate collector of everything from stamps, coins and vinyl records to frogs and leaves and stones. At the age of fifteen his bookshelves were already overloaded with books about spirituality and religion, outer space and the afterlife, ancient civilizations and occult sciences, Freud, Nietzsche, Marx, Einstein, the Greek classics, and anarchist philosophers. I still live with him and his room is still a miniature of a flea market, an intriguing place of inspiration.

His behavior continued to attract attention. I remember him "drying herbs" in the oven and hitting us all when we objected, and police (called by the neighbors because of the strong smell) searching every inch of our house. Knife fights, sirens, police cars, handcuffs for my brother, and injuries for the rest of the family were a frequent show for the neighbors. The police "diagnosed" him with substance abuse. I was declared the sister of a "junkie" and my friends were prohibited by their parents to visit anymore. Gradually, the whole family was ostracized and left to live in frustration, in a new reality. I was in my twenties when I started the visits to police stations, prisons, and psychiatric facilities.

FROM LABELS AND COERCION TO VOLITION, SUPPORT, AND MEANING

My brother's understanding and perception of the real world were frequently considered as sharply and persistently divergent from reality. Sometimes he thought he was Antichrist incarnated while others that he was a cannibal from Papua New Guinea's jungles. After a long delay – of years, not months – he was diagnosed with schizophrenia; however, he never accepted the label. At that time he was studying nuclear physics.

In the eyes of the law he may have upgraded from a "junkie" to a patient; however, in the eyes of society he became a "psycho." At the same time, I also upgraded from the sister of a "junkie" to the sister of a "psycho." For my parents, the dilemma was where he could best receive treatment. The public sector was not encouraging: there were only eight public mental hospitals in all of Greece, which accommodated over 7,000 patients, more than half of whom were over fifty, and 56 percent of whom would stay more than ten years (Bairaktaris, 1994, p. 108). Was this the most suitable point of contact with the psychiatric health system for a young man in his early twenties? Of course not.

At that time a few private psychiatric clinics were also available. My parents chose one of these with the hope it might be something like the nice clinics we see in films on TV, but it was in this clinic that I first saw chained and otherwise restrained and maltreated young service users who begged me in whispers for assistance.

In 1992 a Greek law (Law 2071/1992) was adopted that has been described as an important step towards securing the rights of persons with mental illness. However, the cumbersome procedure of involuntary admission, which does not separate placement and treatment, has led to its frequent circumvention by psychiatrists (see European Committee for the Prevention of Torture and Inhuman or Degrading Treatment or Punishment (CPT), 2019, pp. 9–27). This Law, which is still in force, obliges next of kin of persons with a mental illness to contact a public prosecutor, who would launch an admission procedure and transfer by the police to a public psychiatric ward. I was faced with the dilemma of either acting as an informer or accepting that my suffering brother would become a laughing stock, and I opted for the former more than once.

However, I could see only absurdity and injustice in this. Just like the condemned of Franz Kafka's "In the Penal Colony," my brother did not know why he was arrested; the lack of communication was intentional in order to facilitate *justice*; a hearing was held *in absentia* of all parties; a standardized involuntary commitment judgment was issued by one single judge "weeks after discharge;" there was no legal representation, no information, nothing. In this process, I was first an informer, then an accessory, and later a betrayer (see Greek Ombudsman, 2019 and Stylianidis et al., 2017). Is this the proper way to seek, offer, and receive treatment?

In 1998, a psychiatric unit was established in the public general hospital of my town. My brother was admitted there against his will. Every time my brother was an inpatient there, I felt that nobody should be treated in such conditions; but this situation had become normalized: the law meant to secure the rights of persons with mental illness was not implemented properly, if at all, but it was nobody's individual responsibility to account for it or to do anything (see Fytrakis, 2007).

Even though treatment with psychotropic medications was a one-way road that alleviated his so called positive symptoms, reduced frustration, and made living under the same roof easier for the whole family every time he was discharged from this closed-door open unit, I am confident that my brother would have chosen a different way if he had access to other options. When asked about opportunities to exercise legal agency during admission, he said: "They respect me. Others have problems because they do not know how to behave. It's important to obey and not to show a desire to leave; when you agree to stay you have better chances to leave because doctors think that you are getting better."

Six years ago my brother accepted that he has "melancholy," as he calls his condition. Since then, he developed a volition (as contrasted to compliance) with regard to medication administration, and never misses his fortnightly five-minute outpatient appointments. However, he also now suffers from chronic respiratory failure, adding to his difficulties and increasing his reliance on family support, which he both seeks and welcomes.

Recently we had the following discussion:

> Me: "The CRPD says that when you are not well nobody should decide to take you to the hospital and give you medication against your will. What do you think?"
>
> My brother: "This must not happen. Don't you understand? I need my treatment to be well. This is why you became a lawyer? To use the law to ban me from being treated?"
>
> Me: "No, of course not. Should we act like this even if you object?"
>
> My brother: "Yes. Otherwise I will be like a mad."

Impairments and difficulties, societal barriers, and disincentives prevented him from finding and retaining employment on an equal basis with others. The only time he worked was fifteen years ago when he benefited from a quota system for fixed-term employment of persons with disabilities. Working for two years in the municipal dog shelter seemed to be his happiest time. Since then, his only income has been a modest benefit as a Disabled Adult Child.

Nevertheless, he compares himself favorably to others and says he is happy with his daily routine of going out at certain hours to sit on a bench in the square. He proudly reports that old school mates salute him, that the Mayor calls him Mister, and that his vote helped a former friend to enter parliament. At home, he enjoys listening to music and participating in discussions about our childhood, dogs, and medicinal herbs. The only thing he asks us to remind him of is to take a shower and change clothes. He is happy to contribute to family life from time to time, tidying his bedside table and collecting light groceries from the local shop. When asked if he would prefer to live independently, he strongly objects. "Do you want to get rid of me? This is home, my room, my things, and you're my family. I am an autonomous fifty-six-year-old sick man, and I have a right to family life," he says. In Greece, autonomy does not convey the sense of detachment, nonreliance, or nonsupport that independence does.

Feeling autonomous never prevented him from asking the family for support in making decisions. Family support to enable him to exercise his legal capacity ranged from assisting him to understand that signing an application form for a debit card would only liberate him from banking queues; to supporting him to comprehend the differences between accepting and renouncing our father's property before he chose to sign the act of acceptance of inheritance; to objecting to his placement under a judicial support mechanism proposed by health professionals "for his own good."

My almost forty-year experience of living with my brother with schizophrenia has led me to believe that it sounds utopian to understand from CRPD General Comment 1 (GC1) that everyone can always decide, given sufficient support. The GC1 absolutist approach would make sense within models whereby a disability can never affect a person's decision-making (as Lewis (2019) maintains). When my brother sometimes believes that he is Antichrist incarnated, his decision-making about treatment for the symptoms of his psychosis is temporarily clouded. Until the CRPD Committee comes up with feasible policy suggestions about universally accepted consent standards, I have no alternative but to continue to play the awful role of informer, accessory, and betrayer imposed by the flawed 1992 Law, in order to provide my brother with the medication that has helped him to live a fulfilling life. As for how I feel: caring about and supporting my brother to lead a life he says he enjoys provides the rewarding feeling of complying with the values we both uphold.

THE ROLE AND THE RIGHTS OF THE SUPPORTING FAMILY

The CRPD in preamble para. 24 locates the individual with disability within the family, suggesting that the former must be seen within the context of a family where the rights of other family members must also be addressed if all family members' rights are to be protected. However, the CRPD addresses the role of supporting family briefly and relates to families as an immediate environment or as a facilitator. This may be understood as not paying sufficient attention to the rights of the supporting family.

Moreover, whether family members undertake a caring role willingly and/or because of the lack of available public support, they may feel that their nonrecognition as a separate entity means that they are not adequately protected against discrimination by association. Likewise, the explicit reference of CRPD Art. 28(c) to entitlements only for families living in poverty disproportionately affects families who are not living in poverty, but who desperately need training, counseling, and respite care to contribute better towards the full and equal enjoyment of their disabled family member's rights. Will my seventy-five-year-old mother who has never, ever, had a day off from supporting my brother for the past three decades not be entitled, through the paradigm shift, to respite care because her modest widow's pension is not at poverty threshold?

The revolutionary theory of justice of the CRPD as applied to disability acts favorably towards persons like my brother who have long been not recognized as equals to persons without disabilities or with other disabilities. However, family members of persons with psychosocial disabilities may feel, as I do, another inequality: if the list of the types of organizations enumerated in CRPD General Comment No. 7 (2018) para. 12(d) (GC7) is exhaustive, this could mean that family members of persons with psychosocial disabilities are not recognized as equals to family members of persons with dementia or intellectual disabilities. Couldn't this explicit differentiation of family members by the CRPD Committee also be seen as discrimination both against family members of persons with psychosocial disabilities who want to provide support and against the latter who wish to be supported by their families? (see Flynn and Arstein-Kerslake, 2017). Couldn't this further be seen as being in contradiction with CRPD Art. 12(3) and CRPD GC1? Would be entailed if the CRPD Committee did not recognize united organizations of persons with disabilities and their families, which are recognized as representative organizations by the States?

MY PATH TO GROUP MENTAL HEALTH ADVOCACY

My story is not unique. It is the story of too many. In 1998, I joined some courageous people who wanted to do what the CRPD Committee described twenty years later in GC7 para. 12(d), albeit excluding persons with psychosocial disabilities. We established a local family and user association to assist and empower users to have a voice and take full control of their own lives, and to work to promote and apply supported decision-making processes to ensure and respect the right of users to be consulted and express their views. Later on, some of our family members became persons in the early stages of dementia, and consequently in 2016 we included dementia in our scope.

It has been reported that in mixed groups of users and families, relatives often dominate. However, it is the nature of how and why people come together that defines the relationships they build. Sometimes groups spring from the desire of some to help and improve the lot of others, who in turn look for assistance and support (Gosling & Martin, 2012, p. 35). Our association, SOFPSI.N.Serron, may not be comprised of a majority of users: however, it can be completely directed by them. On the basis of Art. 11 of the statute, the five-member Board can consist of five users. Our ultimate aim has always been to have users take the lead.

Our speaking from the heart spoke to the hearts of other users and family members, and led to the establishment of other mixed associations who joined voices and formed a federation. POSOPSI is the sole second-level national organization conducting group advocacy for mental health and a national member of the National Confederation of Disabled People, which is designated, inter alia, as the Framework for the Promotion of the Implementation of the CRPD in Greece.

On the basis of Arts. 2(4), 4(3), and 12–16 of the Federation's statute, user views not only are not dismissed in favor of third-party representatives, but are considered as at least equal to those of family members. Representing 50 percent of views in the General Assembly and having the possibility to obtain a majority of 63.63 percent in the Board, users are closely consulted and actively involved in influencing public opinion, policy, and service provision, as well as in legal and regulatory frameworks and procedures across all levels and branches of the government.

Even though users and family members have the right to seek election, it does not mean that they all always want to. However, there is no tension between users and family members, nor should there be between the CRPD's emphasis on individual autonomy in decision-making and caregiver representation. In our case, users are not represented by caregivers at the first level, nor at the second. Isn't individual autonomy more likely to result from support rather than nonsupport?

ADVOCACY FOR HEALTH: MOBILIZATION, EMPOWERMENT, AND REPRESENTATION

We dived into efforts to dispel myths, reduce stigma, and create humanized external environments that facilitate internal recovery in which users can grow, such as a four-day festival (SOFPSI.N.Serron, 2013), where 3,000 people, old and young, stigmatized and stigmatizing, mad about somebody, mad at something or in a mad rush, got together as one soul sharing the idea that we are all equal and we may all go mad sometimes, so let's not discriminate against anybody.

I later learnt that the actions our association undertakes are included in the term "advocacy for health" (WHO, 1998, p. 5). Twenty-two years later, the term still precisely depicts the nature of advocacy actions: "Acting by and/or on behalf of individuals and groups to design living conditions that create and support health outcomes and healthy lifestyles," informed by three underlying principles: mobilization, empowerment, and representation (Center for Society Orientation, 2013). Our social actions to gain social acceptance were fruitful in terms of two of these three principles.

Mobilization was achieved: local authorities, health professionals, local media, school boards, and other disability, cultural, and sports associations joined us in our endeavors. This generated a knock-on effect which proved to be a driver for collaboration in fighting the societal stigma of mental health conditions.

Empowerment also produced results. While we knew that peer support is increasingly recognized as a best-practice intervention for rights-based, recovery-oriented mental health care, we had to acknowledge that many users in this part of the world are frequently not even aware that they have rights. Raising awareness about rights is the first step towards claiming them. Improved awareness of their rights as citizens helped many users build their confidence to be peer and self-advocates, and to become protagonists of their own lives once again, including on stage (SOFPSI.N. Serron, 2014). Family members were equipped with approaches to adopt a rights-based model of caring and supported decision-making practices (see Simmons & Gooding, 2017), and provided with psychoeducation and peer support to improve the quality of user-caregiver relationships and promote dignity. Collaboration with Boston University (Center for Psychiatric Rehabilitation) (Global Leadership Institute, 2012) culminated in the organization of training seminars on "rights and recovery" attended by users, caregivers, and mental health professionals who were invited to learn from lived experiences (SOFPSI.N.Serron, 2014).

Over the past twenty-two years, hundreds of people have benefited from our actions – but not my brother. "You can do everything to help people, but without a person's interest in getting better, the help can't work. I want nothing to do with the mad," he says. As a family we wish he could benefit from support and peer groups; however, he has always rejected anything related to "psy." We continue to listen to him if he needs to talk. Sometimes just being there is enough.

However, while our actions helped fight self-stigma and societal stigma to an important extent, as long as structural stigma exists, they can never be a complete solution. To secure political commitment, policy support, and systems support for equity in mental health, something more was needed: representation. Effective representation entails other types of advocacy actions, such as educating legislators; engaging in research to produce relevant resources to present realities based on real peoples' real stories; having a presence in conferences where the future of laws and policies is planned; and lobbying against legislation restricting rights on the basis of psychosocial disabilities.

LAW AND SOCIAL JUSTICE

At this point another issue arose. How can one undertake effective representation actions without a minimal legal background? What could I do to help advance, protect, and fulfill the rights of users? At thirty-three, I entered law school with the hope of learning how to use the law to do social justice work and make a difference to the lives of users. To my disappointment, the closest links with mental health I could find were about how to impose restrictions on the grounds of mental illness and perceived dangerousness. The law I studied at that time failed to prepare me even remotely to serve the interests of users. Legal education in my law school was focused on training lawyers to serve interests that maintain the status quo.

Thus I graduated with no knowledge or skills in lawyering for social justice. Clearly some further legal training and skills were necessary for the promotion of social change to address human rights violations in mental health. I found the international diploma in mental health, law and human rights delivered by the Indian Law Society in Pune, India with the support of the WHO, Geneva. This course aims to equip practitioners with the knowledge to ensure that the rights of persons with psychosocial disabilities are better respected, in accordance with the CRPD and other international standards.

WHO QUALITYRIGHTS

Through our local association SOFPSI N.Serron, I first applied my CRPD knowledge to researching human rights conditions in the same mental health facility where my brother had been a "revolving door patient." The focus was to assess quality of care in this establishment using the human rights model of care promoted by the WHO QualityRights toolkit. The findings (Nomidou, 2013) revealed that different groups expressed different perceptions of what quality of care was: from the users' perspective, quality evaluation was about their personal experience in terms of satisfaction with the support they were getting and the degree to which their needs, preferences, and objectives were met. However, staff did not tend to perceive quality in terms of quality-of-life outcomes, or see human rights as closely related to quality of health services, but tended to emphasize organization of care, or structure, and the influence of organization of care on clinical processes of care as delivered by providers (Donabedian, 2005). Finally, family members perceived care quality as closely related to information, relief, counselling support, and interaction with staff. "I have learnt to listen to them ... When will they learn to listen to me?" a user said, while a psychiatrist stated: "It rests upon the psychiatrist to decide who is going to be informed about his/her right to appeal involuntary admission and who is not."

Empowering users and family members helped them engage in self- and group advocacy. Awareness raising among health professionals helped them reflect on their daily practice through the lens of the CRPD.

Armed with the findings of this report (QualityRights Assessment Greece, 2012), as the association's spokesperson I was better able to advocate for improvements in mental health care settings. I believed – as I still do – in the transformative power international human rights instruments have. I am sure that the full implementation of the CRPD can bring the hoped-for changes in the field of mental health.

However, after eight years of involvement in group advocacy for its implementation on the ground, I am convinced that Greece is still a long way from truly internalizing the paradigm shift it endorsed by ratifying the CRPD. In Greek society, there are widely held beliefs that service users are unable to make their own decisions, leading to practices that discriminate against them and prevent them from enjoying the same opportunities as others. These beliefs are often seen as normal and are propagated even by the victims themselves. Furthermore, these beliefs are actually manifested in Greek laws which preclude users from making their own decisions; in a vicious circle these laws fuel societal attitudes regarding this supposed inability and incapacity. These embedded societal attitudes are expressed in resistance to legal reforms.

The year I completed my report (2012) was the year that Greece ratified the CRPD and it was time for the country to start implementation. At this point I started to wonder what comes first: enforcement of human rights norms under the rule of law, or movement towards attitudes that embrace diversity and inclusivity. My professional experience in Greece and abroad in both low-resource and high-income countries has convinced me that both must be addressed if countries are to truly foster a spirit of inclusion. Whether or not the CRPD becomes reality on the ground in the differing specific circumstances of Greece and other countries, rather than just on paper, is much more dependent on attitudes than on its legally binding character. In order to achieve lasting change, key stakeholders will also have to recognize the gaps in their knowledge and act to overcome them. The CRPD alone cannot magically solve every problem, but changing laws can play a part in changing people's minds.

RAISING AWARENESS OF THE CRPD

In my capacity as the Federation's legal representative and spokesperson, I had opportunities to participate in post-CRPD ratification drafting or reviewing legislation that affects users. To my surprise, many of the legal (see Perlin, 2013) and medical professionals who made up the participating committees were not free of biases or stigmatizing attitudes. Discussions also revealed gaps in their knowledge of the content of the CRPD or its applicability to users, or of the ratification-related obligations of our country to shift the policy gaze away from the medical model and custodial provisions to a more encompassing social paradigm. However, insiders often view with suspicion ideas put forward by outsiders such as myself. I grasped the opportunity to raise awareness of the CRPD, and despite an apparently generalized resistance, some prominent and influential insiders welcomed "these interesting perspectives" and showed genuine interest in knowing more. I started to have new allies in my efforts to influence policy, laws, and regulations through the lens of the CRPD. *Helping those who change laws that can help change people's minds to start by changing their own minds was a significant first step.*

More often than not, a first step is followed by a second, a third, and many more. Being invited by old allies, such as social and community psychiatry professionals (see Stylianidis, 2016) who promote recovery and rights-based practice, and by my new allies to almost all major mental health-related conferences in the country allows me to raise awareness of the CRPD and what its implementation would entail. Given that implementation does not and cannot happen in vitro, I grasp these opportunities to address influential mental health policymakers and professionals, in order to define rights and responsibilities, identify rights holders and duty bearers, and refer to the obligations of the state to recognize all users as full persons before the law. Biases and stigmatizing attitudes also exist among mental health policymakers and professionals (see Corrigan & Watson, 2002). These events are attended by hundreds of influential stakeholders and are a good forum to advocate about the rights-based provision of health and social care services to users. *Helping change the minds of established influential key stakeholders who can help change and implement laws was my second step.*

Work with established stakeholders is vital, but it is tomorrow's generation that will break today's status quo and bring the hoped-for changes in fields that affect users. I believe in the power of the young. Even though biases are also present among students (see Lally et al., 2013), the youth are not yet fully contaminated by the prejudices of the old. In my mental health advocacy journey, I have met inspiring medical educators striving to create a new generation of human rights-oriented professionals and policymakers who recognize empathy and compassionate interactions as central to improvement; see the recipients of health and social care services as the ultimate stakeholders in quality improvement; and believe that the rights-based approach to healthcare will allow them not merely to identify needs and seek ways to address medical situations, but also to defend dignity, help patients exercise agency, and create work spaces in which patients' rights are enacted and enjoyed (see Lionis, 2015). *Helping train this new generation of tomorrow's health professionals and policymakers was my next step.*

Therefore, just like with self-stigma and societal stigma, in order to overcome structural stigma, a whole range of people need to change attitudes and beliefs (Baumann Anja-WHO Regional Office for Europe, 2010). In other words, only a rights-based holistic approach to both law and policymaking and the implementation and monitoring thereof can effectively improve the situation for users both on paper and on the ground. I want to hope that the implementation of the CRPD won't have the same fate as the Greek mental health reform, which is famous for being still incomplete after almost forty years

THE PERFECT ADVOCATE

My whole experience to date has shown me that I will always need to develop further skills. Daily hands-on experience on mental health group advocacy practice shows that in order to change attitudes, skills beyond the legal spectrum are needed: skills that fall within other frameworks, including but not limited to sociology, anthropology, history, political science, social work, diplomacy, communication, cooperation, management, and strategy. I recognize that lifelong learning will always be necessary to equip me with additional skills to help transform power relations and remove formal and informal barriers to human rights-based, recovery-oriented laws, policies, and practices that promote inclusion of users.

The perfect advocate does not exist, and group advocacy too depends on politics and policy prioritizations, and a plethora of other factors. There are still many countries balancing old embedded beliefs and new obligations for change, where professional advocacy is not yet a legal entitlement, where no formal financial assistance for group advocacy and support services is available, and where both the former and the latter are mainly, if not exclusively, resourced by passion, commitment, and resourcefulness. I have learnt to operate in such environments, to inspire hope to users and families and remind the state and other key stakeholders of their obligations.

It has been a long road, but I have finally started to be the mental health advocate I wish I had met forty years ago: one of those advocates who, according to Lewis (2017), "speak up about what they care about and care about what they speak about."

CONCLUSION

Ideally, the CRPD would be fully implemented and there would be public support services available for all users and family members throughout Greece. Ideally, there would also be professional advocates in all mental health and social care facilities, hopefully with knowledge of human rights and adequately equipped with the necessary skillsets to redress power imbalances, empathize with and protect users from abuses, assess their values and goals, and help them exercise their rights in closed-doors facilities. I look forward to the moments of potential friction between them and family members! It would mean that users are not alone within quasi-omnipotent medical contexts. It would also mean that the government will not depend on families anymore to achieve national goals without affording them, including their disabled family members, any support. It would further mean less friction between users and family members on one part, and state authorities, policymakers, and health and legal experts, on the other.

In the meanwhile, users and family members united will continue to demand the burden of obstacles to be confronted; the imbalances of the biomedical model to be balanced; procedural and substantive safeguards to be provided; accountability for human rights violations and abuses to be ensured; the social and underlying determinants for the promotion of mental health to be addressed; and home-based support and community services to be made available throughout the country.

With tactics ranging from dispelling myths and ever-present fears; to helping users help themselves to overcome the obstacles they face; to building confidence in family members to help users help themselves; to informing users of their human rights and raising awareness among others to respect those; to reporting problems and filing complaints; and to advocating for the adoption of human rights-respecting laws and practices, we – users and family members – work together towards enabling fostering user autonomy and honoring healthy interdependence.

REFERENCES

Bairaktaris, K. (1994). *Mental Health and Social Intervention*. Athens: Enallaktikes Ekdoseis [in Greek].

Baumann Anja-WHO Regional Office for Europe. (2010). User empowerment in mental health.

Center for Psychiatric Rehabilitation. https://cpr.bu.edu/.

Center for Society Orientation. (2013). www.cod.rs/en/what-we-do/advocacy-and-lobbying/.

Corrigan, P. W. & Watson, A. C. (2002). Understanding the impact of stigma on people with mental illness. *World Psychiatry: Official Journal of the World Psychiatric Association (WPA)*, 1(1), 16–20.

Donabedian A. (2005). Evaluating the quality of medical care. *MilbankQ*, 83, (2005), 691-729. https://doi.org/10.1111/j.1468-0009.2005.00397.x.

European Committee for the Prevention of Torture and Inhuman or Degrading Treatment or Punishment. (2019). Report to the Greek Government on the visit to Greece. CPT/Inf (2019) 4. https://rm.coe.int/1680930c9a.

Fytrakis, E. (2007). The involuntary commitment today: A black hole in the rule of law. *Greek scientific journal Cahiers Psychiatrics*, 100 (October–December 2007), 109–120. www.academia.edu/6735710/The_involuntary_commitment_today_a_black_hole_in_the_rule_of_law_in_Greek.

Gabriel, J. (1990). Island of Outcasts. Video. www.youtube.com/playlist?list=PL7CB3F677112F3989.

Global Leadership Institute. (2012). https://cpr.bu.edu/resources/ecast/2012-archive/2012-12/.

Greek Ombudsman. (2019). Report on the implementation of the CRPD. https://tbinternet.ohchr.org/_layouts/15/TreatyBodyExternal/Countries.aspx?CountryCode=GRC&Lang=EN.

Lally, J., ó Conghaile, A., Quigley, S., Bainbridge, E., & McDonald, C. (2013). Stigma of mental illness and help-seeking intention in university students. *The Psychiatrist*, 37(8), 253–260. https://doi.org/10.1192/pb.bp.112.041483.

Lewis, O. (2017). From here to home. Valedictory address to graduating students of the international diploma on mental health, human rights and law. Pune, India. https://cmhlp.org/impact/convocation-address/.

Lewis, O. (2019). Why isn't the Committee's interpretation of Article 12 universally accepted? *International Journal of Law and Psychiatry*, 62, 7–8. https://doi.org/10.1016/j.ijlp.2018.09.006.

Lionis, C. (2015). Why and how is compassion necessary to provide good healthcare? Comments from an academic physician. *International Journal of Health Policy and Management*, 4(11), 771–772. https://doi.org/10.15171/ijhpm.2015.132.

Merrit, J. (September 10, 1989). Europe's guilty secret. *The Observer*.

Nomidou, A. (2012). QualityRights Assessment Greece. www.who.int/mental_health/policy/quality_rights/en

Nomidou, A. (2013). Standards in mental health facilities – an in depth case study in Greece using the WHO QualityRights tool. *Journal of Public Mental Health*, 12(4), 201–211. https://doi.org/10.1108/JPMH-06-2013-0046.

Perlin, M., (2013). Sanism and the Law, in *Virtual Mentor*. 15(10) (2013), 878–885. https://doi.org/10.1001/virtualmentor.2013.15.10.msoc1-1310.

Simmons, M., & Gooding, P. (October 23, 2017). Spot the difference: Shared decision-making and supported decision-making in mental health. *Irish Journal of Psychological Medicine*, 34 (4), 275–286. https://doi.org/10.1017/ipm.2017.59.

SOFPSI.N.Serron. (2013). Changing Perceptions ... All Together! Video. www.youtube.com/watch?v=D15hJLO3aJw&t=4s

SOFPSI.N.Serron. (2014). From Vision to Reality. Video. www.youtube.com/watch?v=Zqv84M88500&t=11s.

SOFPSI.N.Serron. (2014). Puppet Theater Group. Video. www.youtube.com/watch?v=Fe7f7u4p2II

Stelios S., Lily E. P., Nektarios D., et al. (2017). Patients' views and experiences of involuntary hospitalization in Greece: A focus group study. *International Journal of Culture and Mental Health*. https://doi.org/10.1080/17542863.2017.1409778.

Stylianidis S., Lavdas M., Markou K., Belekou P. (2016) The Recovery Model and Modern Psychiatric Care: Conceptual Perspective, Critical Approach and Practical Application. In S. Stylianidis (ed.) *Social and Community Psychiatry*. Cham: Springer. https://doi.org/10.1007/978-3-319-28616-7_9.

WHO. (1998). Health Promotion Glossary. www.who.int/healthpromotion/about/HPR%20Glossary%201998.pdf.

25

Users' Involvement in Decision-Making: Lessons from Primary Research in India and Japan

Kanna Sugiura [*]

Abstract

People with psychosocial disabilities experience substituted decision-making, including involuntary admission, regularly. The Convention on the Rights of Persons with Disabilities (CRPD) mandates States parties to respect the will, preference, and autonomy of the person at all times. However, implementing this at policy and practice level in each country is still controversial. To explore will, preference, and autonomy of people with psychosocial disabilities, this chapter aims to understand the types of contexts and relationships service users were engaged in leading up to their participation in admission decision-making. Service users who previously had been involuntarily admitted designed and carried out interviews at psychiatric hospitals in Japan and India. The interviews showed that service users were marginalized through power imbalances and a lack of communication. Service users were discouraged from nurturing autonomy in their everyday lives leading up to admission decision-making. Based on the study, we recommended policies that would give service users the same powers as other stakeholders and encourage open communication between them. Implementing these policies into their everyday lives would enable them to confidently voice their will and preference at the admission decision-making stage, including making direct decisions or effectively using supported decision-making.

1 INTRODUCTION

People with psychosocial disabilities are systematically excluded from decision-making in their everyday lives and experience coercion, including within medical settings. The CRPD declares that the autonomy, will, and preference of a person should be respected at all times and requires that States parties end substituted decision-making. It further encourages direct decision-making and supported decision-making by the person. (United Nations, 2007). To achieve this, the CRPD encourages nations to change attitudes from a medical model, which focuses on biological impairments, to

---

[*] The author would like to thank Dr. Vikram Patel for his advice on design of this study, Dr. Soumitra Pathare for his guidance on the study in India, and Dr. Norito Kawakami for his guidance on the study in Japan.

a social disability model which views disability as being shaped by the interaction between an individual and their social environment. It also emphasizes addressing social barriers and adaptations that affect people with disabilities as a result of society having been designed to meet the needs of those without disabilities. These barriers should be removed. The model also goes on to say that persons with disabilities should be viewed as subjects who can claim their rights and make decisions about their lives, as well as being active members of society. The CRPD also demands that people with disabilities be included in planning laws and policies that concern them.

To foster this spirit, 181 countries have ratified the CRPD to date. However, its implementation is creating tension globally among stakeholders such as policymakers, lawyers, doctors, families, and service users, particularly around CRPD Article 12, relating to "equal recognition before the law" in psychiatric emergencies – namely, when service users are perceived to be in danger of harming themselves and others (Freeman et al., 2015). I believe that the CRPD Article 12 and individual decision-making models (e.g. isolated autonomy, informed consent) are often overly emphasized in isolation from the rest of the Convention's provisions. In order to reflect the actual everyday lives of people with psychosocial disabilities, I believe we need to expand our vision to include Article 19, which relates to "living independently and being included in the community" to the discussion. This chapter looks at the environments and human relationships with which people are engaged. In this view, we also need to reframe autonomy in line with the social model. Relational autonomy recognizes autonomy as an emotional construct which is nurtured in context and relationships, as opposed to the current isolated autonomy models, giving us a better understanding of autonomy and decisions that we arrive at naturally (Walter & Ross, 2014; Dove et al., 2017; Kong, 2015). In this way, we can develop supported decision-making models as encouraged in the CRPD and move away from substituted decision-making practices, such as involuntary admission. The essence of these contextually based models is to support the person to collect information, choose actions, and communicate their will and preference to others, and not dictate decisions for them. These supported decision-making models provide empathic support and advocacy for the person. These models need to be developed and implemented in each country based on their socioeconomic and cultural context (Sugiura, Mahomed, Saxena, & Patel, 2020). To develop supported decision-making models, we need to look at how service users are currently participating in decision-making in each country and to identify where they need to exercise autonomy. This needs to be laid out from the service users' perspective.

2 THE LIVED EXPERIENCE PERSPECTIVES: CASE STUDIES FROM INDIA AND JAPAN

To understand the experiences of people with psychosocial disabilities, when the involuntary admission was decided and the context and relationships they were in when it was decided, we conducted qualitative research using service user-led interviews. In this chapter, I will present case studies conducted in India and Japan where service users who have experiences of involuntary admission were involved in every step of the studies.

2.1 Service User Involvement

Kanna Sugiura (KS) (a female psychiatrist from Japan) sought advice from a senior service user researcher (a female researcher and a service user from the United Kingdom) on the research design. Together, we developed a world view around service users who experienced involuntary psychiatry admission (Figure 25.1). This view formed the guidance for the interview guide and analysis. The senior service user researcher continued to advise throughout interviews, analysis, and reporting.

The four interviewers in Japan and two interviewers in India were chosen by opportunistic sampling from people who had been in involuntary psychiatric admission and who either spoke Japanese in Japan, or spoke the local dialect and English in India. Specifically, KS advertised at a local peer-support group in Japan where four service users volunteered. In India, the participating hospital recommended two service users. The service users signed a non-disclosure agreement, received guidance on the purpose of the study, and practiced basic interview skills. There were some service users who could not acquire the necessary interviewing skills, such as to stay neutral, ask open-ended questions, and stay on the topic. These service users were not selected as interviewers but participated in all the other stages of the study, such as developing an interview guide, analyzing, and reporting. We

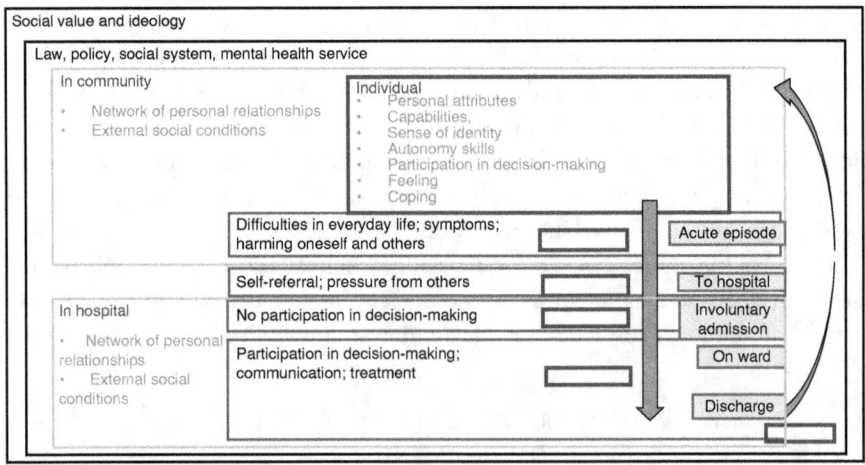

FIGURE 25.1 The world view of a service user
Source: Original research

planned flexible scheduling during the studies, but otherwise, there was no need for special arrangements.

2.2 Context

The study chose one private psychiatric hospital (600 beds, eleven seclusion rooms, eight wards, mainly four beds per room and thirteen doctors) and one psychiatric ward (fifty beds, one seclusion room, mainly individual rooms and nine doctors) in a private general hospital in Japan; and one public psychiatric hospital (550 beds, seclusion rooms not in use, four wards, mainly 100 beds per room and nine doctors) in India, using opportunistic sampling. All the hospitals had peer-supporter programs (i.e. service users who were formerly admitted visited currently admitted service users on wards or outside to share their experiences with medical treatments or stories from their everyday lives). All the participating hospitals in this research were in urban areas and services were covered through health insurance or tax. In Japan, the hospitals were under the National Insurance Scheme. In India, hospital funding varied from public funding to payments by service users at the point of service. Many participants in India told us that they were taken by family members to see religious healers first and then to private psychiatrists. As both of these services are expensive, when they could no longer afford them the service users were taken to the public psychiatric hospital. Admission to private hospitals requires family members or other caregivers to stay with the service user during admission. However, the public psychiatric hospital allowed service users to be admitted alone. The Indian psychiatric hospital was the only public hospital in the state and some service users travelled more than 200 km. The national law in India states maximum duration of involuntary admission is ninety days, and the hospital rules stated that service users needed to have family members present to get discharged. Japan does not have a cap to hospitalization days. In India (Mental Health Act 1987), doctors assess service users; if service users agree, they will be under voluntary admission, and if not they will be under involuntary admission (admission under special circumstances). In Japan (Mental Health Act), doctors assess service users and decide voluntary or involuntary admission based solely on medical assessment. Both India and Japan had two types of involuntary psychiatric admission. The details are shown in Table 25.1. Currently, India's mental health system is governed by the Mental Health Act 2017.

2.3 Participants

The inclusion criteria in this study were adults who had been involuntarily admitted to a psychiatric hospital within the past three months. Doctors on the wards created lists of service users who matched the inclusion criteria. The study used a purposive sampling method to achieve maximum variation. KS purposefully chose the service users from

TABLE 25.1 Criteria for psychiatry admission and frequency

	Subject	Assessed by	Agreed by	Ordered by	Number of cases per year
India: Mental Health Act 1987 (used at time of study)					
Admission under special circumstances	Psychiatric patient who needs hospitalization but who does not agree with it (maximum ninety days)	Two doctors	One relative or one friend	Not necessary	Thirty cases (at the participating hospital in 2016)
Detention of alleged mentally ill person pending report by medical officer	Person who is deemed to have a psychiatric condition (duration can be extended up to thirty days)	Not necessary	Not necessary	One judge	Not counted
Admission by court order	Person who has been admitted under the Act and diagnosed with a psychiatric condition and needs hospitalization or is deemed to be a danger to themselves or others	Two doctors	Not necessary	One judge	127 cases (at the participating hospital in 2016)
Voluntary admission	Psychiatric patient who needs and agrees with treatments in hospital	One doctor	Not necessary	Not necessary	1,413 cases (in 2016)

Japan: Mental Health Act					
Involuntary admission	Psychiatric patient who is a danger to themselves or others unless hospitalized	Two designated psychiatrists	Not necessary	Mayor	Thirty-seven cases (at the participating hospitals in 2017)
Medical protection admission	Psychiatric patient who needs hospitalization, is not a danger to themselves or others, but is not in a condition to make voluntary admission	One designated psychiatrist	One guardian	Not necessary	530 cases (at the participating hospitals in 2017)
Voluntary admission	Psychiatric patient who needs and agrees with hospitalization	One doctor	Not necessary	Not necessary	281 cases (at the participating hospitals in 2017)
India: Mental Health Care Act 2017 (Currently enacted)					
Admission of persons with mental illness with high support needs	Psychiatric patient who is a danger to themselves or others or is putting their health at risk due to neglect (maximum thirty days)	One psychiatrist and one mental health professional/medical practitioner	Nominated Representative has to make the application for admission.	Not necessary	Not counted
Independent admission	Psychiatric patient who needs and agrees with treatments in hospital	One doctor	Not necessary	Not necessary	Not counted

Source: Ministry of Health, Labour and Welfare, Government of Japan (1950); Ministry of Law and Justice, Legislative Department, Government of India (1987, 2017)

the list and asked them whether they were willing to participate in the study. The sample represented our intention to include an equal number of male and female subjects and wide ranges of age groups, diagnoses, and number of admissions. We also purposefully included service users who had requested mental health tribunals in Japan. We recruited new participants until we reached saturation of results. Sometimes the doctors or nurses introduced KS to the service users. In Japan, sometimes KS recruited alone and in India the interviewer "TT" (male, twenties, diagnosed with bipolar disorder and substance abuse; he prefers to be addressed by his initials for this chapter) always translated the interviews into English for KS. All the participants were informed that their participation was entirely voluntary and that they could withdraw their consent at any time. After KS affirmed the purpose of the study and its confidentiality and anonymity, written or thumb-printed informed consent was obtained. If the person could not hold basic conversations during the recruitment and could not follow the informed consent procedure, they were excluded. If the participants were still under involuntary admission, their family member or doctor provided written or thumb-printed informed consent additionally, as required by the ethics committees. About one fifth of the service users declined to participate during recruitment.

Recruitments and interviews were carried out in Japan from September 2017 to December 2017 and from June 2018 to October 2018, and in India from January 2018 to May 2018. In total, forty service users were interviewed (eighteen in India and twenty-two in Japan). The sample had similar numbers of male and female subjects, a wide age range, a wide range of diagnosis, and a wide mix of service users, including those who had been admitted for the first time or who had been admitted several times (Table 25.2).

2.4 *The Interviews*

Based on the worldview above (Figure 25.1), KS developed a thematic interview guide in Japanese and English and the senior service user researcher reviewed it. Then it was used by service user interviewers to practice, and refined for use in Japan and India respectively. The guide started an interview with "What brought you to the hospital?" or "Tell us about the day you came to the hospital," and asked about the interviewee's experience of coming to the hospital, getting admitted involuntarily, and staying on wards. The guide gave flexibility to the interviewers to reorder, skip, or add questions depending on participant's responses.

Kenjiro Horiai (KH) in Japan (male, peer staff, thirties, diagnosed with schizophrenia) and TT in India interviewed throughout the studies. KS also did one interview in India in English, as the participant felt more comfortable talking to a female interviewer. KS introduced herself as a researcher and a psychiatrist who did not influence clinical practices in the hospital. KH and TT introduced themselves as service users who had been involuntarily admitted

TABLE 25.2 Included service users

	Sex	Age	Highest education	Diagnosis (self-report)	Type of admission*	No. of involuntary admissions	Self-harm	Harming others
India (N=18)	Male: 10 Female: 8	20s: 2 30s: 5 40s: 7 50s: 2 70s: 1 Unknown: 1	Illiterate: 4 Primary school: 2 Middle school: 5 High school: 3 College: 2 Unknown: 2	Fever: 1 Low brain: 1 Shadow following: 1 Rolling eyes: 1 *Kenchi* (Seizure): 1 Schizophrenia: 1 Depression: 2 Alcohol abuse: 1 Drug abuse: 1 Unknown: 8	AUSC: 16 ACO: 2	1st: 6 2nd: 4 5th–6th: 3 10th–12th: 2 25th<: 2 Unknown: 1	Yes: 5 No: 13	Yes: 5 No: 13
Japan (N=22)	Male: 11 Female: 11	20s: 3 30s: 3 40s: 6 50s: 2 60s: 3 70s: 2 80s: 3	Primary School: 1 High School: 12 College: 7 Unknown: 2	Schizophrenia: 8 Depression: 3 Anxiety: 1 Bipolar Disorder: 1 Manic: 1 Alcohol addiction: 1 No problem: 6 Bipolar Disorder or Schizophrenia: 1	MPA: 17 IA: 5	1st: 13 2nd: 5 3rd–6th: 4	Yes: 4 No: 18	Yes: 5 No: 17

* AUSC: admission under special circumstance; ACO: admission by court order; MPA: medical protection admission; IA: involuntary admission,
Source: Original research

before. After obtaining informed consent and demographic data, KS sat at a removed distance so the interviewer and the participant could focus on the interview. At the end of interviews in Japan, KS followed up with clarifying questions. The interviews happened in one of the rooms in the hospitals. The participants were happy to talk about their experiences, saying that it was the only occasion an interest had been shown in listening to them. As a result, they reported feeling better about themselves and more composed after they spoke to us. The participants found it made them feel hopeful to meet someone with the same experience who had been discharged, and who was working and functioning in society. TT was reluctant to disclose that he was a service user with experience of admission in the beginning, but after a couple of interviews where he had positive reactions from participants he was more confident to introduce himself as a service user.

2.5 Analysis

All the interviews were audio recorded. In Japan, all the interviews were transcribed verbatim and in India TT listened to the interview recording in local language and did a translation that was faithful to the original dialogue, transcribed in English (there was no original language transcript). All the transcripts were anonymized and managed in NVIVO 12. The analysis followed Thematic Analysis (Braun & Clarke, 2006), as follows:

1) The interview transcripts were read through several times and memos were created around topics.
2) Initial codes were created from the memos and existing literature.
3) These codes were applied systematically through the transcripts.
4) Through comparing transcripts under the same code and codes against codes, the codes were merged, divided, and changed.
5) The refined codes were compared to establish their definitions and the relationships.
6) Once the codes were established for the experiences of service users when the involuntary admission was decided, we focused on included service users in each code.
7) We repeated steps 1 through 5 to establish codes to understand the context and relationships they were in when the admission was decided.

Several researchers and nurses joined in steps 2 to 5, and the service users participated in steps 4 and 5 for consistency and accuracy in reflecting the transcripts onto the codes.

2.6 Ethics and Funding

The study protocol had been approved by the University of Tokyo and all the hospitals involved. Informed consent and informed assent were obtained as described above. The original study protocol planned for peer-to-peer interviews to take place in private. However, the ethics committee asked the researcher/psychiatrist (KS) to remain in the room so that the interview could be stopped in case the participants became distressed while answering potentially sensitive questions (in practice, no participants showed distress). One of the ethics committees in Japan had a representative of service users. The study was funded by Kobayashi Foundation (Fuji Xerox) and the University of Tokyo. The funds were used to compensate the interviewers' and participants' transportation, recording, transcription, and KS's living expenses during her time in India.

2.7 Results

The interviews showed that the services users participated in admission decision-making in five different ways: making their own choices; seeking information and explaining themselves; deliberately withdrawing themselves; being apathetic; or being forced to comply.

2.7.1 Making their Own Choice

This attitude was observed in Japan only.

I need admission to get the help I need. (Japan)
The service users had convinced themselves that they wanted to be admitted irrespective of the outcome of the assessment by the doctor.

> "I asked for the involuntary admission. I might get suicidal again and plan to leave here and, in those situations, I cannot trust my judgments. I need someone to assess me whether I can leave or I should stay." (Japan)
> "I called the ambulance myself. To get to a hospital." (Japan)
> "I am in this kind of condition ... I believe my daughter's judgment is correct. She knows me more than anyone else ... how I usually am and how I can be. She can tell if I am normal or if I am in danger. I trust her judgment and I chose to do what she said." (Japan)

Before being admitted, these service users had been using medical services comfortably. Those who had families had one family member that they strongly trusted. The service users started to develop health conditions they could not manage on their own (i.e. suicidal thoughts, strong anxiety, and physical weakness) and had started to consider hospitalization to a psychiatry ward based on their hospitalization experience before, or based on their physical doctors' suggestions. By the time they reached the hospital, they were already determined to get treatment in hospital. During the admission assessment, the service users requested hospitalization and they were relieved to know that the doctors agreed to it, even though doctors made the admission decision based solely on the medical assessment. Some wanted to reassure their family members by choosing hospitalization. Some of them specifically asked that a certain family member be involved in the decision-making and sign the admission document for them, as they were worried that their own judgment at admission or discharge could be fragmented.

2.7.2 Seeking Information and Explaining Themselves

This attitude was observed in both India and Japan.

Listen to me and explain to me. (India/Japan)
The Service Users felt that families and doctors did not listen to their perspectives. They also felt they were not being informed around their admissions and what would happen to them thereafter.

> "They should discuss no? Why we are admitted. They don't discuss ... This is an injustice done to everyone ... Nobody is happy ... That much I can tell you that nobody is happy." (India)
>
> "Because if that happens we can at least decide and think by our self. But like this if you are not given the choice about self then it becomes very bad." (India)
>
> "I didn't want the admission ... I wanted to start my own business. That was my plan ... finance is more important in our life ..." (India)
>
> "I wanted to hear on what basis they decided this involuntary admission. I made my biggest effort to talk about myself and listen to the doctor." (Japan)
>
> "I was not given any time to say my opinions or my explanation. They don't have time ... or actually they don't want to listen to me. They just process my admission. Maybe they had a document about me to themselves? I don't know ..." (Japan)

In India, on a daily basis, the service users were told by families that they were "mad," even though they did not identify any problems themselves. The service users were forced or threatened with a stick to go to hospital by the outreach team who received referrals from the service users' families. Service users who refused to go to hospital were ignored, with no support from anyone. Arriving at the hospital, service users were directly taken to the wards without explanation or medical assessment. In Japan, before admission, these service users had financial and other troubles that they did not consider health related. They wanted their family to see them as themselves, without focusing only on what their family saw as sickness. They also felt people should have listened to their opinions regarding their treatment plan (e.g no medical treatment, or the type and dose of medication) and some discontinued the treatments. They agreed to come to the hospital with their families or police, but they did not think it would lead to their admission. At hospital they realized that their family was pursuing hospitalization. The admission was decided by doctors and families without the reasoning clearly explained to the service users.

2.7.3 Deliberate Withdrawal

This attitude was observed in both India and Japan.

***I follow others.* (India/Japan)**
Overwhelmed by others and circumstances, the service users knew that the admission was about them but were not given the opportunity to influence the decision.

> "I had faith in God that is how and why I came." (India)
> "Last month I promised [my aunt] that I will stop everything and will get an admission. That is why I came here [this month]." (India)
> "Whatever is happening it is for our good. If they will keep me, then it's okay." (India)
> "They said either your father or you will have to be admitted. I do not have any work but my father is searching for a job. I mean why should I harass him, I am paying for the mistakes I made. Like that, I came instead of him." (India)
> "There was nothing wrong with me. But people around me insisted that I was acting strange. I had to convince myself." (Japan)
> "They said involuntary admission ... The city administration, law, and police were involved ... I could not go against it." (Japan)
> "It was a big deal. Everyone was preparing for admission. I was not myself." (Japan)

In India, service users' health conditions, arguments, violence, or lack of housing brought them to the hospital. Some said it was caused by black magic or poison used by families on them. Some felt they needed medical treatments. One service user felt he needed to accept the admission request from his family and followed them to the hospital but did not expect to be admitted that day. The others who had been admitted several times felt hospital was better than home and asked their families to bring them to hospital. Others were brought to hospital with violent force by police or the outreach team. During the admission assessment at hospital, service users and families spoke with doctors with inhibition, as they felt that the doctors were superior. Service users sometimes felt that people did not explain anything to them, as people presumed that they would not understand. In Japan, these service users had been living comfortably and thought they didn't need advice or control from their families. They felt people around them were "weirder" than them. They had been avoiding medical services as they were unnecessary or costly, or they wanted to avoid medication. They felt their families insisted that they should go to the hospital even though they had no problems. They were overwhelmed to find out that police and law enforcement agencies were all involved in this. They withheld themselves from talking with doctors, they gave up on appealing to the tribunal, and some felt they had been accused.

***I should not be the one who decides.* (Japan)**
The service users blamed themselves for their actions and they felt they should not be the ones to decide what should happen to them.

> "Do I want to decide? It was my fault to attempt suicide so there is nothing I can say." (Japan)
> "It would be nice to decide about myself. But honestly, I do not have the right. After that... after I attempted murder... I do not have the right." (Japan)

These service users in Japan were thinking of divorce or their parents were divorced and had minimum communication with families. They also had limited communication in their communities and they felt lonely. They attempted suicide or harmed families and they blamed themselves for it. As a result of this, they could understand why their families had arranged admission and they felt they should not be the ones to decide. The service user who had hurt his family felt that his family saved him from going to jail by sending him to hospital. They withheld themselves from talking to the doctors and waited for their decisions at the assessment.

2.7.4 Apathetic Engagement

This attitude was observed in both India and Japan.

***It is a routine.* (India)**
The service users had been under involuntary admission numerous times that they didn't mind being constantly admitted and discharged whenever it was convenient for their families.

> "I felt one and the same. When I came this time, it was the regular process." (India)
> "Fifteen years since the last time, my family keeps me here. They also bring me out and they also bring me here." (India)
> "It's been around twenty to twenty-five times... I don't have a problem of living here, they give good food, people are good and I do not have any complaints... There is no one home." (India)

The service users in this category were men with repeated admissions for the past several years, with each admission after spending a couple of days with their families (the law limits the hospital stays to ninety days). Many did not speak about admission in the interviews as it was not their major concern (they spoke more about their lives on ward). They were groggy, ill, angry, or had physical problems and felt they needed treatments.

***I should agree with my family to avoid conflict.* (Japan)**
To maintain good relationships, the service users wanted to agree with their families and doctors even when they felt hesitant to stay in hospital.

> "I do want to decide things about myself including admission. But I have a niece. Do I want to live alone? Disconnect myself from her?" (Japan)
> "My wife decided the admission. It does not have to be me. I leave it up to her." (Japan)
> "Doctors decide based on their assessments. It's not my call. I have no better ways." (Japan)

At home, these service users had been feeling that their general living skills were declining. Their concern about themselves was modest. They felt that their families supported them well and they worried that they might become a burden to them. They wanted to keep good relationships with their families. They also felt that they could not find any other appropriate social supports for themselves. When coming to the hospital, they realized that their family members had chosen the hospital specifically for them and they felt grateful.

2.7.5 Forced Compliance

This attitude was observed in India only.

I was abandoned by my family. (India)
The service users felt they had been left behind by their families and they knew that, without family support, they could not leave hospital.

> "I am scared that what if they [my family] will not take me home. What will I do then?" (India)
> "He [brother in law] kept me here and then he did not even come here to meet me either ... He took my ID Card. Took it. Got me admitted and then he went away." (India)
> "They [family] asked me once to stay in hospital but I said no. They kept me here anyway." (India)
> "My father... he wanted to bring me here forever." (India)

Family members, neighbors, police officers, or hospital staff forced (through methods including lies, chasing, threats, or beatings) service users to come to hospital for a variety of reasons such as sickness, violence, being single, getting divorced, or being a financial burden to the family. They felt no one was supportive. One of the service users believed she got poisoned at home, which made her mad. At admission assessment, many service users had no communication with doctors. Some service users heard doctors telling families that they should go home at the admission assessment, but their families insisted on admitting them and left. Service users also wondered whether their families had bribed the hospital not to discharge them.

I was forced by the police. (India)
The service users had no idea why they were in hospital, other than that they had been forcefully brought in by police with no possibility of leaving hospital.

> "They said that where else should I keep you? They said that you will have to stay here anyhow." (India)
> "I do not know anything at all. That policeman had come and they kept me in the car. Then once again they kept me here." (India)

The participants who came in this category were women with no family, under admission by court order. The service users had lost their family members due to sickness or a major earthquake. They said that their health, black magic, or their violent behavior brought them to the hospital. Police forced them to the hospital, saying that they had no family. They thought police brought them to hospital to provide general protection because they were women. During the admission assessment, one of the service users had no communication with doctors, and the other service users were told by doctors that they should consider the hospital as their home, as they had no family.

3 DISCUSSION

The interviews demonstrated how service users participated in the decision-making process at the admission stage. How they: made their own choices; sought information and explained themselves; deliberately withdrew themselves; were apathetic; or were forced to comply. The interviews showed the service users' will and preference, and how the ways they expressed them were shaped by the context and relationships they were in, such as self-efficacy, awareness of symptoms, financial or housing independence, relationships with families, relationships with medical services, an understanding of their situation and its impact on them, and their prior experiences. The service users were learning how much (or little) they could express their will and preference to participate in decision-making through their interaction with others. Assumptions of incapacity and paternalism by family members, neighbors, police, and medical professionals had created a power imbalance in the interaction, where service users were ignored, oppressed, and marginalized. The lack of communication between service users and other stakeholders exacerbated the marginalization. As the current involuntary psychiatric admission system allows doctors and families to ignore service users' autonomy, will, and preference to make decisions, there were minimal to no efforts from doctors to engage in dialogue or reach a consensus with service users. The interviews also showed that families made decisions without consulting service users and sought interventions at institutions rather than working to find agreeable solutions at home. Those who had felt the need for admission requested hospitalization and agreed to the admission decision made by doctors based on a medical assessment. Some of them specifically asked that a certain family member be involved in the decision-making and sign the admission document for them, as they were worried that their own judgment at admission or discharge could be fragmented. Those service users felt a sense of ownership of the admission decision.

In India, either family members or the police assumed the incapacity of the service users and had already determined admission (even before the outcome of a medical assessment) and brought service users to hospital with force. Under the India Mental Health Act 1987, the patient's will and preference around admission is required to be considered; however, the results show this was not implemented in practice. During the assessment at hospital, service users were not physically present and doctors were authoritative. Sometimes families insisted on admission against a doctor's assessment. "A woman should not be living alone," was often the reason police cited for admission – and doctors agreed. Violence by service users and towards service users at home and on the way to hospital was often a topic throughout the interviews. In Japan, service users were frustrated that the doctors prejudged their situation, did not listen, and did not explain what their treatment plans were, or the reasons behind the decision to admit them. They felt they had been constantly ignored, which resulted in them giving up on expressing their will and preference around their treatment plans. Many wanted to be in a good relationship with families and doctors and some felt that their families wanted them admitted in their own interests, so they did not want to challenge this. Some blamed themselves for the situation and held themselves back from making any decisions. These factors made the service users withdraw their will and preference.

Service users are marginalized every day, including at the decision-making stage around their admission, due to power imbalances and a lack of communication between medical professionals, their families, and themselves. Some service users became repressed and learned to hold back their will and preference, whilst others who had ownership over their autonomy felt comfortable enough to assert it. Often families and others looked at hospitalization as the only solution, even when the service user was dealing with an everyday social problem. Responses to this need to bring in a wider context and adopt an inclusive social model. This means we need to implement CRPD Articles 12 and 19 together, rather than separately, to focus on admission decision-making. Service users need to be heard and respected at all levels, including in terms of social values, the law, and communities – not just at admission decision-making at hospital (Figure 25.1). Service users need to have control over everyday issues of liberty, including hospital admission.

Any support mechanisms the service users can engage with to overcome power imbalances and lack of communication in order to nurture autonomy will be useful for exercising their autonomy throughout everyday life and at the admission decision-making stage. Policies that would help achieve these are the following:

1. Develop social services and community mental health services so that service users and their families have access to support networks in communities and at home. Services that provide support around housing, employment, education, social skills, pensions, health insurance, day care, service user associations, and family associations would also address some of the limitations service users face in this area.
2. Social workers should visit service users' homes to assess and develop action plans in the case of emergencies, instead of police or outreach teams forcefully taking service users to hospital. These agencies should not be allowed to lie to service users.
3. Substituted decision-making, including involuntary admission, needs to be abolished, as this is a reoccurring source of power imbalances and lack of mutual communication.
4. Instead, there should be decision-making models that place equal value on service users' views and styles of reasoning to encourage dialogue. Open Dialogue (von Peter et al., 2019) is a good example, which works with a service user's family and support network to help those involved in a crisis situation to be together and engage in clear and empathetic dialogue. Planning in advance (e.g. Advance Directives, Crisis Plans, Named Person (Sugiura et al., 2020)) will be useful to maintain autonomy and communication in emergency situations.
5. Include other service users, close friends or other support networks who know the service user well when making decisions. The inclusion of a service user interviewer in this study showed that service users are more forthcoming and honest with peers than with professionals or families.
6. Educate mental health professionals. They need to understand that their assessments and treatments can be unidirectional and that excluding service users from decision-making causes suffering, confusion, self-blame, and resignation. Professionals need to be open to spending the time required to listen and explain clearly to service users.
7. Power imbalances and lack of communication always need to be explored when identified. Powerlessness of service users should not be devalued or papered over. A Personal Ombudsman (FuturePolicy.org, 2020) who can advocate for the service user (and who is independent of public services) could also be useful for regulating this.

REFERENCES

Braun, V., & Clarke, V. (2006). Using thematic analysis in psychology. *Qualitative Research in Psychology*, 3(2), 77–101. https://doi.org/10.1191/1478088706qp063oa

Dove, E. S., Kelly, S. E., Lucivero, F., et al. (2017). Beyond individualism: Is there a place for relational autonomy in clinical practice and research? *Clinical Ethics*, 12(3), 150–165. https://doi.org/10.1177/1477750917704156

Freeman, M. C., Kolappa, K., de Almeida, J. M. C., et al. (2015). Reversing hard won victories in the name of human rights: A critique of the General Comment on Article 12 of the UN Convention on the Rights of Persons with Disabilities. *The Lancet Psychiatry*, 2(9), 844–850. https://doi.org/10.1016/S2215-0366(15)00218-7

FuturePolicy.org. (2020). Sweden's personal ombudsmen system. www.futurepolicy.org/rights-and-responsibilities/swedens-personal-ombudsmen-system/

Kong, C. (2015). The Convention for the Rights of Persons with Disabilities and Article 12: Prospective feminist lessons against the "will and preferences" paradigm. *Laws*, 4(4), 709–728. https://doi.org/10.3390/laws4040709

Ministry of Health, Labour and Welfare, Government of Japan (1950). Act on Mental Health and Welfare for the Mentally Disabled. www.japaneselawtranslation.go.jp/law/detail_main?re=&vm=2&id=3480

Ministry of Law and Justice, Legislative Department, Government of India (1987). Mental Health Act 1987. https://legislative.gov.in/actsofparliamentfromtheyear/mental-health-act-1987

Ministry of Law and Justice, Legislative Department, Government of India (2017). Mental Healthcare Act, 2017. www.prsindia.org/uploads/media/Mental Health/Mental Healthcare Act, 2017.pdf

Sugiura, K., Mahomed, F., Saxena, S., & Patel, V. (2020). An end to coercion: Rights and decision-making in mental health care. *Bulletin of the World Health Organization*, 98(1), 52–58. https://doi.org/10.2471/BLT.19.234906

United Nations. (2007). Convention on the rights of persons with disabilities. UN Doc. A/61/611 (2006).

von Peter, S., Aderhold, V., Cubellis, L., et al. (2019). Open Dialogue as a human rights-aligned approach. *Frontiers in Psychiatry*, 10 (May), 1–6. https://doi.org/10.3389/fpsyt.2019.00387

Walter, J. K., & Ross, L. F. (2014). Relational Autonomy: Moving beyond the limits of isolated individualism. *Pediatrics*, 133 (Supplement), S16–S23. https://doi.org/10.1542/peds.2013-3608D

26

Involvement of People with Lived Experience of Mental Health Conditions in Decision-Making to Improve Care in Rural Ethiopia

Sally Souraya, Sisay Abyaneh, Charlotte Hanlon, and Laura Asher

Abstract

A human rights-based approach is required to embed the principles of participation, empowerment and accountability in mental healthcare systems. Involvement of people with lived experience in decision-making is a key element of this approach and an important ingredient of strengthening mental health systems and improving care. Ethiopia represents a case example of a low-income country where both conceptual and practical frameworks of involvement are currently being developed in the context of limited resources. Whilst experiences of involvement and autonomy in decision-making remain limited due to contextual challenges and cultural norms, approaches such as community-based rehabilitation and participatory action research offer potential platforms to promote, facilitate and enhance involvement. To ensure effective implementation, these approaches need to be supported within a pragmatic multi-stakeholder strategy that aims to create a cultural shift, empower people with lived experience, overcome structural barriers (particularly stigma and poverty), provide culturally appropriate resources (including guidance and training) and develop an implementable legislative framework for mental health care.

1 INTRODUCTION

Involvement of people with lived experience of mental health conditions (service users)[1] in decision-making to improve mental health care needs to be addressed in its totality. Involvement can be conceptualised at multiple levels: the *micro level* (e.g. individual care decision-making and management); *meso level* (e.g. in local service planning, monitoring, staff training and input into guidelines); and *macro level* (e.g. policy making and national level planning) (Tambuyzer et al., 2011). Although the

---

[1] For consistency purposes, we used the term 'service users' in this chapter to refer to people with lived experience of mental health conditions, including those who may not be using or ever have used mental health care services. The use of the term 'service users' has also been informed by discussions and reflections with small number of service-users (n=12); caregivers (n=12); and healthcare professionals (n=18) at Sodo District, where the majority preferred this term.

levels appear distinct, one level facilitates the other, and their complementarity is crucial in ensuring comprehensive involvement and human rights-based mental health care.

Empowerment and involvement of service users in strengthening mental health systems is gaining ground as a policy imperative in many countries. There are clear international guidelines and explicit efforts from the World Health Organisation (WHO) to involve service users in advocacy, policy, planning, legislation, service provision, monitoring, research and evaluation (World Health Organisation, 2013). The WHO is working with local governments to ensure that all mental health strategies and interventions are compliant with the Convention on the Rights of Persons with Disabilities (CRPD). There is a particular focus on CRPD Article 12 and General Comment 1, which state that all persons have decision-making capacity. The aim is to eliminate all forms of substitute decision-making by ensuring that appropriate support is in place for service users to make their own decisions. Promoting person-centred and recovery-oriented models of care is vital to support the implementation of service users' rights by focussing on their needs and expectations.

As a complex, multi-dimensional and evolving concept, the involvement of service users remains easier said than done. The implementation of involvement is made challenging by longstanding stigmatising beliefs and discriminatory practices towards service users. Service users have historically been excluded from their right to meaningful participation in decisions that have a direct impact on their lives (Semrau et al., 2016). Their input may be devalued, as they are often believed to have insufficient mental capacity (Perkins et al., 2018). These attitudes and practices often create a vicious circle hindering active involvement (Rose, 2017). As a consequence, service users may feel incompetent and unable to contribute, leaving them with little influence over the care they receive (Faulkner, 2017).

Service user involvement is an essential ingredient to strengthen mental health systems; to scale-up appropriate and quality services; to reduce the treatment gap; and to protect and promote human rights (Saxena et al., 2015). However, the application of service user involvement in low- and middle-income countries (LMICs) has received minimal attention. Local adaptations that respect cultural, social and religious values are needed. A promising opportunity is presenting itself in Ethiopia, where both conceptual and practical frameworks are currently being developed. The experiences from this country may help other LMICs, where resources are limited and availability and accessibility of care are the main priorities.

2 ETHIOPIA – STEPS IN THE RIGHT DIRECTION

Over the last decade, Ethiopia has made huge strides to strengthen the health system and improve health outcomes. Spearheaded by the Health Sector Transformation Plan 2015/16–2019/20 (HSTP), there have been tremendous efforts to expand access to primary healthcare, reorient health services towards prevention and build a compassionate workforce. An emphasis on community engagement in health decision-making is a keystone of HSTP. This includes strategies to promote person-centred care, improve health literacy and involve communities and service users in governing boards to ensure their voices are heard.

There has also been notable political commitment to address gaps in the delivery of mental health care in Ethiopia. Ethiopia has one psychiatrist per 1 million population and 0.68 mental healthcare professionals per 100,000 people (World Health Organisation, 2015). Furthermore, existing services are concentrated in urban centres and hospitals, even though the population remains largely rural. The Ethiopian National Mental Health Strategy (Ministry of Health, 2012) seeks to tackle the shortage of resources by promoting a task-sharing approach, whereby primary healthcare staff are trained to successfully identify and treat people with mental health conditions using an adapted version of the WHO Mental Health Gap Action Programme (mhGAP).

Whilst providing care in a setting with few human and financial resources is a challenging task in itself, the mental health strategy aims to implement mental health services that counter discrimination and human rights abuses and promote informed decision-making, recovery, empowerment and social inclusion. However, given that representation of service users at the national level remains limited, how these concepts can be translated into practice is a critical question.

Ethiopia ratified the CRPD in 2010; however, to date there is no mental health legislation or specialised body to protect the rights of service users. In 2016, the CRPD Committee raised concerns in relation to the lack of support for decision-making in Ethiopia. The committee recommended that Ethiopia develops and implements supported decision-making models that respect the autonomy, will and preferences of people with intellectual and psychosocial disabilities (United Nations Human Rights, 2016).

Efforts to increase access to mental health care in Ethiopia are being supported by rigorous research activities focussed on the development and implementation of evidence-based models of care, and strengthening of mental health systems. Research programmes such as 'Emerging mental health systems in low- and middle-income countries' (Emerald) (Semrau et al., 2015) and the PRogramme for Improving Mental health carE (PRIME) (Lund et al., 2016) have played a key role in the development and promotion of service user involvement by providing funding and platforms to create knowledge, guide practice and build capacity.

This chapter draws on research by Souraya et al. (2018) and Abayneh et al. (2017, 2020) to discuss the current experiences and challenges of service user involvement in rural Ethiopia (see Table 26.1).

Abayneh et al. explored the experiences, perceived barriers and facilitators to service user and caregiver involvement in mental health system strengthening (2017), and then applied a Participatory Action Research (PAR) approach to inform

TABLE 26.1 *Research studies on service user involvement in rural Ethiopia*

Study	(Souraya et al., 2018)	(Abayneh et al., 2017)	(Abayneh, Lempp & Alem et al., 2020; Abayneh, Lempp & Hanlon, 2020)
Aim	Identify factors that influence service user involvement in decision-making relating to individual care planning	Explore the existing situation with respect to service user involvement in mental health system strengthening	Use participatory action research methods to develop and pilot a model of service user involvement in mental health system strengthening
Site	Sodo district, southern Ethiopia	National level and Sodo district	Sodo district
Methods	Focus group discussions; in-depth interviews; member checking	Semi-structured interviews	Theory of Change (ToC) workshops; empowerment interventions for service users (Rai et al., 2018); establishing Research Advisory and Participant Groups (RAG and RPG); participatory prioritisation exercise; developing plan of action; implementing and evaluating, using process indicators and in-depth interviews
Participants	Twenty-eight stakeholders who were RISE pilot participants (people with schizophrenia, caregivers) or involved in the	Thirty-nine stakeholders (policy makers from the Federal Ministry of Health and the WHO, psychiatrists involved in policy	Two ToC workshops: seven and twenty-four stakeholders (service users, caregivers, clinicians, administrators and

TABLE 26.1 (continued)

Study	(Souraya et al., 2018)	(Abayneh et al., 2017)	(Abayneh, Lempp & Alem et al., 2020; Abayneh, Lempp & Hanlon, 2020)
	delivery of RISE intervention (CBR workers, supervisors and health officers)	and service development, health administrators, primary care facility heads, service users and caregivers)	community leaders) RAG: twenty multi-sectoral community representatives (e.g. health administrators, religious leaders and community leaders) RPG: six service users, four caregivers and three health professionals

Source: see table

the development and piloting of a model of involvement in newly integrated primary mental health services (2020).

The experiences of service user involvement in decision-making at the individual care level were explored by Souraya et al. in the context of a community-based rehabilitation (CBR) programme (2018). The aim was to identify key influences on individual care decision-making processes, and to elucidate the role of different stakeholders. The study was nested within the pilot study of the Rehabilitation Intervention for people with Schizophrenia in Ethiopia (RISE) project (See Box 26.1) (Asher et al., 2018).

3 EXPERIENCES AND CHALLENGES OF INVOLVEMENT

3.1 Involvement in Mental Health System Strengthening and Service Planning

3.1.1 Experiences of System-Level Involvement

In Ethiopia, service user involvement in mental health system strengthening is a relatively new concept (Abayneh et al., 2017). To move towards actual involvement of service users, we (1) co-produced a Theory of Change (ToC) model; (2) empowered and equipped both service users and health workers to engage in service

BOX 26.1 REHABILITATION INTERVENTION FOR PEOPLE WITH SCHIZOPHRENIA IN ETHIOPIA (RISE) PROJECT

Rehabilitation Intervention for people with Schizophrenia in Ethiopia (RISE) is a CBR programme delivered by trained lay workers

Structure	Training and supervision	Evaluation
Home visits to person with schizophrenia and caregiver	Five weeks' classroom and fieldwork training	Pilot study to assess the acceptability and feasibility of CBR
Referral to primary care clinic for clinical review and medication	Two non-specialist field supervisors	Cluster-randomised trial to assess effectiveness of CBR in reducing disability
Public awareness raising	Support from psychiatric nurse in complex or emergency situations	
Targeted community mobilisation		

Home visit intervention (manualised)

Four core modules (understanding schizophrenia, preparing for a crisis, human rights and accessing mental healthcare)

Eleven optional modules selected on basis of collaborative goal setting (e.g. returning to work; participating in community activities)

Module delivery through psycho-education, family intervention, basic counselling and problem-solving techniques.

Source: Asher et al., 2018

user involvement; and (3) applied a PAR approach. PAR helps to build understanding of service users' experiences and move beyond prevailing biomedical approaches to generate locally relevant solutions that tap into community resources and address social injustices (Mathias et al., 2019).

A Research Participant Group (RPG) was established comprising service users, caregivers and health workers. Prior to their involvement in the PAR process we used photovoice, combined with a workshop, to empower service users by ensuring they were informed about their rights and equipped to articulate their priorities in involvement activities. In a separate workshop, primary care workers also received training in how to work with service users. To manage power dynamics and hierarchies between participants, the RPG members worked together through facilitated small group discussion, individual dialogues and reflections using nominal group technique, which ensured that all voices were heard. There was minimal facilitation by academic researchers. Stakeholders/RPG members first recognised the challenges to service user involvement, then identified local resources and assets and designed strategies for how these resources could strengthen mental health services (e.g. to raise public awareness about mental health and empower service users). The final step was to develop an action plan, which we are currently assisting the RPG to implement.

3.1.2 Barriers to System-Level Involvement

We found that service user involvement in mental health system strengthening is a complex intervention shaped by intersecting individual, health organization, community and strategic level factors (Abayneh et al., 2017). However, like in many LMICs, strategies, guidelines or models addressing this complexity are lacking in Ethiopia.

We found that low value is placed on service user involvement and there is little experience of stakeholders working collaboratively with service users on their empowerment. Because of their mental health conditions, service users were often not listened to or not considered credible within and beyond the mental health system. They were considered incapable of adding value to service planning; typical attitudes were, 'What value can they add?' Or, '[Their opinion] doesn't really matter to what we do.'

Service users lacked confidence to participate effectively in mental health system strengthening (Abayneh et al., 2017). This may be due to a lack of awareness of their rights, low literacy and/or poor access to social and material resources (adequate healthcare, education or employment) that would enable them to participate and realise their abilities (Lempp et al., 2018). These structural and social factors put service users at a cognitive disadvantage for self-understanding (Newbigging & Ridley, 2018).

Similar to other mental health systems, the needs of service users in Ethiopia tend to be medicalised, rather than understood to be the product of social relations, structures and problems (Kurs & Grinshpoon, 2018). Service users are often excluded from decision-making due to a wrongly presumed irrelevance or lack of expertise and a wrongfully denied capacity as 'knower' (Fricker, 2007). Service users are commonly characterised as bizarre or dangerous, being cognitively unreliable and emotionally unstable. As a result, service providers often underestimate service users' knowledge, insights and capacity for decision-making. Similarly, service users' choices might be seen as incoherent, illogical or lacking credibility.

3.1.3 Benefits of System-Level Involvement

A number of perceived benefits of service user involvement in health system strengthening were reported. These included the opportunity to: advocate for better physical health services and integration of psychosocial support; fight exclusion from civic engagement; improve service quality; and raise awareness of available services (for example, through sharing testimonials about mental health care and living with mental illness) (Abayneh et al., 2017).

By creating a space and opportunity for service users and stakeholders to collaborate together, the PAR process helped: 1) redirect the blame away from service users to the injustices in the social and healthcare systems; 2) acknowledge the capabilities, assets and social resources which exist in Sodo district; 3) identify how these resources can be mobilised to strengthen mental health services and to address intersecting inequalities (e.g., poverty, marginalisation); and 4) initiate stakeholder involvement to address the socio-economic concerns and inclusion of service users.

As a result of the PAR process, the service user RPG members reported a more positive sense of self, better social relations, new insights into their experience of mental ill-health and available resources and an increased willingness to be involved in future mental health system strengthening activities. They also described a sense of empowerment to take actions to improve their living and working conditions.

3.2 Involvement in Decision-Making Related to Individual Care

3.2.1 Experiences of Involvement in Individual Care Planning

We found that decision-making about an individual's care tends to be driven by healthcare professionals and caregivers. The decisions tend to be the major focus, rather than the process itself, which means that service user involvement is often diminished. Decisions not to adhere to medication or to refuse care are often considered irrational by caregivers and healthcare professionals and are typically identified as signs of relapse and lack of capacity rather than legitimate choices. It is implied that 'better' decisions involve adherence to medication and adherence to health professionals' advice (Souraya et al., 2018).

As in many cultures, healthcare professionals in Ethiopia are trusted and expected to assume an authoritative and prescriptive role (Bayetti et al., 2016). Study participants reported that a power dynamic often exists in healthcare encounters in which the knowledge and opinions of health professionals (health officers and CBR workers) is considered more valuable and trustworthy than those of service users (Souraya et al., 2018). Thus, both service users and caregivers often acquiesced to the views of healthcare professionals in decision-making. Even when explicitly asked about their preferences and given the opportunity to decide, some service users delegated health professionals to make the decisions.

Personal autonomy in relation to care needs to be understood in the context of Ethiopian society. Giving a person freedom to decide whether to take psychotropic medication or not might be perceived as irresponsible and even unethical. This is because in rural Ethiopia a collective approach to decision-making is dominant (Hanlon et al., 2010), with the 'smallest autonomous unit' being the family rather than the individual (Alem et al., 2002). The rights of families are commonly not separated from those of service users and value is given to mutual responsibility (Alem et al., 2002). The tendency of some service users to not engage in decision-making may reflect the marginalised role of service users in their community (Mayston et al., 2016), and reveal fears that their access to treatment could be jeopardised if their opinions do not align with those of healthcare professionals (Abayneh et al., 2017).

In common with other LMICs, we found that caregivers in rural Ethiopia are often key decision-makers, rather than a contributor to the process (Hanlon et al., 2010). We identified two scenarios: first, where caregivers completely excluded their relatives and made decisions on their behalf without even informing them. This left some service users feeling frustrated at not being informed or not having choices. Second, where service users trusted caregivers to make decisions on their behalf and considered caregiver involvement legitimate, positive and caring. Both scenarios seemed to arise from a cultural assumption that the responsibility of care lies on the caregivers. Moreover, caregivers were considered to have the right to be the decision-makers as they felt equally affected by the illness burden. Healthcare professionals also prioritised caregiver involvement as they were perceived to be more active (e.g. asking questions and expressing ideas) than service users in the decision-making process. Caregivers also have a key practical role in ensuring service users' access and adherence to treatments. Household finances are typically in the hands of caregivers; therefore, without the family's backing, service users may not be able to access care at all (Alem et al., 2002; Hanlon et al., 2010).

We found that in some cases the caregivers' role went beyond involvement in decision-making and into coercive practices (e.g. physical restraint and mixing medication into food without telling the service user). The use of coercion in this context has been conceptualised as a form of protective care pragmatically employed to ensure individuals receive effective treatment and that they and the wider community are protected from harm (Asher et al., 2017). In our study, even health professionals who felt that coercion is ethically inappropriate argued that its use as a last resort is justified as long as it was used for the benefits of service users. This aligns with the notion that service users' autonomy should not be at the expense of allowing people to go untreated. Administrating treatment without consent is thus argued to show respect for people by ultimately helping to restore their autonomy (Srinivasan & Thara, 2002).

3.2.2 Barriers and Facilitators to Involvement

People with comorbid intellectual disability and those with acute illness were perceived to have low decision-making capabilities and thus tended to be less involved in decision-making about their care (Souraya et al., 2018).

It has been posited that decision-making capacity is considered an 'all or nothing' phenomenon in many African countries, where capacity may not be assessed by healthcare professionals, let alone re-assessed following treatment (Bartlett & Hamzic, 2010). However, we found that healthcare professionals considered the capacity of people with schizophrenia to improve after they had received treatment and had recovered clinically. Health professionals appeared to differentiate their response to service users based on service user adherence to health worker advice. They reported asking service users who were adherent to treatment about what they wanted and respecting their choices, but the same did not apply to service users who were not adherent. A more fixed view of impaired capacity was expressed by caregivers compared to healthcare professionals.

The motivation and expectations of service users appeared to affect the extent of their involvement. Healthcare professionals shared how difficult it was to engage people who lacked motivation and were not willing to express themselves due to their symptoms or as a result of pervasive stigma. Service users' age, position and financial power in the family also appeared to play a role in determining who was involved in decision-making. For instance, a father who is responsible for his family would be given the opportunity to make his own decisions, in contrast with a son or daughter living with their parents who might have less involvement in care planning (Souraya et al., 2018).

Service users were often unable to execute their desired treatment choice due to unaffordable treatment or limited treatment options (e.g. mainly first-generation anti-psychotic medication and limited psychosocial support) (Souraya et al., 2018).

3.2.3 The Role of CBR in Enhancing Involvement

Our findings suggest that CBR holds substantial promise as a low-cost strategy to enhance the participation of people with schizophrenia in decision-making in rural Ethiopia (Souraya et al., 2018). Greater opportunities for involvement were perceived to be available in the context of a CBR programme, compared to primary care. Through a collaborative process of goal setting and crisis planning, most CBR workers tried to involve service users, listened to their needs and respected their opinions. Service users were asked to express their preferences as to what should happen if they became unwell, including how and where they would seek support (for example, holding a family meeting, taking to the health centre for review or contacting a priest for support). CBR workers referred to the crisis plan when needed, but also asked the person about their current wishes. When it was not possible to ascertain preferences, CBR workers supported the family to access treatment at the health centre and advised them to avoid physical restraint if possible. CBR workers advised caregivers how to reduce harm from chaining when it did occur (e.g. to keep service users fed and sheltered, change positions and check for wounds), and continued to support access to treatment.

Effective strategies to facilitate involvement employed by CBR workers included using clear and simple language and giving sufficient time to understand options and express choices (Souraya et al., 2018). CBR workers also supported the enactment of treatment choices, for example by assisting individuals to attend the health centre. Adjustments to CBR delivery, for example tailoring the frequency of home visits, were made as a result of service users being explicitly asked about their preferences. The greater time capacity of CBR workers was perceived to enhance the participation of service users compared to other settings, such as high-workload health centres. Moreover, home visits were perceived to increase confidentiality and offered service users the possibility to interact more freely in the decision-making process (Souraya et al., 2018).

Whilst CBR workers were trained in the principles of shared decision-making and generally demonstrated good communication skills, a minority were found to ignore or override the views of participants (Asher et al., 2018). CBR skills improved with targeted top-up training and a longer period of work experience (Asher et al., 2021).

3.3 Commonalities between Involvement at Individual and System Levels

Involvement of service users in decision-making at individual and system levels are interlinked. Where involvement is limited at the system level, opportunities to implement it at the individual care level become scarce. Our studies (Abayneh et al., 2017, 2020; Souraya et al., 2018) in rural Ethiopia suggest that five shared barriers to involvement exist.

First, there is a lack of motivation and low expectations for service users' involvement among all stakeholders. This is partly due to involvement being a relatively new concept in the healthcare system and thus not being widely recognised as a possibility. Healthcare providers, as well as service users, have limited understanding of the value and relevance of involvement to service users' lives and to the mental healthcare system.

Second, service users are unfairly denied their capacity as 'knower'. They tend not to be considered credible decision-makers and their knowledge, insights and opinions are often underestimated by service providers. Greater value is put on the knowledge and views of healthcare professionals and, in the case of individual care planning, on the opinions of caregivers. Service users' choices and treatment preferences may be dismissed as being incoherent, illegitimate or a sign of relapse. This tendency is underpinned by pervasive stigma towards people with mental health problems, who are perceived as being unreliable, unstable and even dangerous. Service users are largely disempowered and have limited awareness of their rights.

Third, healthcare providers consider involvement as adding to system complexities and detracting from addressing the treatment gap. Their limited time capacity means that attempts at involvement tend to be tokenistic. Moreover, there is an important gap in skills, experience and structures of healthcare providers to work collaboratively with service users, let alone to enable them to participate in decision-making. The lack of guidance and training means that even willing stakeholders may struggle to put involvement into practice.

Fourth, in some cases lack of impetus for involvement may be illness related, with symptoms affecting the motivation and willingness of service users to express themselves. This circumstance in turn may arise through inadequate care, or inaccessible and unaffordable treatment.

Fifth, poverty, low literacy and social exclusion are structural factors that hinder service users from realising their abilities and actively participating in decision-making at both system and individual care levels.

4 FACILITATING AND ENHANCING INVOLVEMENT IN DECISION-MAKING – THE WAY FORWARD

A joint strategy for involvement spanning individual and system levels is required. Both approaches exemplified in this chapter (PAR and CBR) can have an impact on both levels. Implementation of service user involvement demands a pragmatic approach that is grounded in partnership with diverse stakeholders. Clarity about the roles and responsibilities of service users, caregivers and healthcare professionals is fundamental for moving beyond tokenistic participation (Semrau et al., 2016). We propose five cross-cutting approaches to enhance involvement in decision-making in community and primary care settings.

4.1 Promote a Culture Shift towards Valuing Involvement

Service user involvement should be underpinned by a culture change towards human rights and strength-based approaches to participation. Promoting a culture of involvement requires lived experience and knowledge to be judged not simply as desirable but as an essential component in the development and delivery of better care. Involvement needs to be valued and legitimised as being in the best interests of both service users and the mental health system.

4.2 Empower Service Users to Be Aware of and Advocate for Their Rights

Mobilisation and empowerment are key mechanisms to create the necessary cultural and system shifts for service user involvement, enabling people to become aware of their rights and claim them, lobby for improved services and advocate to influence policy and legislative reforms. Empowered service users could have the confidence, self-esteem, resources and skills to be more involved in decision-making at the micro, meso and macro levels (Kleintjes et al., 2013). In Ethiopia there is one newly established service user organisation and one caregiver-led group, reflecting the scarcity of service user movements in LMICs that may result in weak mental health advocacy (Lempp et al., 2018). It is therefore important to tap into community assets, such as community and religious leaders, to assist the process of empowerment and ensure that people have access to information to improve mental health and human rights literacy (Sunkel, 2012). Furthermore, engaging community structures (e.g. schools, cultural and religious institutions) as entry points for awareness raising helps to improve attitudes and reduce stigma by providing social contact opportunities for service users and the community. Equally, promoting self-advocacy and the recovery stories of service users can help to change how they are perceived and treated in the community.

4.3 Create Legislative and Strategic Oversight

A legislative and policy framework aligned with the CRPD is needed to support the operationalisation of involvement in decision-making at individual care planning and system levels. There now exist several examples globally of legislation that recognises the rights and legal capacity of service users, which could be drawn upon. Components could include advance directives and the establishment of the legal figure of a 'guarantor for equality before the law', who is bound to safeguard the personal autonomy of a person with mental health conditions (Sugiura et al., 2020). Family caregivers should not be considered the default to take this role, particularly when relationships are abusive.

It is also essential to develop a national human rights review body with authority to oversee, assess and improve quality and human rights in mental health facilities – for example, using the WHO QualityRights Toolkit. Equally, it is important that the review body monitor the threats to service user autonomy which emerge outside the healthcare system by establishing mechanisms to identify coercive treatment and restraint in community settings. Responses should focus on supporting access to care rather than on penalising caregivers who have instigated restraint.

4.4 Develop Culturally Appropriate Resources to Support Involvement

We propose that skills in supporting involvement in decision-making be considered a key competency for all cadres of healthcare workers, including mental health specialists, primary care workers and community health workers. The ability to support the balance of protection from harm with preservation of autonomy is fundamental.

Core components of guidance and training would include how to support service users to choose their preferred treatments, alongside reassurance that care provision will not be affected by expressing preferences. Decisions that do not accord with healthcare professionals' recommendations need to be recognised as legitimate and be respected, unless they risk harming the person (Souraya et al., 2018).

The mhGAP Implementation Guide 2.0 provides key principles for the involvement of service users in the development of their treatment plans. However, further practical guidance and culturally reflective examples (case scenarios and stories) would be beneficial for healthcare providers.

Acknowledging cultural variations in decision-making norms and values is key. Individual autonomy is not entirely consistent with Ethiopian cultural norms, which perceive rights as being mutual and collective rather than individual; and choices are often influenced by various dynamics (e.g. family position, socio-economic status, gender, age or the authority of healthcare professionals). In particular, guidance should be compatible with the traditionally prominent role of caregivers in care planning.

Collaborative crisis planning could be promoted and integrated in mental health care across all settings, including primary care. Crisis planning should cover where and how service users would prefer to seek care, and the type of treatment they prefer. Plans should also explicitly include the wishes of service users in relation to involuntary treatment if needed and the involvement of their caregivers and broader community.

Decision support tools are a key approach to facilitating change in decision-making practice (Slade, 2017). However, formal decision aids used in high-income countries are mostly delivered online and require resources that are not currently available in Ethiopia. We propose an alternative of brief, context-specific information leaflets to give information and encouragement towards involvement in a clear language that considers the cultural and conceptual framework of decision-making in Ethiopia. Other low-cost, community-based approaches for supported decision-making, such as advocacy, peer support, circles of care and open dialogue, could also be explored in the Ethiopian setting, potentially as adjuncts to CBR (Sugiura et al., 2020). Community resources (e.g. community-based organisations, community leaders and religious and traditional healers) could be leveraged for the promotion of such methods.

A little-explored area is how, and by whom, involvement in decision-making can best be measured. Measurement mechanisms embedded in routine mental health care could provide immediate feedback to healthcare professionals to help them modify their practice. Ideally, this could be through a brief, practical and culturally adapted tool that emphasises the perception of service users regarding their involvement, as well as considering the views of caregivers and healthcare professionals.

4.5 Improve Access to Care and Address Structural Inequalities

Without a strategy that addresses poverty, availability of affordable medications, access to psychosocial care and mental health and human rights literacy, real choices for treatment in the context of mental health care will remain limited in Ethiopia. As a consequence, involvement in decision-making will be tokenistic or immaterial. Better access to good quality care through the integration of mental health into primary care should reduce the need for involuntary treatment, including restraint in the community. Involving service users in health system strengthening, for example using approaches such as PAR, makes it more likely that new services will meet their own needs and therefore promote better outcomes. CBR and similar approaches such as Basic Needs bolster livelihoods by building service users' work skills and supporting income-generation opportunities (Kleintjes et al., 2013). Together, these endeavours may result in a positive feedback loop whereby more accessible and holistic care results in a more motivated and empowered body of service users who are more likely to engage in decision-making at system and individual care planning levels.

5 CONCLUSION

Involvement of service users in decision-making to improve care is limited in Ethiopia. Whilst contextual challenges (limited access to information and care, stigma, discrimination and poverty) are substantial, there are efforts and opportunities to implement involvement at individual and system levels. Effective implementation of involvement would require a pragmatic multi-stakeholder strategy that creates a cultural shift; provides guidance, training, a legislative framework and culturally appropriated resources; and empowers service users. Both CBR and PAR offer promising platforms for the implementation of such approaches. They could have the potential not only to increase involvement in decision-making to improve care but also to address some of the main contextual challenges, such as access to care and stigma, that hinder involvement and affect the lives of people with mental health conditions.

REFERENCES

Abayneh, S., Lempp, H., Alem, A., et al. (2017). Service user involvement in mental health system strengthening in a rural African setting: qualitative study. *BMC Psychiatry*, 17(1). https://doi.org/10.1186/s12888-017-1352-9

Abayneh, S., Lempp, H., & Alem, A. et al. (2020). Developing a Theory of Change model of service user and caregiver involvement in mental health system strengthening in primary health care in rural Ethiopia. *Int J Ment Health Syst* 14(51). https://doi.org/10.1186/s13033-020-00383-6

Abayneh, S., Lempp, H., & Hanlon, C. (2020). Participatory action research to pilot a model of mental health service user involvement in an Ethiopian rural primary healthcare setting: study protocol. *Research Involvement and Engagement*, 6(1). https://doi.org/10.1186/s40900-019-0175-x

Alem, A., Jacobsson, L., Lynöe, N., Kohn, R., & Kullgren, G. (2002). Attitudes and practices among Ethiopian health care professionals in psychiatry regarding compulsory treatment. *International Journal of Law and Psychiatry*, 25(6), 599–610. https://doi.org/10.1016/S0160-2527(01)00112-1

Asher L, Birhane R, Teferra S, et al. (2021). "Like a doctor, like a brother": Achieving competence amongst lay health workers delivering community-based rehabilitation for people with schizophrenia in Ethiopia. *PLoS One*. 16(2). https://doi.org/10.1371/journal.pone.0246158

Asher, L., Fekadu, A., Teferra, S., et al. (2017). "I cry every day and night, I have my son tied in chains": physical restraint of people with schizophrenia in community settings in Ethiopia. *Globalization and Health*, 13(1). https://doi.org/10.1186/s12992-017-0273-1

Asher, L., Hanlon, C., Birhane, R., et al. (2018). Community-based rehabilitation intervention for people with schizophrenia in Ethiopia (RISE): a 12 month mixed methods pilot study. *BMC Psychiatry*, 18(1). https://doi.org/10.1186/s12888-018-1818-4

Bartlett, P., & Hamzic, V. (2010). *Reforming Mental Disability Law in Africa: Practical Tips and Suggestions*. Human Rights Law Centre, University of Nottingham.

Bayetti, C., Jadhav, S., & Jain, S. (2016). The re-covering self: a critique of the recovery-based approach in India's mental health care. *Disability and the Global South*, 3(1).

Faulkner, A. (2017). Survivor research and Mad Studies: the role and value of experiential knowledge in mental health research. *Disability and Society*, 32(4), 500–520. https://doi.org/10.1080/09687599.2017.1302320

Fricker, M. (2007). Epistemic Injustice: Power and the Ethics of Knowing. In *Epistemic Injustice: Power and the Ethics of Knowing*. Oxford University Press. https://doi.org/10.1093/acprof:oso/9780198237907.001.0001

Hanlon, C., Tesfaye, M., Wondimagegn, D., & Shibre, T. (2010). Ethical and professional challenges in mental health care in low- and middle-income countries. *International Review of Psychiatry*, 22(3), 245–251. https://doi.org/10.3109/09540261.2010.482557

Kleintjes, S., Lund, C., & Swartz, L. (2013). Organising for self-advocacy in mental health: experiences from seven African countries. *African Journal of Psychiatry (South Africa)*, 6(3), 187–195. https://doi.org/10.4314/ajpsy.v16i3.25

Kurs, R., & Grinshpoon, A. (2018). Vulnerability of individuals with mental disorders to epistemic injustice in both clinical and social domains. *Ethics and Behavior*, 28(4), 336–346. https://doi.org/10.1080/10508422.2017.1365302

Lempp, H., Abayneh, S., Gurung, D., et al. (2018). Service user and caregiver involvement in mental health system strengthening in low- and middle-income countries: a cross-country qualitative study. *Epidemiology and Psychiatric Sciences*, 27(1), 29–39. https://doi.org/10.1017/S2045796017000634

Lund, C., Tomlinson, M., & Patel, V. (2016). Integration of mental health into primary care in low-and middle-income countries: the PRIME mental healthcare plans. *British Journal of Psychiatry*, 258(S56). https://doi.org/10.1192/bjp.bp.114.153668

Mathias, K., Pillai, P., Gaitonde, R., Shelly, K., & Jain, S. (2019). Co-production of a pictorial recovery tool for people with psycho-social disability informed by a participatory action research approach – a qualitative study set in India. *Health Promotion International*, 35(3). https://doi.org/10.1093/heapro/daz043

Mayston, R., Alem, A., Habtamu, A., et al. (2016). Participatory planning of a primary care service for people with severe mental disorders in rural Ethiopia. *Health Policy and Planning*, 31(3), 367–376. https://doi.org/10.1093/heapol/czv072

Ministry of Health [Ethiopia]. (2012). *Ethiopian National Mental Health Strategy 2012/13–2015/16*.

Newbigging, K., & Ridley, J. (2018). Epistemic struggles: the role of advocacy in promoting epistemic justice and rights in mental health. *Social Science and Medicine*, 219, 36–44. https://doi.org/10.1016/j.socscimed.2018.10.003

Perkins, A., Ridler, J., Browes, D., et al. (2018). Experiencing mental health diagnosis: a systematic review of service user, clinician, and carer perspectives across clinical settings. *The Lancet Psychiatry*, 5(9). https://doi.org/10.1016/S2215-0366(18)30095-6

Rai, S., Gurung, D., Kaiser, B. N et al. (2018). A service user co-facilitated intervention to reduce mental illness stigma among primary healthcare workers: utilizing perspectives of family members and caregivers. *Families, Systems and Health*, 36(2). https://doi.org/10.1037/fsh0000338

Rose, D. (2017). Service user/survivor-led research in mental health: epistemological possibilities. *Disability and Society*, 32(6), 773–789. https://doi.org/10.1080/09687599.2017.1320270

Saxena, S., Funk, M. K., & Chisholm, D. (2015). Comprehensive mental health action plan 2013–2020. *Eastern Mediterranean Health Journal*. https://doi.org/10.26719/2015.21.7.461

Semrau, M., Evans-Lacko, S., Alem, A., et al. (2015). Strengthening mental health systems in low- and middle-income countries: the Emerald programme. *BMC Medicine*, 13(79). https://doi.org/10.1186/s12916-015-0309-4

Semrau, M., Lempp, H., Keynejad, R., et al. (2016). Service user and caregiver involvement in mental health system strengthening in low- and middle-income countries: systematic review. *BMC Health Services Research*, 16(1). https://doi.org/10.1186/s12913-016-1323-8

Slade, M. (2017). Implementing shared decision making in routine mental health care. *World Psychiatry*, 16(2), 146–153. https://doi.org/10.1002/wps.20412

Souraya, S., Hanlon, C., & Asher, L. (2018). Involvement of people with schizophrenia in decision-making in rural Ethiopia: a qualitative study. *Globalization and Health*, 14(1). https://doi.org/10.1186/s12992-018-0403-4

Srinivasan, T. N., & Thara, R. (2002). At issue: management of medication noncompliance in schizophrenia by families in India. *Schizophrenia Bulletin*, 28(3), 531–535. https://doi.org/10.1093/oxfordjournals.schbul.a006960

Sugiura, K., Mahomed, F., Saxena, S., & Patel, V. (2020). An end to coercion: rights and decision-making in mental health care. *Bulletin of the World Health Organization*, 98(1), 52–58. https://doi.org/10.2471/BLT.19.234906

Sunkel, C. (2012). Empowerment and partnership in mental health. *The Lancet*, 379(9812). https://doi.org/10.1016/S0140-6736(11)61270-1

Tambuyzer, E., Pieters, G., Van, C., & Phdà, A. (2011). Patient involvement in mental health care: one size does not fit all. *John Wiley & Sons Ltd Health Expectations*, 17, 138–150. https://doi.org/10.1111/j.1369-7625.2011.00743.x

United Nations Human Rights. (2016). *Ethiopia's record on rights of persons with disabilities faces review by UN Committee*. United Nations Human Rights Office of the High Commission.

World Health Organisation. (2013). *Mental Health Action Plan 2013–2020*. World Health Organisation.

World Health Organisation. (2015). Mental health atlas. *Bulletin of the World Health Organization*.

For EU product safety concerns, contact us at Calle de José Abascal, 56–1°,
28003 Madrid, Spain or eugpsr@cambridge.org.

www.ingramcontent.com/pod-product-compliance
Lightning Source LLC
LaVergne TN
LVHW011754060526
838200LV00053B/3593